*The Films
of
Jeanette MacDonald and Nelson Eddy*

I Married an Angel, 1942

The Films
of
Jeanette MacDonald and Nelson Eddy

Eleanor Knowles Dugan

with

Film Credits and Revisions by
John Cocchi

Music Credits and Discography by
J. Peter Bergman

GRAND CYRUS PRESS
San Francisco

© 2011 Eleanor Knowles Dugan
Revised Edition

All rights reserved.

*Originally published in 1976 by A.S. Barnes and Co., Inc.,
Cranbury, NJ and The Tantivy Press, London*

2006 edition published by Eleanor Knowles Dugan

ISBN 978-0-9790994-5-8
Library of Congress Control Number: 2011920032

Dugan, Eleanor Knowles, 1937–
The Films of Jeanette MacDonald and Nelson Eddy

(MacDonald, Jeanette, 1903–1965)
(Eddy, Nelson, 1901–1967)

Cover design by Tony Thornton.
Front cover photo from *Sweethearts*, 1938.

Grand Cyrus Press
1024 Sacramento St.
San Francisco, CA 94108-2003
(415) 433-7244
grandcyruspress@gmail.com
www.GrandCyrusPress.com
www.jeanettemacdonaldandnelsoneddy.com

To everyone,
past, present, and future,
who finds the world a little more special
for having been touched by the magic
of Jeanette MacDonald and Nelson Eddy.

Although Jeanette MacDonald and Nelson Eddy wore white wigs in only two of their eight films together, and then very briefly, this is the way millions remember them.

Contents

Acknowledgments
Foreword: They Talk, 1

CHAPTER 1 – Jeanette MacDonald: Arch Street to Arc Lights, 3

CHAPTER 2 – They Sing! Hollywood, Wired for Sound, Discovers the Musical, 17

The Love Parade, 21
The Vagabond King, 32
Paramount on Parade, 41
Let's Go Native, 43
Monte Carlo, 51
The Lottery Bride, 60
Oh, for a Man!, 68
Don't Bet on Women, 77
Annabelle's Affairs, 81

CHAPTER 3 – All Talking, No Singing, No Dancing, 88

One Hour with You, 91
Une Heure près de toi, 101
Love Me Tonight, 101
    And related short *Hollywood on Parade*, 102

CHAPTER 4 – From Paramount to MGM via Monte Carlo, 115

The Cat and the Fiddle, 117
The Merry Widow, 129
    And related short *Happy Days Are Here Again*, 129
La Veuve Joyeuse, 146

CHAPTER 5 – Nelson Eddy: What's a Nice Concert Singer Like You Doing in a Studio Like This? 153

Handlebars, 165
Broadway to Hollywood, 166
Dancing Lady, 170
Student Tour, 172
Naughty Marietta, 174

CHAPTER 6 - The Second Most Famous Team, 194

Rose Marie. 206
San Francisco, 228
Maytime, 247
The Firefly, 274
Rosalie, 287
The Girl of the Golden West, 300
Sweethearts, 315

CHAPTER 7 - Celluloid Sweethearts:
    Their Off-Screen Loves and Marriages, 338

Let Freedom Ring, 343
Broadway Serenade, 355
Balalaika, 366
New Moon, 380
Bitter Sweet, 398
    And related short *Miracle of Sound*, 412
Smilin' Through, 412
The Chocolate Soldier, 423
    And related short *We Must Have Music*, 434
I Married an Angel, 434

CHAPTER 8 - Music to Make War By, 458

Cairo, 464
Phantom of the Opera, 475
Knickerbocker Holiday, 488
Follow the Boys, 498
Make Mine Music, 502
Northwest Outpost, 506
Three Daring Daughters, 517
The Sun Comes Up, 529

CHAPTER 9 - The Finale That Never Was, 538

CHAPTER 10 - As They Had Lived, 550

EPILOGUE, 553

Other Notable Film Appearances, 554
Books about Both Stars, 557
Discography, 558
Addenda, 590
Index, 592

Acknowledgments

Many, many people helped make this book. First, thanks to Anna Michalik, who scanned the pages of the 1976 B.C. (before computers) edition into word processing format, a mighty task. Then to her, Diane Flaherty, and Ginny Sayre, all of whom contributed generously with technical support, new information, and additional photos for this new edition. Mary Truesdell has generously contributed selections from her fascinating background research on early scripts and treatments for some of the major costarring films. Elsa Dik Glass has provided genealogical information from her forthcoming biography of Nelson. Pam Winter masterminded the technological aspects. And, finally, David Gasten inspired this new edition.

It is necessary to express my appreciation to many who have helped, some of whom are sadly no longer here to read their names.

The first edition owed much to Charles Shibuk, the original research editor; Earl Anderson, who contributed extensively to the stage histories of film actors and operettas; Diane Goodrich, who provided many rare photographs; Bob Grimes, who was ingenious in tracking down elusive musical credits in his fantastic sheet music library; Julie Illescas, who patiently and cheerfully checked out over a hundred different dates, facts, and record numbers in her personal collection of memorabilia; Don Koll, whose great love of the musical film was the inspiration for this book and whose many contributions and suggestions are its backbone; Andrew C. McKay, who furnished many of the reviews quoted, especially the fascinating Philadelphia ones; Buddy McDaniel, who helped immensely with the music lists.

More recently, a debt is owed to Anita McCreery and Helen Crawford, who made extensive contributions regarding Nelson's opera and concert careers; and to Stephanie Loyd Barr for her hard work, patience, and computer genius.

Deep gratitude for their many contributions and their encouragement is owed to: Yannek AgaKhan; Michael Barr; Sue Baumann; Eric Benson; Bill Berner; Randy Beucus; Gerald Bordman; Mary B. Burgess; Miguel Cao; David Chierichetti; Cathy Clark; Tom Clark; Rose Cocchi; Thelma Cohen; Collectors Book Store, Hollywood; Paul Collins; Jill Coogan; Judith Mary Cox; Monty Crooks of the Academy Cinema, Palo Alto; Carla Librizzi DeGovia; Dan Dugan; Mary Dunphy; the Nelson Eddy Music Club; Marnus Els; William K. Everson; Robert Friess; Marlyse Fuller; Alex Gordon of 20th Century-Fox & Gene Autry Entertainment; Vera J. Gordon of Washington Irving High School; John Hadley; Pierre Guinle; Phil Haggard; Audrey Hsia; Clara Rhoades and Tessa Williams of the Jeanette MacDonald International Fan Club; Miles Kreuger; Shirley Lagasca; Brian Lannes; Al Lareau, Charles Lindsley of the Music and Arts Division of the Los Angeles Public Library; Tom Luddy of the Pacific Film Archive; Leonard Maltin; Gary Mazzeo; Alvin H. Marill; John Martin; Dick Mayfield; Amy Revere McCauley; Dion McGregor; Norman Miller; the Lincoln Center Research Library for the Performing Arts of the New York Public Library; Jennifer Myers; Ken Norton; Joe Pearce; Lucy and the late Perry Pickering of the Nelson Eddy Appreciation Society; Patty Pettit; Kitty Rea; Ken Richards; the San Francisco Institute for Comic Art; the Art and Music Division of the San Francisco Public Library; Ian Shuttleworth of *Theatre Record*; Harold Suber of the U.C.L.A. Film Archive; Tony Thornton; Jack Tillmany; Zarubi Elmassian Vortian; Pippa White; Gunnard Wilson; and Marjorie M. Zimmerman of Julia Richman High School.

Your forgiveness is asked and corrections requested for any errors or omissions that have occurred despite our exhaustive efforts.

Foreword: They Talk!

The Jazz Singer really started something. It premiered on October 6, 1927 at the Warner Bros. Theatre in New York and set a multi-million-dollar industry on its ear.

Ironically, *The Jazz Singer* wasn't the first of anything. It certainly wasn't the first sound film. Films with sound had been shown publicly in many forms since the earliest days of the cinema. (Sorting out the various "firsts" would take a volume twice the size of this one.) And it wasn't the first feature-length sound film. *Don Juan* with John Barrymore, issued a year before, had a complete Vitaphone soundtrack of music and sound effects, and there were claimants for the same honor going back to the turn of the century. It wasn't the first "talkie." D.W. Griffith used a brief talking sequence in his 1921 *Dream Street*, and many others, before and after, had tried to mate sound and image. *The Jazz Singer* wasn't even the first feature-length "talkie," since it employed titles for most of the dialogue.

It was, however, the first sound film to be commercially successful, the first to make Hollywood aware that it was going to have to scrap millions of dollars worth of equipment and invest heavily in a new, unknown medium—this at a time when most major studios were dangerously overextended in theatre-chain investments.

The "talkie" reared its ugly head just as the silent film was approaching its presumed ultimate in artistry. Complicated stories could be told smoothly and fluently with a minimum of titles. The titles themselves could be masterpieces of thought, mood, innuendo, humor, or revelation. Rather than interrupting the flow of the film, they had become an integral part of the rhythmic structure, aiding and heightening the effect of a scene.

The first sound films, and especially the first musicals, had to start over, to create a whole new language of film. Very briefly, actors and singers were immobilized by microphones and stationary cameras in soundproof booths. Early sound equipment in theatres suffered from as many technical weaknesses as early television sets did. Unintelligible or blaring sound added nothing to films already suffering from visual limitations. Lighting, which had become an art in itself in the late twenties, now had to allow for boom shadows. The projected picture was made murkier still by perforations cut in the screen to permit sound to come through. Actors who were accustomed to free movement now had to remember diction, projection, and where the microphone was hidden, causing some stiff performances. Thomas A. Edison echoed the opinion of millions when he said in 1930, "Without improvements, people will tire of the talkies. Talking is no substitute for the good acting we had in silent pictures."

Many people today think of the "Roaring Twenties" as a time of great prosperity. It may have been for bootleggers and film stars, but the man in the street was caught between inflation and periodic recessions. When he felt a pinch, he didn't take his family to the movies.

It was during one of these slumps that Warner Bros., in financial difficulty, made a desperate gamble. To aid ailing box office receipts, they selected one of several sound devices—a disc method evolved by Bell Laboratories and licensed by Western Electric, and AT&T—and set out to make films that would let the smallest town have background music equal in quality to the largest city cinema. They christened it the Vitaphone.

Don Juan, starring John Barrymore and Mary Astor, premiered on August 6, 1926. It had a complete synchronized orchestral soundtrack and sound effects. *Variety* devoted its next edition to the Vitaphone, but theatre owners were reluctant to go heavily into debt for the necessary equipment. Further encouragement was needed.

Warners decided on another sound feature, *The Jazz Singer*, this time with Broadway star Al Jolson recording song inserts. (George Jessel had created the stage role, but wanted extra money for the recordings necessary to do the soundtrack. Warners then turned to Eddie Cantor who refused, saying no one could equal Jessel in the role. Jolson was Warners' third choice.)

Jolson had shied away from the silent films made by so many other Broadway entertainers (Eddie Cantor, Alfred Lunt, W.C. Fields, Will Rogers), feeling his appeal rested on his singing. *The Jazz Singer* is basically a silent film with musical accompaniment, but the irrepressible Jolson turned it into a personal triumph and an entertainment landmark. Between songs, with the mike still on, he ad libbed, "Folks, you ain't heard nothing yet!" and the audience over- whelmingly agreed. Later in the film he sings for his mother, actress Eugenie Besserer, and sets the tone for his series of eleven "mammy" pictures by telling her that he is going to take her to the tunnel of love and hug and kiss her. (Mother love had not yet acquired its bad reputation.) The screen comes alive as Miss Besserer squirms with embarrassed pleasure: "Oh, go on with you." A moment of complete theatrical exaltation had occurred, and the audience would not forget it.

In the hectic days that followed, Hollywood turned to Broadway for people who knew how to sing and talk. In 1929, dozens, perhaps hundreds, of Broadway lights decided to twinkle in Hollywood. Of all the leading ladies of the New York musical stage who made the long train trip west, no one had a longer, more creative film career or reached greater and more enduring popularity than a slender, fair-haired girl from Philadelphia: Jeanette MacDonald.

Classically trained singers didn't meet the instant reception accorded their musical comedy counterparts. Some of the finest opera singers of this century gave excellent performances before the camera, but they aroused more respect than enthusiasm in the American moviegoer. It wasn't until 1935 that a Philadelphia concert singer named Nelson Eddy burst on the scene and made box office history.

1
Jeanette MacDonald: Arch Street to Arc Lights

In December of 1919, a sixteen-year-old schoolgirl entered the backstage door of the Capitol Theatre at 51st Street and Broadway. When she emerged she had gotten her first theatrical job in New York.

Appropriately, the Capitol Theatre was one of the posh new palaces devoted to exhibiting films, and the unlikely looking little chorus girl, who would one day sing from the Capitol screen, was now a "prologue" dancer doing five shows a day between screenings of Eric Stroheim's [sic] *Blind Husbands*.

Under a contract with the new Actors' Equity, won in the long, bitter strike that had just concluded, she would make the magnificent sum of twenty-five dollars per week. The program listed her as "Janette McDonald."

Jeanette Anna MacDonald, as we know her better, was born in Philadelphia on June 18, 1903, the youngest of Daniel and Anna Wright MacDonald's three daughters. Since her later studio biographies set the year at 1907, a few words of explanation may be helpful. Miss MacDonald's school records show her birth date as 1903, making her initial New York stage appearance at the more likely but no less impressive age of sixteen, not twelve. (While a well-developed twelve-year-old might convince a stage manager that she was sixteen, it is unlikely that a three-year-old could convince a school principal that she was really seven.) A listing in a 1909 YWCA show program, crediting her with a song, also makes the 1907 date unlikely.

Throughout her stage career in the 1920s, the date quoted to interviewers moved slowly forward to 1904, then 1906, and was finally frozen at 1907 when she signed with Paramount. The 1903 date was finally confirmed when biographer Edward Baron Turk located Jeanette in the handwritten, chronological ledger, *Register of Baptisms, 1888-1911*, of Philadelphia's Olivet Presbyterian Church. He also confirmed the 1903 date in the *Thirteenth Census of the United States, 1910*.

In our more candid times, when world-famous beauties proudly proclaim their real age, this deception might seem slightly vain, if not downright dishonest. However, Jeanette MacDonald was a child of another age. The shockwaves were still reverberating from the brave announcement by film actress Beverly Bayne

Baby Jeanette. *Courtesy Diane Goodrich.*

that she was married to her leading man, Francis X. Bushman. For an actress to admit that she was married, or nearing thirty, or worst of all a mother, was still pretty daring. How could such a woman hope to be alluring to men who had been brought up to think of actresses as glamorous concubines of the imagination? Youth was all, and Jeanette MacDonald, along with most leading ladies of her time, played the game.

Jeanette was born and brought up in her family's red-brick house at 5123 Arch Street, near 52nd Street, in Philadelphia. Jeanette described her father as a "leading contractor" and politician, but his varied employment was actually more humble, and the family finances were sometimes precarious. A 1928 *New York Times* article claimed Mr. MacDonald was also an actor. This may have been in his youth or just a reporter's way of adding some theatrical color to Jeanette's otherwise very normal middle-class upbringing.

All through her life, interviewers would despair of making copy out of the disgustingly "normal" Miss MacDonald—normal, that is, if anyone with total dedication and absolute strength of purpose can be called normal. All three MacDonald children set their young hearts on stage careers and went at it with Scottish tenacity and Yankee energy. Money was not plentiful (one of Jeanette's earliest ambitions was to be a big star so that she could "take care of mama"), but Elsie, Edith Blossom, and Jeanette were provided with singing and dancing lessons. "Mother and Dad were simply wonderful," Jeanette said later. "They always helped and never stood in my way."

Soon the fledgling prima donna graduated from tap dancing in front of the mirror to dancing lessons with Al White and from imitating her mother's opera records to singing lessons with Wassil Leps. Opportunities to perform at church and school functions were eagerly awaited.

Jeanette lent her clear soprano to *The Kiddie Revue* put on by James H. Littlefield and his wife Caroline at the Academy of Music. She led a chorus in "It's a Bear" while Elsie and Blossom did bits in a doll chorus. Ann Pennington was a fellow performer.

With the same group, she stopped the show at the Pennsylvania Railroad Y.M.C.A. in 1909, singing "Take Me Up with You, Dearie." As she sang, a little boy was lowered from the flies in a miniature airplane (quite a novelty only six years after the Wright Brothers). She joined him in the plane and the song as they "took off" to thunderous applause. Mrs. Minnie Barry, who costumed the children, recalled Jeanette: "She was a lovely child, always quite the lady—a little lady."

If Jeanette's manners were exemplary, her truthfulness managed to get her and her teacher, Al White, in trouble. He organized a group of his better pupils into a Kidland act that played at the

South Broadway Theatre in Philadelphia. It was so successful that he booked them for a Sunday night performance at Minor's Bronx Theatre in New York City. Jeanette was tall and might have passed for fifteen, the minimum legal age for performers. But when an inspector asked how old she was, she answered honestly, causing Mr. White to spend some uncomfortable hours at the police station. He didn't hold a grudge and used her in a novelty act called "Al White's Song Birds" that played vaudeville houses around Philadelphia.

After these junkets, she returned reluctantly to the Dunlap School at 51st and Race Streets.

A young fashion plate.

Jeanette's parents, Daniel and Anna Wright MacDonald. Weekly ice cream making was a ritual with Father MacDonald. When Jeanette married, she and her husband carried on the tradition. *Courtesy Diane Goodrich.*

School seemed a definite waste of time to Jeanette, who especially hated arithmetic. She loved languages and geography, but reasoned that a performer could learn these traveling around the world, not sitting at a desk. She was destined never to finish high school.

The MacDonalds were Scottish Presbyterians, and religion always played an important part in Jeanette's life. When she was twelve, she taught Sunday school classes at the nearby Tennent Presbyterian Church, where she frequently performed in church productions. Her strong sense of what was right sustained her throughout her life, though it occasionally made her impatient with those whose "right" was different from hers.

Jeanette in an early children's act. Although she was usually the youngest member of the company, she generally managed to be the center of attention. That's her in the middle. *Courtesy Diane Goodrich.*

The family group began breaking up when eldest sister Elsie eloped with a young sailor. Mrs. MacDonald had long dreamed of a career as a concert pianist for Elsie and expressed her strong disappointment. She made it clear that marriage and careers didn't mix, and Jeanette never forgot it. Soon Blossom left to go to New York, the Mecca, then and now, for stage-struck girls.

Jeanette recounted later that when her father went to New York City on business (actually seeking work), she played hooky from West Philadelphia High and went along to visit Blossom. Her sister was dancing in the Ned Wayburn prologue called *The Demi-Tasse Revue* at the Capitol Theatre. In November, 1919, without telling her father, Jeanette auditioned and was accepted as a chorus replacement.

The official version of what happened next has long been that he moved his business to New York so he could oversee the careers of his two daughters. However, biographer Turk's research has revealed that actually he was unable to find work or meet his mortgage payments. The Arch Street house was put up for sale, and Daniel and Anna moved into a two-room apartment on West 49th Street already occupied by Jeanette, Blossom, and another young Ned Wayburn dancer. Jobs were scarce, and Daniel never again found real employment. Jeanette and Blossom became the breadwinners of the family. Daniel died a broken man a few years later and was buried in Philadelphia on August 4, 1924. In years to come, Jeanette never acknowledged his failings as a provider and painted him as an important person—as he was in her heart. "I owe much to my father," Jeanette said. "He had a splendid personality and was always ready for fun."

In her first *Demi-Tasse Revue*, "Janette" played an Indian Maiden and a Twinkling Star, the latter to a now-forgotten Gershwin tune, "Come to the Moon." Another unnoticed song on the program was Gershwin's "Swanee," which didn't become famous until Al Jolson picked it up and sang it at the Winter Garden.

It seems delightfully appropriate now that Jeanette took her first dance steps on Broadway on the stage of a movie theatre. The Capitol Theatre had opened a month earlier on October 24, 1919 with an elaborate four-hour show that sent most of the formally dressed audience away, tired but happy, long before the film came on. A highlight of that night was a torrid rendition of "Oh, What a Moanin' Man" by twenty-seven-year-old Mae West, who did a shimmy sitting down—and was banned from further performances. The chorus numbers between the "acts" were overseen by Ned Wayburn, a portly gentleman with pince-nez glasses, who was well known as a "production-creator" for Ziegfeld. He was engaged by the Capitol's guiding light, Major Edward Bowes, to bring miniature Ziegfeld numbers to the movie-going public, who could see a show and film for as little as thirty cents. Jeanette first appeared in the Wayburn revue only two weeks before Wayburn and Bowes agreed to part company.

Jeanette and Blossom stayed on at the Capitol, Jeanette appearing as a four-leaf clover in "Say It with Flowers" and "assisting" in "A Little Bit O' Scotch" through the Christmas holidays.

1920 was a turning point, not only for Jeanette but for America, the American theatre,

A very early publicity portrait.

and the American woman. The War to End All Wars had concluded, and soldiers were still drifting home to few cheers and fewer jobs. Women had cast off six centuries of corsets and gained the right to vote. The chorus girl reflected the startling changes.

Gone forever were the elaborately gowned Florodora Girls and the ladies playing boys to provide an excuse for showing their legs in tights. The new ladies of the chorus exposed their bare legs, although baggy bloomers and mid-calf socks made it mostly a study in knees. Ziegfeld, of course, would make tantalizing near-nudity an art before the 1920s were over. Although Jeanette's costumes at this point were far less revealing than her early film "Lubitsch lingerie" would be, they must have seemed pretty racy to a modest teenager.

She loved to tell of her first encounter with silk underwear that all the chorus girls wore. She was so ashamed of her own sturdy woolen vest and knickers that she spent her first paycheck on fancy lingerie. It is typical of Miss MacDonald that while she was always frugal, she had an instinct for spending money on things that would impress other people.

In late January of 1920, "Jeannette MacDonald" joined the chorus of *The Night Boat*, a Jerome Kern musical that had been running since New Year's. She had kept up her contact with Ned Wayburn by taking classes at his dance studio. When he cast replacements for his production numbers in *The Night Boat*, he remembered the tenacious dancer who performed so briefly in his *Demi-Tasse Revue*.

The Night Boat played at the Liberty Theatre on 42nd Street between Broadway and Eighth Avenue. The block had been the heart of the theatre district for several years, but the presumptuous new movie theaters were starting to press in and soon the "legitimates" would continue their northward trek. The Liberty itself had succumbed briefly to motion pictures, housing the premiere of *The Birth of a Nation* in 1915. However, it quickly returned to normal and was home to several of Jeanette's shows as well as to the Lunts, Gertrude Lawrence, and Noël Coward before becoming an all-night revival house and then a purveyor of erotic cinema entertainment. Happily this block of theatres was restored in the 1990s.

The plot of *The Night Boat* had husbands and wives pursuing each other on a nighttime cruise up the Hudson to Albany. As a member of the chorus, Jeanette got to sing "Some Fine Day," "Left All Alone Again Blues," "Good Night Boat," and "Catskills, Hello," all Kern tunes with lyrics by Anne Caldwell. She also understudied ingenue Stella Hoban. The cast included later film personalities Ernest Torrence and Hal Skelly.

In early August, Jeanette left *The Night Boat* when she landed the featured rôle of Eleanor Worth in the long-running hit, *Irene*. At seventeen she had her first solos on Broadway, singing "Hobbies" and "Castle of Dreams." Besides the lilting title song, the show's best-remembered tune is "Alice Blue Gown," which was sung by the show's star, Patti Harrold. The music was by Harry Tierney (*Rio Rita*) and lyrics were by Joseph McCarthy. After a mere week on Broadway, Jeanette (now billed as "Jeannette MacDonald") was sent to Boston as a road-company replacement. This permitted the management to advertise her as a member of the "Broadway cast."

All through her ten months in New York City, Jeanette had maintained passing grades in school, first at Washington Irving, then at Julia Richman High School. When the tour began, Jeanette informed school authorities that she was "moving to Boston." It wasn't entirely untrue. *Irene* played one week at the Wilbur Theatre there before heading on to Philadelphia. This was to be Jeanette's last encounter with formal education. With her heavy schedule, she had just completed the tenth grade. (When the *Irene* tour reached Chicago, the title rôle was taken over by a young singer named Irene Dunne, later a major film star.)

During the long, hot summer of 1921, Jeanette returned to New York. She eked out a living for a while modeling fur coats in the sweltering heat. The combined earnings of Jeanette and her sister Blossom allowed the family to move to larger quarters at 325 Central Park West.

Another replacement part followed. *Tangerine* had opened in August of 1921 with a new Guy Bolton book after an initial out-of-town failure. The desert island musical starred the lovely Julia Sanderson and dealt with husbands who run away to the South Seas rather than pay alimony. Their wives follow and all are reunited at the end of Act III. In mid-September, Jeanette joined the cast, replacing Edna Pierce as one of the wives, "Kate Allen." Although she was finally "Jeanette MacDonald" and understudied the star, she was pretty much lost in the shuffle. She had one interpolated song by Jean Schwartz, "Man Is the Lord of It All." When the show went on the road, she asked for a raise so that she could bring her mother along. Instead, she got her notice.

Another stretch of unemployment ended in her heading downtown to Greenwich Village, where she joined the cast of an amorphous revue called *Fantastic Fricassee*, based much too loosely on the Franco-Russian import hit, *Chauve Souris*. "An uncooked mess," reported the *New York Post*. The show played at the now departed Greenwich Village Theatre on Sheridan Square. Ben Hecht and Maxwell Bodenheim contributed skits. The show included an ever-changing group of songs and sketches with titles like "Virgins of the Sun," "When the Dead Get Gay," and "Japanese Death Song." At various times, Miss MacDonald delivered "Waiting for You" (by Frankie [W. Frank] Harling) as a duet with Jimmy Kemper, and "A Heart That's Free," probably the song of the same title that she sang in *San Francisco*. She also played in the prologue and in "Brittany Pastoral."

The show failed to generate much excitement until an official of the Prison Reform Association strongly objected to its playing a performance before prisoners at Sing Sing in November of 1922. "It seems incredible that you have selected these naked dancing girls," stated executive secretary Harriet Laidlaw, who also held positions on both the Jewish Welfare Board and the Catholic Welfare Council, a busy lady. *Fantastic Fricassee* was banned at Sing Sing, and the box office thrived.

Zelda Sears saw Jeanette in the show and recommended her to producer Henry Savage, who was putting together his annual vehicle for the sprightly musical comedy star Mitzi. Jeanette got a three-year contract with Savage and the ingenue lead in *Minnie and Me*.

The title referred to a monkey and was soon changed to *The Magic Ring*. Jeanette toured with the show out of town for five months, until it opened on October 1, 1923 to rave reviews. Not all the praise was for its fiery little Hungarian

Backstage at *The Magic Ring*, 1923, with Hazel Gladstone, one of the ladies of the chorus. *Courtesy Diane Goodrich.*

star. The *New York Tribune* reported: "The blonde beauty of Jeanette MacDonald is one of the glowing things to be commemorated like the keepsakes of which she eloquently sings. It is understandable that only a resort to necromancy could drive the hero from her legitimate charms." The *New York Times* said, "Among the merits of the evening must be listed the appearance and voice of Jeanette MacDonald." She was mentioned in nearly every review, and in 1923 there were twelve daily papers in New York City!

The plot concerned a magic ring given to Polly Church (Mitzi), a foundling organ grinder, by a kindly curio-shop owner (Sydney Greenstreet). She uses its powers first for soup and then to go to the ball, on Long Island, of course, where the powers of the ring enable her to win rich Tom Hammond (Boyd Marshall) away from Iris Bellamy (Jeanette). Jeanette sang "Keepsakes," "Milaiya," "Broken Hearts," and "Deep in Someone's Heart," with music by Harold Levey and lyrics by Zelda Sears. The costumes and some of the scenery were designed by young Adrian, who would later make Jeanette one of the best-costumed women in Hollywood.

While Jeanette made her way every night, matinees Wednesday and Saturday, to the West 41st Street stage door, a young blond actor named Raymond Guion was drawing good notices a few blocks away in *The Potters* on West 45th Street. Two years later, in *The Cradle Snatchers*, Guion and juvenile Humphrey Bogart were pursued by matrons Edna May Oliver and Mary Boland. Raymond Guion probably passed Jeanette occasionally on the street before he left for Hollywood and changed his name to Gene Raymond.

The Magic Ring completed ninety-six performances at the Liberty Theater and then went on tour for nearly two years, a common occurrence before radio and movies "killed the road." Miss MacDonald played 641 consecutive performances! After two years, Mitzi signed with another management, the show closed, and Jeanette's contract was sold.

The Liberty was again home base for *Tip Toes*, a George and Ira Gershwin musical that opened on December 28, 1925. Tip Toes herself was played by Queenie Smith, who later played "Ellie" in the 1936 film of *Show Boat*. The sprightly Tip Toes (Miss Smith) is stranded in Florida with her brothers, who decide to marry her off to a millionaire. They borrow money from the brother of Sylvia Metcalf (Jeanette) and outfit Tip Toes like an heiress. Naturally, her true love turns out to be a millionaire in disguise. Jeanette sang "Nice Baby" and "It's a Great Little World" and joined in the finale. The show was filmed as a silent with Dorothy Gish as Tip Toes and Will Rogers as on a brother.

Young George Gershwin was already famous for his "Rhapsody in Blue" and *Lady, Be Good*, but *Tip Toes* was not one of his most memorable scores. Only "Looking for a Boy (to Love)" and "Sweet and Low Down" are still played, but the show earned more money for producers Alex Aarons and Vinton Freedley than their previous hit, *Lady, Be Good*. The *New York Times* said: "Miss MacDonald is truly beautiful."

Jeanette had now sung songs by Jerome Kern, Harry Tierney, and George Gershwin. If the 1930s were Hollywood's "Golden Era," the 1920s were certainly Broadway's "Golden Decade." In the ten years between the Volstead Act and the stock market crash, more money flowed across more ticket counters and more people saw more shows than in any decade before or since. Salaries and costs were lower, more shows were done, and many more people were steadily employed. A Broadway season could count on thirty to forty musicals, compared with a scant half-dozen today.

Nearly every major Broadway composer of the first half of the twentieth century was at work, from Franz Lehár, Victor Herbert, Sigmund Romberg, and Rudolf Friml to Gershwin, Kern, Irving Berlin, Cole Porter, Rodgers and Hart and Hammerstein. The unique new form to be known as musical comedy was being fused from nearly every other musical and theatrical form known to western civilization. America still smugly thought of itself as a melting pot, although the Quota Act of 1921 had effectively ended nearly all non-WASP immigration. However, Broadway in the 1920s made the musical equivalent of a melting pot a reality.

"The Show Business" offered a way up to anyone with guts and talent. So many major artists of the era were of immigrant stock that

A portrait taken in January 1925. *Courtesy Jack Tillmany.*

Indiana-born Cole Porter once said the greatest tragedy in his life was not being born on the Lower East Side. It looked for a while as if even black Americans would be able to enter the "mainstream" through the back door of show business, as the Italians, Irish, and Jews were doing.

Any girl with looks and energy could also hope to find the pot at the end of the rainbow. The salaries were better than anything a shop girl or seamstress could make, but an even bigger attraction was the men they were able to meet and marry.

Marriage, however, was apparently the last thing in the world on Jeanette MacDonald's mind. We try to get a picture of what made her tick, of the factors that produced such clear-eyed ambition and drive in a slender girl with a cloud of golden hair. It is like trying to pinpoint childhood influences in the life of an Einstein or Mozart. They simply existed to do what they had to do. Jeanette seemed to exist to make the absolute most of the talents allotted to her, and with further willpower to turn her limitations into assets.

She possessed a pleasant face, a clear, light voice, a body neither ugly nor especially sensuous. Taken one by one her features were, at best, average, with the exception of her eyes. Even in her earliest photos, her eyes manage to reach out to you. Her nose, however, was much too long, her neck too thick, and her chin definitely too prominent.

Considering all of this, it is with a sense of wonder that we realize she has convinced us that she is utterly, incredibly beautiful. It is a beauty that has been transmitted by some of the plainest but most exciting women in show business. Katharine Cornell had it, and Gertrude Lawrence. Norma Shearer and Sophia Loren project on film a radiance far in excess of their physical attributes. It is an allure, a glow, an outpouring of an electrical energy that comes from within and so overpowers us that we would not notice or care if the lady had a wart on her nose. In the vernacular of the 1920s, Jeanette MacDonald had "it."

"And was she nice?" you ask people who knew her then. They stare at you blankly. "Nice?" It is, it turns out, like asking if the Grand Canyon is "nice." She was cheerful, considerate, hardworking. A string of adjectives follow approximating the Boy Scout ideal. However, when she felt she was being imposed upon, she stood firm. Crossed, she fought back.

Theatre (and performers) live on publicity. Here Jeanette and her friend Amy Revere plug their touring production. The sign reads, "Presenting Boston's Most Favorite Novelties, Jeanette MacDonald – Amy Revere, Stars of Yes, Yes, Yvette and The Electric Red Bug." *Courtesy Amy Revere McCauley.*

And she could hold a grudge for years if necessary. She was a dedicated performer and no false modesty or indecision slowed her steps.

If Jeanette arrived on Broadway at the ideal musical moment, she also picked the ideal physical moment. Until the early 1920s, dancers were generally 5' 2" or shorter, due chiefly to the three-inch heels they wore and the legendary shortness of their male partners. Jeanette was a monumental 5' 5". Fortunately, she found dance directors who were starting to use taller girls as dancers instead of clotheshorses. One of these was Albertina Rasch, who later married composer Dimitri Tiomkin and emigrated to Hollywood, where she choreographed several of Jeanette's films.

Jeanette still played the second female lead in her next adventure, a sprightly trifle based on *Brewster's Millions* called *Bubblin' Over*. The show starred Cleo Mayfield and Cecil Lean, veteran performers who had made a hit the previous year touring in *No, No, Nanette*. Jeanette played "Geraldine Gray, in love with Monty," the somewhat portly Mr. Lean. The songs were by Richard Myers with lyrics by Leo Robin, whose words would brighten a number of MacDonald films, including *Monte Carlo* and *One Hour with You*.

Jeanette sang "Dreams Never Die," "I'm a One Man Girl," "Montezuma," "In an Old Rose Garden," and the title song. (Miss Mayfield had only four numbers, including "Say it with a Uke" and "I'm a Red Hot Cradle Snatcher.") The story concerned a young man who must spend a million dollars in twenty-four hours so he can inherit seven million more. The show thrived in Philadelphia throughout August of 1926 and moved on to Boston, where Miss MacDonald got a new song, "Shake Me and Wake Me." In Boston, the small part of "Jane, a maid" was taken over by teenager Imogene Coca. However, a major upheaval apparently took place at this point, for the show limped into New York, not to Broadway but to Brooklyn. It played a week at the Werba Theatre without Jeanette and quietly died.

Next Jeanette took over the lead and title rôle in *Yes, Yes, Yvette*, concocted by producer H.H. Frazee, who had produced the highly successful *No, No, Nanette*. Frazee repeated the pattern of *Nanette* by sending *Yvette* on a lengthy pre-Broadway tour. *Nanette* had been such a hit on the road that a "road-company road company" spun off and was touring before the show ever saw the lights of Broadway. *Yes, Yes, Yvette* was out on the road for more than a year, drawing warm notices, but when it finally reached the Great White Way on October 3, 1927, the critics turned thumbs down. It ran only forty performances at the Sam Harris Theatre. Jeanette played Yvette Ralston and sang songs by Philip Charig and Ben Jerome with lyrics by Irving Caesar: "My Lady," "How'd You Like To?" and the title song. The cast included young Jack Whiting and veteran Charles Winninger, who left the show just before it folded to create the rôle of Captain Andy in *Show Boat*.

Jeanette was finally a star—in a flop. Her steady progression always seemed to be marked by defeats that would have slowed down a less dedicated performer. Three steps forward, one step back. (Of course, if *Yes, Yes, Yvette* had been a hit along with Gershwin's *La, La, Lucille*, we might still be getting sequels like *Fie, Fie, Francine* and *Wow, Wow, Wanda*.)

Most reviewers were kind, but Goldsmith of the *New York Times* gave Jeanette her first pan: "As for Miss MacDonald, one finds some difficulty in understanding the furor she created among the continental [i.e., Midwest] reviewers. She has, to be sure, a stunning figure, a pretty face and bright hair. She is graceful and pleasant, but her voice has been impaired by a too-long exposure to the rigors of the two-a-day, and she gives full rein to an unfortunate tendency to act coy. If the horrid truth be told, she rolls her eyes!"

J.J. Shubert spotted Jeanette in *Yes, Yes, Yvette*, and she was cast in *The Studio Girl*, a musicalization of George DuMaurier's novel, *Trilby*. Press releases were sent out, but she couldn't get out of her contract with Frazee and the show opened in New York without her.

The Shubert brothers then signed her and sent her on a brief hinterlands tour in a show called first *Sweet Daddy* and then *One Sunny Day* before it settled into the Imperial Theatre as *Sunny Days* on February 8, 1928. It was a musical version of *A Kiss in a Taxi*, which had graced Broadway two years earlier with Claudette Colbert in Jeanette's rôle. The music was derivative, with reviewers citing similarities to recent hits, but Jeanette was well received.

"They have put the dainty Jeanette MacDonald in the part of the shop girl to dance buoyantly and to sing with the best voice in the company," Brooks Atkinson of the *New York Times* stated. The story revolved around a Parisian banker played by Frank McIntyre, who carries on his philandering using the name of his puritanical bookkeeper. Also in the cast was Lynne Overman, a comedian with a loose, laconic, laid-back style. He too "went Hollywood" and provided comic interest

Circa 1928.

in a number of late 1930s and early 1940s musicals.

Jeanette as "Ginette" landed the banker after an evening dominated by the fancy hoofing of Carl Randall, but she managed to sing "Ginette," "Really and Truly," "So Do I," and "Trample Your Troubles," with music by Jean Schwartz and lyrics by Clifford Grey. *Sunny Days* ran 101 performances and went out on tour.

Apparently the increased stature of her rôles plus a contract with the Shuberts made more elegant living quarters a necessity, because she moved in 1928 to a brand new apartment house on 55th Street at 6th Avenue, convenient to the theatre district and complete with canopy and doorman. The building was torn down in the 1960s, along with Joseph Urban's exquisite Ziegfeld Theatre next door and an office building perpetrated on the site. (A wise man has said that we will be truly civilized when theatre lobbies contain small plaques announcing that an office building once stood on the spot.)

Her next show, *Angela*, was a musical reincarnation of *The Royal Family* (not to be confused with *The Royal Family of Broadway*, a takeoff on the lives of the Barrymores). The story, by Captain Robert Marshall, dated back thirty years and told of Princess Angela (Jeanette MacDonald), who must marry an odious King (Eric Blore, later prominent in Astaire-Rogers films) to save the kingdom. Then everyone finds out her real love is actually the missing Prince.

Under the titles *The Queen's Taste* and *The Right Girl*, it toured during the fall and opened as *Angela* at the Ambassador Theatre on December 3, 1928 to terrible reviews. It barely survived through the New Year for forty performances. The large cast also included future film personality Alison Skipworth (see *Oh, For a Man*). "Miss MacDonald brought the only pleasing voice to the comedy and sang pleasantly whatever was set before her," wrote Brooks Atkinson in the *New York Times*. Her songs by Alberta Nichols and Mann Holiner were "Love is Like That," "I Can't Believe It's True...Maybe So," and "You've Got Me Up a Tree."

During the run of *Angela*, film star Richard Dix saw Jeanette and wanted to sign her for his upcoming film, *Nothing But the Truth*, a film version of *Yes, Yes, Yvette*. The Shuberts were never given to generous gestures, and Jeanette couldn't get out of her contract. The film eventually featured Helen Kane, the boop-a-doop girl, plus Berton Churchill (*Sweethearts*) and Ned Sparks (*42nd Street*).

It is intriguing to speculate on what might have happened if Jeanette had made her first picture with Richard Dix. Would her personality have complemented Dix's casual, sardonic style? Would she have been noticed? Or would she have been indifferently received and allowed to return to Broadway, as were dozens of other delightful performers?

Jeanette MacDonald: Arch Street to Arc Lights

Boom! Boom! in 1928. The cast included Archie Leach, later Cary Grant.

After a week's rest, she was next put into *Boom! Boom!*, already touring out of town. Jeanette stepped into Ann Seymour's rôle. It opened on January 28, 1929 at the Casino, where Jeanette had been a chorus girl in *Tangerine* eight years earlier. The show was based on a play called *Oh, Mama*, which had starred Alice Brady (see *Broadway to Hollywood*, p. 166) three years earlier. It, in turn, was based on a French play, *Mademoiselle Ma Mère*. The mania for continental plays would continue until World War II effectively forced America to rely upon its own playwriting resources.

A number of *Angela* people contributed to *Boom! Boom!* including book writer Fanny Todd Mitchell and director George Marion, father of George Marion, Jr. (who created the unforgettable lyrics for Miss MacDonald's 1930 film, *Let's Go Native* and co-authored the screenplay for *Love Me Tonight* in 1932). The music for *Boom! Boom!* was by Werner Janssen with lyrics by Mann Holiner and J. Keirn Brennan. Miss MacDonald as "Jean" sang "What Could I Do?," "Be That Way," and "Messin' Around" to Stanley Ridges, while Frank McIntyre, her paramour in *Sunny Days*, contented himself with singing to the showgirls. A non-singing rôle was allotted to a twenty-four-year-old Englishman named Archie Leach, who later changed his name to the equally unlikely Cary Grant and headed west. (Also in the cast was an actor named Eddie Nelson, utterly unrelated to Nelson Eddy.) The plot concerned a shipboard romance between Jean and a nice young man. A year later she is forced into marriage and finds her husband is the lad's father. Act III and much singing solve everything.

The opening night of *Boom! Boom!* provided more challenges than merely remembering the just-learned lines and routines. Halfway through her first number, Jeanette noticed a stir in the audience and then a commotion that brought the performance to a standstill. A much-publicized naval hero, Captain George Fried, and members of his crew were shown into a box, and the audience rose to applaud them as the orchestra burst into the "Star Spangled Banner." With the National Anthem still ringing in her ears, Jeanette went back to her love scene unflustered and again won glowing praise, especially from young Brooks Atkinson. (Her costumes were by future-great Orry-Kelly.)

Following the Shubert pattern, *Boom! Boom!* ran a mild two months in New York and then set out for Detroit. From there it went to Chicago and the Four Cohans Theatre, where it was playing in May when Jeanette received a telegram. Her Paramount screen test for Richard Dix had been seen by no less a director than the world-famous Ernst Lubitsch. If she could sing, he wanted her for a rôle in his first sound film, *The Love Parade*, opposite the continental sensation, Maurice Chevalier.

This was a brilliant stroke of fortune (if the results of ten years of hard work can ever be termed luck), but not quite the honor we would like to think it was. Chevalier was the star and an unknown but competent actress was all that was needed. Who today remembers his leading lady in his first American film, *Innocents of Paris*? (It was Sylvia Beecher.)

Although Lubitsch had "discovered" fiery Pola Negri (or, as he humorously commented, perhaps vice versa) he was more noted for creating breathtakingly sensuous women from unpromising clay. His selection of Jeanette was an act of choosing raw material rather than a finished product. He got both a fledgling film performer who took to the new medium as if it had been designed for her and a seasoned theatre veteran who was not overwhelmed by the crazy place called Hollywood. In fact, she did not give up her New York apartment until she had completed five films and it looked as if she might stick around the movie capital a while longer.

And so, in June of 1929, as stock prices spiraled higher and higher, Jeanette MacDonald negotiated an end to her Shubert contract and boarded a train for the long journey to Hollywood.

2
They Sing!
Hollywood, Wired for Sound, Discovers the Musical

Hollywood in 1928–29 must have been like Paris during the French Revolution. The changes were so intense, day to day living so precarious, that mere survival became an accomplishment.

Intellectually, we can appreciate the problems that faced producers, directors, and technical people, but the real drama occurred in the lives of the actors and actresses who had used their bodies and faces to reach millions and now were told that they must talk. It was almost as if the ballet dancers of the world were suddenly instructed to sing and recite while performing an arabesque!

Stories abound of famous stars who couldn't talk and of careers that were drastically altered when a dramatic star was found to have a "comedy" voice (i.e., Eugene Pallette, ZaSu Pitts). It was an era of ironies. Who remembers today that Joan Crawford, Gary Cooper, and Garbo were silent stars? Yet, Clara Bow, who starred in more talkies than silents, is firmly enshrined in all hearts as the epitome of the silent flapper queen.

For the most part, sound simply added a new dimension to the types of films Hollywood had already perfected: dramas, comedies, mysteries, adventure yarns, westerns, love stories, and yes, even musicals. *Rose Marie*, *The Student Prince*, *The Merry Widow*, *Carmen*, and *La Bohème* among others had silent film versions (several in the case of *Carmen*), but musicals with music were entirely new.

The tremendous appeal of this new film form was so obvious that almost every major silent star except Garbo ultimately sang before the camera: Joan Crawford, Gloria Swanson, Janet Gaynor, Charles Farrell, Ramon Novarro, Clara Bow, Pola Negri, and even Buster Keaton. Most of them were pretty good or at least immensely likeable, but Hollywood wasn't content.

To "hedge their bet," they offered contracts to almost any Broadway or international singer with a reputation. Some of the stage's greatest talents were lured west with varying results. Three of the most effervescent ladies of the musical comedy—Gertrude Lawrence, Marilyn

1929, still in New York. Jeanette never bobbed her hair. To get a "flapper" look, she wore it in a flat bun at the back of her neck. *Courtesy Diane Goodrich.*

Miller, and Ethel Merman—lost much of their sparkle on the silver screen. The men fared better. Many, like Maurice Chevalier, Eddie Cantor, and Bing Crosby, seemed to have been born for the camera. A few Broadway lights like Ethel Shutta, Dennis King, and Hal Skelly flashed briefly and brightly across the screen and then returned to their beloved stage.

Of all the Broadway musical comedy stars who went to California in 1929, only Jeanette MacDonald survived the various musical cycles to remain a film star for twenty years.

The impact of the sound film also stripped Broadway of the cream of a whole generation of gifted actors—Claudette Colbert, Ann Harding, Spencer Tracy, James Cagney, Barbara Stanwyck, Fredric March, and Edward G. Robinson, to mention a few. Classical concert and opera circles were raided for performers. January 1930 saw the release of a film version of Lehar's *Gypsy Love*, retitled *The Rogue Song*, which introduced Metropolitan Opera baritone Lawrence Tibbett to film audiences. Two months later came *Song o' My Heart*, for which tenor John McCormack was paid $250,000 to play the leading role and sing a selection of Irish ballads. Grace Moore followed, making her screen debut for MGM in a highly fictionalized biography of Jenny Lind, *A Lady's Morals*.

The film musical, understandably, followed the three major formats of the musical stage. The revue form permitted each studio to introduce their now-talking stars to the public, and never have such concentrated entertainment riches reached American audiences in such a short time. Movie goers were treated to Norma Shearer, John Gilbert, and John Barrymore doing Shakespeare, Nancy Carroll tap dancing out of a giant satin slipper, skits with Jack Benny, Ted Lewis, and Bea Lillie, Clara Bow on a battleship, Winnie Lightner singing in a giant bathtub, and Buddy Rogers and Lillian Roth on a giant clock. Rin-Tin-Tin barked for the microphone, and Ruth Chatterton provoked tears in a touching scene about a French tart. Overall quality ranged from superb (*Paramount on Parade*) to turgid (MGM's *Hollywood Revue*).

The magnificent culmination of movie revues came in 1930 when Paul Whiteman hosted *The King of Jazz*. This all-Technicolor delight featured a very young Bing Crosby, the Whiteman band, Gershwin's "Rhapsody in Blue," and the most tremendous musical finale of any film ever made. The film revue has been used only spasmodically and with limited success since then, but it is nice to think that in its brief hour, it captured most of the best of Hollywood.

The second major musical film category was "musical comedy," the new type of stage entertainment that had been emerging by fits

They Sing! Hollywood Wired for Sound

and starts since *A Trip to Chinatown* in 1890, helped along by Jerome Kern's Princess Theatre productions in the late teens, and reaching puberty in the mid-1920s. (Someone has claimed the distinction between operetta and musical comedy is that musical comedy is performed in modern dress. This rule of thumb pretty much holds true, with intriguing exceptions such as *Street Scene* and *The King and I.*)

A number of Broadway musical comedy successes came to the screen in the first two years of sound: *Good News*; *No, No, Nanette*; *Rio Rita*; *Hit the Deck*; *Sally*; and *Sunny*, to name a few. Original musical comedies were created by the dozen, among them *The Broadway Melody* with songs by Arthur Freed and Nacio Herb Brown and *Sunny Side Up* with a DeSylva, Brown and Henderson score.

The super-naturalism of the screen medium was sympathetic to the contemporaneity of the musical comedy, but at the same time it emphasized the unlikelihood of ordinary people suddenly bursting into song. To solve this problem, a new musical film form was invented that is nearly impossible to reproduce on stage: the backstage musical. For all the glamour of the film world, Broadway would be the primary subject of musical films for years to come.

The third stage form to reach the screen intact was the operetta. It had rich visual appeal and heightened melodrama, both qualities that had marked some of the best films of the silent era. There was no reason to think they would not be successful in sound.

Operetta today is frequently regarded as being contemporary with the Gibson Girl era. Actually, the summit of operetta was reached in the jazz-mad 1920s. Sigmund Romberg's *The Desert Song* and *The Student Prince*, Rudolf Friml's *Rose-Marie* and *The Vagabond King*, Jerome Kern's *Show Boat* and Noel Coward's *Bitter Sweet*—all this music was fresh and new when sound films began.

The music was new, but most of the early screen adaptations bogged down hopelessly in ancient stage conventions, conventions that were so venerable that theatre audiences scarcely noticed them. The romantic leads stood stolidly, stage center, surrounded by chorus, to deliver their songs. The accompanying gestures were larger than life, big enough to reach across the orchestra pit to the farthest corners of the balcony. Then there were the comedy routines involving word play between the comic and soubrette, who usually stood "in one"—on the apron of the stage—while the scenery was being changed and the chorus got into their next costumes. Many directors used these necessary stage devices intact in the first film musicals. The very earnest 1929 film version of *The Desert Song* can reduce a contemporary audience to tears (or laughter).

Since casting gifted singers who could also act and do comedy was (and is) nearly impossible, stage librettists wisely wrote in two

An unusual Paramount publicity still of Jeanette, 1930.

A cameraman once told Jeanette that being near-sighted made her eyes photograph better. *Courtesy Paramount Pictures*.

Jeanette poses with director Ernst Lubitsch and his cigar. When he took to calling her "Mac," she called him "Lu." When he switched to "Donald," she gave up. *Courtesy Paramount Pictures.*

sets of lovers: the stalwart operatic principals and the music-hall type second leads. This distinction was so great that many producers interpolated songs by Tin Pan Alley composers into Graustarkian operettas. Gershwin, Gus Kahn, Jerome Kern, and Irving Berlin all contributed songs to shows ostensibly composed by well-known operetta composers.

The early operettas, like their sister musical comedies, came to the movie houses clanking the chains of their stage origin. Direction by a Lubitsch or an original score by Rodgers and Hart could overcome this, but most early screen musicals clung helplessly to their stage ancestors. Even when the original plot was entirely abandoned, as in the Grace Moore-Lawrence Tibbett *New Moon* (1930), the nearly genetic traditions of the stage production were present.

1929 was Hollywood's first year "wired for sound." Each studio had committed itself to an all-out battle for the new talkie market. During 1928, most studios had issued sound films of some sort. Many of them were "monkey-gland" pictures, shot silent and then overhauled with a musical soundtrack and inserted dialogue sequences. Most, if not all, of these are forgotten today, except by film buffs.

The race was on. It was, as Dickens said of another revolution, the best of times and the worst of times. In just a few months, this incredible burst of creativity, of trial and error experimentation in a new medium, would be cut short by a worldwide depression. Until then, Hollywood was the most exciting, and terrifying, demanding and exhilarating place in the world to be, and right in the middle of it was the bright-haired singer from Broadway, Jeanette MacDonald.

The Love Parade

Paramount.
New York premiere November 19, 1929.
General release January 18, 1930.
Produced and directed by Ernst Lubitsch.
110 minutes.

French title: *Parade d'Amour* (Parade of Love)
Spanish title: *El Desfile del Amor* (Parade of Love)
German title: *Liebesparade* (Love Parade)
Swedish title: *Prins Gemålen* (The Prince Consort)

From the play *The Prince Consort* by Leon Xanrof and Jules Chancel. Film story: Ernest Vajda. Libretto: Guy Bolton. Editor: Merrill White. Photography: Victor Milner. Dialogue director: Perry Ivins. Art Director: Häns Dreier. Sound: Franklin Hansen. Songs: Victor Schertzinger, and Clifford Grey. Movietone Recording.

Maurice Chevalier (Count Alfred Renard)
Jeanette MacDonald (Queen Louise)
Lupino Lane (Jacques)
Lillian Roth (Lulu)
Edgar Norton (Major domo)
Lionel Belmore (Prime Minister)

Albert Roccardi (Foreign Minister)
Carl Stockdale (Admiral)
Eugene Pallette (Minister of War)
E.H. Calvert (Sylvanian Ambassador)
Russell [Russ] Powell (Afghan Ambassador)
Margaret Fealy (First Lady in waiting)
Virginia Bruce (Lady in waiting)
Josephine Hall (Lady in waiting)
Rosalind Charles (Lady in waiting)
Helene Friend (Lady in waiting)
Yola d'Avril (Paulette)
André Cheron (Paulette's husband)
Winter Hall (Priest)
Ben Turpin (Cross-eyed lackey)
Anton Vaverka (Cabinet minister)
Albert De Winton (Cabinet minister)
William von Hardenburg (Cabinet minister)
Adolph Faylauer (Noble at opera)
Jean Harlow (Extra in theatre audience and also in box at left)

Oscar nominations:
   Best Picture
   Best Actor: Maurice Chevalier
   Best Director: Ernst Lubitsch
   Best Cinematography: Victor Milner
   Best Interior Decoration: Häns Dreier
   Best Sound Recording: Franklin Hansen

French version: A silent film was, by its nature, an international medium. Titles in any language could be inserted to represent the dialogue. But with the coming of sound, talkies faced a huge dilemma. How to speak everyone's language? European markets were essential for the continued prosperity and growth of Hollywood. For *The Love Parade*, which obviously would have this problem (still unsolved today), it was addressed with a "French version," *Parade d'Amour*, that incorporated the musical numbers in their entirety, plus some dialogue sequences in French that were either dubbed or reshot by Chevalier and MacDonald. The rest of the film employed titles for dialogue, as in *The Jazz Singer*, which was still enjoying tremendous popularity in France. *Variety* wrote, "French version of the Chevalier picture is nothing to write home about. Reproduction was thin and tinny in the musical numbers, and the dialogue had been cut in favor of titles in French, the half-and-half version being very unsatisfactory. Song numbers came through well, however....Business is sensational."

Ernst Lubitsch is universally acknowledged to be a great film director. This is unusual because he created no innovative techniques and, in America, directed no mammoth epics. His only contribution to the screen was *style*. Many of the best "sophisticated" comedies of the late silent era were obvious efforts to match the appeal and panache of his films. Lubitsch worked so closely with his scriptwriters that all his films bear the hallmark of the Lubitsch wit. One of his more daring achievements was *Lady Windermere's Fan*, in which Lubitsch substituted his own trademark visual epigrams for Oscar Wilde's famous verbal ones—successfully.

Sheet music cover. *Courtesy Pierre Guinle.*

The Love Parade

Queen Louise of Sylvania (Jeanette) bathes, attended by her ladies in waiting, including Virginia Bruce (rear, second from left).

His German-Jewish theatre origins are often apparent in European settings and operetta-like plots. He had, in fact, directed the silent version of *The Student Prince*. However, there was something definitely Gallic in his humorous cynicism for the foibles of man, especially man in pursuit of woman. His ingenious ability to convey a complex, frequently sexual, image with a simple, everyday (and uncensorable) gesture became known as "the Lubitsch touch."

In the first year of sound, directors as well as actors found themselves working in an entirely new medium. Many of the better ones needed two or three pictures before evolving the basic techniques, the "language" that would be the sound film. Not Lubitsch. His first sound film bursts on the screen full born. With Lubitsch touches for the ear as well as the eye, *The Love Parade* is as enjoyable today as it was in 1929.

Admittedly, sound film techniques were progressing at astonishing speed. The stationary camera, immobile in a booth—immortalized in *Singin' in the Rain*—still existed, but directors and technicians were at work day and night devising new methods of recording sound while camera and actors were in motion. Some truly incredible camera work appears in late 1929 and, within two years, the camera regained the mobility of the late silent era.

One of the first attempts to liberate the camera (and save money) was to shoot scenes without dialogue on silent film and then intercut them with sound sequences. This was practical when the few sound cameras in existence were

The queen scolds Count Alfred (Maurice Chevalier) for his scandalous doings in Paris and then invites him to dine. Dialogue captions were a charming feature of early stills. This one reads, "It would be the most delightful experience of my life."

being rented around the clock and a studio might not have access to one when needed. But it produced a primitive effect when characters entered in dead silence and then the resumption of sound-film hiss was heard just before they spoke. It was even more disconcerting when the silent sequences were shot at slower speed so that the inserts had a comic speeded-up look.

Lubitsch, however, uses silent footage to devastating effect for an audible Lubitsch touch during the telling of a presumably naughty story. We presume it is, though the camera cuts away to outside the window just as the denouement is reached so we cannot hear, evoking more laughter than any punch line could.

The ladies in Lubitsch films were the European male's Ideal Woman. They were beautiful and displayed as much of their beauty as possible. They were cunning but never intelligent. They could experience great distress but never pain. They were willing and even enthusiastic sex objects and needed only the establishment of

The Love Parade

the superiority of a particular male to end their resistance. Thereafter, they became his devoted slave. Small wonder that America's male population loved Lubitsch heroines.

Jeanette MacDonald's first film appearance under Lubitsch's direction established her as a major movie personality and typed her as a sophisticated sex queen. Her appearance in lingerie was a high point of nearly every film she made until *Naughty Marietta* in 1935.

As a European, Lubitsch's taste in women tended to the *zaftig*. Indeed, the heroines of his German films must be classed as ample. When he saw the slender Miss MacDonald, he ordered her to gain weight. During the shooting, milkshakes were handed to her at every opportunity until she acquired the plump sleekness that looked good in lacy "step-ins."

The Love Parade opens with a pair of male hands turning the pages of a smart French magazine behind the credits. So that there is no doubt where we are, a line of chorus dancers appears, kicking away between giant champagne bottles as "P-A-R-I-S" flashes overhead.

It is the city of love, and Jacques (Lupino Lane), in valet's livery, is enthusiastically preparing for an intimate dinner. He sets the table, describing each step in "Champagne," then whips the tablecloth from beneath the china, flowers, and candles, and does a comic exit.

Behind the bedroom doors of the luxurious suite, a fierce argument is heard in French. Count Alfred Renard (Maurice Chevalier) appears, followed by Paulette (Yola d'Avril), who is furiously brandishing a fancy garter. Alfred gestures that it must be hers, but she raises her skirts, revealing that she has two already. She pulls a tiny gun from her purse, but they are interrupted by a pounding on the door. Her husband! There is only one thing a lady can do. She shoots herself.

Alfred and her husband (André Cheron) stand frozen. Then the husband seizes the gun and revenges his wife by shooting Alfred. A puzzled look comes over Alfred's face. He pats his chest tentatively, then shakes his head. The bullets are blanks. He and the husband kneel beside Paulette who, by this time, is watching the proceedings with some interest. The husband is overjoyed to get his straying lamb back and covers her with kisses.

They reconcile and are ready to go when he notices that her dress is undone. Several moments go by as he fumbles with the tiny hooks. Finally, in exasperation, she flounces over to Alfred, who expertly finishes dressing her. The couple depart and Alfred starts to toss the pistol and garter into a drawer already full of similar souvenirs. He is interrupted by the Sylvanian ambassador (E. H. Calvert), who tells him this scandal will be his last in Paris. As ambassador, he is ordering his military attaché

Alfred weds the queen, but his wedding night is soon disrupted by a 400-gun salute. (Jeanette hated the false eyelashes worn by all film actresses and quietly removed them after several days of shooting. Lubitsch noticed that she suddenly looked better, and she never wore them again.)

back to Sylvania by the first train as punishment. "My wife has told me *everything*," he comments darkly.

"I think," gulps Alfred, "I'd better take the first *airplane*." Jacques begs to accompany his master to Sylvania, where his stories of the Frenchman and the farmer's daughter will be new. Alfred disconsolately consents. He steps out onto the balcony overlooking the twinkling lights of Paris and sings farewell to the ladies of Paris: "Paris, Stay the Same." From the servants' quarters, Jacques reprises the song to the maids in the nearby windows and, finally, from the attic, Alfred's bulldog serenades the sorrowing canines in the bushes below.

We now cut to Sylvania where a busload of American tourists are yawning through a tour guide's description of the royal palace—until he mentions that it cost $110 million dollars. They rise as one to gape at its sudden splendor.

In a gilded bed in a magnificent palace bedroom, Queen Louise is awakened by the drone of an approaching airplane. We get our first screen glimpse of Jeanette MacDonald as she yawns and stretches sensuously in a revealing lace nightgown. With a secret smile, she tells her ladies-in-waiting of her "Dream Lover." (This charming waltz was used as background music in dozens of other Paramount pictures and was heard into the 1970s on Muzak in posh elevators.) The Queen's ladies in waiting, (Margaret Fealy, Virginia Bruce, Helene Friend, Rosalind Charles, and Josephine Hall) join her in the chorus. On the high note, she sweeps off to her bath. (NOTE: The bath sequence is a modified copy of an over-the-top scene in Lubitsch's *Die Austernprinzessin* [*The Oyster Princess*], 1919, in which he spoofs the *nouveau-riche* with a millionaire's daughter who descends into an enormous marble bath, surrounded by a dozen attendants.)

Chest-deep in bubbles in a sunken marble tub, Louise is irritated by her ladies' subtle references to her possible marriage. Marriage! Marriage! That's all she hears! Outside, the band strikes up the wedding march. Didn't she tell the conductor never to play the wedding march again? But this is a *new* conductor, she is told. The old one is getting *married*. Louise splutters her rage into a soapy sponge.

In her council room, she learns that her cabinet has given up all negotiations for her marriage. She is first relieved, then irritated. They hasten to explain that finding someone to be her husband is...rather difficult. He would not be a king, after all, only a prince consort. Prince consorts have nothing to do. That is, they have something to do, but they also have *nothing* to do.

Louise indignantly cites her various charms, ending by displaying the most perfect legs in Sylvania. "Thank you, Your Majesty," sighs an elderly councilman.

Outside, Count Alfred is nervously awaiting an audience. The Major Domo (Edgar Norton) advises him to say as little as possible. His French accent may irritate the Queen. How did he ever acquire such an accent? Count Alfred begins a fascinating tale of a French doctor's wife. This is the scene where, at the crucial moment, the camera cuts outside the palace and through the window we silently watch the Major Domo enjoying the punch line. Count Alfred's fears return when the entire cabinet pours out of the council room, fleeing the Queen's rage. Things do not look good.

The Count is ushered in and stands at attention while the Queen reads a confidential report of his scandalous doings, puffing furiously on Miss MacDonald's only screen cigarette. She smiles. Alfred smiles. She giggles. Alfred giggles. She scowls. Alfred cringes. She disappears behind the report in a cloud of smoke. Suddenly she slams the report down on the table and dashes from the room—to a nearby mirror where she eagerly powders her nose and pats her hair. Gravely, she reappears. She understands that he has been seriously involved with a woman. "No," smiles Alfred, "with *several*."

The hardworking crew pose for a group photo with (left to right) Lupino Lane, Ernst Lubitsch, Jeanette, and Maurice Chevalier.

As punishment, she decides that he shall grow a beard. Count Alfred assures her that he looks terrible in a beard, not dashing as she happily concedes she had anticipated. He has a better punishment to suggest: that he be attached to her personal service, day and night. She is outraged—"You call *that* a punishment"—and invites him to dinner. In a charming duet, he assures her he will do "Anything to Please the Queen."

The palace clock strikes eight, and interested parties gather to observe the momentous occasion. The faithful valet Jacques takes up a post on the terrace where he is joined by Lulu (Lillian Roth), the Queen's maid. He starts to tell her the story of the Frenchman and the farmer's daughter, but Lulu stops him. "But I am the Frenchman." "You are not." "How do you know?" "*I* am the farmer's daughter."

The cabinet gathers in the garden to discuss Alfred's eligibility as a prince consort. It seems his great-grandfather was the illegitimate son of one king and his grandmother was the sweetheart of another. "I had no idea he came from such a distinguished family," murmurs the Minister of War (Eugene Pallette).

The ladies in waiting are outside the dining room keyhole. Jacques and Lulu climb to a nearby tree branch for a better view. We follow the progress of the dinner through the excited

The Prince Consort shows up at the opera to save Sylvania's Wall Street loan before he leaves for Paris to file for divorce. He happily ogles the ballerinas, knowing the Queen dare not cause a scene.

faces and comments of the onlookers. Thus we learn that the Queen laughs, drinks, dines, and finally beckons Alfred to follow her into her boudoir, closing the door behind. "Heaven save the Queen!" cries Jacques and topples backward from his perch.

In her boudoir, the Queen suggests that the Count forget she is a Queen. What would he do if she were a mere woman and he were meeting her for the first time? Nervously, he swallows his glass of brandy, then takes her hand and tenderly kisses the palm. "Oh, but if it's like this at first—what can be left for later?"

"*Plenty*," he assures her. He tells her that she surpasses all other women in his life: "My Love Parade." Louise joins him in song and then in a surge of emotion, he kisses her long and gently. She is stunned, afraid. Then trembling, she orders him to go. He refuses. "Go, now...Alfred!" "Yes...Louise!" he cries, striding exultantly from the room.

In joyous confusion, she leans against the piano, hitting the keys. Suddenly the waiting courtiers hear the Queen singing "Dream Lover." Her search is ended. Their voices join hers in a triumphant duet that evolves into the wedding march.

Count Alfred is being dressed by Jacques for his wedding. He is unnerved to find that one of his medals depicts a cross-eyed king. Whenever he has seen a cross-eyed man, he confides, something terrible has happened. The door opens and a cross-eyed lackey (silent comedy star Ben Turpin) announces that the Queen is ready.

In the throne room, the Major Domo pounds the floor with an enormous staff to announce the entrance of the Queen. In an exquisite gown and pearl tiara, Queen Louise is escorted down a grand staircase by numerous pages and trainbearers, followed by her ladies-in-waiting.

Then the Major Domo taps the floor with a tiny staff to announce the entrance of Count Alfred. All goes smoothly until the clergyman (Winter Hall) asks Alfred if he will be "an obedient and docile husband." There is silence. The cabinet members fidget. The Afghan ambassador (Russell Powell), who disapproves of women dominating men, smirks. Louise implores Alfred with her eyes. He melts. "I do." Everyone breathes again. "I now pronounce you wife and man," intones the clergyman.

The couple's wedding night is interrupted by cannon fire outside the window. Alfred is completely disconcerted, but Louise is transfixed: "Our bridal music!" The cannons fire and recoil, fire and recoil, through the night.

In the garden, Lulu is equally transported. She urges Jacques to make it a double wedding, pointing out the joys of non-noble love: "Let's Be Common." They do one of the funniest and most charming dance duets on film. This delightful sequence emphasizes how wasteful Hollywood was not to make more use of these superb performers.

Four weeks have passed and Alfred's joy in doing "something but nothing" is starting to wane. Louise is busy all day, meeting with cabinet members and reviewing her troops, which she does stirringly to music: "March of the Grenadiers." (This courtyard set was much used at Paramount, and Lubitsch skillfully mixes long shots from an earlier silent film showing the courtyard filled with soldiers and footage of Jeanette and twenty or so of her guard.) Louise returns home to find Alfred sulking and attempts to cheer him up. After the foreign loan is arranged, she will take him to Vienna and buy him some nice new uniforms.

Protocol prevents Prince Alfred from taking any part in the government, although he is full of ideas and plans. The final insult comes when he learns that he can't even eat breakfast without his wife's permission. He stalks off to the palace garden to dine on green apples and accept the consolation of his little bulldog. The dog is the only one in the palace who looks up to him. He sings of his tribulations in "Nobody's Using It Now," which is somewhat confusing since "it" is the only thing anyone *is* using.

> I've sown wild oats,
> I have indeed.
> But now that I've stopped sowing them,
> I'm going to seed.
> (Copyright Famous Music Corp.)

The cabinet informs Queen Louise that unless she and Alfred appear at the opera that night with happy smiles to demonstrate their marital bliss, Sylvania's Wall Street loan is in danger. Without it, they are broke.

Alfred bursts in on the meeting. He has more than a smile to save the country. He has a budget. Protocol prevents anyone from reading it, however, and Louise must go along with the cabinet plan. Alfred is ordered to appear that night in full uniform and in the very best of humor. "If Your Majesty had not already commanded me to smile," he cries bitterly, "I would laugh!" The door slams behind him and his laughter echoes down the hall.

The servants have taken sides in the rift, the women siding with the Queen and the men with the Prince. Lulu and Jacques lead each faction in song: "The Queen is Always Right," and end in a knock-about dance on the kitchen table.

The fatal hour approaches. Alfred appears in a traveling suit. He is leaving at once for Paris. He will attend the opera "only with soldiers and handcuffs."

"Alfred!" Louise wails, but he is gone. She sinks into a chair, alone and weeping. The strains of "Dream Lover" are heard, and she sings through her tears until another melody drowns it out. It is the "March of the Grenadiers." Her guard is waiting. Her duty is clear. Drying her tears and squaring her shoulders, she dons a white fox wrap and starts for the opera, down a grand staircase and through the marble halls (the lobby of the Los Angeles Biltmore) in a truly beautiful tracking shot, her heels clicking proudly, defiantly, to the music.

The opera audience murmurs knowingly when she steps into her box—alone. Louise sits in an agony of embarrassment. The Afghan ambassador leers. Suddenly there is silence.

Louise thinks Alfred has come to make up, but he only wants his pajamas. She must pursue him to his own bedroom on the other side of the castle before he forgets the divorce and takes command of his Queen.

Alfred has appeared behind her in full dress uniform. Everyone rises and cheers. (Jean Harlow can be seen as an extra both in the orchestra and in a close-up of ladies in a box—a busy lady.)

Alfred has come, he tells Louise, because he doesn't want to ruin the woman he once loved. Tomorrow he is leaving for Paris, where he will file for divorce as soon as the loan is secured. She tells him haughtily that he needn't have bothered to come, and he cheerfully gets up to go. She pulls him back fiercely. Very well, he says, he will stay if she begs him. It takes several tries before she can get the proper supplicating tone in her voice. Fully enjoying this change of status, Alfred ogles the ballerinas on stage until Louise threatens to tear the opera glasses from his eyes.

"If you were just a mere woman, you could make a scandal, but you can't," he chortles. "That's what you get for being a Queen." The Afghan ambassador gleefully offers the prince an even more powerful pair of glasses.

Back at the palace, Louise's sobs can be heard throughout the east wing. In the west wing, Alfred is gaily singing as he packs. Louise spots Alfred's satin pajamas hanging over a chair and bawls all the harder. Then she determines to act. She slips on a beaded chiffon robe with fur cuffs and heads for Alfred's room—across the grand hall, up the grand staircase, and along another hallway to his door.

"Alfred," she calls in a tiny voice. "A mouse is in my room." He tells her to call her soldiers. Her sobbing and his singing increase in volume as they try to drown each other out. Suddenly Alfred opens the door and marches cheerfully toward her room. Louise, amazed and then delighted, hurries ahead, doffs her robe and leaps into bed.

Alfred arrives, but it is only to retrieve his pajamas. She pursues him back across the grand hall, up the grand staircase and down the hall into his room. There she locks the door behind her and hides the key in her ample sleeve. "*Where* shall we live in Paris?" she asks tearfully. She will follow him wherever he goes.

Then there's no use for him to leave, he decides. But he must think of a suitable punishment. Louise has one to suggest: that he take command, not only of affairs of state but of her. She shall be attached to him from morning till "—er—from night till morning!"

"And you call that a punishment?"

"Yes...my *king!*"

They reprise "My Love Parade" as Alfred slowly draws the boudoir curtain and the orchestra rises in happy conclusion.

The Love Parade remains one of the most sophisticated (both structurally and esthetically) and enjoyable of the 1929 film musicals. It also proves that the more things change between men and women, the more they remain the same.

The Love Parade was Maurice Chevalier's second American film. It secured him a near-permanent place in Hollywood for many years to come. He was, in fact, almost the only star to continue making musicals during the period when the public stayed away from them *en masse* and movie marquees would advertise, "This is NOT a musical." His first American film, *Innocents of Paris* earlier in 1929, had been quite wooden, but the critics singled him out for praise. Although he was forty years old, Chevalier overwhelmed the screen with youthful vitality and raw sex appeal. As a child performer he had specialized in bawdy songs. The incongruity had shocked audiences into laughter and applause. But as he grew older, he found people no longer laughed at a mature performer singing the same songs, so he perfected the glance, the shrug, the smile, the roll of the eyes that, like the "Lubitsch touch," could say everything and yet nothing. It is a near-tragedy that sound film wasn't perfected fifteen years earlier, so that more of this magnificent performer's early years could have been saved for us.

The Love Parade

The Swedish name for *The Love Parade* translates as *The Prince Consort. Courtesy Anna Michalik.*

English comedian Lupino Lane, a close relative of Ida Lupino, had appeared in several American silents, among them D.W. Griffith's *Isn't Life Wonderful* (1924), and a number of silent comedy shorts. 1929 saw an "English invasion" in Hollywood similar to the "German invasion" of talent in the mid 1920s. English actors could speak. They had, without exception, a thorough stage background.

One of the first quandaries facing the early sound film was, "What is American speech?" What regional accents would be accepted by a country not yet homogenized by radio and television? Because Hollywood drew so heavily on the New York stage, the accents most commonly heard that first year were British, New York, and Brooklyn, with a generous dash of Yiddish. A number of careers changed course because of accents. Johnny Mack Brown's rich Alabama drawl reduced him from sophisticated playboy rôles to farm boys, cowhands, and an occasional Texas oil millionaire. Reginald Denny, on the other hand, could no longer portray heartland Americans when the microphone revealed his elegant British diction.

After a brief flurry, isolationism set in and most British actors departed or stayed on to do character rôles. Ronald Colman, Leslie Howard, and Herbert Marshall were among the few surviving leading men. Lupino Lane made a few more musicals and then returned to a film and stage career in England.

There is a story that Lillian Roth was brought to Hollywood to play Queen Louise, but when Lubitsch heard her Brooklyn accent, he had a comic rôle written for her instead. Lubitsch spoke English like a "Dutch" comic and probably wouldn't have known an accent if it bit him, but he would never have picked the zany comedienne with the winning kewpie doll face for his frosty Queen. The comic pair of lovers was a standard operetta fixture and much of the film's texture depends on the contrasts between the two couples. Like Chevalier, Lillian Roth exhibited great vitality and charm. She did a string of Paramount musicals, including Miss MacDonald's next feature, *The Vagabond King*, but her career would be cut short by personal conflicts.

Reviews

While Chevalier drew most of the acting raves (Lubitsch rated the most space in almost every review), Jeanette was not overlooked in her screen debut. Richard Watts of the *New York Herald Tribune* called it "an entirely winning performance....On the stage Miss MacDonald was regarded as a competent player and singer, but nothing in her past work has given reason for anticipating the skillful and alluring performance she brings to *The Love Parade*. Blessed with a fine voice, a sense of comedy and a definite screen personality, she registers an individual success that makes her future in the new medium an enviable one."

Mordaunt Hall of the *New York Times* attended the premiere in New York City and commented: "Miss MacDonald sings charmingly. In fact, the microphone takes better to her singing than to her speaking and, as she was there [at the premiere] last night and said a few words to the spectators, it was quite evident that the fault lay with the treacherous microphone and not with Miss MacDonald's diction." Amidst the surfeit of musicals that were bombarding the screen, Hall found *The Love Parade* "a delightful entertainment...one that makes the spectator hopeful that the silly diatribes that have so recently been seen on the screen will be cast in the background for this sophisticated, intelligent fun."

Recordings (See Discography for further information)

"Dream Lover" (Jeanette MacDonald)
"March of the Grenadiers" (Jeanette MacDonald)
"Mon Cocktail d'Amour" (My Love Parade) (Chevalier)
"My Love Parade" (Chevalier)
"Nobody's Using It Now" (Chevalier)
"Personne Ne S'en Sert, Maintenant" ("Nobody's Using It Now") (Chevalier)
"Paris, Je T'aime d'Amour" ("Paris, Stay the Same") (Chevalier)
"Paris, Stay the Same" (Chevalier)

Music in the Film

All music is by Victor Schertzinger and all lyrics by Clifford Grey, except ballet music as indicated. In listing performers after each title, "and" denotes a genuine duet, while commas between names indicate a sequence of singers.

Overture: "My Love Parade," "Champagne," "My Love Parade," "Dream Lover"
"Champagne" (Lupino Lane)
"Paris, Stay the Same" (Chevalier, Lane, Jiggs the dog barking)
"Dream Lover" (MacDonald with Fealey, Bruce, Friend, Hall, Charles)
"Anything to Please the Queen" (MacDonald and Chevalier)
"My Love Parade" (Chevalier, MacDonald)
"Dream Lover" reprise (MacDonald, chorus)
"Sylvania's Queen" (chorus)
"Let's Be Common" (Lane and Roth)
"March of the Grenadiers" (MacDonald and male chorus)
"Nobody's Using It Now" (Chevalier)
"The Queen is Always Right" (Roth and Lane with chorus)
"Dream Lover" reprise (MacDonald sobbing), INTO:
"March of the Grenadiers" reprise (male chorus)
"Valse Tatiana" ballet - O. Potoker
Finale: "My Love Parade" reprise (Chevalier and MacDonald)

The Vagabond King

Paramount.
New York premiere February 18, 1930.
Released April 19, 1930.
Produced and directed by Ludwig Berger.
Retakes directed by Ernst Lubitsch.
104 minutes.
Two-strip Technicolor.

French version title: *Le Roi des Vagabonds* (King of the Vagabonds)

Based on the 1925 hit operetta *The Vagabond King* by Rudolf Friml, William H. Post, and Brian Hooker, which was, in turn, adapted from an earlier stage version of the novel *If I Were King* by Justin Huntly McCarthy. Adaptation and dialogue: Herman J. Mankiewicz. Photography: Henry Gerrard and Ray Rennahan. Art Director: Häns Dreier. Editor: Merrill White. Color Consultant: Natalie Kalmus. Wardrobe: Travis Banton. Sound: Franklin Hansen. Movietone Recording.

The Vagabond King

If I Were King and its various descendants offer a highly romanticized biography of the 15th-century French poet, François Villon. A non-musical stage version of *If I Were King* opened in New York in 1901. The operetta version opened at the Casino Theatre on September 21, 1925, starring Dennis King as Villon with Carolyn Thomson as Katherine. *If I Were King* was filmed by Fox in 1920 with William Farnum and by Paramount in 1938 with Ronald Colman and Frances Dee. John Barrymore appeared in another film biography of the poet François Villon, *The Beloved Rogue* (United Artists), in 1927. The operetta was filmed again in 1956 for Paramount with Kathryn Grayson and Oreste. (Brian Hooker, the lyricist, is best known for his superb translation of Edmund Rostand's *Cyrano de Bergerac*.)

Dennis King (François Villon)
Jeanette MacDonald (Katherine de Vaucelles)
O.P. Heggie (King Louis XI)
Lillian Roth (Huguette)
Warner Oland (Thibault)
Arthur Stone (Olivier the barber)
Thomas [Tom] Ricketts (Astrologer)
Lawford Davidson (Tristan, the Major Domo)
Christian J. Frank (Executioner)
Elda Voelkel (Girl)
Dorothy Davis (Brunette)
Thora Waverly (Brunette)
Cecile Cameron ("Raven Hair")
Jean Douglas (Blonde)
Eugenia Woodbury (Blonde)
Rae Murray (Blonde)
Blanche Saunders (Blonde)
Frances Waverly (Blonde)
Gloria Faith (Page)
Theresa Allen (Page)
Sue Patterson (Page)
Virginia Bruce (Tavern wench)

Foreign language versions: After the generally poor reception for musicals dubbed into other languages, *The Vagabond King* was issued in foreign markets as a silent film with intertitles and background music during dialogue sequences plus the original American soundtrack during songs. (*The Rogue Song* with Lawrence Tibbett had enjoyed considerable popularity overseas in this form.) The French version was called *Le Roi des Vagabonds*. Later a German language version was dubbed, using German actors.

Dashing Dennis King repeated his stage rôle as the even more dashing Friml hero. King's impressive Broadway career included the starring roles in Friml's *Rose-Marie* and *The Three Musketeers*, Kern's *Show Boat*, and Rodgers and Hart's *I Married an Angel*. *Rose-Marie* and *Angel* became film vehicles for MacDonald and Eddy.

Restoration: *The Vagabond King*, like many of the 1929/1930 musicals, was filmed in two-strip Technicolor. For almost fifty years, only dark, murky black-and-white prints of *The Vagabond King* were available, and film historians had pretty much written off the film as a stiff and stodgy adaptation of the stage operetta. A few scenes in the original two-strip Technicolor were shown occasionally by the Museum of Modern Art in New York, hinting at visual glories, but the complete color print at the U.C.L.A. Film Archive had become shrunken and too brittle to screen. It was only a matter of time before the nitrate stock turned to powder or goo.

Before time ran out, U.C.L.A. managed to allocate funds to preserve the only known existing print

The king's niece, Katherine (Jeanette), is rescued by the vagabond poet, François Villon (Dennis King), when villains try to kidnap her. The pale yellow of her satin cloak and Villon's dark red tunic stand out against the blue-green light of the Paris dusk. The film is filled with such colorful "stained glass" tableaus.

by rephotographing each frame, one at a time. This restored print was screened on 7/21/91 at U.C.L.A., and for the first time in many decades, audiences were able to appreciate the stunning color canvas created by Director Berger and Art Director Häns Dreier to support Friml's lush score. We discover what the grey blurs of the existing black-and-white prints concealed: the flickering reflections of torches on rough stone, the red explosions of battle, the shimmer of candlelight on gilt and jewels, and the intricate patterns of dancers in brocaded gowns. Each establishing shot is a superb composition of light, shade, and color. Seeing the restored *Vagabond King* elevates it from an historical curiosity to a viscerally exciting film.

Jeanette MacDonald's second film was as typical of the early musicals as *The Love Parade* was not. At first glance, it seemed to have everything going for it. *The Vagabond King*, a romantic musicalization of the life of the fifteenth-century poet, François Villon, had been a big hit on Broadway in 1925. Dennis King was lured to Hollywood to star in the rôle of the dashing poet-scoundrel that he created on the stage. The

The Vagabond King

score was one of Rudolf Friml's best, haunting and fresh to this day despite endless repetitions by amateur vocalists. A neater, more filmic script was fashioned by Herman J. Mankiewicz, and, best of all, the film would be in Technicolor.

Color films had existed from the birth of the motion picture, first in hand-colored prints and then in early Kinemacolor (1909) and Prizma Color (1916). Two-color Technicolor had been on the neighborhood movie screens for several years, mainly as special inserts and finales, but also in features like *The Black Pirate* (1926) with Douglas Fairbanks. Mid-1929 to mid 1930 saw seventeen complete Technicolor musicals, plus color musical sequences in many others.

The marriage of color and music was so perfect that, had there been no Depression, there might never have been another black-and-white musical. However, a color film cost more than three times what a black-and-white film did. Making quality prints was slow and difficult, so that it was hard to produce a large enough quantity to supply the smaller theatres. If the lab erred, colors would fluctuate during a scene. Two-color Technicolor required side-by-side cameras, photographing the same scene through red or green filters onto black-and-white film stock, then running the film through two dye baths, red-orange and blue-green. While a true blue or yellow could not be obtained, an astonishing range of tones could. Anyone who has ever been privileged to see a perfectly preserved color print of this period can testify to its beauty and dramatic excitement.

Tragically, the very nature of film, its unstable nitrate base, has brought about the loss of many early musical films. As sound techniques progressed rapidly in the early 1930s, these early, "primitive" films were relegated to storage where the nitrate began to deteriorate. When TV made a potential new market for some of these forgotten treasures, the studios found they had either cans of jelly or a black-and-white film with the color musical inserts past saving. Slowly, black-and-white copies are turning up and color prints are emerging from European film vaults where they were lovingly preserved, but much has been lost forever.

Ludwig Berger, director of *The Vagabond King*, was, like Lubitsch, another "German invader" of the 1920s. The popularity of his German silent, *The Waltz Dream* (1926), brought him to Hollywood, where he did two silents before directing his first sound film, *The Vagabond King*. He did one more American film, *Playboy of Paris* (1930) with Maurice Chevalier, and returned to Europe, where he continued doing musicals. He was no Lubitsch and both *The Vagabond King* and *Playboy of Paris* suffer from what may be either "Germanic heaviness" or the loss of fluidity that temporarily afflicted so many directors. (Interestingly, Lubitsch directed the 1931 American sound version of *The Waltz Dream,* called *The Smiling Lieutenant*, with Maurice Chevalier and Claudette Colbert.)

The Vagabond King camera is mostly immobile, but there are a few instances when it moves. François Villon scrambles over the rooves of Paris in a scene surpassing the same sequence in John Barrymore's silent Villon biography, *The Beloved Rogue*, three years earlier. There is a nice tracking shot of people swirling down a curved staircase in the outlaws' tavern, and the scenes of Paris on the march against the Burgundians are stirring. But there are also scenes where the principals are clearly hindered by a stationary mike. In one, Warner Oland stands 3/4 turned to the camera, addressing three cutthroats who mirror his posture on the other side of the screen. While they all gesture violently, no one moves a toe, so conscious are they of the camera and microphone. This is the type of scene that later films liked to spoof, and *The Vagabond King* abounds in them.

Dennis King came to Hollywood directly from his stage rôle of d'Artagnan in Friml's *The Three Musketeers,* to recreate his stage triumph

King Louis (popular character actor O.P. Heggie) plans an amusing torture for Villon, who has been singing seditious ditties. Katherine is the bait.

as François Villon. It is a stage performance in every sense, with no attempt made to play to the camera rather than the balcony. Perhaps Berger was too occupied with technical considerations or too in awe of the famous Mr. King to suggest altering what had been so successful on stage, or perhaps King was too nervous in the new medium to give up gestures and intonations that had already brought him acclaim. In any case, the performance is at once incredibly irritating and tremendously exciting.

Jeanette MacDonald was required only to sing, wear exquisite costumes (whose clinging lines make them closer to a 1930s nightclub than a Gothic palace), and intone her lines in the standard operetta speech of the day, an elaborate monotone that sounds like (and frequently is) the cue for a song. The stilted quality of her performance after her ease and warmth in *The Love Parade* is astonishing. If *The Vagabond King* had been her first and last picture, she would be forgotten today.

Lillian Roth at first seems miscast as the hoyden Huguette (who, in the stage version, wears men's clothes and has an affair with an effeminate courtier). However, she brings womanly depth to the rôle. Her haunting rendition of "Huguette's Waltz" and her death scene are dramatic high points of the film.

Warner Oland, later famous as the benign Charlie Chan (he was actually Swedish), continues in his early villain rôles as the evil Thibault. O.P. Heggie, who was a master at portraying kindly, avuncular characters, here attempts the amoral and crafty King Louis, mainly by squinting and cackling.

Behind the credits we see a dramatically lit Gothic archway. A title tells us that the Paris of Louis XI is a city surrounded by Burgundians and wolves. (Explanatory titles were a continuing feature of early sound films and are still resorted to occasionally even today to establish locale.)

The dregs of Paris are gathering in the cellar of the Tavern of the Vagabonds to forget their hunger, cold, and fear in wine and lechery. Through the noise and confusion comes a clear, strong voice. It is François Villon (Dennis King), sitting cross-legged on a planked table reciting a mocking diatribe against the king.

The king's soldiers interrupt his sport and he flees over the rooves of Paris to find sanctuary in nearby Notre Dame. (Although it is night, shafts of golden light stream down from the vaulted roof above.) Clutching his gritty cap in even dirtier fingers, he slips among the worshipers, thinking more of purses than prayers.

Suddenly as the choir voices rise in a beautiful hymn, he sees a vision. Behind the filigreed screen of a small chapel, a golden-haired lady in hooded satin cloak is lighting a candle. The lights seem to make a halo about

The Vagabond King

her head. She finishes her prayer and leaves. Enraptured, Villon follows—just in time to rescue her from three villains.

She is Katherine de Vaucelles (Jeanette), niece of the king. She thanks Villon and continues on her way, but he pursues her with flowery speeches. She suggests that courage rather than rich words are needed to save Paris. Where is the man that will dare all for France? If there were such a man, all her heart and all her love would be his.

Villon can't resist an offer like that. He follows her to the palace and scales a wall to catch a glimpse of her as she sings of the man who will save Paris and win her heart: "Some Day." He is moved to respond with a stirring musical version of the classic Villon poem, "If I Were King," written for the film.

The traitorous Grand Marshall of France, Thibault (Warner Oland), has promised the Burgundians to deliver the King's niece as a hostage. In the "mirror image" sequence described above, he berates his hirelings for being foiled by a single man. Perhaps, before their next try, they had better get rid of Villon.

On a castle battlement, Louis XI (O.P. Heggie) is consulting his astrologer (Thomas Ricketts), as his niece Katherine looks on. Of a more practical mind, she trains the astrologer's telescope on the Burgundian troops. The camera tracks in a complete circle, taking in the red camp fires that completely ring the city. The astrologer predicts that someone will come from the depths to save Louis's throne. Louis is astounded, for he has had a similar dream. In it, he was a pig rooting in the gutter, where he found a priceless pearl. This must symbolize the man he is looking for. But where will he find him? Where?

The Tavern of the Vagabonds is a riot of singing and dancing when Louis and his chamberlain, Tristan (Lawford Davidson), arrive, disguised as merchants. As luck would have it, Villon is leading the people in a decidedly uncomplimentary ballad, "What France Needs Is a King." Behind his cowl, Louis's eyes glitter with hate. Villon will hang—but not just yet.

Several of the "ladies" present, including Huguette (Lillian Roth), engage in a hair-pulling match for the favors of Villon. Graciously, he separates them and tells them of his new love, an angel he has seen in church. His poetic images are so eloquent that even Huguette forgets to be angry. Poetry is thirsty work, and Villon cadges drinks from the two "merchants" at a corner table. One of them questions Villon, who readily admits he'd make a better king than old Louis. "A patriot?" inquires the disguised Louis.

"Just a poor fool with a heart too big for his body," Villon rhapsodizes. He grows more and more eloquent in describing the life of a vagabond until, leaping on a table, he leads the crowd in the rousing "Song of the Vagabonds."

A rose garden provides a convenient spot for the love duet "Only a Rose." Jeanette had another name for this song.

To Louis's surprise, Grand Marshall Thibault arrives with a brigade of soldiers to arrest Villon. In the scuffle, Villon runs Thibault through. The king reveals himself and orders Villon taken to the palace prison. Louis will be revenged.

The stage is set for Villon's punishment. In a scene that is an actor's dream, he awakens from drugged slumber in a canopied bed to find himself washed, shaved, and dressed in an exquisite tunic. He stands before the mirror of his chamber in a scene at once heavily theatrical and utterly delightful. When groups of courtiers, pages, and chefs, all carefully rehearsed, come in to greet him, the wiliness of the gutter replaces the wonder of the poet in his eyes. Louis watches from a curtained balcony, enjoying the spectacle. Perhaps, however, Tristan has overdone it. "This is every beggar's dream of a royal awakening," Tristan assures him.

Villon learns that he is now the "Count of Montcorbier" and that, under his new appointment as Grand Marshall, he is to judge some vagabonds arrested the night before in a tavern riot. They are, of course, his friends. He glories in their awe of the new Grand Marshall, telling each some secret known only to Villon until they are convinced he is a wizard. Louis summons the Lady Katherine to his lofty hiding place to see this new Grand Marshall.

Huguette begs the Grand Marshall for news of Villon and is assured of his safety. Katherine recognizes the name of her rescuer and wants to plead for his release too, but Louis tells her there will be time enough later.

The vagabonds are released, and Louis descends to confront Villon. The King of France and the King of the Vagabonds face each other. Louis wonders if Villon still feels he'd make a better king. He offers him a choice. Villon can return to the gutter—or he can be king for seven days. At the end of that time, he will hang. Villon hesitates. A page announces that the Lady Katherine requests an audience with the new Grand Marshall. "I accept the hazard!" cries Villon.

It is the dead of winter, but fortunately there is a nearby garden with rose bushes in full bloom. There Katherine echoes Huguette's plea for the life of Villon. In his new guise, Villon again woos the lady with flowery speeches. He does not meet with refusal, but her heart is still set on a savior of France. He pledges to be that man and, as a token, she gives him "Only a Rose." (Because all songs in the film were recorded live on the set, with several cameras shooting at once, Miss MacDonald's close-ups include a small portion of Mr. King, who accidentally or deliberately leaned into the shot. Thus this number became known among her fans as "Only a Nose.")

A Burgundian messenger arrives at court to demand the surrender of Paris. Before the entire court, Villon answers his threats with poetic fervor: "When we who drink are dry, when we who glow are frozen, when we who eat are hungry, our answer to rebellious Burgundy will be the same!" He hurls the Burgundian banner at the herald's feet. Katherine realizes she has found her man. She stands on the grand staircase and reprises "Some Day" as the courtiers join her and the church bells chime the news of the savior of France.

Behind the Burgundian lines, the treacherous Thibault, very much alive, tells the Burgundians that he has failed to kidnap the King's niece. Before dawn, he will have a better prize for them—the King himself.

In the Tavern of the Vagabonds, Huguette is waiting for news of Villon. Several men offer to console her, but she wants none of them. She sings of her way of love in the haunting "Huguette's Waltz." Thibault arrives and recruits the willing vagabonds, including Huguette, to "free Villon" by capturing the new Grand Marshall.

Villon's seven days are up tomorrow, but the sword may claim him before the noose.

The Vagabond King

Tomorrow he rides into battle against the Burgundians, but tonight he tells Katherine of his love: "Love Me Tonight." A masquerade fête is held on this, his last night. Louis wonders that François doesn't fear his coming death. Villon replies that he is too happy just being alive. The courtiers are dancing with wild abandon when Huguette and Thibault slip in. Villon spots Thibault behind his monk's hood, but loses him in the snake-dancing throng. Another suspicious-looking monk passes and Villon grabs the tiny wrist. It is Huguette, who finally recognizes Villon without his beard. She tells him of Thibault's plan and Villon nods pensively.

Thibault sends word to the King that a new astrologer desires to speak with him. When the aged King shuffles in, they seize him, only to find they have Villon instead. In the ensuing struggle, Huguette throws herself in front of Thibault's sword to save Villon. The King and his soldiers arrive to capture the traitors, and Villon takes the dying Huguette in his arms. Many have loved her, she tells him, but only one ever took her heart. Cradling her limp body, he speaks her epitaph in the poetry of the original Villon:

The young and yare, the fond and fair.
Oh, God, where are the snows of yesteryear?

There are no more troops to fight the Burgundians. The Grand Marshall furiously orders that the prison doors be thrown open. As François Villon, he will lead the thieves, beggars, and women of the streets against the enemy. Lady Katherine witnesses his unmasking and shrinks from him in horror. With nothing to lose, Villon and the rabble of the streets surge to battle, singing the "Song of the Vagabonds." In a thrilling montage, we see them marching and fighting, the women taking up the crude weapons as their men fall. Villon is at their head, his vivid red tunic slashed until he is naked to the waist.

In Notre Dame, the nobility cower, waiting to learn their fate. Over their chants of "Miserere" comes the jubilant sound of the "Song of the Vagabonds." Villon, bloody but triumphant, leads his army of beggars into the square before the cathedral and drops the vanquished Burgundians' banners at Louis's feet. Villon is the hero of France.

The King has a problem. If he orders Villon's death, he will face a riot. If Villon lives, his popularity is a threat to King Louis. Villon solves the dilemma. In his own capacity as Grand Marshall, he orders himself hanged and then surrenders to the King's guard. The crowd is outraged and turns on the King.

The crafty Louis offers to spare Villon if someone else will step forward to take his place on the gallows. The crowd falls back, silent. "It

The earthy Huguette (Lilian Roth) in the Tavern of the Vagabonds. She loves Villon enough to die for him—and does. Despite her New York accent, Roth delivers the "Huguette Waltz" with heart-rending effectiveness. *Courtesy Ginny Sayre.*

is no news to me, Sire," Villon comments, "that men love the dear habit of living." To a tolling of bells and a dirgelike song, he is marched to the gallows.

But Katherine has heard of his fate. As the rope is placed around his neck, she rushes forward to offer herself in his place. The King cannot hang his own niece, and so Villon must go free. The lovers are reunited on the gallows. Tenderly, they embrace and pledge their love in "Only a Rose," as the entire city of Paris joins in and the sky behind them glows gold.

The Vagabond King was respectfully received by critics and public. The color and the music made any dramatic shortcomings seem less grievous, and there were enough stirring and amusing moments to cancel out some of the heavy staginess. Fortunately for Miss MacDonald, her next film but one would return her to the masterful hands of Ernst Lubitsch.

Reviews

Mordaunt Hall of the *New York Times* found the film "beautiful and often quite stirring" but "lethargic." He praised the efforts of director Berger but noted, "He has not succeeded in eliciting from Miss MacDonald much in the way of acting, and her enunciation never gives the slightest suspicion of belonging to the period.... She, however, sings charmingly."

Outside New York, critics were not so hard to please. Mildred Martin of the *Philadelphia Inquirer* called it "the most successful film operetta to be made so far." She found Berger's direction "outstanding," but Miss MacDonald "somewhat disappointing." She noted that "[MacDonald's] singing voice is pleasing, but her spoken lines are delivered self consciously."

Outlook Magazine liked the picture and predicted a battle between Dennis King and Lawrence Tibbett for future eminence in musical films. They did experience some discomfort, however, and assigned the blame accordingly: "The only real trouble with *The Vagabond King* is a completely blah performance by Jeanette MacDonald, the leading lady, who evidently thinks she is back on Broadway where you can run through musical comedy love scenes as though you were reciting Latin verbs. The movie public wants love scenes it can take seriously." It would not be the last time that Jeanette took the blame for a bad picture.

Recordings (See Discography for further information)

"Only a Rose" (MacDonald)
"If I Were King" (King)
"Song of the Vagabonds" (King)

Although one of the high points of the film is Lillian Roth's poignant delivery of "Huguette's Waltz," Roth's Paramount contract amazingly prohibited her from recording her successful Paramount songs! However, the song was recorded in 1955 by Susan Hayward, who played Roth in the film version of Roth's autobiography, *I'll Cry Tomorrow*.

Music in the Film

All music by Rudolf Friml and lyrics by Brian Hooker except where noted. In listing performers after each title, "and" denotes a genuine duet, while commas between names indicate a sequence of singers.

Overture: "Song of the Vagabonds" (male chorus)
"King Louie" (Dennis King) - by Sam Coslow, Newell Chase, and Leo Robin
"Mary, Queen of Heaven" (chorus) - by Coslow, Chase, and Robin
"Some Day" (MacDonald)
"If I Were King" (King) - by Coslow, Chase, and Robin
"What France Needs" (King, chorus) - by Robin and Chase

"Song of the Vagabonds" (King, chorus)
"Only a Rose" (MacDonald, King)
"Some Day" reprise (male chorus)
"King Louie" reprise (chorus), INTO:
"Huguette's Waltz" [also called "The Vagabond King Waltz"] (Roth)
"Love Me Tonight" (MacDonald and King)
"Nocturne" also called "In the Night" (chorus)
"Song of the Vagabonds" reprise (King and chorus)
"Death March" (Gene Wolff) - by Robin and Chase
Finale: "Only a Rose" (MacDonald and King with chorus)

Songs from the stage production that were used in the film are "Song of the Vagabonds," "Some Day," "Only a Rose," "Huguette's Waltz," "Love Me Tonight," and "Nocturne."

Paramount on Parade

Paramount.
A revue in 20 parts.
Released April, 1930.
101 minutes.
Two-strip Technicolor sequences.
(Jeanette was cut from release print)

In the first big year of sound, mid-1929 to mid-1930, every major studio put out a revue showing off its stars in the new medium. Paramount, with the best line-up of musical and comedic talent, produced the finest of this genre, *Paramount on Parade*. The vaudeville format let Paramount create versions in a variety of languages, interpolating sequences of performers popular in Scandinavia, France, Germany, Japan, and South America.

Amazingly, although dramatic stars like Clara Bow, Ruth Chatterton, and Gary Cooper turned out in the American version to warble before the microphones, and Chevalier, as the studio's top musical star, had three numbers, Jeanette is conspicuously missing.

Yet stills of her exist bearing the film's code number, sparking tantalizing rumors that she had emceed the Spanish version, *Galas de la Paramount*. However, her name did not appear in the extensive cast lists of this version, published in *Variety*. Recently, a print of *Galas* has turned up with nary a frame of Jeanette.

Until 1996, the only available prints of *Paramount on Parade* were missing the color sequences, each of which was a major musical number: "Sweeping the Clouds Away" with Chevalier; "Isidore the Toreador" with Harry Green; "Nichavo" with Dennis King," "Come Drink to the Girl of My Dreams" with an all-star cast; and "Torna a Surriento" with Nino Martini. (Fortunately, "Sweeping the Clouds" survived in a black-and-white version.)

Then the U.C.L.A. Film Archive reconstructed a nearly complete print, using new-found soundtrack recordings and color footage. (One scene has soundtrack only plus still photos, another has image only without sound.)

At the first public screening of the restored version, Nino Martini's gondola floated into view as he sang "Torna a Surriento" (Come Back to Sorrento). Instantly the theatre was filled with excited whispers: "It's *Jeanette!*" This rediscovered color footage reveals a long shot of Jeanette seated in the gondola, matching the existing still photo. However, when the camera cuts to a close-up, it is another actress who does nothing but smile at the singer.

Originally, the song had been a duet, but when Jeanette's part was cut (probably for time considerations), it is likely that Jeanette insisted on removing her image so she wouldn't appear to be a mere extra. This was easy to do in the close-ups, but it was too expensive to reshoot the Venetian canal. Thus the mystery of Jeanette's involvement with *Paramount on Parade* is more or less solved.

The episodic nature of the revue format permitted Paramount to tailor the film for individual markets. Chevalier, whose appeal was greatest in the more sophisticated urban areas of

Gondolier Nino Martini urges Jeanette to abandon David Newell and come back to Sorrento with him.

the United States, had fewer songs in the prints circulating in the hinterlands. Spanish-language sequences were inserted for distribution to the southwestern United States. The popular Jewish comedian, Harry Green, was probably never seen in the wild west, where his humor would have been lost. In fact, after a brief flourish in the late 1920s and early 1930s, Jewish ethnic humor all but vanished from the screen. In April of 1930 the Hebrew Actors' Union issued an edict barring Jewish actors from films. The union feared that their presence on the silver screen would make inroads on the very vital Yiddish theatre in America. It was a wistful gesture, for Jewish dialect actors were already disappearing from films and only top performers like Jolson and Cantor were unaffected. The union might better have served the Yiddish theatre by promoting films that would have widened the appeal of top Yiddish stars. (The few films of personalities like Molly Picon are cherished today.)

Paramount on Parade is still one of the most entertaining films made in 1930. It is really a shame that Jeanette didn't make it out of the cutting room. The increasing discoveries of "lost films" and lost footage in recent years may be cause for hope. Perhaps, in some abandoned film vault in Auckland or Tierra del Fuego, Jeanette is still gliding in her forgotten gondola, singing "Come Back to Sorrento" with tenor Nino Martini.

Let's Go Native
Paramount.
Released August 16, 1930.
Directed by Leo McCarey.
Produced by PARAMOUNT-PUBLIX Corp.

77 minutes.

Original script: George Marion Jr. and Percy Heath. Sound: Harry D. Mills. Dances and ensembles: David Bennett. Montages: Slavko Vorkapich. Photography: Victor Milner. Movietone Recording.

Jack Oakie (Voltaire McGinnis)
Jeanette MacDonald (Joan Wood)
James Hall (Wally Wendell)
William Austin (Basil Pistol)
Kay Francis (Constance Cooke)
Charles Sellon (Grandpa Wallace Wendell)
David Newell (Chief Officer Williams)
Eugene Pallette (Deputy Sheriff Careful Cuthbert)
Richard "Skeets" Gallagher (Jerry, King of the Island)
Rafael Storm (An Argentinean)
Charlie Hall (Charlie, a mover)
Earl Askam (Mover)
Harry Bernard (Mover)
Pat Harmon (Policeman)
Virginia Bruce (Grandpa Wendell's secretary)
E.H. Calvert (Diner eating duck)
Grady Sutton (Diner)
John Elliott (Captain)
Oscar Smith (Cook)
The King's Men (Singing off-camera for movers)

Let's Go Native is one of the most interesting bad films ever made. It is a study in mistimed comedy routines, of gag lines explained and punch lines repunched into insensibility. This is not to say that punch lines can't be repeated effectively. We have all walked in halfway through a film and found the audience helpless with laughter at a seemingly innocuous line. (A superb example is Melvyn Douglas's "coffee" joke in *Ninotchka*, which becomes more and more hilarious with each equally pointless repetition.) But *Let's Go Native* doesn't know when to stop. Over and over again, the delicious bubbles of screwball comedy begin to form, only to be dissipated by heavy writing and heavy directing.

The comic core of the film is the shipwrecking of assorted lovers on a desert island, where they have only theatrical costumes to wear. The "King" of the island is another castaway from Brooklyn who rules over two hundred maidens between the ages of eighteen and twenty-one. The mechanics of getting the group to the island are so elaborate and tedious,

Joan Wood (Jeanette) can't decide which frock to wear for her eviction. The sheriff (Eugene Pallette) and her boyfriend (James Hall) try to advise her.

however, that less than half of the film remains for what should have been the heart of the story.

Director Leo McCarey was plainly still feeling his way with the sound medium. He was responsible for some classic Laurel and Hardy silent comedies, but two of his first three sound films were pedestrian dramas, and the third, *Red Hot Rhythm* (1929), was a slender musical starring Alan Hale. *Let's Go Native* must have been valuable experience for him because three years later he directed the comedy classic *Duck Soup* with the Marx Brothers. His later successes include *Ruggles of Red Gap* (1935), *The Awful Truth* (1937), *Love Affair* (1939), and *Going My Way* (1944).

Miss MacDonald's titular leading man is James Hall, a mildly pleasant young actor. He had made a promising start in silents and starred in *Hell's Angels* in 1930, but did little thereafter.

The real star of the picture is Jack Oakie. This engaging, moon-faced comedian seems to be in half of the musicals Paramount ever made. Despite his rasping voice and baked-potato expression, he could break your heart in a moment of pathos and win the girl in the end.

The songs in *Let's Go Native* are catchy and feature some of the best-worst lyrics ever written. Unfortunately, the dance numbers they inspire feature tired choreography and unimaginative photography.

Let's Go Native

Our story begins in the enormous Hollywood-*moderne* lobby of Joan Wood's costume shop. Through a bit of clumsy exposition, we learn that an Argentine millionaire is importing a Broadway revue with costumes by Miss Wood, and the beauteous damsels promenading about will leave that night for Buenos Aires. Miss Wood has not yet appeared for the dress rehearsal, and a phone call to her apartment reveals only loud crashing noises.

The noise is caused by several burly movers. The Sheriff (Eugene Pallette) is supervising a crew of incompetents in repossessing Miss Wood's furniture. (Compare the wasted motion of this scene with similar sequences in good silent comedies and, of course, the brilliant destructive routines of the Marx Brothers or Laurel and Hardy.) The Sheriff instructs his men to be more quiet. The madame is still in the hay.

"Hey," cries Joan Wood (Jeanette) from the bedroom. "Who stands without? Suitors for my hand?"

"No, miss," replies her maid. "Movers for your furniture." Joan's creditors have thoughtfully arranged it. Joan is starting to dress when her boyfriend, Wally Wendell (James Hall), arrives. He offers his usual solution to her financial difficulties: marry him and live off his rich grandfather. Joan refuses as usual, unless he consents to go to work. She turns to more important things, trying to select a frock from her departing wardrobe. Holding up two elaborate gowns, "the blue?...or the green?," she wavers back and forth until the Sheriff thrusts a fur-trimmed gray dress into her hands.

The departing piano is stopped by Wally for "one last song"—"My Mad Moment":

> At our first meeting, a salad you were eating.
> I sat enraptured and hardly dared to move.
> For grace of movement there could be no improvement
> As you speared a bit of orange with your fork.
>
> And then you smiled. I forgot what home meant.
> My heart went wild. You were my mad moment ....
>
> (Copyright Famous Music Corp.)

The movers (their singing voices supplied off-camera by the King's Men) join Joan and Wally in a chorus, then relentlessly cart the piano to the top of the stairs for its inevitable shattering descent.

The Sheriff accompanies Joan in her roadster so that he can repossess it when they reach her shop. "I don't know when I've seen a nicer paint job," he comments. Joan, who is applying lipstick, takes it as a compliment. He comments on the lack of scars, and she tells him she has never had an operation. In this aura of misunderstanding, the roadster roars off, an accident looking for a place to happen.

Nearby, taxi driver Voltaire McGinnis (Jack Oakie) and his passenger, Basil Pistol (William Austin), are similarly occupied. They find their accident first when Joan's pocketbook falls on her running board. Attempting to retrieve it, Pistol becomes spread-eagled between two moving cars (shades of Harry Langdon), and

Shipwrecked. Voltaire studies the horizon while Joan studies her mirror. (Left to right: James Hall, Jeanette, William Austin, Kay Francis, Jack Oakie.) Some outdoor filming was done at Catalina Island.

causes a monumental traffic jam before Voltaire drives their taxi through the police precinct window. (Again, compare this with the more spectacular silent comedy auto sequences.)

Joan arrives at her shop, oblivious to the havoc she has wrought. She turns her car over to the Sheriff, who promptly runs it into a fire hydrant.

In the shop, we are treated to a musical montage depicting a "dress rehearsal." A title explains that Joan "substitutes for the absent star" by modeling the costumes in musical numbers.

For purposes of plot, Joan learns that she must accompany her costumes to Buenos Aires to collect payment for them.

Wally arrives. He has told his family he is getting married and found they were just going to suggest the same thing. However, it wasn't Joan they had in mind. Their choice is Constance Cooke, a girl Wally hasn't seen since she was fourteen. She rubbed an eclair in his hair, he recalls. Wally, of course, has turned down his family's suggestion and is now disinherited with only $48 to his name.

So that they won't be parted, Joan decides to get him a job on the boat to Buenos Aires. The nice Chief Officer will do anything for her, she decides. Chief Officer Williams (David Newell) obviously has designs on Joan and is delighted to give her boyfriend a job as a "trimmer." Joan is equally delighted. Wally can put the parsley and lemon on the fish during the day, and they will be together every moonlit night on boat deck.

Pistol dashes in looking for his old friend Wally, followed by the irate cab driver, Voltaire. "Not the old French philosopher?" asks Wally. Voltaire explains that when he was born, his mother told the nurses to tell the doctor that his name was Walter. The nurse was Jewish, so the doctor wrote it down the way she pronounced it: "Voltaire."

Pistol needs to borrow $2,800 from Wally to pay for Voltaire's cab. Wally confesses that he is

The entire film is an excuse to "go native," which Jeanette does fetchingly. *Courtesy Jack Tillmany.*

broke. Pistol's dismay is cut short by the arrival of an equally irate policeman bearing the license photo from Voltaire's now-abandoned taxi. He is combing the city for the runaway driver and passenger, and Voltaire looks suspiciously like one of the men he is after.

Voltaire frantically makes a series of faces until he decides the jig is up and relaxes into his own normal expression. The policeman shrugs. "For a moment I thought you were him," he says and departs. Voltaire and Pistol decide the town is too hot for them. They will join Wally as trimmers until things cool down. Joan is introduced to Pistol and Voltaire. "Not the old French..." "No, lady, not the old French photographer."

Wally must join Joan in another "dress rehearsal" number. One of many silent titles tells us that it is an occasion for "panting whirls and whirling pants." Seated on a snow-covered log, they tell us "It Seems to Be Spring." Joan strips off her coat, revealing summer chiffon:

> It seems to be spring, little flowers leap from their beds
> ...and snails with a shout, go sprinting about.
> It seems to be Spring, the cows contentedly moo
> And two little calves in your chiffon stockings I view.
> It seems to be Spring in my heart.
> (Copyright Famous Music Corp.)

The image of the lovers dissolves into that of a pair of comic bears who embrace and cuff one another, then picture disolves back to Joan and Wally, now completely invisible beneath a blanket of snow.

In the posh Wall Street office of Wally's grouchy grandfather (Charles Sellon), a telegram announces that his prospective daughter-in-law, Constance, has run away to South America rather than marry Wally. A second wire from Wally says he and his fiancée are on their way to South America. (Naturally, Wally, Joan, and Constance are all on the same ship.) "Aren't those children cute, fooling us all the time," Grandpa murmurs.

Wally won't be seeing much of either Constance or Joan, however. He and his friends are down in the hold, trimming coal, not fish. Joan is desolate at his unexplained absence and writes him a note begging him to meet her. Voltaire gets the note, thinks it is for him, and tries to keep the assignation. The head stoker won't hear of it. "No wonder the French lines are doing all the business," comments Pistol.

Wally's friends wire his grandfather about his predicament, hoping for their own release. Grandpa Wendell wires the head of the ship line, his old school chum, to put Wally and Constance in the bridal suite. But there is no release for Voltaire and Pistol. Their grandfathers didn't go to school with the head of the line.

Constance (Kay Francis) interrupts the reunion of Joan and Wally. The lovers quarrel over their imagined rivals, Constance and Chief Officer Williams. Pistol and Voltaire are transferred to the dining room, and a series of uninspired comedy routines follow involving the difficulty of eating uncarved duck and a free-for-all that ends with dozens of passengers tossing each others' hats, shoes, and coats overboard. (Compare with similar sequences in late silent comedies like *Two Tars* and *A Pair of Tights*.)

The tedium is relieved when the chorus girls come out on deck to rehearse their number. Voltaire is delighted and leads them in "Joe Jazz," whose zestful arrangement almost succeeds in canceling out some of the dullest, most poorly filmed choreography in early filmdom. (Oakie describes in his 1981 autobiography, *Double Takes,* how the musicians had discovered they could collect overtime by repeatedly making mistakes and how he decided to help them out by spoiling a few takes himself. Thus the number was shot over and over into the night and finally abandoned. The end result is a cut-and-paste photo-montage over one of the music tracks.) The sprightly lyrics go:

Grandpa Wendell (Charles Sellon, center) arrives on his yacht to rescue his grandson and fiancée. The passengers had escaped the sinking ship with only the clothes on their backs and a trunk of Joan's theatrical costumes, contributing to the zany costume party atmosphere. (William Austin, left.)

With all the musical numbers recorded "live," most of the island scenes were done on a soundstage with the orchestra just off camera. (Charles Sellon, far left; James Hall, Jeanette, Skeets Gallagher, center.)

He isn't interested in winning your hand.
If he can win your feet
His evening is complete.
When he yells, "Up and at 'um,"
Well, his anatomy's up,
Because Joe Jazz is taking you.
    (Copyright Famous Music Corp.)

A heavy fog causes a shipwreck, and after another needlessly long sequence (5-1/2 minutes!) full of stock footage, five castaways, happily our principals, reach the desert island where they should have been four reels ago. Native maidens come out to greet them, and Voltaire tries elaborate sign language on one of them without success. "Just call me Voltaire," he shrugs. "Not the old French philosopher?" she cries.

Joan has found a trunk full of her costumes washed up on the beach, surrounded by giggling girls who are trying on the spangled garments. "You likee? Maybe makee purchase?" she asks.

"Well, I should hope to tell ya. This is strictly the bananas," replies the gum-chewing damsel. "I could do damage with that," cries another. "It soitenly brings out me good pernts."

Joan asks if the girls are from Brooklyn. No, they tell her, but the head man is. The King (Richard "Skeets" Gallagher) is borne in on a litter by a bevy of grass-skirted beauties. He is delighted to have visitors. He was marooned here some time ago, himself.

"Shipwrecked?" asks Pistol. No, the King explains, he was a master of ceremonies on a cruise ship, and one night they threw him overboard. (Gallagher had been a master of ceremonies for *Paramount on Parade*.) As far as the King has been able to figure out, they are on one of the Virgin Islands..."that drifted."

The "ersters" offered the hungry castaways for lunch contain enormous pearls. The King apologizes, but they haven't been able to catch any oysters without them. Pistol goes off to lay a golf course and wherever he attempts to dig a hole, oil shoots up. Again the King apologizes. The castaways are trapped forever with untold wealth.

Voltaire offers a solution: "Let's Go Native," and Pistol takes up the second verse:

> Upon some archipelago, put me and watch this fella go.
> Some maiden who's Maylay, I'll waylay.
> No costume bills to pay for her.
> Old nature's making hay for her.
> These girls get their trousseaus with a scythe.
> (And some naughty males
> Always hope the harvest fails.)
>
> (Copyright Famous Music Corp.)

The torrid native dance that follows is weakened by constant dissolves, a flaw of even Astaire-Rogers numbers for several years to come.

The ladies of the island have costumed their jazz band from Joan's ample trunk. To pay for their finery, the King gives Joan the island and his pearl crown, worth half-a-million dollars. It is too small, so she gives it to Pistol as commission for negotiating the sale of the island. Voltaire claims it in payment for his taxi and then runs off to use it to charm Constance.

Connie, in a fetching spangled tutu, listens to his vows of love: "I've Gotta Yen for You." She is moved to reply prettily in song, one of Kay Francis's rare singing appearances. Within a year Miss Francis would be hard at work on the dramatic "women's pictures" that would make her fame, but here she is the essence of the musical heroine, soft, warm, and incredibly beautiful.

Wally's grandfather arrives on his yacht to rescue Wally and Constance. In the process he buys the island from Joan for a million dollars. A crudely simulated earthquake then destroys the island, driving everyone onto the yacht.

Joan returns the million-dollar check to Grandpa and agrees to marry Wally if he gets a job. Voltaire is now rich enough to marry Constance because he has the pearl crown. He models it raffishly, accidentally knocking his own hat off the ship rail. When he leans over to try to retrieve it, the crown follows. The film fades out on Joan and Wally laughing, and we assume that Voltaire and Constance will have to live happily ever after on her money.

Courtesy of the Bob Grimes Sheet Music Collection.

Besides cocoanuts and dancing girls, the island is rich in oil and pearls. Here, the King shows off his "pearl fedora." Left to right: William Austin, Skeets Gallagher, James Hall, Kay Francis, Jeanette, Jack Oakie.

Reviews

"A ludicrous audible film hodgepodge," wrote Mordaunt Hall of the *New York Times*. ("Audible film" was the *Times*' current terminology for sound films.) "Whatever may be the final opinion of this mile or so of merry tomfoolery, it should be set forth that not a few of its hectic adventures were greeted with shrieks of laughter....Miss MacDonald gives as pleasing a performance as possible in such a melange." (Mr. Hall also disliked the Marx Brothers' *Animal Crackers*, which he reviewed the same week.)

Mildred Martin in the *Philadelphia Inquirer* noted that Jeanette "sings a song or two in her usual pleasing fashion but...doesn't seem quite as much at home in this whimsical crazy sort of thing as she does in some of her former pictures." Miss Martin liked the film, however: "sheer delight for those who like slightly mad, light-hearted comedy." She found Jack Oakie "irresistible" and said "Leo McCarey...has shown his deft touch in numerous places."

"This is madness—weird, wonderful madness!" *Photoplay* opined. "Every gag in history turns up somewhere in this insane hash of song, dance, and story....Terrific nonsense—and how you'll scream!"

No Recordings

Music in the Film

All music by Richard A. Whiting and all lyrics by George Marion Jr. (who had been prominent as a writer of clever titles for silent films). In listing performers after each title, "and" denotes a genuine duet, while commas between names indicate a sequence of singers.

Overture: "Let's Go Native" (sung by the King's Men), "It Seems to Be Spring"
"My Mad Moment" (MacDonald and Hall with the King's Men)
"It Seems to Be Spring" (MacDonald and Hall)
"Joe Jazz" (Oakie sings, then dances with ladies' chorus)
"Let's Go Native" (Oakie, Austin, reprised by good unbilled jazz band)
"I've Gotta Yen for You" (Oakie, Francis)
Finale: "It Seems to Be Spring," "I've Gotta Yen for You," "Joe Jazz," "Let's Go Native"

The song "Pampa Rose" apparently was filmed by MacDonald, but cut before release. However, she can be seen dancing in a Spanish costume during the fashion show montage. ("Pampa Rose" was ultimately used in the 1935 film *Coronado.*)

The song "Don't I Do," apparently intended for Oakie to sing to Francis, was also cut, possibly replaced by "I've Gotta Yen for You." Apparently used as background music is "Gotta Be Good" by Victor Schertzinger.

Monte Carlo

Paramount.
New York premiere August 27, 1930.
Released October 4, 1930.
Produced and directed by Ernst Lubitsch.
85 minutes.

From the story *Die Blaue Küste* (The Blue Coast) by Hans Mueller, with an episode adapted from *Monsieur Beaucaire* by Booth Tarkington and Evelyn G. Sutherland. Screenplay: Ernest Vajda. Additional dialogue: Vincent Lawrence. Photography: Victor Milner. Art Director: Häns Dreier. Sound: Harry D. Mills. Movietone Recording.

The 1926 MGM silent called *Monte Carlo* is not based on *The Blue Coast.*

Jack Buchanan (Count Rudolph Farriere, AKA Paul the hairdresser)
Jeanette MacDonald (Countess Helene Mara)*
ZaSu Pitts (Berthe the maid)*
Tyler Brooke (Armand)
Claud Allister (Duke Otto von Liebenheim)*
Lionel Belmore (Count Gustave von Liebenheim)**
John Roche (Paul, the hairdresser)
Albert Conti (Duke Otto's companion)
Donald Novis (Monsieur Beaucaire)
Helen Garden (Lady Mary)
David Percy (Herald)
Erik Bey (Lord Winterset)
Sidney Bracy (Hunchback at casino)
Geraldine Dvorak [Garbo "double"] (Extra in casino)
Billy Bevan (Conductor)
Frances Dee (Receptionist)
Rolfe Sedan (Hairdresser)
John Carroll (Wedding guest officer)

* The American Film Institute directory gives the character names used in the press book, some of which obviously were changed before the film was actually shot. Jeanette's rôle is listed as "Vera von Conti," ZaSu Pitts as "Maria," Claud Allister as "Prince Otto von Seibenheim," and Lionel Belmore as "Duke Gustave von Seibenheim." (Press books are invaluable guides to changes made during production, since they were often prepared well in advance.)

** Lionel Belmore replaced Edgar Norton, who nevertheless received billing as Count Gustave.

"Five more minutes and I would have been married." 1264-8

Countess Helene (Jeanette) escapes from her wedding in only her lace "step-ins." As her maid (ZaSu Pitts) hunts for a dress, she fans herself with relief. Caption: "Five more minutes and I would have been married."

NOTE: A German film called *Melody of the Heart* (UFA Studios), directed by Häns Schwartz, was released in the U.S. the same week as *Monte Carlo*, drawing attention to the fact that both films had almost identical song sequences on a moving train. Although the German film was made a year earlier and had been released in Europe before Lubitsch began filming, he said he had not heard of it, and this was probably a coincidence.

Lubitsch's second musical film with Jeanette MacDonald is a delightful if overly superficial romp through the boudoirs and gambling casinos of the Riviera playland. One of its key songs, "Beyond the Blue Horizon," became a standard that Miss MacDonald recorded three times during the next seventeen years and sang countless times in concerts and on the radio.

Her rôle in *Monte Carlo* is curiously unsympathetic, that of a spoiled "Countess" with no past to speak of, willing to go to any lengths to maintain a luxurious standard of living. When marriage to a rich ninny is too repulsive, she determines to stay solvent by gambling. Unlike

Monte Carlo

the endearing heroine of Lubitsch's *Trouble in Paradise*, she is not even clever enough to steal. We never learn how she got her title, which is not hereditary. Is she a once-wealthy widow? She wears no wedding ring. Or is she a camp follower of the rich, down on her luck? The impersonality of the rôle is accented by the fact that no one calls her by her first name until the picture is almost over.

The rather dry quality of the film is accentuated by the second American film appearance of British music-hall star Jack Buchanan. Buchanan had scored on Broadway in *Charlot's Revue* (with Bea Lillie and Gertrude Lawrence) and came to Hollywood in 1929 to make the all-Technicolor *Paris* with Irene Bordoni. His filmic quality could best be described as "dapper," and he did not win a permanent place in American hearts as so many of his countrymen did. After *Monte Carlo*, he returned to England where he became a national institution, starring in and often producing more than eighteen films and many stage musicals before his death in 1957. He returned to Broadway several times and to Hollywood in 1953 when he played the egotistical director in *The Band Wagon*, arguably his finest film rôle.

Another English actor, Claud Allister, plays Miss MacDonald's booby suitor, and ZaSu Pitts, star of von Stroheim's epic *Greed* (1925), has a minuscule rôle as a maid. (Miss Pitts was a beautiful and brilliant actress in silent films, doing both drama and comedy. When *All Quiet on the Western Front* was previewed, it ran on the same bill with one of her comedies. The audience, having just laughed at her in one film, was still laughing when she had her first dramatic sound sequence as the dying mother. The studio promptly replaced her in the film, and thereafter she was typed as a vague eccentric, which of course she played superbly.)

Lubitsch's use of action behind the credits, when many films still used sign board titles is again in evidence. A pair of hands is seen dealing cards over a whirling strobe-light effect that emphasizes the lilting "Always in All Ways." The music takes on a ceremonial tone and we are present at the preparations for a lavish wedding. The guests in summer finery are assembled as the chorus sings the triumphant "Day of Days." But it is not a good day for a wedding.

The skies open and the ladies' thin dresses are plastered to their bodies, their hair drooping under sodden garden hats. The men scramble for cover, still singing loudly. Worst of all, the bride has vanished, leaving her wedding dress on a chair. No, it is not a good day for a wedding.

The groom, Duke Otto von Liebenheim (Claud Allister), assures the astonished guests that he'll bring the bride back if he has to drag her: "She'll Love Me and Like It."

Her joy is expressed by singing "Beyond the Blue Horizon" as she looks out the window of a racing train. Hundreds of harvesters in the passing fields join in. (The train footage was shot in California's Napa Valley.)

At Monte Carlo, the runaway Countess spurns Count Rudolph (Jack Buchanan), but finds her hairdresser "Rudy" (the Count in disguise) irresistible.

OTTO:
I have a nasty temper though I keep it in control,
For after all, I really am a simple hearted soul.

BRIDESMAIDS:
He's a simp, he's a simp,
   he's a simp-le hearted soul.

OTTO:
But when the seeds of kindliness have failed to bear
   me fruit,
I then become, I must confess, a nasty tempered
   brute.

BRIDESMAIDS:
He's an-ass, he's an-ass,
   he's a nasty tempered brute.
         (Copyright Famous Music Corp.)

At the train depot, Countess Helene Mara (Jeanette) makes her appearance just in time to catch the famous Blue Train. In her compartment, she doffs her fur coat, revealing lace "step-ins" and quite a bit of Miss MacDonald. "Five more minutes and I would have been married," she sighs. The conductor inquires as to her destination and she asks him to suggest someplace. Well, he says, they go to Vienna...Monte Carlo.... "Monte Carlo!" she cries. There she will win her happiness at the green tables!

The rhythm of the train wheels is picked up by the orchestra and, in a montage of clicking wheels, pumping pistons, and jets of steam the music accelerates:

Beyond the blue horizon waits a beautiful day.
Goodbye to things that bore me.
Joy is waiting for me.
        (Copyright Famous Music Corp.)

She leans out the train window to sing to the harvesters in the fields, and from the farthest hilltop they wave back as they join her in the chorus. It is truly a stirring number, although never quite as precisely edited as we like to remember. (Beautiful Napa Valley substituted for the vineyards of southern France.)

Also trying his luck at the green tables is Count Rudolph Farriere (Jack Buchanan). He has a foolproof system. If he is standing next to a brunette, he bets on red. If he is standing next to a redhead, he bets on black. But what, inquires his friend Armand (Tyler Brooke), if he is standing next to a blonde? "I ask her where she lives."

His blonde arrives in the person of the Countess. Rudolph is suddenly shy, but he has a new strategy. He tells Armand to accost her. Then Rudolph can slap his face and rescue the lady. Armand approaches the Countess, who slaps his face herself. Her anger dissipates when she sees a hunchback (Sidney Bracy) farther down the path. Happily, she pays him fifty francs to touch his hump. The lady is superstitious.

Rudolph now decides on a new strategy. He follows her toward the casino in a marvelous

Monte Carlo

"Beyond the Blue Horizon" became a standard. Early sheet music covers were an art form, as this delightful one illustrates. *Courtesy of the Bob Grimes Sheet Music Collection.*

tracking shot, telling her that luck will be hers if she will only stroke his hair—"caressingly." She is intrigued but marches coldly on. As she vanishes through the doors of the casino, Rudolph cries that now she will lose everything. He turns and ponders his next move. Suddenly the door behind him opens a crack. A slender white arm creeps out and tousles his hair and the door snaps shut. If she wins now, Rudolph sighs happily, she is his.

Win she does. Soon her ten thousand francs are five million, and she has engaged a half-dozen more servants. But her good fortune doesn't make her any more disposed toward the brash young Count. She is cool to his flowers and midnight phone calls. In a charming duet, "Give Me a Moment, Please," she keeps hanging up on him until he gives up. Then she hums the final strains of the song into her pillow.

The novice hairdresser attempts his first shampoo. (Lubitsch loved to provide Jeanette with such comic opportunities.) *Courtesy Jack Tillmany.*

(Buchanan's voice was electronically distorted to simulate a telephone voice, possibly the earliest time this was done.)

Rudolph is at his wits' end when he and Armand run into Paul, a gentleman who boasts of living with the Countess. Paul confides that he is utterly devoted to her. Oh, if only they could see her in her negligée as he does! Rudolph is about to thrash the bounder when he learns that Paul is the Countess's hairdresser. The three sing of the delights of the profession: "Trimmin' the Women." Paul (John Roche) is easily persuaded (for a small fee) to take a leave of absence, sending "Rudy" in his place.

The Countess's maid, Berthe (ZaSu Pitts), instructs the new hairdresser ("brand new," he assures her) in his duties. Above all he is not to flirt with chambermaids. "But to avoid any misunderstanding," she simpers, "*I* am not a chambermaid."

The Countess has taken so little notice of the Count that she doesn't recognize the besmocked Rudy. Her recognition takes a different form. She eyes him carefully, then slips out of the room and returns in a far more elaborate, transparent negligée. She tells him she hates the name Rudolph, even Rudy. She will call him "Paul." "Paul's" first job is to bob the Countess's shoulder-length hair. He makes numerous passes with the scissors, but can only bring himself to cut one curl for his watch. Then he performs an elaborate shampoo that leaves the lady spluttering suds. To appease her anger, he gently strokes her forehead. Her delighted moans and gasps of pleasure shock the eavesdropping Berthe. This is something new and they comment on the sensation: "Whatever It Is, It's Grand."

Soon Count Rudolph has replaced the Countess's chauffeur and lackeys. He can't wait, he tells his friend Armand, until she fires her maid. Rudy's charming nature isn't the only reason the Countess is dismissing her servants, however. She is broke again. When "Paul" is told the news, he refuses to leave. He will work without pay.

Monte Carlo

Duke Otto (Claud Allister) finds his fiancée and again proposes marriage to save her from poverty. She tells him she is only marrying him for his money, which delights him no end. Her honesty will make theirs the happiest of marriages.

Duke Otto arrives at this critical moment, seeking his errant fiancée. The Countess reluctantly agrees to marry him, but only for his money. Otto is overjoyed with her honesty. It will make theirs the happiest of marriages. He tells her again: "You'll Love Me and Like It."

Wistfully, the Countess tells "Paul" that now she can keep him. He is horrified at this development and offers to keep *her* with his inheritance. The Countess is insulted. Quickly he changes his story, telling her that he has inherited luck, not money. He will gamble her small pittance into a young fortune. He pledges himself to her: "Always in All Ways."

In a series of dissolves, they set out for the casino. First "Paul" and the Countess climb into the backseat of the limousine, where they sit happily holding hands until they realize there is no driver. Next "Paul" is in the front seat with the Countess in the back, and finally they are both laughing in the front seat.

They find Duke Otto already at the gambling tables, so the pair unreluctantly retreats to the park and the moonlit promenade overlooking the

"So you don't think I'm a *man*—" Rudy snarls and locks the bedroom door.

announces the dawn with a flute reprise of "Always in All Ways." Staggering with sleep, the Countess retrieves the sequence of keys until she can unlock the bedroom door.

She greets "Paul" awkwardly. After all, he must remember the difference between them. The only difference between them, he snarls, is that she is a woman and he is a man. "You're not a man at all!" she retorts. His answer is to lock the bedroom door and carry her to the couch. "All right," he leers sensually, "I'm *not* a man."

"That's what you get for being nice to your servants," whimpers the Countess. She closes her eyes and, breathing heavily, awaits his next move. But "Paul" disappoints her. He storms out, leaving her alone.

She spends the rest of the day searching for "Paul." Night falls. Duke Otto arrives to take her to the opera, but she can't go unless "Paul" does her hair. The duke exits and "Paul" enters. Coyly, the Countess tells him that she hasn't been seeking him in his capacity as a hairdresser. Coldly, he replies that the only reason he has come to dress her hair is so that she will be an advertisement for him at the opera. Then all the women will come to him. The Countess is furious and tears her hair into wild disarray. *This* is the way she is going to the opera. She'll tell everyone *he* did it. She'll *ruin* him!

The opera is half over when she arrives. Duke Otto solicitously inquires after her hairdresser. *Hairdresser*! He is never to mention that word again. Frantically drumming her fingers on the arm of the chair, she leans forward to view the action onstage. The opera is *Monsieur Beaucaire*. "What is it about?" she snaps. Trembling, he tells her that it is about a hairdresser.

It's a silly story, he tells her. A noble lady has fallen in love with a hairdresser. When she finds out who he really is, she throws him out. The Countess comments on the action as the stage lovers act out their story. Lady Mary (Helen Garden) tells the courtiers that if Monsieur Beaucaire should return,

ocean. Hours later, "Paul" goes back to the casino alone with the Countess's stake and she goes home to wait for him.

"Paul" returns with three-hundred-thousand francs he has "won" at the table and dares to claim a kiss. The lady is grateful for the money but scandalized by the kiss. At first she resists. Then to her own astonishment, she returns it passionately. Overwhelmed, she flees to her bedroom and locks the door against him, as he sings plaintively outside: "Give Me a Moment, Please." Unsure of herself, she locks the door key into a drawer, the drawer key into a jewel box, and the jewel box key under her pillow so that she can safely finish the duet from her side of the locked door.

A clock with elaborate mechanical figures has mockingly chimed the hours throughout the night with oboes and bassoons. Now it she'd drive him away again. Otto applauds loudly. Onstage, a messenger arrives and tells the startled court that the mere barber is in reality a prince of France.

"Paul" appears in the box across from the Countess and she begins to suspect. She slips past the dozing Otto and joins him. Can he ever forgive her? Her words are echoed by Lady Mary on stage. Beaucaire (Donald Novis) denounces Lady Mary and leaves her forever. Lady Mary sinks weeping into a chair on stage. In in the box, the Countess is equally distraught.

I don't like that ending," consoles Rudolph. "I like *happy* endings."

Train whistles and the chug-chugging of a steam engine drown out the applause. The lovers are united on the Blue Train, singing "Beyond the Blue Horizon" as Rudolph crouches (somewhat uncomfortably) beside the Countess, whose chiffon scarf streams gaily out the window of the rushing train.

Reviews

Monte Carlo was very well received by the critics. *Outlook* Magazine noted happily that "Jeanette MacDonald slithers in and out of a good deal of expensive lingerie." There were raves for the "Beyond the Blue Horizon" number, and most critics noted it was a musical without a dance number.

Even lesser Lubitsch films were treasured amidst the trash that was appearing on the screen under the title "musical." The *New York World* said, "And now they can preserve the reels of *The Love Parade* and *Monte Carlo* and burn all the rest, and nobody will even notice the loss."

It is only now, with the complete library of Lubitsch works for comparison, that we find *Monte Carlo* wanting. Film historian William K. Everson wrote in program notes for a 1966 screening, "It opens beautifully...we have high hopes for the rest of the film. Alas, they are never quite fulfilled, and, despite charm and typical Lubitsch touches in terms of pantomimic comedy, it remains one of his lesser efforts."

Recordings (See Discography for further information)

"Beyond the Blue Horizon" (MacDonald)
"Always in All Ways" (MacDonald)

Though the other *Monte Carlo* songs remain little known in this country, many became standards in Britain and can still be heard there today.

Music in the Film

All music is by Richard Whiting and W. Franke Harling, all lyrics by Leo Robin. In listing performers after each title, "and" denotes a genuine duet, while commas between names indicate a sequence of singers.

When the Countess thinks "Rudy" is using her to attract other lady customers, she dresses her own hair for the opera. (The fashions of 1930 were in transition between the "flapper" and the long, clinging lines of a few years later.)

Overture: "Always in All Ways," "Beyond the Blue Horizon"
"She'll Love Me and Like It" (Allister, chorus)
"Beyond the Blue Horizon" (MacDonald, chorus)
"Give Me a Moment, Please" (Buchanan, MacDonald)
"Give Me a Moment, Please" fragment reprise (Roche)
"Trimmin' the Women" (Buchanan and Brooke and Roche)
"Whatever It Is, It's Grand" (MacDonald and Buchanan)
"She'll Love Me and Like It" reprise (Allister, MacDonald)
"Always in All Ways" (Buchanan, MacDonald)
"Give Me a Moment, Please" (Buchanan)
"Always in All Ways" reprise (Buchanan, MacDonald)
Monsieur Beaucaire (Percy, Garden, Bey, Novis, with chorus) - operetta fragment based on Booth Tarkington story, contrived by Whiting, Harling, and Robin. (Not the opera by André Messager.)
Finale: "Beyond the Blue Horizon" (MacDonald and Buchanan)
Over closing credits: "Always in All Ways" (orchestra)

NOTE: A preview program dated August 27, 1930 lists a song called "A Job with a Future," sung by Jeanette and Jack Buchanan. This apparently was replaced by "Whatever It Is, It's Grand." The cue for the first song is still heard when "Paul" asks the Countess how long she will employ him.

The Lottery Bride

United Artists.
Released October 25, 1930.
Directed by Paul L. Stein.
Produced by Arthur Hammerstein and presented by Joseph M. Schenck.
80 minutes.
Two-strip Technicolor finale.

Based on Herbert Stothart's story, "Bride 66." Adapted by Horace Jackson. Music by Rudolf Friml, lyrics by J. Keirn Brennan. Supervision: John W. Considine Jr. Continuity and dialogue: Howard Emmett Rogers. Editor: Robert J. Kern. Editorial Adviser: Hal C. Kern. Settings: William Cameron Menzies and Park French. Musical Arrangements: Hugo Riesenfeld. Photography: Ray June and Karl Freund. Sound: J.T. Reed and Frank Maher. Production Manager: O.O. Dull. Assistant directors: Lonnie D'Orsa and Walter Mayo. Costumes: Alice O'Neill. Movietone Recording.

Jeanette MacDonald (Jenny Trondson, Bride 66)
John Garrick (Chris Svenson)
Joe E. Brown (Hoke Curtis)
ZaSu Pitts (Hilda)
Robert Chisholm (Olaf Svenson)
Joseph Macaulay (Alberto)
Harry Gribbon (Battleaxe Boris)
Carroll Nye (Nels Trondson)
Max Davidson (Marriage broker)
Frank Brownlee (Guard)

"I feel so foolish—why did you do it…" says the title. Before they are united, the Count has an unusual punishment for her arrogance.

The Lottery Bride

Paul Hurst (Lottery agent)
Robert E. Homans (Miner)
Eugene Pallette (Miner)
Broderick O'Farrell (Bank cashier)
Torben Meyer (Karl Olson, lottery winner)
Bobby Dunn (Olson's friend)
Budd Fine (Radio operator)
Chuck Hamilton (Radioman)
Charles K. French (Dirigible officer)
Clarence Geldert (Dirigible lieutenant)
Michael Visaroff (Official on dock)
Murdock MacQuarrie (Captain)

* Although many cast lists give Jeanette's family name as "Swanson," the original press sheets say "Trondson." The name is not mentioned during the film.

The Lottery Bride rates a place in film history because it is certainly one of the pictures that contributed to the refusal of the American public to attend any film even sounding like a musical. Rudolf Friml's name and that of noted set designer William Cameron Menzies are about the only things going for it. Both prove misleading.

Friml's songs were apparently culled from the wastebasket, for they are not even bad enough (with one exception) to fall into that appalling category "camp." Menzies' Scandinavian interiors lack only live trolls.

It was becoming nearly mandatory for operettas to be supervised by men who had made their name in silent German cinema, and so Dr. Paul L. Stein occupied the director's chair. *The Lottery Bride* was his fourth sound film, so inexperience was no excuse. He did four more films in America, including Pola Negri's first American sound film, *A Woman Commands* (1932), and then left for England.

Musicals had become a readily saleable product, and every hot market finds someone willing to supply it quickly and cheaply. Despite the big names and Technicolor finale, *The Lottery Bride* marries undistinguished music to a ludicrous plot, and the resultant progeny is a misbegotten mess.

Jeanette as "Jenny." *Courtesy Diane Flaherty.*

Leading man John Garrick was a blond young Britisher who had starred in a number of early musicals for Fox. He didn't survive the first musical "cycle" and, surprisingly, neither did stage veteran Robert Chisholm, who provides the bright moments of the film with his consistent refusal to overact. (Chisholm had just appeared in Friml's *Luana* on Broadway, a show that survived seventeen performances.) Garrick returned to England, subsequently appearing in 28 more musicals including the lavish 1934 *Chu Chin Chow*, and, back in the U.S., *The Great Victor Herbert* in 1939. Silent star ZaSu Pitts, who had played Jeanette's maid in *Monte Carlo*, was hitting her stride in sound films as a comedienne. She appeared in nine other films that year.

Jenny entertains her friends with "Yubla," a tribute to the concertina.

Strolling couples in simple peasant garb of satin and velvet are seen entering a Norse sailing ship, now a landlocked café christened The Jazzy Viking. Inside, the students sing a rousing drinking song, "Come Drink to the Girl that You Love," with much banging of cups on the trestle tables. Bandleader Hoke Curtis (Joe E. Brown) introduces himself to the café proprietress, Hilda (ZaSu Pitts). He has brought his (all black) jazz band from America to fill an engagement at The Jazzy Viking. Just in time, he figures. The number they're doing in the next room isn't so hot. "Oh, they don't work here," Hilda explains. "Just university boys and their girlfriends having a party."

Jenny (Jeanette) appears for her only solo in the film, dancing with a concertina chorus to "Yubla." Hoke admires the collection of pretty girls' pictures being thumbed by a bearded old man in the corner (Max Davidson). The codger, however, is only a marriage broker who arranges to send brides to the men up north.

Jenny and her boyfriend, Chris (John Garrick), are starting into the garden when they run into Alberto (Joseph Macaulay), an unctuous Italian aviator, and Jenny's brother, Nels (Carroll Nye), who looks worried. Alberto assures Jenny that Nels is all right, just working hard at the bank. Jenny and Chris depart, and we learn that Nels *is* worried. He has embezzled money from the bank to pay his gambling debts to Alberto.

In the moonlit garden, Chris tells Jenny that it is natural to worry about brothers. He himself often worries about his big brother, Olaf, who is up north in a mining camp. He soothes her with

The Lottery Bride

the film's love song, "My Northern Light," in which he compares the girl's eyes to the arctic phenomenon.

During the next few days, Hoke takes over more than the bandstand at the café. Soon he is asserting his male prerogative over Hilda, suggesting several changes in business procedures. One is to hold a marathon dance. Jenny thinks it might be fun to enter, but Chris says no. "I think too much of you to let those pretty eyes and little feet of yours get all tired out in such a crazy affair." Nels arrives and privately begs Jenny to enter with him. He is in serious financial trouble and must win the prize. "Chris, I'm entering the contest with Nels. I'll explain later," cries Jenny as she is dragged onto the dance floor. Alberto smirks, enjoying Chris's anger.

The dance begins with a low, sensuous beat, rising steadily in a wall of oboes and saxophones. Hours go by. Only two couples left. Jenny is prostrate during the rest period. "Nels, I can't dance anymore!" Nels begs her to continue. Otherwise, he'll go to jail. Alberto comes to tell them the dance is starting again. "The strain of the dance has not taken any of the beauty from your face," he leeringly tells Jenny.

Nels begs Alberto to lend him enough money to cover the shortage. Alberto agrees...if Jenny will ask him, he replies suggestively. Shuddering, Jenny drags Nels toward the dance floor, but they are met by the police. Jenny helps Nels escape, then faints in Alberto's arms, where Chris finds her.

Operetta tenors are a uniformly doltish lot, only slightly above the Australian tree toad in perception, so Chris chooses to misunderstand the tableau. He storms off, leaving forever, and Jenny is arrested for helping Nels escape. Alberto chuckles with glee as the lights fade on our "first act curtain."

Two months later, Jenny is released from prison. She is met in the waiting room by Hoke and Hilda, who has lost her café. The police closed it because of the marathon dance. Hoke tells the women that everything will be all right. "We still have my brains...and they're good." "Good as new," Hilda mutters, "they've never been used."

Jenny decides she must follow Chris's example: leave Oslo and start all over again. The jailer (Frank Brownlee) announces a visitor, and Jenny's heart leaps. It is not Chris, but the marriage broker, offering Jenny a chance to be a picture bride. "Can you imagine Jenny doing a thing like that?" scoffs Hilda. "I'll go!" cries Jenny.

In the far north, a snowbound tavern. The brides are being allotted by spins of a roulette wheel as the miners chant, "Round She Whirls." Chris has joined his brother, Olaf (Robert Chisholm), a bearded, gentle bear of a man, and they are watching the revelry of their drinking companions. The brothers sing of their friendship in sturdy march rhythm: "Shoulder to Shoulder." In a quick piece of plot development, Chris wins a bride and then turns her over to Olaf without glancing at her picture. It is, of course, Jenny's picture that Olaf holds.

Chris (John Garrick) comforts Jenny during the marathon dance contest she has been forced to enter because her brother (Carroll Nye, second from left) has embezzled money from the bank to pay his gambling debts to the Italian aviator (Joseph Macaulay, left).

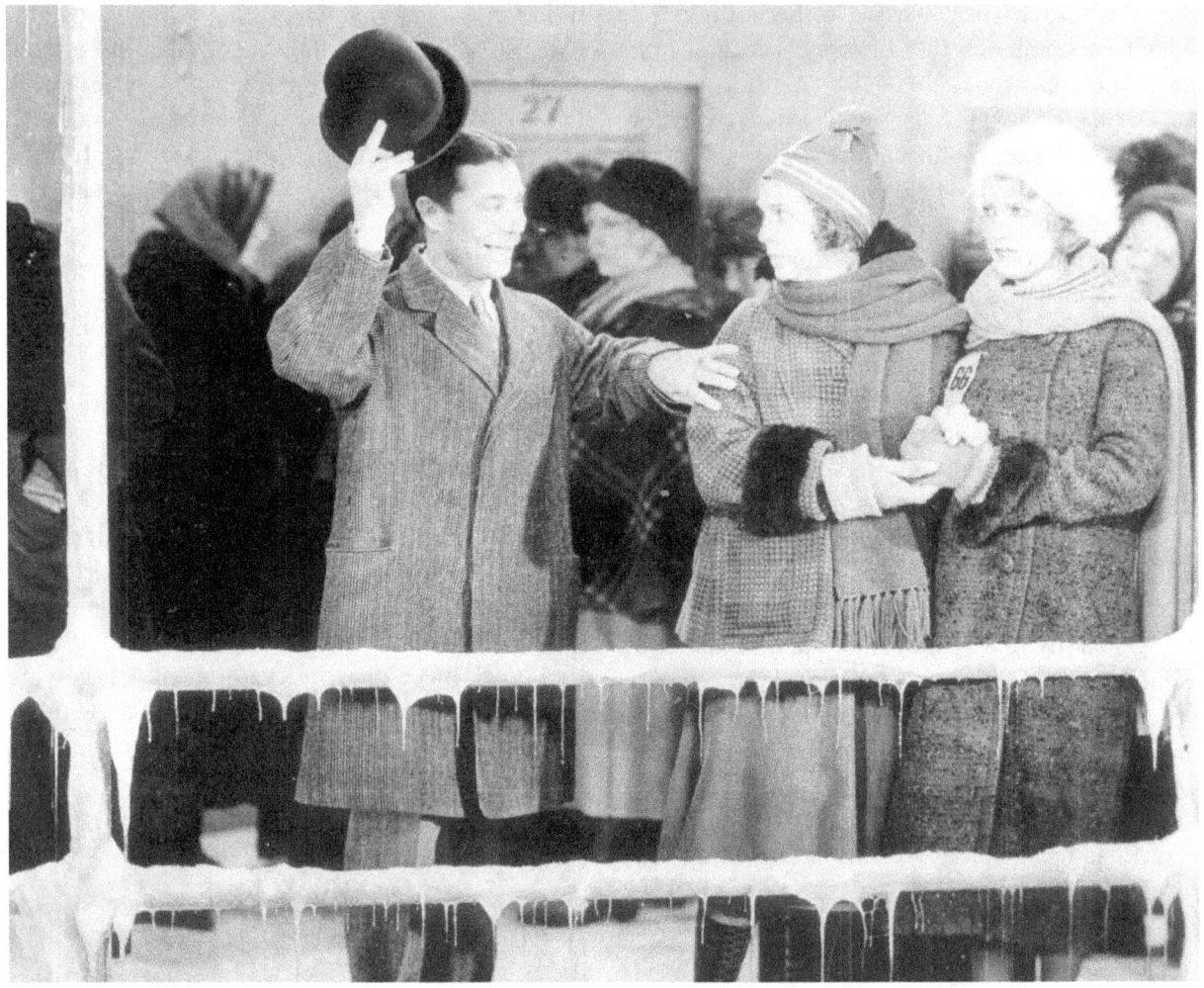

After Jenny gets out of prison, she decides to flee Oslo and start over in the remote north as a "picture bride." Hilda (ZaSu Pitts) has lost her café and Hoke (Joe E. Brown) has lost his black American jazz band, so they join her.

The bride boat is pulling out, and Hilda runs to join Jenny, wanting to get away from Hoke. But Hoke follows her, and so the three are headed for the Arctic Circle. They reach their destination and find the whole town turned out, but not for them. An Italian dirigible is due to land on its route over the North Pole. (Until the Hindenburg disaster, dirigibles were a popular subject for adventure films, e.g., *Dirigible, The Lost Zeppelin*.) Hilda accidentally gets a bride number pinned on the back of her coat, and mountainous miner Battleaxe Boris (Harry Gribbon) claims her, much to her delight and Hoke's dismay.

Olaf arrives to claim his bride, and Chris and Jenny confront each other. They pretend not to know each other, and their icy greetings are cut short by the arrival of the Italian dirigible. Olaf rushes off to direct the mooring, leaving Chris to care for Jenny. Chris refuses a reconciliation and Jenny resolves to be faithful to the good-hearted Olaf.

The Lottery Bride

The crowd welcomes the airship musically with "High and Low." From the comically minute cabin of the dirigible, steps—you guessed it—Alberto! In the necessary recognition scene that follows, all the interrelationships are cited (except that of Chris and Jenny) and Alberto intones: *"Strange* that we should all meet here." Olaf cheerfully invites Alberto to live at his house during the airship's stopover.

Hoke and Battleaxe resolve their rivalry over Hilda. To her disgust, they go off arm in arm to have a drink. The *ménage à quatre* has its problems too. Jenny is flirting with Alberto to spite Chris. "Alberto, do you remember the song I liked so well?" "Of course," he replies and sings eight bars of "Napoli," certainly the shortest tenor aria on record.

Robert Chisholm as Chris's brother provides the only believable moments in the film. Both he and Joseph Macaulay had just appeared in Friml's short-lived Broadway musical *Luana.* In 1934, Chisholm played "Macheath" in the first American production of Kurt Weill's *The Threepenny Opera.*

Back at the tavern, Hoke and Battleaxe are deep in the bottle, singing an incredibly tedious ballad of snakes and sotted illusions: "Two Strong Men."

Olaf is oblivious to the tensions in his little household. He tells Jenny how much he loves her: "You're an Angel." He casually exits the fantastically paneled room on his high note and Chris bitterly reprises the song.

The dirigible at long last is taking off for the North Pole. Chris has secretly joined the crew to get away. He tells Olaf he wishes him and Jenny all the happiness in the world and boards the ship. Jenny arrives just in time to see Chris waving from the rising dirigible. As the miners chant "High and Low," Jenny runs after the departing airship, with an effective point-of-view shot of her falling farther and farther behind as the dirigible picks up speed. The scene is strongly reminiscent of Renée Adorée's pursuit of John Gilbert in *The Big Parade* (1925). At last, Jenny falls weeping and exhausted into a snow bank. Her hand dislodges some loose snow, which plops on the miniature houses supposedly in the valley below.

Olaf is finally catching on. He wanders disconsolately about his cabin, finding a photo of Chris and Jenny under the pillow in her room. Naturally, he sings of his sorrow: "I'll Follow the Trail."

The dirigible isn't doing too well, either. It ices over and crashes. This scene is intercut with another tedious comedy sequence in which Hoke tries to promote Battleaxe as a prizefighter, only to have him licked by the smallest man in town.

With the dirigible down, Olaf tries to commandeer an icebreaker to get to Chris. Its captain tells him, "There's nothing out there but *death."* "My *brother's* out there!" intones Olaf. He sets out with a dogsled, refusing to take Jenny. Soon he too is lost. Meanwhile, Chris and Alberto leave the crash scene to go for help.

Back at the mining camp, Jenny leaps on a table and begs for volunteers to man the icebreaker. Hoke says he has a reputation for following women, so he might as well live up to it. "I'll go," cries a miner. "Let's all go," shouts another. They surge off in perfect operetta chorus fashion.

In the cardboard wasteland, Olaf happens upon Chris and Alberto, and amidst much panting, Jenny's innocence is revealed. Behind the *papier-maché* ice blocks upon which our heroes are reclining, we see a miniature icebreaker, a trickle of smoke coming from its smokestack. It trembles through the tiny paper icebergs, but our heroes are too far gone to see it. The camera cuts back and forth between the oncoming icebreaker and the fading adventurers, slowly at first, then faster and faster. The music grows louder and louder.

From the deck of the full-sized icebreaker, Jenny spots Chris. "Chris!" she cries. "Jenny!" he answers. The screen bursts into a Technicolor blaze of northern lights as the lovers wave to each other and the strains of "My Northern Light" rise in a grand climax.

Reviews

"Arthur Hammerstein's first talking and singing musical movie is pretty good as to score, but so altogether bereft is it of imagination in libretto, mounting, or approach, that it must take its place along toward the end of the class," reported the *New York Herald Tribune*.

Variety said "there isn't a worthwhile performance in the entire cast," and noted that "only don't-care theatres can safely venture this one in their bookings." The *New York Times* was becoming more respectful in reviewing the theatrical stepchild, cinema, and Mordaunt Hall was polite: "Rudolf Friml's musical compositions in *The Lottery Bride*...are thoroughly enjoyable, but, like most film operettas, the story, the dialogue and, to some extent, the acting, are quite another matter. It is a pictorial contribution that causes one to wish that the performers would sing more and talk considerably less."

"Your eyes are like the glory of the northern lights at play"—Friml was too often at the mercy of inferior lyric writers.

No Recordings

Music in the Film

Music by Rudolf Friml and lyrics by J. Keirn Brennan, except as noted. In listing performers after each title, "and" denotes a genuine duet, while commas between names indicate a sequence of singers.

Overture: "You're an Angel," "My Northern Light"
"Come Drink to the Girl that You Love" (chorus)
"Yubla" (MacDonald)
"My Northern Light" (Garrick, MacDonald)
Marathon music (orchestral) - authorship uncertain

The Lottery Bride

"Round She Whirls" (male chorus)
"Shoulder to Shoulder" (Garrick and Chisholm with male chorus)
"High and Low" (chorus)
"Napoli" (Macaulay)
"Two Strong Men" (Gribbon and Brown)
"You're an Angel" (Chisholm)
"High and Low" reprise (chorus)
"I'll Follow the Trail" (Chisholm)
Finale: "My Northern Light"

Trivia

The studios created "press books" to help theatre owners publicize each film. Besides special promotion ideas (like building fake igloos in the lobby or sending a knight in armour galloping around town), these large magazines contained ads that could be reproduced and news releases that the local press could print verbatim. A combination of facts, fantasy, and purple prose, they were sometimes issued before the film was completed and so described scenes that were never filmed or cut, or cast members who ended up on the cutting room floor.

Director Paul L. Stein poses for a publicity photo with Jeanette and possibly the dialogue director. Behind them are some of designer William Cameron Menzies' cardboard icebergs.

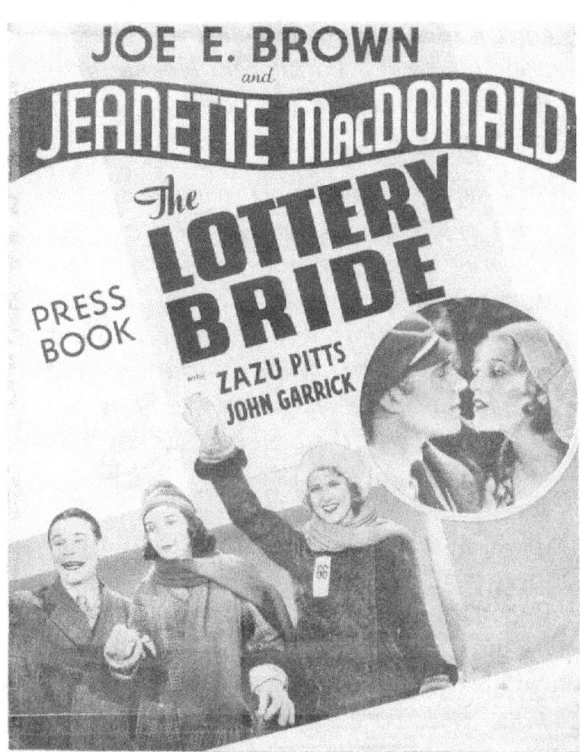

Press book cover. *Courtesy Anna Michalik.*

From *The Lottery Bride* press book:

> As many as nine exposures were made on a single film for the Technicolor sequence in order to present visions as they might appear in the minds of men.... The colorful scenes, set to music by Rudolph Friml, foremost living composer, represent the vision of three men lost in the arctic ice fields after a dirigible crash and who are resigning themselves to an icy death.
>
> John Garrick sings a love song, and the ice fields dissolve into the scenes of his native Oslo, where he sees himself being wedded to Jeanette MacDonald while beautiful little girls strew flowers and peasants turn out in holiday attire.
>
> Then Robert Chisholm joins in the singing and the vision changes to their

earlier life—a great ice carnival, a great army of skaters, ski jumpers leaping from the heavens and disappearing over the horizons.

Joseph Macaulay, portraying an aviator, sings of his native Rome. An extravagant vision of the city appears in the sky; there is music of a three-day Lenten carnival, the music of Holy Week, and processions merging into one that vanishes over a distant hill. The magnificence of is the result of experts. these blurring, dissolving, intermingling scenes

Little of this is visible in the final film, of course.

Reportedly, producer Arthur Hammerstein set up his own sound camera and simultaneously filmed his own personal copy of the picture.

Oh, for a Man!
Fox.
Released December 14, 1930.
Produced and directed by Hamilton MacFadden.
86 minutes.

French release title: *L'Amant de Minuit* (Midnight Lover)
Spanish release title: *¡Mio Seras!* (Mine alone!)

Based on the short story "Stolen Thunder" by Mary T. Watkins, published in the *Saturday Evening Post*, June 7, 1930. Screenplay: Philip Klein. Dialogue: Lynn Starling. Photography: Charles Clarke. Art Director: Stephen Goosson. Music Director: Arthur Kay. Sound Recording: E. Clayton Ward. Costumes: Sophie Wachner. Editor: Al De Gaetano. Movietone Recording.

The film was announced in September 1930 as a forthcoming vehicle for the popular Fox team of Janet Gaynor and Charles Farrell.

The only known surviving print of this film, missing reel 7, is at the Museum of Modern Art in New York.

Jeanette MacDonald (Carlotta Manson)
Reginald Denny (Barney McGann)
Warren Hymer (Pug Morini, the "Walloping Wop")
Marjorie White (Totsy Franklin)
Alison Skipworth (Laura, Carlotta's maid)
Albert Conti (Peck)
Bela Lugosi (Frescatti)
André Cheron (Costello, the voice coach)
William B. Davidson (Kerry Stokes)
Bodil Rosing (Masseuse)
Donald Hall (Backstage admirer)
Evelyn Hall (Pushy dowager with daughter)
Althea Henley (Dowager's daughter, June)
Mary Gordon (Flower seller)
Gino Corrado (Signor Ferrari)

With the fading of the film musical in late 1930, Jeanette continued to be dead wood at Paramount. They had no use for her, so, after *The Lottery Bride* at United Artists, she was lent to Fox for the remainder of her two-year contract.

Jeanette as Isolde. *Courtesy Patrick Kuster.*

Oh, for a Man!

The unsuspecting Carlotta (Jeanette) doesn't know that romance is about to come into her life in the person of an opera-loving burglar, Barney McGann (Reginald Denny).

The three films she made there disappeared during Fox's stormy merger with Twentieth Century Pictures in 1935, and they were believed lost until 1969, when portions turned up during a preservation program initiated by Alex Gordon. His efforts also located many of Fox's musical gems of the 1929–30 period, including *Fox Movietone Follies of 1930*, *Sunny Side Up*, and George Gershwin's *Delicious*, the latter two with Janet Gaynor.

Two of Jeanette's films at Fox were considered then and now as Bs, programmers to round out the new double bills. As with many Bs of the period, their very economy of length and "production value" make them the entertainment equals of heavier, more pretentious works.

Oh, for a Man! isn't a lost classic, but it has enough sparkle and historical interest to be worth saving. It's the first film in which Jeanette sings opera (the "Liebestod" from Wagner's *Tristan und Isolde*!). A fast and funny comedy, slim but refreshing as a summer lemonade, its sophisticated battle-of-the-sexes tale is nicely handled. It's Jeanette's picture all the way, and she tears a passion to tatters with elegance and great good humor. Her performance is almost balletic, her body, her arms, hands, fingers, eyebrows posed theatrically at every moment, a culmination of her stage training and her Lubitsch film technique. But never, even in the hands of Lubitsch, had she been more lovingly photographed or more stunningly gowned.

Director Hamilton MacFadden dealt mainly in Bs and westerns (later he did Charlie Chan vehicles), and it shows in his quick, simple style and bluff approach to situations that Paramount would have nursed for innuendo.

Jeanette's leading man is Reginald Denny, an elegant Englishman who had an impressive silent career, mainly as a zany romantic comedian of the Cary Grant school. Only recently have some of his early films become available, allowing a renewed appreciation of his flawless comedic timing.

Carlotta muses on the special talent of her handsome burglar. Her maid is played by Alison Skipworth, who appeared on stage with Jeanette in *Angela*.

Carlotta promises Barney that she will give up her career if he will give up his. Their honeymoon leaves them unoccupied during the day, and they soon long to return to work. *Courtesy John Martin.*

In the early days of sound, Denny maintained leading man status, appearing opposite Grace Moore in the fictionalized Jenny Lind biography, *A Lady's Morals* (1930), and as the errant husband of the exquisite Kay Johnson in Cecil B. DeMille's only musical, *Madame Satan* (1930).

However, his casting as the befuddled and discarded husband in Noël Coward's *Private Lives* (1931) was more typical of the rôles that would keep him in sound films for the next thirty-five years. His career encompassed more than 153 films.

The cast of *Oh, for a Man!* includes two bright ladies from Broadway. Bouncy, blonde Marjorie White's wisecracking and boisterous song and dance delivery had made her a staple of the early Fox musicals (*Sunny Side Up, Fox Movietone Follies of 1930, Just Imagine*), but, as with Jeanette, the demand for her talents was diminishing. Magnificent grand-dame Alison Skipworth plays Jeanette's motherly companion. She had begun as a Gaiety Girl and had a distinguished stage career behind her as did most of the notable Hollywood character actors of the 1930s. On Broadway, Skipworth had appeared briefly with Jeanette in the ill-fated *Angela* in 1928. Her elegant British diction and benign truck-driver face brought her dozens of rôles in good to middling films, including *Tillie and Gus* and *If I Had a Million*, before she retired from the screen in 1938, but she never got the one really memorable rôle she deserved.

Oh, for a Man! opens with Jeanette singing "The Liebestod" from Wagner's *Tristan and Isolde* behind the credits, the first time she sang opera on the screen. A program tells us that we are in the New York Opera House. Stage center, Carlotta Manson (Jeanette) is singing the famous aria over the body of her dead lover. High above, two stagehands ignore the drama below and match pennies on a catwalk. One jogs the spotlight with his elbow, and the lady finds herself in near darkness on her high note. Her cries of outrage bring them back to their job and Carlotta, exquisitely gowned in sequined chiffon, dies long and languidly, her voice revealing a surprisingly dark lower register for this early in the MacDonald career. The curtain descends on the prostrate Carlotta, and she springs to her feet, denouncing the electricians, her tenor, the management, everyone. She then instantly composes her features for a triumphant curtain call.

Backstage is just as hectic. She thanks an admirer for his recent gift of pearls and learns that he sent emeralds. A gushing patroness of the opera is waiting in her dressing room, hoping to arrange an audition for her giggling daughter. Fortunately, Carlotta's maid-companion, Laura (Alison Skipworth), announces that the diva's calendar is entirely filled and shows them out. While Carlotta suffers fools badly, she still considers herself a friend of struggling artists. She is very sympathetic to a young composer who shoves through the crowd at the stage door to speak with her, and she promises to hear his songs.

In Carlotta's elegant drawing room, several formally dressed men wait uneasily for the lady. From the next room come her ever-rising moans of pleasure. "It won't be long now," Laura comments. "She's loudest at the end."

Sure enough, the lady emerges ecstatically in a filmy peignoir. We are quickly set straight, for Carlotta is followed by her masseuse (Bodil Rosing), who is explaining she won't be able to come the next day. Her sister is having a baby. Carlotta is thrilled at the news, her arms making exultant arcs in the air. How marvelous! How splendid! She will be godmother and the christening will be held right here.

She turns on her waiting admirers. "Everyone cries, 'Carlotta, give me a song,'" she declares grandly. "No one ever cries, 'Oh, Carlotta, give

Jeanette's films were so popular in Europe that authorized novelizations were published. This French paperback runs 92 pages and contains 32 photos. *Courtesy Pierre Guinle.*

me a baby!'" Thus inspired, Kerry Stokes (William B. Davidson) stays and proposes. Carlotta tells him quite touchingly that she plans to sing and sing until she's eighty and then be a lonely old lady. He shakes his head sadly. "You always win," he says. "Why not?" she replies. "No one ever offered me enough opposition."

He departs, and, in the awaited negligée sequence, she prepares for bed in the seductive half-light. Laura tucks her under her satin coverlet and opens the French doors for air as Carlotta snuggles happily into her pillow.

We fade in on a man's wristwatch set at 3:00. French doors open onto a moonlit balcony (beyond which hangs a solid black velour curtain, a holdover from the stage convention). An arm sporting the same wristwatch comes over the edge of the balcony, and a shadowy figure pulls himself up and enters the room. His flashlight wanders about until it settles on a jewel box. "They're not real," Carlotta tells him calmly. The figure rushes at the bed and tries to slip a chloroformed rag over her face. She announces that she is Carlotta Manson and shrilly orders him to stop at once. "Do you want to ruin the world's most beautiful voice?"

The malevolent figure draws back. Why, he gasps, he always goes to the opera when she is singing! Good opera inspires him to do his best work. Carlotta is fascinated and soon charms him into removing his bandana mask and cap. The bed light reveals a chiseled profile that goes nicely with his muscular body. (Denny was frequently cast as a boxer in silents, although here, nearing forty, he was getting a bit chunky. Denny's American boy-next-door image had been shattered when sound revealed his British origin, and directors were still not sure what to do with him. Here, he attempts to be "American" with a somewhat erratic Irish brogue.) Carlotta studies the interloper. "Why, you're *much* too good looking to be a burglar!" she gushes.

"I've been pretty nice to you," he says suddenly. "Now you're going to do something for me." The lady's little shiver of happy horror turns to amazement when he explains that he wants her opinion of his voice. She must make allowances, of course. His night work is pretty rough on the throat. "We singers understand," she nods. He launches into a high-powered rendition of "Believe Me If All Those Endearing Young Charms." The tone is good, but the high notes are deliberately strained and off key. (Denny was announced for the rôle of Danilo in the planned 1930 film version of *The Merry Widow* and could really sing.)

Nevertheless, Carlotta finds herself strangely stirred by the handsome robber. It must be his singing, she decides.

At this moment, Laura pounds on the door. "Who's singing?" she calls. "I am," Carlotta replies. The knowing Laura makes a perfunctory fuss about Carlotta having a man in her room and leaves. Carlotta confides that they won't be bothered again and turns her attention to her burglar's career. She can just see him in tights, she thrills, happily hugging herself. She will arrange everything. Tomorrow night her very own conductor and manager will audition him. The burglar is cynical. Suppose they turn out to be police officers? She gives him her pearl ring as a sign of faith. And what is his name? she cries as he starts toward the balcony. "Never ask a burglar his real name," he says, "but you can call me 'Barney McGann.'" Then he kisses her long and hard. She comes up for air spluttering angrily. "I might have taken a lot more than that," he laughs and leaves.

Carlotta rages silently at the window, her body writhing in fury. The arch of her back slowly changes to a catlike sensuality, and her clenched fists uncurl to make little stroking gestures in the air. She turns and dances slowly across the room, crooning to herself. Then, purring, she flings herself on the bed with a happy convulsion: "Oh, Carlotta, this is *life*!"

Barney arrives belligerently the next day to audition for Peck (Albert Conti) and Frescatti (Bela Lugosi, already famous for his stage

Oh, for a Man!

Barney runs into his old friends, Totsy (Marjorie White, seated) and Pug Morini, the "Walloping Wop" (Warren Hymer, far right). Their boisterous ways irritate Carlotta, and soon the honeymooners part. Here, a scene from the lost reel, which included a song by White. She was a Fox jazz baby who delivered hot numbers in many early musicals.

portrayal of Dracula and shortly to appear in the film version). Barney tells them he doesn't know what his song is about because it is in German. He belts out a very loud, very Germanic art song. Peck and Frescatti's faces are a study, but Carlotta is radiant. "What do you think?" she cries when Barney has left the room. "Well, what do *you* think?" asks the kindly Peck. Carlotta rages that they are prejudiced, that they won't give a young singer a chance. She wants no less than an opera contract for the coming season. Barney can start in the chorus and work up. It will only cost them one-hundred dollars a week (quite a salary in those days when a family could live comfortably on thirty dollars a week). Peck sees the value of this investment in Carlotta's tranquility and consents.

Barney agrees to give up his night work—"You can't afford to expose that marvelous throat"—and begins his lessons. Carlotta's very own teacher, Costello (André Cheron, the irate husband in *The Love Parade*), takes on the job, but is soon at the end of his wits. Although Barney dutifully swallows the raw eggs Carlotta brings him, he can't get his vocalizing right. He tells Costello to keep his shirt on and the little man explodes. "All right, take it off," Barney says. "Run around in your B.V.D.s."

Costello storms that Barney will never be a singer and stalks out. Carlotta turns on Barney. How does he expect to be a singer? "I *don't*," he replies. He's always had his freedom—"except for two years and six months"—and he isn't going to give it up now. He'll send her a check to pay the maestro for the lessons. He has never owed a woman anything, he says, picking up his cap.

Carlotta realizes that desperate measures are called for and flings herself in his way. "I couldn't live without you," she says tremulously. "Forget everything except me...I *love* you." She moves her face closer to his, and he kisses her. "I want to marry you," she sighs, clinging to him. Barney laughs harshly.

He won't be the husband of a prima donna. Why, he'd end up carrying her luggage around and fetching her things and walking her dogs while she performed. He'd be known only as her husband. Carlotta knows her own mind. She'll quit. She's always loathed this life and now she has the courage to give it all up. "You kinda like me?" Barney asks. She exults in his embrace, head back, arms extended. "Ah, this is *life*!"

She rushes about, preparing for her new life. Barney must call her chauffeur, Laura must get her coat, and Peck must call the opera house. Barney reluctantly goes to look for the chauffeur, Peck dashes for the phone, and Laura more sensibly announces that she is quitting. Carlotta is too excited to notice. "My heart is like a singing bird," she cries and exits with a grand flourish.

In a beautifully lit night shot on a boat deck, Carlotta and Barney are being seen off to Italy. Laura comes trudging up the gangplank, much to Barney's dismay. "What is that sister of Satan doing here?" he growls. Carlotta airily assures him that she can't live without Laura and thrusts her two Pomeranians into his arms while she poses for photographers. As Barney sulks, someone cries, "Oh, there's Carlotta Manson's husband." His gloom deepens.

A title over a lake and mountain scene tells us: "In Sunny Italy—'Love works its magic spell.'" Barney is awakened in his fantastic brocaded bed by the sound of Carlotta vocalizing in the next room. He expresses his displeasure by going to the punching bag incongruously sitting in one corner and whamming away. Carlotta is then revealed lying in her bed next door. She sits up in astonishment and vocalizes even more insistently. The volley of noise from Barney's room increases. The sound mixing on this scene, indeed the sound quality in the whole picture, is superb.

Carlotta shouts inaudibly to Laura to tell Barney to stop, but Laura's pounding on the intervening door is lost in the sounds of Barney's anger. Carlotta flees to her dressing room, and Laura notices Barney's slippers at the foot of

"Find him!" Carlotta orders her manager (Albert Conti). She has finally realized that her adoring public can't provide what Barney can.

Oh, for a Man!

Carlotta's bed. With an air of studied distaste she picks them up between thumb and forefinger and, holding them at arm's length, slips Barney's door open and drops them inside.

Breakfast is laid on the terrace, and Barney's bad day continues. The newspaper is all in Italian, a language he doesn't understand. Laura dumps his breakfast on the table. The soft-boiled egg comes apart in his hand. Then the Pomeranians come out to yap at him. He scares them away by pounding on the ground with a large loaf of Italian bread just as Carlotta sweeps out in another fabulous negligée. "If you must be brutal," she says icily, "why don't you attack someone your own size?" "I haven't seen someone my own size since I got here," he cries.

She begins reading the newspaper, clucking happily over the news of the opera world. "Is there anything in there to interest me?" he growls. Yes, she replies tartly. A jewel robbery. They quarrel until she has him near the point of striking her, then they kiss passionately. "Oh, darling," she sighs, "I don't believe I've ever been so happy." They nuzzle affectionately. "These perfect days," Carlotta murmurs, "and the nights are even more wonderful."

Doesn't she miss her fine friends? he asks. Oh, no, she replies. There's no one else in the world but Barney. At these words, a car pulls up and a group of her friends pour out, talking volubly in Italian. She carries on an animated conversation with them, introducing Barney. They depart, still talking, and she tells him she has been asked to sing at a charity bazaar that night. She simply can't refuse. Then, of course, they must go away at once or her friends will never leave them alone. Unfortunately, she has friends in all the interesting places, so she's not sure where they can go.

The bazaar takes place on the huge "Long Island estate" set used in *Sunny Side Up*. Barney is discovered sullenly wadding bits of chocolate cake into balls and tossing them at a statue of Venus, where they form "buttons" down her ample bosom. Suddenly he is recognized by an

A Spanish poster for *Oh, for a Man!* The title means "Mine Alone!" *Courtesy Anna Michalik.*

old friend, Totsy Franklin (Marjorie White). She also is in Italy on her honeymoon. She has married Barney's friend, Pug Morini, the "Walloping Wop" (Warren Hymer). Pug dashes over to greet Barney just as Carlotta is introduced on stage.

Wearing an enormous and very becoming horsehair garden hat, Carlotta struggles through her art song, "On a Summer Night," disconcerted by the bursts of laughter from Barney and his friends.

She finishes and comes coolly to meet them. He tells her that Totsy is a singer too, and Totsy asks innocently, "Oh, do you sing?"

"I was just trying to," Carlotta replies, "but you probably didn't hear me through all the din and excitement." She and Barney tiff, and he tells her to stay with her high-hat friends. He is going home with Totsy and Pug.

Reel 7 is still lost, but in it we presume that Carlotta returns home to find a boisterous revel in progress. We know from contemporary reviews that Totsy sings a red-hot number called "I'm Just Nuts about You." Apparently this is the source of more friction, for reel 8 begins with Carlotta weeping on her bed. "My lover has left me," she wails, flailing the pillows. "I'll *kill* myself!"

"Yes, darling," Laura replies matter of factly, "but not today. Never kill yourself when you're miserable." She suggests that Carlotta lose herself in her work, but the lady is set on more histrionics. "I want to stay here and dream of my lost love!"

Laura continues her good-humored advice until Carlotta's anguish subsides. Her body sags, then stiffens with resolve. She has been a traitor to her public. Now she will make amends. She will sing. "This is *life*!" she cries, tears streaming down her face.

Another title tells us that it is "New York City—opening of the opera season." Carlotta rushes into her dressing room in a fantastically jeweled and low cut "Juliet" costume. Why is she doing all this? she demands of Laura. "Three thousand dollars," Laura replies. "*Dust and ashes!*" wails the prima donna. There hasn't been a word from Barney, but Laura suspects that the six-foot flower-covered heart in the corner is not from one of Carlotta's aristocratic friends. Carlotta grabs the attached note: "Hope you knock 'em cold tonight."

She decides Barney must be in the opera house and sends Peck to watch the exits. Find him, she orders, bring him back. Peck promises and sprints off.

At her apartment, Carlotta paces the floor, waiting. A knock, and Peck appears. She looks eagerly past him, but he is alone. She sends Peck away and begins stalking the room. She loathes the world! She wants to get away from it.

"How about Mars?" suggests Laura languidly. Carlotta has another idea. "I'll become a nun!" she cries happily. Laura will follow her to Mars, but not into a convent. She leaves Carlotta, who has assumed a radiant, prayerful attitude in the moonlit bedroom.

Carlotta has slipped into bed when a familiar arm reaches over the balcony. "Barney...is that you?" she calls.

"How many burglars do you know?" replies a familiar voice. He had a job down the block and so he stopped in to see how she was. He admits he saw her sing. The first part was okay, but the last act was "punk." Her heart wasn't in it, she sighs. "Artists like you and me," he says sternly, "never get anywhere unless we keep our minds on our jobs." He starts toward the balcony.

"Wouldn't you like to stay a little while?" she calls, plucking at the coverlet.

He turns. "Longer than that if someone should ask me." He sinks down on the bed and they kiss for a fadeout that surprisingly is unaccompanied by music. We assume they are reunited happily if not peacefully ever after.

Reviews

Variety reported that the film was "a frothy farce... one of those physical romances nicely shaded through Hamilton MacFadden's suave direction and capable performances by Jeanette MacDonald and Reginald Denny. Picture is hardly of deluxe house caliber, but should get by nicely in the neighborhoods. Miss MacDonald handled several comic situations with finesse and sings two interpolated songs, one operatic, to set her among the best of the screen sopranos."

Mildred Martin in the *Philadelphia Inquirer* thought Jeanette's Isolde was "self conscious... fortunately picture audiences are not as exacting as operatic ones." She conceded that "[Carlotta's] tantrums, her vanity, and her power of self-dramatization are amusingly handled by Miss MacDonald."

No Recordings.

Music in the Film

In listing performers after each title, "and" denotes a genuine duet, while commas between names indicate a sequence of singers.

Overture and opening sequence: "The Liebestod" from *Tristan und Isolde* (MacDonald) - Richard Wagner
"Believe Me If All Those Endearing Young Charms" (Denny) - traditional music, lyrics by Thomas Moore
German art song (Denny) - composer uncertain
"On a Summer Night" (MacDonald) - William Kernell
"I'm Just Nuts About You" (White) - William Kernell
No finale, film ends in silence

Don't Bet on Women

Fox.
Released: February 15, 1931.
Produced by Fox Films.
Associate Producer: John W. Considine Jr.
Directed by William K. Howard.
70 minutes.

British release title: *More Than a Kiss*

Based on the original story "All Women Are Bad," by William Anthony McGuire. Screenplay and dialogue: Lynn Starling and Leon Gordon. Staged by: Henry Kolker. Photography: Lucien Andriot. Editor: Harold Schuster. Costumes: Sophie Wachner. Sets: Duncan Cramer. Sound: Albert Protzman. Movietone Recording.

The only known surviving print of this film is at the Museum of Modern Art in New York.

Edmund Lowe (Roger Fallon)
Jeanette MacDonald (Jeanne Drake)
Roland Young (Herbert Drake)
J. M. Kerrigan (Chipley Duff)
Una Merkel (Tallulah Hope)
Helene Millard (Doris Brent Fallon)
James T. Mack (Sommers, Fallon's valet)
Henry Kolker (Butterfield)
Louise Beavers (Maid)
Cyril Ring (Jeanne's dancing partner)

Don't Bet on Women is the second of Jeanette's three "lost" films for the Fox studios, believed to have been destroyed in a vault fire. Fortunately, a print has been found, adding to our understanding of this critical period in the history of Hollywood and the career of Miss MacDonald.

The film turns out to be a typical "programmer" of the early 1930s. Director William K. Howard (*The Cat and the Fiddle*) had not yet mastered the talkie form, and the film is pictorially sluggish. Edmund Lowe (who had played "Quirt" to Victor McLaglen's "Flagg" in *What Price Glory?*, the sizzling 1926 war story) was more at home in rugged he-man rôles. Here, he is stuck in a drawing room comedy. Roland Young (*One Hour with You*) plays his usual dry, acerbic character. (It takes a great suspension of disbelief to imagine any romantic feelings between his character and his on-screen wife, Jeanette.) Una Merkel *(The Merry Widow)*, one of the unsung treasures of Hollywood, glitters as Jeanette's comedic best friend.

It was Jeanette's first non-singing rôle, although at one point she actually sits down at

Jeanne (Jeanette) and her husband (Roland Young) are happy until he decides to gamble. *Courtesy James Robert Parish.*

the piano and strums the keys. Possibly a song was cut so the studio could advertise, as so many did, "This is not a musical!"

Contemporary viewers labeled it a stylish drawing room sex comedy of the type done so well by Lubitsch at Paramount. The film opens late at night in a swank Manhattan bachelor's apartment. Sommers, the valet (James T. Mack), is fielding phone calls from ardent females and making excuses for his absent master, ladies' man Roger Fallon (Edmund Lowe). Roger returns home from a night on the town with his rotund friend, Chipley "Chip" Duff (J.M. Kerrigan). He congratulates Sommers on protecting him from his over-eager girlfriends. Just then, his greedy ex-wife bursts through the door.

Doris (Helene Millard) wants more money so she can afford to marry her new beau, only her second marriage since she and Roger parted five years before. Roger readily agrees. He owes it to her. Once he loved and worshipped her, but she has educated him, teaching him that "all women are bad—for *me*."

Because his own lawyer might think he'd turned sentimental, Roger goes to Chip's lawyer, Herbert Drake, to have the agreement drawn up. The pompous Herbert (Roland Young) doesn't approve of divorce. It is invariably the man's fault. Women, he says, are like children—sometimes sweet, sometimes naughty. They require a man to guide them. Herbert primly describes his unvarying and utterly boring daily routine. "Must be very exciting for your wife," jokes Roger. "I try *never* to excite my wife," says Herbert smugly. "It's not good for her."

They debate the nature of women. "All women are bad," declares Roger amiably. Herbert disagrees: "My wife and I have absolute trust." Roger grins. "There's *nothing* a woman resents so much," he tells Herbert. "It's a dreadful comment on her charm."

That evening, Roger and Chip are on board Roger's yacht in Long Island Sound, preparing to head for the high seas and anywhere they won't run into women. Just then, they hear cries

Her husband bets playboy Roger Fallon (Edmund Lowe) that he can't kiss the first woman who walks in the room. The black maid is first, so they agree it shall be the *second* woman. Jeanne enters.

for help. A swimmer in distress. And female! "Women are *always* in trouble," says Chip. He's for letting her drown, but Roger gallantly hauls her onboard. Their sputtering mermaid is the beautiful if daffy southern belle, Tallulah (Una Merkel). Chip is examining her for injuries in a strictly pre-Code and enjoyable fashion when a motor launch pulls alongside, piloted by Tallulah's anxious friend, Jeanne Drake (Jeanette).

Jeanne is invited on board and Roger soon forgets his eagerness to get away from women. Jeanne, however, is cool to his advances. She's married, she says, and suggests he is the kind who only pursues unavailable women. "Are you insinuating I enjoy forbidden fruit?" asks Roger. "I should say an apple a day was your diet for years," she replies.

Chip is making much better progress with Tallulah, who invites both men to Jeanne's big party that evening. Jeanne seconds the invita-

Don't Bet on Women

tion. "You tempt me frightfully!" smiles Roger. "Aren't I lucky?" teases Jeanne. "I haven't had a good temptation in years." When Roger learns that Jeanne is Herbert Drake's "perfect" wife, he promises to attend.

At the party, Tallulah discovers that Chip was born in Limerick, Ireland and dazzles him with a limerick of her own:

There was a young lady from Athens
Who hand-painted china just lovely.
When people said, "Oh,"
She said, "I don't care.
You don't get paid much for it anyway."

Roger and Herbert again trade quips and barbs about women's virtue, while an orchestra plays in the adjoining ballroom. "Kisses," opines Roger, "are the food of love....If women don't have a good cook at home, you can't blame them for going out for their meals."

"You mean no woman can resist you," sneers Herbert. He so detests Roger's cynical attitude

Roger discovers that Jeanne is in love with him. Worse yet, he is in love with her.

that he proposes a wager. He will pay Roger $10,000 if Roger can get the next woman to walk in the room to kiss him within forty-eight hours. "Agreed!" cries Roger. They look toward the door. The black maid (Louise Beavers) enters.

With a shrug, the two men move to the veranda and start over. Tallulah approaches. Roger turns her away. Then suddenly Jeanne steps away from her dancing partner and crosses the threshold with a smile.

Roger chivalrously suggests that Herbert won't want to go through with the bet, but Herbert insists. Roger will be their houseguest for the next two days.

As Herbert and Jeanne prepare for bed that night, he tells her about a hypothetical bet a friend has made about his wife's virtue. Jeanne thinks it is revolting. "But the husband has nothing to worry about," she says. Herbert beams. "Unless the man is attractive," she adds. Herbert groans softly.

The next morning, Tallulah, tipped off by Chip, tells Jeanne about the bet. Jeanne vows to have her revenge on both men for this insult. Besides, she's curious what her own reactions will be: "There's no virtue in a woman being good if she's never had a chance to be bad." To Herbert's horror, Jeanne insists on going through with the bet. "Oh, what an opportunity for a good woman!" she exults.

Far from avoiding Roger during the next two days, she tells the now-sheepish gamblers, she intends to spend every moment with him to test herself. She and Roger prepare to go horseback riding. Herbert nervously insists on joining them, but is prevented by the arrival of Butterfield (Henry Kolker), an important client seeking a patent on an umbrella.

On a remote, romantic hillside, Jeanne ridicules Roger's skillful lovemaking. She will enjoy observing his methods, she says tartly. He squirms with embarrassment, but continues, growing more and more eloquent. Eventually she is moved. The lady is starting to weaken.

Jeanne's friend Tallulah (Una Merkel) discloses the bet. Before the "Code" began in 1934, screen heroines could spend much of their time in lovely lingerie.

Romance is in the air. Chip and Tallulah announce their engagement. The two couples will dine with Roger at his apartment that night to celebrate. Later, Herbert quizzes Jeanne about her day as they dress for this party. She playfully tells Herbert how much she admires Roger's prowess—with horses. Herbert replies defensively that *he* was in the cavalry. Jeanne taunts Herbert by quoting his infantalizing comments about women. The quarrel escalates, until Herbert says he won't go. Jeanne says she will go alone. Herbert, sulking, refuses to kiss her goodbye. "Too bad," says Jeanne. "This is one night I feel like being kissed!"

After the celebratory dinner at Roger's apartment, Chip and Tallulah depart to see *Outrages of 1931*. Jeanne has seen the show, so she and Roger stay behind alone. She sits at the piano and begins playing. A song seems imminent. Then, heartbreakingly, she turns away. ("This is *not* a musical.")

The couple flirt and spar. "Woo me, try me, test me," she challenges. He does, and she cannot help herself. She confesses she loves him. He starts to kiss her, then pushes her away. He genuinely loves her. Jeanne is hurt and dumbfounded. In a fury, she denounces him and slaps his face, just as Herbert walks through the door. "A triumph for right thinking!" Herbert cries.

Roger gives Herbert his check for $10,000, but Herbert tears it up. He is content, he says, to have shown Roger how wrong he has been about women. As Herbert and Jeanne exit, she impetuously kisses Roger. Alone, Roger laughs sardonically. "Don't bet on women!" he says.

Reviews

The New York papers were divided. The *New York Post* said, "Save your money." Mordaunt Hall in the *New York Times* called the film "an excellent comedy sketch, bubbling with bright lines and originality. It is worked with real skill and directed imaginatively by William K. Howard. The two players who furnish most of the amusement are Miss Merkel and Mr. Young. Miss MacDonald is quite effective in her part."

Variety noted that drawing room comedies rarely did good business. "All it has besides the players' names is a magnificent technical production and a good deal of smart literary quality which are poor substitutes for entertainment punch....an inept story superlatively acted. Jeanette MacDonald plays the heroine charmingly." They also picked out Una Merkel and Roland Young as the outstanding performances.

No Recordings or Songs

Annabelle's Affairs
Fox.
Released June 14, 1931.
Associate Producer: William Goetz.
Directed by Alfred L. Werker.
76 minutes.

U.S. prerelease titles: *Two Can Play; Good Gracious Annabelle*

Adapted from Clare Kummer's popular 1916 play, *Good Gracious Annabelle*. Adaptation and Dialogue Director: Leon Gordon. Contributing Writer: Harlan Thompson. Costumes: Dolly Tree. Photography: Charles Clarke. Editor: Margaret Clancy. Assistant Director: Horace Hough. Sound Engineer: Al Bruzlin. Art Director: Duncan Cramer.

In 1919, Ms. Kummer's play became a silent film, also called *Good Gracious Annabelle*. It starred Billie Burke and Herbert Rawlinson. Sigmund Romberg composed a musical version, *Annie Dear*, in 1924, which also starred Billie Burke, along with Ernest Truex. (The 1938 film *The Affairs of Annabel* with Lucille Ball and Jack Oakie is unrelated to this film.)

The U.C.L.A. Film Archive has the only known surviving footage, reel 3, of this lost treasure.

Victor McLaglen (John Rawson, AKA Hefty Jack)
Jeanette MacDonald (Annabelle Leigh)
Roland Young (Roland Wimbledon)
Sam Hardy (James Ludgate, the butler)
William Collier Sr. (Wickham)
Ruth Warren (Lottie, the maid)

Miner John Rawson (Victor McLaglen) discovers his wandering wife, Annabelle Leigh (Jeanette), checking into a posh New York hotel. (Bellboy Robert Parrish later became a director. Cyril Ring, right.)

Sally Blane (Dora)
Joyce Compton (Mabel)
George André Beranger (Archie)
Walter Walker (Walter J. Gosling)
Ernest Wood (McFadden)
Jed Prouty (Bolson)
Hank Mann (Summers)
Wilbur Mack (Vance, the assistant. hotel manager)
Louise Beavers (Ruby)
Robert Parrish (Bellboy)
Cyril Ring (Desk clerk)
Ward Bond (Butler)*

* First time that Ward Bond and Victor McLaglen played a scene together in the same film. They were later leading members of John Ford's stock company.

The last of Jeanette's three "lost" Fox films may be truly lost. Only one reel is known to have survived and it now reposes in the archives of U.C.L.A. The fragment reveals a fast-paced, lightweight comedy, certainly superior to Jeanette's other Fox efforts, but because the film features no legendary stars (Garbo, Dietrich) or director and the one reel has no commercial value whatsoever, it may be doomed to turning to jelly in the can.

The film reunited Jeanette with two *Don't Bet on Women* players, Roland Young and Louise Beavers. Young was very well received in *Annabelle's Affairs* for his portrayal of an inebriated millionaire ("Gorgeously amusing"—

Philadelphia Inquirer). Victor McLaglen also scored nicely in one of the diamond-in-the-rough rôles he had gravitated to in American films (*The Cock-eyed World, The Black Watch*). He managed to mask his British accent sufficiently to be believable as a Montana miner. Jeanette, of course, had a bath and lingerie scene.

Clare Kummer's popular 1918 play, *Good Gracious Annabelle*, provided the basis of the

Annabelle doesn't recognize her husband after he follows her to New York City and undergoes a transformation at the barber shop.

film. The story, as reconstructed from contemporary synopses and reviews, is this: Annabelle Leigh, played by Jeanette ("an extravagant but adorable minx," *New York Post*), is thrown from her horse and twists her ankle. She takes refuge in the shack of a miner, John Rawson (Victor McLaglen), and jokingly suggests that their spending the night together has compromised her. He rushes off and returns with a minister. To her astonishment, they are married on the spot. She departs in the morning, but John insists on sending her fat support checks each month.

Annabelle is the type of girl who can't live without a hotel suite and a charge account at the modiste, so she doesn't object. When the checks stop eight years later, she gets a loan on fifty shares of "worthless" mining stock from millionaire playboy Roland Wimbledon (Roland Young). Then her lawyer informs her that the stock is now worth several million dollars. It is at this point that the surviving reel begins.

Annabelle is racing distractedly across a posh hotel lobby, swathed in furs and sporting a very becoming end-of-the-cloche hat with angled brim. Her husband, John, pursues her and introduces himself. She recognizes neither the name nor the face, but he persists. (He has undergone an amusing metamorphosis at the local barber shop and outfitted himself in "city slicker" clothes.) He is from Montana, from "the mines out there." She races on, and he follows. Does she know anything about mines? "No, not much, except they used them in the war."

He tells her he has a message from her husband, and she stops short. "He told me all about you," John says expansively. "How indelicate," she snaps. "He told me you had the prettiest eyes and the sharpest nails of any woman east of the Rockies...I'm inclined to agree about the eyes."

Annabelle softens and invites him to join her and her friends for lunch. She asks him to wear a sprig of lily-of-the-valley from the ample bouquet pinned to her furs, and he happily agrees. She immediately changes her mind (undoubtedly an unexplained plot device), but he insists. She tells him coyly that he can supply something she and her friends lack at lunch. What that is becomes obvious in the next scene.

John entertains Annabelle and her friends, Dora (Sally Blane), Mabel (Joyce Compton), and Archie (George André Beranger), with tales of her husband's despair after she left and of his subsequent education at the hands of an English school teacher. "She must have had large hands," Annabelle scoffs. John demonstrates her husband's rough and ready style on anemic little

Fox maintained the image that Lubitsch had created for Jeanette, that of a pampered, adorable, but empty-headed sex object living in a luxurious fantasy world. Louise Beavers plays her maid. *Courtesy Anna Michalik.*

Archie. When he begins a second anecdote, Archie shrinks back out of reach, and John is forced to twist a silver platter into a tube instead.

A telegram is delivered to Annabelle announcing that her husband is in town. She rushes off to phone her lawyer. Passing swiftly down the row of payphones, she matter-of-factly feels in each coin-return until she finds the necessary nickel and drops it in the slot. (She is obviously used to cutting corners.) While she is placing her call, Ludgate (Sam Hardy) stops at the next phone to call the Genteel Employment Agency. He is seeking a cook, a gardener, and two parlor maids. "Do they also handle sea captains?" he inquires.

Annabelle dashes after him and asks archly if he is seeking "an artiste de la cuisine." "A what?" "A cook." Ludgate admits that he is, on behalf of Mr. Wimbledon of Rock Point, Long Island.

"The man who bought my stocks!" she cries. "I beg your pardon?" says Ludgate. "Don't mention it," she replies.

Ludgate lists the luxurious accommodations and simple duties that make up the job. "But you're not a cook," he decides, gazing at her lavish costume. "How dare you!" she snaps. She describes several gourmet dishes until Ludgate's

Annabelle's Affairs

DRESSED: Pals Dora, Mabel, and Annabelle (Sally Blane, Joyce Compton, and Jeanette).

UNDRESSED: Annabelle, Dora, and Mabel in a pre-Code moment.
Both photos courtesy Anna Michalik.

mouth is watering, his eyes rolled back in ecstasy. She is hired. Before she leaves for Long Island, she tells him, she will need a hundred dollars. Better yet, split the difference and make it two hundred. Ludgate offers to drive her down as soon as he locates some additional servants. "What kind of car?" she asks. "Rolls Royce." "Color?" "Sort of a...dark black." "Satisfactory." All these exchanges are in light, rapid-fire style that makes even simple statements read like punch lines.

The mining shares change hands several times before Annabelle discovers that the man she has grown to love is her husband. (Sam Hardy, second from left.)

Annabelle tells Ludgate she has an excellent gardener and two "unbelievable" parlor maids for him. They are lunching with her right this minute in the Gold Room, she explains, and she goes to get them. "The *Gold* Room?" Ludgate murmurs incredulously. These must be very wealthy servants.

Back in the Gold Room, Annabelle's friends are trying desperately to leave John with the check, obviously Annabelle's original intention. First Dora excuses herself to wash her hands. Mabel says she had better go help. "She always forgets to take off her gloves."

Finally Archie lets out a loud groan. His foot has gone to sleep. Maybe, suggests John, he should walk on it. Archie does so...and keeps going. The table is deserted, and the waiter presents the bill: lunch–$45; platter–$22.50.

In the lobby, Annabelle hastily explains her plan to her co-conspirators. Archie protests he knows nothing of being a gardener, but she assures him he can read a book on their way down. She introduces herself to Ludgate as "Mrs. Annie Butterfield" and assigns false names to her friends. Ludgate begins listing their wages just as the reel ends.

John follows this motley crew to Rock Point and becomes captain of Wimbledon's yacht. Wimbledon's only requisite for this job is that the applicant be able to dance the hornpipe.

Wimbledon is a jolly soul who spends all his time drunk. This leads to several slapstick sequences. In one, he drives his car, full of singing cronies, through hairbreadth escapes. In another, his servants place crockery around his unconscious form, knowing that when he wakes from a drunken stupor he likes to smash things.

With John and Annabelle both after the mining shares, the shares change hands throughout the rest of the film. Sam Hardy as the butler who is fired every few minutes and Ruth Warren (of the vaudeville team "Wayne and Warren") as a drunken maid both drew nice press notices. Annabelle finally gets the shares of stock back. She tells John she loves him but must, in honor, return the shares to her husband. He then reveals his identity with a bear hug.

Reviews

All reviews of *Annabelle's Affairs* were so favorable that, even allowing for "dating," it is clear that a very pleasant little comedy has been lost. The gist of *Variety*'s review was that Jeanette did "an Ajax" "holding up [the film] practically alone" with her comic skill. *Variety* liked the film a lot and said: "This picture gives every indication of winning for Miss MacDonald as many followers as her previous screen efforts combined. She romps here and delightfully. A splendid farceur and, on this effort, the best

Annabelle's Affairs

Bathing was rarely a solitary activity in pre-Code films or done above floor level. Here, Dora (Sally Blane) and Mabel (Joyce Compton) admire the plumbing. *Courtesy Anna Michalik.*

among the femme contingent on the coast." High praise indeed!

Time Magazine ran a picture of Jeanette in satin "step-ins" and commented "she undresses well." Of the film, they said "it is hilariously funny farce of a sort rarely seen in the cinema."

The New York reviewers loved Jeanette: "... plays the part admirably"–*New York Post*; "... does a first rate job"–*New York World-Telegram*. But her hometown critic, Mildred Martin of the *Philadelphia Inquirer*, continued to be very cool to Jeanette's abilities: "[The film's] chief defect is Philadelphia's own Jeanette MacDonald who...is a bit too consciously coy and looks down her nose rather too obviously for complete enjoyment."

No Recordings

Music in the Film

Fox's cue sheet lists one song in the film, "If Someone Should Kiss Me Tonight," by James Hanley. However, no available review mentions a song, so it may have been cut before release, used only as background music, or sung by a minor character. Even if Jeanette did have a song, it did little to stop the bizarre rumors racing through the European press.

3
All Talking, No Singing, No Dancing

One has only to sit through two or three of the worst musicals of 1929–30 to understand why the American filmgoer turned *en masse* from this form of entertainment. A good musical of the stage or screen can get by on the slenderest or most illogical story as long as the "numbers" are terrific. A strong story with well-integrated melodies can get by without any hit tunes. But when the entire product becomes a slapdash effort to cash in on a moneymaking trend, the results can be monstrous beyond belief. An evening made up of *The Lottery Bride* plus *Golden Dawn*, a jungle epic with Vivienne Segal and Walter Woolf King, or *Sweet Kitty Bellairs*, an olde Englishe romp with Walter Pidgeon and Claudia Dell, would cure anyone except the most rabid film buff of ever wanting to see a musical again.

Not only were musicals of appalling quality being dumped on a glutted market, but the dramatic film was maturing at astonishing speed. 1930 films like *Anna Christie*, *The Blue Angel*, *Little Caesar*, *Morocco*, and *All Quiet on the Western Front* stand today simply as classic films, not as representatives of a quainter era.

The musical, which had contributed so many innovations in the first "thousand days" of sound film, became, in the hands of lesser talents, simply a pallid rehash of its earlier vitality. Still clinging to the stage tradition of a dozen different songs or, worse, one weak song done over and over, the musical suddenly appeared dated. Even the better musicals of 1929–30, films like *The Broadway Melody* (an Oscar winner), *Sunny Side Up*, and *Whoopee*, seemed to date so quickly that they vanished into the studio vaults. There are of course musical classics from this time, but most of them were passed over when they appeared beside their flashier sisters.

The Love Parade, Rouben Mamoulian's *Applause* with Helen Morgan, the Marx Brothers' *The Cocoanuts*, or *The Dance of Life* with Nancy Carroll and Hal Skelly can hold any audience today. Yet *Applause* was hissed off the screen when it premiered in London and withdrawn after two days.

But the harm had been done. There were more than sixty musicals in 1929, over seventy-five in 1930. Fewer than ten were released in

All Talking, No Singing, No Dancing

Jeanette's beloved voice teacher, Grace Adele Newell, became a member of the family. She outlived Jeanette, dying at age 92 in 1966. *Courtesy Anna Michalik.*

1931. Completed musicals were yanked back to have their songs snipped out, leaving a string of song cues ending in blackouts.

The trains that had carried the Broadwayites to Hollywood now were filled with top-name movie stars departing Hollywood for vaudeville and public appearances to bolster their incomes and popularity.

Although Miss MacDonald had made a good impression as a straight comedienne, she was still considered a singer and found herself "at liberty." 1931 was a bad year to be unemployed. Broadway was at its lowest ebb in this century. Barely a dozen musicals were on the boards, compared with more than seventy per season during the 1920's. However, Harriet Parsons reported happily that Jeanette had stage offers from Earl Carroll, Ziegfeld, Schwab and Mandel, and Ray Goetz.

Jeanette's films with Chevalier and Jack Buchanan had brought her a devoted following on the Continent and in England, so she decided that an overseas concert tour would reinforce this popularity and quite possibly bring stage and film offers in a part of the world more appreciative of her talents. A rather bizarre series of rumors also may have sparked the tour.

Apparently the story began in Belgium when a couple were injured in a car accident. They were taken to a hospital where they refused to give their names. The Italian consul arrived to talk to them and the couple eventually slipped away. Meanwhile scandal magazines had reported that Crown Prince Humbert of Italy was seeing an American film actress. The two stories became integrated, and now it was Miss MacDonald who had been involved in a car accident with her lover, the Prince. When it was learned that the car duo were actually an Italian banker and his mistress, the locale was changed to Monte Carlo and it was the Prince's wife, Princess Marie-José, who found the erring couple and either threw acid in the singer's face or shot her with a pistol, blinding her in one eye.

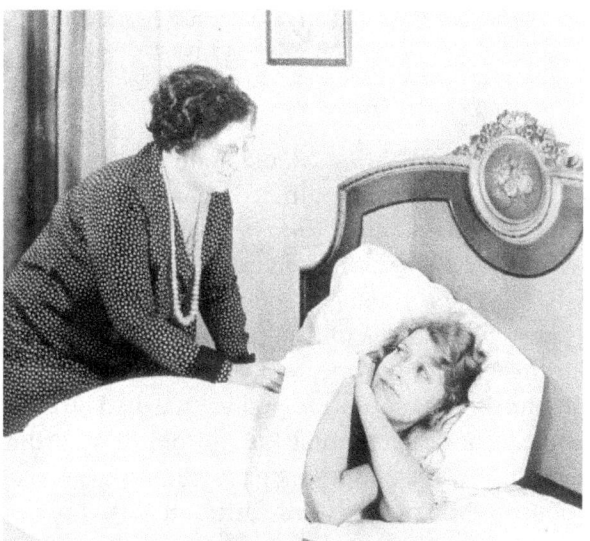

Jeanette lived with her mother in Hollywood and here posed a typical early morning awakening. *Courtesy Paramount Pictures.*

A fanciful 1931 French novella claimed Jeanette had been disfigured by her royal lover's jealous wife and her place taken on the screen by her look-alike sister. Courtesy Pierre Guinle.

To explain Miss MacDonald's continuing appearance in films, albeit a non-singing one, a weekly magazine, *Fantasio*, printed an imaginary interview with Jeanette's sister, Blossom, who claimed to have taken over her film work. (These bogus tales of film stars were very popular throughout Europe, and Garbo was currently attempting to sue a magazine that had used a copy of her signature at the bottom of a sordid letter. However, long distance suits with backroom publications were difficult.) A French publisher issued an obviously fictional account, *Jeanette MacDonald? Les Documents Secrets*, in 1931. (It included the poignant misstatement that comedian Fatty Arbuckle, then barred from movie making, was still one of Hollywood's biggest stars.)

The European press took up the scandalous story without bothering to wire Hollywood, where Miss MacDonald was hard at work, neither blind nor disfigured. The American press was more skeptical and ran the story as an example of the credulousness of their foreign counterpart.

The stories provided a colorful background for a triumphant concert tour during which Miss MacDonald could not only entertain her fans, but also prove to the more morbid that she was still alive. Before sailing from New York, she made two broadcasts. The medium of radio would be her second home in the late thirties and throughout the forties. (She had made her radio debut in March of 1930 on the Paramount Publix Hour.)

Her arrival in Paris was reported in the American press to have sparked more excitement than Lindbergh's landing. This is surely an exaggeration, but an indication of the French affection for the star of *Parade d'Amour* who could charm them in her Berlitz French. She opened for a two-week run at the Empire Theatre in Paris on September 4, 1931, with Chevalier himself in the audience, and in London on September 21 for another two weeks at the Dominion Theatre. *The London Times* reported: "Miss MacDonald was a little nervous about her ability to please [a stage audience], but the applause did not sag during her performance and when, flushed with the appreciation of her most stirring film song, ["March of the Grenadiers"] and, with glinting hair falling in waves to her shoulders, she took a succession of final curtains, there could be no question of her success."

She did receive stage and film offers including a bid to do *The Merry Widow* in French on the Paris stage and also a film, *The Queen's Affaire*, for producer Herbert Wilcox. Negotiations collapsed and Anna Neagle played

One Hour with You

the film rôle. Fortunately, Paramount called Jeanette back for *One Hour with You* and then the ultimate musical, *Love Me Tonight*.

Critics are fond of citing the 1933 blockbuster *42nd Street* as the film that revived the musical. But how then do you explain 1932, the year of *Love Me Tonight*? Perhaps the sophisticated and often multilingual European musicals of 1930–31 like *Le Million*, *Die Drei von der Tankstelle/Le Chemin du Paradis*, *Il Est Charmant*, and *Der Kongress Tanzt/Le Congrès s'amuse* were restoring the faith and interest of the better directors in this country. Perhaps the improved sound equipment made recorded music sound better. And perhaps the writers, composers, directors, singers, and American public had all matured together and were ready for 1932 and *Love Me Tonight*. But first came *One Hour with You*.

Rumors of a romance flew when Jeanette stayed at Chevalier's French villa during her continental tour while he was finishing a picture in America. European fans considered Jeanette and Chevalier a couple, despite his being married to Yvonne Vallee.

One Hour with You
Paramount.
New York premiere, Feb. 24, 1932.
Released March 25, 1932.
Produced by Ernst Lubitsch.
Directed by Ernst Lubitsch and George Cukor.
90 minutes.
Color-toned print.

Filmed simultaneously with a French cast as *Une Heure près de toi*. (See page 101.)

From the 1909 play *Nur ein Traum* (Only a Dream) by Lothar Schmidt [Goldschmidt] which premiered in Munich. *One Hour with You* is a remake of Lubitsch's 1924 silent comedy classic, *The Marriage Circle*, for Warner Bros.

In London, Jeanette signed to appear with Herbert Marshall (left) in a film for director Herbert Wilcox (center), but this intriguing combination was not to be. Wilcox's future wife, Anna Neagle, starred in his 1933 UK production of *Bitter Sweet*, later remade in Hollywood by Jeanette and Nelson.

Screenplay: Samson Raphaelson. Photography: Victor Milner. Editing: William Shea. "Dialogue Director": George Cukor. Songs: Oscar Straus or Richard A. Whiting. Lyrics: Leo Robin. Gowns: Travis Banton. Sound: M.M. Paggi. Cameramen: William Mellor, William Rand, Guy Roe, Lucien Ballard. Art Director: Hans Dreier. Set Decorations: A.E. Freudeman.

Maurice Chevalier (Dr. André Bertier)
Jeanette MacDonald (Colette Bertier)
Genevieve Tobin (Mitzi Olivier)
Charlie Ruggles (Adolph)
Roland Young (Professor Olivier)
George Barbier (Police Commissioner)
Josephine Dunn (Mlle Martel)
Richard Carle (Detective Henri Poirier)
Charles Judels (Policeman)
Barbara Leonard (Mitzi's maid)
Florine McKinney (Guest saying "good night")
Donald Novis (Singer at party)
Charles Coleman (Marcel, the butler)
Eric Wilton (Butler)
George[s] Davis (Cabby)
Bess Flowers, Bill Elliott (Extras at party)
Sheila Manners [Sheila Bromley, Sheila LeGay] (Colette's downstairs maid)
Leonie Pray (Colette's upstairs maid)
Kent Taylor (Guest greeted by Colette)
Lita Chevret (Guest)
Mae Questel (Office worker)
Guests & extras: Pat Somerset, Jack Byron, James Ford, Jack Chefe

Oscar nomination: Best Picture.

One Hour with You is generally described as "bright," "sophisticated," and "witty," yet it is a curiously unsatisfying film. It brought director Ernst Lubitsch, Miss MacDonald, and Chevalier together for the first time since *The Love Parade* three years earlier. Lubitsch had directed Miss MacDonald in *Monte Carlo* and Chevalier in *The Smiling Lieutenant* in the interim. However, his exact part in *One Hour with You* is a bit clouded.

Officially he is listed as director and George Cukor as "dialogue director." Dialogue directors were common in the early days of sound,

A gendarme catches Colette (Jeanette) and André (Maurice Chevalier) doing what is forbidden in Paris.

especially when the director himself had a slim command of English as Lubitsch did. Cukor was not an old hand like Lubitsch, but he had made some snappy films. *The Royal Family of Broadway* (with Cyril Gardner), starring Fredric March, and *Girls about Town*, starring Kay Francis and Lilyan Tashman. He wasn't a Lubitsch, but then Lubitsch wasn't a Cukor.

In his later years, Cukor stated variously that he directed all of the film after Lubitsch was taken ill, and that he directed part of it before Lubitsch returned and took over. Whatever occurred, the resulting film bears testimony to the lack of a strong, single overall hand.

Some of the film's unevenness must be traced directly to the script, and, since Lubitsch is acknowledged to have done all preproduction work and script supervision, his overwhelming tendency to "third act" his films is highly evident. With no other film director has a theatrical background produced so strong an effect. Lubitsch historically co-authored his films, and since they all share the same trademark, we must assume that this, too, is a "Lubitsch touch." The story inevitably reaches a point that, on stage, would be the second act curtain. The lovers are

One Hour with You 93

Colette and her doctor husband, André, are happily married. Then Colette learns that her best friend, Mitzi, is coming to visit. (Leonie Pray as the upstairs maid.)

Mitzi (Genevieve Tobin) takes one look at André and feels the need of a doctor. André is reluctant to provide the cure she desires. *Courtesy Anna Michalik.*

her childhood sweetheart and live happily ever after.

Lubitsch lavished great care on the mechanics of building up to his "second act curtain," and then occasionally seemed to lose interest in the third act. *One Hour with You* is a notable example. Not only is the ending weak, but (unforgivable for Lubitsch) it is also dull.

Lubitsch had dealt deftly with the joys of infidelity in his silent *The Marriage Circle*, based on the same source as *One Hour with You*. Here, however, no one except the stylish Genevieve Tobin seems to have much fun. Her stodgy husband is played by Roland Young in a tight-lipped version of the rôle he would perpetuate in *Topper*. Charlie Ruggles plays the expansively repressed Adolph with enough intensity to make us hope he will ultimately succeed in his amorous endeavors.

The credits again show Lubitsch's insistence on style from the first moment. The hands of a giant clock revolve, printing and erasing the title credits. Curiously, Lubitsch never took this to its next logical step, unfolding the opening parted or the "wrong" lovers paired. In *Ninotchka*, comrade Garbo returns to Russia. In *Trouble in Paradise*, heiress Kay Francis agrees to marry jewel thief Herbert Marshall, leaving his accomplice Miriam Hopkins to her own devices. In *The Love Parade*, the prince returns to save his queen's good name before divorcing her. In *The Merry Widow*, the widow learns Danilo has been ordered to make love to her and ends their "romance." Each needs the third act to straighten things out and provide a happy American ending.

Europeans traditionally favored the ironic or downbeat ending, so much so that a number of Hollywood films had both "American" and "European" endings. In the European version, the heroine usually died of tuberculosis or became a streetwalker, while the American ending always had her recover in time to marry

Colette looks among her dinner guests for the cause of André's agitation, not realizing it is beside her.

sequence of the film behind the credits as is commonly done today.

The Paris police commissioner (George Barbier) is instructing his patrolmen poetically in a scene duplicating the police station sequence in René Clair's 1930 musical classic, *Le Million*. However, it is not criminals they seek but lovers who are clogging the park benches, leaving no room for tourists.

> The situation is not funny.
> Our best cafés are losing money.

"Cleaner parks and more prosperity" the chief tells his men, and they rush off chanting, "Cleaner parks, cleaner parks,"

A likely pair of culprits is quickly found. "You can't make love in public," the gendarme growls. "Oh, but officer, he can!" cries the lady. "Darling!" cries the man and they sink back into their embrace. They are, the officer learns, Dr. and Madame Bertier (Maurice Chevalier and Jeanette). As the only married couple in the park, they are ordered to leave.

In the French-language version, André is equally stoic. *Courtesy Anna Michalik.*

A French-language version was filmed simultaneously. Here, Lili Damita as Mitzi, happily cuddling with Colette before cuddling with Colette's husband. *Courtesty David Chierichetti.*

"Well, there's only one place to go," sighs the lady. Collecting top hat and furs, they make their less than reluctant way to a snug little townhouse with vast art-deco interiors. The bedroom door is opened. They enter. The door closes. The door opens again. Dr. André Bertier reappears, and, in a continuation of the style of directly addressing the film audience that Lubitsch-Chevalier had begun in The Love Parade, he tells us that it is *not* what we think. They *are* married. "Dar—ling..." calls Colette Bertier from the next room. "Vive la France!" says the doctor and exits.

On a white satin bed, the pajamaed lovers sing "What a Little Thing Like a Wedding Ring Can Do."

ANDRÉ: I don't have to stop when I kiss your hand.
COLETTE: It's lawful.
ANDRÉ: It's grand!

They turn out the light. Pause. "Oh, darling," says Colette. "I forgot to tell you." The light goes on, and she asks him to guess who's coming for lunch tomorrow. He tells her to tell him tomorrow and turns off the light. A few moments of darkness. The bed light is again turned on, and Colette, holding the light chain, tells him that it is Mitzi, her old school chum from Lausanne. Several more exchanges take place in the double bed during which the light goes on and off. Finally André unscrews the bulb and tosses it out the window. "Mitzi, kitzi, itzi, bitzi..." he coos in the darkness.

A painting of a lady clad in gauze: "So that's Mitzi?" says an admiring voice. "My wife," agrees Professor Olivier (Roland Young). "When I married her she was a brunette, but now you can't believe a word she says." The art connoisseur is a detective (Richard Carle), hired by the disgruntled professor to obtain evidence for a divorce. In Switzerland, he explains, they have a peculiar law. When a husband shoots his wife, they put him in jail. Therefore he has brought his wife to Paris where the law is not so disagreeable. Mitzi (Genevieve Tobin) won't make him wait long. At that moment, a spring shower is driving her into a waiting taxi, waiting of course for André who chivalrously offers to drop her. She makes more progress than she realizes, for after several minutes André leaps from the cab to walk home in the downpour.

Mitzi arrives and the friends romp through the rooms, exchanging giggling confidences in rhymed dialogue, underlined with music:

> COLETTE: Oh, Mitzi, my darling, how have you been?
> MITZI: I'm much wiser now, thanks to several men.
> COLETTE: How's the composer you went with so much?
> MITZI: He's gone but he had such a marvelous touch.
> COLETTE: And the painter who painted you all draped in gauze?
> MITZI: One night I found *out* what an artist he was!
> COLETTE: How's the Professor?
> MITZI: Which one do you mean?
> COLETTE: The one that you married.
> MITZI: Oh, he's still on the scene.
> COLETTE: You don't sound so happy.
> MITZI: Unless you're well mated, this business of marriage is much overrated.
> COLETTE: Oh, Mitzi, you don't know how sorry I feel.
> As for André and me, well, it's just too ideal.

And she sings of the joys of married love, "We Will Always Be Sweethearts":

> Day after day we will always be sweethearts,
> The same as the day we began.
> (Copyright Famous Music Corp.)

André arrives home somewhat damp from his walk and is introduced to Mitzi. "My very best friend," sighs Colette happily, placing their hands together, "and my very, very husband." Lunch is announced, and the ladies exit. André turns to the camera and tells us that he is determined not to weaken. "We'll see," he says hopefully and goes to join the ladies.

Paris doesn't agree with Mitzi. She soon requires a doctor. Naturally she phones Dr. Bertier. André is reluctant to mix business with Mitzi, but Colette insists. André kisses Colette goodbye, squares his shoulders and marches off to a martial tune.

Mitzi, reclining in a ravishing peignoir on a chaise lounge, receives Dr. Bertier and suggests a complete examination. André counters with various remedies, all to be taken "Three Times a Day."

> ANDRÉ: This tonic ought to help you.
> MITZI: I know a sweeter way.
> ANDRÉ: Oh, no, madame, I couldn't see you *three* times a day.
> (Copyright Famous Music Corp.)

Professor Olivier discovers them in the midst of the examination. "Madame is in a very serious condition," André hastily assures him.

One Hour with You

Colette causes some agitation of her own. André's best friend Adolph (Charlie Ruggles) wants to be more than a friend to her. (The title song was introduced during this scene, but not by the stars.) *Courtesy Anna Michalik*

"Why shouldn't she be," replies the professor genially. "Conditions are bad everywhere."

Colette, in Jeanette's now-compulsory satin step-ins, is trying to dress for her dinner party while answering numerous phone calls. One caller is Adolph (Charlie Ruggles). He inquires with fierce intensity if he will be sitting next to her. She replies that he is her husband's closest friend, but that is as far as she'll go. Adolph tells her he is coming as Romeo. "What? What? Not a costume party?" He hangs up and summons his butler. Why was he told it was a costume party? "Ah, monsieur," murmurs the smirking Marcel (Charles Coleman, the eternal butler), lowering his eyes to Adolph's knobby knees, "I did so want to see you in tights."

André is having his own problems. Every time he slips into the dining room to rearrange the place cards so that he is *not* sitting next to Mitzi, Colette catches him. She, of course, assumes that he is trying to sit next to the scantily gowned Mlle. Martel (Josephine Dunn).

Mitzi, in an equally revealing gown, takes leave of her loving husband after being assured that he won't be home all night. Her reluctant maid is also ordered to take the night off. At the party, Colette confides her fears about Mlle Martel to Mitzi who sets her mind at ease. She won't let André out of her sight. All will be well.

Adolph bursts in and rushes about in search of Colette so that he can say "How do." Dinner is served, and, to the strains of a hired orchestra, the party sweeps in to dine. Mitzi has now reswitched the place cards so that André *is* sitting next to Mlle. Martel. André is mortified, and Mitzi gives Colette a knowing shrug. Colette is furious and decides to flirt with Adolph. "Let's be happy. Let's be gay," she cries. "Are you talking to me?" gasps Adolph. "Romeo!" coos Colette.

The orchestra launches into the melting "One Hour with You" for after-dinner dancing. Adolph doggedly pursues Colette around the dance floor. "When are we going to be gay?" Colette is too busy watching the mechanics of Mitzi "rescuing" André from Mlle. Martel. Mission accomplished, Mitzi gives Colette an enormous wink over André's quivering shoulder, and they swirl off to the music. "Right *now!*" cries Colette, and Adolph takes her in his arms.

Interestingly, neither Chevalier nor Miss MacDonald introduced the classic title song. It was young Donald Novis, the tenor of the opera sequence in *Monte Carlo*, as vocalist with the orchestra. The four principals then sing or talk the lyrics as they circle the dance floor. (The song was later used with nonsense lyrics as the Klopstockian love song in *Million Dollar Legs* (1932) with Jack Oakie. Eddie Cantor took it up as the theme song for his radio program, and it has been identified with him ever since.)

Mitzi drags André onto the terrace and undoes his tie. André is horrified. He can't tie a tie. Mitzi can, she assures him, and slips off into the inviting darkness of the garden. André is in a dilemma. He turns to the audience and outlines his alternatives. If he goes inside and Colette sees his tie, he gets into trouble. If he goes into the garden, he gets into trouble but he gets his tie fixed. What shall he do? He breaks a sprig from a bush and plucks the leaves, daisy fashion,

André tries to persuade Colette he is innocent, but she tearfully refuses to believe him. He decides to prove her right—but with the wrong woman.

reciting the choices, concluding with "I get my tie fixed." He follows Mitzi into the moonlit garden.

A close-up of André's tie. The camera pulls back to reveal that it is tied around Mitzi's ankle. André thinks better of his decision and flees once again. The moon is affecting Adolph too. He tells Colette that if it weren't for his splendid education, he'd yield to the animal in him. Colette has no ear for his proposals. She goes in search of André, only to find him having his tie tied by the obliging Mlle. Martel. It is Colette's turn to rush off into the garden, sobbing bitterly.

The party is over. Mitzi shakes André's hand and whispers that she will be waiting in a taxi at the next corner. "Five minutes." "Impossible!" he replies. "Ten minutes." "Ridiculous!" "All right, fifteen minutes." "Positively...maybe."

One Hour with You

Everyone is gone. André wonders how it all happened in "Oh! That Mitzi." His indecision is resolved when Colette angrily orders him from the house. "My compliments to Mlle. Martel," she sneers as the door slams. He is gone.

"André!" she cries, and runs in search of him. Someone is standing in the shadows by the door to the garden, waiting for her. It is Adolph. He seizes her:

> I'm dying *for* one hour with you.
> I've got to *pour* my love out to you.
> I'm just insane with desire.
> I'm on fire. Have a heart."
> (Copyright Famous Music Corp.)

He kisses her triumphantly. "André!" she cries. "You'll have to call louder than that if you want André to hear you," Adolph murmurs, "...but if you want Adolph, all you have to do is whisper."

Colette sinks down on the couch sobbing, not over Adolph, but André. "Sorrow makes you even more beautiful," says Adolph. "Thank you, Adolph," sobs Colette. Adolph can hardly contain himself: "Any man who would leave a woman like you on a night like this with a man like me...*deserves* it."

Colette learns that Mitzi has left her husband, but who can her new lover be? André rejects each of her excited speculations. *Courtesy Anna Michalik.*

Colette tells him that it was *she* who was wrong. "You have a right to be wrong. You're a woman. Women were born to be wrong. I like my women wrong." Colette escorts Adolph to the door and maternally gives him a good night kiss on the forehead. Across town, the lights go out in Mitzi's apartment where something of a similar nature is taking place.

The next morning, André comes home to find Colette awaking from a nightmare. She tells André in song that she dreamed Adolph kissed her. He laughs at the absurdity and they reprise "We Will Always Be Sweethearts." They are reconciled.

The day brings other changes in the lives of the principals. The professor receives a "Daily Report on the Nights of Mlle. Olivier." Mitzi is seen departing from her residence. lock, stock and nude portrait, as her husband beams approvingly from the window above. His arm is around the waist of the now obliging maid (Barbara Leonard).

At the office of the divorce court, the lady clerks, with knowing smiles, sign, seal, and stamp a summons. André has just received this summons when Professor Olivier is announced. The professor toys with André at great length until Colette comes in. The professor departs and Colette speculates at equal length on why he and Mitzi have separated. André slips into the garden for a musical respite: "What Would You Do?"

> Do you think you could resist her?
> Do you think you wouldn't have kissed her?
> Would you treat her like a sister?
> Come on, be honest mister!
> (Copyright Famous Music Corp.)

Colette must be told. At length André tells her. "My husband and my very best friend," she says unbelievingly. She again orders André from the house. "From now on, you're nothing but a doctor to me!"

Adolph walks in on them, inspiring Colette with a plan for revenge. "What's your one hour," she tells André, "compared with my twenty-five minutes?" André laughs in disbelief. Furiously, Colette turns to Adolph to verify her account of their torrid tryst. Behind her back, André condescendingly motions Adolph to agree to everything she says. Adolph does, and Colette announces triumphantly that now she and André are even.

They turn to the audience and explain that, despite the confessions, they are crazy about each other. What would you do? Well, that's what they do too! The orchestra launches into a lively rendition of "One Hour with You."

Reviews

The film was still a director's medium, at least as far as Lubitsch's films were concerned, and every review dwelt on his contribution. "The result is something so delightful that it places the circlet of gilded laurel leaves jauntily upon the knowing and wise head of Hollywood's most original and knowing director of sophisticated comedy," rhapsodized Mildred Martin of the *Philadelphia Inquirer*. She felt that Genevieve Tobin had nearly stolen "stellar honors...right before the wide and beautiful eyes of Jeanette MacDonald."

The *New York Times*, too, gave first honors to Lubitsch and second place to Chevalier. "This latest Lubitsch production, aided by M. Chevalier and his supporting cast, is filled with scintillating wit of the Parisian variety... The fair and graceful Miss MacDonald is in her element in this offering...*One Hour with You* is an excellent production with Lubitsch and Chevalier at the top of their form." Jeanette was still, more or less, window dressing.

Recordings (See Discography for further information)

"Oh! That Mitzi" (Maurice Chevalier)
"Oh, Cette Mitzi" (Maurice Chevalier)
"One Hour with You" (Jeanette MacDonald; also Jimmie Grier and the Cocoanut Grove Orchestra with vocal by Donald Novis)
"Une Heure près de Toi" ["One Hour with You"] (Jeanette MacDonald)
"We Will Always Be Sweethearts" (Jeanette MacDonald)
"Coeur contre coeur" [We Will Always Be Sweethearts] (Jeanette MacDonald)
"What Would You Do?" (Maurice Chevalier)
"Qu'auriez Vous Fait?" ["What Would You Do?"] (Maurice Chevalier)

Music in the Film

Music mostly by Oscar Straus or Richard A. Whiting, lyrics by Leo Robin. In listing performers after each title, "and" denotes a genuine duet, while commas between names indicate a sequence of singers.

Overture: "One Hour with You," "We Will Always Be Sweethearts"
Police station talk song (Barbier, male chorus) - John Leipold.
"What a Little Thing Like a Wedding Ring Can Do" (Chevalier and MacDonald) - Straus and Robin.
Mitzi-Colette talk song (MacDonald and Tobin) - Straus and Robin.
"We Will Always Be Sweethearts" ["Day after Day"] (MacDonald) - Straus and Robin
"Three Times a Day" (Chevalier and Tobin) - Whiting and Robin
"One Hour with You" (Donald Novis, Chevalier, Tobin, MacDonald, Ruggles) - Whiting and Robin.
"It Was Only a Dream Kiss" - talk song (MacDonald and Chevalier) - Straus and Robin. INTO:
"We Will Always Be Sweethearts" reprise (MacDonald and Chevalier)
"What Would You Do?" (Chevalier) Whiting and Robin.
Finale: "One Hour with You"

Love Me Tonight

Sheet music for the simultaneously filmed French language version. *Courtesy Pierre Guinle.*

Une Heure près de toi

A French version of *One Hour with You*, called *Une heure près de to*i (One hour near you), was shot simultaneously on the same set and with many of the same performers.

French script by Léopold Marchand. French lyrics by André Hornez (the French equivalent of Lorenz Hart). Debut at the Paramount Theatre, Paris, June 1, 1932.

Chevalier and MacDonald play the leads in both English and French versions. Josephine Dunn and Richard Carle repeat their rôles as Mlle Martel and a detective. Other principals in the French version are:

Lili Damita (Mitzi Olivier)
Ernst Ferny (Professor Kurt Olivier)
Pierre Etchepare (Adolphe)
André Cheron (Prefét de Police)
Richard Carle (Detective)
Josephine Dunn (Mlle. Martel)

Extensive inquiries in France have failed to locate an existing print, but there is always hope. After being assured for years that "*La Veuve Joyeuse* n'existe plus" (Jeanette's simultaneously filmed French version of *The Merry Widow* no longer exists), it turned up. Miracles can happen!

Recordings (See Discography for further information)

"Coeur contre coeur" [We Will Always Be Sweethearts] (Jeanette MacDonald)
"Oh, Cette Mitzi" (Maurice Chevalier)
"Qu'auriez Vous Fait?" ["What Would You Do?"] (Maurice Chevalier)

Love Me Tonight

Paramount Publix.
Released August 26, 1932.
Produced and directed by Rouben Mamoulian.
104 minutes.

French title: *Aimez-moi ce soir!* (Love Me Tonight)
Swedish title: *Din för i kval* (Yours for an Evening)
German title: Schloss im Mond (Castle in the Moon)

Story by Léopold Marchand and Paul Armont, based on their play, *Le Tailleur au Château* (The Tailor in the Castle), Paris, 1924. Screenplay: Samuel Hoffenstein, Waldemar Young, and George Marion Jr. Music: Richard Rodgers. Lyrics: Lorenz Hart. Photography, Victor Milner. Art Director: Hans Dreier. Sets: A.E. Freudeman. Orchestra Arrangements and Music Supervision: Nathaniel Finston. Costumes: Edith Head and Travis Banton. Cameramen: William Mellor and Guy Roe. Sound: M.M. Paggi. Editor: Rouben Mamoulian. Cutter: William Shea. Western Electric Noiseless Recording.

Maurice Chevalier (Maurice Courtelin)
Jeanette MacDonald (Princess Jeanette)
Charlie Ruggles (Vicomte Gilbert de Vareze)
Charles Butterworth (Count de Savignac)

Myrna Loy (Countess Valentine)
C. Aubrey Smith (Duke d'Artelines)
Elizabeth Patterson (Aunt)
Ethel Griffies (Aunt)
Blanche Frederici (Aunt)
Joseph Cawthorn (Dr. Armand de Pontignac)
Maj. Sam Harris (Bridge player)
Robert Greig (Major Domo Flammand)
Ethel Wales (Mme Dutoit, the dressmaker)
Marion "Peanuts" Byron (Baker's wife)
Bert Roach (Emile)
Tyler Brooke (Composer)
Clarence Wilson (Shirt maker)
William H. Turner (Boot maker)
Tony Merlo (Hat maker)
Rolfe Sedan (Taxi driver)
Gordon Westcott (Credit Official)
George (Gabby) Hayes (Grocer)
Mary Doran (Madame Dupont)
George[s] Davis (Pierre Dupont, the chauffeur)
Edgar Norton (Valet)
Cecil Cunningham (Laundress)
Herbert Mundin (Groom- cut from print)
Rita Owin (Chambermaid)
Mel Kalish (Chef)
Tom Ricketts (photo of Jeanette's dead husband)
Carrie Daumery (Guest)

Hollywood on Parade

Jeanette appeared in at least two Paramount publicity one-reelers, in one of which she did a specially filmed promo for *Love Me Tonight*. The series was called *Hollywood on Parade*, and consisted of specially filmed scenes or interviews combined with newsreel-type footage, actual scenes from films, and even screen tests.

In *Hollywood on Parade*, Number 5, Jeanette sings a steamy version of the title song, "Love Me Tonight." This short opens with Roland Young (Jeanette's costar in *Annabelle's Affairs*, *Don't Bet on Women*, and *One Hour with You*) who displays his toy penguin collection. Then cowboy star Ken Maynard examines an outdoor sculpture of a roundup that he has commissioned to dress up a vacant lot and playfully rides one of the cement horses. Next, page girls appear with a giant magazine cover of Jeanette which dissolves to an orchestra, conducted by Nat Finston. We see Jeanette in a tufted satin bed. She rises, dons a negligée, and then leans over the foot of

Jeanette's ice-princess character in *Love Me Tonight* was belied by a steamy rendition of the film's title song, shot separately for *Hollywood on Parade*. Courtesy Patrick Kuster.

the bed, gazing directly into the camera, as she sings both verse and chorus of the title song. Then the scrapbook pages turn again, introducing the final segment with Maurice Chevalier who sings "Louise," apparently a screen test.

In *Hollywood on Parade*, Number 8, Jeanette is seen in newsreel footage entering a costume party. Frankie Darro, playing a fan, asks for her autograph, but she denies her identity: "Tonight I'm Anna Held." Nevertheless, she signs graciously.

Both these *Hollywood on Parade* one-reelers are currently in the U.C.L.A. Film Archive, and seen occasionally on the American Movie Classics television channel.

If you ask "noted authorities," critics, film writers, and just plain musical nuts to agree on the ultimate musical, *Love Me Tonight* will top nearly every list. They might prefer a Judy Garland vehicle, adore a Busby Berkeley spectacular, sway to memories of Fred and Ginger, or become misty-eyed over a MacDonald-Eddy operetta, but it is *Love Me Tonight* that all musicals are measured to and from, like some kind of international film musical dateline.

Love Me Tonight

Unlike any other film hit, *Love Me Tonight* has had no imitators because, well, it is inimitable (unless you count the Wheeler and Woolsey parody in *Diplomaniacs* with Bert Wheeler mimicking Jeanette).

Director Rouben Mamoulian, like Lubitsch, had created a classic with his first sound film, *Applause* (1929), with Helen Morgan. He had done only two films after that, *City Streets* (1931) and *Dr. Jekyll and Mr. Hyde* (1931), which won an Oscar for Fredric March. In between films, he had been active on the New York stage. Over the years, his stage successes included *Marco Millions*, *Porgy and Bess*, *Oklahoma!*, and *Carousel*.

Love Me Tonight was the third MacDonald-Chevalier film, with Charlie Ruggles doing a ne'er-do-well aristocratic playboy, quite a change from his rôle in *One Hour with You*. The top-notch cast included Myrna Loy in one of her ever-more-frequent Caucasian rôles, C. Aubrey Smith, and the ultimately wistful comedian, Charles Butterworth. Chevalier's bubbly performance is even more remarkable when one realizes that he was still profoundly depressed over the death of his adored mother.

Love Me Tonight represents the fusion of centuries of stage artistry and artifice with the unique infant, film. Like nearly every classic, its whole is greater than the sum of its parts. The characters are actually caricatures, two dimensional representations of all the stock stage personalities of operetta, yet the human qualities they mirror are so strong, we must identify with each of them.

The Princess in the tower is a pathetic remnant of aristocracy, doomed never to marry because there is no one left who is her social equal. (Compare this to the situation of predominantly female European royal houses after World War I who could find no princes for their eligible daughters.) The commoner is a hard-working tailor, poor because the aristocracy cannot pay its bill (social unrest, Bolshevism, unionism—all forces in the 1930s). The three witches or fairy godmothers of legend are the maiden aunties in the tower, providing a Greek chorus of comment and response to the action. Add to this the irascible uncle, the booby suitor, the playboy comedian, and nymphomaniac comedienne, all stock characters.

One of the script writers was George Marion Jr. who created the unforgettable lyrics for *Let's Go Native*. He had been a prominent title writer in silent days on such great films as *It* with Clara Bow and *The Son of the Sheik* with Rudolph Valentino. He later scripted *The Gay Divorcée* for Fred Astaire and Ginger Rogers.

The songs of *Love Me Tonight* are superb and inseparable from the story line, each advancing the action, or, in the case of "Poor Apache," establishing a character more specifically and hauntingly than any dialogue. (Curiously the one song in the film that is "thrown away" is the immortal "Lover," a song that has enjoyed constant rediscovery with new arrangements and performers.) Rodgers and Hart created the original film score as they had for *The Hot Heiress* (1931) in the earlier musical cycle. (Five of their stage musicals were also

The count (Charles Butterworth) is unable to entertain Princess Jeanette after his accident. He fell flat on his flute.

converted to the screen in 1929–30.) The songs "Mimi," "Isn't It Romantic," and "Lover" are standards and several others should be.

All these ingredients were brought together under the direction of a man with the strength of steel and the lightness of a flower, and called *Love Me Tonight*.

Paris at dawn. Silently we look out over the jumbled rooftops to the Eiffel Tower in the distant haze. The city begins to come slowly to life. The plunk of a pick. The swish of a broom. The scrape-plop of a shovel. The squeak-shush-squeak of a grinding wheel. The sounds cross each other in subtle rhythms, each new one adding an element to the fugue until a charming soubrette drops the needle on her phonograph and an orchestra joins the sounds. The city is awake. (Mamoulian used a similar sequence in his first New York stage production, the Theatre Guild's *Porgy*.)

The camera tracks to an empty window. A hat rack can be seen supporting a straw hat, and a crack on the wall looks suspiciously like the profile of our hero. A figure appears, struggling into a turtleneck sweater until the head, boyish and tousled, emerges. It is Maurice Courtelin (Maurice Chevalier). (Performing stars, as opposed to acting stars, almost invariably retained their first names in early films. Al Jolson, Harry Richman, and Eddie Cantor were generally "Al," "Harry," and "Eddie.")

Maurice joins the city of Paris in "The Song of Paree." In what Lorenz Hart lovers cherish as a "Hart lyric" he tells us:

> It has taxi horns and claxons
> To scare the Anglo-Saxons.
> That's the song of Paree.
> (Copyright Famous Music Corp.)

Maurice dons his jacket and emerges on the street, greeting merchants and passersby in song:

> How's your business?
>   How can it fail?
> How's your grandpa?
>   He's back in jail.

> (To a pretty girl) Hello, my coy friend,
> Some other boy friend?
>   (Her escort, sternly) This is my wife!
> (Fleeing) How are you?
> Bonjour, Monsieur Cohen.
> How are things goin'?
>   (with Yiddish accent) Comment ça va?
> (Maurice, laughing, to the whole world) How
>   are you?
> (Copyright Famous Music Corp.)

Maurice enters a tailor shop, vanishes into a dressing room, and reappears in a flawless cutaway and striped pants. He is a tailor. Business will be brisk this morning. First Emile (silent comedian Bert Roach) comes to claim his wedding clothes. A flurry of activity outside attracts their attention.

It is the Across-Paris run. The crowd cheers the racers as they flash past the window. But one of the racers is dropping out. He is coming into the shop. It isn't a racer at all. It is the Vicomte Gilbert de Vareze (Charlie Ruggles), dressed in boxer shorts and clutching a fruit peddler's price sign to his chest. It seems a husband had arrived home unexpectedly...does Maurice have any of his suits ready that he can wear in this emergency? Proudly Maurice opens a closet revealing a dozen finished suits. Gilbert chooses a suit, borrows some ready cash, and departs, shirtless and tieless.

Emile emerges from the other dressing room in his wedding clothes. "A tailor's art for your sweetheart...the love song of the needle united with the thread. Isn't it romantic?" Sitting before the dressing room mirror, Maurice and his three images elaborate on his romantic ideal:

> Isn't it romantic?
> On a moonlit night she'll cook me onion soup.
> Kiddies are romantic,
> And if we don't fight, we soon will have a troop.
> We'll help the population.
> It's a duty that we owe to France.
> Isn't it romance?
> (Copyright Famous Music Corp.)

Love Me Tonight

Emile leaves the shop, happily humming the catchy melody. The song is taken up in turn by a nearby taxi driver (Rolfe Sedan) and his composer passenger (Tyler Brooke) who is on his way to the railroad station. The train wheels throb rhythmically as the composer begins jotting down the melody, surrounded by soldiers on their way to rural maneuvers. They join him in the chorus, then, to a military beat, they march across the fields, declaring the romance of being a soldier. A passing gypsy hears the song and rushes to a firelit grove where his violin pours out the romance of the night. On the balcony of a nearby château, the beautiful Princess Jeanette (Jeanette) hears the melody and is moved to burst into song. Her idea of romance is somewhat different from Maurice's:

> Brought by a secret charm
> Or by my heart's command,
> My prince will ride in arm—
>   or just to kiss my hand.
>   (Copyright Famous Music Corp.)

Her reverie is interrupted by a ladder thumping against the balcony. It is the Count de Savignac (Charles Butterworth), come to join her in a little chat before dinner. Jeanette, however, has had another fainting spell and is going straight to bed. The Count offers to entertain her with his flute, but Jeanette isn't up to it. Nor is she up to any more of his lovemaking. He is about to leave when he loses his balance and topples backward, ladder and all. "Ohhh," he calls from below. "I'll never be able to use it again."

"Oh, Count, did you break your leg?"

"No, I fell flat on my flute."

The camera leaves this little scene and tracks around the castle to a tower window. There we discover three elderly ladies (Elizabeth Patterson, Ethel Griffies, Blanche Frederici), like the weird sisters in *Macbeth*, crouched over a steaming kettle. They are mixing a cure for the Princess's fainting spells.

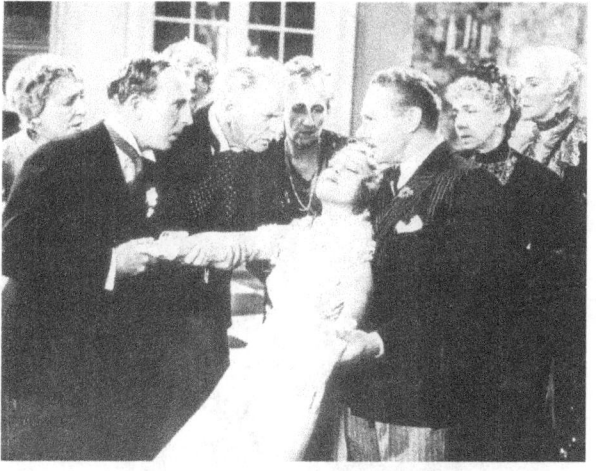

The princess has mysterious fainting spells. Her doctor prescribes marriage, but no one of equal rank is available. He then suggests exercise. Left to right: Extra, Butterworth, Daumery, Smith, Griffies, MacDonald, Ruggles, Patterson, Frederici.

Downstairs the elderly Duke (C. Aubrey Smith) is tending to more practical matters. A vivacious young lady archly informs him that he can be rid of her for twenty thousand francs. She is, however, merely his niece, Valentine (Myrna Loy), asking for an advance on her allowance. The Duke refuses, saying she'll only go back to Paris and her frivolous life. They are interrupted by the major domo (Robert Greig) announcing the new footmen. Valentine inspects each of the venerable old men. "Can't we ever get a footman under *forty* in this place?" she snorts and exits.

There is very little under forty in the entire château. The drawing rooms are filled with yawning ancients playing bridge. ("A Hot Time in the Old Town Tonight" is played as a dirge behind this scene.) Suddenly a flurry of violins announce the arrival of the Vicomte Gilbert. He has apparently spent what Maurice gave him for he orders the taxi to wait while he borrows money from his uncle. Encountering the dozing Valentine on the grand stair, he urges her to lend him the money, and they can both return in the taxi to their beloved Paris. Valentine tells him

Under director Rouben Mamoulian, Jeanette continued the Lubitsch lingerie tradition.

Love Me Tonight

that she is already over her allowance and Uncle won't let her have any more.

Gilbert is confident that he can get around the Duke. "I'll tell him I need the money for charity... to provide good homes for bad stenographers." The Duke overhears and sends the taxi away, furiously threatening to cut Gilbert off if he runs up any more debts. Several of these debts are about to come home to roost, however. Upstairs, the Princess is asleep on her satin pillow, a mournful look on her pretty face.

Back in Paris, Maurice is surrounded by his fellow tradesmen, the hat maker (Tony Merlo), the shirt maker (Clarence Wilson), and the bookmaker (William H. Turner), who have done work for the Vicomte Gilbert on Maurice's recommendation. They want their money. Maurice assures them that the Vicomte's trade will make all their reputations. Sure enough, a distinguished gentleman (Gordon Westcott) arrives to inquire if Maurice has made suits for the Vicomte. He is not a potential customer, however, but a bill collector. He has come to warn Maurice that the Vicomte *never pays*.

They are all ruined! Angrily the tradesmen plan a course of action: "Let's go down and storm the château like in the old days," but Maurice cries that he will do it alone. "I'll be a one man French Revolution!"

The whole neighborhood turns out to see him off. Maurice is resplendent in one of the Vicomte's best suits plus his own inevitable straw hat. An obliging neighbor (Mary Doran) tells Maurice that her husband must deliver his employer's car to Biarritz and would love to drop Maurice at the Chateau. "Pierre, tell Maurice you'd *love* to drop him." "I'd *love* to drop you," growls Pierre (George Davis.) Maurice departs to the cheers of the throng.

The cheers fade into a steady tap-tap. The elegantly garbed Maurice is seated on a log while Pierre lies under the car, trying to make repairs. A distant melody is heard. It is the beautiful Princess, out for a carriage ride through the woods—and she is singing:

Lover, when you find me
Will you blind me with your glow?
Make me cast behind me
All my—whoa!
(Copyright Famous Music Corp.)

The road is narrow, and as she attempts to pass the stranded car, the rear wheels slip off the road. Her horse rears, the lady tumbles into the ditch, and Maurice leaps into action. He rescues the lady, losing his straw hat in the process.

She is more or less grateful until he begins to make love to her: "Give me just a moment to sing to you...Mimi." She tells him archly that her name is not Mimi, but he launches into the song that would become a Chevalier standard. The fellow is insolent, but the Princess Jeanette hears him out, even repressing a smile at his audacious charm. But when he tells her he'd like to have "a son of a Mimi," she becomes indignant. She drives off in her now-righted carriage, the wheel neatly dissecting Maurice's straw hat. Pierre whoops with glee at this desecration of the ubiquitous boater, but

Maurice rescues the princess when her carriage overturns in a ditch, losing his most precious possession in the process. The two songs delivered in this scene, "Mimi" and "Lover," both became classics. *Courtesy Patrick Kuster.*

Maurice, undaunted, pulls a fresh one from his luggage. "Now we can go on."

Jeanette gets only as far as the foyer of the château before she faints again, collapsing daintily on the floor. Everyone rushes to her side, the three aunties uttering little birdlike chirps of distress. Gilbert seeks help from Valentine, napping on a nearby settee. "Valentine, could you go for a doctor?" She rouses, smoothes her hair, and gives him a dazzling smile. "Certainly, bring him in."

The doctor (Joseph Cawthorn) arrives, all whiskers and efficiency. In song ("A Woman Needs Something Like That"), he asks the Princess to remove her clothes which she does with élan. After he and the camera have had their fill of her lingeried charms, he questions her as to her love life, in verse of course. It seems the sad lady has been a widow for three years, at sixteen she was wed. Her bridegroom dear was seventy-two!

> PRINCESS: Why do I lie awake in bed?
> And why does blood rush to my head?
> DOCTOR: At night?
> PRINCESS: Quite right, at night.
> And why does music make me sad?
> And why do love songs drive me mad?
> DOCTOR: At night?
> PRINCESS: Quite right, at night.
> (Copyright Famous Music Corp.)

The doctor's diagnosis is simple: "With eyes and red lips and a figure like that...you're not wasting away. You're just wasted!" The cure is obvious. The Princess, he tells her anxious relatives, ought to be married...to a man of her own age.

The Duke explains that there are only two men in France of equal rank to the Princess. One is eighty-five and the other will be twelve on his next birthday. The doctor prescribes the only alternative: "Exercise!"

The plaintive little Count seizes this opportunity to urge the Duke to consider him as a prescription. After all he *would* have been a prince if his family had not been badly gypped during the Crusades, and besides... He whispers in the Duke's ear, and the old gentleman draws back with respectful astonishment: "*Marie Antoinette?*" Impressed the Duke consents to the Count continuing his suit...but not this afternoon. The Count makes a half-completed little gesture of triumph, reminiscent of Harry Langdon. "Of course, but that's me—always impetuous."

To a martial strain, the repaired limousine arrives at the enormous doors of the château. After several futile knocks, Maurice slowly opens the door and finds himself in the mammoth foyer. Hesitantly, he starts across the marble floor, slowly at first, then with the spirit of the chase, more and more eagerly as he searches for signs of life. No one is in sight. To a happy gallop, he starts up the grand staircase, finding deserted hallways at each landing. Finally in a burst of speed, he completes the stairs and has reached the attic. With a shrug and a skitter of violins, he returns to the main floor where the somnambulant bridge players are just emerging from a side room.

Valentine spots this exciting stranger and rushes up to him. "Are you alone? In life, I mean?" He assures her he is unmarried and she dashes off upstairs to change. The major domo directs Maurice to the drawing room in his search for the Vicomte Gilbert.

On his way, he passes the three aunties, sitting formally together like a row of china pug dogs, stitching on a tapestry. "Do we bore you with our sewing?" "Sewing?" "Quite so." "Oh, no! A needle is magnetic." "How true! And how poetic!" He has won them over completely and their burbles of approval can be heard as he continues down the hall.

In the drawing room, Maurice discovers an old man polishing a suit of armor. Never use silk, Maurice tells him. Always flannel. They are happily conversing when Gilbert walks in and pales. Maurice has been chatting with the Duke. Maurice pales too, but the Duke assures him he is the first of Gilbert's friends the Duke has liked.

Gilbert pulls Maurice to one side and begs him not to tell his Uncle about the bills. Maurice is adamant. He won't leave without the money. Then stay a few days, Gilbert urges, until he gets his next allowance.

Valentine and the aunties swarm in, and Gilbert introduces his friend "Baron Courtelin." All urge Maurice to stay, but he refuses...until the Princess appears. He has found his "Mimi." "I'll stay!" he cries to the obvious joy of everyone but the Princess.

The sun rises the next morning on quite a different group of people. The exuberance of the visiting "Baron" has melted even the frosty Duke. He leaps from bed and begins singing "Mimi." Down the hall, Gilbert takes up the strain as he deftly lathers his face and shaves with a flourish. The three aunties are back at their embroidery, giggling and singing "Mimi" with Elizabeth Patterson managing a Chevalier imitation. Finally, the Count, in silk pajamas, accompanies his devastatingly funny morning workout with miniature dumbbells and a final chorus. He finishes and takes up a giant hunting horn, giving it a practice bleat. The noise and image dissolve into an imposing huntsman sounding the call against a blazing sky. The hunt is forming.

The Count, however, has decided to do his hunting in the library. He has never heard of the Courtelins, he tells the Duke. He has gone through eight volumes of French genealogy before breakfast and not a Courtelin. Of course, there are still thirty-six more volumes to go.

Maurice appears for the hunt wearing Gilbert's riding habit which he has altered to fit himself. His mount is less conventional—a bicycle. Maurice has never been on a horse in his life. The Count offers him a mount "worthy of a Courtelin"—Thunderbolt. Maurice is trying to refuse the offer gracefully when Princess Jeanette rides up and announces that she has also selected a horse for him—Solitude. He is saved. Happily he accepts her offer. Gilbert whispers grimly that the horse is called Solitude because it always come home alone.

A frantically bucking horse is brought out and saddled. But this is only Thunderbolt. Solitude is still kicking the sides out of the fortress that serves as his stall. Finally he is saddled. Jeanette's eyes burn through Maurice. With a swallow, he squares his shoulders and mounts. Jeanette's disdain turns to genuine fear, but it is too late. At top speed, Solitude is gone, Maurice clinging to his back.

To a rollicking melody, the stag, dogs, and horses leap, scramble, and gallop over the sunlit countryside. The dogs close in on the door of a rustic cottage. Jeanette thrusts them aside and enters. Maurice is feeding the stag a pan of oats. She upbraids him furiously for mocking the tradition of the hunt. "You need some lessons!"

And *she* needs lessons in being a woman, he tells her. She knows everything about etiquette and tradition, but nothing about style, charm... love. Her hair is too prim, her riding habit is not in the mode. He closes his eyes and smiles. He is thinking of her without these clothes. "Open your eyes at once!" she orders. In *different* clothes, he explains.

The hunt arrives, and Maurice urges them to go back, quickly and quietly because the stag is asleep. Laughing, they take off in slow motion. Maurice and Solitude have parted company, so he joins one of the aunties on her horse for the languorous gallop back o the château.

The Count has found no Courtelins in the genealogy volumes, not even among the better class illegitimates. The Duke turns on Gilbert, but Gilbert bluffs his way through. "I don't think I better tell you. It wouldn't be safe." He implies that the Baron is royalty incognito. "He has the Hapsburg lip," nods the little Count.

At a costume ball in the "Baron's" honor, the guests waltz with dirgelike slowness. The Duke asks the Count to entertain, but he replies that he has been helpless since his accident: "I fell flat on my flute."

The "Baron" appears, and the bored company comes to life. His costume is the most novel of all, a common *Apache*. (He is wearing the clothes he wore in the opening scene of the film.) "How unusual!" "How intriguing," the ladies cry. The Princess is not impressed: "How common!" She detests the *Apache* and his attitude toward women. That is only because she doesn't understand, says Maurice, and offers to explain, to the delight of the other ladies present.

> I'd love to treat her pretty
> And take her round the city,
> But what's a poor Apache to do?
> With one deep sigh,
> I must black her eye.
> While other men are dancing
> And tenderly romancing,
> I've got to throw her body around.
> The spot that no one dares touch,
> The spot that only chairs touch,
> Is frequently touching the ground.

He tells them of the life of the *Apache* as his shadow growing taller on the wall behind him:

> I was found in a basket in front of a church
> But my childhood was not very sainted.
> I didn't know my mother who didn't know
>   my father.
> My parents were not...well acquainted.

And of his career, his shadow now huge, dominating the room:

> And when at last I'm led off
> To where they'll chop my head off,
> I'll tell the executioner this:
> "Nuts to *you*."
> And then I'll close my eyes of blue.

He bends forward, and, with a jerk, his cap falls from his head in heart-stopping imitation of the guillotine:

> Sad but true,
> That's what a poor Apache must do.
>   (Copyright Famous Music Corp.)

The audience shudders, then shaking off the grimness of the moment, bursts into delighted applause. Valentine is in hot pursuit of the "Baron," but he eludes her and follows the Princess into the garden. She has fled the crowded ballroom and runs along the leafy paths until she faints in a conveniently secluded bower. Maurice finds her, starts to revive her, then sinks down and kisses her. She awakes and slaps his face. He kisses her again. She slaps his face again. "How dare you! Why did you do that?"

"Because I love you," he says simply. She flings herself into his arms and returns his kiss passionately. They love each other. He warns her that his hands are empty, but she tells him his arms need never be empty of her. But what, he asks, if he were not what she thinks him to be? "Whoever you are, whatever you are, wherever you are, I *love* you."

"Then," he says, "Whatever happens tomorrow, *love me tonight*." The camera pans discreetly up to the brilliant moon, then dissolves to the sleeping Jeanette, now smiling on her satin pillow as her voice on the soundtrack sings "Love Me Tonight." Maurice's voice joins hers, and the screen

The "Baron" Maurice shocks the guests at a fancy-dress ball with his "Apache" costume—actually his real clothes. Left to right: Loy, Chevalier, MacDonald, Butterworth.

Love Me Tonight 111

An all-star line-up of Paramount performers: left to right, C. Aubrey Smith, Charlie Ruggles, Maurice Chevalier, Myrna Loy, Jeanette MacDonald, Charles Butterworth, Elizabeth Patterson, Blanche Frederici, Ethel Griffies.

divides to show him in his own bed, also smiling in his sleep. In his dream he confesses he is only a tailor. "A tailor!" she thrills. "Isn't it romantic!" They both snuggle happily into their pillows.

The next morning, Jeanette has taken Maurice's advice to heart. She sends for him to inspect her new riding habit. His admiration for its wearer is cut short when he notices that the collar rides up. Professionally he rips it off and begins taking the jacket apart. The dressmaker, Mme Dutoit (Ethel Wales), is scandalized and takes her leave. Never mind, Maurice tells the clinging Jeanette, he will make her a riding habit that will tame Solitude.

The dressmaker's cries of outrage rouse the castle. "Mme Dutoit has been insulted," wail the aunties, rushing down the hall like a trio of yipping Pekingese. "At *her* age? Remarkable!" says the Count. "Some men have no taste," sneers Valentine. "The old girl must have something," says Gilbert agreeably.

The Duke leads the assembling crowd to find out what has happened. They discover Maurice embracing the lingerie-clad Princess. Frantically she tries to hide behind the detached collar of the

The "Baron" takes an interest in the princess's wardrobe. When he is exposed as a common tailor, she is horrified.

jacket. The Count is all for killing the "Baron," who tries to explain that he was only fixing her riding habit. He'll prove it. Give him two hours and he will remake the entire habit. Gilbert accepts the Count's fifty-thousand-franc bet that Maurice will fail, and the Duke reluctantly agrees to the challenge. Illogically but necessarily, Jeanette and Maurice are left alone.

But rather than making love, Maurice begins measuring the astonished Princess. Two hours later the new riding costume is finished. "It's perfect," cries Jeanette joyfully. Then bewilderment sweeps over her face. How she asks was he able to do it? "Because...I *am* a tailor."

She is dumbfounded, laughs hesitantly, then realizes he is telling the truth. He reminds her of her pledge in the garden, but she runs from the room in horror. The aunties rush in, and he repeats his confession. They go off amidst an ever-rising chorus of little yelping sounds. In a long overhead shot, we see Maurice slowly pull the tape measure from his neck and drop it to the floor.

"Help, yelp," squeak the aunties, informing the Duke and the entire château that the "Baron" is actually a tailor. With a gigantic outpouring of scorn, they heap abuse on the impostor: "The Son of a Gun is Nothing but a Tailor." In a delightful patter song, we learn that the servants are even more outraged than the Duke. They have been waiting on an equal! The chambermaid (Rita Owin) moans:

> I used to flirt until it hurt
> While he stood there in his undershirt.

and the laundress (Cecil Cunningham) rages over her washboard:

> Down upon my hands and knees
> Scrubbing out his B.V.D.s
> Is a job that hardly pleases me.
> If I'd 'a known, I woulda tore
> The buttons off his panties, for
> The son of a gun is nothing but a tailor.
> (Copyright Famous Music Corp.)

Upstairs, Jeanette paces her room to the melody. "Nothing but a tailor!" she cries in anguish. Maurice is seen crossing the grand foyer with his suitcase. A whispered chant follows him: "Nothing But a Tailor." In her room, Jeanette recalls her vow of love the night before. Superimposed over her tear-stained face, we see the distant figure of Maurice walking toward the railroad station. A train is heard over the music. He boards it, and the train pulls out as Jeanette hears her own voice singing "Love Me Tonight." It is too much.

The double image vanishes. To a cacophony of train whistles, Jeanette runs downstairs and out to the stable. The roar of driving train wheels punctuates the cross cutting between Maurice on the train and the Princess on a galloping horse, Faster and faster, the music races as we cut from pounding hooves to driving pistons. Jeanette pulls abreast of Maurice's window. "Stop the train! I'm going *with* you." "No, I love you too much," he shouts. She gallops ahead to the engine and repeats her order. "What's the trouble?" calls the engineer.

"I love him!"

Love Me Tonight

"*That's* not a railroad problem," he replies shaking his head.

With a mighty burst of speed, Jeanette turns her horse aside and cuts across the field, reaching the far curve of tracks a minute before the train. She leaps from her horse and stands on the tracks, hands on hips, head high, silhouetted against the sky as the music pounds majestically. The engineer frantically blows his whistle, but she will not move. The train screeches to a stop just in front of her.

Maurice runs down the gravel beside the train and takes her in his arms, lifting her to safety beside the engine. A great burst of steam engulfs them as they embrace.

Back in the castle, the three aunties have finished their embroidery. "Once upon a time there was a Princess and a Prince Charming... who was not a prince...but who *was* charming." They shake out their tapestry to reveal a Prince on a white horse beckoning to a Princess high in the tower above, and we assume the two will live happily ever after.

Love Me Tonight was to be Miss MacDonald's last film at Paramount. The most perfect of film musicals had required little of her. Indeed her part could have been played effectively by someone possessing the thespian skills of the average debutante. Her costumes were unbelievably dowdy, and she was frequently badly lit. Possibly these factors made her want to seek greener pastures elsewhere.

Rodgers and Hart remained at Paramount to write *The Phantom President* starring George M. Cohan and then did *Hallelujah, I'm a Bum*, an overlooked classic with Al Jolson, for United Artists. For MGM they wrote Nelson Eddy's second screen song, "The Rhythm of the Day," in *Dancing Lady*. Eleven years later, Rouben Mamoulian would stage Rodgers' first post-Hart effort, *Oklahoma!*

In early 1933, a bombshell called *42nd Street* burst over the box offices of the nation's theatres. Warner Bros. had come up with a new musical formula and regained the musical ground they had lost since their early success with *The Jazz Singer*. Basically, the new formula was a perfection of the fast-paced backstage story plus ultra-stunning production numbers by Busby Berkeley. Their equally bright *Gold Diggers of 1933* followed four months later.

A minor player in both films, Ginger Rogers, then went to RKO in the fall for another great musical, *Flying Down to Rio*. In it she partnered a prominent Broadway dancer, who had been badly underused in his previous film, MGM's *Dancing Lady*. (Also nearly unnoticed in *Dancing Lady* was baritone Nelson Eddy.) Fred Astaire and Ginger Rogers were only supporting players in *Flying Down to Rio*. The romantic leads were played by Dolores Del Rio and Gene Raymond. Four years later, Jeanette would become Mrs. Raymond.

Jeanette's departure from Paramount didn't leave them musically destitute. Mae West made her first starring vehicle that year and young Bing Crosby was catching on. Late in 1933, Paramount produced a delightful descendant of the sung dialogue in *Love Me Tonight*, the classic *Duck Soup* with the Marx Brothers. It would be their last Paramount film also. Like Miss MacDonald they would go to MGM for their greatest success and eventual decline.

Reviews

Most reviewers were disappointed that Lubitsch was not at the helm of *Love Me Tonight*. "A strange alliance," said Mildred Martin of the *Philadelphia Inquirer*. She found Mamoulian "merely an unoriginal and uninspired substitute"!

Mordaunt Hall of the *New York Times* was a voice for the minority when he said that Mamoulian "gives to his scenes a charming poetic suggestion," although Hall too felt that "he may not reveal Ernst Lubitsch's satire and keen wit or René Clair's clever irony." It would take a number of years before *Love Me Tonight* (and Mamoulian's earlier *Applause*) would get the reappraisal they deserved.

Recordings (See Discography for further information)

"Isn't It Romantic" (MacDonald, also Nat Finston and the Paramount Orchestra, also Eddy with Gale Sherwood in 1964)
"Love Me Tonight," (MacDonald)
"Mimi" (Chevalier)
"N'est-ce-pas poetique?" [Isn't it Romantic] (MacDonald)
"Poor Apache," (Chevalier)
"Je suis un méchant" [I'm a bad one - Poor Apache] (Chevalier)
"Veux tu m'aimer," [Do you want to love me? - Love Me Tonight] (MacDonald)

Music in the Film

All music is by Richard Rodgers and all lyrics by Lorenz Hart. In listing performers after each title, "and" denotes a genuine duet, while commas between names indicate a sequence of singers.

Overture: a lovely melody not used elsewhere in the film.
"Song of Paree" (Chevalier)
"How Are You?" (Chevalier, Marion Byron, "Gabby" Hayes, and others.)
"Isn't It Romantic" * (Chevalier, Roach, Sedan, Brooke, male chorus, gypsy violinist, MacDonald)
"Lover" (MacDonald)
"Mimi" (Chevalier)
"A Woman Needs Something Like That" (MacDonald and Cawthorn) **
"Mimi" reprise (Smith, Ruggles, Patterson, Griffies, Butterworth)***
"The Hunt" (orchestral)
"Poor Apache" (Chevalier)
"Love Me Tonight" (MacDonald, Chevalier)
"The Son of a Gun is Nothing But a Tailor" (Smith, Loy, Griffies, Patterson, Frederici, Butterworth, Greig, Norton, Owin, Kalish, Cunningham, MacDonald)
"Love Me Tonight" reprise (Chevalier and MacDonald)
Finale: "Love Me Tonight"

* The melody of the verse for "Isn't it Romantic?" is lifted verbatim from the verse to "Now I Believe" from the 1931 Rodgers & Hart stage musical *America's Sweetheart*. The lyrics of another *America's Sweetheart* song, "You Ain't Got No Savoir Faire," contain the rhyme "chairs touch" and "dares touch" which Hart used again in *Love Me Tonight* for "Poor Apache."

Compare Mamoulian's spread-the-song sequence to a similar one in the 1930 film, *Congress Dances*, directed by Erik Charell, in which Lilian Harvey sings from a moving carriage, her song taken up by each group she passes. Two years later, Mamoulian did Charell one better, having the song move on its own. (The dramatic ending of Mamoulian's eve-of-Waterloo ball scene in *Becky Sharp* also seems to have been influenced by a similar scene in *Congress Dances.)*

** "The Man for Me" (MacDonald and Chevalier), cut from release prints, was positioned here. The song was a pleasant, rather syncopated melody in which Princess Jeanette attempts to write a letter to her friend Marie. Maurice interrupts repeatedly, dictating a glowing description of himself. It is probably fortunate the song was cut, for it eliminates the awe of the humble tailor for the Princess, a very necessary ingredient for the "fairy tale."

*** In the March 1973 issue of *Film Fan Monthly*, Myrna Loy is quoted in an interview with David Chierichetti as saying that she, too, sang a verse of "Mimi." However, when the film was reissued in 1950, the scene was cut, apparently because her navel showed through a sheer nightgown.

4
From Paramount to MGM via Monte Carlo

After the success of Oscar-nominated *One Hour with You* and the classic *Love Me Tonight*, Miss MacDonald again sailed for France, staying at Chevalier's villa in Cannes while he was working in Hollywood. Chevalier was divorcing his first and only wife, and this increased the romantic rumors that he and Jeanette were engaged, although Miss MacDonald was officially betrothed to her handsome business manager, Robert Ritchie.

It is difficult to imagine two temperaments or lifestyles more different than those of the quixotic, womanizing Chevalier and the proper, somewhat prim Miss MacDonald, but stranger combinations have occurred, and their devoted fans hoped for the best.

The trip proved to be a turning point in many ways. First of all, there was a flurry of offers. The press reported that she would make *The Merry Widow* at Paramount's Joinville studios in France, although MGM claimed the American rights, having filmed the silent version with John Gilbert and Mae Murray. She was also reported to have signed a contract with United Artists-British Dominion Films to do a picture with Herbert Marshall, directed by Herbert Wilcox (possibly *Bitter Sweet*). The *New York Herald* listed the film as *The Queen* and the director as Richard Wallace, with Marshall still as costar. All these were put aside in favor of an offer from MGM, which was on the verge of seizing the musical crown from Paramount.

Cannes was a lively place in the winter of 1932-33. The *Paris Daily Mirror* reported that Miss MacDonald was "partying" with Vilma Banky, Rod LaRocque, Gloria Swanson, Harold Lloyd, and Clara Bow. One can almost see the generally frugal Miss MacDonald calculating the career potential of this social fling.

Two other important vacationers were MGM's young guiding genius, Irving Thalberg, and his wife, actress Norma Shearer. Miss MacDonald, according to Bosley Crowther in *The Lion's Share*, lent Miss Shearer her unique chauffeur-hairdresser (shades of *Monte Carlo*!), and a friendship was cemented. Thalberg persuaded Jeanette to sign with MGM to make *I Married an Angel*. It was exactly her type of picture, a Moss Hart script based on a Hungarian play about an angel who loses her wings on her wedding night. With a fabulous score by Rodgers and Hart, it would be the perfect successor to *Love Me Tonight*.

However, once back in Hollywood, things did not go according to plan. MGM was getting nervous about public pressure for "family" pictures. *I Married an Angel* was shelved and eventually made its way back to Broadway in 1938, where it was a hit. In 1942 it finally reached the screen as the team's last picture together.

MGM hustled the dubious Miss MacDonald into a recently acquired property, the Broadway hit *The Cat and the Fiddle*.

About this time, a song dedicated to Jeanette was published in Argentina.

¡Oh, Jeannette!

Words by Franco Amenabar. Music by Juan Giterman. Dedication: "To Jeannette Mac Donald of the Celestial Voice." (The following English translation is by Edward Baron Turk.)

At the movies I saw
The film of your passion
With your subtle song
Like a pleasing illusion.
Your soft rhymes
Gave cordial consolation
To the shadowy pain of my heart.
Beautiful woman of the film,
With your songs I felt happy.

Jeannette,
Divine actress,
Sing your verses.
I don't know if what you are living is a dream,
    Jeannette.
If it's not true that your soul is far away
I can go to your heaven.

Courtesy Gary Mazzeo.

Jeannette,
I dreamed an enchanting love.
I don't know if this happy, starry love
Is a movie illusion.
Your voice alone I hear
In my loneliness.
I feel in my solitude
Your voice, your song of love alone.

I saw you with Chevalier
Enjoying a beautiful love
And your harmony was
A nightingale's song.
In your delicate face of a slender woman
The faithful star of art shined its splendor.
Because of your celestial voice
I felt sad and sentimental.

No copyright date on sheet music. Published by Américo A. Vivona, Cochambamba 2362, Buenos Aires, Argentina.

The Cat and the Fiddle

MGM.
Released February 16, 1934.
Directed by William K. Howard.
Retakes by Sam Wood.
Produced by Bernie Hyman and William K. Howard.
92 minutes.
Finale in three-strip Technicolor.

French title: *Le Chat et le Canari* (The Cat and the Canary)

From the operetta by Jerome Kern and Otto Harbach. Screenplay: Samuel and Bella Spewack. Music Director: Herbert Stothart. Art Director: Alexander Toluboff. Interiors: Edwin B. Willis. Gowns: Adrian. Photography: Harold Rosson and Charles Clarke. Editor: Frank Hull. Assistant Director: Lesley Selander. Technicolor Photography: Ray Rennahan. Technicolor Art Direction: Natalie Kalmus. Sound: Douglas Shearer. French Choral Director: M. Farrell.

The stage version opened at the Globe Theatre in New York City on October 15, 1931, and ran 395 performances there and later at the Cohan Theatre. The cast included Odette Myrtil, Georges Metaxa, Bettina Hall, Eddie Foy Jr, and Jose Ruben.

Ramon Novarro (Victor Florescu)
Jeanette MacDonald (Shirley Sheridan)
Frank Morgan (Jules Daudet)
Charles Butterworth (Charles)
Jean Hersholt (Professor Bertier)
Vivienne Segal (Odette Brieux)
Frank Conroy (Theatre owner)
Henry Armetta (Taxi driver)
Adrienne D'Ambricourt (Concierge)
Joseph Cawthorn (Rudy Brieux)
Earl Oxford (Singer)
Yola d'Avril (Shirley's maid)
Armand Kaliz (King in "A New Love Iis Old")
Frank Sully (Actor)
Irene Franklin (Lotte Lengel)
Arthur Hoyt (Man in box seat)
Christian Rub (Messenger in play)
Paul Porcasi (Club proprietor)
Herman Bing (Drum major)
Leonid Kinsky (Violinist)
Georges Davis (Henri, the musician)
Sterling Holloway (Messenger with flowers)
Max Davidson (Old man)
Leo White (Prompter)
Billy Dooley (Electrician)
The Albertina Rasch Ballet
Enrico Ricardi (Novarro's stand-in)
Dulcie Day (MacDonald's stand-in)
Otto Fries (Piano mover)
Sumner Getchell, Harry Swailes, André Renaud, Jack Chefe (Music students)
Robert Graves (Diner)
Henry Kolker (Theatre manager)
Alice Carlisle (Vegetable seller)
Grace Hayle (Lettuce seller)
Germaine De Neel (Maid)
Harry Depp (Opera singer's husband)
Polly Bailey (Ballet mistress)
Frank Adams (Musician)
E. Alyn Warren (Orchestra leader)
Phil Tead (Reporter)
Charles Crockett (Rudy's secretary)
Harold Minjir (Manager of travel bureau)
George Le Guere (Elevator operator)
Jacques Vanaire (Singer)
George Nardelli (Singer's assistant)
Dewey Robinson (Arabian singer)
J.H. Peters (Stage manager)
Reginald Barlow (King's aide)
Bits: Rolfe Sedan, David Reese, Eugène Borden, Ludovico Tomarchio, Freddie Ford, Geneva Williams

After the huge theatrical success of his *Show Boat* in 1927, Jerome Kern had continued his attempt to push the American musical toward a sophisticated operatic perfection. While *Porgy and Bess* was still a gleam in Gershwin's eye, Kern sought to create the Great American Opera. Musically, he succeeded with *The Cat and the Fiddle*, full of strikingly modern melodies, but always redolent with Kern's traditional "odor of sachet." However, he was done in by a clumsy and unmemorable libretto.

The principal dramatic tension of the stage version hinges on whether the heroine has been "ruined" when trapped overnight in the villain's apartment. She says no, but the hero refuses to believe her and discards her as unworthy until outside proof supports her undefiled virginity.

Songwriter Shirley Sheridan (Jeanette) comes to Brussels to study with Professor Bertier (Jean Hersholt, right). Both impresario Daudet (Frank Morgan, left) and composer Victor Florescu (Ramon Novarro) hope to score with her.

(Modern audiences would boo the sexist pig off the stage, and this musically exquisite work is rarely revived.)

The film was cobbled together just as the Code and the Hays Office were coming into power. Snipped and hacked, with unmatched retakes inserted here and there to cover the gaps, the supposedly sanitized version ends up implying that the boy and girl are living in sin! (The basic problem with most censorship is that it often creates unintentional naughtiness far worse than what it is trying to eliminate.)

Nevertheless, there is still enough youthful fire in Novarro's performance and enough dazzling Jerome Kern score to make *The Cat and the Fiddle* enjoyable. Jeanette, despite Thalberg's professional promises, is still a costar. The film is a vehicle for Ramon Novarro, hero of the classic *Ben Hur* and one of MGM's top moneymakers for a decade. He was growing a bit old for his screen persona of a spirited juvenile, and this would prove to be one of his last films at MGM. However, his youthful enthusiasm is still infectious and undiminished.

The vamp of the piece is played by Broadway star Vivienne Segal, making one of her infrequent film appearances. She would later star on Broadway in *I Married an Angel*, subsequently a film vehicle for MacDonald and Eddy. Director William K. Howard (*Don't Bet on Women*) was noted mainly for his strong dramatic films—the silent classic *White Gold*, a Germanic western with psychological overtones, and *The Power and the Glory*, Spencer Tracy's *tour de force* about a hated tycoon.

The film comes as close as MGM ever got to the Paramount style of light sex comedy. It is genuinely funny, and the superb music that rarely stops for more than a minute or two makes one forget the plot deficiencies—almost. Every song in the original score is used, although several get new lyrics ("Poor Pierrot," "One Moment Alone").

The simple stage plot undergoes some revamping. In the stage version, an American girl with one hit song to her credit comes to Brussels to study music. There she meets a serious young composer who is being aggressively pursued by a violin-playing musical comedy star (thus the title). Odette Myrtil played the role of the violinist, and, oddly, the name of the stage performer was inherited by her singing film counter-part.

The composer writes an operetta, *The Passionate Pilgrim*, for the star, but it is terrible. It remains for the girl to write a hit and save the boy from the vamp's clutches. Georges Metaxa created the role of Victor Florescu, as he already had that of Carl Linden in *Bitter Sweet* in London. (He also played the band leader in the Astaire-Rogers film *Swingtime*.)

The film story becomes a somewhat illogical tale of living in sin in Paris and Brussels. Considering the flak that the proposed *I Married an Angel* incurred, it is astounding that *Cat* raised not one eyebrow. The lively overture is liberally laced with concertina passages and finally a piano theme that continues over the credits into a Brussels café. Composer-music

The Cat and the Fiddle

student Victor Florescu (Ramon Novarro) is playing for his supper.

He and the café owner (Paul Porcasi) each feel they have been shortchanged by the other. Amidst the ensuing tumult, Victor escapes in a passing military parade, its ever-quickening rhythms carrying him from the pursuing restaurateur into a passing taxi. It is, of course, the cab of Shirley Sheridan (Jeanette), who has just arrived in Belgium and is heading for the *pension* next door to Victor's. An enthusiastic type, Victor immediately makes love to Shirley. She wisely ignores him.

The cab arrives at their destination and Victor gallantly offers to pay her cab fare. As Shirley sweeps haughtily up the steps of her *pension*, her suitcase bursts open, strewing her lingerie across the pavement. Victor leaps to her assistance, pocketing a lacy souvenir.

The cabdriver (Henry Armetta) must be paid, and Victor has no money. He offers his hat, his coat, his pants. The driver shakes his head: "They crease in front. I like mine to crease on the sides." Instead, the driver seizes Victor's music portfolio, promising to exchange it anytime for the twelve-franc fare. Victor will have no trouble finding him, the cabby calls as he drives away. His cab "Theresa" has a very distinctive horn.

Disconsolately, Victor enters his *pension*. His old music teacher, Professor Bertier (Jean Hersholt, the "Dr. Christian" of radio and films), is waiting for Victor in his room with tremendous news. Daudet, the noted music patron, has agreed to listen to Victor's music. If he likes it, he will commission an operetta. The appointment is at 5:00 that afternoon. And where is Victor's music? Victor reaches in his pocket and produces a lacy chemise.

He has lost his portfolio, but surely he can remember his own songs. Frantically, he tries to pick out the melodies on the piano, as the professor grows more and more angry. They are all wrong. The old professor is heartbroken that Victor has ruined this opportunity with his philandering. He leaves, and Victor settles down at the piano to reconstruct his lost melodies.

His playing is interrupted repeatedly by a rival pianist across the courtyard, playing jazz. They pound away in counterpoint until Victor screams in rage. His tormentor yells back. It is Shirley.

Instantly, Victor is the lover again. He risks life and limb to clamber across to her window. Hanging by one hand, he gallantly offers to

MGM hoped to create a new, romantic singing team, one with international appeal, by pairing Jeanette with Ramon Novarro.

return her lacy undies. As his grip loosens, Shirley relents and hauls him in. He stays to help her write the song she has been working on, "The Night Was Made for Love." Wearing a singularly unattractive Adrian frock, Shirley joins Victor in a duet of the lovely song.

Shirley tosses Daudet's roses out the window. They land on Charles (Charles Butterworth), who is looking for a harp lesson.

(Although Adrian would make her one of the best-costumed ladies in Hollywood, his heart was obviously not in his work here. He had not yet evolved his bag of tricks for dealing with her singer's ribcage and muscular but long neck.)

Transported by love, Victor rushes off to get his portfolio back. He will use force if necessary. Racing through the streets of Brussels, he hears the unique horn of "Theresa" and throws himself in front of the cab, begging the driver to return his music. Their argument takes place in the middle of a funeral procession. A top-hatted gentleman leans from one of the carriages and gently chides them for detaining his late uncle. He becomes interested in the dispute and offers to advance Victor the cab fare because he himself likes music. "Do you know why I like music?" "No, why?" "I don't know. That's why I asked you."

With dialogue like that, it must be comedian Charles Butterworth, the wistful Count of *Love Me Tonight* who "fell flat on his flute." In this epic, he plays "Charles." He is happy to lend Victor the money since he has become rich at a single stroke. His uncle had the stroke two days ago. Now Charles is looking forward to buying a harp.

Victor has no time for conversation. He exchanges the francs for his precious music, thanks Charles profusely, and darts off. "Not at all," Charles calls after him. "I hope I have a chance to do a favor for *you* sometime."

Outside the conservatory, Victor crashes into a distinguished-looking gentleman. They exchange heated words until Professor Bertier introduces the gentleman as Jules Daudet, the man Victor has come to see. "Charmed!" cries Victor instantly, all smiles.

Daudet (Frank Morgan) is *not* charmed. He refuses to stay. Victor mounts the steps and calls after him, "I don't care!" It doesn't matter that he has made an enemy or lost his career. He has met the most glorious girl in the whole world! He would not trade all the success, money, and fame in the world for one of her smiles. What do they matter? He has found love! The gathered students burst into applause, and Daudet returns to hear his music.

Victor is playing for Daudet and the entire student body when Shirley arrives. She tries to explain to Professor Bertier that she has come to audition, but everyone keeps shushing her. To see the cause of their intense interest, she climbs on a chair and peeks through a transom. The chair slips and the door crashes open. The startled listeners look up to see a pair of dangling legs and a slim body. Without seeing the rest of Shirley, Daudet decides that this must be why he came to Brussels.

Victor exuberantly introduces Shirley as his fiancée, which she vehemently denies. Daudet absently agrees to produce Victor's operetta and turns to more important things. What, he asks Shirley, does she want most in life? "Me!" cries Victor. Ignoring him, Shirley explains that she has come to audition and she is quickly seated at the piano. She sings "The Night Was Made for Love" and then plays "Impressions in a Harlem Flat." Professor Bertier is unmoved by Shirley's unclassical approach, but Daudet warmly offers to publish her songs. Shirley wonders if his enthusiasm is entirely professional.

The Cat and the Fiddle

Victor woos Shirley by singing, "She Didn't Say 'Yes'"—and the lady doesn't say, "No."

On a dark, rainy night, Shirley is alone in her garret playing the piano. A messenger boy (Sterling Holloway) arrives with an enormous bouquet of white roses from Daudet. The note reads: "The night was made for love." The messenger comments that it seems a stupid message, but he guesses it would be all right if you did it inside. Shirley heaves the roses out the window and returns to her playing. The roof begins to leak in a dozen places and the orchestra echoes the drip, drip as Shirley puts her few bowls around on the floor.

Victor arrives with an armload of pots. He once lived in her room, he tells her, and slept in her bed. The raindrops make a counterpoint as he sings her his new arrangement of their song, "The Night Was Made for Love." He asks her to be "comrades," to "live, love, laugh, sing, eat, starve" with him. She is still unconvinced.

A knock is heard at the door. It is Charles, covered with roses (although it is more than five minutes since Shirley threw them out the window). She apologizes, but Charles tells her it could have happened to anyone. If she has a window, he'll throw them out again. He has come looking for Victor to claim a harp lesson. His harp is downstairs.

"Tomorrow," Victor pleads, trying to ease him out the door. His efforts are in vain, for suddenly a full operetta chorus of quaint types comes surging in, complete with musical instruments. They sing and dance around the surprisingly spacious garret. Victor has told them that he and Shirley "belong together," and she ponders this in "She Didn't Say 'Yes.'"

Daudet arrives in the midst of the tumult and takes Shirley outside onto the shabby landing for a private conversation. Skillfully he makes her an offer and tactfully she refuses. Has he come too late? he inquires. "Perhaps," she replies. To test Shirley's affection, Daudet tells Victor he must leave that night for Paris with Daudet in order to have his operetta produced.

In a whirl of "The Night Was Made for Love" ("La Nuit il faut aimer") sheet music covers and currency, we dissolve to an elegant Paris hotel, where Victor and Shirley are living on Shirley's earnings. Victor awakens Shirley

The inimitable Charles Butterworth. *Courtesy Anna Michalik.*

Frank Morgan was transitioning from handsome leading-man rôles to comic character parts—in which he would also excel. *Courtesy Anna Michalik.*

from a lovely dream: that they were so rich that Victor walked around in a golden jacket. "And nothing else?" "I don't think so," she replies.

Daudet phones to find out if Shirley will have his song finished that afternoon. Shirley promises, and she and Victor put the finishing touches on "I Watch the Love Parade."

Victor is unhappy. He can't work in Paris. Shirley tells him he must go and entertain their guests (left over from the night before?), especially Odette. Odette's husband is scandalously rich, and she is dying to go back on the stage. Of course, says Shirley, if Victor is unhappy, they can return to Brussels at once. Daudet interrupts them to say their guests are waiting. Victor goes off to find Odette, and Shirley tells their "employer" that she and Victor are returning to Brussels together.

The Cat and the Fiddle 123

The "cat" of the title is Shirley's rival, Odette, played by Broadway star Vivienne Segal. She starred in four 1930 Technicolor film musicals. Left to right, Ramon Novarro, Frank Morgan, Segal.

In the drawing room, the sensuous Odette (Vivienne Segal) is vamping Victor, singing his new song, "A New Love Is Old." Odette introduces Victor to her husband, Rudy (Joseph Cawthorn), who knows only one song: "Pop Goes the Weasel." Charles offers to play his harp, which he has brought with him. "Do you mean to tell me you came here just to play that thing?" Rudy asks. "I thought I'd get a little drunk too," Charles replies.

Daudet tells Victor that Shirley is inside packing, that she plans to give up her career for Victor. "Are you going to let her wreck her career?" "Why not?" Victor smiles. But he has second thoughts. In Brussels, Shirley would still be supporting him. That's fine with Shirley, who proposes marriage. Victor panics and plays the compulsory renunciation scene, making Shirley believe he no longer loves her. He then sings "A New Love Is Old," nearly breaking down.

He is gone, and Shirley wanders disconsolately about the overdecorated suite, listening to the chandelier tinkle in the breeze as the orchestra softly plays "I Watch the Love Parade." She flings herself sobbing on the bed.

Victor apparently finds time to finish his operetta, *Le Chat et Le Violin* (The Cat and the Fiddle), apparently stays in Paris, and apparently

Victor leaves Shirley, takes up with the glamourous Odette, and writes his operetta. But when Odette walks out as the star on opening night and Victor faces jail for writing a bad check, Shirley must return and save him and the show.

is being financed by Odette, for we next see him at a rehearsal, where Odette is singing "Hh! Cha! Cha!" Victor is summoned to Odette's dressing room, where she is draped seductively on a *chaise longue*. He protests that he respects her husband too much. "Help me," she croons, holding out her arms. As he is helping her, her husband enters. Assuming the worst, Rudy withdraws his backing and his wife from the show.

The theatre owner (Frank Conroy) demands immediate payment of the rent in advance to protect himself. Victor gives him a bad check, figuring that if the show is a hit he can make it good. If it is a failure, he might as well be in jail.

He calls the cast together and tells them their salaries may not be forthcoming for awhile. The male lead and the orchestra walk out, but everyone else stays. Charles bemoans the fact that now he won't be able to afford a new pair of shoes. Lining his old pair with newspapers, he spots an item about Shirley's engagement to Daudet. He tries to tell Victor, but Victor is on the phone trying to reach Professor Bertier in

The Cat and the Fiddle

Brussels. The professor must come to Paris with his students to form the new orchestra.

Charles slips away and calls on Shirley to ask her to replace Odette. Shirley is in the process of moving, and he follows her into a freight elevator. Seating himself at a convenient grand piano, he plays Victor's new song "Try to Forget." As the elevator goes up and down over and over, Shirley sings the song and breaks down in tears.

Backstage, Victor is putting the finishing touches on the production for the opening night. He will play the hero, and Charles has called to say he is on his way with a new leading lady. Professor Bertier and his students arrive to complete the company. Charles returns, not with Shirley, but with Mlle. Lotte Lengel (Irene Franklin). "Lotte Lengel!" cries the delighted old professor. "She was a star when I was a child."

Charles explains to the horrified Victor that it will be necessary to change the story slightly. The heroine will no longer be his sweetheart, but his mother. In despair, Victor decides to cancel the show, but Professor Bertier reminds him of the students. They paid their own way and will be stranded if he lets them down. "Start the overture," says Victor.

Onstage, the chorus is singing "We Belong to the Queen's Hussars." Backstage, Mlle. Lengel has a problem. She has been gargling with rum for her sore throat. "I think she swallowed a little of the gargle," Charles observes. Mlle. Lengel is consumed with self-pity. She is old, she tells Charles, and ugly. She is a grandmother. "Is that so?" says Charles agreeably. "Congratulations."

From the stage, a familiar voice is heard in song. It is Shirley. She has saved the show. Backstage, she tells Victor that she is still marrying Daudet. This time she will do the walking out. She goes to make her costume change while Victor follows, protesting his love. Daudet is waiting in her dressing room. It is he who insisted Shirley come, so that she wouldn't

A Technicolor finale unites the lovers.

feel guilty later. He asks Victor to leave while Shirley is dressing, giving us the anticipated lingerie sequence. Victor is surprised. Has Daudet forgotten what he and Shirley have *been* to each other? (Hollywood shorthand for s-e-x.) "There's something about the theatre that's gotten in my blood," Charles murmurs as Shirley undresses.

Shirley and Victor begin rehearsing their upcoming scene, but Victor keeps interjecting his personal pleas. Shirley tears herself away and runs onstage to sing "I'll Bring You a Song in the Springtime." (Note that Jeanette's Adrian-designed costume in the finale was originally made for Joan Crawford for the "Let's Go Bavarian" number with Fred Astaire in *Dancing Lady*, 1933.)

The second act curtain rises in three-strip Technicolor on a huge, snow-covered tree. (The year 1934 saw the introduction of this advance over the earlier two-strip Technicolor. It was capable of registering yellow, red, and purple, in addition to the original blue-greens and red-oranges.) A passerby (Christian Rub) asks Victor if "she" will appear, and he replies sadly that "she" has passed him by. Suddenly "she" does appear, and they join in a final duet to the melody of "Poor Pierrot." The snow magically melts, and the tree blossoms with lush green leaves and pink blossoms. The music surges to a climax, and we assume the lovers live happily, one way or another, ever after.

Reviews

William Boehnel of the *New York World-Telegram* (who would dislike the later MacDonald classic, *The Merry Widow*) found *The Cat and the Fiddle* "by far the most tuneful, charming and thoroughly entertaining operetta the screen has offered in years....Jeanette MacDonald [is] more attractive than ever." The *New York Times* thought the film captured "much of the [stage version's] original charm and spontaneity....There are clever performances by Ramon Novarro and Jeanette MacDonald."

The *New York Herald Tribune* was more perceptive (from our viewpoint) when they commented: "After great effort has been expended on making the score an integral part of the plot, rather than something superimposed upon it, you suddenly discover that the plot hasn't really been worth all the trouble."

Variety was harshest of all: "For better or worse, the original *Cat and the Fiddle* stage script has been so altered by the film adapters that the only thing of merit remaining is the music. In place of the café scene in which the lovers reunited, so well done in the Max Gordon stage production, the picture uses the stock finish for most backstage stories: the heroine shows up at the last minute to play the leading role in the show-within-the-show and saves it. Even though the heroine is just a music student and, as far as the picture tells, has never before appeared on a stage....There are times when Miss MacDonald and Novarro seem to be of dual height, other times when Novarro looks about an inch taller, still others when he's two or three heads above the former Chevalier leading lady."

Recordings (See Discography for further information)

"Try to Forget" – (MacDonald)
"Essayons D'Oublier" [Try to Forget] – (MacDonald)

Music in the Film

All music by Jerome Kern and lyrics by Otto Harbach, except where noted. In listing performers after each title, "and" denotes a genuine duet, while commas between names indicate a sequence of singers.

Like its stage ancestor, the film version of *The Cat and the Fiddle* is one continuous melody line that occasionally forms itself into "songs." There are a number of recurring orchestral themes without specific names, one of which turns up in the film with two sets of lyrics.

Overture: based on themes used in stage overture, EVOLVES INTO: Victor's piano concerto, based on recurring orchestral themes
March (orchestral) - possibly caricaturing the can-can theme from *La Belle Hélène* by Jacques Offenbach
Musical piano battle (Victor and Shirley each playing their half-finished compositions) - based on similar scene in stage play
"Finaletto" to Act I, containing fragments of "Peer Gynt" by Edvard Grieg and "Impressions in a Harlem Flat" (See below)
"Funeral March" - by Fredric Chopin
Victor's audition - recurring themes, especially from Act I, scene 2

The Cat and the Fiddle 127

Ramon Novarro was one of MGM's biggest silent stars in such films as *Ben Hur* and *The Student Prince*. A singer and composer, he often put on concerts and was involved in musical stage productions.

"The Night Was Made for Love" (MacDonald and Novarro)
"The Breeze Kissed Your Hair" (Novarro) - as in the stage play, the verse for:
"One Moment Alone" (Novarro and chorus)
"The Night Was Made for Love" reprise (MacDonald)
"Impressions in a Harlem Flat" (piano) - based on melody in Kern's "Finaletto"
Concertina melody (chorus vocalizing) - based on "La Jeune Fille Est Malade," Act I, EVOLVES INTO:
"Poor Pierrot" (dance with chorus vocalizing)
"She Didn't Say 'Yes'" (chorus and MacDonald)

"Don't Tell Us Not to Sing" (chorus) - originally "Don't Ask Me Not to Sing." Song was cut from stage play, but used in film. (Kern reused the song during the fashion show sequence in the stage version of his *Roberta*, but it was not sung in the film version with Astaire and Rogers.) EVOLVES INTO:
"The Night Was Made for Love" success montage (MacDonald and chorus in English, chorus in French, music box reprise)
"I Watch the Love Parade" (Novarro, MacDonald)
"A New Love is Old" (Vivienne Segal)
"A New Love is Old" reprise (Novarro)

"The Crystal Candelabra" (orchestra with MacDonald humming "I Watch the Love Parade") - identical to stage sequence
"Hh! Cha! Cha!" (Earl Oxford and Segal with chorus)
"Try to Forget" (MacDonald)

Le Chat et le Violin (Victor's operetta):
    Overture: identical to film overture
    Chorus based on recurring theme ("This is the day that the masses...") - lyricist uncertain
    Chorus based on bridge in "I Watch the Love Parade" ("We belong to the Queen's hussars...") - lyricist uncertain
    "A New Love is Old" reprise (MacDonald)
    Waltz - a recurring theme in stage play
    "I bring you a song in the springtime..." (MacDonald) - based on recurring theme, lyricist uncertain
    "Try to Forget" reprise (Novarro)
    "Try to Forget" reprise with new lyrics (MacDonald and male chorus)
    Musical bridge based on Act II, Scene 6 theme in stage version
    "I Watch the Love Parade" (Novarro, MacDonald)
    "Poor Pierrot" with new lyric ("Long, long ago...") (MacDonald, Novarro, chorus)

Finale: fragments of "She Didn't Say 'Yes'" and "The Night Was Made for Love"

Songs from stage version used in the movie were "One Moment Alone," "The Night Was Made for Love," "She Didn't Say 'Yes,'" "I Watch the Love Parade," "A New Love Is Old," "Hh! Cha! Cha!" and "Try to Forget." "Poor Pierrot" was used with new lyrics.

Trivia

Jeanette and Nelson nearly appeared in a Kern musical together. According to research by Amy Asch, Jerome Kern and Oscar Hammerstein II copyrighted at least four unpublished songs on 4/30/35, written for a proposed MacDonald-Eddy film, *Champagne and Orchids*: "Dance Like a Fool," "Singing a Song in Your Arms," "Champagne and Orchids," and "When I've Got the Moon" (AKA "Banjo Song"). The index of Kern manuscripts at the Library of Congress notes that "Dance Like a Fool" was also intended for but not used in a film called *Rise and Shine*.

The Hammerstein papers at the Library of Congress also contain a "temporary complete" screenplay for *Summer Breeze*, dated 3/8/35, labeled "MGM Production #1790" (or #1796). Story, dialogue, and lyrics by Hammerstein with music by Kern. The characters were "typed" for Jeanette, Nelson, Wallace Beery, Clifton Webb, Elizabeth Patterson, Constance Collier, Vilma Ebsen, Buddy Ebsen, and Donald Meek.

The plot involved a small town with financial troubles that hopes to capture tourist trade by setting up a summer theatre. The plot, borrowed directly from the plot of the Kern/Hammerstein hit *Music in the Air*, has an estranged leading lady (Jeanette) and leading man (Nelson) accepting parts without realizing that they'll be working with each other. Two local sweethearts get romantically involved temporarily with the older couple, the boy with the actress, the girl with the actor. Songs were to be "Summer Breeze," "Happy Am I" (a comedy song), "Dance Like a Fool" with a big production number, and various untitled solos and duets for the Jeanette and Nelson characters.

Another Library of Congress file for an untitled Kern/Hammerstein project contains songs assigned to "Ross," "Tibbett," "Jeanette," "Beery," "Webb," "Parker" (no first names listed) and chorus. The cast and the song titles— "Summer Breeze," "Bone of Contention," "Whispering Chorus," "Volunteer Fireman," "Production Number," "I Can't Sing," "Opera Wardrobe," "Duet Rehearsal," "Reprise Duet," "Reprise in Show," "Finale"—suggest some overlap.

The Merry Widow

MGM.
Released November 2, 1934.
Directed by Ernst Lubitsch.
Produced [uncredited] by Irving Thalberg and Ernst Lubitsch.
110 minutes. (Current running time: 103 or 99 minutes. See "Censorship Cuts" below)

French version: Filmed simultaneously in English and French. See, *La Veuve Joyeuse*, page 146.

American TV title: *The Lady Dances* (to avoid confusion with the 1952 Lana Turner/Fernando Lamas remake)

Based on the operetta *Die Lustige Witwe*, with music by Franz Lehár, book and lyrics by Victor Leon and Leo Stein. Screenplay: Samson Raphaelson and Ernest Vajda. Contributions to script: Ernst Lubitsch and Lorenz Hart. New Lyrics: Lorenz Hart and Gus Kahn. Photographer: Oliver T. Marsh. Art Direction: Cedric Gibbons and Frederic Hope. Sets: Edwin B. Willis and Gabriel Scognamillo. Editor: Frances Marsh. Assistant Directors: Joseph Newman, Joe Lefert. Costumes: Ali Hubert. Miss MacDonald's Gowns: Adrian. Sound: Douglas Shearer. Musical Adaptation: Herbert Stothart. Orchestrations: Charles Maxwell, Paul Marquardt, and Leonid Raab. Dance director: Albertina Rasch. MacDonald's Waltz Instructor: Bob Spencer.

Lehár's operetta premiered in Vienna on December 30, 1905. It opened in New York on October 21, 1907 at the New Amsterdam Theatre, produced by Henry W. Savage and starring Ethel Jackson and Donald Brian.

First adapted to the screen in 1907 as a 14-minute Swedish short, *The Merry Widow* has been filmed at least five times in the United States. In 1912, there was a one-reel version starring Wallace Reid and Alma Rubens for Reliance Majestic. Essanay did a two-reeler in 1913. The famed Erich von Stroheim silent in 1925 starred Mae Murray and John Gilbert. Both the 1925 MGM silent and the 1934 MGM film were photographed by the very talented Oliver T. Marsh, brother of the great silent actress Mae Marsh. MGM remade *The Merry Widow* in 1952 in Technicolor, with Fernando Lamas as Danilo and Lana Turner as a non-singing American Widow. Joseph Pasternak produced and Curtis Bernhardt directed. Una Merkel, who had played the Queen in the 1934 version, appeared as Miss Turner's companion.

Ernst Lubitsch, Jeanette, and Maurice Chevalier prepare to start their fourth—and last— collaboration. *Courtesy Anna Michalik.*

Trailer: The trailer for the 1934 film version is a visual and historical delight. It contains footage of Franz Lehár himself wielding a baton and begins with an entrancing shot of Danilo and Sonia waltzing atop a spinning earth against a star-studded sky.

Happy Days Are Here Again: In a companion promotional short, Lehár addresses American audiences in English: "I greet you on the thirtieth anniversary of my *Merry Widow*!" We also see behind-the-scenes footage of production of the film.

Censorship Cuts: American TV prints and the commercial video of *The Merry Widow* have five major cuts, made by television censors in the early 1960s. Missing are:

1. In the garden, Danilo boasts that there isn't a window in Marshovia he hasn't jumped out of, not a husband he hasn't gotten around, but here he is bluffed.

2. Danilo produces his own key to leave the Queen's locked bedroom. (He can still be seen pocketing it as he emerges.)

The Widow (Jeanette) at the gate of her estate in the mythical kingdom of Marshovia. Cedric Gibbons won an Oscar for set decoration.

3. Danilo asks a Maxim's girl, "Do you still cry when you love someone?"

4. A close-up of Lulu's garter and its inscription, "Many Happy Returns."

5. Sonia explains that Fifi's method of "committing suicide" was to take a cold bath: "You'd be *surprised* what a cold bath can do."

A 1993 Laserdisc contained these segments, but they are missing from commercial videos and DVDs.

Maurice Chevalier (Count Danilo)
Jeanette MacDonald (Sonia)
Edward Everett Horton (Ambassador Popoff)
Una Merkel (Queen Dolores)
George Barbier (King Achmed II)
Minna Gombell (Marcelle)
Ruth Channing (Lulu)
Sterling Holloway (Mischka, orderly)
Henry Armetta (Turk)
Barbara Leonard (Sonia's maid Melissa)
Donald Meek (Valet)
Akim Tamiroff (Maxim's manager)
Herman Bing (Zizipoff)
Lucien Prival (Adamovitch)
Luana Walters, Sheila Mannors [later Sheila Bromley], Caryl Lincoln, Edna Waldron, Lona André (Sonia's maids)
Barbara Barondess (Frou Frou, Maxim's girl)
Eleanor Hunt (Margot, Maxim's girl)
Patricia Farley, Shirley Chambers, Jeanne Hart, Maria Troubetskoy, Dorothy Wilson, Dorothy Granger, Jill Dennett, Mary Jane Halsey, Peggy Watts, Dorothy Dehn, Connie Lamont (Maxim's girls)

The Merry Widow

Charles Requa, George Lewis, Tyler Brooke, John Merkyl, Cosmo Kyrle Bellew (Escorts)
Roger Gray, Christian J. Frank, Otto Fries, John Roach (Policemen)
Gino Corrado (Waiter)
Perry Ivins (Waiter)
Katherine Burke [later Virginia Field] (Prisoner)
George Baxter (Ambassador)
Paul Ellis (Dancer)
Leonid Kinsky (Shepherd)
Evelyn Selbie (Newspaper seller)
Wedgwood Nowell (Lackey)
Richard Carle (Defense attorney)
Morgan Wallace (Prosecutor)
Frank Sheridan (Judge)
Arthur "Pop" Byron (Doorman)
Nora Cecil (Woman with goat in court)
Winter Hall (Priest)
Matty Roubert (Newsboy)
Ferdinand Munier (Jailer)
Dewey Robinson (Fat lackey with spray)
Russell Powell (Lackey)
Billy Gilbert (Lackey)
Arthur Housman (Drunk in carriage)
Johnny [Skins] Miller (Drunk)
Hector Sarno (Gypsy leader)
Bella Loblov (Gypsy violinist)
Jan Rubini (Violinist)
Jason Robards Sr. (Arresting officer)
Albert Pollet (Headwaiter)
Rolfe Sedan (Gabrielovitsch)
Jacques Lory (Goatherd)
Lane Chandler (Soldier)
Extras: Joan Gale, Earl Oxford, Florine McKinney, Arthur Jowett

Actors listed with the Screen Actors Guild as having contracts, but who do not appear in release print:
Claudia Coleman (Wardrobe mistress)
Lee Tin ("Excited Chinaman" [sic])
Tom Francis [Tom Herbert] (Orthodox priest)

Oscar for Interior Decoration: Cedric Gibbons and Frederic Hope.

The Merry Widow was presented on "The Railroad Hour" (radio), 3/7/49, with Jeanette and Gordon MacRae.

The Merry Widow was the world's first hit musical. The tremendous acclaim that accompanied its premiere in Vienna on December 30, 1905 brought instant fame to its thirty-five-year-old composer, Franz Lehár, and began an international success. In the century since, there has scarcely been a night without a performance somewhere in the world.

Working in the genre of "little opera" begun by Von Suppé and brilliantly perfected by Johann Strauss Jr., Lehár turned out a musical romance centering on the obligatory waltz theme. However, his waltz and its staging were different from the "production number" types so in vogue. "The Merry Widow Waltz" begins slowly, sensuously, teasingly, as the hero takes the reluctant heroine in his arms and moves her around an empty stage. Only when she responds does the waltz break into dazzling gaiety. It was

The Merry Widow enjoyed international appeal. Here a poster in Chinese. Often the dialogue was dubbed, while the songs remained in English.

Various versions of *The Merry Widow* have spun off fashions in their respective eras. Here, Jeanette's coiffure is touted by a Hungarian beauty salon in Budapest. *Courtesy Patrick Kuster.*

a moment audiences waited for, and, when Donald Brian took Ethel Jackson in his arms each night in the American production, there was an audible sigh of fulfillment.

Nor was *The Merry Widow*'s popularity limited to its music. The enormous picture hat worn by Ethel Jackson swept the fashion world, so much so that editorials and sermons decried it and several local governments passed ordinances against "Merry Widow hats" as unsafe, unhealthy, and immoral. (Mae West, in her evocation of the Gay Nineties, ignored the tiny hats actually worn at the time and used the giant "Merry Widow" hat of a decade later.)

The *Widow* plot was slender enough not to intrude on the glorious melodies that have become part of the musical heritage of half the cultures of the world. Not since the works of Gilbert and Sullivan had the theatres of the Western world seized on a musical entertainment with such delight. Exact statistics are nearly impossible to come by, but, when releasing their 1934 version, MGM boasted that the stage *Widow* had played over a quarter-of-a-million times in twenty-four languages and, in one year, racked up 18,000 performances. The saga of the *Widow* deserves a book in itself.

The fantastic popularity of the *Widow* and the equally fantastic opportunity to make lots of money from the show brought about an incredible maze of pirated productions, overlapping rights, and ownership disputes that would keep some lawyers busy for their lifetimes. It also made formulating international copyright laws an absolute necessity.

Lehár, Fritz Stein, and Victor Leon had sold "forever all rights to make motion pictures" of *The Merry Widow* to Herman Tausky of Paris. He sold this right in 1923 to New York producer Henry Savage (one of Jeanette's early bosses). Savage, in turn, sold the rights to MGM, which had made an extravagant silent version in 1925, directed by Erich von Stroheim and starring Mae Murray and John Gilbert. MGM looked forward to a sound version, but the courts ruled with illuminating ingenuousness that "talkies" were not necessarily "motion pictures."

MGM repurchased the rights in 1929 from Lehár, Stein, Leon B. Hershmensky, and Ludwig Doblinger. But these rights concerned only the stage story and the "Doblinger score" used on the Continent. Slightly different scores were being used in England and America. If the motion picture used a note of these other two scores, MGM was warned, they could be sued.

MGM had already been sued successfully by a real Prince named Danilo when the 1925 *Widow* was released. The Prince had collected $4000 for libel and was still living modestly near Nice when the remake was planned. Libel suits had been a sore point for MGM since Prince Youssoupov had collected $250,000 from them for allegedly defaming his wife in the biographical *Rasputin and the Empress* in 1932. To save any legal action, Prince Danilo became a mere captain and the date of the story was changed from 1905 to 1885.

In the midst of these obstacles came a claim by von Stroheim to ownership of certain plot features that he and Benjamin Glazer had written into the silent version. Thus the 1930 talkie version, which had scheduled Sidney Franklin as director and Albert Lewin and Ernest Vadja as adapters, was scrapped. The lawyers went back to their toils for three more years, safely missing the musical Sahara of the early 1930s. When the *Widow* finally made her sound film appearance, it was under nearly ideal conditions.

The Lubitsch *Widow* comes close to being one of the most perfect film musicals ever made, flawed only by Lubitsch's overwhelming tendency to "third act" his films. (See *One Hour With You*.) The film has been described as both "an enormous success" (*The Hollywood Musical* by Clive Hirschhorn) and a "flop" (*American Magazine*, September 1937), and it was both. Critically it was acclaimed, and it stands today as the summit of the Lubitsch-Chevalier-MacDonald triumvirate. Financially it was less than box-office dynamite. While giving Miss MacDonald some of her funniest lines, it did not yet put her in the permanent "star" category. Had *The Merry Widow* been her last film, she would be remembered today by a small but enthusiastic cult of "sophisticates" who treasure the more obscure joys of the past.

MGM, one of the most prominent studios in the closing days of the silent era, had been getting stiff competition from Paramount. They responded by hiring away Paramount talent, including Miss MacDonald, Chevalier, and Lubitsch. Chevalier was an established international star, and, as such, was not rushed into an expedient vehicle as Miss MacDonald had been with *The Cat and the Fiddle*.

MGM had always planned *The Merry Widow* as a major musical film, and now, finally, all legal obstacles were cleared away. For the title role, Chevalier wanted Grace Moore. She was one of the few women in history to accomplish a musical career "backward"—from music hall to true eminence in grand opera (a feat Miss MacDonald would later try to repeat). Miss Moore's increased stature in the music world plus her blonde beauty and elegant carriage made her an ideal "prestige" candidate for the world-famous role of the Widow.

Born in Tennessee in 1901 (or 1898), she was in several musical comedies as well as several editions of *The Music Box Revue* (1923 and 1924) on Broadway. There, she attracted the attention of Otto Kahn, Chairman of the Board of the Metropolitan Opera, who helped to finance a year's study for her in Europe. She made her debut at the Metropolitan Opera in 1928 as Mimi in *La Bohéme*. Irving Thalberg, always seeking "quality" performers for MGM, wanted a genuine prima donna from the Met. Miss Moore was more attractive than most, and the voice that introduced "What'll I Do" and "All Alone" in *The Music Box Revue of 1924* did have appeal. She made her screen debut in MGM's fictionalized Jenny Lind biography, *A*

Sonia confides her disturbing thoughts to her diary. The scene caused bruises on her shins as Lubitsch hid under the table, whacking her with a stick.

Lady's Morals (1930). Although she sang two arias from the Lind repertoire, "Casta Diva" from *Norma* and "Chacun le Sait" from *La Fille du Regiment*, with great competence, the film was a disaster.

As a second film, she and Lawrence Tibbett were costarred in a bizarre version of *New Moon* (1930), with a contemporary Russian setting and shorn of much of its original score. Thus ended Miss Moore's early Hollywood career. Three years later, considerably slimmed down and with a Broadway musical success (Millocker's *The DuBarry*) behind her, she returned to Hollywood and once again interested the movie moguls. She wanted most of all to do *The Merry Widow*, which was about to go into production at MGM. Chevalier approved, but Thalberg remembered the early fiascoes.

Miss Moore's very revealing autobiography, *You're Only Human Once*, describes how she spent an afternoon trying to persuade Irving Thalberg, even offering to do the role for nothing. "Finally Thalberg told me bluntly that Lubitsch didn't want me, didn't believe in me, was sold on another girl...Thalberg tried to ease the blow by offering me an option on a future picture....Well, they should have believed me. *The Merry Widow* was a flop."

Chevalier's version of the incident was that billing presented an insoluble problem. He wanted no more than star billing in his first MGM picture, and Miss Moore would take no less. So the rôle went to MacDonald. We can appreciate Chevalier's refusal to surrender status. (As Spencer Tracy said when asked why he always insisted on billing over his female costar: "This isn't a lifeboat. It's a Goddamn movie.")

We can also see from our vantage point how Chevalier's continued insistence on noncompetitive costars frequently led to weak pictures, a hubris he shared with Mae West. He was very reluctant to "team" again with Miss MacDonald, fearing the loss of identity that, ironically, would befall Miss MacDonald when she latter teamed with Nelson Eddy.

So Grace Moore signed with Columbia Studios and made *One Night of Love*, a box-office hit and an Oscar nominee. This film almost single handedly made opera acceptable in general entertainment pictures. At a time when even the most successful films seldom played more than one week as first-run engagements in a metropolitan city, *One Night of Love* played the same theatres for months.

At the Los Angeles premiere, Moore, never one to be modest, told Thalberg: "I bet *this* will top *The Merry Widow*." He replied, "Try and top [this film] yourself." She made four more Hollywood films and a French version of the opera *Louise*, but she never did top *One Night of Love*. However, from the release of the film in September 1934, until *Naughty Marietta* came out six months later, Grace Moore had scored the biggest success of any classically-trained film singer and was probably the best-known and most popular singer of serious music in the world. It was a type of mass fame not to be known again by an opera singer until 1951, when Mario Lanza made *The Great Caruso*.

The Widow was a role that Jeanette had long aspired to, having learned the entire score in French for a Paris stage appearance that never came off. If the Paris appearance had proved successful, Paramount was planning a French film version, but then Jeanette had to return for shooting on *Love Me Tonight* and the whole project was abandoned. Now she was finally *The Merry Widow*.

It is difficult to know how much of the tremendously exciting crosscurrents between Chevalier and Miss MacDonald on screen were generated by their off-screen personalities and how much was Lubitsch. The fact remains that the film possesses the single most important ingredient for a successful sex comedy—what D.H. Lawrence called (in another context) "the dumb, dark, bitter belly-tension between a man and a woman." Without it, we are laughing at cardboard cutouts. With it, we are laughing at ourselves.

The Merry Widow   135

Lubitsch idealized Jeanette and created her early screen persona. He once proposed to her. At his death, the brilliant director was planning a film version of *Der Rosenkavalier* for her. *Courtesy Fay LaGalle.*

Thalberg's fine hand is clearly visible in the quality of all aspects of the production. Music underlines nearly every passage of dialogue, prompting the characters to pensiveness, joy, anger, or ardor. Art director Cedric Gibbons was apparently given free rein and came up with an Oscar-winning Never-Never Land of sets that might best be described as Metro-Goldwyn-Mittel-Europa.

Just as MGM had taken considerable liberties with the stage plot in their 1925 silent version (the Widow's husband was a foot fetishist and didn't die until the film was nearly two-thirds over), so the first musical film version elaborated very effectively on the simple plot.

In the first act of the stage version, the rich Widow meets a former suitor at a ball in Paris. He had jilted her years ago for a richer girl, and she had gone on to marry and survive the richest man in Pontevedrino. She disdainfully rejects Danilo's conveniently rediscovered passion until he sweeps her into one of the several luscious waltzes. We know she won't maintain her resistance for more than three acts.

Act II of the stage version takes place in a garden of the embassy of Pontevedrino, giving everyone a chance to dress in exotic peasant costumes and the Widow a chance to sing the simple folk song, "Vilia." She also piques Danilo's interest by trading places with a married woman who is trapped in the gazebo with her lover. Act III takes everyone to Maxim's for a can-can and a conclusion. In between, the action is stopped frequently for comic interludes between various eccentric government officials who seek to promote the Widow's marriage to a Pontevedrinian so that her money will stay in the country.

The Widow has had many names The original, "Hannah Glawari," probably wasn't considered glamorous enough.. Mae Murray, the 1925 film Widow, was "Sally," an American dancer. The 1952 version found Lana Turner playing a songless Widow, also an American, named "Crystal." (Her Danilo, Fernando Lamas, delivered the traditional soprano aria, "Vilia.") In Jeanette's French-language version, she is called "Missia Palmieri," possibly a way to explain her accent.

But our 1934 English-version heroine is named "Sonia," and she is Marshovian through and through. And where is the kingdom of Marshovia? Following the credits, we are shown a map of Central Europe. No Marshovia. A large magnifying glass swings into place, and there it is.

The smaller the country, the gayer the uniforms, for we next see the resplendent troops of Marshovia marching through the winding cobblestone streets, pushing reluctant cows out of their way as they sing the spirited "Girls, Girls, Girls!" The girls are there to applaud, not

Tormented by curiosity, the womanizing Count Danilo vows he will see what lies behind the Widow's veil. Sausage is one of his weapons.

the tune, but the dashing captain. Squeals of "Danilo! Danilo!" and we see our star (Maurice Chevalier) as he leads his men in song. Not everyone is appreciating our handsome hero. A carriage sweeps by, bearing the mysterious, veiled Widow. Danilo gives her his most dazzling smile, but she turns away, perturbing him no end. He must do something about this.

It is night, and a glorious MGM moon illuminates the garden of the Widow's white château. The simple folk are gathered, humming a haunting melody underlined by a cimbalom. Wistfully, the Widow Sonia (Jeanette) wanders through this scene of what must have been her past happiness. Her widow's weeds are immensely becoming, depicting vaguely the 1880s. (To costume designer Adrian, this meant a soft, bias-cut 1930s evening gown with a delicate bustle beginning four inches lower than any self-respecting nineteenth-century bustle. And no corsets, of course.)

The Widow's reveries are interrupted by a visitor who leaps over the garden wall. The handsome officer has brought her a confidential letter. She reads with growing amazement: "Madame Sonia—if you should ever meet Captain Danilo, let me tell you, he is terrific." Modestly, the officer confesses that he is Danilo and begs her to remove her veil. She tells him to leave immediately or she will report him to the King. "Let me stay," he pleads, "and you can recommend me to the *Queen*."

Sonia assures him that she would remove her veil if there were the *slightest* temptation—but there isn't. Perhaps, Danilo splutters, she can't see him very well. The Widow sweeps grandly from the garden, pausing at the door. "Not terrific...not even colossal," she says. Danilo runs after her and shouts that their romance is over.

Pensively, the Widow returns to her boudoir. A maid in simple peasant frock of satin and chiffon takes her widow's veil and hangs it in a cupboard full of similar black bonnets. Another maid places her black dress in a closet of black dresses. Her black shoes and corset join their *confrères,* and finally her little black lapdog takes his place on a cushion. The french doors to the balcony are thrust open to reveal Sonia in a filmy black negligée, reclining on a *chaise longue,* her golden hair loose on her shoulders.

The throb of the cimbalom rises from the garden. Standing on the moonlit balcony, Sonia sings "Vilia," one of the best-known songs in the score. (Interestingly, in no version of *The Merry Widow* does "Vilia" have any bearing on the plot, being a pseudo-folk song dragged in for its sheer beauty.) As Sonia sings, a distant tenor voice joins her, and she clutches her heart in a surge of emotion. The tenor is revealed to be Danilo's homely valet, Mischka (played delightfully by Sterling Holloway). Danilo obviously hasn't given up his conquest, as he "conducts" Mischka's bobbing Adam's apple (and dubbed voice).

"There's a limit to every widow!"

Retiring to her fantastic white satin bed, the Widow starts to dismiss her maids. As a seeming afterthought, she asks that they check the address of a certain Count—oh, yes—Danilo. Gleefully the trio tells her his street, house number, and floor—"Apartment B." Danilo, it seems, is very democratic.

Alone, Sonia takes out her diary. She flips slowly past a year's worth of empty pages that have accumulated since her widowhood, then rushes to her writing table. Hours later the book is full, the inkwell empty, and the Widow muses on the irony of love: "Tonight Will Teach Me to Forget."

This was Miss MacDonald's first experience with miming ("lip-syncing") to a prerecorded soundtrack, and she had considerable trouble starting at precisely the right moment. Lubitsch finally got a long stick and gave her legs a sharp whack under the table at the moment she was to begin. Prerecorded songs freed the performer from worrying about vocal production while emoting and made possible infinitely more complex "numbers" in terms of camera movement. The process also deprived the musical film of the "live performances" that made so many early musicals more exciting than later, glossier productions.

Days pass. The Widow's diary announces, "I have forgotten him" and then "I am forgetting him..." Finally, it is too much! Sonia orders her servants to get everything ready. She is going to Paris as soon as possible: "There's a limit to every widow!"

In a burst of music, the closet of black widow's weeds dissolves to brightly colored gowns, the black veils to gay bonnets, even the little black dog is replaced by a white one. We get our last on-screen glimpse of Jeanette MacDonald in lingerie as she dresses. Then, in a dazzling taffeta gown and ravishing little hat, the Widow sweeps off to Paris.

To King Achmed of Marshovia (George Barbier), the departure of Marshovia's richest citizen is a source of imminent disaster. His valet (Donald Meek) warns him that the shepherds have been grumbling. If conditions don't improve, they are talking of organizing a black sheep movement. The King learns that they are east-side shepherds and dismisses them contemptuously as "intellectuals."

Achmed's beautiful wife, Dolores (Una Merkel), is more interested in how long her portly husband will be away than in national bankruptcy. A telegram from Paris warns that the Widow may marry one of her many suitors and leave the country flat broke. Achmed is off to a cabinet meeting to select a Marshovian to meet foreign competition—someone charming and irresistible, so that the Widow will fall in love with him and return to Marshovia. Dolores wrinkles her pretty nose at the various candidates that her husband puts forth, especially Gabrielovitsch. They will have to do better than that!

To a purposeful reprise of "Girls, Girls, Girls!" Achmed departs for the cabinet meeting. The guard on duty, Danilo, salutes as he leaves, then lets himself into the Queen's boudoir. The doors close softly.

Halfway down the grand staircase, Achmed realizes that he has forgotten his sword and belt. He returns to the boudoir, and the door closes

To keep the Widow and her fortune in Marshovia, King Achmed (George Barbier) makes up a list of eligible bachelors to woo her. He counts on the considerable experience of Queen Dolores (Una Merkel) for recommendations.

behind him as the music swells in agitated warning. Seconds pass. The door opens again and Achmed reappears, carrying a sword belt. The music relaxes as he starts down the stairs again, trying to buckle the belt. He is baffled to find that the belt is too small.

Slowly, a light of understanding spreads across his face. He races back to those perfect "Lubitsch touch" doors, throws them open, and bursts inside to confront the lovers. His fury is quickly dissipated when he realizes that he has found the perfect candidate for the Paris assignment. He tells the Queen that "With my brains and your contacts, Marshovia can't miss."

Danilo glories in his return to Paris. His valet Mischka urges him to report immediately to the embassy, but Danilo has other plans. Tomorrow is soon enough. Tonight is his; he sings. "I'm going to Maxim's."

In another room of the hotel, we find Sonia also preparing for a big evening, when she hears Danilo singing of Maxim's in the street below. She echoes his song wistfully to the horror of

The Merry Widow

When the Widow decamps for Paris, Danilo (Maurice Chevalier) is ordered to pursue and marry her. Here they meet at Maxim's. (Minna Gombel as Marcelle, right.)

her waiting escorts: "Her face must not be shown there, and we are too well known there."

Maxim's is a burst of gaiety and music, complete with a seductive can-can. Danilo is hardly in the door when he is greeted with a kiss by a flashily dressed girl named Lulu (Ruth Channing) on the arm of an elderly gentleman. The gentleman takes exception. Words are exchanged, then blows. Lulu rushes off for a policeman. "My seconds will call on you," announces the irate gentleman (Edward Everett Horton), and they solemnly exchange cards. As they glance down at their respective cards, each bursts into a happy smile. They are hugging and kissing when Lulu returns with a gendarme. "I wouldn't bother," the officer advises her.

Ambassador Popoff (for it *is* Ambassador Popoff) drags Danilo into a private lounge and begins outlining Danilo's duties. "Tell me, have you ever had diplomatic relations with a woman?" Danilo is to meet the Widow the following night at an embassy ball, but tonight belongs to the ladies of Maxim's. With squeals of delight, they leave their "dates" and swarm around him. "Oh, it's great to be in love," he cries.

Sonia enters, having eluded her straitlaced escorts, just in time to see Danilo in their midst. The headwaiter (Albert Pollet) mistakes her for one of the girls and instructs her to join a customer and order lots of champagne. Marcelle (the magnificent Minna Gombell) also takes her

Danilo mistakes Sonia for a Maxim's girl and takes her to a private dining room. The new film censors were concerned about what Jeanette did with her foot during the steamy love scene.

The Merry Widow

for a fellow employee. "Any Americans tonight?" Sonia inquires, surveying the patrons. Meanwhile, Danilo is literally being carried onto the dance floor, where he breaks into an impromptu can-can.

Spotting his old friend Marcelle, he dances over to her and kisses her soundly. Marcelle brandishes the souvenir of their last meeting, a jeweled garter inscribed "Many happy returns." Sonia is mortified, but Danilo has turned his attention to her and she cannot escape. She decides to go along with him, telling him her name is Fifi. Isn't he the man who gave her this bracelet? she asks sweetly, pointing to one of the dozen on her arm.

Danilo persuades her to join him at a table, even though, she tells him, she was just in the mood for a banker...which he is not. Danilo is completely disconcerted by this uncooperative Maxim's girl, but he decides to have a go. He steals her slipper and retreats upstairs to a private dining room. Not too reluctantly, she limps after him.

Alone with him, she struggles with her own feelings as the violins throb "Tonight Will Teach Me to Forget." Danilo grows tired of her indecision and storms out. The strains of "The Merry Widow Waltz" are heard below. Danilo returns for his drink and sits sullenly as Sonia begins dancing sensuously around him, dipping, bending, brushing past him, until he can ignore her no longer. Rising suddenly as she passes, he takes her in his arms and they dance together. Sonia sings the world-famous "Merry Widow Waltz" as they glide around the room.

Danilo gently guides Sonia to the velvet-covered couch and they sink into an ardent embrace. (The Breen Office concluded reluctantly that Monsieur Chevalier could lie on top of Miss MacDonald on a couch as long as she kept one foot on the floor—out of camera range!) "Do you love me?" murmurs the willing Sonia. "Certainly," he replies absently, nibbling her neck. Sonia realizes her great moment means nothing to him.

Danilo reports for duty and finds the Widow he must marry is his lost "Fifi." Ambassador Popoff (Edward Edward Horton) is baffled by their cryptic conversation.

She rushes to the door and furiously calls in all the other girls. "Here they are," she tells him. "All your little tonights...and not a *tomorrow* among them." (Note the lady in the black dress, a prominent Broadway actress named Barbara Barondess, who was obviously intended for a speaking part that got lost in the editing.) As the ladies try to console him, Danilo realizes he really wants Fifi. But she has driven off in her carriage, singing of her disillusionment.

A printed title announces the embassy ball. Sonia has recovered her composure and is dazzling the assemblage, singing as she waltzes with each of the officers present. All except Danilo. Poor Mischka is at Maxim's, attempting to dress Danilo, who has tried to forget Fifi in champagne bubbles. The girls all pitch in to help, commiserating with Danilo for being ordered to marry. "I've never heard of such a thing," mutters one girl, "and I've been with the army all my life." Another girl tells him that if Fifi really loves him, she'll come back. "But she's a lady..." protests another. "Aw, I once knew a lady who came back twice."

Learning that Marshovia will be broke and Danilo shot if he doesn't marry the Widow, the girls load him into a carriage and drive him to the embassy. There Ambassador Popoff works

The embassy ball. The seductive strains of "The Merry Widow Waltz" prove irresistible to the quarreling lovers.

frantically to sober him up while Danilo declares that he can't marry the Widow. He is already in love. Nevertheless, Danilo is brushed, groomed, sprayed with cologne, and made ready for the big moment.

Popoff sweeps in with the Widow to "accidentally" discover Danilo in the drawing room. Danilo also discovers that the woman he must marry is his lost Fifi. Their conversation is understandably cryptic. Sonia is an immovable iceberg. She tells him Fifi is dead. She committed suicide by jumping into a cold bath. The horrified Popoff runs off to send a telegram to King Achmed, leaving Sonia and Danilo alone. Sonia spurns all attempts at reconciliation until, again, the strains of "The Merry Widow Waltz" do their magic.

Swaying slowly, gently, they come together, then, faster and faster, they waltz as the music builds. In one of the most exciting dance sequences of the screen, they swirl through a deserted ballroom, until suddenly dancers burst through every doorway, sweeping in great circles around them. Again, in a mirrored hall, they are alone until a virtual battalion of waltzers comes revolving over the marble floor, echoed and reechoed in the mirrors as the music soars. The rhythms of music and movement blend into brilliant patterns over and over, until, at last, Danilo and Sonia are alone. They cling to each other as the violins softly complete the melody.

Popoff gets an angry telegram from the King saying that all Europe knows what Danilo told the Maxim's girls, a tribute to their stamina and contacts. If the Widow finds out, everything is lost. She and Danilo must be married tonight!

Sonia has just decided to believe Danilo and trust him. Just then, Popoff is heard in the nearby ballroom announcing their engagement. Danilo angrily denounces Popoff, but Sonia realizes that it has all been a plot. She has been made ridiculous before everyone. Never again can she believe anything Danilo says. Sadly but proudly, Danilo takes his leave, tells the crowd the engagement was a mistake, and marches off under guard to take his punishment.

Brushing the tears from her eyes, Sonia rushes laughing onto the dance floor. As the camera speed slowly accelerates, she swirls from one partner to another, her wild laughter echoing through the empty entrance hall as Danilo is led away to prison.

Our "third act" takes us back to Marshovia, where Achmed and Dolores, fearing the worst, are packing. Wrapping his crown in old newspapers, the King is startled by cannon shots. The new guardian of the King's bedchamber, Count Gabrielovitsch (whose lovemaking the Queen had disparaged), tells them that it's not revolution, just the opening of Danilo's trial.

Danilo is led into the courtroom to the applause of all the ladies present. He thoroughly enjoys this acclaim as the bailiff unlocks his gold handcuffs, engraved "Dolores to Danilo." The evidence is interrupted by the Widow herself, who has come from Paris to "defend" Danilo. He lied to her and deceived her, she tells the court emotionally. They shouldn't put him in jail. They should give him a medal! Danilo pleads with Sonia to believe he loves her, but she is adamant.

Angrily, Danilo turns to the courtroom and "confesses" in an emotional speech. "Any man who can dance through life with hundreds of women and is willing to walk through life with one, should be hanged!" The men in the courtroom rise to applaud him.

In a rather weakly motivated finale, the Widow comes to jail to visit Danilo. She finds his cell empty. He is busy elsewhere. "There's a party in the women's ward," one pretty inmate tells her. When Danilo returns, he and Sonia exchange barbed comments until they find themselves locked in. Outside, Achmed, Popoff, and the entire cabinet have gleefully assembled. We view the reconciliation, alternating between the suppositions of those outside and the reality inside the cell. A gypsy orchestra is brought in to play..."The Merry Widow Waltz." Iced

Danilo is court-martialed for failing to marry the Widow. She decides to visit him in jail and finds herself locked in. Outside, a gypsy orchestra begins playing "The Merry Widow Waltz."

champagne is sent through the cell's revolving food shelf. Cologne is sprayed through the peephole.

Once again, the waltz softly invades the room. Danilo and Sonia ignore each other, pacing aimlessly about the small cell until, inevitably, they come together. A minister's face appears in the peephole. "Captain Danilo, do you take..." "Certainly," murmurs Danilo. "Of course," sighs Sonia. The music rises as they kiss.

The Merry Widow was to be Lubitsch's last musical until *That Lady in Ermine*, just started when he died in 1947. It also represented a turning point in Chevalier's career. His disputes with the studio had earned him the reputation of being difficult. He left MGM and made one more Hollywood film, but his appeal was waning. Nearing fifty, he moved and looked like a man of thirty, but that wasn't enough. Youth was taking over, rejecting the favorites of their elders. He returned to undiminished stardom in France, not to make another American film until he played Audrey Hepburn's father in Billy Wilder's *Love in the Afternoon* in 1957. In 1958, his U.S. star status was solidly reclaimed with the musical *Gigi*.

In 1937, an article in *American Magazine* noted the irony of the respective MacDonald-Chevalier careers. In 1929, Chevalier had been an international star, Miss MacDonald an unknown. Now. eight years later, she was one of the ten top box-office stars of the year, while Chevalier was "through." Thirty years later, their positions would again be reversed.

Reviews

The prestige publications rushed to heap glory on *The Merry Widow*. The *New York Times* described it as "witty and incandescent...heady as the foam on champagne, fragile as mist, and as delicately gay as a good-natured censor will permit." They said that Chevalier "has never been in better voice or charm," and that Miss MacDonald "is in the twin possession of a captivating personality and lyric voice."

Time Magazine called it "the third and by far the best cinema version of Franz Lehár's famed operetta. Lubitsch [has the] ability to improve a story by telling it as if he didn't mean it."

The trade publication *Variety* assured theatre owners that it was "undoubtedly a stick of dynamite for the box office...from now on, if the Lubitsch *Merry Widow* lead is followed, operetta is in the bag for Hollywood. Maurice Chevalier and Jeanette MacDonald are aces as Danilo and Sonia. The former Paramount pair once again work beautifully in harness together, with this one a cinch to enhance Miss MacDonald's already high rating as a singer and a looker and a good bet to regain much of the ground lost by Chevalier in the last couple of years."

The *New York Post* said, "It is a Merry Widow Waltz in 6/8 time, brittle and continuously

The Merry Widow

stimulating....it is aided by Miss MacDonald's eminently satisfying voice and Chevalier's delightful acting."

Only one New York paper found fault with the film, but it was a fault that would be echoed in small-town papers across the country. The *New York World-Telegram* reported that, "The Merry Widow, as amended for the talking and singing screen, is no great improvement on the original. Indeed, on the whole it is just a torpid affectation. Lukewarm is the best this cinema thermometer can register for it." Although millions in middle America may not have known what "torpid" meant, they knew what they liked, and they stayed away from the theatres in large enough numbers to make *The Merry Widow* a financial albatross for MGM.

Recordings (See Discography for further information)

"Vilia" (MacDonald) - English and French recordings
"Tonight Will Teach Me to Forget" (MacDonald)
"The Merry Widow Waltz" (MacDonald)
"L'Heure exquise" ["The exquisite hour" - The Merry Widow Waltz] (MacDonald)

Chevalier did not record any songs from *The Merry Widow*.

Music in the Film

All music is by Franz Lehár and all English lyrics by Lorenz Hart (although Richard Rodgers is also credited), except where noted. In listing performers after each title, "and" denotes a genuine duet, while commas between names indicate a sequence of singers.

Lehár's *The Merry Widow* is laced with dozens of familiar melodies, almost all of which are used in the film score, superbly arranged by Herbert Stothart. (The only missing melody is "Wie eine Rosenknospe.") The English titles given below are the copyrighted 1934 titles. To indicate the original verse or chorus melody on which the movie song is based, the German first line is given also. Just about every minute of the film is richly underlined with music, so only the main themes are listed.

Overture: first few bars are identical to stage overture; then "Bei mir daheim ist's nicht der Brauch" from Act I; then "Es Waren Zwei Koenigskinder," Danilo's Act II aria, INTO:
"Girls, Girls, Girls!" (Male chorus, Chevalier) - based on "Weib, Weib, Weib" ("Ja, das Studium der Weiber ist schwar")
Pensive Widow in garden and humming chorus with Bella Loblov playing violin - based on "Und nun das Glück gekommen," Camille's song in Act II, INTO:
"Vilia" (MacDonald, Allan Rogers dubbing for Sterling Holloway, chorus) - based on "Vilja"
"Tonight Will Teach Me to Forget" (MacDonald) - based on "Sieh dort den kleinen Pavillion" sung by Camille, Act II. English lyric by Gus Kahn.
"Melody of Laughter" (orchestra bridge) - based on "O Kommet doch, O kommt, Ihr Ballsirenen," sung by Danilo in Act I
"Maxim's" (Chevalier) - based on "Da geh' ich zu"
"Melody of Laughter" reprise (MacDonald, eight suitors, four maids), INTERMINGLED WITH:
"Maxim's" reprise (Chevalier, MacDonald, eight suitors), INTO:
"The Girls at Maxim's" (orchestral can-can) - based on "Das hat Rrrrass! / So tralalalala!" finale of Act II, also "Rintantou, Rintantirette" from Act III
"Girls, Girls, Girls!" reprise (Chevalier)
"The Merry Widow Waltz" (MacDonald). The section that Jeanette recorded is based on "Bei jedem Walzerschritt"
"Maxim's" reprise (MacDonald, tearfully leaving Maxim's)
Embassy ball - begins with overture to Act II, INTO:

"If Widows Are Rich" (MacDonald, male chorus) - based on "Geigen erklingen, locken so suess" from Act I

Russian dance (Albertina Rasch Ballet) - based on "Mi velimo dase dase velisimo," opening of Act II. (The lyric is in the imaginary language of the Widow's home country.)

"The Merry Widow Waltz" (orchestra reprise with chorus) - employing the waltz section listed above, plus "Melody of Laughter" and "Wie die Blumen im Lenz erblüh'n" sung by Danilo in Act I

"Melody of Laughter" reprise (MacDonald, male chorus)

Trial scene: underlined by overture and "The Merry Widow Waltz"

Finale: "The Merry Widow Waltz"

La Veuve Joyeuse
(*The Merry Widow*)
105 minutes.

Filmed simultaneously in Hollywood with the English-language version. All production credits as in *The Merry Widow* except: French dialogue: Marcel Achard. French Lyrics: André Hornez. Montage: Adrienne Fazan. Footage and characters without dialogue were, for the most part, identical in both films.

Maurice Chevalier (Captain Danilo)
Jeanette MacDonald (Missia Palmieri)
Marcel Vallée (Ambassador Popoff)
Mme. Danièle Parola (Dolores)
André Berley (General Achmed)
Fifi D'Orsay (Marcelle)
Pauline Garon (Loulou)
Georges Davis ("L'ordonnaire" - Mischka)
Akim Tamiroff (Turk)
Albert Petit (Maxim's manager)
Emile Dellys (Zizipoff)
Georges Renavent (Adamovitch)
Lya Lys (Maxim's girl)
Georgette Rhodes, Odette Duval, Anita Pike, Barbara Leonard (Missia's maids)
Fred Cavens, Sam Ash, Harry Lamont (Policemen)
George Nardelli, Constant Franke, Jacques Vanaire, George Jackson, George Renault, Marcel Ventura (Escorts)
Max Barwyn, Georges De Gombert, Arthur de Ravenne, Gino Corrado (Waiters)
Jean Perry (Valet to Achmed)
Fred Malatesta (Ambassador)
George Colega (Ambassador)
Adrienne d'Ambricourt (Newspaper seller)
Eugène Borden (Defense attorney)
Jules Raucourt (Prosecutor)
André Cheron (Judge)
Eugene Beday (Doorman)
Juliet Dika (Wardrobe mistress)
Carrie Daumery (Woman with goat in court)
August Tollaire (Orthodox priest)
Gene Gouldeni (Priest)
Alice Ardell (Kiki)
André Verrier (Jailer)
Jacques Lory (Newsboy / goatman)

The major difference between the English and French versions of *La Veuve Joyeuse* is that King Achmed and Queen Dolores are demoted to General Achmed and his wife Dolores. The French version is slightly sexier, but has had all political humor and references to royalty removed. This is not surprising, because the French government of the time would not have been especially sympathetic to monarchies.

After the credits, a title tells us the film is dedicated to Franz Lehár and his great melodies. The film opens with a magnifying glass revealing "Marsovie" on a map of Europe. There, Captain Danilo is leading his marching men in singing "Femmes, Femmes, Femmes!" ("Girls, Girls, Girls!"), as a disinterested Widow sweeps by in her carriage.

Danilo pursues the Widow to her garden, where he tells her he has bribed her servants and fed her watchdogs "saucisson de Constantinople" (Turkish sausage). When Missia is unimpressed and refuses to remove her veil, he complains that he has "lived in every armoire (closet) in Marsovie, jumped out of every window, but here I'm stopped by 20 centimeters of material." (Unlike the English version, he does not suggest that she recommend him to the Queen.)

Missia spurns him: "Pas de tout 'oh oh,' même pas 'eh eh.'" (Not at all 'oh oh,' not even 'hey hey.'") Danilo retreats over the wall and tells his "ordonnance" Mischka: "La romance est termineé" (the story is ended).

On her balcony, Missia sings "Vilia." After learning that Danilo is well known to her maids, she seizes her diary—"Mon Journal"—and writes as she sings:

> Mon coeur est las, mon coeur est lourd.
> Vainement, jour apres jour, j'attends l'amour.
> C'est un reve que je poursuis.
> Il m'enchante et puis s'enfuit.
> Il vaut mieux souffrir d'amour
> Que souffrir d'espérer pour toujours.
>
> [My heart is weary, my heart is heavy.
> Vainly, day after day, I wait for love.
> It's a dream that I pursue.
> It enchants me, then flies away.
> It's better to suffer from love
> Than to suffer from hoping forever.]

She then exhausts the inkwell, telling her diary of this strange new agitation. Days go by, and, she writes, she is still forgetting Danilo. Finally it is too much. She announces to her maids that they are all leaving for Paris. "Toute veuve a ses limites!" ("Every Widow has her limits!")

As she dresses, she sings: "I want to laugh, I want to live, I want to be courted, told silly things." (English title: "Melody of Laughter").

Next, a scene not in the English version: The camera shows the portrait of a baby, then pulls back to reveal the name plate on the frame: "Maximilien III de Marsovie." A title tells us "Le roi Maximilien s'interessant plus à sa jolie nourrice qu'à ses dames d'honneur, c'etait son Excellence le général Achmed qui gouvérnait la Marsovie." ("Since King Maximilien is more interested in his pretty nurse than in ladies-in-waiting, it is His Excellency General Achmed who governs Marshovia.")

The valet brings General Achmed his suspenders and tells him that the street sweepers are talking of sweeping away the government. (The sweepers are "shepherds" in the English version.) "Are they boulevard sweepers or side-street sweepers?" asks Achmed. "Left-bank sweepers." "Ah!" snorts Achmed. "*Let* them talk."

Achmed is getting ready for a council meeting where a man will be selected to lure the Widow back from Paris by making love to her. His wife, Dolores, "Madame la Generale," watches him from their sumptuous bed. She dismisses both his suggestions, Sinkovitch and Gabrielovitsch.

Danièle Parola as Dolores is much slicker than her American counterpart, Una Merkel, very Parisienne, and has a more specific

Poster for *La Veuve Joyeuse*, French version of *The Merry Widow*. *Courtesy Jill Coogan.*

background. While Achmed dresses, she insists on knowing the time he will return "within 15 minutes." Achmed is annoyed: "If you don't shut up, I'll send you back where I got you." Dolores is unconcerned: "If you wish, I can go back to the circus. I can still do the *trapeze de la mort* and carry a man with my teeth." (She addresses her husband with the formal "vous," which is unusual.) This is serious, Achmed tells her: "If the Widow takes her wealth out of the country, even France won't lend us money."

Achmed leaves, but returns for his sword and finds Danilo in his wife's bedroom. In his rage, he threatens to have Danilo's tongue cut out (English version: "ears cut off"). "I need time to find a punishment," Achmed roars. Danilo replies, "Take your time. Patience is a soldier's virtue."

"You have cost me my reputation," Achmed tells Dolores. "I wanted to be 'Achmed the Great.' Now I'll be called 'Achmed the Little' because of you." Dolores struggles to explain: "But I can't find the words in the language of the court." (She refers to high-class language.) Achmed sneers, "You can't say *anything* in the language of the court."

Suddenly, Achmed realizes he has found the best man to send to Paris. "Can you speak French?" he asks Danilo. This works easily in the English version, but, in French, Danilo replies that he speaks Marshovian, German, Russian, French and English. "Say something in English," orders Achmed.

"Her ladyship is the most marvelous woman I ever saw. I'm telling you, she is just gorgeous," replies Danilo in English. He departs for Paris via a montage of French advertising signs seen from a train window.

In Danilo's hotel room, Mischka (Georges Davis) tells his master that two women were talking about Danilo on the streetcar: "They were so funny that two other ladies asked for your address."

"We'll have to move again," sighs Danilo. He must report to the Marsovie ambassador, but first he is off to Maxim's. As he sings the praises of the Maxim ladies—"Je m'en vais Chez Maxim's" (I'm Going to Maxim's)—the English "Lolo, Dodo, Joujou, Cloclo, Margo, Froufrou," which don't sound French to the French, become "Manon, Ninon, Lison, Franchon, Suson, Toinon." In her nearby hotel room, Missia reprises "Melody of Laughter":

Je veux être l'oiseau que l'on délivre.
Je veux rire. Je veux vivre.
Adieu peine et tristesse, adieu Marsovie.
Quel bonheur de connaître la grande vie.
Je veux qu'on me courtise, qu'on me grise,*
Qu'on me dise des bêtises,
Car je veux être adorée.

[I want to be the bird that you set free.
I want to laugh, I want to live.
Goodbye, sorrow and sadness,
    goodbye, Marshovia.
What happiness to know the good life.
I want to be courted, dazzled,*
Told silly things,
Because I want to be adored.]

* NOTE: "grise" literally means "drunk," but has alternate meanings such as tipsy, light-headed, exhilarated—"it goes to my head."

Meanwhile, Danilo reprises "Maxim's": "It's a happier place than the Comédie Française." Missia's maids warn her in song not to follow Danilo to Maxim's: "That's where ladies smoke cigarettes!" (In English: "dance the can-can.") Missia completes the song: "To please the men, we need to be rag dolls!"

Danilo arrives at Maxim's. In the foyer, he flirts with an old girlfriend, Loulou (Pauline Garon). Her escort is outraged, and a fight follows until each discovers the other's identity: Danilo has been slapping the Marshovian ambassador, Popoff (Marcel Vallée). They hug each other enthusiastically, just as Loulou returns with a gendarme, who consoles her: "In your place, I wouldn't bother your gall bladder." The hat check attendant asks Loulou: "Who is that old camel?"

La Veuve Joyeuse

Fifi D'Orsay (right) plays Marcelle in the French-language version, *La Veuve Joyeuse*, filmed simultaneously on the same Hollywood sets with a different supporting cast.

Popoff tells Danilo how he will introduce Danilo to the Widow at the embassy the following night. In the English version, he concludes with, "And *you* come over the garden wall!" There is then a dissolve to Danilo entering Maxim's. The French version continues the foyer scene for several more unnecessary lines. "I'm not too sure about climbing the wall," Danilo replies. Popoff says, "Then you can arrive by car and ring the bell. The butler will take your saber. You wait in the anteroom, and I will introduce you to the Widow." Finally, Popoff and Danilo exit into the main room.

Danilo's arrival thrills the Maxim's girls, but a Turkish gentleman (Akim Tamiroff) is disconsolate. He tells his pretty companion: "I had a very well-equipped harem. Then I invited Danilo. He killed my married life—twenty-seven times."

Danilo greets his favorites and some of the exchanges are different from the English:

DANILO: Did you fix the springs in your couch? (Girl nods.)

GIRL: I gained five kilos!
DANILO: I'll help you lose them!

DANILO: (to another) Does your landlady still take as long to answer the door?

Missia follows Danilo to Maxim's and is mistaken for a Maxim's girl. One of the ladies, Marcelle (Fifi D'Orsay), shows her a garter Danilo gave her which is inscribed "Joyeuse Pentecôte." (Happy Pentacost—in English it was "Many happy returns.") This is a somewhat remote *double entendre*, possibly referring to the Feast of the Ascension and Danilo's ability to rise to the occasion.

Missia tells Danilo her name is "Fifi," and they are soon in a private dining room upstairs. However, Missia suddenly gets cold feet, and Marcelle finds Danilo sulking in the hall. Irate, Marcelle storms in and denounces "Fifi": "Listen to me. I'll have you boycotted because you must know you can't come and disgust the clients with an honest woman's tricks!"

Missia relents and, as the magic strains of "The Merry Widow Waltz" fill the room, she lures Danilo to dance with her:

> L'heure exquise m'a conquise,
> Brusquement tu m'emportes,
> Que m'importe si tu mens.
> Car...Je sens tout à coup
> Que rien n'existe non plus,
> Rien que nous.

> [This magnificent moment overwhelms me.
> Suddenly I am carried away by you.
> It doesn't matter if you are lying,
> For all at once I feel
> That nothing exists anymore,
> Nothing except us.]

In the French version, Danilo carries Missia to the couch. In the American version, she walks. (It may be censorship, or perhaps the French version was filmed first, and Chevalier declined to lift the healthy Miss MacDonald a second time.)

As their love scene progresses, Missia switches from the intimate "tu" to the formal "vous," indicating she wants Danilo to stop

A French newspaper ad. *Courtesy Anna Michalik.*

being playful and reply seriously to her questions. Danilo rises. "Now I know who you are *not*. May I ask who you *are*?"

Missia realizes he doesn't love her. She runs to the door and summons the Maxim's girls. She tells Danilo: "Toutes vos petites amies d'un soir—aucune parmi elles ne songe au lendemain." ("All your little evening friends—none of them is thinking about tomorrow.")

Missia leaves Maxim's in tears, singing a tribute to its girls in a reprise of "Maxim's": "Your hearts are made of cardboard."

At the embassy the next night, Missia is being courted by all of Paris. As she dances she sings: "A man who insists that his wife has wit, he will always be rich."

Danilo has tried to drown his sorrows at losing "Fifi" and is tracked down in an upstairs room at Maxim's. Mischka and the sympathetic

Maxim's girls carry him to the embassy. There he is sobered up and presented to the Widow. While the two lovers spar verbally, Popoff receives a telegram from General Achmed back in Marsovie. It is read to him by his aide, Zizipoff. In English, this was a comic interlude of rolled r's by comedian Herman Bing. French comedian Emile Dellys delivers this speech in a high-pitched staccato monotone, equally funny.

The brief English-version scene in which Popoff instructs an aide to hide his bottle of poison is missing from the French film. However, the French version is more specific about how the secret of Danilo's mission got around: "The Maxim's girls told all of Paris, the French Ambassador told his wife's maid, she told the butler, he told the Ambassador's wife, she told Sinkovitch, he told Madame Gabrielovitsch, Madame Gabrielovitsch reconciled with her husband, Gabrielovitsch told Dolores. Dolores didn't know Gabrielovitsch was married so they had a big fight. Achmed walked in too early as usual."

Missia and Danilo declare their love for each other, but her happiness is cut short when she learns he was ordered to make love to her. (It's hard to be hysterical in another language and, as Jeanette tearfully denounces Danilo, she completely loses her French accent.)

Danilo is led away to jail for failing in his duties. Missia resumes her dancing, singing with frantic gaiety: "Love is a duty in Paris; One must love in Paris."

Back in Marsovie, the trial of Danilo begins as revolution threatens the country. The delightful scene in which King Achmed wraps his crown in newspaper, however, is missing from the French version.

Although the Widow comes to testify on his behalf, Danilo demands punishment: "Celui qui a la chance de plaire assez aux femmes pour pouvoir en changer et est assez fou pour en aimer une seule, mérite d'être fusillé." ("Any man who has the luck to please women so much that he can exchange one for another–and then falls in love with just one–should be shot.")

Back at the palace, Achmed and Dolores learn that the Widow has gone to visit Danilo in jail., "I bet..." Dolores begins eagerly. "We don't have time to bet!" says Achmed sharply:

At the jail, Missia finds Danilo's cell empty, but a woman appears at the barred window: "Tell Danilo they have good red wine in the women's ward and lots of laughs." (Jeanette tangles her tongue on the French tongue twister "*rigolera*," meaning "will laugh.")

Missia jumps on Danilo's bed to escape a scurrying mouse, just as Danilo returns. She tells him she was chased by a mouse. "All the way from your estate to the jail? It must have been a *rabbit*!" She indignantly tries to leave, but the door is locked.

A Spanish-language poster. *Courtesy Anna Michalik.*

A Dutch cinema program for "The Jolly Little Widow." *Courtesy Anna Michalik.*

Outside the cell, Popoff and Achmed are congratulating each other. "Even Napoleon would not have thought of this," says Popoff. Musicians arrive and begin playing "The Merry Widow Waltz." Inside the cell, Danilo and Missia are drawn irresistibly into each other's arms. Missia teases him by repeating his statement at the trial: "Any man who has the luck to please women so much that he can exchange one for another—and then falls in love with just one..." Danilo corrects the ending: "should be...*married!*"

Review

Comedia, 2/2/34, reported [author's translation]:
"The Merry Widow—just the name is sufficent to evoke a flood of appealing memories. [It] has returned to Paris, fully as captivating, still possessing the secret of eternal youth and beauty. In the past, it succeeded in seducing all those who saw it, and it won't fail to conquer us all yet again. This delicious idyll of Missia and Danilo is now playing at the Cinéma Madeleine. Marcel Achard has written the dialogue, sparkling with his usual talent and verve. He knows how to provide equal amounts of comedy and charm.

"Jeanette MacDonald portrays the Widow with grace and great beauty. The memory of her pretty figure and marvelous voice remain unforgettable. Maurice Chevalier has created a remarkable characterization, a dazzling Count Danilo.

"In this enchanted world, redolent with the sweet accents of wondrous music, we are soon caught up in the most intoxicating of waltzes. The Merry Widow is new again, proving the adage about 'Precious old wine in brand new bottles.'"

Recordings (See Discography for further information)

"Vilia" (MacDonald) - both English and French recordings
"L'Heure exquise" ["The exquisite hour"] - Merry Widow Waltz (MacDonald)

5
Nelson Eddy: What's a Nice Concert Singer Like You Doing in a Studio Like This?

Nelson Eddy's singing partner of fourteen years, Gale Sherwood, was once asked if he was difficult.

"Difficult? No. Bad tempered, yes," she replied with a smile. The twinkle in her eye and the affection in her voice implied that she was mocking Eddy's own concern that his perfectionism was hard on those around him.

If Eddy's exacting standards and dedication were hard on his coworkers, they were never heard to complain. The overwhelming impression one gets of Eddy's life is of the intense loyalty of nearly everyone who knew him. When he died in 1967, his secretary, Mildred Hudson, had been with him for nine years; his nightclub partner, Gale Sherwood, for fourteen years; his wife, Ann, for twenty-seven years; and his accompanist and friend, Ted Paxson, for thirty-seven years.

Nelson Eddy started life in Providence, Rhode Island, where he was born on June 29, 1901. His father, William Darius Eddy, was a machinist and toolmaker who moved from city to city, so that young Nelson attended school in Providence and Pawtucket, Rhode Island and New Bedford, Massachusetts. He was a redhead in those days, earning the nickname "Bricktop." In his early thirties, his hair began turning silver, producing an unusual "blond" effect.

Music was a major part of his life from the first. His mother, Atlanta-born Isabel Kendrick Eddy, was a soloist at the Church of the Transfiguration in Providence. His grandmother, Caroline Ackerman Kendrick, had been a distinguished oratorio singer. His father did stagehand and extra work with the Providence Opera House at night following a ten-hour shift at Braun and Sharp Manufacturing Company.

Nelson's official MGM biography made much of his paternal New England roots, but little has been known about his maternal line. To start with, how did an Atlanta beauty meet and marry a Yankee? Researcher Elsa Dik Glass, in her forthcoming biography of Nelson, answers this question and chronicles Nelson's gifted maternal ancestry, which undoubtedly was the major contributor to his musicality:

> Steady employment wasn't the strong suit of [Nelson's father] William Eddy, the somewhat gray sheep in a venerable New England family that has produced many politicians and scientists. Three years [before Nelson's birth], when twenty-four-year-old William had enlisted for the Spanish-American War, he listed his occupation as "stage mechanic," rarely regarded as a steady career. He joined the First Rhode Island Regiment on April 29, 1898, and a month later was appointed Sergeant-at-Arms-Drummer in a military band. However, he never saw action because he soon became ill. He was on sick leave off and on through July 1898 when he had surgery for an "inguinal right bubo" (hernia). He continued on medical disability status until November when he was granted a four-day furlough to stay with his aunt, Mrs. Daniel Kendrick in Philadelphia. It would be a most fortuitous visit for Nelson Eddy fans, because there he met his future wife, a Southern belle named Caroline Isabel Kendrick.
>
> Isabel, as she was more commonly called, was born in Atlanta, Georgia on July 7, 1879, daughter of Caroline Ackerman and Edward Stillman Kendrick. Caroline's father, Joseph Ackerman, was a Jew of Russian descent born in New York City while her mother, Belinda, was a New Jersey-born Methodist. Joseph's father (Nelson's great-grandfather) had emigrated to America from Holland, and his grandfather (Nelson's great-great-grandfather) originated in Russia. This

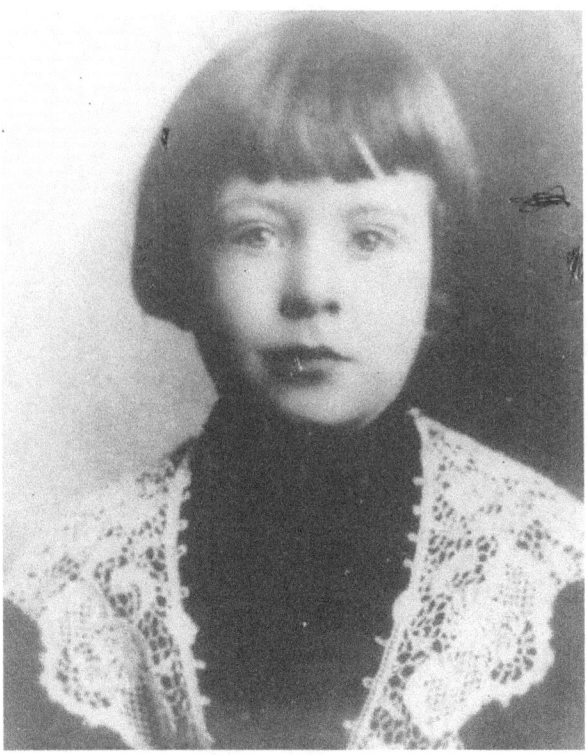

Young Nelson. His bright red hair earned him the nickname "Bricktop." *Courtesy Anna Michalik.*

"Dad" Eddy also sang in the church chorus and in local shows like *H.M.S. Pinafore*, working occasionally as a stagehand.

Nelson's boyhood homes in Providence no longer exist. In 1901, his family resided at 96 Hartford Avenue, which was replaced by a post office in the 1960s. By 1911, the family had moved to 42 Common Street, razed for Interstate 95 about the same time as his earlier home. The Mayor of Providence, Vincent Cianci, reports with regret that there are no known photos of either home.

The Eddys traced their lineage back to President Martin Van Buren and to John Eddye, who came over from England to settle in colonial Massachusetts in 1650. When Governor Winthrop toured the colony making an early census of his taxpayers' occupations, he was stumped by Eddye and listed him finally as "John Eddye, Gentleman."

Russian heritage may explain Nelson's exceptional skill in the Russian repertoire.

Isabel's grandfather Joseph worked as a tailor in the cloth factories of Newburgh, New York. Just before the Civil War, he moved his wife and two children to Mobile, Alabama. There his wife, Belinda, taught piano, directed a choir, and gave birth to two more children. The younger was Caroline, Nelson's maternal grandmother.

Caroline Ackerman grew up to be a headstrong and determined young lady. Charmed by a handsome traveling salesman, Edward Stillman Kendrick, she followed him to Atlanta and married him there on Christmas Day, 1877. They had three children: Clark, Isabel (Nelson's mother), and Edward Jr. Edward Sr continued his travels, moving his family from Atlanta to New York City, back to Atlanta, and finally to Philadelphia, where he hoped his brother, William, would help him obtain employment. Whether Edward Sr found a job or not is uncertain, but his penchant for the ladies and gambling interfered with his home life. He pawned Caroline's beloved piano and then deserted his family in 1897.

The loss of the piano was both an emotional and financial blow because Caroline, inheriting her mother's musical ability, had been supplementing the family finances by teaching piano and singing. Fortunately, her eldest child, Clark, was working at the Mott Iron Works in Philadelphia, where his uncle was a foreman. The eighteen-year-old Clark managed to reclaim the pawned piano so his mother could continue earning a living. (Clark, in turn, would later provide a job at Mott for *his* struggling nephew, Nelson.)

Seventeen-year-old Isabel had also been working as a clerk at the Iron Works for a year....

In the winter of 1898/9, William Darius Eddy, on medical furlough, visited his aunt in Philadelphia. There, he met young Isabel, a distant relative by marriage. A year later, on December 23, 1899, they were married at the Naval Home in Philadelphia, with her mother as attendant. The young couple then left for Rhode Island where they lived for two years at five different locations.

© 2001, Elsa Dik Glass

Nelson sang in the boys' choir at St. Stephen's Church and then as a soprano soloist with Grace Church and All Saints Church. He said later that he had encountered religion in so many different versions that he was never able to accept the doctrine of any single church.

Fourteen-year-old Nelson moved with his mother to Philadelphia after his parents divorced. *Courtesy Anna Michalik.*

Instead he evolved his own very deep belief in God—and a religious philosophy that extended into everything he did. In later years he loved to discuss theology with people like Will Durant. ("A great philosopher—he knows all the angles and subscribes to what I feel.")

Singing wasn't Nelson's only musical talent. At the Grove Street School in Pawtucket, he played trap drums in the school orchestra and seemed likely to become a drummer. His father had played bass drum in the First Regimental Band of the Rhode Island National Guard, and his grandfather, Isaac N. Eddy, had pounded the same instrument for more than fifty years with Reaves' American Band.

Many weekends of Nelson's early days were spent with his paternal grandparents, Isaac and Martha Gardiner Eddy, in Pawtucket. His grandmother, he said, taught him "gentleness, kindness, and the value of simple living."

When Nelson was fourteen, his parents separated, and Nelson moved with his mother to Philadelphia. The need to work ended his formal education, although the rest of his life was literally spent in study of one kind or another. Eventually Nelson's parents were divorced. Unlike many people in such circumstances, he maintained a warm relationship with his father in later years and with his father's second family, Mrs. Marguerite E. Eddy and Virginia, Nelson's "kid sister," twenty-five years his junior.

In Philadelphia, Nelson went to work at the Mott Iron Works, a plumbing supply house where his uncle, Clark Kendrick, was a supervisor. Nelson's first position was as a telephone operator for $8 a week, a very good wage for a boy in 1915. (Perhaps Kendrick was employing a bit of mild nepotism to help his sister and her son.) Eddy was soon promoted to the shipping department at twelve dollars per week. At night he voraciously read books on history, economics, and philosophy.

One day Eddy decided to quit his job. It is difficult to imagine the conscientious Eddy just

Young Nelson had to quit school and take a job in his uncle's factory. *Courtesy Helen Crawford.*

quitting anything. Perhaps he was fired for having his mind too much elsewhere or perhaps family tensions made it impossible to continue working for his uncle. Most likely he simply decided that the mail room was not for him and set out to do what he truly wanted to do. At this point in his life, it was to be a reporter and so, after weeks of searching, he landed an $8 a week job with the *Philadelphia Press* as night clerk. In his spare time he tried writing obituaries on a commission basis. He begged the *Press* editor for a reporter's job, but at sixteen he was considered too young.

And so he began what was to become an Eddy custom. One afternoon he walked into the office of the *Evening Public Ledger* and convinced them that he was eighteen and a great reporter to boot. He got the job but a staff cutback soon put him out on the street again.

Eddy soon decided that a sober appearance was useful in the business world. *Courtesy Diane Goodrich.*

This time it was the *Evening Bulletin* that received a surprise visit, and soon sixteen-year-old Nelson was covering police news. Murder, violent death, and the lowest doings of humanity became everyday occurrences in his life. He also covered trials and political happenings. A fellow employee, Lou Mogelever, recalled that Eddy was fired for always singing on the job. In any event, he was switched to sports news. He didn't dare confess that he had never seen a professional baseball game in his life, although he had played as a kid. Apparently his bluff worked, for he replaced the regular sportswriter and soon was interviewing Connie Mack and Ty Cobb. After this, he had a stint on the rewrite desk, where his headlines were more famous for fitting the space than anything else.

Again he seemed to have reached a dead end, so he called on N.W. Ayer Advertising in November of 1920. He left their offices with a copywriter's job that would last five months. Thereafter the George Edwards Agency got to hear Eddy singing while he worked.

All this time, he also continued singing in local churches. (A few years ago, the Episcopal Cathedral Church of the Saviour at 3723 Chestnut Street still had a photo on display of young Nelson in the church choir. A parishioner recalled that both Nelson and his mother had also sung in another church across the street.)

In his spare time, Eddy found himself more and more serious about his singing. For amusement he sang along with opera records until he had mastered the strange languages and phrasing. (His ear was phenomenal. The author has met Russians who insist he must have been raised in a Russian-speaking home to have such a flawless accent in his Russian arias.) He imitated the voices of Ruffo, Scotti, Amato, Campanari, and Werrenrath, noted baritones of the day. Finally the urge became so great that he paid another afternoon call, this time on David Bispham, the former Metropolitan Opera singer, who was now a teacher. The sixty-three-year-old Bispham listened to the nineteen-year-old Eddy as he launched into an Italian aria he had memorized. The next day Eddy received a photograph from Bispham autographed "To Nelson Eddy, the coming baritone—or I miss my guess."

Nelson began lessons with the great Bispham, cautiously keeping his job. Their association was short-lived, for Bispham died suddenly on October 2, 1921. Eddy found another teacher and began supplementing his income with guest appearances. His first paying job was for the Colonial Dames of the Art Alliance. A lovely lady, he recalled, asked him to sing a few songs for them and afterward gave him a check for $25. It was the first indication that he might someday be able to make a living by singing.

Though he got in trouble for singing around the office, he began getting some amateur singing engagements. *Courtesy Diane Goodrich.*

His first stage appearance was in Mrs. George Dallas Dixon's society theatrical called *The Marriage Tax* at the Philadelphia Academy of Music in January 1922. He played the "King of Greece." The omission of his name from the program proved to be a lucky accident. He was well received in the rôle and everyone wanted to know who the mysterious "King of Greece" was. Thus he was on the receiving end of newspaper publicity for the first time, even if it was on the society page. (Noted music critic Max de Schauensee was a fellow performer.)

Eddy followed this with rôles in several amateur Gilbert and Sullivan productions with the Savoy Company at the Broad Street Theatre. In May of 1922 he played Strephon in *Iolanthe* and the Major-General in *Pirates of Penzance*. He also made two appearances with a little theatre group called "Plays and Players."

In 1924 he entered a musical competition and took top prize, a chance to appear with the Philadelphia Opera Society. He made his operatic debut on 2/11/25 as Amonasro in *Aida*, performed at the Academy of Music. The *Philadelphia Record* reviewed its former rival reporter royally: "Nelson Eddy as Amonasro had an electrifying effect on the audience. A young singer with that indefinable gift so seldom seen of arresting the audience's interest and holding it continuously, Mr. Eddy was a star from the moment he appeared on stage."

William von Wymetal was the group's producer at this time, in association with Fritz Reiner, who later directed the Philadelphia Symphony Orchestra. Wymetal joined Eddy years later in Hollywood and created the opera sequences in *Maytime* and *Phantom of the Opera*.

Nelson appeared as Tonio in *I Pagliacci* on 12/11/24 with the Philadelphia Civic Opera Company. The group's musical director, Alexander Smallens, began giving Nelson serious coaching, and his repertoire grew to more than thirty rôles, including parts in *Roméo et Juliette, Aida, Secrets of Suzanne, l Pagliacci* (where, Max de Schauensee commented later in the *Philadelphia Bulletin*, he occasionally had trouble with the A-flat in the Prologue), *La Bohème, Manon Lescaut, Faust, Samson et Dalila, L'Elisir d'Amore*, and *L'Amore dei Tre Re*. De Schauensee recalled that Nelson sang "an especially beautiful 'Ode to the Evening Star' in *Tannhäuser*."

Also with the company was a singer, Edouard Lippé, who would later become Eddy's teacher and close friend. Baritone Lippé had suffered a spinal injury that made it difficult for him to continue his career, so he turned to teaching. Eddy was still working by day, taking correspondence courses by night, and singing at every opportunity. Lippé sternly warned him

An early professional portrait. *Courtesy Anna Michalik.*

that if he continued with his heavy schedule, he would lose not only his voice but his health. Eddy gave up his job and trained with Lippé.

Lippé taught Eddy for several months and then sent him to his own teacher, William Vilonat, who was about to leave for Dresden. Vilonat recommended the only course open to serious American singers at that time: Eddy must go to Europe to study. (World War II, of course, brought some of the finest European teachers to America while forcing America to rely on its own home-grown resources, and the tradition ended.)

Eddy borrowed money and accompanied Vilonat to Europe in 1927. Eddy felt that he never really "saw" Europe, although he visited London, Paris, and Berlin. During the day he practiced and studied languages, while every night for relaxation he attended the opera to memorize the great rôles. In Dresden, he lived with a German family. There he was offered a position with the Dresden Opera, but he had become homesick and turned it down, much to Vilonat's distress.

When Eddy got back to America, he felt he was ready for a singing career. He auditioned for manager Arthur Judson of Columbia Concerts and was put under contract.

His first appearances in 1928 were small-town recitals, oratorios, and orchestra engagements. He began to be noticed. People asked for more appearances by the tall, good-looking baritone with the beautiful voice. He moved into a spacious apartment at 13th Street and Chestnut.

During his vocal studies in Germany, Nelson posed in lederhosen. *Courtesy Judith Mary Cox.*

Tonio in *I Pagliacci* was one of Nelson's more than thirty opera rôles. *Courtesy Ken Howard.*

Only the distinctive nose and chin reveal Eddy beneath his makeup as Manfredo in *L'Amore dei Tre Re* in 1928.

When Dr. Frank Sill Rogers of the Mendelssohn Club in Albany, New York came to New York City to sign up singers for their season, he visited Columbia Concerts and was told about the exciting new singer. "I don't know much about his singing," someone in the office told him, "but I do know that every time he visits the office, none of my lady typists can do any work." Rogers engaged Eddy for two very successful appearances with the Club. Eddy was scheduled to appear with them for a third season, but sent a telegram explaining that he would be in Hollywood. He had just signed a movie contract. However, he would be happy to pay the fee of an equivalent singer as a replacement. Rogers wired Eddy back that the only equivalent artist he could think of was Lawrence Tibbett, then the top singer in America. If Eddy wished to send Tibbett as a replacement, the Mendelssohn Club would be happy. Flattered (or perhaps unable to afford Mr. Tibbett), Eddy made the long trek back to Albany for a third appearance that brought him a standing ovation.

Vilonat, like Eddy's earlier teacher Bispham, died without seeing his student reach full professional recognition. Eddy returned to studying with the diminutive Lippé, who would be his main teacher (although in later years he would turn to a wide variety of teachers to work on different aspects of his technique). Several years later, when Eddy faced his first feature rôle in *Naughty Marietta*, he summoned the little man from the East Coast to coach him. Lippé both rehearsed Eddy in his songs and took the of rôle of the landlord the in the film. He stayed on with Eddy for many years in Hollywood.

Eddy continued to appear with the Philadelphia Civic Opera, singing in the only American performance of *Feuersnot* by Richard Strauss on December 1, 1927 and in the first American performance of Strauss's *Ariadne auf Naxos* on November 1, 1928. In *Ariadne*, Eddy sang the rôles of the Wigmaker and Harlekin in the original German. Also in the cast, in her first opera appearance, was Helen Jepson, later a leading interpreter of French rôles at the Metropolitan Opera.

In 1928, Eddy sang for a music club in Norristown, Pennsylvania. The club's accompanist was a twenty-year-old pianist named Theodore Paxson. They hit it off, and Eddy engaged him to play for several more dates nearby. Then in 1929 he asked Paxson to go on tour with him. Paxson was Eddy's accompanist, friend, and advisor for the rest of Eddy's life. In 1941, Paxson and George Brown combined to manage Eddy, succeeding Eddy's first manager, Calvin Franklin. Paxson was at the piano in 1967 when Eddy was fatally stricken on stage.

Important conductors began using Eddy. Leopold Stokowski, then conductor of the Philadelphia Symphony Orchestra, was on the podium for the American premiere of Alban Berg's *Wozzeck*. The sets were by the innovative stage designer, Robert Edmond Jones. Eight months later, Eddy sang the rôle of the Drum Major (a tenor part) when the opera was presented on 11/24/31 at the Metropolitan Opera House in New York.

On another occasion Eddy sang for the great maestro, Arturo Toscanini. He had been recommended for the baritone rôle in Respighi's *Maria Egiziaca* (Mary in Egypt), which the maestro planned to premiere with the Philharmonic Society. Young Eddy auditioned for the part of the elderly Abbot Zosimo, his voice trembling in simulation of age—and possibly with just a bit of nervousness. Toscanini heard him out, then patted his shoulder and said he would do. Illness prevented Toscanini from completing the season, and it was Respighi himself who conducted the Christmas performance in 1931. Years later, when Toscanini visited the MGM lot in Culver City, Eddy greeted him by singing a few bars of *Maria Egiziaca*.

Like Jeanette MacDonald, Nelson Eddy entered his chosen field when it was going into a period of rapid growth and change. Several mechanical devices had contributed to a national interest in music greater than at any previous time in our country's short history. The first of these was obviously the phonograph, which brought "good" music for the first time to a hundred million Americans who had rarely heard more than the church organ or the local dance-hall pianist.

The second important factor in the rapid development of the concert circuits was the automobile. When Eddy was born in 1901, the railroads were the nation's arteries. Twenty short years later, America's muddy lanes were fast becoming a network of paved roads that permitted ease of movement and ready access to small towns that would have been undreamed of at the turn of the century. The "mainstream of culture" that had been dammed up in the big cities now went sloshing out along the highways and byways to middle America. The retreat from the land was in full swing in the 1920s, and more and more people were settling into towns and cities, seeking the amenities that this type of living offered. Continental expansion had ended with statehood for Arizona and New Mexico in 1912, the Native Americans were suppressed, and now the country could turn to cultural pursuits. Even the smallest towns began boasting societies dedicated to great literature, art, and music. The small-town music circuit, like the minor leagues of baseball, prepared hundreds of talented beginners for the big time.

The third mechanical contrivance that opened America to the joys of music, classical and otherwise, was the radio. The airwaves had first vibrated to the human singing voice when Vaughn De Leath crooned into a microphone high over Times Square in December 1919. She was promptly ordered to stop by a brand new kind of public official, a radio inspector. He felt that entertainment had no place on the airwaves. Enough people disagreed to advance the radio in less than a decade from the crystal set to an imposing appliance housed in a wooden edifice, the prestige status symbol of the newly affluent. The radio became so popular that it brought about another twentieth-century invention: installment buying.

On 2/6/24, Eddy's baritone was heard on the ether over station WOO, Philadelphia. He was just twenty-three years old. During the next twenty years he sang for Newton Coal, Dutch Masters, General Motors, Ford, the Voice of Firestone, Vicks Open House, Screen Guild, Chase & Sanborn, the Lux Radio Theatre, Old Gold, the Electric Hour, the Bell Telephone Hour, and the Kraft Music Hall.

In 1936, he hosted the Chase & Sanborn Hour with Edgar Bergen and Charlie McCarthy. It was here that the "Shortnin' Bread" legend was born. Versions of the song were staples of the concert repertoire since the white music world discovered (and began to write their own) black music in the late nineteenth century. Eddy had undoubtedly sung it at his early concerts, but Charlie McCarthy's constant teasing about the number associated the singer and the song for life. "Shortnin' Bread" even served as an in-joke in *Make Mine Music* when Willie the Operatic Whale (sung by Eddy) was described as "casting his shortnin' bread upon the waters."

Shifting social patterns and television ended live radio programming in the early 1950s, just as the movies and radio had ended the dynamic concert circuit of the 1920s and early 1930s. Eddy, who had given the best of his considerable talents to the concert stage, films, and radio, suddenly found himself a trouper without a stage. Several alternatives were open to him and he made a difficult decision, very wisely as turned out. However, let's get back to the decision in his life that is the reason for this book.

On February 28, 1933, Eddy flew from San Diego to Los Angeles to replace soprano Lotte Lehmann, who had canceled an appearance due to illness. The magazine *Saturday Evening* reported that he "dashed on stage" at the Philharmonic Auditorium "with typical American collegiate candor. He started his recitative, spoken before it could be realized that

Nelson as Amonasro in *Aida*, a blue-eyed Ethiopian king. This would prove to be his final opera rôle on stage—to rave notices with the San Francisco Opera.

As Abbot Zosimo in the world premiere of Respighi's opera *Maria Egiziaca* (Mary in Egypt), with Charlotte Bowden, March 1932 at Carnegie Hall. Arturo Toscanini conducted. *Courtesy Anna Michalik.*

The image of a serious young concert singer. *Courtesy Diane Goodrich.*

this was the opening of his program and not a preliminary announcement. His listeners responded so warmly that encores started early in the evening....joy of singing and camaraderie go far toward making Nelson Eddy an idol of the American public which he may well become."

The *Musical Courier* reported that Eddy "scored a series of cordial successes." (Prophetically, the same page headlined "happy rumors" from Hollywood that a revival of filmed operetta was imminent. Prominently mentioned was a celluloid version of *The Merry Widow*, possibly starring Jeanette MacDonald and Lawrence Tibbett, with Irene Dunne in a featured rôle.)

Hollywood was contemplating another try at operetta. In the audience that fateful night at the Philharmonic Auditorium was Ida Koverman. She urged her boss, Louis B. Mayer, head of MGM, to try to sign the impressive baritone. (Miss Koverman was Mayer's "private secretary," which was the contemporary feminine title for a brilliant executive assistant.) Nelson also reportedly got offers from Paramount and RKO.

Eddy had a major career decision to make, and he went about it with thoughtful caution. His final decision to give up the concert stage temporarily for the bright lights of Hollywood was certainly not motivated by the glamour of the place and probably not even by the money. He had too often given up more lucrative work to do what he really wanted to do. He thought the offer over carefully before accepting the twenty-eight week MGM contract with seven-year renewal options.

Two things, he said later, influenced his decision. First was his interest in the new medium of talkies, which, like radio, was only a few years old. He had a lifetime fascination with electronic gadgets, and, besides, he could sing for millions instead of hundreds of thousands, a great plus for any performer. Second, and perhaps even more important, was the fact that for the first time in his adult life he would have a real home base—a house, a garden, books, dogs, family, and friends who would be there when he returned from the concert tours that he hoped to keep making.

In Eddy's mind, films always remained incidental to his music. They represented a way of becoming better known, just as radio had, and thus attracting more people to hear his concerts and the songs he loved to sing. The idea of being a "star" probably did not occur to him, and if he had known some of the tribulations he would face when the movie-going public conferred the title on him, he might have chosen to go happily on with his concerts.

The movies *did* have the desired effect on his concert tours. George Brown, his manager, recalled the days when Eddy made fees of $50 to $100 per evening. When he finally got $500 for an oratorio performance, Nelson confided that his dream was to be able to make $10,000 per year by singing. Soon a single concert would bring in more than that at the box office.

Handlebars
MGM.
Released August 25, 1933.
Produced by Pete Smith.
Directed by Jules White.
10 minutes.

Pete Smith (Narrator)
Nelson Eddy (uncredited singer)
Gordon Elliott* (uncredited 1900 cyclist)
Dick Dickinson (uncredited 1869 cyclist)

* Later western great Bill Elliott.

After MGM rushed to sign Nelson to a film contract, he left his hectic concert tour and took up residence. But then he had to wait many frustrating months with nothing to do before filming a brief scene in his first film, *Broadway to Hollywood*. Or was that his first film?

In 2003, Nelson Eddy Appreciation Society co-president Anna Michalik ran across a Canadian radio interview from the 1960s. In it, Nelson casually mentions that his first MGM film

Only the most knowledgeable Nelson Eddy fan would have recognized his voice on the soundtrack of this 1933 Pete Smith short, made before Nelson gained national fame. (Gordon [Bill] Elliott as the male cyclist.) *Courtesy Diane Flaherty.*

was "a Pete Smith bicycle short." After some research, the author tracked down a copy of a likely candidate: *Handlebars*, just one of seven one-reel comedy shorts produced and narrated by Pete Smith in 1933. It's a humorous history of the bicycle since 1819, and there, unmistakably, is Nelson's voice! As a Gay Nineties couple ride along, he sings one 32-second chorus of "Bicycle Built for Two."

Probably, someone at MGM arranged this anonymous quicky recording session to provide Nelson with something to do so he wouldn't go stir-crazy. And because the short had come and gone long before the general public was familiar with his voice, the film has only just been added to his filmography.

Music in the Film

"Bicycle Built for Two," also called "Daisy Belle" (Nelson Eddy) - Harry Dacre.

Broadway to Hollywood
MGM.
Released September 15, 1933.
Directed by Willard Mack.
Retakes directed by Jules White.
Associate Producer: Harry Rapf.
89 minutes.
"March of Time" ballet in 2-strip Technicolor

Prerelease titles: *Show World* and *March of Time*.

The following information about the relationship between the unreleased 1930 film *The March of Time* and the 1933 film *Broadway to Hollywood* was provided by archivist Yannek AgaKhan:

The original shooting title on Sept 14, 1929 was *From Broadway to Heaven*. Filming of "The Past" sequences began Dec 1, 1929. This was the vaudeville section with Weber and Fields, Louis Mann, Fay Templeton, William Collier Sr, DeWolf Hopper, Josephine Sabel, Marie Dressler and Barney Fagan. This first section was completed Feb 1, 1930. (Beth and Betty Dodge, the Dodge Sisters, were hired Feb. 7, 1930.)

"The Present" and "The Future" sections and the 2-strip Technicolor numbers were completed on June 14, 1930. The film was never released in the U.S., but a version was released in Germany (3/27/31) as *Wir Schalten Um Auf Hollywood* (*We're Switching Gears to Hollywood*).

In 1933, Metro re-opened production, severely editing the "past" segment and part of the "present" into a new story with new players called *Broadway to Hollywood*. All costs were billed to the original production code number, 462, for *The March of Time*.

Original screenplay: Willard Mack and Edgar Allan Woolf, and Moss Hart. Editors: William S. Gray and Ben Lewis. Musical arrangements: Dr. William Axt. Art Director: Stanwood Rogers. Interior Decorations: Edwin B. Willis. Photography: William Daniels and Norbert Brodine. Dance Supervision: Sammy Lee and Albertina Rasch. Assistant Director: John Waters. Sound: Douglas Shearer. Cameramen: Al Lane and Bill Riley.

Alice Brady (Lulu Hackett)
Frank Morgan (Ted Hackett)
Madge Evans (AnneeAinsley)
Russell Hardie (Ted Hackett Jr)

Jackie Cooper (Ted Jr as a boy)
Eddie Quillan (Ted Hackett III)
Mickey Rooney (Ted III as a boy)
Tad Alexander (David)
Edward Brophy (Joe Mannion)
Ruth Channing (Wanda)
Jean Howard (Grace)
Jimmy Durante (Jimmy, a Hollywood character)
Fay Templeton (Singer - sound film debut)
May Robson (herself, a 50-year veteran)
Nelson Eddy (John Sylvester)
Una Merkel (Flirt in audience)
Barney Fagan (Soft-shoe dancer)
Maggie Cline (Singer)
Josephine Sabel (Singer)
Helen Parrish (Cousin)
Russ Powell (Diamond Jim Brady)
Ed Piel (Stage manager)
Edwin Maxwell (Rockwell, the producer)
Forrest Taylor (Director Conway)
Charles McAvoy (Lincoln actor)
Moe and Curley Howard (Clowns)
Muriel Evans (Girl)
The Albertina Rasch Dancers
Entertainers: Tom Nawn and Company, Rice and Cady, Ed Foster, Billy Sullivan, Leo White, Claire DuBrey, Claudelle Kaye (Bits)

In Nelson Eddy's first three on-camera appearances, he did one number with little or no relation to the story. This was a common practice for "screen testing" newcomers for appeal, and films of the 1930s are often spotted with songs, frequently in a nightclub setting, by performers who appear nowhere else in the film. If the number was terrible, it could be snipped out without any reshooting. If the performers "clicked," they would get a buildup and a bigger part in their next picture. (It was also a convenient way to use black performers. Their footage could be excised from prints for southern distribution without any strain, e.g., Ethel Waters in *On with the Show*.)

Broadway to Hollywood is technically an altered version of the unreleased 1930 epic, *The March of Time,* which started filming in 1929. Both have the same production code number.

The original film, a monolithic accumulation of mammoth two-strip Technicolor production numbers with a skeletal plot, was completed June 14, 1930, just as the bottom dropped out of the musical market.

Over the years, MGM recycled bits of the original film in shorts like the 1933 *Nertsery Rhymes* with the Three Stooges, which used "A Girl, a Fan, and a Fella" by the Dodge Sisters. (Beth and Betty Dodge's "Lock Step" number was used in *That's Entertainment III* in 1994.)

In 1933, when musicals started to regain popularity, MGM decided to refilm the plot segments, add some of the original color sequences converted to black and white, and release it as a new film. Many of the musical numbers filmed for *The March of Time* are used, including the "March of Time" ballet with 500 Albertina Rasch dancers, though some songs are drastically edited. For example, Fay Templeton's "Come Down, Ma Evening Star" is heard as background for other business, whereas it was spotlighted in the original.

The plot concerns three generations of one family, a popular literary and stage theme of the 1920s, and, due to cultural lag, of the screen in the thirties. (Many of the brighter films of the 1930s—*Holiday, The Awful Truth, A Bill of Divorcement, Anna Christie*—were Broadway plays of the 1920s.)

The first generation of a noted vaudeville family, the Hacketts, are played by Frank Morgan and Alice Brady. Morgan was a matinée idol of many years who came to films fulltime in the 1930s after occasional appearances since early silent days. His rôles were repeats of his stage image, a sophisticated mature lover (as in Jeanette's *The Cat and the Fiddle*) or the wronged husband of a young wife. His genius for the unfinished sentence, the uncompleted gesture of frustration, brought him more and more comedy parts as his red hair faded to gray. In *Naughty Marietta* and again in *Sweetheart*s the transition was complete, and today he is best remembered as the Wizard of Oz.

Eddy's first on-screen appearance lasts ten seconds. Here, he is resting between takes with Alice Brady, who starred in *Broadway to Hollywood* along with Frank Morgan and Mickey Rooney.

Alice Brady came from a famous theatrical family and was regarded as one of Broadway's finest tragic actresses. She had appeared in silent and early sound films, mostly in a serious vein, but like Morgan, she would soon slip into comedy parts and become an outstanding exponent of the vague but darling loony before her untimely death in 1939. Two other grand dames of the stage, Fay Templeton and May Robson, also have small roles in *Broadway to Hollywood*, so it is a nostalgic treat for theatre buffs. As further esoterica, two of the Three Stooges, Moe and Curley, appear in clown makeup in a scene with Russell Hardie.

Ted and Lulu Hackett start out in vaudeville in the 1880s. As the medium begins to slip, their son, Ted Jr (played first by Jackie Cooper, then Russell Hardie), leaves the act for the musical stage and its attendant wine and women. His overindulgence causes the accidental death of his dancer wife (Madge Evans), and he enlists to fight in the World War, being killed in France.

His son, Ted III (first Mickey Rooney, then Eddie Quillan), goes to even further extremes by becoming a movie actor. He also takes up with ladies and liquor until Grandpa Hackett straightens him out.

The picture closes with Ted and Lulu Hackett watching their grandson on a movie set. Ted slumps forward in his chair, and Lulu sits quietly holding his hand, tears streaming down her cheeks, as Ted III dances on before the camera.

Eddy, singing "In the Garden of My Heart," has less than six seconds on screen before the scene switches to a loud backstage family argument. Through the dressing room din, Eddy fans can hear him gallantly continuing on the now forgotten stage.

Review

The film got mild comments from the press. Only his hometown *Philadelphia Inquirer* made note of Eddy's on-camera debut: "Nelson Eddy

A rare still of the legendary Fay Templeton in a scene cut from the final film. *Courtesy Yannek AgaKhan.*

makes an unfortunate debut as a 'ham' vaudeville singer."

Music in the Film

In listing performers after each title, "and" denotes a genuine duet, while commas between names indicate a sequence of singers. An asterisk (*) marks numbers originally filmed for *The March of Time*.

Overture: "When Old New York Was Young" - Gus Edwards, Howard Johnson; "Sidewalks of New York" - James Blake; "Ma Blushin' Rosie" - John Stromberg, Edgar Smith
*"Hansom Cab Drivers" orchestral - Howard Johnson, Gus Edwards

"We Are the Two Hacketts" (Brady, Morgan) - Al Goodhart
"We Are the Two Hacketts" reprise (Morgan, Brady, Hardie)
"The Honeysuckle and the Bees" (Evans, girls) - Max Penn, Abbe Fitz
*"Snow Ballet" - Dimitri Tiomkin
"Come Down, Ma Evenin' Star" (Templeton) - John Stromberg and Edgar Smith
"Ma Blushin' Rosie" (Hardie) - John Stromberg and Robert Smith
*"The March of Time" (chorus) - Lou Alter, Howard Johnson
*"Bedelia" (Sabel) - William Jerome and Jean Schwartz
"There'll Be a Hot Time in the Old Town Tonight" (Sabel - Theodore A. Metz and Joe Hayden)
"Ma Blushin' Rosie" reprise (Templeton, chorus)
"Poor Little G-String" (Hardie, Evans) - Fred Ahlert and Roy Turk
*"Melody in F" (Albertina Rasch Ballet) - Anton Rubinstein
"In the Garden of My Heart" (Eddy) - Ernest R. Ball and Caro Roma
"Knee Deep in Rhythm" (girls, Quillan) - Al Goodhart and Gus Kahn

Dancing Lady

MGM.
Released November 24, 1933.
Directed by Robert Z. Leonard.
Executive Producer: David O. Selznick.
Associate Producer: John W. Considine Jr
94 minutes.

From the novel by James Warner Bellah, published July 1932 and serialized in the *Saturday Evening Post,* April 30 to June 4, 1932. Screenplay: Allen Rivkin and P.J. Wolfson. Special Effects: Slavko Vorkapich. Photography: Oliver T. Marsh. Incidental Music and Music Conductor: Louis Silvers. Dances: Sammy Lee and Eddie Prinz. Assistant Director: Red Golden. Art Direction: Merrill Pye. Editor: Margaret Booth. Interior Decorations: Edwin B. Willis. Gowns: Adrian. Sound: Douglas Shearer and Paul Neal.

Joan Crawford (Janie Barlow)
Clark Gable (Patch Gallegher)
Franchot Tone (Tod Newton)
May Robson (Dolly Todhunter)
Winnie Lightner (Rosette Henrietta La Rue)
Fred Astaire (Himself)
Robert Benchley (Ward King)
Ted Healy (Steve)
The Three Stooges - Moe and Curly (Jerry) Howard, Larry Fine as Harry (Stagehands)
Art Jarrett (Art)
Grant Mitchell (Jasper Bradley Sr)
Nelson Eddy (Himself)
Gloria Foy (Vivian Warner)
Maynard Holmes (Jasper Bradley Jr)
Sterling Holloway (Pinky, the author)
Florine McKinney (Grace Newton)
Bonita Barker, Dalie Dean, Shirley Aranson, Katharine Barnes, Lynn Bari (Chorus girls)
Jack Baxley (Barker)
Frank Hagney (Cop arresting Janie)
Pat Somerset (Tod's friend)
Charlie Williams (Arrested in burlesque house)
Ferdinand Gottschalk (Judge)
Eve Arden ("Southern" actress)
Matt McHugh (Agent)
Charlie Sullivan (Cabby)
Harry C. Bradley (Author's pal)
John Sheehan (Author's pal)
Stanley Blystone (Traffic cop)
Charles C. Wilson (Joe, club manager)
Bill Elliott (Café extra)
Larry Steers (First nighter)
C. Montague Shaw (First nighter)
Nella Walker (Miss Allen, Bradley's secretary)
Frank Morgan (cut from release print)
Mildred Carroll (singing voice for Crawford in "Rhythm of the Day")
Jean Howard, Jean Malin (Bits)
Matty Roubert (Burlesque candy seller)
Leo Willis (Fresh burlesque patron)
The Hughes Kiddies (Specialty)

Speaking of teams, *Dancing Lady* was the fourth of seven films in which Joan Crawford and Clark Gable appeared together. After her earlier

Dancing Lady

Courtesy Anna Michalik.

silent flapper image, Miss Crawford had gone dramatic, and *Dancing Lady* represented a change of pace for her. Gable was already established as a misogynistic stud, and his next film, *It Happened One Night*, would confirm superstar status. Franchot Tone had had an illustrious stage career that included creating the role of Curly in the pre-*Oklahoma!* non-musical *Green Grow the Lilacs*. His film roles consisted mainly of repetitions of his *Dancing Lady* character, the millionaire playboy with the smile of an appealing child and the soul of a snake.

MGM was still trying to do backstage musicals, hoping to capture some of the glory (and box-office receipts) from Warner Bros. Admittedly, they tried a mildly pleasant imitation of Berkeley's style (overhead shots, "featured" showgirls), but depended most heavily on cinematic effects in the production numbers. The audience was supposed to forget Busby Berkeley, but *Dancing Lady* only served to strengthen the comparison. Berkeley, as his imitators and rivals were constantly learning, was inimitable. Fortunately MGM discovered the musical romance centered on the operetta form, and they gave up the "Let's put on a show" genre until Judy Garland and Mickey Rooney transferred it from Broadway to barn and made it fresh again in the late 1930s.

Dancing Lady concerns a hoofer with a heart of gold (Joan Crawford) who prefers dancing to romancing. She tells her playboy admirer (Franchot Tone) that she will only marry him if she fails on stage. The playboy promptly bribes the backer to cancel the production. Of course, the hard-boiled dance director (Clark Gable) puts up his own dough to save the show.

In trying to make a lady out of Miss Crawford, Tone instructs her: "Don't say 'them things'" and "Don't buy shoes with ribbons on them." Miss Crawford opts for ribbons and Clark Gable at the fadeout.

The song standard that came out of the show is "Everything I Have Is Yours," by Harold Adamson and Burton Lane. Rodgers and Hart contributed one song, "Rhythm of the Day," which Nelson Eddy delivers energetically, if briefly. He charges into a mass of bewigged court dancers who are doing a placid minuet and advises them to be more modern. They then dance through an archway, stage center, and emerge in modern dress on the other side—a mild substitute for imaginative choreography. Miss Crawford makes the transition from horse-drawn carriage to limousine, and Eddy is promptly replaced by tap dancers. His "pep" song was far better suited to a "jazz singer," but he registers nicely in his small bit.

Fred Astaire was also more or less wasted in the film. He has a brief top-hat sequence with Miss Crawford, but his principal number is a clog dance in lederhosen, "Let's Go Bavarian." To be completely fair, it is reminiscent of the "Triplets" song that he had done so well in the stage version of *The Band Wagon*, but still a very minor effort. Art Jarrett got some of the songs, and the delightful Winnie Lightner, her film career waning after a fast start in the 1929 musical rush, delivered one number. All three of the Three Stooges provided the "comedy."

Review

The theme that Nelson had somehow sold out and prostituted his art was beginning. A review in the *Philadelphia Inquirer* noted: "Nelson Eddy, Philadelphia baritone, who made good in opera and concert, and turned a willing ear to Hollywood's siren song, is to be seen and heard in one musical number as a typical revue singer."

Music in the Film

Of the eight songs in the score by various composers, the one standard to emerge was "Everything I Have Is Yours" by Burton Lane and Harold Adamson. Nelson sang "Rhythm of the Day" by Richard Rodgers and Lorenz Hart, a strident pep number ill-suited for his voice or personality. Mildred Carroll dubbed Joan Crawford's voice in this number only.

Student Tour

MGM.
Released October 5, 1934.
Directed by Charles F. Reisner.
Produced by Monta Bell.
87 minutes.

Original story: George Seaton, Arthur Bloch, and Samuel Marx. Screenplay: Ralph Spence and Philip Dunne. Music Director and Synchronization: Jack Virgil. Photography: Joseph Valentine. Art Director: Cedric Gibbons. Art Associates: Arnold Gillespie and Edwin B. Willis. Editor: Frank Hull. Dances: Chester Hale. Assistant Director: Sandy Roth. Sound: Douglas Shearer.

James [Jimmy] Durante (Hank Merman)
Charles Butterworth (Prof. Ethelred "Lippy" Lippincott)
Maxine Doyle (Ann Lippincott)
Phil Regan (Bobby Kane)
Florine McKinney (Lilith Lorraine)
Douglas Fowley (Mushy)
Monte Blue (Jeff Kane)
Betty Grable (Cayenne)
Fay McKenzie (Mary Lou)
Bobby Gordon (Jakie)
Mary Anita Loos (Dolores)
Pauline Brooks (Peggy)
Herman Brix [later Bruce Bennett] (Hercules)
Nelson Eddy (Himself)
Florence and Alvarez (Dancers)
Mary Jane Irving, Dorothy Short, Jean Seal, Edna May Jones, Susanne Thompson, Joan Sheldon, Maxine Nash, Joan Arlen [later Ann Rutherford], Vivien Reid, June Storey, Ercell and Clarice Wood (twins), Dixie Dean, Linda Parker, Margo Early, Mary Dees, Jerry Frank, George Bruggeman, Bryant Washburn Jr, Dale Van Sickel, David [Dave] O'Brien, Jack Lubell, Dudley James, Carlyle Blackwell Jr, Lyman Williams (Students)
Lynn Cowan (Master of Ceremonies)
Helen Chan (Sun Toy)
Eddie Hart (Steward)
Dutch Schlickenmeyer (Officer)
Herbert Prior (Grouch)
Minerva Urecal (Wife)
Carl Stockdale (Dean)
Arthur Hoyt (Assistant to Dean)
Dora Clemant (Wardrobe woman)
Dewey Robinson (Chinese warlord)
Nick Copeland (Waiter)
Frank Tang, Luke Chan (Chinese prisoners)
Sam Flint (Captain)
June Gittelson (Fat girl)
Tom Tamerez (Indian prince)
Arthur Wanzer (Elderly man)
Florence Roberts (Elderly woman)
Red Berger (Mailman)
Harry Strathey, Larry Wheat (Businessmen)
E. Alyn Warren (Saga)
Robert Stevenson (Bartender)
Fred Malatesta (French manager)
Dick Farham (Assistant manager)
Charles Fallon (Croupier)
Sherry Hall (Radio announcer)
Mischa Auer (Sikh policeman)
Edward LeSaint (Old graduate)
A. Barr Smith (English coxswain)
Robert Adair (English trainer)
Herbert Evans (English coach)
Neville Clark (Captain of English crew)
Otto Frisco, Eddie Daas, James Bell (Indian fakirs)
Sam Lewis (Jewish Hindu)
Jamiel Hasson (Indian policeman)

After going unnoticed in two small parts, Eddy finally got a real showcase in *Student Tour*. It was his final "guest appearance" before being "discovered" in *Naughty Marietta*. The film was a college musical and distinctly a B, employing MGM's superb second-string character actors in principal roles. Like all MGM B's it had the gloss of a major production, but a lower payroll, fewer sets, and, in this case, a story that became episodic through lack of strong supervision between script and cutting room.

A philosophy teacher at a small west-coast college (Charles Butterworth, the ingenuous comedian of *Love Me Tonight* and *The Cat and the Fiddle*) flunks the college rowing team. The team must pass in order to go on a round-the-world tour to England to compete in a rowing match. The captain of the team (Phil Regan) is loved by the professor's ugly duckling daughter (Maxine Doyle), who of course removes her glasses before the end of the film and becomes beautiful.

The professor agrees to accompany the team as they sail around the world, coaching them in philosophy on the way. Naturally he shares a stateroom with Jimmy Durante, the crew's trainer. (MGM was again trying to mate Durante's boisterous style with that of a quieter comedian as they had done disastrously with Durante and Buster Keaton.) The daughter attends a shipboard masquerade ball in a Pierrette mask and is unrecognized by the team captain, who falls in love with her.

The college vamp (Florine McKinney) convinces the captain that she was the masked girl and so the professor's daughter has a conspiratorial scene with a mustachioed gentleman (Eddy) who agrees to help her. It seems the professor's daughter has done a bit of nifty tap-dancing while masked and her rival can't do so much as a time step.

Each exotic port-of-call on the tour provides the excuse for a production number, and Monte Carlo is next. Eddy helps the heroine by singing "The Carlo," a dramatic bolero by Arthur Freed and Nacio Herb Brown ("Singin' in the Rain," "Broadway Melody") and she goes into her dance. The captain realizes his error in time for the heroine to act as coxswain and lead the boat crew to victory with a rousing song.

Nelson got a real showcase in *Student Tour* (with Jimmy Durante and Charles Butterworth), singing the senuous "The Carlo."

Review

"Nelson Eddy is worked into the final scene at a Monte Carlo party, effectively doing a baritone solo." (*Variety*)

Music in the Film

Six of the songs were by Arthur Freed and Nacio Herb Brown, including Eddy's number, "The Carlo." Eddy introduced this new dance, "performed by fifteen teams." One additional song, "I Say It With Music," was written for the film and performed by Jimmy Durante.

Naughty Marietta

MGM.
Released March 29, 1935.
Directed by W.S. Van Dyke II.
Produced by Hunt Stromberg.
106 minutes.

French title: *Le Fugue de Mariette* (The Escapade of Mariette)
Danish title: *Letsindige Marietta* (Licentious Marietta)
German title: *Tolle Marietta* (Out-of-control Marietta)

Based on the 1910 operetta by Victor Herbert with book by Rida Johnson Young. Screenplay: John Lee Mahin, Frances Goodrich, and Albert Hackett. Musical Adaptation: Herbert Stothart. Art Director: Cedric Gibbons. Art Associates: Arnold Gillespie, Edwin B. Willis. Orchestrations: Paul Marquardt, Jack Virgin, Charles Maxwell, Leonid Raab, and Wayne Allen. Sound: Douglas Shearer. Costumes by Adrian. Assistant Director: Eddie Woehler. Photography: William Daniels. Editor: Blanche Sewell.

Naughty Marietta was originally presented on Nov. 7, 1910 at the New York Theatre, with Emma Trentini and Orville Harrold. It ran 136 performances before going "on the road," a highly respectable run in the days when production costs were a fraction of what they are today, and a producer could recoup his investment in a month!

Nelson got his first big screen break as the dashing mercenary Captain Dick in *Naughty Marietta*.

Jeanette MacDonald (Princess Marie de Namours de la Bonfain, AKA Marietta Franini)
Nelson Eddy (Captain Richard Warrington)
Frank Morgan (Governor Gaspard d'Annard)
Elsa Lanchester (Madame d'Annard)
Douglass Dumbrille (Uncle of Marietta, Prince de Namours de la Bonfain)
Joseph Cawthorn (Herr Schuman)
Cecilia Parker (Julie)
Walter Kingsford (Don Carlos de Braganza)
Greta Meyer (Frau Schuman)
Charles Bruin (Dockside troubadour)
Akim Tamiroff (Rudolpho)
Harold Huber (Abraham - "Abe")
Edward Brophy (Ezekial "Zeke" Cramer)
Olive Carey (Mme Renavent)
William Desmond (Havre gendarme chief)
Mary Doran, Jean Chatburn, Pat Farley, Jane Barnes, Kay English, Linda Parker, Jane Mercer (Casquette girls)
Arthur Belasco, Tex Driscoll, Edward Hearn, Edmund Cobb, Charles Dunbar, Ed Brady (Mercenary scouts)
Dr. Edouard Lippé [Nelson's music teacher] (Landlord)
Cora Sue Collins (the child Felice)
Helen Shipman (the real Marietta Franini)
William Burress (Bouget, pet shop keeper)
Catherine Griffith (Prunella, Marie's maid)
Billy Dooley (Drunk, Marietta's "brother")
Guy Usher (Ship's captain)
Walter Long (Pirate captain)
Harry Cording, Frank Hagney, Constantine Romanoff (Pirates)
Henry Roquemore (Herald)
Mary Foy (Duenna)
James C. Morton (Barber)

Naughty Marietta

Jeanette disliked the small hat that Adrian had designed for her and persuaded director Van Dyke to let her wear this one instead.

Louis Mercier (Dueler)
Robert McKenzie (Town crier)
Charles Bruin (Singer on dock)
J. Delos Jewkes (Priest on dock)
Zarubi Elmassian (Suzette - voice only)
William Moore [later Peter Potter] (Suitor Jacques)
Harry Tenbrook (Suitor at convent)
Ben Hall (Mama's boy)
Ed Keane (Major Cornell)
Roger Gray (Sergeant)
Ralph Brooks (Marie's suitor at cottage)
Edward Norris (Marie's suitor at cottage)
Richard Powell (Herald)
Wilfred Lucas (Herald at ball)
Jack Mower (Nobleman)
Lawrence Grant, Craufurd Kent (New Orleans aristocrats)
Bits: Robert Graves, Richard Hemingway, Margaret Bloodgood, Judith Vosselli, Vessie Farrell, Olin Howland, Pat Flaherty, Beatrice Roberts, Milton Douglas, Elena Ulana, Georgia Caine, Kit Guard, Mary Loos.
Marietta (Cocker spaniel puppy - actually a litter)

Oscar for sound recording: Douglas Shearer.
Oscar nomination for Best Picture.

Other Awards: Voted one of the Ten Best Pictures of 1935 by the New York film critics. Photoplay Gold Medal Award as Best Picture of 1935 (beating out *Mutiny on the Bount,y* which won the Oscar). Selected by the National Registry of Films, 2004.

Naughty Marietta was presented on Cecil B. DeMille's Lux Radio Theatre 6/12/44 with Jeanette and Nelson, and on the Railroad Hour 1/17/49 with Jeanette and Gordon MacRae.

The first film made by Jeanette MacDonald and Nelson Eddy together was nearly an accident. At least it acquired that reputation in the myths that grow up around any unprecedented success. The two singers and their director were a most unlikely combination for making screen history.

Jeanette was one of a handful of survivors of the earlier musical cycle. Of the genuine "29ers," Chevalier, Harry Richman, Jolson, and Cantor were still hanging on, John Boles was playing Shirley Temple's father, Grace Moore was making a comeback, Bing Crosby was rising, Bebe Daniels was about to depart for England where she would become an institution with her husband Ben Lyon, Joan Crawford had gone dramatic, and Dietrich was—Dietrich. The slick sex comedies that were Jeanette's forte were dying at the box office. The public, reflected by the Hays and Breen Offices, wanted "family" pictures. The delightful *Merry Widow* had brought little money to the MGM coffers. A few more flops would undoubtedly have sent Jeanette back to Broadway.

Nelson Eddy was an expensive novice. His "blond" good looks and classically trained baritone had caused MGM to lure him from a lucrative concert career to an even more lucrative film contract—this in the depths of the

With "naughty" in the title, early publicity stills and ads naturally played up Jeanette's saucy image as the lingerie queen. *Courtesy Patrick Kuster.*

Depression when most stars were taking salary cuts. The seven minutes of singing he had done on the screen in no way justified his salary and everyone knew it. He was the subject of many conferences, and it looked as if he were on his way out, a fact that did not dismay him. He missed the warm response of facing a live audience and was uneasy on the impersonal soundstages.

Director W.S. (Woody) Van Dyke II was a rugged outdoorsman. He was also one of Hollywood's lifeblood directors. He turned out competent and frequently very good films in record time, under budget, and without elaborate demonstrations of his own importance. Thus he has been completely ignored by the cultists who prize the work of the more colorful if less productive men behind the megaphones. He started in the silent era, directing Tim McCoy westerns. Because of his reputation for location work and no-nonsense efficiency, he replaced Robert Flaherty (*Nanook of the North*) on the Tahitian-based production of *White Shadows in the South Seas* when the studio feared its investment was in jeopardy. His credits included *Tarzan, The Ape Man* and the classic *The Thin Man*, with Myrna Loy and William Powell, which he reputedly shot in sixteen days. His only venture into the musical film was *Cuban Love Song* (1931), an interesting offbeat story with magnificent singing and acting by Lawrence Tibbett, pleasant slapstick by Jimmy Durante, an appealing performance by Lupe Velez, and endless repetitions of "The Peanut Vendor."

The idea of pairing Jeanette MacDonald and Nelson Eddy existed for more than a year before the vehicle was decided upon. In July of 1933, MGM announced that they would both appear in *The Prisoner of Zenda*. This was later amended to *Americans Can Sing* and then to *I Married an Angel*. However, the stricter code made the story of an angel who loses her wings on her wedding night too risky. Finally a safe vehicle was chosen.

Naughty Marietta

As soon as the strong appeal of both the film and Nelson Eddy became obvious, the ads quickly dropped sexual innuendo and were changed to include his photo and to emphasize the adventure and romance. Jeanette's days as the lingerie and bubble bath queen were at an end—just in time as Hollywood adopted a strict on-screen moral code.

Naughty Marietta was a most improbable blockbuster. The Victor Herbert operetta dated back to 1910 and was a favorite of studio head Louis B. Mayer. It had been bought as a vehicle for Marion Davies, who had scored in the silent *The Red Mill*, and then abandoned when musicals lost their box office appeal. (Also shelved was Miss Davies's unfinished version of *Rosalie*, in which Nelson Eddy would later star.)

Louis B. Mayer had been a small-town impresario in his youth, booking road companies of *The Firefly* and *Rebecca of Sunnybrook Farm*. He always loved the old standbys and guessed (rightly as it turned out) that his audiences did too. Several people pointed out with dismay that *Naughty Marietta*'s key song, "Ah, Sweet Mystery of Life," was the theme song of Forest Lawn Cemetery. Mayer was adamant. Perhaps to minimize the cost of the impending disaster, "one-take" Van Dyke was selected as director and Hunt Stromberg assigned as producer. The stage was now set for the rebirth of screen operetta.

Naughty Marietta became Jeanette MacDonald's third film to win an Oscar nomination for Best Picture. Its light, breezy style of comedy and richly romantic music made it one of the most popular pictures of 1935 and started a cycle of operetta pictures that would last until World War II.

A Danish program cover. Major movie theatres offered handsome photo-filled programs for new films, similar to Playbills for theatre.

The backbone of the screen's first operetta classic was a tightly written script that stripped away the extraneous eccentric characters of the stage version, as well as the past life of the heroine that provided the title. Gone was the gypsy girl in love with the Governor's effeminate son who is secretly a pirate. The final curtain of the stage version finds the heroine comfortably ensconced in New Orleans. The MGM Marietta abandons idleness and riches for a life in the wilderness with the man she loves, a theme that has stirred the heart since prehistory.

Other assets were superb musical arrangements and added music by Herbert Stothart, and briskly casual direction by Van Dyke so that the film never seems to take itself seriously. Indeed, much of the charm may come from the outdoorsy feeling Van Dyke got by shooting most of the exteriors in natural sunlight. The strong light is occasionally unflattering to our heroine, but the fresh-air spontaneity more than makes up for it. Working quickly and economically with standard sets, stock footage of sails unfurling, and some rear projection, Van Dyke gets a sense of immediacy in *Naughty Marietta* that is lacking completely in the lavishly produced *New Moon* which the trio would make five years later.

Van Dyke was noted for his "one-take" policy. Film novice Eddy was understandably stiff and a bit terrified at his first encounter with heavy acting and caused numerous retakes in his first tense days on the set. On the stage he was able to establish an immediate rapport with his audience. Admittedly, he had always been uncomfortable with the melodramatics necessary in some grand opera roles. Critic Alexander Smallens recalled that "acting" was definitely

A French poster. *Courtesy Diane Flaherty..*

Naughty Marietta

Princess Marie (Jeanette) slips away from the palace to visit her old singing teacher (Joseph Cawthorn, a matinee idol of twenty years earlier) and his wife (Greta Meyer). Marie and "Schumy" try to write down the mysterious melody of the cathedral bells. *Courtesy Jack Tillmany.*

not Eddy's strong point, but that, in "straight" roles, his singing and warm manner conquered the audience. Eddy himself remembered his favorite roles as Wolfram in *Tannhäuser* and Papageno in *The Magic Flute*. Wolfram's chief emotional projection is dignified concern and Papageno is a broad comedy part, perfectly suited to Eddy's own sense of fun.

In those days opera acting, as well as the more traditional forms of stage acting, were still based on a system evolved by François Delsarte in the nineteenth century. Delsarte had tired of the frantic arm waving and scenery chewing that passed for dramatic acting and, after studying people in real-life situations, he formalized a catalogue of gestures that fit motion to emotion: back of wrist to head to express dismay, hand to heart to indicate passion. His method is the heart of classical ballet and would serve concert and opera singers throughout the first half of the twentieth century, but it was hardly the technique for a screen hero.

Van Dyke used on-set pranks to loosen up Eddy and reveal his natural charm. At one point, Van Dyke learned that the nervous Eddy was repeatedly flubbing a high note at a recording session. With nearly a hundred musicians and technicians staring icily at him, Eddy was not likely to calm down. On the next take, Van Dyke arranged for an enormous blast of sirens to go

Her cruel uncle (Douglass Dumbrille) has arranged her marriage to a Spanish "powder puff" (Walter Kingsford) so she can remain at court and become the king's mistress. Marie has other ideas.

off just as the fatal note was reached. Everyone laughed including the astonished Eddy, and his next take was perfect.

The opening shot of *Naughty Marietta* is of a trilling lark on a slender finger. A voice echoes the bird's song, and the camera pulls back to reveal the Princess Marie de Namour de la Bonfain (Jeanette) in a pet shop. She has slipped away from the palace to purchase some songbirds and to visit her old singing teacher nearby. Bringing a big-eyed puppy as a gift, she finds Herr Schuman (Joseph Cawthorn, the doctor in *Love Me Tonight*) hard at work. He is trying to write down the mysterious melody of the bells from the nearby church. Just as Marie starts to help him, they are interrupted by the pranks of her former fellow students. Together, they all swirl up the stairs from floor to floor, singing the spirited "Chansonette" as the little spaniel clambers determinedly after them.

Back at the palace, things are far from gay. Marie's doltish fiancé, Don Carlos (Walter Kingsford), has arrived with his three cadaverous sisters, bearing a gift of wedding clothes—all black. Marie's ominous uncle (Douglass Dumbrille) orders her to be nice to Don Carlos, but she knows the marriage has been arranged only to make her accessible to the lecherous Louis XV. The alternative is prison and possibly death. In despair, she picks out the notes of the unfinished song on the piano.

She is interrupted by a serving girl, Marietta (Helen Shipman), who has come to say goodbye. Marietta is too poor to marry her Giovanni, so she is going to the New World as a Casquette Girl with a dowry from the King. There she will marry a trapper or planter and begin a new life.

A new life! Princess Marie decides to change places with Marietta. She gives the girl a dowry so she can marry her sweetheart. As a final gesture, Marie throws open the doors of her aviary, letting the birds fly free.

The king's messengers are searching the countryside for her, but the new Marietta is nearly unrecognizable among the raw-boned brides. In a simple homespun dress, she crosses her eyes behind wire-rimmed glasses and distorts her face by stuffing her mouth with bread, chewing elaborately. When a suspicious sentry questions her, she points out a reeling

Pirates attack the ship, kill the crew, and seize the women. (Mary Foy, left; Cecelia Parker, right.)

Marie trades places with her maid and escapes as "Marietta" in a boatload of brides bound for Louisiana. She stuffs her cheeks with bread to avoid being recognized. *Courtesy Diane Flaherty.*

drunk on the dock (silent comic Billy Dooley) as her "brother." She waves him such a tearful farewell that he decides to go with her. Fortunately, he and the ship sway in different directions. As the ship prepares to sail, a dockside troubadour (Charles Bruins) sings the mocking love song of "Antoinette and Anatole." Amidst the tears of the old people and children left behind, the ship pulls out into the harbor, taking the young girls to an unknown fate. Their voices rise in the moving "Prayer" (based on a Victor Herbert piano piece).

Off the coast of Louisiana, the girls discuss what kinds of husbands they hope for, but Marietta is hard at work on her song. "I'm not going to marry," she tells them. She comforts the timid Julie (Cecelia Parker) when the other girls tease her and tells Julie she will find a fine young man in the New World. "But what about you, Marietta? Don't *you* want a fine young man?"

They are interrupted by pirates who kill the crew and cart the girls off to their camp in the bayou. Facing death or worse at any moment, the girls hear a distant song. It is Captain Dick Warrington (Nelson) and his scouts!

They come "Tramp, Tramp, Tramp"-ing out of the woods and demolish the pirates. The girls take quite a liking to their colorful rescuers, but

The Casquette Girls are rescued just in time by handsome Captain Dick Warrington (Nelson) and his scouts. Marietta decides that the men of New Orleans are more interesting than the men of Versailles. (Cecelia Parker as Julie, center)

Dick Warrington assures them they will be delivered untouched to New Orleans. Marietta instantly dislikes the brash captain, and he, in turn, resents her superior airs.

Around the campfire, Dick charms the girls with his rich baritone rendition of "The Owl and the Bobcat." Marietta pretends disinterest. Dick can't understand what brought such an attractive girl to the wilderness to seek a husband. "Surely nothing short of a wooden leg."

He takes advantage of the moonlight to sing the lushly romantic "'Neath the Southern Moon." Marietta is not impressed. She snaps her fingers in his face and walks off disdainfully—right into a tree.

In New Orleans, the Casquette Girls are welcomed enthusiastically by the entire population, led by the Governor (Frank Morgan in his first role without a mustache since 1928) and his haughty wife (Elsa Lanchester). Soon the girls

Naughty Marietta

A scene cut from the film. Surrounded by alligators, the scouts steer their precious cargo in flat-bottomed boats to New Orleans. *Courtesy Jack Tillmany.*

are promenading in the garden of a nearby convent, interviewing prospective husbands. "Can I have a blonde, mother?" "'*May* I have a blonde,' son."

Dick and the Governor are enjoying the sight of all these pretty girls when a disturbance erupts. Marietta is refusing several very persistent young men. The Governor reminds her of her contract, but she insists it was "lies, all lies." Certain that he has seen her somewhere before, the Governor reads her contract in search of the lies. Marietta agrees to the truth of each statement—her age, health, hometown—until he reaches "is of excellent character, entirely above reproach."

"*That's* it!" she cries, as Dick eyes her in disbelief. "Surely," she asks, lowering her eyes, "you have a place in New Orleans for someone who doesn't wish to marry but who likes to be charming…"

Amidst his wife's splutters of rage, the Governor orders the gendarmes to take Marietta away and "find her a home somewhere." His wife eyes him coldly. "And *you* thought you *knew* her."

Dick again rescues Marietta, this time from the gendarmes, who hope she plans to charm *them*. He finds her a place to live in the Bohemian quarter and invites himself to dinner. "I never cooked in my life," she tells him, "and I'd *die* before I cooked you a radish."

"You don't *cook* radishes," he replies, "you eat them alive." Marietta is just about to throw Dick out when a group of singers from Rudolpho's Marionette Theatre come by the balcony window. Dick loves to be sung to, and chides Marietta for not being as agreeable and talented as the troupe's dark-eyed soprano. Marietta gleefully eclipses the lady with a spirited rendition of "The Italian Street Song," giving an extra emphasis to the "Ah-*ha-ha*" refrain for Dick's benefit.

Several gentlemen who have followed Marietta from the convent arrive with something less than marriage on their minds. Dick agrees with their declaration that Marietta should have the best among them, thanks them for their compliment, and closes the door in their faces. He turns to find out more about this decidedly puzzling Casquette Girl, but she has fled.

The leader of the gendarmes, Major Cornell (Ed Keane), is infuriated by the continued presence of Dick's scouts within his jurisdiction, but Dick insists on keeping his men in town "for a rest" while he looks for Marietta. A chance visit to the Marionette Theatre reveals Marietta in a doll costume, singing "Ship Ahoy."

In New Orleans, Marietta escapes marriage and sets up housekeeping alone. Her landlord is played by Edouard Lippé, Eddy's singing teacher.

Marietta escapes Dick's attentions too and gets a job at Rudolpho's Marionette Theatre. (Akim Tamiroff as Rudolpho on lamppost.)

Backstage Rudolpho (Akim Tamiroff) warns Marietta that Captain Warrington is notorious as a heartbreaker.

Nevertheless, Dick manages to persuade her to accompany him on a tour of the town. They argue good naturedly until they pass an outdoor café and Marietta realizes she is hungry. At a nearby table are two members of Dick's rustic regiment, Abe (Harold Huber) and Zeke (Ed Brophy), loudly slurping their soup. This charming interlude is interrupted by a messenger on horseback. A ship is in the harbor bearing Don Carlos and Marie's uncle, who is offering a large reward for "Marietta Franini." (The original stage "Marietta," Emma Trentini, was from Naples to justify her accent, and the vestigial name remains.)

Dick sends the crowd off to the Marionette Theatre and escapes with Marietta in a small boat. Drifting in the bayou, he tells her he has a song for her, "I'm Falling in Love with Someone." She has a song for him too, but she doesn't know the words yet. "It's all so mysterious," he says. The gendarmes are waiting for them in Dick's camp. Dick offers to fight their way out, but Marietta fears for his

Naughty Marietta

Dick finally tracks her down. Though warned by Rudolpho that Dick is a "notorious heartbreaker," Marietta agrees to a tour of the town with him.

Dick and Marietta run into two of his rustic scouts (Harold Huber, left, and Ed Brophy). Alone later, Marietta tells Dick about her unfinished song.

Marietta is exposed as a runaway princess and taken to the home of the governor (Frank Morgan) and his wife (Elsa Lanchester). Dick is ordered never to see Marietta again on pain of death, but he returns to hear her song.

Dick forces his way into the ball for Marietta. His friend the Governor (Frank Morgan, right) tries desperately to stop him. *Courtesy Anna Michalik.*

life and quickly consents to return to France with her uncle and Don Carlos.

At the Governor's house, the ladies of New Orleans who had spurned Marietta now vie with each other to meet the Princess Marie. She is elaborately dressed and coiffed for the ball in her honor. Don Carlos has been convinced by her uncle that her running away was just a girlish prank to entice him.

Julie, now married to a young man in the Governor's service, tells Marietta that Captain Warrington has been ordered to leave town immediately on pain of death. Even as they speak, they hear the scouts passing in the road on their way up-river.

Dick has been forbidden entrance to the ball, but Major Cornell is eager to even old scores and lets him in. Dick finds Marietta. Terrified for his safety, she lies to him, telling him that she will see him tomorrow even though her ship is leaving that night. She is trying to persuade him to leave when her uncle discovers them together. "Don't be silly, Uncle. This young man only came to say goodbye."

The guests beg for a song. Across the crowded ballroom floor, Marietta sees Dick leaving and knows she will never see him again. The words for her song fall into place. She sings and he knows that it is just for him: "Ah, Sweet Mystery of Life." The "secret of it all" is love. Dick realizes this is farewell, and forgetting his safety, he returns to sing with her. She pauses halfway up the stairs and turns to sing the emotional duet.

The song ends. Marietta rushes upstairs in tears. Her uncle furiously places her under guard. But Dick is waiting in her room to take her away "to the land beyond the mountains." As they slip down the backstairs, her uncle discovers she is gone and rushes out on the balcony.

"Arrest them," he cries to two nearby gendarmes. He orders the prisoners taken to the Governor's office.

"At once!" cry the menacing gendarmes, and they do a smart about-face. It is Abe and Zeke. "We know a *better* way to the Governor's office," comments Abe. "Yeah," murmurs Zeke. "Through the woods. Kinda pretty..."

Lovely Elsa Lanchester. *Courtesy Anna Michalik.*

Naughty Marietta

The guests beg the Princess for a song. Suddenly, she realizes her song is complete. Marietta knows the words she must sing before she sends Dick away forever.

The closing scene shows Marietta, once again in homespun, riding into the West in the arms of Captain Warrington as the scouts sing "Tramp, Tramp, Tramp" and the lovers' voices soar in "Ah, sweet mystery of life, at last I've found thee."

It was apparent from the beginning that *Naughty Marietta* was going to be a hit. The premiere was held in Washington, D.C. on March 8, 1935, and the formally dressed audience included Supreme Court judges, cabinet members, thirty-five senators, and the Russian ambassador. The film opened at the Capitol Theatre in New York (the site of Miss MacDonald's first stage appearance), where it had a record run. Rereleased in 1945, it ran five weeks at New York's Plaza Cinema as a single feature, and has it enjoyed revivals ever since.

Reviews

Ed Sullivan reported in the *New York Daily News*: "It's terrific. MacDonald-Eddy are the new team sensation of the industry. Their duet of

"But I haven't seen a man I *could* love…"

"I will not enter into that life of degradation…"

"What do you care as long as I do what you want?"

'Sweet Mystery of Life' is the grandest thing ever recorded!" Regina Crewe proclaimed in the *New York American*: "Superlatives for Naughty Marietta! It's the top, the super-stratosphere of musical motion picture entertainment! In Nelson Eddy, who debuts so auspiciously as Jeanette MacDonald's hero, the screen has found a thrilling thrush, possessed not only of rare vocal tone but of personality and form and features cast in the heroic mold. A madly enthusiastic audience applauded each song."

The *New York Times*'s Andre Sennwald was just as enthusiastic: "A screen operetta which would have delighted its composer. W.S. Van Dyke has made a photoplay which is gaily romantic and rhapsodically tuneful. Such fortissimo singing as Mr. Eddy and Miss MacDonald provide for those rapturous love songs has not been heard in a motion picture theatre since One Night of Love." (The Oscar-nominated *One Night of Love* with Grace Moore had scored a huge hit several months earlier.)

Venerated critic Richard Watts Jr wasn't sparing with superlatives for his review in the *New York Herald-Tribune*: "Virtually perfection of cinema light opera....The triumph of Naughty Marietta is registered by Nelson Eddy who has a brilliant baritone voice."

"Great entertainment! An exquisite film so rich musically and strong in story, it makes the average musical movie seem tawdry. Handsomely produced and skillfully directed, it features the splendid voices of soprano Jeanette MacDonald and baritone Nelson Eddy. The story is dramatic, its tender charm contrasted with the stirring scenes of action and suspense." Bland Johanneson, *New York Daily Mirror*.

"A great screen operetta sung to perfection. Possessed of a brilliant baritone voice, handsome Mr. Eddy has a way about him which, with his singing ability, should make him one of cinema's outstanding figures. MacDonald's is a stunning performance, both vocally and dramatically." William Boehnel, *New York World-Telegram*.

Even *Time* magazine unbent long enough to offer faint praise: "This preposterous scrap of Americana is well suited to the needs of sentimental cinema....a worthy example of what operatic cinema can amount to....[Nelson Eddy is] as personable a singer as his most serious Hollywood rival, Lawrence Tibbett."

Indeed, newcomer Nelson eclipsed the established Jeanette in the rave department: "A new movie star emerged from the Capitol [NYC] screen when Nelson Eddy appeared opposite Jeanette MacDonald in Naughty Marietta...his fine, full powered voice is admirably suited to the Herbert score" wrote Kate Cameron in the *New York Daily News*.

"Those advance enthusiasms were justified. Nelson Eddy is a find, and Metro-Goldwyn-Mayer has wisely put him in a part well suited to his acting ability and magnificent voice. Jeanette MacDonald is at the top!" reported Eileen Creelman in the *New York Sun*. *The New York Journal* reported that "Naughty Marietta is a personal triumph for Nelson Eddy. Already famous on the concert stage, Mr. Eddy is established as a definite screen personality."

Recordings (See Discography for further information)

The superb MGM arrangements of these old tunes done by Herbert Stothart were not used for the RCA recordings, so millions know most of these MacDonald/Eddy favorites only in their rather flat recorded versions.

"Ah, Sweet Mystery of Life" (Recorded both separately and together by both MacDonald and Eddy, plus as a duet between Eddy and Nadine Conner)
"Italian Street Song" (MacDonald)
"Chante Italienne" [Italian Street Song] (MacDonald)
"I'm Falling in Love with Someone" (Eddy)
"'Neath the Southern Moon" (Eddy)
"Tramp, Tramp, Tramp" (Eddy and male chorus)

Eddy also recorded songs from the original *Naughty Marietta* that weren't used in the film: "It Never, Never Can Be Love," "Live for Today" (with Nadine Conner), and "Naughty Marietta."

"Ah, Sweet Mystery of Life," with "Indian Love Call" on the reverse, received a Gold Record for selling a million copies, a major accomplishment when the nation's population numbered only 160 million.

Music in the Film

All music by Victor Herbert. Original lyrics by Rida Johnson Young. New lyrics by Gus Kahn. In listing performers after each title, "and" denotes a genuine duet, while commas between names indicate a sequence of singers.

An asterisk (*) indicates author's working title for material crafted for the film. No copyright records have been located for these songs. (The bird call that opens film is used as a calling theme between lovers Gene Raymond and Loretta Young in the poetic film *Zoo in Budapest*, 1933.)

Overture: Roll of drums, "Italian Street Song" (MacDonald, Eddy, male chorus), "Ah, Sweet Mystery of Life."
"Chansonette" (MacDonald and chorus) - based on "Punchinello," arranged by Herbert Stothart, lyrics by Gus Kahn.
"Antoinette and Anatole" (Charles Bruin and women's chorus) - based on "Dance of the Marionettes" from stage score, lyrics by Gus Kahn.
"Prayer"* (Delos Jewkes, chorus, MacDonald) - based on a Herbert piano solo, "Yesterthoughts" (1900), lyrics by Gus Kahn. (Also sung as "Wonderful Dreams" by Allan Jones and Mary Martin in *The Great Victor Herbert*, Paramount, 1939.)
"Tramp, Tramp, Tramp" (Eddy and male chorus) - Lyrics by Rida Johnson Young and Gus Kahn. (The verse about "wading in blood to the knee" is happily omitted.)
"The Owl and the Bob Cat"* (Eddy and male chorus) - based on "If I Were Anybody Else But Me" from original stage production, lyrics by Gus Kahn.
"'Neath the Southern Moon" (Eddy) - Lyrics by Rida Johnson Young. (Originally a contralto aria for the gypsy lover of the Governor's effeminate son.)
"Mon Ami Pierrot" fragment (contralto) - traditional French folk song.
"Italian Street Song" (Zarubi Elmassian, Eddy, MacDonald with chorus)
"Ship Ahoy" (MacDonald, M. Sankar, Countess Sonia, Alexander, Bokefi, William Sabot) - music identical to "Antoinette and Anatole," based on "Dance of the Marionettes" from stage version, lyrics by Gus Kahn.
"I'm Falling in Love With Someone" (Eddy) - Lyrics by Rida Johnson Young.
"Ah, Sweet Mystery of Life" (MacDonald, Eddy, violin obligato by Jan Rubini) - Also known as "The Dream Melody," lyrics by Rida Johnson Young. (There is a popular but untrue legend that the song, used as an entr'acte in the stage production, had lyrics put to it after the show opened. Both versions were copyrighted simultaneously and used from the beginning.)
Finale: "Tramp, Tramp, Tramp" (male chorus) sung contrapuntally with "Ah Sweet Mystery of Life" (MacDonald, Eddy)

Songs from the original stage production that were used in the film are: "Italian Street Song," "'Neath the Southern Moon," "I'm Falling in Love With Someone," "Tramp, Tramp, Tramp," and "Ah, Sweet Mystery of Life." New words were put to the melodies of "Dance of the Marionettes" and "If I Were Anybody Else But Me."

Naughty Marietta

"If you run out of names for boys, you can use mine—Richard."

"I've waited two days for that smile."

"At last, I know the secret…"

Script History
Contributed by Mary Truesdell

A March 1930 draft of the script in the MGM archives, intended for the adorable and feisty Marion Davies, depicts Marietta as a Parisian laundress with aspirations to be a singer. Her beau is a baker, "heavy, clumsy, but nice and honest." The supporting male lead is a gawky music student from the provinces, lusted after and eventually kept by an aristocratic siren. Marietta, in turn, is tempted by a well-to-do villain, but eventually the principals achieve career success and true love together.

The next script adaptation has Marietta still in Paris, wooed simultaneously by a poor Gypsy named Dumaine and a rich villain named Etienne. Dumaine ultimately wins her heart by singing "Ah, Sweet Mystery of Life" under her window, and they go off to a life of poverty and happiness.

With the Motion Picture Code in effect in 1934, Felix Feist prepared a new version, still intended for Davies. It reverts to the New Orleans stage location, but with Marietta, still feisty and adorable, arriving from France to escape an arranged marriage. She rebels at the marriage auction block, and Dick, intrigued by her feisty adorableness, carries her off, tied and gagged. This script was further adapted and refined into the MacDonald-Eddy version we know today.

Trivia

Seeking appropriate future vehicles for the burgeoning MacDonald-Eddy team, MGM advertised a forthcoming production of Reginald de Koven's operetta *Robin Hood*. Eddy certainly had the opera credentials, but it was hard for some to picture him leaping about in tights. When Warner Bros. released a non-singing saga of Sherwood with Errol Flynn in 1938, the opera project was shelved.

Movie Goofs

Movie magic sometimes comes about because scenes are routinely shot out of sequence and then rearranged in the editing process or parts of the same scene are shot on different days. Costumes may change within the same scene, props appear and disappear. The continuity person (called a "script girl" in the old days) tried desperately to prevent these mistakes, but sometimes they slipped in. Here are some favorites spotted by sharp-eyed fans.

The spot on the head of the cute puppy following Jeanette up the stairs in the opening scenes keeps expanding and contracting—indicating they used a whole litter to film the scene. (Molly Yeckley)

After Princess Marie puts the bird in the aviary, she places its carrying cage under a small table. But when the real Marietta comes in to say goodbye, the cage is not there. (Anna Michalik)

Nelson's pinkie ring is off and on from scene to scene. (Tricia Lutz)

While Dick is singing "The Owl and the Bobcat" to Marietta, the tie on her cloak keeps tying and untying itself. And the sail on the small boat in the bayou keeps furling and unfurling as he sings "I'm Falling in Love with Someone" to her. (Anna Michalik)

Jeanette's hairstyle in the scene before the gypsies appear keeps switching from smooth curls to tight curls. (Stephanie Loyd)

Jeanette carries white gloves in her hand as she leaves her bedroom, but a second later, as she descends the stair to the ball, she is wearing medium-colored gloves with several bracelets firmly clasped over them. (Author)

At the ball, when the guests ask Marietta to sing, her uncle is at her left. But when the camera cuts to a medium shot, he is at her right. (Minami Pennington)

Notice the microphone boom shadow following Nelson and Jeanette in their farewell scene on the horse as they ride away into the mountains. (Elsa Dik Glass)

A Spanish poster for *Naughty Marietta*. Note the spelling "Jeannette." *Courtesy Anna Michalik.*

6
The Second Most Famous Team

Audiences left *Naughty Marietta* keenly aware that they wanted more. But more what? Not just more operetta. The success of a lace-valentine operetta was as astonishing to cynical Depressionites as it would be today. Not just more Jeanette MacDonald. She was a film veteran of six years standing. And not just more Nelson Eddy, although his appeal was an essential ingredient of the new phenomenon. What audiences wanted and got was the combination, the union of talents, the *team*.

Even before MGM realized what was happening, the public knew that a new entity had been born. The studio was not far behind, of course. Hollywood has always been a multimillion-dollar industry run with machinelike efficiency and Ouija-board fancifulness. The marriage of art and commerce has led to some bizarre goings-on, but one doctrine has emerged: Don't tamper with a winning combination.

We can all understand MGM's mystification. The magic, the charisma, the chemistry of a "team" is good for several hundred thousand words, most of it balderdash, but basically it can be expressed by the principle that the whole is greater than the sum of the parts.

"Jeanette-MacDonald-and-Nelson-Eddy," to their mutual astonishment, became a single legend, a household "word" surpassed only by the worldwide recognition accorded Laurel and Hardy (who made more than 100 films together). By happy accident, Jeanette and Nelson joined with director W.S. (Woody) Van Dyke to create a world where the illogical ideals of goodness rewarded and integrity triumphant obtained a temporary reality in the emotional surge of music. While millions in Europe were responding to blood-quickening martial music, Americans found emotional release in the stirring melodies of love.

They made only eight pictures together, yet there is hardly anyone who does not know of Jeanette MacDonald and Nelson Eddy, even if they have never seen their films. The legend lives on in countless television skits, funny and unfunny, loving and unloving. A classic of this genre is "You Be Nelson and I'll Be Jeanette," performed by Carol Burnett and Julie Andrews. Rick Besoyan's musical, *Little Mary Sunshine*, a spoof of their hit *Rose Marie*, ran nearly three years in New York and is still performed by theatre groups around the country. And in 1970, when the Canadian Mounted Police retired their classic red-jacketed uniform, hundreds of newspapers accompanied their story with a picture of Nelson Eddy as Sgt. Bruce in *Rose Marie*, made thirty-four years earlier! The "singing sweethearts" have taken a place in our cultural heritage that they could never have guessed at.

Naughty Marietta, the film that started it all was certainly regarded more as a convenient way to meet production quotas than as a major artistic effort. In the days when a studio had to turn out eighty or more pictures a year to supply their chain of allied theatres, a good number of films were assembly-line efforts. Happily Jeanette's fifteenth film succeeded beyond anyone's expectations. Her reputation for sexy comedy may have made her the obvious choice for a film called *Naughty Marietta* (the early publicity showed her provocatively hoisting her long skirts to her knees), but an entirely new Jeanette emerged. Lubitsch had created her film image: the cool beauty awakened to the joys of earthly love by a charming rascal. It was a rôle she had repeated with variations until *Naughty Marietta*. She had been the aloof foil to Chevalier's mercurial charm, but Nelson Eddy was a solid, trustworthy, big brother type, not a ravishing rake.

Remarkably but necessarily, the MacDonald image did a complete about-face. Now she was the vivacious one. With Chevalier, her screen response had been guarded, laced with good-humored skepticism. Eddy's screen personality demanded no such defenses.

While the screen Chevalier might bound through a lady's bedroom window at night, Eddy would stand outside and sing of his passion. The new screen MacDonald responded with a more appealing warmth and vulnerability.

Nelson with his mother, Isabel Eddy, in 1938. She was also a singer, and they sang duets on one of his radio shows. *Courtesy Anna Michalik.*

Without this essential personality change, the genuine sentimentality of the MacDonald-Eddy films would not have been possible. Where the Lubitsch heroine functioned in an insulated world of champagne and witticisms, the new MacDonald could pray, love children, face death. The strict new standards of the Hays Office may have made this change ideal for filmic survival, but the "new" MacDonald also rang a tremendous note of response with the public.

The public reaction to Nelson Eddy was also phenomenal, indeed almost too phenomenal for comfort. The studio recognized that they had a potential gold mine and proceeded to give him the biggest publicity buildup since Anna Sten, even allowing co-billing with an established star. This kind of buildup often produces its own backlash as with Miss Sten, but Eddy miraculously overcame it. The critics rushed to outdo each other in praise of the newcomer:

"A new star emerged on the Capitol screen." -*New York Daily News*.

"The screen has found a thrilling thrush, possessed not only of a rare vocal tone, but of a personality and form and features cast in the heroic mould." -*New York American*.

"Eddy is a brilliant baritone, masculine, engaging and good looking."-Richard Watts Jr in the *New York Herald*.

It was the kind of praise that must either be lived up to or lived down. As Eddy put it, "I knew I was good, but I wasn't great." The same critics who devoted so much lush prose to his virtues would discover shortly that he wasn't

1936

much of a dramatic actor and would dip their pens in vitriol. "I was expected to live up to a success that had not been earned, but which had merely happened," Eddy later lamented.

He knew he wasn't an actor and the public took one look at him and knew he wasn't an actor. It was, indeed, a major part of his charm. Eddy had stepped from the rarefied world of the "serious" singer into the cozy warmth accorded the film entertainer. On an opera or concert stage, a performer faces an audience comparable to that of a gladiator in ancient Rome or a trapeze artist performing without a net. Basically the audience is waiting for the fatal slip. A tension grips the assemblage that is released in applause only when the gladiator, the aerialist, the *singer* survives the performance.

1936

The Second Most Famous Team

1938

A film singer approaches his audience in an entirely different way. He is no longer a distant speck in a spotlight, but a living, breathing, charming human being with warts or a chipped tooth or a crooked tie—just like us, only bigger, somehow more lifelike up there on the screen. He has become a friend long before he opens his mouth to sing, and, when he does, it is like discovering that the terribly nice guy you met at a party has a beautiful voice. You are surprised, thrilled, delighted. If the world's greatest singer has not succeeded in making you like him before he opens his mouth, it doesn't matter what comes out.

Critics of "serious" music have traditionally taken a dim view of this easy acceptance by the lowly film audience. Max de Schauensee of the *Philadelphia Bulletin* gave a classic demonstration of this phenomenon when he wrote, "Though Nelson Eddy took the *easy road* and made his fame and fortune in other channels, we who lived in Philadelphia during the late 1920s will not easily forget that he was a fine opera singer as well." (author's italics.)

Much of Eddy's appeal, and he had considerable appeal, as his fan mail testified, came initially from his very lack of "acting." He possessed that magic third dimension on the screen, the ability to communicate standing still that has always separated "stars" from those who are merely brilliant actors. (Indeed a "star" frequently does not need to be even a competent thespian.) Eddy projected a quality of tremendous warmth, intelligence, and good humor that overcame any temporary awkwardness. He was a good friend suddenly required to emote in front of the camera, and we shared his nervousness and liked him all the better for it.

The romantic bond between the MacDonald and Eddy screen characters was heightened by the fact that they sang together. Rarely had Miss MacDonald sung duets with her leading men,

1935

In 1939, columnist Ed Sullivan declared Tyrone Power and Jeanette MacDonald winners of a movie goer's survey for the King and Queen of Hollywood. Jeanette replaced previous Queen Myrna Loy.

and, when she did, they generally took alternate lines or verses. Fan magazines would write reams on the perfection of this new combination, each voice distinct unto itself yet blending perfectly. Of course Douglas Shearer's excellent Oscar-winning sound recording helped.

Musically, the pair were a study in contrasts. Jeanette could play the piano, transposing keys on sight. Eddy, for all his background in "serious" music, could play only the drums. When the script called for him to play a piano, he just faked it. (He did, however, hold an honorary musicians' union card in the Hollywood local—as a peckhorn player.) He was widely read although his favorite casual reading was musical scores, and his field of interests was catholic. Jeanette concentrated intensely on what interested her, and occasionally her lack of general education was revealed in startling *faux pas*. At a San Francisco concert in 1948 she mispronounced the name of a French composer when introducing a song and then sang it in flawless French. On another occasion she referred to Richard Strauss as "the waltz king." (It was Johann Strauss Jr).

Another intriguing difference was their diction. For all her popular musical stage background, Jeanette employed the "European" enunciation so dear to classical singers' hearts. (American English was still not regarded as "cultured.") Jeanette could and did get five or six syllables out of a word like "mystery," while classically trained Eddy sang some of the most flawless American English to come along until Sinatra seized the title.

The chemistry of a "team" is as unpredictable as it is indefinable. Why was it that William Powell and Myrna Loy made thirteen films together without ever being regarded as a team? Olivia de Havilland and Errol Flynn costarred eight times, frequently in lush costume epics, and were never a "team." Yet, Jeanette MacDonald and Nelson Eddy were already a team before their second picture together was completed. They made fewer co-films than any other team—Laurel and Hardy, Astaire and Rogers, Wheeler and Woolsey, Janet Gaynor and Charles Farrell, Abbott and Costello, Martin

Nelson proudly shows off his top of the line Cadillac, probably a Series 62 Club Coupe. The license plate says 1938.

1938

A candid catches a bespectacled Nelson at the stable where he kept his horse. *Courtesy Jeanne Murphy.*

after being hailed as a comedienne. Unlike Miss MacDonald, she would succeed.

Nelson Eddy, like Fred Astaire, came to Hollywood about five years into the sound era after a career before live audiences. Two years older than Eddy, Astaire had been a major light on Broadway with his sister, Adele, until her marriage in 1932 ended their partnership. He and Eddy both had small rôles in *Dancing Lady* (MGM 1933), but their talents were wasted in unsuitable numbers. (Astaire had previously made one silent and one sound short with his sister, and Eddy had had one on-screen guest appearance.) Astaire then went to RKO where his supporting rôle in *Flying Down to Rio* with Ginger in his arms made them both stars. The

A publicity photo. Nelson wrote an article called "I Bought a Horse," recounting his humorous experiences with the equine species.

and Lewis—with the exception of Dick Powell and Ruby Keeler, who appeared opposite each other in only seven films. Fred Astaire and Ginger Rogers made ten films together and had completed six of them when *Rose Marie,* the second MacDonald-Eddy film, confirmed the MacDonald-Eddy coupling in 1936.

A comparison of the two most famous musical duos is intriguing. Ginger Rogers, like Jeanette, worked on Broadway in the late 1920s and went to Paramount in the first days of sound. Unlike Miss MacDonald, she was still only a featured player when the movies spotted her. Nor did she start out in films as a star. She had to do a large number of shorts and Bs before achieving that status. Jeanette was a leading lady if not a star right from her first film rôle. Like Jeanette, Ginger Rogers would try for recognition in more prestigious, "serious" films

Robert Taylor, Jeanette MacDonald, and Paul Muni broadcasting on "America Calling" in 1938.

Nelson chatting with soprano Lotte Lehmann. She later trained Jeanette for her opera debut.

Diva Amelita Galli-Curci and Nelson arrive for the opening of the Los Angeles Opera, 1939.

Although he was a fine musician, Eddy never learned to play a musical instrument. The Hollywood musicians' union local gave him an honorary card anyway—as a peckhorn player. Here he clowns on a French horn on the set of *Maytime*.

nominal stars of that film were Dolores del Rio and Jeanette's future husband, Gene Raymond. Eddy had to wade through one more small part before *Naughty Marietta* made him a star.

Astaire made only one film without Ginger before 1940, while she appeared in seventeen without him. During the same period, Jeanette and Nelson each made three non-team pictures. Both teams separated after seven years. Astaire and Rogers parted in 1939, each going on to major screen careers as individuals. Astaire partnered other lovely ladies, and Miss Rogers did some excellent comedy and dramatic work in the 1940s and 1950s. They were reunited more or less by accident when Judy Garland was taken ill and could not appear in *The Barkleys of Broadway* (MGM 1949). MacDonald and Eddy made their last MGM film together in 1942 and their fans waited impatiently for a reunion.

And what did stardom do to the lives of Jeanette MacDonald and Nelson Eddy? Both of them had decades of hard work, training, and trouping behind them. Their "overnight success" found them emotionally secure, stable, and able

The Second Most Famous Team

Conductor Eugene Ormandy and Nelson with the Philadelphia Orchestra at the Academy of Music, rehearsing for a benefit for the orchestra pension fund, 1939. *Courtesy United Press International.*

to see the lavish adulation in perspective. Miss MacDonald, as a longtime resident of Hollywood, had evolved all the personal mechanisms of defense necessary to handle the acclaim, pressures, and demands of press agents, fans, charitable institutions, aspiring young singers, and onetime acquaintances who suddenly decided they were her dearest friend. She was noted for her graciousness in the face of a barrage that would have sent a lesser person to the nearest desert island.

Eddy did not yet have these defenses. He was made miserable by the sudden overpraise and criticism. He resented having to lay his private life, thoughts, and feelings before anyone with the price of a ten-cent movie magazine. He could not go out without being hounded by screaming fans. If he so much as went for a haircut, the shop would fill with giggling, hovering females waiting to snatch bits of his hair from the dirty floor. (A few over-exuberant ones, repeatedly hiding in his dressing room or hotel room to leap out at him, would today be classified as "stalkers.") He could easily have withdrawn entirely from his fans as many performers have been forced to do, but once again his "perfectionism" prevented his retreat. The admirers (predominantly female) who crowded his dressing room after concerts and nightclub appearances or stopped him on the street could almost always count on recognition and a welcome.

Suddenly having more money than he had ever had before also required some adjustments for Eddy. He acquired the house he had always wanted, with a tennis court and swimming pool, but he resisted the Hollywood preoccupation with fancy cars and clothes. He wore gray suits and drove a black coupe. He was rarely seen in nightclubs. His new wealth enabled him to indulge his interest in pewter. He bought several ready-made collections. Then, with his basement full of barrels of old pewter, he realized that he had been acquiring, not collecting. It was a realization that some of us are never fortunate enough to make. He gave the pewter away, and thereafter collected his artworks one at a time, with care and thought. His collection eventually included pieces by Rodin, Epstein, and Maillol. He preferred seventeenth-century English artists "because they are so solid and satisfying" and

Nelson with Metropolitan Opera stars Lily Pons, left, and Gladys Swarthout— clowning at a party in 1938. *Courtesy United Press International.*

modern French painters "because they give you a sense of excitement." He kept his own sculpting hobby a secret until he was more proficient than some professionals because he did not want the phony praise so often heaped upon a performer's efforts in other fields.

Eddy didn't desert the opera stage until his "discovery" in *Naughty Marietta* made his presence on stage more of a distraction than an asset. In 1934, when he was still "unknown," he sang Wolfram in *Tannhäuser* with the San Francisco Opera on December 8. Marjory M. Fisher of the *San Francisco News* wrote, "Nelson Eddy made a tremendously fine impression. His voice was rich and resonant, and his singing interesting and effective from the histrionic as well as from the vocal standpoint. He has not had the stage experience of his better known confrères, but he left no doubt in the minds of discerning auditors that he belongs in that fine group of baritones which includes Lawrence Tibbett, Richard Bonelli, and John Charles Thomas and which represents America's outstanding contribution to the contemporary opera stage."

On May 20, 1935, he had a small rôle in Howard Hanson's *Merry Mount* in Ann Arbor, Michigan, with Rose Bampton in the cast. On

Nelson sang "Silent Night" with Shirley Temple at her radio debut, Christmas Eve, 1939 on Screen Guild Theatre.

November 11 of that year he sang Amonasro in *Aida* with the San Francisco Opera. Elisabeth Rethberg, Giovanni Martinelli, and Ezio Pinza were in the cast. Miss Fisher was again enthusiastic: "It is news when one sees a handsome Amonasro who is every inch a king, and hears him sing with the suave beauty of tone that Nelson Eddy brought to the rôle of the Ethiopian king." Opera quietly faded from Eddy's schedule as films and highly lucrative concerts claimed more and more of his time.

Eddy allowed himself another "indulgence," if it can be called that. He built a complete recording studio in his home, where he recorded songs and dialogue from the film he was doing to polish his performance. He also experimented with multiple recording techniques. As early as 1935, he was recording his own voice over and over to produce the effect of a chorus. This may have inspired the phenomenal multi-voiced track of his later film, *Make Mine Music*. On numerous evenings, his voice teacher, Dr. Edouard Lippé, would come for a lesson and end up puttering around the studio with Eddy into the late hours. Eddy also had a large musical library that he personally catalogued and drew on over the years for material to use on radio and in concerts. His extensive collection of scores, books, and sheet music is now at the Occidental College in Los Angeles for use by scholars. In 1969, his wife presented a collection of his stills, scripts, scrapbooks, and transcriptions of radio programs to the U.C.L.A. Theatre Arts Collection. This "Nelson Eddy Collection" is available to students.

Soon after Eddy had signed with MGM, his friend and accompanist, Ted Paxson, decided to take a crack at Hollywood too. He and his bride, Helen, stayed with Eddy and his mother on their arrival, and Helen became Eddy's first secretary.

Jeanette and her longtime secretary, Emily (Wentz) West, first met in the late 1920s on Broadway. They were appearing in nearby theatres at the same time and ate together on matinée days. Jeanette invited Emily to her wedding and promised her work in the studio chorus if she would stay.in Hollywood. Emily joined a growing group of actors and technicians whom Jeanette requested on her pictures. Later, during World War II, Miss West was working in a defense plant when Jeanette asked her to become her "girl Friday." Jobs were frozen, and it was necessary to cut some red tape, but the charming Miss MacDonald succeeded. Emily became Jeanette's secretary, then Gene's, and a part of the "family" for life.

Circa 1940

Another member was Grace Adele Newell, Jeanette's beloved singing teacher. Jeanette's sister Blossom and husband, Clarence (Warren) Rock, who married in September, 1926, had emigrated to Hollywood after years of touring in vaudeville as "Rock and Blossom." Blossom used the name Marie Blake (Jeanette's character in *San Francisco*) and had a running rôle as Sally, the Telephone Girl, in the *Dr. Kildare* film series. Later, Blossom used her married name, Blossom Rock, for numerous appearances

Circa 1937

in films and on television, where she is best remembered for playing Grandma on "The Addams Family."

The third MacDonald sister, Elsie, had started a talent school outside Philadelphia, and, in 1939, she married businessman Bernard J. Scheiter. Nanette Wallace, Elsie's granddaughter, was a favorite of Jeanette's.

Jeanette had planted her footprints in the concrete outside Grauman's Chinese Theatre in 1934, but it was not until 1938 that Nelson took part in the Hollywood tribal rite. Officially, he had begun a regime of acting lessons, but some sources reported that the studio frowned on this activity. They knew they had a "winner" without knowing why and hesitated to tamper with any of the ingredients. As one studio executive put it: "Nelson always has a profitable following. If he makes an extraordinary picture, if we happen to find an unusual story for him—the returns on it, of course, are unusual. But no matter what he makes, there seems to be a basic return we can always count on."

And thus the seeds of decline were sown, not only for Eddy, but for Miss MacDonald. Ironically, almost any of her earlier rôles could have been played by a sophisticated, mature woman. Now that she was approaching her mid-thirties, her rôles became younger and younger. Eventually both she and the already-graying Eddy would be required to play characters almost half their ages, a fact apparent to the most casual filmgoer.

But now, both performers were at the peak of their powers and about to shoot one of the screen's most popular musical films, *Rose Marie*.

Rose Marie

MGM.
Released January 31, 1936.
Directed by W. S. Van Dyke II.
Produced by Hunt Stromberg.
113 minutes.

TV title: *Indian Love Call* (an attempt to avoid confusion with the 1954 remake).

Based on Arthur Hammerstein's production of the operetta *Rose-Marie* by Rudolf Friml, Otto A. Harbach, and Oscar Hammerstein II. Screenplay: Frances Goodrich, Albert Hackett, and Alice Duer Miller. Music Director: Herbert Stothart. Camera: William Daniels. Editor: Blanche Sewell. Totem dance staged by Chester Hale. Operatic sequences staged by William von Wymetal. Sound: Douglas Shearer. Art Director: Cedric Gibbons. Art Director's Associates: Joseph Wright and Edwin B. Willis. Gowns: Adrian. Assistant Director: Joseph Newman. *Roméo et Juliette* dance staged by Michael Val Raset. Technical Advisor: William Brennan. Vocal Coach: Paul Lamkoff. Montages: Slavko Vorkapich.

The stage *Rose-Marie* (with a hyphen) opened on September 2, 1924 at the Imperial Theatre, starring

Rose Marie

Dennis King and Mary Ellis, with Arthur Deagon as the Mountie, Sgt. Malone. It ran 557 performances.

MGM made *Rose-Marie* as a silent in 1928, now feared lost. Filming, directed by Lucien Hubbard ,began with Renée Adorée in the title rôle, but she was replaced by Joan Crawford, who starred with James Murray as Kenyon and House Peters as the Mountie. Our 1936 version dropped the hyphen and discarded the stage plot. MGM made a third, also hyphen-less version in Cinemascope and Technicolor in 1954, with Ann Blyth, Howard Keel, Fernando Lamas, Marjorie Main, and Bert Lahr, directed by Mervyn LeRoy. It used much of the stage plot.

Jeanette MacDonald (Marie de Flor)
Nelson Eddy (Sergeant Bruce)
Reginald Owen (Myerson)
Allan Jones (Roméo, also Mario Cavaradossi)
James Stewart (John "Jack" Flower)
Alan Mowbray (Premier)
George Regas (Boniface)
Robert Greig (Café Manager)
Una O'Connor (Roderick, Marie's maid)
Lucien Littlefield (Storekeeper)
David Nivens [later "Niven"] (Teddy, a suitor)
Herman Bing (Mr. Danielle)
James Conlin (Joe, the piano player)
Dorothy Gray (Edith)
Mary Anita Loos (Corn Queen)
Aileen Carlyle (Susan)
Halliwell Hobbes (Mr. Gordon, opera manager)
Paul Porcasi (Emil, the chef)
Gilda Gray (Belle)
Bert Lindley (Pop)
Edgar Dearing (Motorcycle policeman)
Pat West (Traveling salesman)
Charles Bruin (Man shaving in his BVD's)
Milton Owen (Stage manager)
David Clyde (Doorman)
Russell Hicks (Commandant)
Rolfe Sedan, Louis Mercier (Admirers in hall)
Jack Pennick (Brawler)
Leonard Carey (Louis)
David Robel, Rinaldo Alacorn, Joseph Chorrie, Bill Cody, Iron Eyes Cody (Dancers)
Matty Roubert (Newsboy)
Major Sam Harris (Guest)
Ernie Alexander (Elevator operator)
James Mason [American silent film villain, not British star] (Trapper)
John George, Lee Phelps (Barflies)
Fred Graham (Corporal)
Olga Dane (*Roméo et Juliette* singer)
Agostino Borgato, Adrian Rosley (Opera fans)
Delos Jewkes (Butcher at hotel)
Bits: Duke York, Julie Laird, Linda Parker, James Young, Tony Beard, Alesandro Giglio, Gennaro Maria-Curci, Doris Atkinson, Bill Steele, Margaret Zitt, Edith Holloway, William Stack

Rose Marie was presented on Screen Guild Theatre (radio), 6/29/47, with Jeanette and Nelson.

One of the twenty-five top-grossing films of 1935-1936.

Stand on any street corner with a microphone and ask passersby to name a Jeanette MacDonald-Nelson Eddy musical. Nine out of ten will mention *Rose Marie*. In most minds this film characterizes operetta and "the team" more than anything else they did together. Any recreation of the "golden age" of film, comic or nostalgic, will inevitably include a singing Mountie and a lavishly gowned soprano.

The director, producer, and most of the writers, designers, and technicians for *Rose Marie*

Jeanette as Juliette. She later sang the rôle on stage.

Jeanette as a temperamental prima donna, Marie de Flor, discusses her contempt for men with her maid (Una O'Connor). The title rôle was first intended for the volatile diva Grace Moore.

were the same people who created *Naughty Marietta*. The cast included a generous sprinkling of prominent "character actors" from MGM's well-stocked stable, plus three interesting new faces.

English actor David Nivens didn't attract much attention as Rose Marie's rejected suitor. It was his fourth featured rôle in American films, and it would take several more pictures to establish his name as the more familiar "Niven."

A twenty-eight-year-old American actor fared better in the difficult but touching rôle of Rose Marie's kid brother. Jimmy Stewart, with only one previous film rôle under his belt, made a tremendous impression and reached "leading man" status within a year.

Young singer Allan Jones, who does two opera sequences with Jeanette, was making his mark so quickly that pictures in which he was featured were being released before films in which he had near walk-ons. Two years later, he would be Jeanette's leading man in *The Firefly* and a personal friend off screen. He and his (then) wife, Irene Hervey, often visited with Jeanette and her husband, Gene Raymond.

The 1936 *Rose Marie* departs drastically from the stage and earlier film-version plots. In the stage and 1928 silent film versions, the Mountie was an incidental character who solves a murder and frees the hero to marry the heroine. Dennis King, Miss MacDonald's costar in *The Vagabond King*, was the lead in the stage *Rose-Marie*. The two sound-film *Rose Marie*s made the Mountie the hero, although the 1954 Howard Keel-Ann Blyth version harked back to the Saskatchewan Hotel setting and used some of the eccentric characters of the stage version.

In our 1936 interpretation, Rose Marie is a singer, but not in a backwoods hotel. She is an opera star, Canadian vintage. The rôle was originally prepared for Grace Moore, but when the film was ready for shooting, she was not available until after Eddy was scheduled to leave on his annual concert tour. Since so much of the film was to be shot on location at Cascade Lake and Emerald Bay, Lake Tahoe, during the summer months of 1935, there was no possibility of delay, and the rôle fell to Miss MacDonald. The plot line, the character of the temperamental prima donna, even the choice of opera sequences, were all holdovers from a Moore vehicle. (Miss Moore had sung the rôles of Juliette and Tosca at the Met.)

We first see our heroine on stage as Juliette in Gounod's opera *Roméo et Juliette*. An intriguing matte shot permits the stage action to "revolve" while the proscenium and orchestra remain stationary. In a brief montage we meet her handsome Romeo (Allan Jones), hear her sing "Juliet's Waltz," and watch the Capulets and Montagues slugging it out, Friar Lawrence marrying the lovers, and their final death scene followed by tumultuous curtain calls. Although not credited on screen, the montage bears the

Rose Marie

Planning to ask the Premier (Alan Mowbray, right) to pardon her brother, she invites him back to her hotel suite. Her harried chef (Paul Porcasi) must prepare dinner for ten in fifteen minutes.

hallmark of Slavko Vorkapich, the noted montagist who contributed to *Romeo and Juliet*, *The Good Earth*, and many MacDonald-Eddy films.

On stage, our prima donna, Marie de Flor (Jeanette), is a radiant sunbeam. Backstage she bitches at everyone in sight, in a near duplicate of the opening sequence of *Oh, for a Man!* Her ardent millionaire suitor, Teddy (David Nivens), who has pursued her from New York, is thrown out of her dressing room. What, she asks her maid Roderick (the Abbey Theatre's Una O'Connor, best remembered as Frankie's mother in *The Informer*), does she need with men when she has her career, money, everything she wants? Everything, Roderick replies, struggling valiantly with a French accent from somewhere west of Cork, everything but *love*. Men are stupid, silly boys, Marie declares. The only one worth caring about is her brother, Jack, who is in prison.

It becomes obvious that her deep distress is causing her display of temper and temperament. She is even rude to her manager, Myerson (Reginald Owen), until he tells her the Premier has been in the audience and would like her to sing for him privately.

The premier! Perhaps a parole can be arranged. The premier (Alan Mowbray) and his entire family are swept off for dinner at Marie's hotel suite, much to the horror of her chef (Paul Porcasi), who has only a few minutes to prepare a feast.

Marie fills the gap by singing "Pardon Me, Madame." The melody is taken up by the hotel guests and staff as it travels over the transom and along phone lines to the switchboard girls, by bellhops, by butchers cheerfully hacking carcasses to the beat, by a man (Charles Bruin) shaving in his undershorts who joins the throng in the hallway, and finally by the crowds in the street below.

The premier is delighted, as well as sympathetic to whatever is obviously troubling the beautiful lady. He will be happy to see her later to discuss her problem.

As they start in to dinner, a mysterious messenger arrives, bearing her brother Jack's ring. Boniface (George Regas) tells Marie her brother has been wounded escaping from prison and needs help. She starts to call the premier, but

Marie sets out to find her fugitive brother in the wilderness, accompanied by Boniface (George Regas).

Her brother's photo on a wanted poster. *Courtesy Jack Tillmany.*

Sergeant Bruce (Nelson). Leading a squadron for a casual trot, he delivers the famous melody in excellent voice. The effect is somewhat lessened by the fact that his men are on a rear projection screen. Considering that some superb location footage was shot for this film and the songs were prerecorded, it is occasionally irritating to jump back and forth in the same scene between genuine exteriors and studio shots with obvious rear projection.

At Mountie headquarters, Sergeant Bruce learns that his next assignment is to track down the killer of a fellow Mountie. He studies the poster: "John Flower, no known relatives, believed to be hiding near Lake Chibougam." He assures the Commandant (Russell Hicks) that he won't fail and rides off to a vigorous reprise of "The Mounties."

Marie and Boniface have reached the outpost nearest Lake Chibougam. A steady stream of Indians passes on their way to a big festival that night. The town itself is a beehive of activity. The local café is doing a good business in drinks

Boniface stops her. A pardon will do no good. Jack has killed a Mountie.

Marie half faints with horror, but family loyalty is too strong. She borrows all the cash she can from the unsuspecting Myerson and prepares to follow Boniface into the wilderness.

(Here, a charming scene is deleted from the final release print. Marie, modestly dressed, makes her way unnoticed through the adoring crowd outside the hotel. All are staring up at her window. "We've been friends for years," brags one man to another, looking Marie straight in the eye and not recognizing her. A taxi driver is reluctant to leave the scene to take her to the train station: "She may sing again," he protests. "I assure you she won't," snaps Marie.)

To the ominous pounding strains of "The Mounties," we see stock footage of uniformed Mounties in training formation—how much better to have implied that they were on Jack's trail—dissolving into our first glimpse of

When her guide absconds with her money, Marie must sing for her supper or starve. She is quickly upstaged by a local songstress. (Jimmy Conlin at the piano.) *Courtesy Jack Tillmany.*

and fights, so Marie decides she isn't really hungry. She passes on to the general store. There she chooses a wardrobe of boots, pants, and heavy woolen shirts, then finds her purse is missing from her pocketbook. Boniface is also missing.

The storekeeper (silent comedian Lucien Littlefield) urges her to report her loss to the new Mountie on duty. Sergeant Bruce is a crack man, he tells her, sent out after the death of their last constable. He'll get her money back!

But Marie is understandably reluctant to run into the Sergeant. She dashes off in search of Boniface, and the first thing she sees is a WANTED poster with Jack's picture. She races on, the music churning in a nightmare sequence punctuated by leering faces and shoving crowds. Imposed over the images is a succession of imaginary newspaper headlines ending with "Flower Hangs." At last, exhausted and starving, Marie returns to the lights of the café. A woman is singing inside.

Marie seeks out the manager (Robert Greig) and asks him for a job. The only kind of job they have, he explains, is dishwashing. Any singing done in his place is strictly on an amateur basis. He points to the evening's songbird who is happily collecting the loose change thrown to her. Swallowing her pride, Marie agrees to try.

The piano player (James Conlin) suggests "something hot." "Could you put it up a key?" she asks. "That's the only key I know!" She waits pathetically for the crowd to quiet down. When it becomes obvious they have no intention of doing so, she raggedly launches into "Dinah." The beat is too fast for her, and she hurries along, several notes behind the music. She is mortified, but the piano player encourages her. He pulls another piece of music from the pile and she does better with "Some of These Days," another revival from the days of "coon songs." (Sophie Tucker, the famed "coon shouter" of twenty years earlier, had just been signed by MGM and her picture appears prominently on the sheet music covers in Jeanette's hand.)

Marie's singing rival is Belle (Broadway star Gilda Gray). According to legend, Gray named the "shimmy" dance when she lispingly told a reporter she was shaking her chemise. *Courtesy Anna Michalik.*

Sergeant Bruce enters and is quickly surrounded by admiring females including Belle, Marie's singing rival. The Sergeant's attention is diverted by the peculiar songstress trying to be heard over the roar of the café. Belle (stage star Gilda Gray, queen of the "shimmy") decides to show up this decidedly uncompetitive competitor and delivers her very loud and very physical rendition of the song. Poor Marie is momentarily nonplused, then tries to mimic Belle's vocal phrasing and gyrations. She is finally eclipsed and flees the café, followed by the Sergeant.

Sgt. Bruce (Eddy) enjoys some of the comforts of civilization before going into the wilderness to search for his comrade's murderer. Left to right, Robert Greig, Bert Lindley, Gilda Gray, Eddy, unidentified extra.

He commiserates with her, telling her that she has a beautiful voice and that Belle was just jealous. "If she ever got lumbago, she couldn't sing a note." Marie tries desperately to lose the Sergeant, but he has heard about her robbery. He ushers her into the small cabin that serves as his office. "Name?" he asks. Her battered suitcase belongs to Roderick and bears a prominent R. "Rose," she blurts out.

"Rose...Marie de Flor," he murmurs. "I always thought your name was just *Marie* de Flor." He recognized her voice the minute he heard her sing. She decides to admit her identity and try a different tack. He must know how it is when one's every move is watched. She has come up here to meet "someone." She lowers her eyes suggestively.

The Sergeant is sure they will find Boniface and her money at the Indian festival that night. Crossing the moonlit lake in a canoe, he deplores helping her get to another man. What's he like? he asks. A big banker? A poet? A polo player? "He's an Italian tenor," she tells him sarcastically. "I'm not Italian," he replies, "but

Rose Marie

as for the singing..." He serenades her with the lushly romantic "Rose Marie," ending with a glowing high note.

She compliments him on his composing skill, and he launches into a reprise: "Oh, Caroline, I love you." "Ah, ah, ah. It was 'Rose Marie' a moment ago." "What did I say?" "'Caroline.'" It seems he fits each new name to the rhythm, courting nearly every girl in the neighborhood. But it doesn't work with some names, he tells her. "It didn't work with Maude—but then nothing worked with Maude."

They reach the Indian camp where the Sergeant is greeted by many of the revelers. He finds "Rose Marie" a safe perch on a tree branch to view the "Totem Tom-Tom" dance. Choreographed by Chester Hale and staged out of doors, this dance can't quite decide whether it is a recreation of an Indian dance or strictly Hollywood fantasy, and it loses slightly on both counts. However, it is quite effective, a joyous hymn to the harvest that avoids the sex-and-sadism trademark of Busby Berkeley's "Totem Tom-Tom" in the 1954 remake.

Though "Rose Marie" tries desperately to avoid the Mountie, Sgt. Bruce recognizes her as the famous Marie de Flor. He insists on taking her to the Indian festival in search of Boniface. In the canoe, she gets quite a surprise.

Rose Marie ignores the romance of the evening and the Sergeant's inclinations and goes in search of her guide. Suddenly she spots him and he tries to hide. The Sergeant collars the suspicious-looking "half breed," but Rose Marie carefully denies knowing him. She suggests that she wander alone through the crowd while Sergeant Bruce attends to business. Unknown to her, he is questioning the Indians about John Flower.

She finds Boniface again and demands that he take her to her brother or she will turn him over to the police. He must pick up supplies and meet her at the wharf in an hour. Sergeant Bruce escorts her back to the inn and begs her to wait there a week until he returns from his duties in the mountains. To get rid of him, she agrees.

Quickly she gathers up her things to leave, but then a voice is heard outside the window. It is the Sergeant, serenading her with "Just For You." It is impossible to get away, so she settles down to enjoy the haunting love song. He finishes and warbles an exultant "*Au revoir, Rose Marie...*" toppling backwards from his perch on a pile of barrels.

Relaxing on location at Lake Tahoe.

"Totem Tom-Tom." *Courtesy Anna Michalik.*

Whistling happily, Sergeant Bruce (we never learn his first name!) returns to Mountie headquarters, where an old friend, "Pop" (Bert Lindley), is waiting to say goodbye in case they never see each other again. Bruce laughs off the premonition, his thoughts on "Rose Marie de Flor." Pop laughs. "Sounds like some kind of soap," he comments. "It's Spanish," Bruce replies. "Means 'flower.' Rose Marie Flower. — *Flower!*"

Rushing back to the inn, he finds that she is gone. "Anything wrong?" inquires the innkeeper who is also the café owner—a small town indeed. "Couldn't be better," Bruce assures him.

Deep in the wilderness, Boniface uses a small map to show Rose Marie where they are headed. His mother is hiding Jack in her cabin, just outside Hayman's Landing, several days' journey away. While waiting for Boniface to tend to the horses, Rose Marie discovers the echo from the nearby cliffs. With childish bravado, she joins herself in a round of "Three Blind Mice." Sergeant Bruce hears her from across the valley and smiles to himself.

Rose Marie and Boniface head on until stopped by a rushing river. She urges crossing it rather than going around. It will save them time, although she has never swum a horse before. Sergeant Bruce reaches the crest of a nearby hill just in time to see Rose Marie swept from her struggling horse. Boniface starts to rescue her, then sees the descending Mountie and flees into the forest. Rose Marie is pulled from the water and revived by the somber Sergeant.

He insists she wear his coat to avoid a chill. Haughtily, she refuses his offer of further assistance and sits down on a rock to await Boniface's return. Bruce makes camp a few yards away and soon the smell of food is too much for her. It is dark. Her horse and guide are gone. She is lost, alone with Sergeant Bruce. Robbed completely of her pride, she must depend on him for her existence.

She gobbles the offered beans and humbly apologizes for her behavior. Bruce leaves the circle of firelight to check on the horses, and she panics. She rushes after him and into his outstretched arms, but the threatening creature she heard in the underbrush is only a soft-eyed doe.

From across the lake comes a floating call, distant, mysterious, like a strange wild bird. "Just an Indian," Bruce tells her. "Listen." From far away comes an answering feminine call.

It is an old Indian legend, he tells her. Years ago two lovers from different tribes met here. Their families were enemies, sort of a Romeo and Juliet affair. They were discovered and sentenced to die, but their spirits still live. When a lover gives the call, their spirits echo it, sending it on until it reaches the one he loves. Rose Marie is moved by the beauty of it. She stands at the edge of the lake and gives the haunting call. Sergeant Bruce takes it up and sings the classic "Indian Love Call."

It is late. The Sergeant gives Rose Marie his tent and insists she pass her damp clothing out to

The haughty Marie, now "Rose Marie," loses her guide and horse and must accept the Sergeant's help. Soaked, she reluctantly borrows his coat and eats his canned beans.

him to hang by the fire. As she hands him each garment, he searches it carefully, but she has kept the map. The events of the day have not stifled her feminine instincts either. Behind the tent walls, she can be heard delicately tearing a strip from her camisole to make rag curlers for her hair. Bruce nods in amusement. In the stillness of the night, Rose Marie hums the "Indian Love Call." Beside the campfire, Sergeant Bruce quietly hums the response.

The next morning brings a splendid view of the countryside and the news that they will have to travel together for the next three days. The nearest place where Rose Marie can pick up a guide is Hayman's Landing. With throbbing heart, Rose Marie follows Bruce into the pines. Soon she is an experienced "trail hand," saddling the horses and cooking over a campfire. The time is gone too soon.

On their last night together, they stand on a cliff overlooking the valley where tomorrow she will find Hayman's Landing and her brother Jack. The setting sun moves the Sergeant to quote Shakespeare: "And this, our life, exempt

The beauty of the wilderness brings the two together.

from public haunts, finds tongues in trees, books in running brooks, sermons in stones and good in everything." He is such a contradiction. Rose Marie doesn't understand how he can spend his life tracking down poor creatures. She gestures to the majesty around them. Doesn't this make him more charitable? Nature, he tells her, is far from charitable. Everyone must pay for what they do. The cruelty is when others must pay for it too.

Rose Marie begs him to give up being a Mountie and let her help him become a singer. "I belong up here," he says simply. The Indian call is heard from below. Tonight there is no answer. Bruce asks her about the man she is going to. She must love him very much. "Yes...I do," she chokes. The call is heard again and she asks him to return it. He answers and then they sing it together. Each knows that whatever happens tomorrow, they will never again be together without something between them.

They admit they love each other. Both are willing to accept the moment. She asks him to come to her if she ever calls him, and he promises. Then reality returns. Bruce rises abruptly. They will go on to Hayman's Landing immediately.

He delivers her to the trading post and coldly takes his leave. When she gets back to the city, he tells her, she won't want to see him. Rose Marie protests, but he silences her: "You'll remember me for what I am—a policeman."

Rose Marie

Eluding Sgt. Bruce, Marie finds her brother, Jack (Jimmy Stewart). *Courtesy Anna Michalik.*

Hours later, she reaches the remote cabin and has a tender reunion with Jack (Jimmy Stewart). He promises her he will start fresh with the money she has brought, but his restlessness and need for excitement are evident to anyone but the most loving sister. He tells her he has been thinking of going to China. Desperately she begs him to stay in touch with her. "You're all I have left in the world. You'll be good, won't you?" "I'll give it a fling," he smiles.

Sergeant Bruce appears suddenly in the doorway, gun in hand. Quickly he handcuffs the cringing Jack. Rose Marie begs him to let Jack go. "He's my *brother*!"

"I know," Bruce replies quietly. He takes Jack to a waiting horse and starts along the path, leaving Marie sobbing hysterically. She tries to call them back, singing the "Indian Love Call," but Bruce's oath is stronger than his promise.

Later on the trail, Jack asks the Sergeant about the excitement his arrest will cause. He always did like excitement, Jack tells the sergeant in a touching vignette. The scene fades.

Somewhere in the world, Marie is on another opera stage performing the last act of *Tosca*. The drama of the scene may be partially lost on those not familiar with the opera, but the general plot comes through. The famous actress ("La Tosca") has been tricked into thinking she can escape with her lover, Mario, after he undergoes a "mock" execution. She tells Mario (Allan Jones) of the plan and happily rehearses him in his phony death scene. "What an artist!" she exclaims as he topples from the all-too-real bullets. The firing squad departs, and she calls to him to rise. He is dead. Trapped on the parapet by the soldiers of the man she has murdered trying to make good Mario's escape, she leaps to her death. It is not exactly a direct operatic parable, but it does give a strong sense of the irony of death and of Marie's feelings about her brother's execution.

A tasteful but powerful parallel might have been drawn if Marie had "seen" her brother's face over that of the opera hero during the stage

But Bruce has trailed her. She begs him not to arrest Jack and take him back to be hanged. Can Bruce put duty before love?

The opera sequences were sung by Jeanette and tenor Allan Jones. Here they do the last act of *Tosca*. Jones was just starting in films. A few years later, he would star in MGM's film version of Rudolf Friml's *The Firefly* with Jeanette.

execution. Instead, for no dramatically valid reason, she keeps hearing the voice of Sergeant Bruce singing "Indian Love Call." The intermingling of Puccini and Friml is intriguing. Finally, the lady hits a perfect high note and collapses in the middle of the stage.

Now the finale. Does Marie forgive Sergeant Bruce and go in search of him, calling to him across the incredibly beautiful pine forest where they first fell in love? Does he answer her and gallop to her side? Are the lovers reunited in music, clinging to each other in the sunset? No. It is as if location money ran out, and the final moments occur on a soundstage with all the wild romance of an afternoon tea.

Marie retires to an elaborate hunting lodge *cum* nursing home, complete with soundstage snow swirling outside the window. In a bit of exposition with Myerson, we learn that she has been reclining on the chintz-covered chaise lounge for six months, not singing a note, not caring about anything. Myerson departs, saying how disappointed he was not to hear her voice echoing through the (blizzardy) hills when he arrived. This is apparently the lady's cue, for she takes up the first strains of the "Indian Love Call."

Sergeant Bruce, prompted by Myerson, steps out of the foyer where he has been hiding and joins her in the chorus on the chaise lounge. A very pallid ending for a picture that has built so well and so dramatically to a much more satisfying conclusion.

The public responded enthusiastically to the good in the picture, and the fan magazines now proclaimed the existence of a "team." The studio began preparing another operetta for the "Singing Sweethearts," this time by the third major operetta composer of the twentieth century, Sigmund Romberg. But Miss MacDonald, perhaps fighting the team image, had another idea. She wanted to keep her own identity and was willing to shoot for the moon, Hollywood variety.

Preparing to shoot a publicity still on location at Lake Tahoe. *Courtesy Gene Arceri.*

Reviews

The popular press rushed to herald the "team" and Nelson Eddy. "Rose Marie stars make perfect team," wrote Kate Cameron in the *New York News*. "Judging by the reception accorded him, the tall, blond and husky concert baritone, Nelson Eddy, has become a serious threat to Clark Gable for the honor of being the movies'

The finished still.

No. 1 matinee idol" - Rose Pelswick, *New York Journal*.

The more staid *New York Times* reported: "As blithely melodious and rich in scenic beauty as any picture that has come from Hollywood. To paraphrase Fletcher, let Jeanette MacDonald and Nelson Eddy sing an operetta's love songs and we care not who may write its book. In splendid voice, whether singing solo or in duet, they prove to be fully as delightful a combination here as they were in Naughty Marietta."

Variety praised the new libretto, the director, the stars, and just about every major scene in the film. "A box-office honey." However, they deplored the unflattering effect of the Mountie hat on Eddy. "From Bill Hart down, the kiddies never could quite look very Romeo underneath that hunk of Stetson."

Recordings (See Discography for further information)

"Indian Love Call" (with "Ah, Sweet Mystery of Life" from *Naughty Marietta* on the reverse) sold over a million copies—the only song from the stage score that Jeanette recorded.
Nelson also recorded an album of the stage songs with Dorothy Kirsten:
"Door of My Dreams" from stage score (Eddy)
"I Love Him" from stage score (Eddy, Kirsten)
"Indian Love Call" (with MacDonald and, again, with Kirsten)
"The Mounties" (Eddy)
"Totem Tom-Tom" (Eddy and Kirsten)
"Pretty Things" from stage score (Kirsten)
"Why Shouldn't We?" from stage score (Kirsten)
MacDonald also recorded "Juliette's Waltz" ("Je veux vivre dans ce rêve") from Gounod's *Roméo et Juliette*.

Music in the Film

In most minds, composer Rudolf Friml is synonymous with *Rose Marie*, so it is surprising to learn that Herbert Stothart wrote most of the score of the 1924 stage production before he became MGM's musical director in the 1930s. He is credited with the numerous bits of incidental music ("Prelude," "Opening," "Wanda's Entrance," etc.), three songs ("Hard Boiled Herman," "Why Shouldn't We," and "Only a Kiss"), and as co-composer of "The Mounties" and "Totem Tom-Tom."

In listing performers after each title, "and" denotes a genuine duet, while commas between names indicate a sequence of singers.

Overture: "Indian Love Call" (chorus, MacDonald), "Rose Marie" INTO:
Scenes from *Roméo et Juliette*, music by Charles Gounod, libretto by Jules Barbier and Michel Carré. *
    Opening of Act I, Capulet's Ball (chorus)
    Roméo's entrance recitative (chorus, Allan Jones as Roméo, baritone as Mercutio)
    "Je veux vivre dans ce rêve" (MacDonald)
    Act I finale montage (chorus)
    Act III duel
    Act IV with Friar Lawrence (bass)
    Act V death scene (MacDonald and Jones)
"Tes Yeux" (MacDonald) - music by René Alphonse Rabey
"Pardon Me, Madame" (MacDonald and chorus, nine soloists including Delos Jewkes, Pat West) - music by Herbert Stothart, lyrics by Gus Kahn
"The Mounties" (Eddy, male chorus) - originally "Song of the Mounties," music by Friml and Stothart, lyrics by Otto Harbach and Oscar Hammerstein II
"The Mounties" reprise (men's chorus, baritone dubbing for Graham, Eddy)
"St. Louis Blues" fragment (Gray) - by W. C. Handy

Rose Marie 221

Director Van Dyke asked Eddy to get more spring into a running leap onto a horse. On his next try, Eddy sailed clear over the horse and landed in some bushes. His head reappeared: "Too much spring, huh?"

"The Indian Love Call" reunites the lovers. *Courtesy Jack Tillmany.*

"Dinah" (MacDonald) - music by Harry Akst, lyrics by Sam Lewis and Joe Young

"Some of These Days" (MacDonald, Gray) - by Shelton Brooks

"Rose Marie" (Eddy, MacDonald sings two lines in comic reprise) - music by Friml, lyrics by Hammerstein and Harbach

"Totem Tom-Tom" (chorus) - music by Friml and Stothart, lyrics by Hammerstein and Harbach

"Just for You" (Eddy) - adapted from Jim's melody line in "Finaletto" sextet, music by Friml, adapted by Stothart, new lyrics by Gus Kahn

"Three Blind Mice" (MacDonald with echo) - traditional

"Indian Love Call" (Eddy, MacDonald) - originally "The Call," music by Friml, lyrics by Harbach and Hammerstein. Sung four times:

1. Earl Covert, tenor, unknown soprano, MacDonald gives "call," Eddy sings.
2. MacDonald hums; Eddy hums.
3. Soprano, Earl Covert give call; MacDonald and Eddy sing duet.
4. MacDonald, sobbing, sings to departing Eddy.

Tosca, Act III, from Tosca's entrance (MacDonald as Tosca, Jones as Mario, bass, tenor**) - music by Giacomo Puccini, libretto by Giuseppe Giacosa and Luigi Illica. Interpolated fragment of "Indian Love Call" (Eddy).

"Indian Love Call" reprise (Eddy joined by MacDonald)

* Pay records indicate Olga Dane sang and acted, Alesandro Giglio recorded only.

** Pay records indicate that Earl Covert, voice of the lovesick brave, also recorded a bit for the *Tosca* sequence.

Songs from the stage version used in the film are "Indian Love Call," "Rose Marie," "Totem Tom-Tom," and "[Song of] The Mounties." "Finaletto" was adapted into "Just for You." Many will mourn the omission of the lovely "Door of My Dreams" from the 1936 film. It was included in the 1954 remake.

Script History
Contributed by Mary Truesdell

Producer Hunt Stromberg was in charge of following up the 1935 smash hit *Naughty Marietta* with a film starring Nelson and diva Grace Moore, writes Mary Truesdell in her 2003 monograph. Since it would have been ludicrous to cast Moore as the naïve peasant girl of the stage and silent versions, Stromberg's idea was to force a spoiled opera singer out of her element and into a New World where she would meet a "real man," the Mountie.

A gimmick in several preliminary scripts was the Singing Waterfall where "Roget" (later Marie) would meet "Sgt. Bruce Marlowe." There, he tells her about the Indian lovers who flung themselves over the falls when their tribes forbade them to marry. Script conferences indicate a debate about whether Jimmy Stewart's character should nobly sacrifice himself and aid the romance by going over the falls in a canoe, so that Bruce wouldn't be responsible for turning him in to hang. One version even had the distraught heroine return to the falls after her brother's death and contemplate suicide before she hears the Mountie's call! Wiser heads prevailed.

Movie Goofs

Movie magic sometimes comes about because scenes are routinely shot out of sequence and then rearranged in the editing process or parts of the same scene are shot on different days. Costumes may change within the same scene, props appear and disappear. The continuity person (called a "script girl" in the old days) tried desperately to prevent these mistakes, but sometimes they slipped in. Here are some favorites spotted by sharp-eyed fans.

The handkerchief in the pocket of Jeanette's suede jacket keeps disappearing and reappearing. When she takes off her boots to dry, Nelson puts his pipe in his pocket. Yet a moment later he is puffing on it. (Anna Michalik)

One of the most frequently noticed goofs is the hotel manager's nightshirt. In the hall, it is a solid medium color with a few horizontal stripes at the hem. As he steps through a doorway, it becomes white with vertical dark stripes. (Elsa Dik Glass and Julie Illescas)

Also, the same actor, Robert Greig, plays the saloon manager with one accent, and then later in the film, appears as the hotel manager with a different accent. Since, with moral restrictions of The Code, MGM certainly didn't want to imply that Jeanette was renting a room over a saloon, this was probably an oversight in casting. Actors like Greig worked so often on so many films that perhaps no one noticed he was on screen in two roles in the same film! (Author)

When Nelson sings "Rose Marie," there is a distinct, moving shadow under his arm, apparently the rocking mechanism for the canoe. Also, the many references to the time of day rarely correspond to the shadows! Like when Nelson makes beans and bacon for supper, and the sun is directly overhead. Also the first two 'Wanted' posters for Jimmy Stewart list his height as 6'1" but the third says 5'8." (Tricia Lutz)

When they roll in the huge drum in preparation for the Indian dance, they tip it on top of a black iron pot that has a fire under it. Nevertheless, in the next scene they are dancing on top of it with no evidence of smoke or fire. (Dorothy Hill)

Trivia

The November 1929 *Photoplay* reported that Carlotta King, heroine of the 1929 film *The Desert Song* opposite John Boles, had been signed to a five-year contract by MGM. "She will next be heard in the sound version of *Rose-Marie*." (MGM had just made a silent version with Joan Crawford.)

Pierre Berton's excellent book, *Hollywood's Canada,* points out several errors in Canadian geography, history, botany, and anthropology in *Rose Marie*. "The Indians, [Eddy] adds, come from miles around to take part in [the festival]. And they certainly do. The dance that follows seems to borrow something from every Indian culture: there are Plains headdresses, Mexican shawls, Aztec breech clouts…west-coast totem poles, drums twelve feet high, and the Great Spirit knows what else—an aboriginal mulligan stew that makes a joke of Canadian Indian culture." Berton also indicates that, given an understandable lack of enthusiasm for Hollywood's misguided stereotypes and often egregious errors, the much-publicized cooperation of the Royal Canadian Mounted Police was far less enthusiastic than MGM indicated.

Berton further notes that of the hundreds of Hollywood films depicting Mounties, at least thirty have the Love-versus-Duty theme. Of these, *nine* require the Mountie to bring in his sweetheart's brother.

While the area of location shooting was called Lake Tahoe in that summer of 1935, the official name for the lake itself from 1883 to 1945 was actually Lake Bigler, named after California's third governor. (E.B. Scott's *Saga of Lake Tahoe* has a good section on the different names Lake Tahoe has had over the years.) The name Tahoe may come from an Anglo distortion of the Washoe word "Da ow a ga," or "lake of the sky." (Thanks to Sara Larson, Executive Director of the North Lake Tahoe Historical Society.)

A Rose Marie Honeymoon

A faded 1935 newspaper clipping describes the adventure of a young couple at Lake Tahoe:

> Honeymooning on a shoestring almost proved disastrous to a young Los Angeles couple, Mr. and Mrs. Jimmy de Fremery. They found themselves stranded and penniless at Lake Tahoe, facing a long hitch-hike home until they met Col. W.S. Van Dyke, the director. De Fremery, who is 21 years of age, chanced to stroll into Van Dyke's film camp at the lake where he is making "Rose Marie" with Jeanette MacDonald and Nelson Eddy. He bared his story "to that big, tall guy." The director was impressed by Jimmy's story and his appearance and hired him as assistant property man. Then he summoned the bride and put her to work as an extra.

James and Eileen de Fremery never forgot the kindness of the Hollywood film company to young newlyweds. Although Jeanette and Jimmy Stewart both posed for James' camera (Jeanette confidently and professionally, Stewart with a typical "aw-shucks" slouch). Nelson was either too busy or too shy to pose. De Fremery's only shots of Nelson are all long-distance over the camera crew's shoulders while Nelson is hard at work.

James de Fremery's on-location snapshots. Here, Jeanette and the pet fawn used in the film.

All photos courtesy James de Fremery.

Jimmy Stewart during filming at Lake Tahoe.

The set for "Totem Tom-Tom," with Emerald Bay beyond. The area is now totally grown over with trees. One of the decaying totem poles resides in a nearby junkyard.

Over the years, many more film projects were proposed and planned than could ever be made. Sometimes, ideas were announced to gauge public response or just to keep the stars' names in print. Here is a trade magazine ad for the operetta *Robin Hood*. The copy reads: "The dashing, thrillingly romantic story of Robin Hood, the heroic marauder of Sherwood Forest. His exploits, packed with hazardous adventure and chivalrous pursuit of the girl whom he loves, provide the screen with one of its most exciting stories, set against a gala background of rural England in the Middle Ages." Of course, the image of Nelson Eddy leaping about in tights must have given some studio execs pause. Wiser heads tailored his vehicles to emphasize what he did best: sincerity and gentlemanliness. In any event, Warner Bros. soon did a non-musical, Technicolor version with Errol Flynn that was such a hit that MGM would not have risked comparison. *Courtesy Tom Linehan.*

RIGHT: Nelson always considered himself a serious musician who did films on the side. His film contracts guaranteed him time off to go on his concert tours. Movie fans who rushed to his performances thinking they'd be hearing Friml and Romberg instead got a full evening of the vocal classics. He sang his film hits only as encores—of which there were many. *Courtesy Alex Soto and Marlyse Fuller.*

Rose Marie

San Francisco

MGM.
Released June 26, 1936.
Directed by W.S. Van Dyke II.
Produced by John Emerson and Bernard H. Hyman.
115 minutes.

German titles: *San Franzisko*, reissued as *San Francisco, Stadt der Sünde* (San Francisco, City of Sin)

Story: Robert Hopkins. Screenplay: Anita Loos. Cinematographer: Oliver T. Marsh. Recording Engineer: Douglas Shearer. Film Editor: Tom Held. Art Director: Cedric Gibbons. Costumes: Adrian. Musical Director: Herbert Stothart. Dances: Val Raset. Mob scene directed by D.W. Griffith. Additional Dialogue: Erich von Stroheim. Special effects (unbilled): James Basevi. Assistant Director: Joseph M. Newman. Third-unit Director: Earl Taggert. Montage Effects/Second-unit Director: John Hoffman. Art Associates: Arnold Gillespie, Harry McAfee, Edwin B. Willis. Opera sequences staged by William von Wymetal. Vocal instructor: Paul Lamkoff.

Clark Gable (Blackie Norton)
Jeanette MacDonald (Mary Blake)
Spencer Tracy (Father Tim Mullin)
Jack Holt (Jack Burley)
Ted Healy (Matt)
Margaret Irving (Della Bailey)
Jessie Ralph (Maisie Burley)
Harold Huber (Babe)
Al Shean (Professor)
William Ricciardi (Baldini)
Kenneth Harlan (Chick)
Roger Imhof (Alaska)
Frank Mayo (Dealer)
Charles Judels (Tony)
Russell Simpson (Red Kelly)
Bert Roach (Freddy Duane)
Warren B. Hymer (Hazeltine)
Edgar Kennedy (Sheriff Jim, process server)
Shirley Ross [AKA Bernice Gaunt] (Trixie)
Tandy MacKenzie (Faust)
Tudor Williams (Mephistopheles)
Spec O'Donnell (Man praying)
Bob McKenzie (Messenger)
Adrienne d'Ambricourt (Madam Albani)
Nigel de Brulier (Old man)
Mae Digges, Nyas Berry (Dancers)
John Kelly (Stagehand)
Tom Mahoney (Police captain)
Jim Farley (Charlie, a policeman)
Wilbur Mack (Bartender)
Pat O'Malley, Ortho Wright (Firemen)
Gertrude Astor (Drunk's girl)
Tom Dugan [cut from print] (Drunk)
Belle Mitchell (Louise, Mary's maid)
Fred M. Fagan (Waiter)
James Brewster, Samuel Glasser, John Pearson (Stooges)
Jason Robards Sr (Father)
William (Billy) Newell (Man in bread line)
James Macklin (Young man)
Tom McGuire (Bartender)
Harry C. Myers (Forrestal, a reveler)
Vince Barnett (Drunk)
Edward Hearn (Parishioner)
Henry Roquemore (Dave, a drinker)
G. Pat Collins (Bartender)
Harry Strang (Soldier)
Vernon Dent (Fat man)
Irving Bacon (Picnicker)
Orrin Burke (Pompous man)
David Thursby (Man)
John "Skins" Miller (Man on stretcher)
Helen Shipman (Bit)
George Goul, Edward Earle (Bit men)
Maude Allan (Elderly woman)
Jack Baxley (Kinko, campaigner)
Carl Stockdale (Salvation Army man)
Anthony Jowitt (Society man)
Jane Barnes (Girl)
Richard Carle, Oscar Apfel, Frank Sheridan, Ralph Lewis (Members of Founders' Club)
Chester Gan (Jowl Lee)
Jack Kennedy (Mike, old Irishman in Church)
Cy Kendall (Headwaiter)
Don Rowan (Barbary Coast type)
Sherry Hall (Well-wisher)
Ben Taggart (Cop)
Long Beach Boys' Choir (Choir)
St. Luke's Choristers (Choir) *
Dennis O'Keefe (New Year's celebrant)
Charles Sullivan (Fire spectator)
Beatrice Roberts (Forrestal, a guest)
Bruce Mitchell (Heckler)
Sidney Bracy (Burley's butler)

San Francisco

Tommy Bupp (Bill, a newsboy)
Bill O'Brien (Waiter)
Sam Ash (Orchestra leader)
Bud Geary (Man restraining Blackie after the quake)
George Magrill (Marine)
Walter Huston, J. Delos Jewkes, Homer Hall, Douglas McPhail ("Battle Hymn of the Republic" singers)
Hector V. Samo ("San Francisco" singer)
Ben Hall (Club patron)
Philo McCullough (Father, "Battle Hymn of the Republic")
Moyer Bupp, Henry Hanna, Jasper Sock (Boys)
Marilyn Harris, Elaine Von, Helen Westcott (Girls)
Edgar Edwards ("The fire's out!")
Bits: King Baggott, Rhea Mitchell, Flora Finch, Fritzi Brunette, Helene Chadwick, Naomi Childers, Rosemary Theby, Jean Acker, Donald Hall, Dave Marks, Mary MacLaren, Myrtle Stedman

* With W. Ripley Door. Another source also credits the Mitchell Boys' Choir.

Oscar for Best Sound Recording: Douglas Shearer
Oscar nominations: Best Picture, Best Actor (Spencer Tracy), Best Director, Best Original Story (Robert Hopkins), Best Assistant Director (Joseph Newman)
New York Film Critics' "Ten Best" list
Film Daily's "Ten Best" list
Photoplay's Gold Medal Award, 1936
One of the twenty-five top-grossing films of 1935-36

San Francisco was nominated for an Oscar and named one of the ten best films of 1936 by *Film Daily*. Its near-Cecil B. DeMillian blend of sex and religion, happy sin, and last reel retribution made it an all-time box-office smash. It remains a glorious blockbuster from the "golden age," and if its obligatory theme of divine punishment for sinfulness (i.e., drinking, gambling, exposing female legs) has lost a bit of its punch, the tremendous earthquake sequence has not.

Jeanette MacDonald now had two top box-office films with Nelson Eddy behind her. MGM was readying the old Romberg operetta, *Maytime*, for her and Eddy, but, wanting to ensure her reputation as a single personality, she chose to wait for Clark Gable to finish another

Gable was reluctant to make a film with Jeanette, fearing he'd just be standing around while she sang.

assignment so that he could appear with her in *San Francisco*.

Writer Robert Hopkins had brought the story idea to Jeanette and asked her help in getting it before the bosses. She liked the story and recommended it to Ed Mannix and then to Louis B. Mayer. Gable, they felt, was ideal for the tough café owner, but he was understandably reluctant. All he would have to do was stand there while Jeanette sang, not his idea of a good picture. The film was rewritten to give him plenty of "Gable" scenes, and he relented. However, his displeasure was still such that he showed up on the set for his first love scene reeking of garlic. When Mary Blake pales and clings to Blackie's lapels after their first screen kiss, it may not have been entirely acting.

San Francisco is widely touted as being Spencer Tracy's first "good guy" role. Actually

Mary Blake (Jeanette) is a small-town girl who comes to San Francisco for an operatic career and ends up auditioning for a job in a Barbary Coast dive run by Blackie Norton (Gable, left). Matt (Ted Healy) is skeptical, but Blackie hires her.

MGM itself had "type-cast" Tracy in gangster parts after signing him as a "backup" to Gable under its policy of having a similar type player under contract in case a major star became difficult or ill.

Tracy's newly discovered "spirituality" had already shown strongly in such earlier films as *The Power and the Glory* for Fox and the classic *Man's Castle* at Columbia. Interestingly, Tracy and Gable were both originally spotted by Hollywood while playing Killer Mears in stage versions of *The Last Mile*. (Preston Foster played the role in the 1932 film.)

MGM's research department, under the direction of Nathalie Bucknall, did a Herculean amount of digging into surviving records of the 1906 earthquake (or, as San Franciscans archly insist, the "1906 fire"). This was the heyday of the research department, when studio income permitted a vast outlay in the interests of authenticity. All details down to the screw holding on a doorknob (with the obvious exception of the women's costumes and hairstyles) could be certified absolutely historically correct. This would continue until World War II took the money and technicians necessary for great historical epics. Never again

San Francisco

would authenticity be the servant of such rousing good filmmaking.

The stark reality of the earthquake-fire sequences in *San Francisco* comes ultimately from the brilliance of the images, not their actual occurrence in history. Although uncredited, the superb special effects are the work of James Basevi, who created some of the screen's finest cataclysms (i.e., the plague of locusts in MGM's *The Good Earth*, the hurricane in United Artists' *The Hurricane*).

The tone of the film is set by an opening title: "San Francisco, guardian of the Golden Gate, stands today as a queen among seaports ...industrious, mature, respectable...but perhaps she dreams of the queen and city she was... splendid and sensuous, vulgar and magnificent... that perished suddenly with a cry still heard in the hearts of those who knew her at exactly 5:13 AM, April 18, 1906." The parchment on which this pronouncement is inscribed bursts into flames.

Missing from the final release print is an opening flashback showing Clark Gable and Spencer Tracy as newsboy chums twenty years earlier. Only a vestigial title remains, returning us to 1905. It is New Year's Eve, and, in a dizzying display of cutting room pyrotechnics, we join the revelers swirling through the snow of confetti and streamers, laughing, dancing in the streets, cheering an elegantly gowned lady mounted on a carriage horse, and filling mugs of wine from Lotta's Fountain (still standing on Market Street). Freddy Duane (Bert Roach), the king of the local wine merchants has opened his warehouse.

Duane is congratulated on this advertising coup by a passing gentleman in opera cape. The gentleman turns toward the camera, and we discover our hero, Blackie Norton (Clark Gable). He is apparently well known in this section of San Francisco for he is warmly greeted by everyone, including a carriage full of seductively clad ladies from a local establishment, presided over by the regal Della (Margaret Irving).

A horse-drawn firetruck streaks through the crowd heading for the Barbary Coast, and Blackie leaps aboard. It isn't his joint that is on fire though, just an old rooming house. Blackie stays to see the last occupants, two children, leap into a net and then saunters on down the crowded sidewalk. In the crowd, he pushes past a tired young lady with a small valise.

Blackie enters one of the brighter nightspots, the Paradise, with an air of authority that proclaims him the owner. On the raised stage at one end of the crowded room, the ladies of the chorus are heralding the new year, led by Trixie (Shirley Ross, who would achieve immortality of sorts when she and Bob Hope introduced "Thanks for the Memory" in *The Big Broadcast of 1938*). Blackie's relationship with Trixie is made clear when she wipes his shoes clean and docilely accepts his snatching a rhinestone dog collar from her neck because he thinks it

A German poster. *Courtesy Anna Michalik.*

French sheet music. (Jo Bouillon was a top bandleader who later married Josephine Baker.) *Courtesy Anna Michalik.*

looks cheap. "Blackie doesn't like it," he chides, giving us his life's philosophy in four words. Another of Blackie's old flames is a society lady at one of the tables. She kisses him passionately, then introduces her husband, who is nuzzling a giggling dancer.

On stage, Matt (Ted Healy) attempts to warble a ballad and is interrupted by flying fruit. Babe the Bouncer (Harold Huber, Nelson Eddy's sidekick in *Naughty Marietta*) quickly collars the culprit and drags him toward the door. Learning that he is from Los Angeles, Babe surreptitiously slugs him and totes him in a fireman's carry to the entrance. (The drunken customer, Vince Barnett, was actually knocked out by Huber, who apologized with tears in his eyes.)

Babe is just straightening his tie when he is accosted by the same young lady we noticed outside. Mary Blake (Jeanette), just been burned out in the rooming house fire, is looking for a job as a singer. She tried "uptown" without success and now has turned to the Barbary Coast.

Babe appreciatively escorts her to Blackie's box. Blackie asks first to see her legs, then if she knows the song the band is playing. She picks up the last few bars of "Love Me and the World Is Mine." Twice her voice breaks under Blackie's gimlet-eyed appraisal, but she squares her shoulders and hits the final notes full blast. Blackie offers her $75 a week. She faints. "Give *me* $75 a week," Matt informs the astonished Blackie, "and I'll drop dead!"

Later that evening, Mary is finishing a hearty meal in Blackie's apartment over the Paradise. Blackie dismisses the Chinese servant in attendance and begins questioning Mary from the other room while he changes into "something more comfortable" for the evening's conquest. Mary tells him that her father was a country parson in Colorado. "*Was?* Oh, he got *on* to himself." No, she explains, he died four years ago. Her mother financed her singing studies and her trip to San Francisco.

Laughingly, Blackie acknowledges her tale as he carefully locks his watch and gold cufflinks in a dresser drawer. "Well, after all, Mr. Norton," she tells him simply, "there *are* such people as country parsons. Sometimes they *do* have daughters."

Blackie promises her some swell new clothes in the morning and closes in. Mary pushes him away, grabs her suitcase, and heads for the door. He blocks her way, saying she doesn't have to stall him if she has a "john on the string." If there's anything he admires, he tells her, it's a woman you can trust out of town. Tomorrow he'll advance her the train fare to send for him. In the meantime she can bunk on the couch.

San Francisco

Being embraced by the sexiest man in Hollywood had one drawback.

Mary stands dazed and undecided until Blackie elaborately leaves the key to his bedroom on her side of the door. As he dons black satin pajamas, he hears the key turn in the lock and shrugs with amusement. He turns out the light, pauses, then turns it back on again, leaning forward to look at himself in the dresser mirror. "Good night, sucker," he says.

In the parlor on the other side of the door, a set decorator's dream of bric-a-brac and bordello-bred bad taste, Mary finds the elaborate settee too short for sleeping comfort. She tosses some pillows on the floor and settles down, but the metallic embroidery on one fringed cushion cuts her cheek. With a sigh, she heaves it across the room where its tinselly letters glint ironically at her in the dark: *Welcome to San Francisco.*

The next morning, we see yet another facet of Blackie Norton, the man among men. He is sparring at the gymnasium with an old friend. A group of Barbary Coast businessmen parade in as he finishes and ask him to run for supervisor. It's the only way they can get decent fire laws. Blackie's sparring partner returns, now dressed as a priest.

"You've always liked a fight, Blackie," comments Father Tim Mullin (Spencer Tracy). Blackie and his friends troop across the back

Mary makes it clear which of her services Blackie is paying for. He decides she must have "a john on the string."

alley to the Paradise for a drink to seal the bargain.

Mary is rehearsing in the empty hall, singing "San Francisco" in slow tempo like a hymn. Blackie stalks over to the upright piano. "Heat it up," he orders and pounds out a tempo version of the tune. "That's the way you're going to sing, or you're not going to sing for Blackie!" He decides to sign her to a contract.

Mary's voice continues in the new tempo, and we see her in a white sequined dress and "can-can" bonnet on the stage of the crowded Paradise. The enthusiastic throng is soon augmented by two elegant gentlemen from "uptown." Jack Burley (silent film star Jack Holt) is slumming with Signore Baldini (William Ricciardi), maestro of the Tivoli Opera. Entertainment isn't Burley's only goal. He has come to suggest that Blackie give up running for supervisor.

In Blackie's private box, they are interrupted by the silver-haired "Professor" (vaudeville star Al Shean of Gallagher and Shean) who played under the maestro twenty years before in Dresden. Excitedly he urges the great Baldini to listen to the singer he has discovered, a singer with *such* a voice! Quietly Blackie orders the "Professor" to stop holding up the show and the little man scuttles away.

Mary's voice is heard over the hubbub in a "classical" number, "A Heart That's Free." Matt is all for dragging her off the stage, but Blackie notices Baldini's great interest and motions Matt to be still. Burley is interested too and sends his card, requesting the honor of meeting Mary. She comes shyly to the box, telling Signore Baldini that they might have met under more favorable circumstances. She once sat for six days in the outer office of the Tivoli Opera, hoping for an interview.

Burley is sure the Tivoli can use her now. Blackie smiles as he apologizes for having Mary under a two-year contract. The two men understand that they are now officially antagonists, and not just politically.

San Francisco

Blackie's childhood friend, Father Tim (Spencer Tracy), hopes Mary will be a good influence on Blackie.

Blackie sends Mary to sing a number at a place around the corner. The "place" turns out to be Saint Anne's Mission, run by Blackie's friend, Father Tim. The number is "The Holy City," which she sings with a boys' choir. The parishioners consist of some of the superb types that MGM seemed always able to call up—derelicts with the weariness of poverty and hunger etched deeply in their faces. In the last row, two tarts, preparing for their evening's work, sit raptly under the spell of the music.

Father Tim invites Mary to his study for some coffee before she returns to the Paradise. There, in his big "spiritual" scene, he tells how he and Blackie were newsboys together and then took different paths. Blackie is a tremendous force. If only he were a force for good instead of evil. Father Tim has tried to change him without success. "Maybe," he says significantly, looking at Mary, "I'm not the right one." Mary blushes beneath his gaze.

Father Tim tells us enigmatically that Blackie "is as unscrupulous with women as he is ruthless with men" and yet he "has never taken an underhanded advantage of anyone." (A study in semantics, this Blackie!) Father Tim assures Mary that she has nothing to fear unless she's afraid of herself. She is in the wickedest, most corrupt, Godless city in America. "Sometimes I wonder what the end is going to be." With his portent ringing in our ears, the coffee boils over.

The hiss of the scalding liquid is drowned by the noisy brass band and shouts of an outdoor political rally for Blackie Norton. Della, as a prominent local businesswoman, assures the crowd of the support of the "ladies" of the Coast. Then Blackie, extremely jaunty in a Norfolk suit and cap, moves the crowd to cheers with his fiery rhetoric and a knockout punch to the jaw of a heckler sent by Jack Burley. The ever-hopeful Trixie rushes to congratulate him, but he tells her to wait for him by the beer truck.

Quickly, he seeks out the "Professor" and asks his help. Trixie, he claims, is hanging around the beer truck, getting stiff. He would consider it a favor if the "Professor" would take her back to town. Mary has been standing between them, watching the exchange like a spectator at a tennis match, but Blackie doesn't notice her until the "Professor" explains he has been acting as her escort. Blackie expresses astonishment at her presence and offers to see that she gets home all right. The band music changes into an oom-pah-pah version of "*Would You?*" as they waltz, Mary losing more and more of her determination.

During their carriage ride home, they have a confrontation about God. Blackie doesn't go for that "sucker competition." He's got to be number one boy. Mary tells him that people who believe in something can love each other more. He says he won't hold it against her, and, taking this for agreement, Mary accepts his arm around her shoulders.

In the gloomy daytime Paradise, Mary sits amidst upturned chairs and mopping scrub ladies, rehearsing the dreamy ballad "Would You?" The Paradise band is truly remarkable, for although it consists entirely of brass, her voice is supported by a dozen violins.

A poker game in the next room again reveals Blackie as a good guy, tossing $100 to a player

Opera impresario Signor Baldini (William Ricciardi, right) and civic leader Jack Burley (Jack Holt, second from left) go slumming on the Barbary Coast and hear Mary sing. They want her for the opera, but Blackie refuses to release her. *Courtesy Anna Michalik.*

he has just cleaned out. Burley arrives and offers to buy Mary's contract. She is summoned from rehearsal and told that Baldini thinks she is ready for the Tivoli. Flushed with joy, she turns to Blackie, and a long look is exchanged. She asks if he wants to sell her contract. "Nope." Then she can't accept.

Blackie is nearly crowing as he shows Burley out and then invites Mary into a private inner office. There, bursting with boyish enthusiasm, he shows her the trophies won by the Paradise the last three years at the Chickens' Ball. The wine agents, he tells her, put on a competition and give a $10,000 prize for the joint that puts on the most artistic show. "Artistic achievement!" he enunciates proudly. He's going to win again this year and use the money for his campaign fund for "the little mugs down here on the Coast."

He turns from trophies of the past to the live one at hand and soon is making love to her. She naturally resists, but not too vigorously. In a "Gable scene" that is a whirlwind of logic and he-man poetry he besieges the lady: "How does it feel to feel like a woman and be afraid of it?" Still dubious, she is swept into a passionate kiss.

He takes this for affirmation and jubilantly leads the dazed and smiling Mary out through the Paradise toward his apartment upstairs for "some chop suey." On the way, they pass through a rehearsal, and Trixie stops mid-step at the sight of Blackie with his arm around Mary.

San Francisco

He orders champagne for everyone, and it is obvious this is a familiar custom. "Nice going, sister," sneers Babe. "Here's to you, darlin', and I wish I had me youth!" toasts one faded belle. "I wish I'd never *had* mine," Trixie mutters darkly. Blackie chucks her under the chin consolingly.

He misses Mary in the crowd and assumes she's gone ahead to the apartment, which has an outside entrance. Out in the street, he is stopped by Father Tim. Mary has asked the priest to say goodbye for her. She is going to work at the Tivoli. She's safe with Burley, Father Tim tells Blackie, because she doesn't *love* him. Shrugging, Blackie invites Father Tim upstairs for some chop suey.

Backstage at the opera house, the overture to *Faust* can be heard. In Mary's dressing room, Burley proposes. He leaves without waiting for an answer and begins checking the opera house to see that everything is in order for this most important night. The actors nod to him as he passes through the backstage hallways. Emerging into his box, he greets his mother, a silver-haired lady of noble features (Jessie Ralph), then strolls into the lobby. Dowagers draped in jewels and satin murmur their best wishes, which he graciously acknowledges. The

"Heat it up!" Blackie orders, demonstrating how to do it on the Barbary Coast.

Director W.S. Van Dyke (left) shooting Jeanette in her first rendition of the title song. *Courtesy James Parish.*

Tivoli is his as much as the Paradise belongs to Blackie Norton.

Among this elite audience are Blackie and Babe, who have brought a process server (silent comedian Edgar Kennedy). They have come to close the show, but Mary's singing is so moving that Blackie can't go through with it. Midway through Mary's final scene, Babe notices that the process server has tired of waiting and gone backstage. Blackie rushes after him and prevents any interruption of the music by neatly clipping the officer with a handy belaying pin.

The performance concludes to triumphal applause. Mary is swept along backstage by a throng of well-wishers to her dressing room where Blackie is waiting. Making her excuses to her singing teacher (Adrienne d'Ambricourt), the "Professor," and the rest, she shuts the door behind her. Mary and Blackie are alone for the first time since she left.

He loves her, he concedes, and he's only "sprung that line once," twenty-five years ago. He hasn't seen the girl lately though. She's up in San Quentin.

As Violetta in *La Traviata*. Jeanette's on-screen opera sequences made her yearn for the real thing.

"Will you marry me, Blackie?" Mary blurts out. If that's the only thing that will make her happy, he jokingly agrees. Their kiss of reconciliation is interrupted by Father Tim, and Mary happily tells him the news. Burley walks in and is understandably irritated at this further invasion of his territory.

Blackie explains with elaborate casualness that he is just visiting his fiancée. Burley pales, and Mary tries to soften the blow, but Blackie is rushing on with his plans. Mary must hurry and dress so they can get back to the Paradise. The gang is all waiting to hear her sing "San Francisco."

Even Mary is astonished. She stands in close-up between them, looking from one to the other as Blackie asks her what she wants: "Me...or this?" Her anguished face slowly fades and with a blare of "Ta-Ra-Ra Boom-dee-ay" we are back at the smoke-filled Paradise.

Mary, in a stunning costume that reveals her legs in sheer black tights, is waiting in her dressing room with Blackie when Father Tim is announced. She grabs for a cape to hide her scandalous outfit and begs Blackie to set a date for their wedding so that they can tell Father Tim. The priest is far too disturbed by Mary's legs to care about a wedding date. Blackie assures him that Mary will be queen of the Coast. He's got five thousand posters announcing her return and ten thousand little ones for trolley cars and ash cans!

Father Tim orders Mary to leave immediately. "You can't marry a woman and sell her immortal soul," he tells Blackie. Blackie's territory and possessions are again being challenged, this time by the deity. He defends himself by socking Father Tim in the nose. We see him start the swing, Mary's horrified face as a blow sounds, Blackie's reaction to what he has done, Father Tim with blood dribbling from his mouth, and then Mary's face again, going from shock to square-jawed resignation. She gathers her cape about her and marches with Father Tim from this den of sin, as impatient customers begin breaking up the furniture.

Mary returns to Jack Burley and goes home with him to meet his mother. Home is a Nob Hill mansion and the regal Mrs. Burley is an Irish immigrant who came around the Horn in the winter of '51 to work as a washerwoman near Portsmouth Square. In a very moving scene, Maisie Burley tells Mary that she too had a Blackie Norton in her life. She begs the girl to marry her son and raise fine kids for the future of San Francisco. Otherwise, where will all this wickedness end?

Burley's campaign to win Mary goes one step further. Blackie's Paradise is closed down for selling liquor without a license, a charge that will put him in jail for a year. It is obviously a political move to keep Blackie from running for supervisor. Blackie's former supporters send word that they aren't going to fight Burley any longer. Blackie is alone.

San Francisco

Blackie lures Mary back to the Paradise and into the costume that causes the San Francisco quake.

Character actress Jessie Ralph gives a moving performance as Maisie Burley, the immigrant mother of Mary's socialite suitor.

He is granted a few hours to raise bail for his performers, and then he sadly turns out the lights and locks the Paradise for the first time since it was opened. He has until 6:00 AM to report to jail.

Outside, a newsboy is hawking papers. On the front page is a photograph of Mary in *La Traviata*. We don't have time to consider that newspaper photographs were almost unknown in 1906, for the picture comes to life, and we are on stage at the Tivoli as Mary triumphs with "Sempre Libera."

Afterward, Burley announces that he is taking her to the Chickens' Ball. Don't worry, he smiles, Blackie won't be there. To the robust strains of "At a Georgia Camp Meeting," they thread their way through the crowded tables at the ball. Further evidence of the city's sinfulness, if any were needed, is provided by a patron who drags a giggling dancer from the dressing room as his wife cheers him on.

Mary, in shimmering white, is above all this. On stage, an exuberant minstrel dance is in progress. Della appears behind Burley and drops into the chair next to him. As she tells Burley what she thinks of him, Mary learns what has happened to Blackie and her fellow performers.

The black dancers make their strutting exit and are replaced by the "Golden Gate Trio," who warble the "Philippine Dance." (A line in the authentic period song, fortunately obscured by the ensuing dialogue, tells us we "ought to see the darkies prance.")

As all roads lead to Rome, so all paths on this fateful night are due to cross at the Chickens' Ball. Blackie comes in to return Della's jewelry. Hocking it will do no good. His performers are being held without bail. He spreads open the handkerchief full of jewelry and absently picks through the lady's lifetime acquisitions. "Say," he picks up one ring. "Didn't I give you this?" "Yeah," replies Della, with a catch in her voice, "you were just a kid..."

Blackie is just exiting down the stairs as Freddy Duane announces that, since no contestants have come forth for the Paradise, the show is over. Mary leaps to her feet. "*I* represent the Paradise!" Burley forbids her, grabbing her arm, but she shakes him off and strides to the stage. The delighted Della sends a waiter to catch Blackie.

The crowd's cheers redouble when Mary announces her selection: "San Francisco."

After her triumph in *Faust*. Left to right, Belle Mitchell, Adrienne d'Ambricourt, Jack Holt, Jeanette.

Standing quietly stage center, she sings the verse straight, then, with a pregnant pause, launches into a torchy version of the chorus as it was never torched before. Sauntering and swaying gently, she teases the audience through a full chorus, then drops to one knee in an imitation of a minstrel singer, throbbing voice, gestures, and all. The audience joins in at her urging, and she becomes a glittering dynamo, writhing in the glow of the footlights, her voice soaring over the din as the crowd responds, creating a total theatrical experience. (Miss MacDonald bet director Van Dyke $500 that this "hot" version of "San Francisco" wouldn't work. To his surprise, he received her check. To her surprise, he cashed it.)

The vote for the contest winner is a mere formality. Mary is happily struggling to lift the trophy cup full of gold pieces when Blackie strides onto the stage. He seizes the cup from Mary and hurls it across the floor. "I don't need this kind of dough."

Mary stands trembling, and the audience murmurs their astonishment. Blindly Mary stumbles from the stage, accepting her cape from a now obliging Burley. She threads her way toward the door, fighting her tears.

Blackie's infamy is too much for the San Andreas Fault. A low moan is heard, building to a roar. The revelers freeze as glasses tremble on the tables. A sharp upward shot shows plaster splintering from around the swaying chandelier. As the intensity of the quake increases, the images flash by faster and faster. The floor begins to lurch. A woman clings to the edges of the table before her, trying to maintain her balance and her dignity. Panic begins among the patrons. The wall behind Blackie shudders, then bursts apart. Mary screams and reaches desperately toward him, but Burley has her in his arms, bearing her away down the stairs. We see her faint and then disappear in a cloud of plaster dust.

The balcony at one end of the room sags away from the wall, sending patrons, tables, and

At the Chickens Ball, Mary learns that her fiancé (Jack Holt) has had the Paradise closed and its employees jailed. Now, she knows what she must do. *Courtesy Jack Tillmany.*

chairs cascading to the floor below. The screams of terror mingle with the cries of the injured and the roar of the earth. Then, as suddenly as it started, it stops.

There is an appalling silence, punctuated by low moans. Blackie, half buried in bricks, pulls himself painfully to his feet. (At the previews of *San Francisco*, the scene of Blackie being buried by a wall of prop bricks was so unbelievable that the audience burst into laughter, and the scene was scissored as the wall starts to break up. Actually, Gable was trapped beneath the debris and narrowly escaped smothering. So much for verité.)

Blackie pauses momentarily beside the body of the faithful Della, then turns to the living. He pulls a waiter from under a beam.

"San Francisco!" *Courtesy Ken Richards.*

San Francisco

In the street outside, people in nightclothes are milling about, crying out for the missing. A hoarse voice calls to Blackie from under a pile of debris. Two of his friends are trapped there. He grabs a husky passerby, and they begin heaving at the timbers. Suddenly another tremor begins. The house in front of them sways dangerously. The stranger drags the struggling Blackie to safety as the stone front of the building collapses, hopelessly burying his friends under tons of rubble.

A piano crashes through the window of a store, landing on the street in an explosion of keys and wires. The facade of a house drops away, hurling a woman and baby from the eerily exposed third floor. Then quiet again, broken by distant screams and the yelping of a dog.

Blackie begins his quest for Mary. One girl tells him she has seen Jack Burley. She points numbly to a fallen wall where Burley's head and arm protrude. A scrap of white feather from Mary's dress is in his limp hand. Blackie plucks frantically at the bricks, imploring people for help. One man hesitates, then rushes on, crying, "Irene!" As Blackie digs faster and faster, he hears the man's voice break into a sob: "Irene." He turns to see him cradling a lifeless body in his arms.

The brick pile yields nothing, and Blackie plunges on through the ruined city. In an unforgettable visual moment, he steps over a small crack in the street that instantly spreads into a huge fissure with broken pipes spurting water. One man topples into the hole and another clings desperately to the edge. Live wires drop onto splintered wood in the streets, and the debris explodes with electric fury. Flames shoot the length of the street, eagerly consuming the wooden houses. Fire trucks rush clanging through the streets, but the hydrants yield only a pathetic trickle. The mains are broken. There's no water to fight the fires.

Evacuation begins. The army moves in and starts dynamiting a fire lane to prevent the flames from spreading. Blackie watches the mammoth explosions moving up Nob Hill toward the Burley mansion. He finds Mrs. Burley hobbling down the hill, clutching a pathetically small valise of possessions, while servants tug at a tiny cart loaded with a few pieces of furniture. Behind them, the incredible Burley mansion, a monument to moneyed Victorian architecture, stands highlighted by the flames below.

Blackie doesn't need to tell Mrs. Burley that her son is dead. She has sensed it already. She buries her head in his shoulder as he strokes her hair. A soldier orders them to move on. They reach the bottom of the hill as an explosion rips the air behind them. Mrs. Burley turns to see the turrets of her home toppling. "My son was born there," she murmurs. A second blast turns the structure to toothpicks. She parts from Blackie: "It's God's help we both need now."

We look out over the burning city, and the light changes from day to night. Blackie is still searching for Mary, going from cot to cot in the aid stations and peering frantically into faces at the soup kitchens. Everywhere he asks about a red-haired girl in a white dress. "God help you to find her, brother," replies one man fervently.

Van Dyke was a reserve officer in the U.S. Marine Corps and engaged a company of Marines to help with the precision staging of the spectacular earthquake and fire sequences.

The earthquake survivors, including Mary, gather on a hilltop, waiting for the fires to end.

Blackie looks for Father Tim and is directed to an aid station at the car barn. There, amidst cots and cable cars, he finds Matt dying. He begs the nearby nun to stay with Matt and goes on from bed to bed. We see an old Italian man writhing with pain as his wife clings helplessly to his hand. The limp, shattered form of a young woman goes by on a stretcher. A nun pulls a sheet over the face of a wizened old man.

At the back of the car barn, Blackie finds Father Tim soothing a small girl. "You haven't found Mary yet, have you?" Blackie shakes his head numbly. "Well, you can't want her for the Paradise, Blackie, that's gone." Blackie tells him he wasn't thinking of the Paradise. Father Tim turns to the little girl for a moment, then grabs Blackie's arm. He is taking him to Mary.

They pick their way through Golden Gate Park after the fire. A platoon of soldiers marches across their path. Another soldier is ordering people to the hospital tent for inoculation. The park is a tent city of rescued furniture, blankets strung on ropes, and families gathered around small cooking fires. The children are romping, untouched by the tragedy. Women are hanging things to dry on improvised clotheslines. Life is going on.

From the crest of the hill comes the sound of singing. Blackie recognizes Mary's voice in "Nearer, My God, to Thee." The drama of the moment is not entirely spoiled by the rag-tag refugees who accompany her in perfect four-part harmony. Mary is comforting the mother of a dead child (a child who inconsiderately twitches quite a bit during the scene). Mary's emotion is real. However, her dress a memory of its former glory, her hair matted and hanging loose. Blackie is overcome. As we have anticipated throughout the film, he finds God, and drops to his knees.

Through her tears, Mary sees Blackie kneeling in the dirt below. She goes to him and they stand a few feet apart, silently looking at each other.

A cry is heard: "The fire's out!" The people around them come to life, jubilantly calling out the news. "We'll build a new San Francisco!" shouts a youth. "Hallelujah!" cries a woman.

Over the din of shouts and cheers, we hear the first strains of "The Battle Hymn of the Republic," slowly, then building as the crowd turns and begins marching. We don't know quite where they are going, but the effect is so stirring that we fall right in with them. In the midst of their ranks are Blackie with his arm around Mary and Father Tim just behind them.

The camera is trained on the bare crest of a hill silhouetted against a brilliant sky. As the music thunders, a solid wall of humanity marches into view. They gaze out at the smoldering ruins and to the strains of "San Francisco" we see a montage of the new 1936 San Francisco rising on the ashes: the skyscrapers, the new Bay Bridge, the automobiles and buses, the soaring towers of the Golden Gate Bridge majestically spanning the harbor although still without benefit of roadway. (This touching tribute to the rebuilt San Francisco was sadly eliminated from the 1948 re-release prints and replaced by a single shot of the contemporary

San Francisco

skyline in an effort to "modernize" the film.) Jeanette's voice soars like the spires of the bridge and we know we have indeed seen a movie!

If the four principals (counting the earthquake) make *San Francisco* a memorable film, the other members of the cast provide a fascinating behind-the-scenes story. In the seven years that had gone by since sound films took over, many silent film actors had fallen on hard times. It was certainly a source of embarrassment to the studios that players who had once been their biggest moneymakers were now on relief. In a burst of benevolence (and publicity), MGM announced a policy of hiring as many old timers as possible for the film. Jack Holt, of course, was a silent star who had hung on during the sound era and continued to star in many B films. Al Shean (the Professor) was the surviving half of the immortal vaudeville team of Gallagher and Shean. Edgar Kennedy (the process server) was a former Keystone Kop and later comedy star in his own right, specializing in the famous "slow burn."

The supporting and bit players included King Baggott, who starred in over two hundred pictures prior to 1920, and Rhea Mitchell, who costarred with him in the 1918 serial *The Hawk's Lair*, directed by Van Dyke. Vernon Dent, who menaced Buster Keaton in so many comedies, Flora Finch, who had been John Bunny's leading lady, Naomi Childers, a star at Vitagraph, Fritzi Brunette from Yankee Films, Helene Chadwick of Astra-Pathé, Rosemary Theby of Vitagraph, Jean Acker (Rudolph Valentino's first wife), Harry C. Myers, Donald Hall, Jason Robards Sr, and dozens more participated. This attention to "old-timers" produced one touching incident.

D.W. Griffith, the father of the silent film, appeared on the set one day to visit his old employee, W.S. Van Dyke. Van Dyke had come to Griffith's attention twenty years earlier when he was a "captain" of extras in the Babylonian mob scenes for Griffith's mammoth masterpiece, *Intolerance*. Now Griffith "directed" a mob scene for Van Dyke as a lark, probably not realizing or caring what a pathetic story the MGM publicity department could make of it.

San Francisco made *Film Daily*'s Ten Best Films list, but curiously was nowhere to be seen on the similar list issued by the *New York Times*. After its earlier enthusiasm, the *Times* had already come to regard musicals as a lesser branch of filmdom and would pass up musicals entirely, including such all-time greats as *Singin' in the Rain* and *An American in Paris,* until 1955 when they grudgingly named *Oklahoma!* and *It's Always Fair Weather*(!)

Jeanette's personal success, as well as the tremendous smash made by *San Francisco*, made her the top box-office attraction of the year. Her next film was *Maytime*, a film that would be interrupted by the untimely death of the young guiding genius of MGM, Irving Thalberg.

Reviews

Variety reported that the manager of the Paramount Theatre in San Francisco, Allen Warshauer, was responsible for the finale of the general 1936 release version. Fearing local hostility to the film, "Warshauer had a cameraman take special pan shots of the city. These were shown at the mention of the dream city of the future which ends the picture and had audiences standing to cheer. John Emerson, who aided Bernie Hyman in producing the picture, attended the first showing and okayed the new ending, saying he would recommend its use on all prints. W.S. Van Dyke, the director, also flew here for the opening."

Variety also referred archly to "the constant singing of Jeanette MacDonald," but then added that "she has never looked better nor sung better and being in a sock picture is an aid to her appearance and performance." Spencer Tracy got most of their praise for playing the tricky rôle of a priest who says "mugg" and "sucker" without giving offense.

The *New York Times* review is worth quoting only to show the strong element of self-importance that was beginning to dominate film reviews: "Out of the gutsy, brawling, catastrophic history of the Barbary Coast early in the century, MGM has fashioned a prodigally generous and completely satisfying photoplay. Astonishingly, it serves the virtues of the operatic film, the romantic, the biographical, the dramatic, and the documentary abundantly well, truly meriting the commendation as a near-perfect illustration of the cinema's inherent and acquired ability to absorb and digest other art forms and convert them into its own sinews." They added that "Miss MacDonald's voice seems more melodious than ever."

More typical of the praise lavished on *San Francisco* was that of William Boehnel in the *New York World-Telegram*: "There comes a time in every motion picture reviewer's life when he is afflicted by a sense of remorse for having squandered his stock of adjectives, for having abused such words as 'great,' 'magnificent,' 'superb,' because when a truly notable film comes along, he really has nothing left with which to describe it." He acknowledged that the film is "good old fashioned hokum....a pretty obvious shilling-shocker dressed up in five pound notes....In the role of Mary Blake, Jeanette MacDonald is superb. Looking more attractive and appearing in better voice than ever before, she plays the part with uncommon charm, forbearance, and emotional depth. Not only does she give the finest performance of her screen career, but she has never sung more thrillingly than she does here."

Recordings (See Discography for further information)

All recordings by Jeanette MacDonald. Intriguingly, she never recorded the film's hit song, "Would You?" The song was later featured in the 1952 "twenties" musical, *Singin' in the Rain*, which consisted of Freed-Brown songs.

"The Battle Hymn of the Republic"
"The Holy City"
"Air des bijoux"
"Nearer, My God, to Thee"
"San Francisco" *

* Those who thrilled to Jeanette's fiery interpretation of this song in the film may be disappointed in the rather tepid—but only—recording she made more than fourteen years later in 1950.

Music from the Film

In listing performers after each title, "and" denotes a genuine duet, while commas between names indicate a sequence of singers.

Overture: "San Francisco," "Would You?"
"Happy New Year" (Shirley Ross and female chorus) - music by Bronislau Kaper and Walter Jurman, lyrics by Gus Kahn
"Noontime" specialty (Ted Healy) - written by Ted Healy
"There'll Be a Hot Time in the Old Town Tonight" (Healy, heard behind conversation) - music by Theodore A. Metz, lyrics by Joe Hayden
"Love Me and the World is Mine" (MacDonald) - Ernest R. Ball and David Reed Jr
"San Francisco" (MacDonald) - Music by Bronislau Kaper, lyrics by Gus Kahn *
"A Heart That's Free" (MacDonald) - A.J. Robyn and T. Railey
"The Holy City" (MacDonald and Long Beach Boys' Choir) - Stephen Adams and F.E. Weatherly
"San Francisco" reprise - (MacDonald and chorus)
"Would You?" (MacDonald) - music by Nacio Herb Brown, lyrics by Arthur Freed

Scenes from *Faust*, music by Charles Gounod, libretto by Jules Barbier and Michel Carré. Vocals include:
- "Me voilà toute seule" (Tandy MacKenzie as Faust) - behind dialogue
- "Air des bijoux" [The Jewel Song] (MacDonald)
- "Soldiers' Chorus" fragment, Act IV (chorus)
- "Il se fait tard" fragment (MacDonald and MacKenzie)
- "Anges Purs" (MacDonald, MacKenzie, Tudor Williams as Mephistopheles)

"Sempre Libera" from *La Traviata* (MacDonald with MacKenzie) - music by Giuseppe Verdi, libretto by Francesco Maria Piave

"At a Georgia Camp Meeting" (orchestral, minstrel show) - by Kerry Mills

"The Philippine Dance" (male trio) - by Bob Carleton

"San Francisco" reprise (MacDonald, chorus)

"Nearer, My God, to Thee" (MacDonald and chorus) - music by Lowell Mason, lyrics by Sarah F. Adams

"The Battle Hymn of the Republic" (MacDonald and chorus) - music by William Steffe, lyrics by Julia Ward Howe

Finale: "San Francisco" reprise - chorus

* After copyrighting this world-famous version during pre-production, Kaper, Jurman, and Kahn then wrote and copyrighted a second title song, an obviously hokey satire on "place" songs. Fortunately, the song we know and love was chosen for the finished film.

Research by Miles Kreuger of the Institute of the American Musical indicates that, under "male quartettes," the MGM pay records list The Highlanders (Howard Chandler), The Uptowners (Homer Hall), and Doug Steade. Zarubi Elmassian and Nick Angelo are listed as recording a few bars from *Il Trovatore*, either not used in the film or a mistaken reference to *La Traviata*.

Trivia

Young singer Douglas McPhail, later in *Sweethearts* and star of *Babes in Arms*, is an extra, standing just behind Jeanette on the crest of the hill in the finale.

Tandy MacKenzie, well-known Hawaiian tenor, made many recordings and was still singing in the 1950s. He dubbed for Walter Woolf King in *A Night at the Opera*.

A 1991 production of *San Francisco* was scheduled to open in London in October 1992. Martin L. Marcus optioned the rights from Turner Entertainment and engaged Rob Bettinson as director, Tim Prager, book, and Geoff Morrow, music and lyrics. "This will be like an operetta," Marcus said, but the production, to be produced by award-winning Nica Burns, never jelled.

Maytime

MGM.
Released March 26, 1937.
Directed by Robert Z. Leonard.
Produced by Hunt Stromberg and Robert Z Leonard.
132 minutes.

French title: *Le Chant du Printemps* (The Song of Spring)
Swedish title: *Engånge I Maj* (Once in May)
Dutch title: *Het Was in de Mei* (It Was in May)
German title: *Maienzeit* (Maytime)
Danish title: *Det var i maj* (That Day in May)
Spanish/Italian/Portuguese title: *Primavera* (Spring)
Finnish title: *Toukokuun päivää* (Days of May)
Portuguese title: *Primavera* (Springtime)

Based on the 1917 operetta with music by Sigmund Romberg and book and lyrics by Rida Johnson Young. Screenplay: Noël Langley [and Claudine West]. Music adapted and directed by Herbert Stothart. Photography: Oliver T. Marsh. Editor: Conrad A. Nervig. Adaptation of French Libretto: Gilles Guilbert. Vocal Arrangements: Léo Arnaud. Opera Sequences: William von Wymetal. Art Director: Cedric Gibbons. Associate Art Directors: Fredric Hope, Edwin B. Willis. Gowns: Adrian. Sound: Douglas Shearer, James Brock. Assistant Directors: Joseph M. Newman and Marvin Stewart. Music Recording: Mike McLaughlin. Montages: Slavko Vorkapich. Dances: Val Raset, assisted by

Paul Foltz and Harvey Karels. Makeup: Jack and Lyle Dawn. Technical Advisor: George Richelavie.

(Ironically, while the "adaptation of French libretto" is credited to Gilles Guilbert, the creators of the original English libretto, young Bob Wright and Chet Forrest, are not credited at all.)

The stage *Maytime* opened on August 16, 1917 at the Shubert Theatre and ran 492 performances. The Shubert brothers routinely bought the rights to European musicals and revamped them for American consumption, usually keeping the European settings. When World War I made German imports unpatriotic, they had Romberg rework Walter Kollo's German hit, *Wie einst im Mai* into *Maytime*, moving the locale to old New York. The stage production starred Peggy Wood, Richard Moran, and Charles Purcell. The stage plot formed the basis of a 1923 film for Preferred, directed by Louis Gasnier and starring Harrison Ford (popular leading man of stage and screen, but no relation to the current star) and Ethel Shannon. Clara Bow had a small part.

A French *Maytime* poster. *Courtesy Anna Michalik.*

Jeanette MacDonald (Marcia Mornay / Miss Morrison)
Nelson Eddy (Paul Allison)
John Barrymore (Nicolai Nazaroff)
Herman Bing (August Archipenko)
Tom Brown (Kip)
Lynne Carver* (Barbara Roberts)
Rafaela Ottiano (Ellen)
Charles Judels (Cabby)
Paul Porcasi (Trentini)
Sig Rumann (Fanchon)
Walter Kingsford (Rudyard)
Grace Hayle (Fat lady at opening May Day fair)
Edgar Norton (Secretary)
Guy Bates Post (Emperor Louis Napoleon)
Iphigenie Castiglioni (Empress Eugenie)
Anna Demetrio (Madame Fanchon)
Frank Puglia (Orchestra conductor)
Adia Kuznetzoff (Dubrovsky, Czaritza's minister; also student in café)
M. Morova (Czaritza's Nurse)
Joan Le Sueur* (Maypole dancer)
Russell Hicks (Monsieur Bulliet, voice teacher)
Frank Sheridan (O'Brien, an opera director)
Harry Davenport, Harry Hayden, Howard Hickman, Robert C. Fischer (Opera directors)
Harlan Briggs (Bearded opera director)
Billy Gilbert (Drunk in café)
Ivan Lebedeff (Empress's dinner companion)
Leonid Kinsky (Student in bar)
Clarence Wilson (Waiter)
Maurice Cass (Opera house manager)
Douglas Wood (Massilon, hotel manager)
Bernard Suss (Assistant manager)
Henry Roquemore (Publicity man)
Alexander Schonberg (French proprietor)
Mariska Aldrich (*Czaritza* contralto)
Paul Weigel (*Czaritza* prompter)
Jack Murphy, Blair Davies, Agostino Borgato, Alberto Morin, Ben Welden, Jose Rubio (Students)
Kirby Hoon [later Kirby Grant] (Student singer)
Christian Frank (Gendarme)
George [Georges] Davis (Usher at *Les Huguenots*)
Pat Somerset (Gossiper)
Ian Wolfe (Court official)
Gus Leonard (Concierge)
Brandon Hurst (Master of Ceremonies)

Maytime

Eric Lonsdale, Guy D'Ennery (Aides)
Claude King (Noble)
Forbes Murray (Aide)
Fred Graham, Frank O'Connor (Servants)
Barlowe Borland (Stage doorman)
Charles Requa (Stage manager)
Arthur Stuart Hull, Harold Entwhistle (Roués)
Frank Elliot (Aide)
Jacques Lory (Drunk)
Belle Mitchell (Marcia's maid)
Hans Joby (Doctor)
Christian Rub (Sleeper outside café)
Genaro Spagnoli (Chef)
Paul Cremonesi, Eric Mayne (Opera critics)
Oscar Rudolph, Herta Lind (Peasants at fair)
Jolly Lee Harvey (Fat woman)
Armand "Curley" Wright (Bow-and-arrow booth)
Sidney Jarvis, Albert Pollet (Cabbies)
Francisco Maran (Gendarme)
Bobs Watson, Helen Parrish ("Merry Month of May" singers)
Ed Goddard (Juggling clown)
Joan Breslaw (Queen of the May)
Nan Merriman, George London (*Les Huguenots* chorus)
The Don Cossack Chorus (Singers at court)
Delmar Watson, Buster Slaven (Boys by Maypole)
Earl Covert (acts De Nevers in *Les Huguenots*)
Alexander Kandiba (*Czaritza* priest)
Nick Asgelo, Dick Dennis (Success montage tenors)
Bernice Alstock (Success montage contralto)
Meglin Kiddies, Bud Murray Children (by Maypole)
Ludovico Tomarchio ("Santa Lucia" singer at St. Cloud festival)
Geneva Hall, Leda Nicova (St. Cloud festival gypsy dancers)
Tudor Williams (sings De Nevers in *Les Huguenots*)
Zari Elmassian (Singer)
Bits: Luke Cosgrave, Diana Dean, Allan Cavan, Sarah Edwards

* Note: Lynne Carver's first appearance under her new screen name. She had been in films since 1935 as Virginia Reid. Film debut of Joan Le Sueur, three-year-old niece of Joan Crawford.

Oscar nominations: Herbert Stothart for Best Score. One of thirty-six top-grossing films of 1937.

Maytime was presented on Cecil B. DeMille's Lux Radio Theatre, 9/4/44, with Jeanette, Nelson, and Edgar Barrier.

German cinema program. *Courtesy Anna Michalik.*

If *Maytime* didn't make any "Ten Best" lists, it was probably because of the competition. It was a year for blockbusters. Prominent on such lists were *Lost Horizon, Camille, Stage Door, The Good Earth, A Star is Born, Romeo and Juliet, Dead End, Captains Courageous, The Life of Emile Zola* (the Oscar Winner), and *The Awful Truth*.

Irving Thalberg died on September 14, 1936 at the age of thirty-seven. The death of a man whose name had traditionally not appeared on any film in his lifetime seems a strange beginning to the story of one of the screen's greatest musicals. Thalberg, however, had guided many of MGM's "quality" productions to

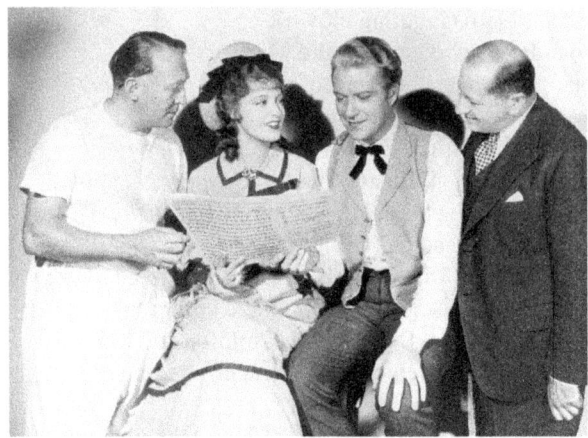

The "first" *Maytime*, later abandoned. Noted director Edmund Goulding poses with MacDonald, Eddy, and composer Sigmund Romberg.

the screen, films such as *Grand Hotel, Mutiny on the Bounty, Romeo and Juliet*, and *The Barretts of Wimpole Street*. Since he had already assumed charge of production on *Maytime*, his death had a profound effect on the film itself. That he was personally going to supervise *Maytime* was an honor of the first order. A mystique had grown up around him and the people who worked with him which somehow demanded and got the very best that anyone could do. However, *Maytime* had major birth pains. Thalberg was reported to have spent a half-million dollars trying to get a workable script—highly unlikely, but an indication of the problems involved. The film eventually cost $1,500,000.

Several scenes were shot, including an elaborate opera sequence (Act II of Puccini's *Tosca*) and a crowd scene on a Manhattan-Brooklyn ferry boat. However, Thalberg was still unsatisfied with the story when he contracted pneumonia and died suddenly.

It was necessary to divide his projects up among the other producers at MGM. A power struggle developed, most typical of film studios and banana republics. Shooting stopped. Director Edmund Goulding (*Grand Hotel, Riptide*) was replaced by Robert Z. Leonard (*Dancing Lady, The Great Ziegfeld*), and Hunt Stromberg (*Naughty Marietta, Rose Marie*) was named producer.

If the subsequent film had been weak, this midstream changeover would have provided ample reason. However, *Maytime* emerged on the screen as "the most entrancing operetta the screen has given us" (*New York Times*). That it did so amidst the changes in nearly every facet of production is a source of unending amazement and satisfaction.

The original story of the stage *Maytime* concerned three generations of lovers in old New York. Peggy Wood, best remembered by today's audiences as Mama in the television series "I Remember Mama" and as the Mother Superior in the film *The Sound of Music*, created the stage heroine. (She also created the rôle of Sari in the original London *Bitter Sweet*. Both she and Mary Martin spent their lives watching others do the screen versions of rôles they had created on the stage.)

The first "Goulding script" bears almost no resemblance to the *Maytime* we know. Margaret and Ed are young opera singers played by

Nelson as Scarpia and Jeanette as Tosca in Act II of *Tosca*, filmed for the first version of *Maytime*.

Jeanette and Nelson. They want to marry, but Ed chauvinistically insists that Margaret give up her career and be a housewife (a recurring theme in films of the 1930s). They seek the advice of an elderly diva, Peggy, who tells them the story of her youth. In a flashback, we see the diva as a young girl, now played by Jeanette. She has had a similar argument with her beau, Richard Wayne (Nelson). Both are employed by a second-rate touring company managed by Herman Bing. The pair split up through personal weakness and vanity. Peggy marries her maestro (Paul Lukas) out of spite, and Richard marries Alice, Peggy's accompanist (noted stage actress Julie Haydon), who bears him two sons. Richard and Peggy are reunited years later but have just agreed to part when Peggy's husband catches them necking in the garden and tries to shoot Richard. The bullet is stopped by Richard's faithful wife, who survives. This puts a crimp in the lovers' relationship, and they don't meet again for another ten years, when they find they don't care much about each other any more. So, the old diva tells the young lovers, get it while you can. This shoddy tale might have undergone transmutation in the hands of Goulding and Thalberg, but it all sounds rather tacky.

Jeanette said later that everyone connected with the film was relieved when the script was discarded. Even then, she recalled, they felt that *Maytime* had the potential of being a superb film.

The footage already shot was shelved, and a new script credited to Noël Langley made fate the lovers' enemy rather than their own frivolity. In the new version, both the aging diva and her younger self were played by Jeanette, while Nelson appeared only in the flashback—more logical if less symbolic. *Maytime*, which had been merely a title of the first script, became the leitmotif of young love in the second. Of the original Romberg score, only "Will You Remember" remained, plus a snatch of "Road to Paradise" in the background. "Farewell to Dreams," which was recorded by Jeanette and Nelson along with "Will You Remember," never appeared in the second version, probably because the only spot for its obvious insertion would have held up the flow of the story.

Costume test of Nelson as Count di Luna in Verdi's *Il Trovatore* for the first *Maytime*. *Courtesy Anna Michalik.*

And *Maytime* does flow. Although 132 minutes long, it seems barely to have started when suddenly the two lovers are singing the final duet. As critic Frank S. Nugent of the *New York Times* commented: "It might be possible to snip a minute out here and there, but I can't think of a spot."

Maytime is spring incarnate, with even the credits spelled out in flower petals on a drifting stream. We open at a 1905 May Day festival, pre-comrade variety, with beribboned tots dancing around a May pole, a flowered goat cart hauling laughing children, a Punch and Judy show, and general springtime gaiety. Through the crowd of onlookers comes an elderly lady with a cane. Miss Morrison (Jeanette) responds

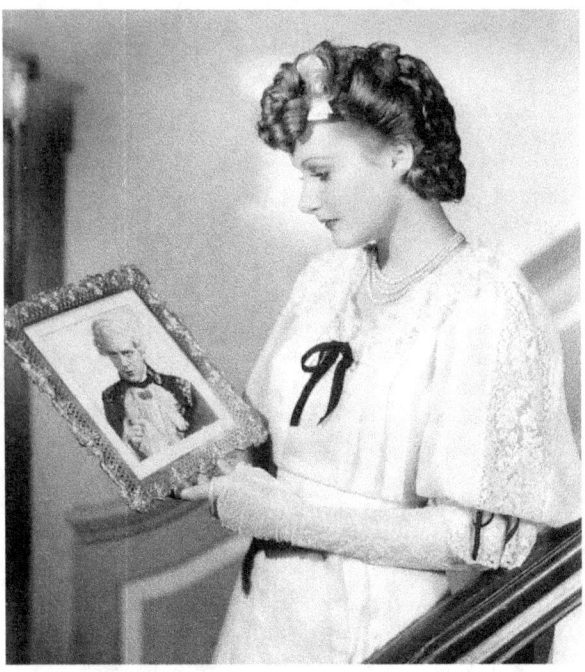

Ingénue Lynne Carver poses with an "in joke" prop, a photo of Nelson as Scarpia from the first version of *Maytime* which can be seen in Miss Morrison's home, supposedly a souvenir of her operatic career. *Courtesy Anna Michalik.*

Miss Morrison walks slowly home and is greeted by her elderly maid, Ellen (Rafaela Ottiano). She shouldn't have gone out, today of *all* days, Ellen says. Sadly, Miss Morrison tells her that May Day now seems the same as any other day—sometimes. As Ellen prepares tea, Miss Morrison stands gazing into the garden full of blossoms. A baritone voice grows out of the music of the birds:

> Do you remember the day
> When we were happy in May?
> (Copyright G. Schirmer & Co.)

She sits on a bench beneath an apple tree, smiling sadly. Her reverie is interrupted by the harsh quarreling of Kip and Barbara just outside the back fence. They agree never to see each other again and Kip storms off, leaving Barbara in tears. She turns to Miss Morrison for consolation, but remains adamant. She wants a chance to be a great singer like Tetrazzini or pleasantly to those she chats with, but she has an air of reserved sadness. (Jeanette's makeup, walk, and voice inflection were so perfect that many of her fans failed to recognize her.)

She shares a bench with young Kip (Tom Brown), who also is not joining in the festivities. His beloved Barbara (Lynne Carver) is considering going to New York to be a great opera star. (No character in a 1930s film ever became anything less than a "great opera star." No hardworking nonstars or chorus members existed in Hollywood fiction.)

Barbara arrives, bubbling with the news that the dashing impresario on her arm (Russell Hicks) considers her worthy of a career. She will visit Miss Morrison later that afternoon to tell her all about it. The impresario eyes the departing old lady quizzically, but Barbara assures him that she is just a sweet, sheltered old lady.

The enigmatic Miss Morrison (Jeanette), a "sweet old lady" with a passionate past. *Courtesy David Chierichetti.*

Maytime

An incredible evening! American singer, Marcia Mornay (Jeanette), and her impresario, Nikolai Nazaroff (John Barrymore), arrive at the court of Louis Napoleon. The Emperor invites her to sing, and a famous composer agrees to write an opera for her. A third surprise awaits her.

Jenny Lind—or *Marcia Mornay*. Miss Morrison takes a deep breath. For the first time she is going to tell Barbara about herself because—*she* was Marcia Mornay.

"It was many years ago. I was very young. It was Paris, in the court of Louis Napoleon!" The wrinkled face vanishes and we are at a splendid court ball. There is a triumphant blast of trumpets, then a rollicking mazurka as the ladies in hoop skirts and the gentlemen in court dress promenade gaily, presided over by Louis Napoleon (Guy Bates Post) and his beauteous Eugenie (Iphigenie Castiglioni).

The trumpets sound again as an elegant carriage pulls up to the massive steps outside. A distinguished man in court dress (the ancestor of our evening tails plus knee breeches and buckle shoes) hands out a lady dressed in glistening white net. The camera cuts to a medium shot, and we see an unbelievably radiant Marcia Mornay (Jeanette) surveying the palace with awe and wonder. She is incredibly nervous at this first venture into the world of royalty, although her escort sarcastically belittles Louis Napoleon's origin. Nicolai Nazaroff (John Barrymore in one of his last coherent film performances) tells her that he presents his singers at court when they are fit to be presented. If she mistrusts his judgment...

Nervously she powders her nose, using the breastplate of a sentry on the stairs for a mirror, then graciously sweeps into the ballroom. She is presented to the emperor, then, on Nicolai's arm, she glides gracefully down the marble staircase and along the columned arcade toward the orchestra at the far end of the hall. As they pass, the comments of the bystanders fill us in on their background. She is Nicolai's latest protégée, although another word might be more fitting, one gentleman murmurs. Nicolai is known for driving singers unmercifully, but one simpering lady assures her companion that he *can* be quite human.

Marcia's first song is "Les Filles de Cadix," which she sings with such saucy good humor that the crowd turns to see the emperor's reaction. He is smiling, so they relax and smile too. Her second song, the martial "Le Regiment de Sambre et Meuse," rouses the guests to patriotic fervor, as they join Marcia and the Don Cossack Choir in the chorus. She is the hit of the evening.

Nikolai (John Barrymore) asks a very high price for his services.

At dinner, she is seated next to the great composer, Trentini (Paul Porcasi). Nicolai has undoubtedly arranged it, for through subtle psychology he persuades the egotistical Trentini to write an opera for Miss Mornay. It is truly the night of her life!

Back home, the now-young Ellen takes Marcia's wraps as she swirls ecstatically around the enormous drawing room. Nicolai has one more surprise for her. Tonight is the culmination of their hard work together. She has always obeyed him, let nothing stand in the way of her career, and until now he has never demanded anything of her. To the gratitude glowing on Marcia's face is added a small element of fear. "I owe all my success to you," she replies. "If there *is* anything I can do to repay you..." Her eyes drop against her will and then are forced back to his.

"Poor Marcia," he answers. "I'm asking a very high price. I want to marry you." Astonishment and relief flash in quick succession on her face. She will be very happy to marry him. Nicolai orders her to get some rest. It is after midnight, and she has a performance the next day. But Marcia can't sleep. The excitement has been too much for her. Spotting a row of horse-drawn carriages parked across the street, she gets dressed again over Ellen's protests and slips out for a ride. The carriage driver (Charles Judels) mistakes her purpose and tells her cheerfully that her husband will have calmed down by the time she returns. The fatigue of the day, the rhythm of the swaying carriage, and the glimmering lampposts gliding past all have their effect. She dozes off.

The sound of church bells chiming 3 AM brings her back to reality. Quickly she orders the carriage to go back and the driver pulls sharply on the reins. The ancient harness snaps and "Jenny" goes trotting off down the twisting cobblestone street while her driver gallops comically after her. Marcia finds herself in the Bohemian quarter of Paris. In a nearby café, voices can be heard boisterously raised in song,

Maytime

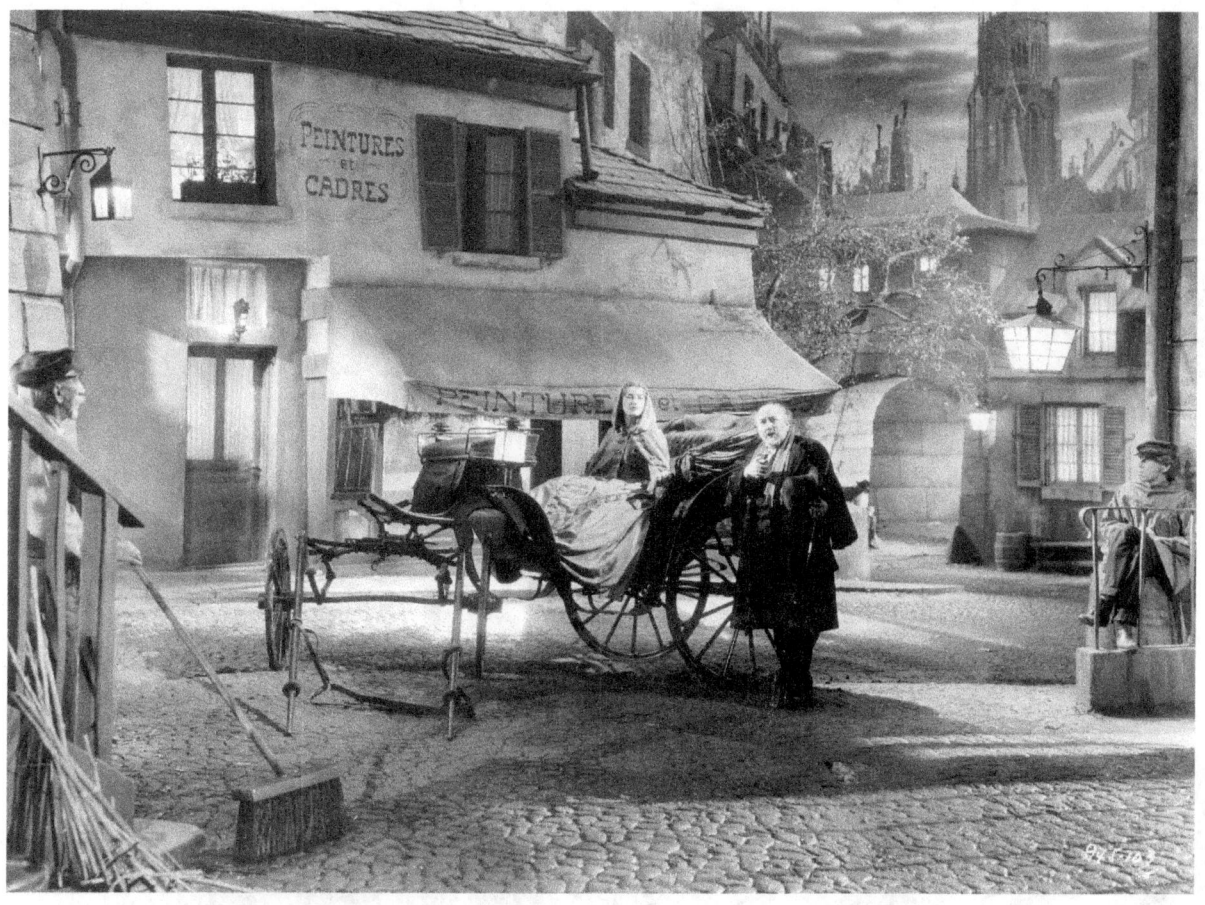

Paris, the student quarter, as created on an MGM soundstage. Marcia's midnight drive comes to an abrupt end when the horse runs away, to the consternation of the cabby (Charles Judels). *Courtesy Jack Tillmany*

and the leading singer has a decidedly beautiful baritone. Marcia can't resist peeking in.

A tall, blond singer is perched on a counter at one end of the smoky cellar, entertaining the colorful neighborhood types with a French student song, "Plantons la vigne." The customers beg for another, and he obliges them with "Vive l'opera," accompanying his tale of the "fat prima donna" by drawing a charcoal cartoon of the lady on the cellar wall. Concluding his tale with an impromptu can can step, the baritone hits a lengthy high note and collapses full length from the counter into the arms of his obliging audience. They dump him into an empty chair, and Paul Allison (Nelson) is sitting face to face with Marcia Mornay.

She begs him to sing again, and he realizes that he has discovered a fellow American. He's been starved for the sound of an American voice and here she is, not only American, but *beautiful*. She laughingly refuses his request to see her again. She is, she tells him slyly, a prima donna, and he doesn't like prima donnas. She gestures to the grotesque sketch on the wall. He assures her he *adores* prima donnas. She in turn assures him that she likes him and that he has a wonderful voice, but she is much too busy ever to see him again.

Paul Allison (Nelson) is an American opera student who prefers singing in congenial surroundings.

Her driver reappears just as the crowd recognizes Marcia Mornay and calls for a song. Ignoring every film tradition, Paul rescues Marcia and escorts her to her carriage. There, he steadfastly refuses to let go of her hand until she agrees to have lunch with him. He points to his apartment across the street. She is alarmed at his insistence and orders her driver to continue. Paul clings precariously to the side of the swiftly moving carriage until she fearfully agrees.

He springs to safety with a whoop that begins an operatic hodge-podge happily entitled "Ham and Eggs." With snatches of melody from a dozen operas, he boasts of the menu he plans, borrows money from his cronies for the groceries, and awakens most of the neighbors who, of course, sing of their anger from their respective windows. Gendarmes who are not so musically inclined eventually break up the concert, and Paul races up several flights of stairs to his garret, hitting the final high note as he bursts through the door.

The vibrato of the note is matched by the quivering of the fat little man in nightcap, asleep in a large easy chair. He is Archipenko (Herman Bing), Paul's music teacher and roommate, who has been waiting up for Paul. He rages over Paul's late hours, but Paul is oblivious. He has met the loveliest woman in Paris. "*Again?*" Archipenko asks with raised eyebrows.

Archipenko's list of grievances against Paul grows so lengthy that Paul drops to the piano bench and underlines each with a chord. As the little man turns to pleading, Paul plays a high pitched trill. But Archipenko's concern turns to amazement when Paul informs him, to the tune of the "William Tell Overture," that Marcia Mornay is coming to lunch.

At her apartment, Marcia tries to slip in quietly. Nicolai is waiting for her in his dressing gown, a cigarette smoldering ominously in his fingers. He has stood there, Ellen whispers, since he discovered she was gone. She tries to explain, but he cuts her short, implying that she has gone to meet another man. Dismayed, she tells him he can ask the cab driver to verify her story. He is waiting downstairs since she forgot her money. The cabby apologizes for the accident, and Nicolai vastly overpays him.

Paul is out shopping for groceries bright and early the next morning. He pauses before a poster announcing *Les Huguenots* that night at the opera, with Marcia as the page, Urbain. A voice from a nearby sidewalk café interrupts his reverie. It is Monsieur Fanchon (Sig Rumann), bragging of the pair of first-row seats he has. Paul tells him he will be there too, in standing room. Fanchon scoffs. The line is around the block already. He pulls his two tickets from his wallet and flaunts them at Paul, crowing at his luck in getting them.

The waiter (Clarence Wilson) brings Fanchon's change and somehow a glass of wine is overturned in Fanchon's lap. Gallantly Paul leaps to rescue the gentleman's wallet, which has slipped under the table. Fanchon departs, leaving the clumsy waiter no tip and Paul, with a furtive grin, produces the two precious tickets from under the table.

Marcia joins Paul and his teacher (Herman Bing) for a lunch of Virginia ham and eggs. The two homesick Americans end up at the piano.

At noon, Paul and Archipenko are busily preparing the luncheon, Paul tossing his sheet music into the stove when they run out of fuel. Archipenko makes a terrible discovery—they have only two plates. The doorbell rings and in their rush to answer, one of the plates is lost. It is Marcia, come to tell Paul that she can't come. But the ham is ready, Paul tells her, *Virginia* ham. Wavering, she sees all their preparations. With a little sigh, she submits and soon is draped in an enormous apron, helping fry the eggs. The last plate is lost in a masterpiece of fumbling by Paul and Archipenko.

Dissolve to the feast—served in saucers. After comical toasts, laughter, and good talk, the dishes are being cleared. Paul is happily humming, and Marcia slips away to the piano in the living room. As the song is echoed from the next room, Paul tosses away the dishtowel and joins her in a duet of "Carry Me Back to Old Virginny." It is a moving moment in the film, touching on the homesickness of the two Americans far from home.

Archipenko applauds loudly. Paul would be such a great singer, he tells Marcia, if *only* he'd study. Perhaps Mlle Mornay will urge him to give up his late hours and work hard. But why should he listen to her? Marcia asks. "I can think of a lot of reasons," Paul replies.

The clock strikes, and Marcia realizes she will be in terrible trouble if she doesn't leave at once. Grabbing her bonnet, she bolts to the door. "It's been fun, but it's all over now, goodbye," and she flees down the stairs. Paul watches her drive away from the window, fingering the two tickets for *Les Huguenots*.

The overture can be heard from the resplendent foyer of the opera as Monsieur Fanchon and his large wife (Anne Demetrio) irately order the usher (George Davis) to show them to their seats. Fanchon has lost the tickets, but he can remember the seat numbers: seven and eight. "Three and four," corrects Mme Fanchon. The usher has no authority to let them in, and Fanchon storms off in search of the

Paul pursues Marcia to the opera house. Here she begs him to leave her dressing room before Nicolai finds him there. (Rafaela Ottiano, right.) To get rid of him, she agrees to meet him at the May Day fair.

manager. Inside in the first row (seats three and four), Paul is glorying in the music, but Archipenko keeps glancing nervously up the aisle.

Marcia makes her entrance in a very handsome "page" costume and delivers her aria (Recitative: "Nobles Seigneurs, salut"; aria: "Une Dame Noble et Sage") to thunderous applause. As she is taking her bows, she watches Paul and Archipenko being escorted up the aisle by a formidable manager. Backstage, she finds Paul waiting in her dressing room. Nicolai is due any minute, and, in her haste to get rid of him, she again promises to meet him, this time for the May Day festival at Saint Cloud.

The elated Paul dashes from the dressing room, straight into Nicolai. Marcia makes light of her visitor: just a silly young man from the gallery who wanted to boast that he had met her. Nicolai sternly reminds her that it is the critics who sell orchestra seats, and ushers them in.

It is May Day in the country, and Paul is waiting impatiently by the road as the festive couples hurry by on their way to the fair.

Maytime

Paul and Marcia set out for a day of fun and romance that must last them all their lives.

Saint Cloud, California style. (Note the eucalyptus trees in the French countryside.)

Competing on the high notes of "Santa Lucia." (Ludovico Tomarchio, right.)

Dancing to the lilting strains of "Road to Paradise."
Courtesy Dolores Baird.

Maytime

Filming the swing sequence.

"Where's your sweetheart?" calls one young man. "You can't have any fun without a sweetheart." Finally, Paul spots Marcia's carriage on the road and runs to meet it. "I was mad to come," she tells him, but Paul takes her hand and pulls her along. "You're going to forget who you are and what you are and everything else," he orders, "except that it's May Day and the sun is shining and we're going to have fun!"

They plunge into the happy crowd, and, in a glorious blend of music and images, we follow them through the joyous day. They swing, play games, watch tightrope walkers and gypsy dancers, and join an Italian tenor in the final few bars of "Santa Lucia," gleefully outlasting him when he tries to hold the high note longer than they.

Finally, to the lilting melody "Road to Paradise," they waltz in a leafy pavilion. Peasant couples swirl around them, passing flowered hoops and tossing handfuls of petals in the air. As Paul and Marcia turn in each other's arms, a Slavko Vorkapich mood montage begins. We see a bouquet of flowers rise and come together, tied with a ribbon bow as birds twitter in the trees and the sun makes a cascade of diamonds reflected in a sheet of water.

Paul and Marcia have climbed to a nearby hill and sit beside a stream (an obvious sound stage set and possibly the only weak element in the film). There, Paul tells her he will sing her a song about sweethearts so that she will remember this day: "Will You Remember." Marcia is moved to join him and then, unhappily, to admit that she loves him too.

It had been such fun. She had hoped it would end like that, but now—there is someone else. Nicolai. She isn't just marrying Nicolai because he's kind and he needs her. She owes him everything. For four years he has sacrificed for her, never breaking a promise, never letting her down. Now she can't fail him, even for something she wants far more. Why don't she and Paul just remember this day? "I'll always love you." Paul says.

"And I'll always...remember your song," Marcia replies.

> Sweetheart, sweetheart, sweetheart,
> Will you love me ever?
> Will you remember the day
> When we were happy in May?
> (Copyright G. Schirmer & Co.)

She rushes off, and, in another masterful Vorkapich montage, we see the bouquet come untied, the blossoms scattering. On a split screen, we see the two lovers standing alone in their rooms. A metronome superimposed over the stern face of Nicolai fills the screen, and the saga of Marcia's career begins. In a succession of opera scenes, rushing trains and carriages, rising and falling curtains, close-ups of sheet music and opera posters, Marcia changes from a lovely young girl to a mature woman, applauded by everyone, yet alone in the spotlight. In the wake of the boat carrying her back to America, Paul's face appears as a few bars of "Will You Remember" weave through the operatic strains. But the cheering reception at the dock overwhelms the melody, and a regal Marcia is seen waving politely, the dapper Nicolai at her side.

Marcia is a dutiful wife to the demanding Nikolai until, years later, fate throws her and Paul together again. Left to right, Walter Kingsford, Jeanette, Nelson, Herman Bing, John Barrymore.

At her hotel, she quietly greets the manager (Douglas Wood) and retires to take a hot bath before her first rehearsal. Nicolai comes to tell her that he will take care of the Board of Directors who are due momentarily. Is she glad to be back in America? he asks. She certainly doesn't show it. Dully Marcia tells him that she's not awfully excited about anything. She pats his hand absently. It is too much for Nicolai who seizes her and kisses her passionately. When he finally lets her go, she sits motionless, staring into space. With a sardonic half bow and click of his heels, he apologizes. "I'm sorry. I should have remembered that *that* excites you less than anything else." He has no right to say that, he acknowledges. She has been a perfect wife, faithful, loyal, obedient, and affectionate. But never once in all the years that they have been married has he felt that he completely possessed her. It has made him love her too much. He kisses her hand and, in a bit of Barrymore scene stealing, rolls his eyes elaborately toward the door so that we follow his exit rather than watching the silent Marcia.

The Board of Directors happily informs Nicolai that they have prepared *La Traviata* for Mme Mornay. "Tra-vi-a-ta?" trills the Barrymore voice in deep disdain. He applauds their efforts. Unfortunately Mme Mornay's choice is *Czaritza*, the opera written for her by the great Trentini. But, objects one bearded director (Harlan Briggs), *Czaritza* needs a baritone. They do have Paul Allison, interjects another, but he is not well enough known. "The public," Nicolai states icily, "will come to hear Mme Mornay." And so it is decided.

Marcia is about to dress when Nicolai calls the news to her through the door. She sways slightly and stands stunned for a moment. Then, her voice cracking into a girlish register, she asks if they couldn't get someone better known. Nicolai assures her that Allison has a fine reputation. She must hurry or they'll be late for the rehearsal.

On the vast opera stage, dotted with chairs and folded scenery, a rehearsal piano pounds out the ominous measures of *Czaritza*. The chorus and principals of the new opera are studying their scores by the flickering work light as Mme Mornay and party enter. They make their way between the sheet-draped seats to the temporary ramp over the orchestra pit. Marcia greets the conductor (Frank Puglia) graciously, but her eyes dart hesitantly toward the stage. She turns to be presented to the company. Paul is standing before her. "How do you do?" she murmurs. "It is an honor, Madame, to sing with you," he replies, gently taking her hand. They stand like that for several moments until the next member of the company is presented. Nicolai eyes Paul strangely.

Through the back doors of the stage bursts Archipenko, resplendent in fur-collared coat and silk hat. He is overjoyed to see Marcia. All these years he has been saying little prayers for her because of what she did for Paul. Stepping sharply on Archipenko's fancy boot, Paul explains to Nicolai that when he was a student in Paris, Mme Mornay was kind enough to encourage him with his career. The rehearsal begins. One of the directors congratulates Nicolai on the choice of *Czaritza*. It is just the chance young Allison has been waiting for. "Yes," Nicolai replies darkly, "I'm *sure* it is."

The singers take their positions on the dim, cluttered stage and begin the final scene of the opera. As the chorus intones a dirge-like Russian chant, the scene dissolves to the performance. The stage is now a room in the Czaritza's palace. This *Czaritza* sequence is Tchaikovsky's Fifth Symphony, made excitingly fresh by its conversion to an opera. William von Wymetal, former producer of the Philadelphia Opera Society, followed young Eddy to Hollywood, where he first directed the *Rose Marie* opera sequences and then created this superb "opera."

The Czaritza (Marcia) is preparing to wave to a waiting crowd from the balcony when her lover, Petrov (Paul), is dragged in by soldiers. Her minister (Adia Kuznetzoff, also an extra in the café sequence) reminds her of her duty and presents her to the throng below, who respond joyously, accompanied by pealing church bells. Petrov proudly proclaims his guilt in seeking the liberty of the people, and here Eddy makes good use of his classic Delsarte training. The Czaritza reluctantly signs the death warrant and tells Petrov that her heart will die with him.

Paul is now a famous baritone. During a passionate duet, they realize they still love each other. (The made-up "opera" *Czaritza* used musical themes from Tchaikovsky's Fifth Symphony.)

Marcia begs her husband to set her free. He does, but not in the way she had hoped.

Left alone, they sing of their love to Tchaikovsky's most romantic love themes. As the music builds and builds to a heart-stopping climax, Paul and Marcia are unable to keep up the pretense any longer. They kiss passionately, oblivious to the roar of applause, the conductor's astonishment, and Nicolai's contorted face in the wings. Paul tells Marcia that she is never going back to Nicolai. He will take her away that night.

In Marcia's dressing room, Nicolai is again all icy reserve. "I brought you two together again. It has its humor." Marcia is too drained to pretend or argue. She sends word to Paul to wait until he hears from her, and she and Nicolai return to the hotel. There she quietly begs Nicolai to set her free. He agrees, but his control vanishes when he has left her. He sinks against his bedroom door in a beautiful example of a Barrymore "mad scene," his eyes rolling, his face terrible to behold. Suddenly, determination puts new life in the sagging body. He strides to the closet for his coat and hat, then opens a small case in his dresser and pockets the contents.

In her room, Marcia is sitting numb and unbelieving when she hears a door slam. Puzzled and alarmed, she goes to Nicolai's room and sees the empty case—a gun case. With a stifled cry, she rushes out into the street after him. The strains of the love theme now pound ominously as we cut from Nicolai striding purposefully through the lightly swirling snow to Marcia racing after him, unsure of her footing on the icy sidewalk.

As Nicolai reaches Paul's door, the love theme continues from inside. Paul is at the piano playing when he realizes Nicolai has let himself in and is standing in the darkened doorway. "I'm giving Marcia her freedom," Nicolai announces calmly, "...and you yours." Marcia is halfway up the stairs when she hears a sharp sound.

Nicolai appears at the top of the stairs, a gun dangling in his hand. Marcia stares unbelievingly, then pushes past him into the apartment. Paul is trying to pull himself up on the piano bench. As Marcia cradles his head in her lap, he tells her that their one day did last him all his life. He dies in her arms, and she collapses in tears as the camera pans up to the snow swirling against the window.

The snow changes to drifting white blossoms, and we are back in Miss Morrison's garden. Barbara promises to visit her much more often so that she won't be lonely, and then sets out to make up with Kip. Smiling, Miss Morrison leans back against the apple tree. We hear the first notes of "Will You Remember" as her eyes slowly close. Paul's voice takes up the song.

Young and straight, he appears before her. From the frail old body on the bench the young Marcia rises and takes his hands. Their ephemeral forms pause and look down the lane at the reunited Kip and Barbara, then turn and walk along under an archway of flowering trees. Slowly they cease being transparent. Marcia's head is against Paul's shoulder as they sing:

> ...though our paths may sever,
> To life's last faint ember,
> We will remember
> Springtime, love time, May.
>   (Copyright G. Schirmer & Co.)

Maytime was Miss MacDonald's personal favorite among her films. Not only was it an

Maytime

The lovers are reunited in a finale guaranteed to put a lump in the throat of the most jaded moviegoer. (In major theatres, a pink-colored gel was sometimes put in front of the projector lens for this scene.)

acting *tour-de-force* for her, but her singing was probably never better. Recording techniques and her voice had both reached perfection almost simultaneously. Paying homage to the electronic advancement, the *New York Times* wrote: "Jeanette MacDonald could not be so beautiful a soprano as the picture would have us assume. Opera would have claimed her. But the bright young men at the sound controls do for her what a dozen maestros could not do: they have lined her throat with velvet and coated her mouth with gold. Miss MacDonald emerges through their magic as the screen's loveliest singer." (This review also demonstrates the condescending attitude still maintained by some critics toward the theatre's stepchild, cinema).

Miss MacDonald *did* want to sing opera. If sheer determination and exhaustive efforts could make her a film star, why couldn't the same make her an opera star, despite a very late start and an unlikely background as a Broadway ingénue? Nelson Eddy, after all, was basically a classical singer. (His scenes in *Maytime* were all done in the first weeks of shooting to release him for his four-month concert tour.) Miss MacDonald began training for an operatic career, with Lotte Lehmann among others, with a singularity of purpose that must overcome any physical limitations.

John Barrymore's performance in *Maytime* is extremely touching, possibly because the character was so close to the real Barrymore—a ruin of a man so recently handsome and eloquent. In a very short time, Barrymore's film rôles would be limited to productions in which the director was willing to turn on the camera, hoping to catch a performance. This worked well in films like *The Great Man Votes* (RKO 1939), but dogs like *The Great Profile* and *Hold That Coed* are tragic to watch. During the filming of *Maytime,* Barrymore married (and separated from) Elaine Barrie, after receiving his divorce from Dolores Costello. In one scene of the film, Eddy fluffed a line as he begged Jeanette to give up Barrymore. With the cameras

Sheet music cover. *Courtesy Fay Holming.*

rolling, he grabbed her shoulders and said, "You can't marry him! I'm going to marry him myself!" "Not if Elaine has anything to say about it," quipped Jeanette.

The superb *Maytime* confirmed the stardom of the team, although irate letters to the editor in *Picture Play* from Eddy fans indicated that they had seen the film with a stopwatch and thought it an outrage that he had so much less time on the screen than Jeanette.

MGM reasoned that anyone who would pay to see them together would most likely pay twice to see them separately and decided to split them. Nelson was teamed in *Rosalie* with Eleanor Powell, fresh from a personal triumph in *Broadway Melody of 1936*, and Jeanette delayed wedding plans to star alone over the title for the first time in *The Firefly*.

Enough credit cannot be given to musical director Herbert Stothart for the success of the

MacDonald/Eddy films. After the personalities of the stars themselves and the good scripts of their early films, it was Stothart's subtle and sensitive selection and arrangement of musical numbers that made the films so delightful. After teaching music at Wisconsin University, Stothart wrote songs for several Broadway shows, *Always You* and *Tickle Me*, both 1920 and both with lyrics by Oscar Hammerstein II. He also collaborated with prominent composers. He contributed to *Song of the Flame* (with Gershwin) and *Wild Flower* (with Vincent Youmans), but his best remembered interpolations were in Friml's *Rose-Marie*. In 1929, he went to MGM as musical director. Between then and his death in 1949, he worked on every MacDonald/Eddy film at MGM except Eddy's *Let Freedom Ring* and Jeanette's final film, *The Sun Comes Up*. He wrote original music ("Pardon Me Madame" in *Rose Marie*, "High Flyin'" in *Broadway Serenade*), made fresh arrangements for hokey old war-horses and balanced the musical menu in each film like a superb chef creating a feast for the ear.

Maytime brought two twenty-year-olds together for the first time. Bob Wright and Chet Forrest wrote new lyrics for venerable melodies. They would do so admirably for eight MacDonald/Eddy films before going "legit," forging stage works out of the works of classic composers: *Song of Norway* out of Grieg and *Kismet* out of Borodin.

Another steady contributor to the MacDonald/Eddy films was comedian Herman Bing. He had come to Hollywood as assistant to the great director F.W. Murnau (*Sunrise*). When Murnau was killed in an auto accident in 1931, Bing turned exclusively to acting. The doughty little man with the z-zauerr-r-r-kraut accent had a lively song number in the film. As the director and technicians fought desperately to keep from cracking up, he turned his Germanic energies loose on an original *Maytime* song, "Jump Jim Crow" ("Ar-r-r-round you go").

Before he got through with the r's in that one, a great number of takes were required because the crew kept collapsing helplessly to the floor with laughter. The scene never reached the screen and resides in some film heaven along with the *Tosca* sequence. A decade later, the little man who had made millions laugh died tragically, by his own hand, in 1947.

Reviews

The *New York Times*, as previously noted, thought *Maytime* "the most entrancing operetta the screen has given us." They continued: "It establishes Jeanette MacDonald as the possessor of the cinema's loveliest voice—this with all deference to the probably superior off-screen voices of Lily Pons, Grace Moore, and Gladys Swarthout—and it affirms Nelson Eddy's preeminence among the baritones of filmdom. The screen can do no wrong while these two are singing. *Maytime* is the most joyous operetta of the season, a picture to treasure."

The *New York Herald Tribune* echoed the *Times*' praises, but stood alone in finding fault with the length (132 minutes). *Variety* also

Shooting the finale.

Nelson Eddy and Jeanette MacDonald. *Courtesy Dennis & Pat Taylor.*

Maytime

thought the film guilty of "dull interludes," but praised the stars as "splendid" and the musical direction as Stothart's "best Hollywood film musical achievement," extolling every phase of production.

Recordings (See Discography for further information)

"Will You Remember" (MacDonald and Eddy; also MacDonald alone)
"Farewell to Dreams" (MacDonald and Eddy) - recorded for first film version, but not sung in final film
"Les Filles de Cadix" (MacDonald)

Music in the Film

In listing performers after each title, "and" denotes a genuine duet, while commas between names indicate a sequence of singers.

Overture: "Will You Remember," "Road to Paradise"*
"Now is the Month of Maying" (children's chorus) - traditional melody, lyrics by Thomas Morley
"Summer Is Icumen In" (children's chorus) - medieval song
"Love's Old Sweet Song" ["Just a song at twilight..."] (chorus) - music by J.L. Molloy, lyrics by G. Clifford Bingham. COMBINES WITH:
"Will You Remember" fragment (Eddy and chorus)
Mazurka from "Les Sylphides" (orchestral) - by Frederic Chopin with unusual arrangement by Herbert Stothart
"Napoleonic Waltz" (orchestral) - source uncertain, arranged by Herbert Stothart
"Les Filles de Cadix" [The Maids of Cadiz] (MacDonald) - music by Leo Delibes, French lyrics by Alfred deMusset
"Le Regiment de Sambre et Meuse" (MacDonald, Don Cossack Choir, chorus) - by Robert Planquette
"Plantons la vigne" [Come, plant the vineyards] (Eddy) - Breton folk song
"Vive l'opera" (Eddy and chorus) - French folk song with English lyrics by Bob Wright and Chet Forrest
"HAM AND EGGS" MEDLEY: (Eddy, assorted soloists, and chorus) - a medley of opera melodies compiled by Herbert Stothart, with new lyrics on the subject of ham and eggs by Bob Wright and Chet Forrest, containing:
"Caro Nome" from *Rigoletto* by Giuseppe Verdi
"Largo al Factotum" from *The Barber of Seville* by Gioacchino Rossini
"O, Du Mein Holder Abendstern" (Oh, Evening Star) from *Tannhäuser* by Richard Wagner
"Largo al Factotum" reprise
"La Donna e Mobile" from *Rigoletto* by Giuseppe Verdi
"Soldiers' Chorus" from *Faust* by Charles Gounod
"Chi Me Frena?" sextet from *Lucia di Lammermoor* by Gaetano Donizetti
"Anvil Chorus" from *Il Trovatore* by Giuseppe Verdi
William Tell Overture by Gioacchino Rossini
"Carry Me Back to Old Virginny" (Eddy and MacDonald) - by James Bland (composer of "Oh, Dem Golden Slippers" and "In the Evening by the Moonlight")
Scene from *Les Huguenots*: Recitative "Nobles Seigneurs, Salut" and aria "Une Dame Noble et Sage" (MacDonald with Tudor Williams and male chorus) - music by Giacomo Meyerbeer, lyrics by Eugène Scribe and Émile Deschamps
MAY DAY MONTAGE: "Road to Paradise" (orchestral); "Will You Remember" (orchestral)
"Santa Lucia" (Ludovico Tomarchio, MacDonald and Eddy) - by Teodoro Cottrau
"Will You Remember" (Eddy, MacDonald) - music by Sigmund Romberg, lyrics by Rida Johnson Young

OPERA CAREER MONTAGE: **
    "Miserere" from *Il Trovatore* by Giuseppe Verdi (MacDonald, baritone, male chorus)
    Prison scene from *Faust* by Charles Gounod (MacDonald, tenor, baritone)
    "Liebestod" from *Tristan und Isolde* by Richard Wagner (MacDonald)
    "Sempre Libera" from *La Traviata* by Giuseppe Verdi (MacDonald, chorus)
    "Triumphal Chorus" from *Le Prophête* by Giacomo Meyerbeer (orchestral)
    "I Dreamt I Dwelt in Marble Halls" from *The Bohemian Girl* by Michael William Balfé (MacDonald)
    "The Last Rose of Summer" from *Martha* by Friedrich von Flotow, actually an old Irish folk song (MacDonald) ***
    "Chi Me Frena?" sextet from *Lucia di Lammermoor* by Gaetano Donizetti (MacDonald, mezzo, two tenors, baritone, bass)
(MGM pay records list Nick Angelo, tenor; Dick Dennis, tenor; Earl Covert, baritone; Allan Watson, bass; and Bernice Alstock, contralto, as singers in the above opera sequence.)
ORCHESTRAL MEDLEY: "Will You Remember" reprise; "Columbia, the Gem of the Ocean" by Thomas E. Williams; "Sidewalks of New York" by Charles B. Lawlor
Czaritza, a manufactured opera with music from the Fifth Symphony of Peter Ilich Tchaikovsky, libretto and original English lyrics by Bob Wright and Chet Forrest, French lyrics by Gilles Guilbert (MacDonald, Adia Kuznetzoff, Mariska Aldrich, Eddy, and chorus). The sequence was intended to be in English, but after Wright and Forrest had finished it, someone decided that opera shouldn't be in a language the audience can understand, so a French translation of the Wright-Forrest libretto was made! MGM pay records list M. Morova as singing and acting the role of the nurse and Alexander Kandiba, bass, acting the Black Priest.

Makeup for 1930 film heroes meant mandatory lipstick and eye shadow—one reason that villains of the period fare better with modern audiences. Even Humphry Bogart got the full beauty treatment when he wasn't playing a gangster.

Finale: "Will You Remember" reprise (Eddy and MacDonald)

* In *Deep in My Heart*, MGM's 1954 film bio of composer Sigmund Romberg, Vic Damone sings "Road to Paradise." He and Jane Powell also sing "Will You Remember."

** It is necessary to note that the opera montage in *Maytime* showing Marcia Mornay's rise to fame has aroused incredulity and occasional laughter from opera buffs since the film's initial release. Snippets from *Il Trovatore*, *Faust*, *Tristan und Isolde*, *La Traviata*, *The Bohemian Girl*, *Marta*, and *Lucia di Lammermoor* are

Maytime

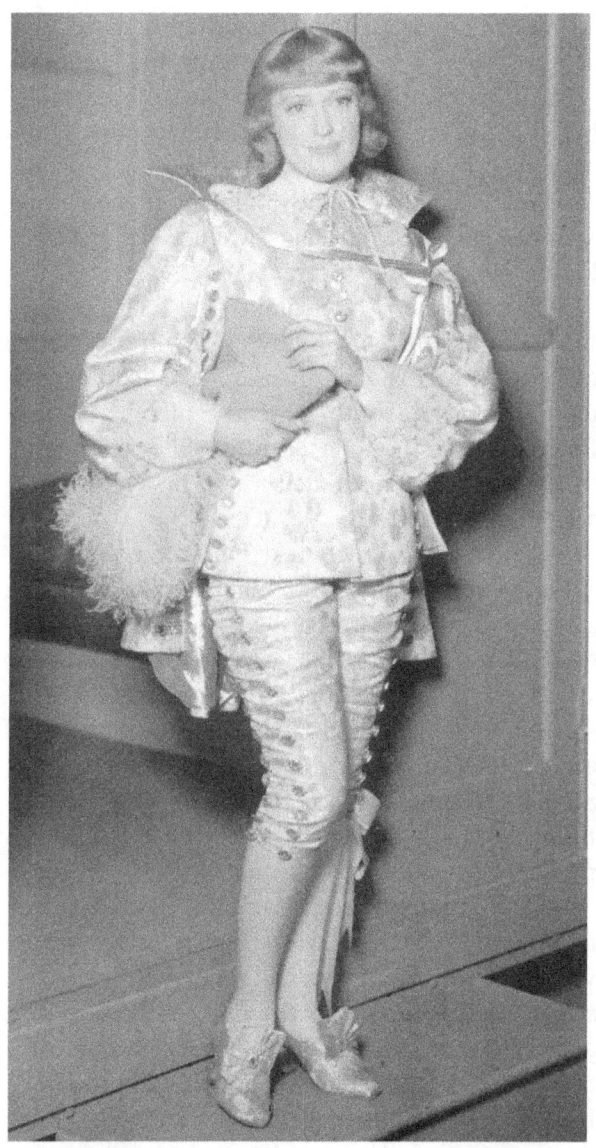

Adrian's fetching costume for Jeanette as Urbain, the page, in the opera sequence from *Les Huguenots*. *Courtesy Anna Michalik.*

heard and visualized. Posters and scores indicate that Marcia Mornay also triumphed in *Tannhäuser*, *Maritana*, *Le Prophête*, *Lohengrin*, *Norma*, *Don Giovanni*, and *The Barber of Seville*. It is one of Vorkapich's most brilliant montages—if *only* the operas had been selected more carefully. At the time the film was released, there were only two internationally known opera stars who might have sung such a repertoire, Lilli Lehman and the American Lillian Nordica. Each started out in the lighter, more brilliant coloratura rôles and progressed to the heavier rôles of Wagner, Bellini, or Mozart. The rôles were never sung simultaneously as they are in the montage. (In modern times both Maria Callas and Joan Sutherland have sung such disparate rôles as Wagner and the Bel Canto repertoire, but never one after the other.) There are an infinite number of operas within Jeanette's vocal range that might have proved more believable than *Tristan*, *Tannhäuser*, *Lohengrin*, *Norma*, or *Don Giovanni*.

*** Nelson's grandmother, Caroline Kendrick, recorded this song for Columbia Records in 1904.

Baritones Joseph Bjorndahl and Douglas McPhail are listed in MGM pay records as doing separate recordings of "M'Appari," the latter with Miss MacDonald. This song does not appear in the film and is a tenor aria. Nelson recorded "Il Balen" from *Il Trovatore* by Verdi, and both principals recorded scenes from Act II of *Tosca* by Puccini which included the classic soprano aria, "Visi d'Arte."

Original stage songs used in the film were "Will You Remember" and an orchestral version of "Road to Paradise." "Farewell to Dreams" was recorded and released in conjunction with the earlier version of the film. "Jump Jim Crow" was filmed with Herman Bing, but cut from the released version.

Script History
Contributed by Mary Truesdell

At least sixteen different writers tried their hand at a film script of *Maytime* for MGM, starting in the 1920s. Some used themes and personalities that fortunately never made it into the final film.

In a 1935 draft by director Edmund Goulding and Franz Schulz, the hero Richard (Nelson) is a drunken, tobacco-chewing, tattooed Irish sailor, given to singing and brawling. That same year, the noted scriptwriter Frances Marion shaped a more tasteful vehicle intended for Grace Moore in which the heroine marries another out of love for her crippled father—thus introducing the theme of self sacrifice for duty as in *Rose Marie*. The Marion version had three generations of lovers, from pre-Civil War to modern times.

In early 1936, famed playwright Moss Hart submitted a breezy modern story with lots of snappy dialogue. However, Irving Thalberg remained committed to a period piece full of sentiment about "tenderness, mingled with charm, humor, sentiment, and romance."

Multi-talented director Edmund Goulding usually contributed highly colorful and dramatic touches to the scripts of his films, but after Thalberg's death, the project was assigned to producer Hunt Stromberg. Needing to "get on with it," MGM assigned Goulding to another film and replaced him on *Maytime* by workmanly W.S. Van Dyke.

In *Maytime*. Courtesy John Cocchi.

Screen credit for the second and final version of *Maytime* goes to twenty-four-year-old Noël Langley, who, according to official MGM publicity, came up with a complete new script in little more than a week following Irving Thalberg's death. Actually, the production files, archived at the Fairbanks Center for Motion Picture Study, tell a different story.

Thalberg died on September 14, 1936. Just twelve days later, Claudine West, a forty-six-year-old English writer, submitted a 32-page treatment that presents an outline nearly identical scene for scene with the finished film. (She was one of many who had contributed to the first "Goulding script" of *Maytime*.)

The question becomes: Did someone order West to produce this new treatment within hours after Thalberg's death on the assumption that the Goulding production would be jettisoned? If so, who? Or, almost equally cold-bloodedly, had she previously been assigned to come up with a completely new script? Minutes of the crucial production meetings for this period are missing from the Fairbanks Center's files, so we will probably never know.

The Claudine West treatment is identical to the finished film up until the lovers part in Paris, with just two differences. There is no proposal scene because the heroine and her impresario are already engaged when the flashback begins. And the ham-and-eggs lunch is merged with the May Day fair scene into a single picnic, eliminating the intervening *Huguenot* aria and subsequent meeting backstage. At this point, the heroine chooses the impresario over the penniless student because Nazaroff can further her career. The Code of Honor theme is not yet present.

West then returns the lovers (named "Janice" and "Richard") to New York years later, where their love is reconfirmed by a series of meetings, including one at a student party that includes the already-filmed "Jump Jim Crow," possibly a sop to economy because the original recorded soundtrack could be used. The big musical reunion is not yet present. The heroine *does* ask for a divorce and Nazaroff *does* agree, then goes to murder the hero, making it look like suicide. The heroine is devastated, leaves her husband, and retires to a small town where she advises a lovelorn maiden to marry the man she loves. (The young girl has not been offered an operatic career, so the career versus love theme is not yet present.)

Within days of this treatment, both producer Stromberg and new director Robert Z. Leonard added many of the additional features, mainly musical insertions, that figure in the final film.

West's other script credits are impressive, including the two sound versions of *Smilin' Through, Random Harvest, Mrs. Miniver, The Chocolate Soldier, Goodbye Mr. Chips, The Good Earth,* and *The Barretts of Wimpole Street.*

Trivia

"*Don't* Carry Me Back to Old Virginny." Nelson Eddy on CNN? Yes! When the state of Virginia decided to seek a new state song, "Inside Politics" on CNN, 1/31/97, played a brief clip of Nelson and Jeanette singing the James Bland classic in *Maytime*: "The song's references to 'darkies' and 'ole massa' recall a painful time for many Virginians," said the announcer. "Rather than bowdlerize the lyrics (as is commonly done when the song is sung today), the legislature has decided to find a song more expressive of modern Virginia."

Los Angeles Examiner, 11/2/36: "Virginia Reid, who started out life as a protégé of Irene Dunne and never got anywhere under the very eyes of our moguls, suddenly leaps into the ingénue lead [of *Maytime*]." She also changed her name to Lynne Carver.

Sunday Oregonian, 9/6/36: headline—"Stanley Morner to Play Eddy's Son in *Maytime*"—"To Stanley Morner, singing protégé of Mary Garden [and later renamed Dennis Morgan], falls the unusual assignment of playing Nelson Eddy's son and 'carrying on' in song for

Maytime is regarded by many as the best MacDonald/Eddy film. It was Jeanette's favorite.

the baritone when, cinematically, he becomes too old to sing in the new Irving G. Thalberg's *Maytime*....Elaborate musical spectacles punctuate the dramatic story, such as 'Sweethearts' ['Will You Remember'], a hit in the original stage show, 'A Windy Day on the Battery,' and new musical numbers by Romberg and Gus Kahn. Frank Morgan, Ted Healy, Mary Philips, and Julie Hayden have also been chosen for the cast."

Movie Goofs

Movie magic sometimes comes about because scenes are routinely shot out of sequence and then rearranged in the editing process, or parts of the same scene are shot on different days. Costumes may change within the same scene, props appear and disappear. The continuity person (called a "script girl" in the old days) tried desperately to prevent these mistakes, but sometimes they slipped in. Here are some favorites spotted by sharp-eyed fans.

Nelson's suspenders can clearly be glimpsed throughout the café scene, but when he launches into "Ham and Eggs," they have vanished. (Tricia Lutz and Bonnie Morton)

At the May Day fair, Jeanette carries various "doll" prizes, but never all of them at once. Guess she keeps giving them away. And what happens to the flowers Jeanette is sniffing when Nelson starts to sing "Will You Remember"? And when John Barrymore arrives at the New York hotel, his overcoat is removed without putting out his cigarette. (Anna Michalik)

Eucalyptus trees, native to Australia and transplanted to California a hundred years ago, are clearly visible in the "French" landscape of the May Day St. Cloud fair. (Author)

German cinema program for *The Firefly*, renamed *Tarantella*. Courtesy Anna Michalik.

The Firefly

MGM.
Released November 5, 1937.
Directed by Robert Z. Leonard.
Produced by Hunt Stromberg and Robert Z. Leonard.
131 minutes. (Previewed at 140 minutes.)
Issued in "Sepia-Platinum."

French title: *L'Espionne de Castille* (The Spy from Castile) [Ironic—Castile is never mentioned]
Czech title: *Spanelská vyzvedacka* (Spanish Investigator)
Dutch title: *De Spionne van Castillie* (The Spy from Castile)
Italian title: *La Lucciola* (The Firefly)
German title: *Tarantella*
Portuguese title: *O Vagalume* (TheFirefly)

Screenplay: Frances Goodrich and Albert Hackett. Adaptation: Ogden Nash. Music Director: Herbert Stothart. Editor: Robert J. Kern. Photography: Oliver Marsh. Gowns by Adrian. Assistant Director: Joseph M. Newman. Treatment: Claudine West and Alice Duer Miller. Montages: Slavko Vorkapich and Elmer Sheeley. Art Direction: Cedric Gibbons. Art Associates: Paul Groesse, Edwin B. Willis. Music Arranger in Mexico: Leonid Raab. Chorus Coach: Enrico Ricardi. Dances: Albertina Rasch. Sound: Douglas Shearer. Music Recording in Mexico: Mike McLaughlin. Technical Adviser: George Richelavie.

The stage version, with music by Rudolf Friml and book and lyrics by Otto A. Harbach, opened at the Empire Theatre in Syracuse on October 14, 1912, and at the Lyric Theatre in New York City on December 2, 1912. It starred Emma Trentini as Nina, with Craig Campbell, Melville Stewart, and Audrey Maple (who later worked with Jeanette in *Sunny Days*).

Jeanette MacDonald (Nina Maria Azara)
Allan Jones (Don Diego Manrique de Lara AKA Captain François André)
Warren William (Colonel De Rougemont)
Douglass Dumbrille (Marquis DeMelito)
Leonard Penn (Etienne)
Billy Gilbert (Innkeeper)
Belle Mitchell (Lola)
Tom Rutherfurd (King Ferdinand)
Henry Daniell (General Savary)
George Zucco (St. Clair, French Secret Service Chief)

The Firefly

Ien Wulf [Ian Wolfe] (Izquierdo, Minister)
Manuel Alvarez Maciste (Pedro, the coachman)
Robert Spindola (Juan, his son)
Zeni Vatori (Waiter in café)
Frank Puglia (Pablo)
John Picorri (Café proprietor)
James B. Carson (Smiling waiter)
Milton Watson (French officer)
Peter DuRey (Officer)
Maurice Black (Pigeon vendor)
Maurice Cass (Strawberry vendor)
Sam Appel (Fruit vendor)
Rolfe Sedan (Hat vendor)
Mabel Colcord (Vendor)
Inez Palange (Flower vendor)
Theodor von Eltz (Captain Pierlot)
Pedro de Cordoba (Spanish general)
Monya André (Civilian wife)
Frank Campeau (Beggar)
Stanley Price (Joseph Bonaparte)
Guy D'Ennery (Spanish general)
Robert Wilber (Dying soldier)
Sidney Bracy (Secretary)
Roy Harris [Riley Hill] (Lieutenant)
Eugene Borden (Captain)
Jean Perry (Major)
Corbett Morris (Duval)
Ralph Byrd (French lieutenant)
Eddie Phillips (Captain)
Bentley Hewlett (Major)
Paul Sutton (Spanish civilian)
Capt. Fernando Garcia (Napoleonic officer)
Karl Hackett (Spaniard)
Boyd Gilbert (Aide)
Russ Powell (Stablehand)
Lane Chandler (Captain of the Guards)
Agostino Borgato (Peasant)
Matthew Boulton (Duke of Wellington)
Edward Keane (Colonel, Chief of Staff)
Victor Adams (Jail guard)
Harry Worth (Adjutant, Secret Service)
Lew Harvey (Officer)
Jason Robards Sr (Spanish patriot)
David Tihmar (Madrid café dancer)
Soledad Gonzales (Extra)
Robert Z. Leonard, Albertina Rasch (Extras in Bayonne café)
Dennis O'Keefe, Raphael [Ray] Bennett (Soldiers in Bayonne café)

Czech sheet music cover. *Courtesy Anna Michalik.*

Jac (Jacques) George (Orchestra leader, Bayonne)
Joe North, Colin Kenny, Brandon Hurst, Pat Somerset (English generals)
Donald Reed, William Crowell, Drew Demorest, Lester Dorr, Hooper Atchley, John Merton, Ramsay Hill, Anthony Pawley (French officers)
Frank Yaconelli, Harry Semels, Charles Townsend, Frederic MacKaye, Roger Drake, Jacques Lory, Alan Curtis (French soldiers)
Gabriel Munoz, Carlos Ruffino (Gypsies)
Pilar Arcos (Old gypsy woman)
St. Luke's Choristers
St. Brendan's Boys Choir
Our Lady of the Angels Choir

One of sixteen top-grossing films of 1937-1938.

The Firefly was Jeanette MacDonald's first solo starring picture for MGM. Director Robert Z. Leonard repeated the somewhat leisurely pacing that had made much of *Maytime* so lovely. The scenes build slowly and beautifully, establishing mood in an unhurried manner, somehow as Spanish as our heroine is supposed to be.

The stage plot of *The Firefly*, concerning a New York street singer who follows her millionaire sweetheart to Bermuda on his fiancée's yacht, disguised as a cabin boy, was utterly abandoned. Much of the score was retained, stuck in at any and every opportunity. (Both *The Firefly* and *Naughty Marietta* scores had originally been written to order for the popular star Emma Trentini, and both plots explained her Italian accent.)

In the film *Firefly*, our heroine is a Spanish Mata Hari in the days of Napoleon. The early scenes in the café, the "Donkey Serenade" sequence, the moonlit night in the garden, and the debut at Bayonne are all masterful pieces of mood, texture, and atmosphere. We are glorying in this atmosphere when we realize that we have been sitting a terribly long time and almost nothing has happened.

As if to rectify this, the screen suddenly launches into the entire British campaign in Spain. Our hero and heroine must choose between love and patriotism, a dramatic situation that is dissipated by permitting the war to consume the last two reels of the film until the lovers can be tidily if illogically reunited at its conclusion. Jeanette as Nina Maria performs some modest bits of spy subterfuge, but then is required by the script to explain them so elaborately to her enemies (and the audience) that their effect is lost.

The Firefly was not the only MGM film in 1937 that got bogged down in historical pageantry. The studio always had a penchant for epics backed up by a good story: *Ben Hur*, *The Four Horsemen of the Apocalypse*, *Mutiny on the Bounty*. The long-awaited *The Good Earth*, which Thalberg had been working on at his death, finally reached the screen that year, winning Luise Rainer her second Oscar. But other top MGM talents fared worse at the hands of history. Greta Garbo and Charles Boyer floundered in the leaden accuracies of a

A recording session with Jeanette and Allan Jones. Both Friml's *The Firefly* and Victor Herbert's *Naughty Marietta* were originally written for the fiery Italian stage star Emma Trentini.

Napoleonic epic called *Conquest*, and Clark Gable and Myrna Loy graced the graceless biography *Parnell*. The film industry was becoming so convinced of its own importance that it was reverting to a genre of film not seen since the works of some of the "master directors" of the silent era—the kind of film in which historical characters pop on and off the screen with dazzling speed to emphasize the significance of the production.

The Firefly suffered from this elephantiasis of the spirit. As with so many films that miss, the blame descended by default on the shoulders of its hapless star. True, Miss MacDonald has one especially weak dance number toward the end of the film, and she performs the incredible dramatic climax with a fervor that made it even worse. A better script and a long session in the cutting room might have made *The Firefly* a really good movie if not a great one, for Jeanette had rarely looked lovelier or performed with more sparkle. Perhaps it was because she was engaged to be married when the picture was completed. Certainly photographer Oliver Marsh (brother of D.W. Griffith star Mae Marsh) also contributed with his genius for making women as beautiful as they ought to be.

Jeanette's Don Diego is tenor Allan Jones, who had done the opera sequences with her in *Rose Marie*. His career had skyrocketed so fast that films like *A Night at the Opera* (in which he replaced the fourth Marx Brother, Zeppo, as romantic lead) were already in release before films in which he had near walk-ons. (Students of Hollywood incongruities treasure the moment in *The Great Ziegfeld* when singer Stanley Morner, later rechristened Dennis Morgan, opens his mouth to sing "A Pretty Girl is Like a Melody," and Jones's voice emerges.) In 1936 Jones got the plum role of Ravenal opposite Irene Dunne in *Show Boat* when MGM refused to lend Universal their first choice, Nelson Eddy. Jones had a nice tenor voice, a breezy manner, and he looked terrific in tight Spanish pants. He and Miss MacDonald played extremely well together and became good friends off screen.

The Firefly was issued entirely in sepia-platinum, printed on film stock that produced a rose-brown and white image on the screen. (This same process had been used for inserts in the first release prints of *Maytime*.) MGM was the last major studio to produce a Technicolor feature, and they probably hoped that this much less expensive process would save them the expense. However, the reduced contrast annoyed many, and, since it cost more than black and white, it soon died out. Sepia-Platinum was used in 1938 for another Jeanette/Nelson film, *The Girl of the Golden West*. Its best applications were for the Kansas sequences in *The Wizard of Oz* (1939) and for *Cabin in the Sky*, the 1943 all-black musical. Thereafter it was generally relegated to westerns.

The film opens with an elaborately loving treatment of King Ferdinand's triumphal entrance into Madrid. (He marches on "Spanish Street" and into "Verona Square," sets built for the Shearer-Howard *Romeo and Juliet* and used for many years. "Spanish Street" was also used for Monterey in *The Girl of the Golden West*.) The people adore their young King, but the mood is somewhat dampened by the ominous presence of French troops.

At a conference, the crafty French General Savary (Henry Daniell) soothes the new Spanish king, Ferdinand (Tom Rutherfurd). He assures him the French troops are only occupying Spain to "protect" it from the English. Since all Napoleon wants is peace in Europe, a meeting between him and the king should take place as soon as possible. Watching the smirking French general and the ingenuous king is the steely-eyed Marquis DeMelito (Douglass Dumbrille, Jeanette's tyrannical uncle in *Naughty Marietta*).

The festivities continue with dancing, feasting, and fireworks. In a nearby tavern, the star attraction is Nina Maria Azara, the "Mosca del Fuego" (a bizarre mistranslation of "firefly"). She is dazzling the customers, including many French officers. One of them, Etienne (Leonard Penn), is suspicious when Nina Maria (Jeanette) says she is too tired to see him after the show. He'll kill anyone he finds with her, he warns. Since the Marquis DeMelito is picking her up, this is somewhat inconvenient.

She decides to make Etienne think her newest admirer is someone in the tavern. Singing "Love is Like a Firefly," she spots a brash young Spaniard in the audience and flirts

Café singer Nina Maria Azara (Jeanette) has a hard time getting rid of Etienne, a romantic French officer (Leonard Penn). Her maid (Belle Mitchell) is familiar with this kind of scene.

Another admirer is Don Diego (Allan Jones). His attentions threaten to interfere with her own romantic activities—as a Spanish spy. A kiss gets rid of him.

with him coyly from behind her fan. Don Diego (Allan Jones) responds joyously, singing "A Woman's Kiss." Nina Maria is delighted and, whirling about to the exciting melody, she obeys the lyrics by giving him a long kiss. Etienne is convinced of her faithlessness and Don Diego of her interest.

The Don pursues her to her dressing room, where she explains that she only kissed him to get rid of the French officer. Through the window, Don Diego spots Etienne lurking outside. She hasn't succeeded. "I think you'd better try again," he says, getting in position for another kiss.

Nina Maria begs him not to fight Etienne, who is an expert marksman, and departs to meet the Marquis. Lola, her hawk-faced maid (Belle Mitchell), sees Nina Maria and Don Diego to the door. "Good night, Senorita. *Goodbye*, Senor!"

Nina Maria's "date" with the Marquis turns out to be business. She is using her job to get information from the French. The Marquis orders her to go to Bayonne, a French city near the Spanish border, where the conference between Napoleon and Ferdinand is to take place. He suspects a trap. Nina Maria readily accepts the assignment, although two agents have already been caught. The Marquis is pleased as always with his employee—no moods, no entanglements. "I can't imagine any man as exciting as this service to my country," she replies.

The next morning, her mule-driven coach is winding its way along a dusty mountain trail. The driver's small son (Robert Spindola) hops out to urge the mules up a hill by playing on his flageolet. He dances ahead, whistling a jaunty melody on his small pipe. Suddenly the driver (Manuel Alvarez Maciste) spots a lone horseman silhouetted against the ridge. Bandits!

With Nina Maria and Lola clinging to each other in the swaying coach, they take off at full gallop. The rider descends the perilous mountainside at even greater speed and finally catches up with the frightened party. (Allan Jones—for it is Don Diego—rode his own horse for this sequence.)

Don Diego has come to tell Nina Maria that he didn't fight the duel. He overslept. Nina Maria is furious at the fright he gave them and orders the driver to continue. Don Diego trots alongside as an uninvited escort. She picked him to get rid of the French officer, Nina Maria tells Lola, but how does she get rid of *him*?

Don Diego pursues Nina Maria's coach when she is sent on a mission, giving him a chance to sing "The Donkey Serenade," written for the film.

The Marquis DeMelito (Douglass Dumbrille) gives Nina her instructions. She assures him that no man could ever be as important to her as her patriotic duty. *Courtesy Anna Michalik.*

Don Diego offers to sing to entertain her on the journey, but she tells him she is going to sleep. The driver's small son again plays his "mule song." To the clip-clop of their hooves, Don Diego sings the now-classic "Donkey Serenade," written especially for the film. The catchy rhythms and counter-rhythms rouse even Nina Maria from her pretended slumber.

At the inn in Vittoria, their first night's stop, she thanks Don Diego for making the journey so pleasant and says goodbye. In her room she is contacted by an agent who tells her the King has already started for the conference at Bayonne. If, as they suspect, a trap has been arranged, she is to send word through a poultry seller in the Bayonne market place.

The quiet evening Nina Maria has planned is interrupted by the persistent Don Diego. In a beautiful mood piece, they dine together and stroll through the moonlit garden, redolent with jasmine. She stops at the stable to check on her driver and then starts back to the inn. Diego delays her, seating her on a straw-covered cart. In an amusing interlude, he tries to convince her they are riding in a Venetian gondola. As proof,

Diego turns a barnyard wagon into a Venetian gondola, singing the love song "Giannina Mia." *Courtesy Anna Michalik.*

he sings the lushly romantic "Giannina Mia." Her reserve softens in the fervent warmth of the music.

Reluctantly, she confesses that she was moved by his song. At the spot, just before the high note, she was wondering—but she'd better not tell him. He insists. "Just before the high note, I was wondering—" "Yes?" "I was wondering if you were going to make it!" More honestly, she tells him that perhaps when she returns from Bayonne she won't be so discouraging.

Bayonne is a dazzling triumph. In Miss MacDonald's most exciting tour-de-force number since "San Francisco," she thrills the French officers with "He Who Loves and Runs Away." (Among the extras are director Robert Z. Leonard, choreographer Albertina Rasch, and future star Dennis O'Keefe.) Nina Maria has eyes only for a distinguished older man at a center table. As she sings, she happily fingers his brand new Colonel's insignia. He is the one she wants.

Her flirtation is interrupted by the sudden entrance of Don Diego. Startled, she pulls herself together and responds to the military turn of the music by seizing the Colonel's bicorn hat and cocking it fetchingly on her own head. She salutes him soldier-fashion, and then, as the officers' voices take up the martial tattoo, she struts elegantly on the stage, the camera sweeping after her in a glorious moment of sight and sound.

As intended, Colonel De Rougemont (Warren William) attempts to retrieve his hat in the lady's dressing room, but they are repeatedly interrupted by notes and flowers from the jealous Don Diego. However, the Colonel succeeds in making a luncheon date with Nina Maria—*tête-à-tête*. Nina Maria tells him she wants to hear all about Napoleon. "If you only *knew* how I felt about Napoleon," she gushes.

The next morning, Nina Maria stops at the stall of a poultry vendor (Maurice Black) to buy two pigeons—carrier pigeons for notifying the waiting Marquis DeMelito. She and Lola then

The Firefly 281

Nina Maria dazzles the French officers in Bayonne. Her black velvet costume, designed by Adrian, was one of Jeanette's most beautiful. (Jac George conducts the orchestra.)

Colonel De Rougemont (Warren William) thinks Nina Maria is just what he has been looking for. She feels the same—about his secret dispatches.

stroll on among the vendors until they spot Don Diego trying on hats. One looks so comical that Nina Maria laughingly forgives him and consents to a sightseeing tour. He points out the house where Don Diego spent a night of torture after Nina Maria rebuffed him. "Funny, I don't see a tablet," she scoffs. They walk on, buying flowers, strawberries, and chestnuts from various stalls. Finally, crossing a rustic drawbridge, they settle on a bank beside a mill pond. Here director Leonard attempts a series of folksy cameos of French country types that comes off as unbearably arch.

Diego tells Nina Maria he doesn't want her to have lunch with Colonel De Rougemont. She smiles at his jealousy and assures him the Colonel is a very important man. Diego admires the locket she is wearing. She opens it to show him pictures of her mother and father. They are dead, she says, killed twenty years before when the French invaded Spain. He thinks that should make her very bitter toward the French. "Oh, no," she replies unconvincingly.

They toss the last of their chestnuts to the ducks, and Diego pretends to feed his finger to one obstreperous drake. Soothing his "injured" hand, she sings "Sympathy."

Their little love scene is interrupted by Napoleon himself, marching into Bayonne. Nina Maria leaps up to keep her lunch engagement. Diego begs her not to go, but she insists. As a pledge of her love, she leaves him the locket, then rushes off to her apartment to change.

A message is waiting there from the Colonel. He is leaving Bayonne for several days and cannot keep their date. Nina Maria guesses he is on his way to Vittoria, the halfway point in King Ferdinand's journey. He will promise Ferdinand anything to get him on French soil, but what are his orders if the king refuses to come?

She dresses in her loveliest frock and arrives at the Colonel's apartment as he is packing. Coyly she serenades him on the spinet while he dresses in the next room: "When a Maid Comes Knocking." The crucial dispatch arrives. She snatches it, playfully scolding it for taking the Colonel from her. Then, flinging herself into his arms, she manages to read the message through

Her locket contains her secret. This photo is from a vintage cigarette card. *Courtesy Anna Michalik.*

The Firefly

When her life is in danger, she turns to the one person she hopes she can trust. He also has a secret.

the envelope by the light of the window. (Quite a trick!) "Order for Arrest" is the heading.

Very reluctantly, the Colonel rides off. Nina Maria returns to her rooms to send this news to the Marquis. But the pigeons are not the ones she bought. Someone has switched their birds for hers. If she had sent the message, the French would have evidence against her.

Who can help her? Lola urges her to go to Don Diego. He can ride to Vittoria with the message. Nina Maria hesitates. Perhaps *he* is the one who is doing all this. Instead, she returns to the market place and learns the poultry seller has been taken away by the police. There is no one else to turn to.

From his window, Don Diego sees her coming. The Chief of the French secret police (George Zucco, the eternal villain) is at his elbow. Diego must get Nina Maria to confess while the Chief and his men hide in the next room. Grimly, Diego admits Nina Maria.

She makes tensely casual small talk, then asks him to deliver a message to Vittoria. He agrees, and she jots it down on a piece of paper. The paper is snatched from her hand by the gleeful Chief. But the message is a request for dinner reservations several days hence. Diego is revealed to be Captain François André of the secret police, who has been pursuing Nina Maria for months. Just to be sure the audience has understood the subtleties of the double-cross, the characters are forced to explain it again, and then Nina Maria is ordered to leave the country.

At the border, Don Diego stops her carriage to return the locket. Just when some kind of dramatic conclusion is called for, a second story begins. We are treated to a Slavko Vorkapich montage showing the oppression of the Spanish by the French. Nina Maria and the Marquis watch Napoleon's brother, Joseph Bonaparte (Stanley Price), make a triumphal entrance into Madrid as the new Spanish ruler. Nina Maria regrets that all this was caused by her failure, but the Marquis tells her she will have another chance. She is to drop out of sight for a while.

Disguised as a gypsy camp follower.

Nina Maria is captured with an incriminating map and sentenced to be shot.

The montage continues with peasants marching under a cloudless sky, a sea of scythes, hoes, and rakes against the guns of the French. Amidst the billows of gunsmoke, the Union Jack appears. A few bars of "The British Grenadiers" and we see Wellington marching to save the day. Symbolically, his line of troops and the peasant militia move down separate forks of a road to join in one great mass; symbolically, they march, and in a double image we see great rocks, carved with the names of Spanish victories, explode.

In a brief camp sequence, the Marquis advises Wellington (Matthew Boulton) that they cannot continue until they hear from a very special spy who is now behind the French lines. The military drums dissolve into a thumping dance rhythm. A group of wild Spanish gypsy girls is entertaining the troops around a campfire. One of them is Nina Maria. The delightful raw tones of the gypsy players evolve into a full orchestration of Rimsky-Korsakov's "Capriccio Espagñole." In a weakly choreographed number, Miss MacDonald whirls before the flames. The passing Colonel De Rougemont spots her.

On the Colonel's orders, Nina Maria is brought to headquarters where she is "caught" with a map of the French lines. The intelligence officer on duty is, of course, Captain André, the former Diego. He translates the coded message, and Nina Maria is imprisoned to await execution. The map shows the positions of the French troops and asks for verification. In the same code, Captain André writes on the map that all is correct except that the French center is weak. The Colonel orders half of each flank to the center, then releases one of Nina Maria's pigeons with the message attached to its leg. From the headquarters window, André watches the bird rise, circle, and fly off.

From her prison window, Nina Maria also watches the bird, but with strange exultation. André visits her cell, and, as the Spanish troops close in, Nina Maria again explains. Her job was to get caught with the message. The Spanish know that any message they receive will have been sent by the French. They will attack whichever area is designated as the strongest, knowing it will be the weakest. André runs off to be with his men, but is waylaid by some unconvincing smoke pot bombs. Nina Maria sees him fall. In a somewhat incongruous reprise of their love song, she thrusts her arms through the bars toward him, singing "Giannina Mia" with tears streaming down her face.

The rumble of explosions fades before the triumphal chorus of victory, and in another montage we see the French flag fall into the dust. The symbolic peasant of Spain rises up and casts off his shackles, backlit by a glorious sunrise. America was very concerned with the Spanish Civil War in 1937, and this was supposed to be stirring stuff, but it is hard to believe that much of the audience found it more than a cliché.

The Marquis enters Nina Maria's cell as the battle concludes. The cheers outside are for her, he says. She goes immediately to the open air hospitals, seeking her Don Diego. She finds him, bandaged and delirious, and sinks down beside him. Dissolve to the lovers, healthy and together

The Firefly

in a mule-drawn wagon as they sing the "Donkey Serenade" and a few bars of "Giannina Mia."

Reviews:

Variety thought that "when trimmed to proper length which will tighten the story interest, *The Firefly* will be a money getter." They also found the sepia tone "monotonous and not nearly so effective as the conventional natural tone....Some radical deletions of footage will be necessary before it is ready for commercial distribution." (Alas, the deletions were never made.)

William Boehnel of the *New York World-Telegram* compared the film to its predecessors: "Done in the manner of old-fashioned operettas, it throws right out the window all the crusading work done by directors such as W.S. Van Dyke, Rouben Mamoulian, and others in trying to convert the screen operetta into a realistic, pungent, believable medium."

A happy ending.

The *New York Times* reported that "[*The Firefly*] is told with such uninspired dialogue and transparency of intrigue that only the superb voices of Jeanette MacDonald and Allan Jones save the production from downright and beautifully photographed dullness. Miss MacDonald's songs seem far too few and her dances far too many. She is neither actress enough nor dancer enough to do all the dissembling and dervishing that... this production requires of her. Miss MacDonald needs a Van Dyke or a Mamoulian to direct her, and it may be too that she needs rescuing from the kind of picture in which people write with feathers." (Jeanette's next film would return her to the hands of Van Dyke and provide her with a modern dress story for one of her more successful films, *Sweethearts*.)

Archer Winsten in the *New York Post* felt that Jeanette did too *much* singing, showing how hard it is to please all the critics all the time. "The scientific aspect of Miss MacDonald's larynx is not wholly clear to this department, but surely something is there, perhaps high frequency if there is such a thing, that records better than other soprano voices. It is clear, rounded, and effortlessly melodious." But he felt there was too much music before the story had been properly developed.

Almost alone among the reviewers, *Time* magazine found the film "excellently directed by Robert Z. Leonard. The present version will be supremely satisfying to devotees of Friml, of Allan Jones, and of Miss MacDonald's beautifully denticulated soprano."

Recordings (See Discography for further information)

Both MacDonald and Jones made separate recordings of these two songs:

"The Donkey Serenade" (This song became an
 Allan Jones standard for fifty years.)
"Giannina Mia"

Between Adrian's costumes and Oliver Marsh's photography, Jeanette had never been more beautiful. It helped that she was in love.

Jeanette is visited on the set by her fiancé, Gene Raymond, during shooting of *The Firefly*, just before their wedding in June 1937.

Rosalie

Music in the Film

All music is by Rudolf Friml and lyrics by Otto A. Harbach unless otherwise indicated. In listing performers after each title, "and" denotes a genuine duet, while commas between names indicate a sequence of singers.

Overture: "Giannina Mia," "He Who Loves and Runs Away"
"English March" (chorus) - by Friml, Bob Wright, Chet Forrest
"Danse Jeanette" (orchestral) - Herbert Stothart
"Love is Like a Firefly" (MacDonald, male chorus)
[The Magic of] "A Woman's Kiss" (Jones, male chorus with MacDonald) - originally "A Woman's Smile" in stage version, new lyrics by Wright and Forrest

Italian sheet music cover. *Courtesy Gary Mazzeo.*

"The Donkey Serenade" (Jones, Robert Spindola, with guitar and flute solos; guitar played by Manuel Alvarez Maciste) - based on Friml's 1920 piano piece, "Chanson," arranged by Stothart, lyrics by Wright and Forrest. ("Chanson" was recopyrighted in 1923 as "Chansonette.")
"Para la Salud" (Maciste, male singers) - arranged by Stothart
"Ojos Rojos" (Maciste playing guitar and singing) - Argentinean folk song arranged by Maciste
"Giannina Mia" (Jones) - lyrics by Otto Harbach
"He Who Loves and Runs Away" (MacDonald and male chorus) - music by Friml, source uncertain. Mrs. Friml believed this was written for the film. Lyrics by Gus Kahn.
"Sympathy" (MacDonald, Jones) - lyrics by Otto Harbach with Gus Kahn
"When a Maid Comes Knocking" (MacDonald with Warren William) - lyrics by Otto Harbach with Wright and Forrest
"Gypsy Dance" (quartet of instruments) - source uncertain, INTO:
"Capriccio Espagñole" (orchestral dance number) - Nicholas Rimsky-Korsakov
"Giannina Mia" reprise (MacDonald)
Triumphal chorus (chorus) - Friml, Wright, and Forrest
Finale: "The Donkey Serenade" and "Giannina Mia" (MacDonald and Jones)

Rosalie

MGM.
Released December 24, 1937.
Directed by W.S. Van Dyke II.
Produced by William Anthony McGuire.
122 minutes.

German title: *Hoheit tanzt inkognit* (The Princess Dances in Disguise)

Based on the Romberg/Gershwin Broadway musical with book by William Anthony McGuire and Guy Bolton, but filmed with all new songs by Cole Porter. Screenplay: William Anthony McGuire. Photogra-

German cinema program. *Courtesy Anna Michalik.*

pher: Oliver T. Marsh. Art Direction: Cedric Gibbons. Set Decoration: Edwin B. Willis, Joseph Wright. Music Director: Herbert Stothart. Sound: Douglas Shearer. Dances: Albertina Rasch. Montages: Slavko Vorkapich. Editor: Blanche Sewell. Assistant Directors: William Scully, George Yohalem. Musical Presentation: Merrill Pye. Music Arrangements: Roger Edens. Orchestra and Vocal Arrangements: Léo Arnaud, Murray Cutter, Leonid Raab, Paul Marquardt. Costumes: Dolly Tree. Dances for Cadets: Dave Gould, Frank Floyd. Assistant Dance Director: George King. Music Recording: Mike McLaughlin. Technical Adviser: Count Andrey Tolstoy. Music conductor: Georgie Stoll.

The stage *Rosalie,* produced by Florenz Ziegfeld, ran for 335 performances beginning January 10, 1928 at the New Amsterdam Theatre. Sigmund Romberg composed eight numbers for the show and George Gershwin seven. (Gershwin's best song in the score was "How Long Has This Been Going On?") The original stage Rosalie was Marilyn Miller, the undisputed queen of the American musical in the 1920s. Her Lt. Richard Fay was Oliver McLennan, and Frank Morgan was the original King.

Nelson Eddy (Dick Thorpe)
Eleanor Powell (Rosalie Romanikoff)
Ray Bolger (Bill Delroy)
Frank Morgan (King Frederic Romanikoff)
Ilona Massey (Brenda)
Edna May Oliver (Queen)
Billy Gilbert (First Officer Oloff)
Reginald Owen (Chancellor)
George Zucco (General Maroff)
Virginia Grey (Mary Callahan)
Tom Rutherfurd (Prince Paul)
Janet Beecher (Miss Baker)
Clay Clement (Captain Banner)
Oscar O'Shea (Mr. Callahan)
William Demarest (Army's coach)
Rush Hughes (Announcer, as himself)
Wallis Clark (Major Prentice)
Richard Tucker (Colonel Brandon)
Jerry Colonna (Second Officer Joseph)
Wilson Benge (Steward)
Pierre Watkin (Superintendent of Academy)
Tommy Bond (Mickey, the mascot)
Purnell Pratt (Ship captain)
Ricca Allen (Schoolteacher)
Al Shean (Herman Schmidt)
Frank Du Frane (Superintendent's aide)
Ocean Claypoole, Katharine [Kay] Aldridge [later a Republic serial and western star] (Ladies-in-waiting)
Edward Earle (Navy officer)
George Magrill (Assistant Army coach)
Lane Chandler (Army coach)
Phillip Terry, William Tannen (Cadets)
George Humbert (Carlo, peasant)
Max Davidson (Chamberlain)
Harry Semels, Roy Barcroft [later a top villain at Republic], John Picorri, Sidney Bracy (Conspirators)
The Albertina Rasch Dancers
Gene Conklin, Tudor Williams (Soloists)
Joe Marks (Puck)
Alexander Canepari (Town crier)
George Boyce, Harry Masters, Dave White (Specialty dancers)
Donald Sadler (Dancer)
Marie Arbuckle, Bernice Alstock, Elinor Coleson, Grace Neilson, Barbara Whitson (Vassar soloists)

One of seventeen top-grossing films of 1937-1938.

Rosalie

The principal problem with the film version of *Rosalie* is William Anthony McGuire's adherence to his original flimsy book. The film becomes a pastiche of nearly every established musical form.

First there is the college musical, which had grown in usage after Mittel Europa ceased being relevant to modern American culture. College students were our new royalty, since only the rich could afford to attend. Of course, as with royalty, the poor boy or girl could always hope to get a scholarship (go to the ball) and marry the prom queen or football captain (princess or prince). A further advantage was that college kids were younger, more athletic, and more inclined to sing and dance than their courtier counterparts—a definite musical plus. Mixed with the rah-rah-sis-boom-bah in *Rosalie* are generous doses of operetta princess facing an unwelcome marriage, a stroll on West Point's Flirtation Walk that had already proved so profitable for Dick Powell and Ruby Keeler, the romance of an aviator (who is seen in his plane for fewer than ten seconds), and production numbers of jazzy splendor.

The film is so chockfull of musical and choreographic plums that it seems ungrateful to ask for a single moment of emotional identification with the characters. But ungrateful we are as one splendid but impossibly motivated number follows another. No matter what the locale, we know we are on a sound stage and keep wishing the director would call a break for lunch so we could see everyone relax and be "real people."

MGM had originally bought the stage play as a vehicle for the delightful Marion Davies. According to an interview with Miss Davies by Malcolm H. Oettinger in the May 1930 *Picture Play*, the film was completed and then scrapped. Miss Davies had earlier worked for seven weeks on *The Five O'Clock Girl*, which was never released, and had completed a full silent version of *Marianne* before remaking it with some cast changes as her first talkie.

Stills exist from *The Five O'Clock Girl* and the silent *Marianne* showing the cast, but only portraits of Miss Davies are known to have survived the scrapped *Rosalie*. Who was in the cast, whether the Gershwin-Romberg score was used or if it was ever completed is uncertain. However, some footage in the 1937 *Rosalie* is patently from an earlier period and may be from the unreleased Davies version. The preposterous court set becomes understandable if it has to match the old footage that featured the Albertina Rasch Dancers writhing to Tchaikovsky and Borodin. And the elaborate finale is an obvious process shot against a fantasy background. The rest of the film contains no big sets except a nightclub (established briefly in a long shot) and some echoing sound stages set with lonely statuary for the dance numbers.

Nelson and Eleanor Powell. *Courtesy Anna Michalik.*

The fifteen Gershwin-Romberg stage songs were discarded, and Cole Porter was engaged to write new ones. Two of his Broadway successes, *The Gay Divorce* and *Anything Goes*, had been made into hit films, and his original score for *Born to Dance* was a special favorite of studio head Louis B. Mayer. Mayer asked Porter to compose a title song that sounded as much like "Rose Marie" as possible. Porter wrote five versions before the sixth became the one finally used. The song ultimately sold half-a-million copies, although Porter never liked it.

Porter, noted as the most "sophisticated" of the Big Five composers (Gershwin, Kern, Rodgers, and Berlin were the others), turned out another standard for the film, "In the Still of the Night." Eddy reportedly hated the song, thinking it wasn't right for his voice. Porter also wrote a delightful song for Miss Powell, "I've a Strange New Rhythm in My Heart," which never got the popularity it deserved.

Eddy, in his first "solo" after three films with Jeanette MacDonald, was paired with a very bright new star indeed, Eleanor Powell. The studio reasoned, not illogically, that some of the MacDonald/Eddy magic would be generated by casting an effervescent leading lady opposite the more reserved Eddy. They also hoped that the grosses on "single" films by MacDonald and Eddy separately would come close to the tremendous profits on a "team" picture, thereby doubling their return. Thus Jeanette soloed in *The Firefly* with Allan Jones and Eddy in *Rosalie* with Miss Powell.

Eleanor Powell had come to Hollywood to repeat her Broadway success in *George White's Scandals of 1935* at Fox. MGM quickly grabbed her and gave her a loving buildup in what is undoubtedly her best film, *Broadway Melody of 1936*. Her costar was a singing Robert Taylor, and much of the joy of the film was generated by Buddy Ebsen (*Girl of the Golden West*), accompanied by his sister, Vilma. Miss Powell followed this with two other films, *Born to Dance* (with Cole Porter score) and *Broadway Melody of 1938* (in which young Judy Garland got considerable attention), before making *Rosalie*.

Ilona Massey (née Hajmassy) played a small rôle as confidante to the princess. She was one of several actresses Mayer had signed while on a talent hunt in Europe the previous year. (His judgment was astute. Three of the others were Hedy Lamarr, Greer Garson, and Rose Stradner, who gave up a promising career to marry Joseph L. Mankiewicz.) Miss Massey had one irrelevant song, but she was pleasantly received. In her second film, *Balalaika* (1939), she was teamed with Eddy.

Broadway hoofer Ray Bolger got more footage but less attention than the blonde Miss Massey. His second released film rôle required him to kill a lot of time with dance routines that were supposed to spark up flat places in the script. His next film, *Sweethearts*, gave him a single showcase number, and, of course, 1939 brought his classic rôle as the scarecrow in *The Wizard of Oz*. The wizard himself, Frank

Two typical Vassar girls: Princess Rosalie (Eleanor Powell, left) and her lady-in-waiting, Brenda (Ilona Massey). *Courtesy Anna Michalik.*

Rosalie

The thirty-six-year-old Eddy trained diligently and managed to look at home in a West Point football uniform. He doesn't suspect that the very American Rosalie (Eleanor Powell) is a Mittel-Europa princess in disguise.

Morgan, recreated his *Rosalie* stage rôle as the King. Like Bolger, he was depended upon for too much comedy without enough material.

Our hero, Dick Thorpe (Nelson), is not only a West Point cadet but a football hero playing his last game against Navy. ("Thorpe" was probably thought more masculine than "Fay," the original stage name, possibly because of the success of football player Jim Thorpe.) It is Dick's last chance for glory, but he begs the coach (William Demarest) to let his buddy, Delroy (Ray Bolger), go in instead. The coach demurs until Dick is injured after racing sixty-five yards with the ball. Delroy gets his chance, much to the delight of his girlfriend, Mary (Virgina Grey), in the stands.

Also in the stands are Rosalie (Eleanor Powell) and her girlfriend, Brenda (Ilona Massey). Rosalie is cheering for Navy, although Brenda thinks they ought to cheer for Army since their kingdom of Romanza has no navy. Thorpe returns to the game and Rosalie announces prophetically that she hates him for his conceited airs. Delroy fumbles the ball with six seconds to play, but Dick saves the day.

The team's cute mascot, Mickey (Tommy Bond of *Our Gang*), claims Dick's helmet, since Dick will never wear it again. Dick makes him a present of it. "The only helmet I'll wear from now on will be a steel one."

In the locker room, poor Delroy gets an irate note from Mary saying she won't let him humiliate her again. She is leaving for Europe immediately with her father. Cheer up, Dick urges. There will be a lot of girls at the party that night—*Vassar* girls.

In dress uniform, the cadets march to meet the girls, caroling "The Marine Hymn." At the party, they encounter their defeated rivals and serenade them with "Anchors Aweigh." Rosalie is just confiding to Brenda that she hates Dick Thorpe because all the other girls like him, when Dick sweeps her onto the dance floor. Her sarcasm stimulates Dick's interest no end. She tells him that she never misses an Army game, but not because *he* is playing. She just likes to watch the soldiers parade. They remind her of her own soldiers. "Your soldiers?" Dick asks. "My *dream* soldiers," she replies hastily.

Rosalie inquires mischievously what he can do besides play football. Well, he replies, he can fly a plane, he's good with a gun, and he can sing. Would she like to hear him? "No, not again." And what exactly does she do when she's not ribbing him? he counters. She's a good swimmer, she answers, and she rides beautifully and can dance. Would he like to see her? "No, thanks."

We next see Dick polishing his airplane, newly rechristened "Rosalie." We are all set for a lovely airborne love scene with Dick serenading Rosalie among the clouds, but the plane turns out to be an earthbound prop. He

After meeting Rosalie, Dick Thorpe (Nelson, right) rechristens his plane "Rosalie." When Rosalie leaves Vassar mysteriously, Dick decides to fly the Atlantic to find her. He assures Delroy (Ray Bolger) that "people are doing it every week now."

Rosalie

Courtesy Anna Michalik.

must take more conventional transportation to reach Vassar.

In her dormitory, Rosalie does the best number in the film, explaining her agitation with "I've a Strange New Rhythm in My Heart," as she taps from room to room. A few bars of "Night and Day" are interpolated in case we doubt Porter's authorship.

Although it is bedtime, a visitor arrives to see Rosalie. General Maroff (George Zucco) has brought a message for Princess Rosalie from her father, the King. Americanized Rosalie rejects the General's formal greeting and hugs him. And how is her father, who so hates being King? How is his juggling? The General tells her the King has tired of juggling and taken up ventriloquism. Indeed, he has become quite attached to his dummy and spends most of his time amusing the court. However, the General is getting away from the purpose of his visit. He has come to escort her home. Her mother has arranged her marriage to the son of the popular Chancellor in order to save the kingdom. They will leave in the morning.

Reluctantly, Rosalie consents. It is her friend, Brenda, of course, who loves the Chancellor's son, while Rosalie will miss more than just her girlfriends when she leaves America. Dick arrives beneath her window at that moment.

First, he tries some opera at Delroy's urging. The windows are ominously dark. Then he turns to "Rosalie." The lights go on, and the entire dorm applauds. Rosalie sends them off to bed and greets her "dream soldier, reporting for duty." See, he tells her triumphantly, she said he wouldn't go around the block to find her, and he has come thirty miles. She replies that a better test would be four thousand miles. How would he like to meet her in Romanza for the spring festival? She will be dressed as Pierrette.

Dick determines to fly the Atlantic, much to Delroy's horror. "Why there's nothing to it anymore," Dick assures him. "They do it every week now." Delroy decides to go by boat and meet Dick when he lands. Then Delroy can pretend he has faced death to fly to Mary's side.

In Romanza, Princess Rosalie is acknowledging the cheers of her subjects as she parades on horseback through the flower-decorated streets. On a horse at her side is her fiancé, Prince Paul (Tom Rutherfurd). They are in animated conversation, but it is football, not love, that consumes their interest.

While Rosalie attends to official duties, her father, the reluctant King (Frank Morgan), is entertaining the court with his dummy, "Nappy." His indomitable wife, the Queen (Edna May Oliver), and his Chancellor (Reginald Owen) are impatient for him to sign a proclamation announcing the Spring Feast Day and granting amnesty to political prisoners. The King recalls that when he signed such a proclamation the previous year, a poor misguided fellow put a poor misguided bullet through his hat. If it had been an inch lower, it would have gone through his head. "You'd never have felt it, Frederic,"

Delroy (Ray Bolger) wants to impress his girl, but he is afraid of flying. He takes a ship and turns up at the Romanza airport so he can pretend he was in Dick's plane when it lands. "Comic relief" is provided by local officials (double talking Jerry Colonna, left, and sneezing Bill Gilbert, right). *Courtesy Anna Michalik.*

his wife assures him, holding out the paper for his signature.

The King has promised Rosalie that Paul can marry Brenda, but the Queen and the Chancellor, Paul's father, soon put an end to that nonsense. In her room, Rosalie refuses to dress for the festival. The last train has arrived without Dick. Brenda, happy in her expectation of marrying Paul herself, tries to cheer Rosalie up.

Overhead, Dick is having trouble finding Romanza. The airport radio is manned by two idiots, one double-talking (Jerry Colonna) and one sneezing (Billy Gilbert). They do an interminable comedy scene with Delroy, who is waiting in his flying suit to join Dick when he lands. Delroy has to hide when his girlfriend, Mary, and her father (Oscar O'Shea) show up to await his arrival. Dick manages to locate the airport after seven minutes and twenty seconds of this tedium.

The starving peasants of Romanza are near revolt, as well they might be, considering that the palace has rooms the size of airplane hangars and the decor of a Byzantine mausoleum. While we are supposed to be enjoying a people's feast day, the musical numbers are presented in splendid isolation on a vast floor, with the King and Queen viewing them, equally isolated on a monumental dais at one end of the mammoth room. First Brenda tells us "Spring Love is in the Air," accompanied by nymphs and satyrs, but more is ahead.

If Rosalie cares for her people, the Queen tells her rather surprisingly, she will dance for them. It doesn't matter that there is not a "people" in sight, except a group of uninspired dancers gyrating dully to some exciting Borodin music. (This may be an insert from the Davies' *Rosalie*.) The General interrupts to announce that an American flier is about to land. Rosalie leaps up. She will dance. She wouldn't want to break her promise to her father, just as he mustn't break his promise to her. She refers to his promise that she won't have to marry Paul, and he splutters as she goes off to dance. At his wife's insistence, he has already arranged for the announcement of Rosalie's engagement to Paul.

At the airport, Dick lands, and Delroy manages to get through the crowd and emerge from the plane door in time to convince his girlfriend Mary that he actually has flown the Atlantic. The King greets Dick and invites him to the festival. Dick confides that he has flown to Romanza to find a girl. The King offers to help. He has quite a few addresses. Dick thanks him but thinks he will just wander the streets until he finds his Pierrette.

Back at the palace, Dick and Delroy are treated to a musical number involving dozens of Pierrettes. How will Dick ever find her, the King wonders. Cymbals crash and a group of giant

The Queen of Romanza is played by the delightful character actress Edna May Oliver. *Courtesy Anna Michalik.*

The King of Romanza (Frank Morgan) welcomes the American flier and offers him his own little black book to aid in his search.

drums is rolled out, followed by a masked Pierrette in tap shoes. Dick has found her.

Rosalie does an elaborate production number to her namesake song, tap dancing over and through the drums to rhythms more appropriate to Broadway than the Balkans. In a thrilling finale, she spins down a ramp, bursting through cellophane-covered hoop after hoop. It is a splendid number, but totally unrelated to a princess dancing for her people on a religious feast day.

Afterward in the moonlit garden, Dick tells Rosalie again that he loves her: "In the Still of the Night." The tower bells begin to chime, and the Chancellor arrives to escort Rosalie to her betrothal ceremony. Dick thinks she has been mocking him again and departs in a rage. Rosalie tries to run after him, but the Chancellor blocks her way.

Rosalie has told Dick that she will be dressed as Pierrette. He finds several dozen masked girls in Pierrette costumes, but then one of them begins to tap dance. *Courtesy Anna Michalik.*

Delroy is also distraught. He has received another note from Mary. She won't let him humiliate her again. She is leaving for America immediately with her father. However, to cheer Dick up, Delroy does some tap dancing over and around the boxes of fireworks that Mary bought to celebrate his arrival. Naturally they go off. The revolutionaries think it is a signal. To the same music that marked the battle sequences in *The Firefly*, the Romanzans storm the palace. "Why don't these things ever happen in the daytime?" moans the sleepy King. The Chancellor suggests they flee to Vienna, but the King prefers America. "Over there, when people get mad, they just sit down," he says, referring to the sit-down strikes of the 1930s.

This would be a good point for a happy ending, but we are not so fortunate. With more than thirty-seven minutes to go, we still have two Eddy songs and one Powell dance, interspersed with innumerable "comedy" routines. All the principals except Dick return to America by boat, talking all the way. The royal family visits West Point, and Rosalie asks for Dick as her escort, even though he is being held for court-martial for going AWOL.

Dick gives Rosalie an icily formal tour of West Point, including Flirtation Walk. When he fails to do any flirting, she cries, "I hate you!" and runs off. "I love you," Dick whispers after her.

Paul and Brenda are doing somewhat better in the romantic locale when Dick discovers them. He tells Paul that Rosalie has gone looking for him, and Paul hurriedly departs, leaving the sympathetic Brenda to plead Rosalie's case to Dick.

Left to ponder the complications of his love affair, Dick is surrounded by a group of passing cadets. He joins them in "It's All Over But the Shouting," and then, still marooned on an echoing soundstage in front of some West Point statuary and shrubbery, Dick delivers the dramatic "To Love or Not to Love."

The King and Delroy have taken quite a liking to each other since they held a mutual insult contest on the boat. A ball is being given in the King's honor, but he is nervously pacing up and down outside. Delroy suggests that the King abdicate and become just plain Fred. Just then, the Queen announces that Rosalie has run away and drags the King off to help find her. Dick is also ordered by his superior officers to search for her without alarming anyone.

Rosalie has decided that the safest thing to be at West Point is a cadet and so is togged out in a uniform and wig that Delroy has provided. A group of cadets begin to suspect, and so Rosalie leads them in a drill and tap routine.

Dick finds her, and she urges him to run away with her. "Prince Dick Thorpe," he scoffs. But he loves her and reprises "In the Still of the Night." Delroy arrives to find Dick kissing a cadet who, fortunately, is Rosalie.

Delroy tells them that their troubles are over. Tonight the King's ventriloquist dummy has been replaced by little Mickey, the team mascot. The befuddled King gets a lecture from his dummy on his kingly duties. He recognizes the substitution, but agrees with Mickey's arguments. He will abdicate. Rosalie can marry Dick, and Brenda can marry Paul, and no one

Revolution breaks out, and Rosalie follows Dick to West Point where she must masquerade as a cadet.

Dick gets to sing at his own wedding. Some shots in the film appear to be from the Marion Davies *Rosalie*, made in 1930 and never released.

will shoot at him anymore. Of course, he is still stuck with the Queen.

In a stupendous wedding finale, Dick and Rosalie march beneath dozens of crossed swords to a medley ending in "Rosalie." The splendid set appears to be a matte shot, possibly from the earlier *Rosalie*. Thus ended Nelson Eddy's first non-team vehicle.

Reviews:

While most of the reviewers had forgiven Jeanette for the weaknesses in *The Firefly*, the same gentlemen (and ladies) of the press found Eddy's first solo effort "embarrassing" *(New York World-Telegram)* and reported that he "sings as well and inopportunely as can be imagined" *(New York Times)*.

The *New York World-Telegram* continued that it was "a long-winded and artificial operetta....If the film had not been directed by W.S. Van Dyke II, its defects might be easier to understand."

Variety called the film "a 250 lb. elf," and the *Times* continued: "[it is] deploying its formidable phalanxes of talent in one of the most pretentious demonstrations of sheer mass and weight since the last Navy games." (They were referring to battleships, not football.) "Eddy...looks adorable in his cadet uniform. For sheer length, breadth, weight and thickness, [Rosalie] is wearying."

Rosalie

Recordings (See Discography for further information)

"In the Still of the Night" (Eddy)
"Rosalie" (Eddy)
"Oh, Promise Me" (Eddy)

Music in the Film

The original stage score by George Gershwin and Sigmund Romberg was entirely abandoned. All music and lyrics are by Cole Porter, except where noted. In listing performers after each title, "and" denotes a genuine duet, while commas between names indicate a sequence of singers.

Overture: "The Caissons Go Rolling Along" fragment, "Rosalie," "Caissons" reprise

Nelson Eddy and Eleanor Powell.

Marches at football game: "On, Brave Old Army Team," "Anchors Aweigh" (orchestral)
"On, Brave Old Army Team" (Eddy and male chorus) – by Philip Egner, INTO:
"The Caissons Go Rolling Along" (Eddy, male chorus, Ray Bolger) – by Edmund L. Gruber, INTO:
"Anchors Aweigh" (same singers) – music by Charles A. Zimmerman, lyrics by Capt. Alfred H. Miles
"Who Knows?" (unknown soprano)
"Who Knows?" reprise (Eddy)
"I've a Strange New Rhythm in My Heart" (Eleanor Powell dubbed by Marjorie Lane, female chorus) with interpolated fragment of Cole Porter's "Night and Day"
"M'Appari" [Ah, so pure] (Eddy) – from *Martha* by Friedrich von Flotow
"Rosalie" (Eddy)
"Why Should I Care?" (Frank Morgan)
"Spring Love Is in the Air" (Ilona Massey and chorus)
"Polovetsian Dances" (orchestra with Albertina Rasch Dancers) – from *Prince Igor* by Alexander Borodin, INTO:
"Swan Lake," Act II (orchestra with Rasch Dancers) – by Peter Ilich Tchaikovsky, INTO:
Tchaikovsky's Symphony No. 6, 2nd movement, Allegro con grazia
"Rosalie" reprise (orchestra with chorus, Powell dances)
"Close" (orchestral behind garden scene)
"Goodbye" ("Addio") fragment (Eddy) – by Francesco Paolo Tosti
"It's All Over But the Shouting" (Eddy and male chorus), INTO:
"To Love or Not to Love" (Eddy, male chorus)
John Philip Sousa medley (Powell dances) – contains "Washington Post March," "Stars and Stripes Forever," "Sempre Fidelis," "El Capitan," "Parade" by Herbert Stothart, reprises of "El Capitan," "Stars and Stripes Forever," and "Who Knows?"
"In the Still of the Night" reprise (Eddy)
Finale:
"Wedding March" – from "A Midsummer-Night's Dream" by Felix Mendelssohn

"Gaudeamus Igitur" (Eddy and male chorus) - traditional
"Oh, Promise Me" (Eddy) - music by Reginald DeKoven, lyrics by Clement Scott
"Rosalie" reprise (Eddy and chorus with organ)
"It's All Over But the Shouting" reprise (orch.)

"It Wasn't Meant for Me" by Cole Porter was copyrighted for the film but not used. "Close," also copyrighted, appeared only as background music. Porter wrote six different versions of the title song before one was chosen.

The Girl of the Golden West

MGM.
Released March 18, 1938.
Directed by Robert Z. Leonard.
Produced by William Anthony McGuire.
120 minutes.
Issued in "Sepia-Platinum."

French title: *La Belle Cabaretière*
   (The Beautiful Saloon Keeper)
Danish title: *Pigen frå det gyldne Vesten*
   (Maiden from the Golden West)
Swedish title: *Flickan från gyllene västern*
   (Girl of the Golden West)
German title: *Im Goldenen Westen*
   (In the Golden West)
Portuguese title: *A Princesa de Eldorado*
   (The Princess of Eldorado)

Based on the 1905 play by David Belasco. Music: Sigmund Romberg. Lyrics: Gus Kahn. Screenplay: Isabel Dawn and Boyce DeGaw. Musical Director: Herbert Stothart. Photography: Oliver Marsh. Gowns: Adrian. Dances: Albertina Rasch. Montage: Slavko Vorkapich. Editor: W. Donn Hayes. Asst. Directors: Robert A. Golden, George Yohalem. Art Director: Cedric Gibbons. Art Associates: Eddie Imazu, Edwin B. Willis. Music Presentations: Merrill Pye. Musical Director: Reginald LeBorg. Tinting and Toning: John M. Nickolaus. Orchestra and Vocal Arrangements: Leonid Raab, Léo Arnaud, Murray Cutter, Paul Marquardt. Sound: Douglas Shearer, James Brock. Music Recording: Mike McLaughlin. Translator and Instructor for Spanish Lyrics: Z. Yaconelli.

The stage play by California-born David Belasco opened in 1905 at the Belasco Theatre in New York City, starring Blanche Bates, Robert Hilliard and

German cinema program. *Courtesy Anna Michalik.*

Frank Keenan (grandfather of Keenan Wynn). It ran 224 performances. An opera version, *La Fanciulla del West* by Giacomo Puccini, had its world premiere at the Metropolitan Opera on December 10, 1910, with a cast headed by Emmy Destinn, Enrico Caruso, and Pasquale Amato. Belasco himself was stage director and Arturo Toscanini conducted.

The Girl of the Golden West was filmed in 1914 by Cecil B. DeMille, with Mabel Van Buren in the title role for Paramount. The 1923 film version, directed by Edwin Carewe for Associated-First National, starred Sylvia Breamer as the "Girl," with J. Warren Kerrigan and Russell Simpson. In 1930, Warners remade the work as a talkie with Ann Harding and James Rennie, directed by John Francis Dillon.

Jeanette MacDonald (Mary Robbins)
Nelson Eddy (Ramerez / Lt. Dick Johnson)
Walter Pidgeon (Sheriff Jack Rance)
Buddy Ebsen (Alabama)
Leo Carrillo (Mosquito)
H.B. Warner (Father Sienna)

The Girl of the Golden West

Cliff Edwards (Minstrel Joe)
Leonard Penn (Pedro)
Monty Woolley (Governor)
Priscilla Lawson (Nina Martinez)
Ynez Seabury (Wowkle)
Robert Murphy (Sonora Slim)
Olin Howland (Trinidad Joe)
Billy Bevan (Nick)
Victor Potel (Stagecoach driver)
Brandon Tynan (The Professor)
Nick Thompson (Billy Jackrabbit)
Tom Mahoney (Handsome Charlie)

In Prologue:
Charley Grapewin (Uncle Davy)
Noah Beery Sr (General Ramerez)
Bill Cody Jr ("Gringo," Dick as a child)
Jeanne Ellis (Mary as a child)
Phillip Armenta (Long Face)
Chief Big Tree (Indian chief)
Russell Simpson (Pioneer)

Armand "Curley" Wright (First renegade)
Pedro Regas (Second renegade)

Gene Coogan (Manuel)
Sergei Arabeloff (Jose)
Alberto Morin (Juan)
Joe Dominguez (Felipe)
Frank McGlynn (Pete, the gambler)
Cy Kendall (Hank, the gambler)
E. Alyn Warren (First miner)
Francis Ford (Second miner)
Hank Bell (Under-Sheriffr)
Dell Henderson, Frank O'Connor (Passengers in coach)
Ronnie Rondell, Joe Popkin, Bob Pierce (Members of Ramerez's gang)
James Farley, Edward Peil Sr (Men in Sheriff's office)
Forbes Murray (Man)
Hal LeSeuer (Adjutant)
Harry Semels (Peon Servant)
Walter Bonn (Lt. Johnson)
Richard Tucker (Colonel)
Virginia Howell (Governor's wife)
Carlos Ruffino, Rodolfo Hoyos Sr ("Mariachie" soloists)
Donald Sadler (Dancer)
St. Luke's Choristers (singing "Ave Maria")
Father Lani's Choir (acting "Ave Maria" choristers)

Cut from release print:
Carol Tevis (Trixie LaVerne)
Ray Bolger (Happy Moore)

One of seventeen top-grossing films of 1937-38.

Danish poster. *Courtesy Anna Michalik.*

"Jeanette MacDonald and Nelson Eddy are like tapioca," wrote Frank Nugent in the *New York Times*. "Either you like them or you don't." He had just seen *The Girl of the Golden West*. With this film, the public began dividing into two camps: those who loved the splendid entertainment Jeanette and Nelson promised in a good film and the more devoted who would be content to watch them read (or sing) the proverbial phone book.

David Belasco's theatrical potboiler had a long, happy history of profits for its author-

Swedish poster for *The Girl of the Golden West*. Courtesy Anna Michalik.

producer when MGM decided it would be a fitting vehicle for its "team." Belasco's plays may not be considered literature today, but as the foremost stage director of his time, he knew how to create a series of hits.

MGM's *Girl* wasn't the first time the western epic had been set to music. No less a composer than Giacomo Puccini had been moved to write an opera based on the story of Minnie and Ramerez. When he visited New York in 1906 to supervise the first American performance of his *Madame Butterfly* (also a Belasco play), Puccini attended Belasco's production of *The Girl*. Although he knew little or no English, Puccini knew a strong dramatic situation when he saw one. The scene in the girl's cabin with the blood and the poker game seemed to him ideal as a second act curtain for an opera.

La Fanciulla del West premiered on December 10, 1910 at the Metropolitan Opera. Belasco was stage director, Arturo Toscanini conducted, and Enrico Caruso was in the cast. Sung in Italian, the opera featured hordes of cowboys singing "Doo-da, doo-da," and heroine Minnie had an aria, "Benvenuta fra noi, Johnson de Sacramento" (Welcome among us, Johnson of Sacramento), all of which may have sounded odd to American ears. Nevertheless, the opera was a success and remained so as long as strong casts were available. However, it didn't have any of the lush melodies for which Puccini was famous and fell from favor until recently. While it is unlikely that it will ever become a "standard," the opera is enjoying new popularity, and a major critic, Robert Lawrence, considers it Puccini's greatest masterpiece.

Musically, the 1938 film *Girl* abounds in some of the loveliest melodies Sigmund Romberg could write, and musical director Herbert Stothart outdid himself in vibrant orchestrations. Unfortunately, MGM also dramatized incidents only mentioned in the stage versions and made maximum use of soundstage exteriors. The phoniness of the plaster rocks and *papier maché* forests seems very jarring to the contemporary eye, but at the time it was regarded as the summit of film craft. Lighting and sound could be completely controlled on a set without the harsh inconveniences of dragging equipment, actors, and crew into the woods to obtain footage easily spoiled by weather, wind, and extraneous background noise. Also it was possible to do "pick-up shots" after a film was completed and the real location under a foot of snow. The advantages of set over nature were so many that it took the demise of the studios (and their vast soundstages) and the super-realism of television news coverage to end the practice.

Belasco had made the play and opera successful with his stagecraft wizardry. The audience forgot they were in a theatre watching a play. The blizzard became real. The 1938 film suffers greatly from being studio-bound, while the earlier film versions were shot outdoors and are infinitely more credible.

The Girl of the Golden West

To explain how our hero and heroine ended up as a bandit and a saloon keeper, the film adds a prologue showing them as children. Here little Mary (Jeanne Ellis) travels to California by covered wagon with her Uncle Davy (Charley Grapewin). *Courtesy Anna Michalik.*

Little Gringo (Bill Cody Jr) is adopted by a Mexican bandit (Noah Beery) when his pioneer parents are killed. Father Sienna (H.B. Warner) urges a less bloodthirsty lifestyle, but the death of Gringo's foster father dictates a life of crime for the child. *Courtesy Anna Michalik.*

Because more than half of the MacDonald-Eddy *Girl* enacts events that occurred before the opening of the stage versions, the film consumes two hours, even after a subplot with Ray Bolger and Carol Tevis was cut. Also apparently trimmed was a song delivered by Cliff Edwards ("Ukulele Ike") of radio and record fame. He is briefly glimpsed holding his uke, but no more.

The Girl herself, Minnie, was rechristened "Mary," probably due to the popularity of two other Minnies, the mouse and the moocher. Miss MacDonald plays her with tomboyish strides and western drawl that are first affected, then affecting. The appeal of the *Girl* is the appeal of the child-woman, a girl raised from birth "without seeing another white woman," completely unaware of her own femininity. Of course, the stage, opera, and film *Girls* all had an Indian companion, Wowkle, but in the sensibilities of those days she was a "native" and didn't count. Fortunately, the MacDonald *Girl* is not required to brag repeatedly that she has never been kissed, as Doris Day was in the 1953 *Calamity Jane*.

Nelson Eddy is delightful when leading his troop of bandits or courting the Girl in quiet conversation, but he is clearly uncomfortable in the heavier, more melodramatic sequences, and his makeup is singularly unattractive. MGM was so sure of the appeal of their property that they no longer were careful to work around his deficiencies.

Walter Pidgeon, too, has problems. The script never decides whether Jack Rance is villain, protagonist, or kindly "other man," and Pidgeon plays each scene tentatively, as if he is not sure what the next day's shooting will require him to do.

In a wagon heading west, we meet little Mary (Jeanne Ellis), who has been brought along by her Uncle Davy (Charley Grapewin) after the death of her gambler pa in Kentucky. She is a chip off the family tree, betting her Uncle a dollar that the Indian tom-toms in the distance don't scare her a bit. That night, the little band huddles around a campfire, and Uncle Davy tries to cheer Mary, blowing a tune on a convenient jug. She joins him in the lovely "Shadows on the Moon."

A tall figure steps suddenly out of the darkness into the firelight. It is Father Sienna (H.B. Warner), come to welcome them and give them a map of the trail through the mountains. Hiding in the darkness, watching the scene, are the fierce bandit Ramerez (Noah Beery Sr) and his little Gringo (Bill Cody Jr).

The bandits seize the mission for a hideout. There, Ramerez teases his adopted son for mooning over the blonde little señorita. We learn that the boy was stolen from his parents by Indians and later found by Ramerez's soldiers. Now he and Ramerez are both "Soldiers of Fortune." When a terrified servant protests that there is no more food, little Gringo shoots one of the mission sheep with a bow and arrow. The beast falls dead at the feet of Father Sienna.

Ramerez happily rewards the boy with a medal from his own highly decorated chest. But Father Sienna speaks so movingly of the rights of others and of the settlers that have come in peace that Gringo is ashamed. Ramerez snatches back his medal, explaining to Father Sienna that if he does not reclaim them when Gringo is bad, he would have none to give him when he is good. Father Sienna gives Gringo a different kind of medal, a religious one.

At the Padre's urging, the local Indians decide to ride down and make peace with the wagon camp. Ramerez follows them at Gringo's insistence. The settlers see Indians coming and fire blindly. Ramerez falls. He is carried back to his own camp where he begs Gringo to sing "Soldiers of Fortune" once more. As the boy sings, Ramerez dies and a new Ramerez is born.

In a Slavko Vorkapich montage, we see the progress of his "career" as WANTED posters offer higher and higher bounties for him, dead or alive. The adult Ramerez (Nelson) appears at the top of the canyon concealing his camp. Leading his band back from a successful expedition, he steers his horse down the twisting path, singing a full-throated version of "Soldiers of Fortune."

His comic sidekick, Mosquito (Leo Carrillo), is quickly surrounded by señoritas seeking presents. Ramerez tells him that bandits have no time for love, but then gives some trinkets to Nina (Priscilla Lawson, Princess Aura in the *Flash Gordon* serials), oblivious to her obvious adoration and jealousy. He is glad to be back in camp with food, wine, and the trees talking to each other overhead. Idly, he begins to sing the song he heard so long ago: "Shadows on the Moon."

Far away through the pines, another voice is singing the same song. Mary (Jeanette) stands on the porch of her cabin, rocking a baby and crooning the haunting lullaby:

> Shadows on the moon are saying summer's on the wane.
> The sun will soon give way to autumn rain.

(Copyright 1938, Renewed 1965 Metro-Goldwyn-Mayer, Inc. Rights controlled by Leo Feist, Inc. Used by permission.)

Ray Bolger, right, and Carol Tevis, center, had a song and a dance, but the film ran too long and their scenes were cut. (Billy Bevan as bartender.)

The Girl of the Golden West

Mary, the "Girl" (Jeanette), is serenaded by Alabama (Buddy Ebsen) in her mountain retreat.

The baby belongs to Mary's Indian companion, Wowkle (Ynez Seabury), who is helping Mary pack for her yearly trip to Monterey. Their conversation reveals that the Girl now owns the Polka Saloon, inherited from her Uncle Davy—"The only saloon in Cloudy, run by the only woman in town."

A whistle outside announces the arrival of Alabama (Buddy Ebsen) on a mule. His piping flute and her coloratura combine in the delightful "Wind in the Trees." Alabama has come to fetch Mary to the Polka where the Sheriff is waiting eagerly with a surprise. ("Cloudy Street," on which the Polka is situated, was also used for *Anna Karenina* and *Balalaika*. In 1943 it was bombed for *Song of Russia,* and what was left was used in the Technicolor remake of *Rose Marie*.)

At the Polka, Mary checks on the customers, including a gentlemanly old drunk, the "Professor" (Brandon Tynan). A miner deposits his gold with her for safekeeping and she adds it to the already overflowing safe. If Wells Fargo doesn't get through soon to pick it up, Ramerez may hear of it. Sheriff Jack Rance (Walter Pidgeon) assures her the money is safe as long as he is on the job. He saunters out, and the grinning miners crowd around Mary. The

Sheriff Jack Rance (Walter Pidgeon) has his eye on the only woman in Cloudy—Mary. *Courtesy Anna Michalik.*

surprise is revealed to be a white piano. "Sure has got pretty teeth," cries a grizzled codger.

Mary rushes out to thank Jack. "Only cost five thousand dollars," he demurs. He asks Mary if she will be ashamed of running the Polka when she gets to Monterey and meets all those fancy people. Mary is startled. Is *he* ashamed? "With you in it, the Polka's a church!" he replies. Mary can't imagine Jack Rance in church. Unless, he tells her ardently, it's to marry her. He wants to take her back East and stake her as a singer. Mary lightly refuses. She loves Cloudy too much to leave.

Inside, the boys are banging away on the poor piano. With great dignity, the "Professor" rises and staggers to the keyboard. The rowdy laughter subsides as his aimless passes at the keys turn into "Liebestraum." The Girl sings as the camera shows an assortment of Cloudy citizens held in rapt attention by the music. In a voice choked with emotion, the "Professor" announces that the last time he played this song was in London before an audience of two thousand people—and the *King*.

Mary departs for Monterey with a bodyguard of Rance's best men. They are good men, but not good enough for Ramerez, who, with bandanna and Mexicano accent concealing his true origin, robs the coach and woos the lady. The lady's fiery resistance spurs Ramerez's interest. When she slaps his face, his fate is sealed.

He sends his men back to camp while he and Mosquito follow Mary to Monterey. Is it safe for bandits in Monterey? Mosquito asks. They'll go as honest men, Ramerez replies. But what, asks Mosquito, if honest men like them meet some bandits?

In Monterey, Mary happily presents Father Sienna with the gold she has brought to the mission, hidden with the papoose during the robbery. He thanks her. If it weren't for her and the mysterious stranger who drops a large bag of gold in the poor box each month, he doesn't know what the Indians would do. Always the mystery gold is wrapped in bark with a message scratched on it: "Return this to your Indians. After all, it rightfully belongs to them."

Father Sienna turns to the organ to rehearse Mary in the song she will sing at mass tomorrow

Another scene cut from the finished film. Mary leads the miners in singing "Oh, Susannah." Left to right, Robert Murphy, Jeanette, Buddy Ebsen, Walter Pidgeon, Olin Howland. Foreground, Cliff "Ukulele Ike" Edwards with banjo. *Courtesy Anna Michalik.*

The Girl of the Golden West

On her trip to Monterey, Mary is held up by the bandit Ramerez, who honors her beauty by returning her jewelry. He tells her where he'd like to dangle. (Frank O'Connor, center; Ynez Seabury, right.)

morning. The Governor is coming down for the fiesta and will be in attendance. The Governor! Mary is nervous, but begins singing "Ave Maria."

The scene dissolves to the choir loft of the old Spanish church where she is singing, accompanied by a boys' choir. The Governor (Monty Woolley in one of his earliest film roles) is delighted with her voice and sends word, asking her to sing for him at the Mariachie.

The big night arrives, and Mary is scared stiff. As the merrymakers whirl past her window, she practices curtsying for the momentous meeting. It's just no good, she decides. She'll bungle it. Couldn't Father Sienna tell them she doesn't feel very well? "Do you want me to lie, Mary?" He cheers her up, and, when her escort is announced, she steadies her bobbling hoopskirt and marches to her fate.

Her fate is a handsome officer, "Lt. Dick Johnson," whom she doesn't recognize without a mask. Ramerez has borrowed a uniform, leaving its occupant in his underwear. With Mosquito as coachman, he drives Mary through the festive streets, joining the throng in singing the romantic "Señorita." On such a night there is plenty of time to get to the Governor's rancho. The horse stops to rest beside the moonlit ocean, giving Dick a chance to reprise "Señorita."

> Pity me, señorita.
> I was free, señorita.
> Then you happened along
> With your smile and your song
> And I knew...
> That as long as there was love in my heart
> I would love only you.
>
> (Copyright 1938, Renewed 1965 Metro-Goldwyn-Mayer, Inc. Rights Controlled by Leo Feist Inc. Used by Permission.)

The Girl happily listens to his song and his compliments (that her eyes are like "two spoonfuls of blue Pacific"), but when he tries to steal a kiss, he gets another slap in the face. She commandeers Mosquito's carriage and arrives at

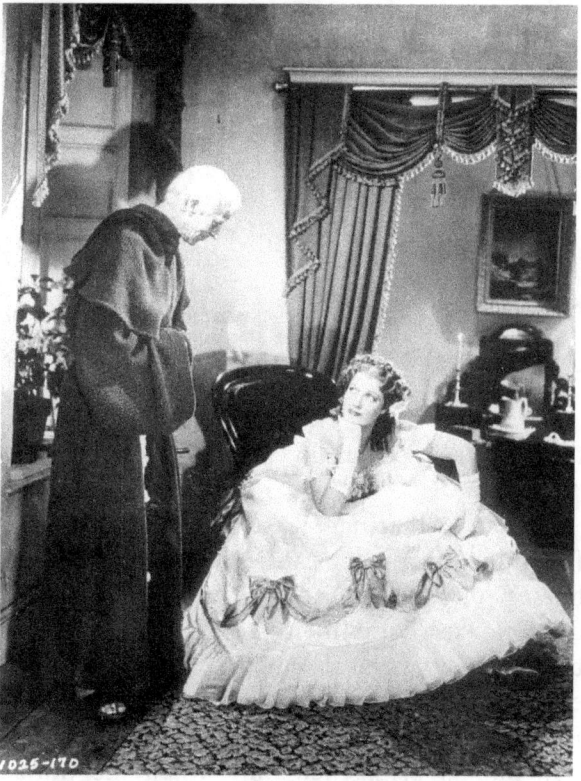

Tomboy Mary is rehearsed in ladylike behavior by Father Sienna (H.B. Warner) in preparation for the Governor's ball.

Her escort is the handsome Lt. Dick Johnson, AKA Ramerez. Unknown to her, he has borrowed his uniform, and its former occupant is calling out the militia. As they sing the "Mariachie," soldiers interrupt and the bandit escapes on a high note.

the Governor's rancho just in time to sing "Mariachie."

In an Albertina Rasch dance spectacle fraught with unintentional symbolism, galloping horses circle a cluster of writhing female dancers, who are then snared by enormous bullwhips wrapped around their waists. Despite enough Freudian overtones to keep three Busby Berkeley numbers going, the dancing gets pretty dull and is brightened only when the police discover Dick, who has followed Mary. He has time for only one chorus before he must depart with the irate constabulary in hot pursuit. Puzzled, Mary returns to Cloudy. We are now more than halfway through the film and have just reached the point where the stage version begins.

Ramerez also travels to Cloudy to hold up the saloon safe. He doesn't suspect that Mary is the Polka's owner and guardian. As part of the bandits' strategy, Mosquito interrupts a tedious song assigned to Alabama ("The West Ain't Wild Anymore") and implies that he is Ramerez.

The real Ramerez is at the Polka asking for whiskey and water. "I'm sorry, sir," answers the bartender (Billy Bevan). "We don't serve no

Nelson Eddy as Ramerez. *Courtesy Sue Baumann.*

fancy drinks." Ramerez arouses Jack Rance's suspicion, but Mary appears just in time to vouch for him. Jack doesn't like anyone trying to jump another man's claim and figures Dick can see all he wants of Cloudy in an hour.

Meanwhile, Mosquito's ruse has worked. Alabama rushes into the Polka gasping that the bandit is up at his blacksmith shop. With a $10,000 reward on the culprit's head, the saloon is emptied in no time. Mary is concerned about the gold she is guarding for the hardworking prospectors and asks Dick to help her lock up. The gold may not be hers, but bandits would have to take *her* before they could take *it*. She tells Dick of finding a dying prospector and promising to send his stake to his family back East. (The basically touching story is couched in such euphemistic terms for death and told with so much eye-batting that it becomes maudlin.)

Mary goes to close the shutters, the signal for Ramerez's men to ride down from the hills. He stops her. "*Don't* do that! If you do..."—he catches himself—"You'll shut out the moon." He abandons his plan to rob the Polka and, like Dante, asks for one hour with his Beatrice. Unlike Dante he gets it, serenading Mary with "Who Are We to Say?" beside a mountain stream.

At her cabin, Mary makes a terrible discovery. *Courtesy Anna Michalik.*

The hour is up, and Dick must leave. Of course, Mary tells him, if he is not too far away tomorrow night, she'll be fixing supper in her cabin up the hill. "All tonight I'll be saying 'tomorrow,'" he says. "And all tomorrow I'll be saying 'tonight,'" Mary replies.

Back in the bandits' camp, Ramerez is oblivious to the hostility around him. His men are furious because his lovemaking has cost them their prize. Nina is also furious and slips away to have her revenge.

A snowstorm is just beginning the next evening, but nothing could keep Dick away. Wowkle is putting the finishing touches on the stew when he arrives. She and Dick exchange pleasantries in Indian dialect. Mary wants to know what was said. "Him say get out now so he can be alone with you," Wowkle says, pulling on her blanket. Dick looks sheepish. "I tell him you say same thing before he come," Wowkle continues. Dick grins.

Ramerez follows Mary back to the Polka where she warmly welcomes him as her handsome lieutenant. *Courtesy Anna Michalik.*

The Girl of the Golden West

Jeanette MacDonald as the Girl. David Belasco's stage heroine was named Minnie, but the screen Girl underwent a name change. *Courtesy Anna Michalik.*

Shot by Jack Rance. Mary must make a terrible bargain for Dick's life. *Courtesy Anna Michalik.*

With the wind howling outside, Ramerez discovers that Mary is the girl he has always remembered from his childhood, and they declare their love. Suddenly, Jack Rance and the boys from the saloon are heard shouting outside. Dick panics and hides. Mary covers for him, thinking he fears Jack's jealousy. But Jack makes it clear that the fancy gentleman at the saloon was really a bandit. Ramerez's girlfriend is waiting at the Sheriff's office to collect the reward. Mary is stunned at this news, but recovers herself and mocks Jack for having the bandit right in front of him and not recognizing him.

Jack strides out to his horse, but Alabama lingers behind. He asks if there is anything he can do. In his hand is the smoldering cigar Ramerez left on the mantelpiece. The Girl thanks him and he quietly leaves.

Mary orders Ramerez to come out and account for himself. She could forgive him his profession, but not his girlfriend. Hysterically, she orders him out of the cabin. He is gone only a few moments when shots are heard. He staggers back in and the Girl relents. She hides him in the loft as Jack pounds on the bolted door. He is sure he saw Ramerez enter the cabin, but Mary convinces him he was wrong. "If you say he didn't, Girl, that's good enough for me," he says. A trickle of blood falls on their clasped hands.

Jack Rance hauls Ramerez out of hiding and is ready to turn him over to a lynching party. He'd have gambled his life that Mary was the last person in the world to help a rat like that.

The Girl challenges him to a bet. She'll play him three hands of poker. If he wins two out of three, he gets Ramerez—and her too. If he loses, he doesn't get either. Jack Rance's character and the nature of his interest in the Girl have been so tenuously established that it seems mere plot convenience when he consents to the game.

Each wins a hand. Then Mary cheats and wins the third game. Jack concedes like a gentleman, then notices that she has thumbnailed the cards. In a fury, he tells her that he'd kill her if she were a man. Tearfully Mary asks him to let Ramerez go and keep her. The scene has now changed focus so many times that we are not astonished when Jack says yes. "I don't cheat, Girl, and I never lie," he tells the Girl proudly. The lengthy cabin sequence that should have been the dramatic high point of the film ends, not with a bang but a whimper and a few bars of "Liebestraum."

Mary is seen bidding the boys at the Polka goodbye. She and Jack are off to Monterey to be wed. The boys beg for a farewell song. She tries to sing "Who Are We to Say?" but chokes on her tears.

In Monterey, Father Sienna is anxiously awaiting the bridal couple when a "man" is announced. It is Ramerez, come to ask the Padre's help in returning to the ways of the boy, Gringo, whom the Padre knew so long ago. The priest happily consents, but first he must perform a wedding. He leaves Ramerez in the garden and goes to greet Mary and Jack. Jack is escorted to the office to sign the register, and Mary wanders into the garden. Jack sees her and Ramerez together from the window and makes a graceful, if utterly illogical, exit, leaving them to sing a final reprise of "Señorita."

The Girl of the Golden West was the first weak MacDonald-Eddy vehicle and didn't bring much glory to anyone. While it was one of the top moneymakers of the year, the split between the general public and the "fans" was beginning. The uncritical enthusiasm of the latter only served to reinforce the opinion of the former that all MacDonald-Eddy films were "silly." On top of the cool critical reception of *The Firefly* and *Rosalie*, their previous solo films, *Girl* represented a distinct minus for their careers.

The film was one of five that Walter Pidgeon walked through at MGM that year. Pidgeon was a silent film actor whose rich baritone made him the leading man in a number of early musicals: *Kiss Me Again* with Bernice Claire, *Viennese Nights*, Rodgers and Hart's *The Hot Heiress*, and *Sweet Kitty Bellairs* with Claudia Dell. After the first musical cycle he returned as a "straight" actor, but didn't attain star status until he scored in *How Green Was My Valley* in 1941.

Buddy Ebsen had earned a warm response in *Broadway Melody of 1936* with his hominy-grits drawl and white-tie-and-tails tap dancing. He was cast as the Tin Man in *The Wizard of Oz*, but was poisoned by the aluminum makeup and replaced by Jack Haley after shooting had begun. Twenty-five years later, *The Beverly Hillbillies* and *Barnaby Jones* on television would make his face known in every corner of the "civilized" world.

Another *Girl* performer, Cliff Edwards ("Ukulele Ike") was also lost in the shuffle. He is best remembered today as the voice of "Jiminy Cricket" in *Pinocchio*. Although he was a well-known singer and recording star, his footage was snipped and he ended up as an "extra" in the final release version of *Girl*.

Now that Jeanette and Nelson were established at the box office, a newer set of names began to sparkle on the marquees. MGM had bright newcomers Judy Garland and Eleanor Powell, as well as Allan Jones and Ilona Massey. Deanna Durbin was musical queen at Universal, and Betty Grable, who had been in films since 1930, was finally getting the attention she deserved, as were Sonja Henie and young Alice Faye. As a possible Eddy backup, MGM signed nineteen-year-old Douglas McPhail, a handsome baritone with boyish charm who, ironically, would play Eddy's understudy in his next film, *Sweethearts*.

Uneasy lies the head that wears the crown!

Reviews:

The foremost criticism of *Girl* was the length combined with the weak plot. *Variety* thought it was twenty minutes too long, the *New York Post*

Father Sienna prepares for Mary's wedding to Jack Rance. *Courtesy Anna Michalik.*

United happily, despite obstacles, for a final duet. *Courtesy Ken Norton.*

said thirty minutes, and the *New York World-Telegram* acknowledged that there may have been longer films, but "few others have seemed as long." The *World-Telegram* continued, "the story is neither distinctive nor sturdy, and hasn't been helped much by the diffused direction."

The *New Yorker* saw no reason why the *Girl* plot "should have to be hauled out." The *New York Times* felt it was "dated as a tin bathtub, but redeemed by the singing of its stars." The *New York Herald Tribune* suggested the original plot offered "rich material for a farce or a satire," and thought "the [film] version at the Capitol [Theatre] comes perilously close to being funny now and then."

About the performances, the press was equally divided. Generally, like the *New York Post,* they thought Eddy's casting as a dashing bandit "a bit too thick," but that "his rich and glorious baritone almost saves the situation for him." Jeanette's singing also drew uniform raves, but opinions on her characterization were divided: "excellent" said the *New York Post*; "a little bit embarrassing" said the *New York World-Telegram.*

The *World-Telegram* summed up the film: "If you are one of those fans who simply cannot get enough of Jeanette MacDonald and Nelson Eddy, then this film will be right up your alley."

Recordings (See Discography for further information)

Jeanette MacDonald recorded nothing from the film, but Nelson Eddy did a 78 RPM album with four songs:
"Señorita"
"Soldiers of Fortune"
"Sun-up to Sundown"
"Who Are We to Say?" ["Obey Your Heart"]

Music in the Film

All music is by Sigmund Romberg, with lyrics by Gus Kahn unless otherwise noted. In listing performers after each title, "and" denotes a genuine duet, while commas between names indicate a sequence of singers.

Overture: "Sun-up to Sundown," Indian theme, "Señorita," "Camptown Races" by Stephen Foster, EVOLVES INTO:
"Sun-up to Sundown" (Chorus, Jeanne Ellis)
"Shadows on the Moon" (Ellis)
"Soldiers of Fortune" (Noah Beery, Bill Cody Jr dubbed by Raymond Chace, male chorus)
"Soldiers of Fortune" reprise (Cody, Eddy, male chorus)
"Shadows on the Moon" reprise (Eddy, MacDonald)
"The Wind in the Trees" (MacDonald, flute)
"Liebestraum" ["Dream of Love"] (MacDonald) - music by Franz Liszt, English lyrics by Gus Kahn, arrangement by Herbert Stothart
"Ave Maria" (MacDonald, sung by St. Luke's Choristers, acted by Father Lani's Choir) -

Sweethearts

music by Johann Sebastian Bach and Charles Gounod, traditional Latin lyrics
"Señorita" (Eddy, chorus)
"Mariachie" (MacDonald, Eddy, chorus) - additional lyrics by Carlos Ruffino
"The West Ain't Wild Anymore" (Buddy Ebsen)
"Who Are We to Say?" ["Obey Your Heart"] (Eddy)
"Who Are We to Say?" reprise (MacDonald)
Finale: "Señorita" reprise (MacDonald and Eddy)

"There's a Brand New Song in Town," sung by Ray Bolger and Carol Tevis, was cut from the film. The song "Girl of the Golden West" was copyrighted and issued as sheet music, but used only as background music in the film.

Script History
From a monograph by Mary Truesdell

"The original Belasco theme of redemption almost gets lost in a welter of comic and melodramatic additions to this film version. With all the money MGM was spending on research, you'd have thought they'd *first* get the script set. But no—they apparently preferred a pattern of 'many writers, many revisions,' to their detriment, a good deal of the time.

When the film was being planned as a Technicolor production, an opening scene was written that has Mary's stagecoach returning from Sacramento when it is stopped by a Wells Fargo representative. Surrounded by the beauty of the Sierras, she descends and wanders joyfully into a field of radiant spring poppies and lupines. Dick Johnson (actually the bandit Ramerez) gallops up, having just robbed another stagecoach down the road. They engage in their typical flirtatious quips and he stoops to pick her a bouquet before riding off.

Thus we quickly establish the lead characters and introduce the conflict, avoiding the long prologue about their meeting as children, which mainly sought to justify Dick's life of crime.

Trivia

Joan Crawford reportedly campaigned to show off her singing skills opposite Eddy in *Girl*.

Sweethearts

MGM.
Released December 30, 1938.
Directed by W.S. Van Dyke II.
Retake Director: Robert Z. Leonard.
Produced by Hunt Stromberg.
114 minutes. (Originally 120 minutes.)
Three-strip Technicolor.

Spanish title: *Enamoradas* (Lovers)
French title: *Amants* (Lovers)
Portuguese title: Canção de Amor (Song of Love)

Based on the 1913 operetta *Sweethearts*, music by Victor Herbert, book and lyrics by Fred deGresac, Harry B. Smith, and Robert B. Smith. Screenplay: Dorothy Parker and Alan Campbell. Cameramen: Oliver Marsh and Allen Davey. Music adaptation: Herbert Stothart. Costumes: Adrian. Special Lyrics: Bob Wright and Chet Forrest. Dances: Albertina Rasch. Art Direction: Cedric Gibbons. Editor: Robert J. Kern. Assistant Directors: Hugh Boswell, Charles O'Malley, Ted Stevens. Contributing Writers: S.J. and Laura Perelman. Montages: Slavko Vorkapich, John Hoffman. Art Associate: Joseph Wright. Technicolor Director: Natalie Kalmus. Set Decorations: Edwin B. Willis. Musical Presentations: Merrill Pye. Orchestrations: Paul Marquardt. Sound: Douglas Shearer.

The original stage production of *Sweethearts* opened on September 8, 1913 at the New Amsterdam Theatre in New York City, where it ran for 136 performances. It starred Christie MacDonald and Edwin Wilson. (It is obvious from the short New York runs of many world-famous hits that a show could recoup its investment quickly in the big city and then "hit the road," occasionally for decades.)

Jeanette MacDonald (Gwen Marlowe)
Nelson Eddy (Ernest Lane)
Frank Morgan (Felix Lehman)
Ray Bolger (Hans, the dancer)
Florence Rice (Kay Jordan)
Mischa Auer (Leo Kronk, *Sweethearts'* playwright)

A Spanish poster. *Courtesy Anna Michalik.*

Fay Holden (Hannah, the dresser)
Terry Kilburn (Junior Marlowe, Gwen's brother)
Betty Jaynes (Una Wilson, Gwen's understudy)
Douglas McPhail (Harvey Horton, Ernest's understudy)
Reginald Gardiner (Norman Trumpett, Hollywood agent)
Herman Bing (Oscar Engel, *Sweethearts*' composer)
Allyn Joslyn (Dink Rogers)
Raymond Walburn (Orlando Lane)
Lucile Watson (Mrs. Marlowe)
George Barbier (Benjamin Silver)
Kathleen Lockhart (Aunt Amelia Lane)
Gene Lockhart (Uncle Augustus Marlowe)
Berton Churchill (Sheridan Lane)
Olin Howland (Appleby, the box office man)
Gerald Hamer (Harry)
Marvin Jones (Boy in lobby)
Dorothy Gray (His girlfriend)
Emory Parnell (Fire inspector)
Maude Turner Gordon (Dowager)
Jac George (Violinist)
Roger Converse (Usher)
Reid Kilpatrick (Radio announcer)
Wilson Benge (Second valet to Ernest)
George Ernest (First callboy)
Billy McCullough (Second callboy)
Lee Phelps (Doorman at St. Regis)
Pat Gleason, Ralph Malone, David Kerman, Jack Gardner (Reporters)
Ralph W. and Rollin B. Berry, Chester and B. Berolund (Lawyer twins)
Mira McKinney, Grace Hayle (Telephone operators)
Hal K. Dawson (Morty, the stage manager)
Forrester Harvey (Tailor's assistant)
Gayne Whitman (Commentator)
Margaret Irving (Vendeuse)
Irving Bacon (Assistant director)
Barbara Pepper, Marjorie "Babe" Kane (Telephone operators)
Jimmy Conlin (Property man)
Dick Rich (First stagehand)
Ralph Sanford (Second stagehand)
James Flavin (Theatre doorman)
Richard Tucker, Edwin Stanley, Edward Earle, Brent Sargent (Men in lobby)
Betty Ross Clarke, Dorothy Christy, Suzanne Kaaren [Mrs. Sidney Blackmer], Lulu May Bohrman (Women in lobby)
Hal Cooke, Jenifer Gray (Mr. Silver's secretaries)
Fred Santley (Music vendor in lobby)
Don Barclay (Taxi driver from Bridgeport)
Arthur "Pop" Byron (Policeman)
James Farley (Carriage starter)
Bruce Mitchell (Stagehand)
George Cooper, Frank Mills (Electricians)
Mary Howard, Joan Barclay, Sharon Lewis, Vivian Reid, Lucille Brown, Valerie Day, Ethelreda Leopold (Chorus girls)
Lester Dorr (Dance director)
Anne Wigton (Saleswoman)
Dalies Frantz (Pianist playing "Badinage")
Paul Marquardt (Conductor of Marine band)
Paul Kerby (Orchestra conductor)
Joe A. Devlin (Taxi driver)
Ralph Brooks, Brooks Benedict (Extras in radio audience)
Toby Wing (Telephone operator)
Cyril Ring (Waiter)

Sweethearts

Philip Loeb (Samuel Silver)
Charles Sullivan (Tommy, a fighter)
Dick French, William Worthington (Men in theatre)
Estelle Etterre, Bess Flowers (Women in theatre)

Oscar nominations:
    Best Sound Recording: Douglas Shearer
    Best Score: Herbert Stothart
Special Oscar citation to Oliver Marsh and Allen Davey for Color Cinematography, a brand new field
Photoplay Gold Medal Award as best picture of the year

Sweethearts was presented on Screen Guild Theatre (radio), 3/25/46 and 12/15/47, with Jeanette and Nelson.

Sweethearts is a happy, delicious bonbon of a musical, rich and utterly satisfying. If one's diet has consisted entirely of "meaningful" films, then one may experience some pangs of guilt at so heartily enjoying its socially insignificant delights. MGM's first feature-length three-strip Technicolor picture is a visual joy. Costumer Adrian threw aside all the "rules" for dressing redheads that made them the pariahs of the fashion world and costumed Jeanette in yellow, shell pink, and fire-engine red.

The story of a pair of Broadway stars—the Lunt and Fontanne of musical comedy—is bright, fast-moving, and liberally decorated with Dorothy Parker-Alan Campbell quips, underscored by frequent sardonic bits of background music. More than a dozen of MGM's best character actors strut their stuff, and the production numbers are glorious.

The original 1913 stage *Sweethearts* provided an improbable story of a foundling, raised by the proprietor of the Laundry of the White Geese, who discovers before the final curtain that she is really the Crown Princess of Zilania and therefore eligible to marry the prince whom she had earlier rejected because of her lowly station. Even true MacDonald-Eddy enthusiasts would have found this a little difficult to accept in 1938. Victor Herbert, however, had created one of his loveliest scores. The problem was solved brilliantly by the Parker-Campbell script, which permitted numbers from *Sweethearts* to be performed without ever bothering about the plot of the show-within-a-show.

The film opens with the camera tracking over the Broadway rooftops where flashing marquees spell out the current successes: Lunt and Fontanne in *Idiot's Delight*—third smash year; Helen Hayes as *Victoria Regina*—fourth year; five years for *Tobacco Road*; and finally *Sweethearts* starting its sixth year tonight! The comments of the enthusiastic ticket buyers in the lobby indicate that it has become an institution.

In the box office, happily surveying the evening's receipts, are producer Felix Lehman (Frank Morgan) and his press agent, Dink (Allyn Joslyn). There hasn't been an empty seat since opening night, comments Appleby, the cashier

A French cover. *Courtesy Anna Michalik.*

Jeanette, who had danced on Broadway, enjoys a romp with Ray Bolger in front of a stage windmill and thousands of brightly colored tulips. Jeanette's copper hair and green eyes seemed made for Technicolor.

(Olin Howland). And it looks like it will run another six years, he says—if Felix can hang on to his stars, Gwen Marlowe and Ernest Lane.

Don't worry, Felix assures him. His kiddies would never leave him. He knows just how to handle them. Why, he doesn't even have a contract with them.

His confidence turns to horror when he spots Hollywood agent Norman Trumpett (Reginald Gardiner) slipping through the lobby. It is Trumpett's annual attempt to sign Marlowe and Lane to a movie contract, and he's not at all discouraged by Dink's efforts to get rid of him. He strides into the theatre, all British accent and oily confidence.

Hot on his heels is another tall, dapper gentleman, Leo Kronk (Mischa Auer). In his fur-collared coat and monocle, the *Sweethearts* playwright sweeps grandly into the lobby, only to be stopped by a pudgy doorman from Brooklyn (James Flavin). Leo's cries of outrage are overheard by Dink, who assures the doorman that this weird scarecrow is indeed the author of the show inside. Dink explains to Leo that this doorman is new, only there a year.

The composer of *Sweethearts*, Oscar Engel (Herman Bing), has beaten his collaborator to the theatre by an hour and is conducting the orchestra on this festive night. Oscar is as short, round, and ringleted as Leo is tall, slender, and sleek. The two old friends catch sight of each other and exchange grimaces as if they had bitten into an unripe kumquat. The houselights dim, Oscar raises his baton, and the stage comes to life.

A giant windmill dominates the action with pathways plunging down to the apron of the stage through brilliant beds of tulips. Twenty-four blue-and-white-clad Dutch girls burst happily onstage and skip down the paths in their wooden shoes. The lead dancer, Fred (Ray Bolger), sings "Wooden Shoes" with an updated lyric by Wright and Forrest:

> Nanette and I have got a plan.
> Here's hoping nothing wrecks it.
> While you make all the noise you can,
> Nanette and I will exit.
> (Copyright G. Schirmer, Inc.)

(The original lyric referred to "Jeanette" and was changed to avoid confusion.) A runway juts out into the audience, so Fred leaps over Leo's tousled head and does a merry tap dance the length of the mirrored span in his own wooden shoes. He returns to the stage in a staccato of clicks, just in time to join the chorus as they turn expectantly toward the windmill door.

The orchestra exhales a few excited chords, and a lovely voice joins them. Its owner, Gwen Marlowe (Jeanette), sweeps into view in the doorway, a breathtaking vision of red hair and green eyes. She follows this magnificent entrance with a musical account of another eloping couple and then does a jaunty clog dance with Fred that ends with his carting her piggy-back off stage. The number uses the basic staginess of

A scene cut from the film. Gwen as the Dutch heroine of the stage operetta sings "The Angelus."

Albertina Rasch's choreography to superb advantage.

The vigilant Felix spots an usher bearing a message from Hollywood agent Trumpett to Gwen and Ernest. He wrests it from the startled usher's hand. Inside the envelope is a note chiding Felix for being so nosy.

On stage, the "Angelus" sequence (cut from the film) begins and ends within seconds. There is a quick glimpse of a roadside chapel set, and then the curtain revolves again to reveal a massive staircase, lined with forty soldiers holding glittering spears. Our hero, Ernest Lane (Nelson), is at the top of the stairs in a blue and silver uniform, singing the dramatic "Every Lover Must Meet His Fate." Entranced, Dutch-girl Gwen starts up the stairs as officer Ernest descends to meet her. Just as the two are about to meet, a discordant note from the orchestra arouses the soldiers who leap between them in a bristle of spears. Still singing, the lovers are forced apart for a grandly melodramatic curtain. This gentle spoofing of the old-time operetta lets the filmgoer fully enjoy the fine old tunes without fretting about the plot they originally decorated.

The camaraderie backstage is revealed in several incidents. Gwen and the chorus girls excitedly open a telegram announcing that a baby girl has been born to one of the dancers on leave. Gwen instructs the dour stage manager (Hal K. Dawson) that the quota of dancers will be increased to twenty-five when the girl returns in the spring—"and the baby can have my part any time she wants it." Ernest, striding skillfully between the shifting scenery, is intercepted by the prop man (Jimmy Conlin), who shows him six kittens just born to the theatre cat. Six kittens on the sixth anniversary. Press agent Dink will get the story in every paper in town. Ernest strokes one of the tiny creatures and shakes his head. "Aw, let the lady have her privacy," he urges.

In her realistically cramped and grimy dressing room, Gwen is confronted by her businesslike secretary, Kay Jordan (Florence Rice), who is rattling off a pile of important invitations for parties after the show. Gwen instructs Kay to decline them all. Gwen Marlowe has a very important date. Next door, Ernest Lane also tells Kay he "regrets." He has a previous engagement that he wouldn't break for anything in the world. Fortunately Kay has foreseen this development and has already refused the invitations.

The shrill ring of the telephone brings the nightly call from Ernest's regal Aunt Amelia (Kathleen Lockhart) and Uncle Sheridan (Berton

The production numbers of the show-within-a-show made perfect use of the charming Victor Herbert songs without involving the viewer in the dated operetta plot.

Sweethearts

In MGM's first three-strip Technicolor feature, Jeanette and Nelson play their first husband and wife roles, Gwen Marlowe and Ernest Lane, stars of the long-running Broadway show, *Sweethearts*.

Churchill). Aunt Amelia congratulates Ernest on the anniversary. Of course, *she* sang *Iolanthe* two thousand times—and has told *him* about it two million times, Ernest mutters.

The phone in Gwen's dressing room is also ringing. It is her mother (Lucile Watson) and Uncle Augustus (Gene Lockhart, husband of Kathleen), with similar felicitations and stories of past glories of their theatrical family. Gwen and Ernest barely make it on stage for the big "Sweethearts" number.

Gwen, in shell-pink tulle, and Ernest, in Dutch jacket and pants, are discovered at the top of a forty-foot "wedding cake" mountain. The entire cast surges onstage to sing the gloriously schmaltzy finale of the operetta—everyone, that is, except understudies Harvey Horton (Douglas McPhail) and Una Wilson (his real-life wife, Betty Jaynes). We know they are the understudies because they are wearing duplicates of the stars' costumes, a simple visual expedient for the film, but utterly unlikely. They stand disconsolately in the wings. In six years they have never had a chance to go on. (Normally understudies are regular cast members in smaller roles.)

The cheering audience demands a curtain speech. Gwen and Ernest look at each other expectantly, then launch into separate speeches ending in unison with "thank you" and a burst of laughter. They are not very good at speeches, Ernest tells the audience. Maybe they'd better just sing. Swaying to the "Sweethearts Waltz," they move out along the runway, shaking hands and gesturing to the audience to join them. "If you don't know the words, sing anyway!" calls Gwen. All over the theatre people take up the song—a pair of teenagers in the orchestra, an elderly couple in the balcony, then the entire audience. The orchestra switches to "Auld Lang Syne" and another piece of genuine if manufactured nostalgia has occurred.

Exhausted and happy, Gwen returns to her dressing room for another nightly ritual. A

After an exhausting evening, the couple comes home to family squabbles. (Walburn, Eddy, Kilburn, and MacDonald.)

The hectic Marlowe-Lane household consists of a secretary (Florence Rice, left) and their combined families (some of Hollywood's top character actors: Terry Kilburn, Gene Lockhart, Berton Churchill, Raymond Walburn, Kathleen Lockhart, and Lucile Watson).

folded note comes sliding under her door. She opens it and reads: "Six years with you are like six minutes. Six minutes without you are like six years." She places it in a wall safe filled with hundreds of similar notes. Pausing sentimentally, she reads two others in the pile: "If you want the moon, my darling, let me fetch it for you" and "All the world's asleep, but we're the ones who are dreaming."

Gwen's special date, of course, is Ernest. It is six years since the show opened—and since their elopement. Wearing the clothes they were married in (although Jeanette's navy suit is absolutely 1938 with padded shoulders), they prepare to slip off to their favorite little honeymoon restaurant.

Their happy nuzzling is interrupted by bellows of rage outside the dressing room door. Leo and Oscar are being separated by Dink and Felix. "His music is killing my lines," screeches Leo. "It's a mercy killing, toots," consoles Dink. Leo denounces the mundane world of musical comedy. After all, he is the author of the world's greatest play! Felix, who has read the opus, winces at the memory, then spies Gwen and Ernest going out the back way. He sprints after them. Aren't they coming to his little party? No, they cheerfully inform him, they have other

Sweethearts

Singing for their supper on an impromptu coast-to-coast hookup—"Pretty as a Picture."

plans. Felix sags against the stairs, doing a splendid performance of a crushed old man abandoned by his friends. Skeptical at first, Gwen and Ernest are finally won over. They insist on going to Felix's little party—a party at which they find several hundred people, an orchestra and chorus, and "just a little coast-to-coast radio hookup."

Hollywood agent Norman Trumpett (Reginald Gardiner) makes a very tempting offer. *Courtesy Anna Michalik.*

Gwen and Ernest resign themselves to singing for their supper. Ernest seats himself at a small upright piano in the center of the glistening dance floor, Gwen beside him in a clinging pink gown. They sing "Pretty as a Picture" while the chorus promenades down a little impromptu runway ("Must have taken two weeks to build," mutters Ernest).

During the number, Miss MacDonald pays homage to the new musical form of the late 1930s by "swinging" the song—very successfully. Then she and Eddy waltz around the room as the chorus takes up the song, the hundreds of tiny Fortuny pleats in her skirt opening to swirling fullness. (Studio publicity hailed this as Eddy's first film dancing, conveniently forgetting his minuet in *Naughty Marietta* and his far more vigorous waltz in *Maytime*.)

In his hotel room, Norman Trumpett is listening to their song on the radio when his call to studio boss Benjamin Silver comes through. Silver (George Barbier) recounts the disasters at the studio—bad weather, illness, and exhaustion. Trumpett *must* sign Marlowe and Lane. "It's a *fait accompli*," Trumpett assures him. When Gwen and Ernest emerge from their "quiet little party," Trumpett is waiting for them in his limousine.

On their way home, he tells them of the leisure and rest that would be theirs in Hollywood. They are half persuaded. Gwen has always wanted a garden. "Yes," Ernest murmurs happily, "to put on overalls and get out and chop down your own fruit trees..." They reach home just as the rear-window projection screen shows them passing through Times Square.

Their home turns out to be not a Broadway hotel, but an incredibly spacious East Side townhouse with an equally incredible assortment of relatives. We again meet Gwen's mother and uncle and Ernest's uncle and aunt, plus Gwen's appalling little brother, Junior (Terry Kilburn). They are in the midst of further reminiscences about their stage successes and insist the exhausted pair join them.

Gwen and Ernest sit numbly over glasses of "lemon juice for the voice" until Uncle Augustus begins playing a beautiful old waltz from *The Prince of Pilsen*, "My Heart's True Blue." They join in and then the entire family does a spontaneous cakewalk to "Keep it Dark." Gwen is balancing precariously on Ernest's knee in a "finale" pose when secretary Kay Jordan enters. Her bathrobe indicates she has been aroused from her bed, and she wonders why Gwen and Ernest aren't in bed too, considering their heavy schedule the next day.

What schedule? they ask. In a flurry of explanations, they learn that their families have committed them to such a variety of guest appearances during the coming week that they must record and broadcast almost simultaneously the following afternoon. No attempt to rearrange the schedule will leave them a minute to themselves. The exhausted pair starts up the stairs to bed, but they are stopped again.

"Sweethearts who need no crown or throne." The giant revolving-spiral set for the show-within-a-show was also used in *The Great Ziegfeld. Courtesy Anna Michalik.*

Cousin Orlando Lane (Raymond Walburn) bursts through the door, followed by the entire cast of his touring *Pirates of Penzance* company. They have run out of money and come to stay until they can get backing to continue on tour. Grimly, Kay pays the cabdrivers who have brought them from Bridgeport, Connecticut. It is too much! Ernest runs upstairs to write Orlando a check.

Gwen's mother is upset that Ernest is willing to back Orlando. Why not send *her* out in a revival of *Dolly Varden*? Amelia pooh-poohs her. Orlando is a member of the first family of the musical stage. The two families wrangle until Gwen explodes. She has to have quiet and a life of her own, and she and Ernest know where they can get it! They are going to *Hollywood*! She runs upstairs to tell Ernest and finds him just hanging up the phone. He's arranged everything with Trumpett. They are going to *Hollywood*!

The next morning in Felix's office, Dink is answering a forest of telephones, denying the silly rumor. Leo, Oscar, and Appleby sit disconsolately. Felix fights his way through the reporters to the inner office. No one can change Gwen and Ernest's minds, he tells them. His kiddies are leaving. Dink and Appleby shove him toward the door to try again. Didn't he tell them he was a lonely old man? Didn't he tell

Panicked that their meal tickets are leaving them, Leo (Mischa Auer, rear left) and Oscar (Herman Bing, rear right) hatch a plan to keep Gwen and Ernest from going to Hollywood. Felix (Frank Morgan, center) protests. (Olin Howland, left; Allyn Joslyn, right.)

them how he was a father to them? What did they say? "They said they were going shopping," Felix replies.

We are next treated to a delightful "fashion show" sequence in which Gwen tries on a dozen Adrian outfits in colors never before dared by redheads. One plaid suit especially catches her fancy, and she orders a matching suit made up for Ernest. She slinks and clowns her way through the costume changes until she realizes that Kay should be ordering things for Hollywood too.

Kay breaks the news that she and the Statue of Liberty don't go west of Hoboken. Gwen is thunderstruck. What will she and Ernest do without Kay after all these years? A phone call from Ernest sends Kay off to rescue him. He is caught without taxi fare in the midst of his hectic schedule.

Gwen holds the fort for him at Radio City, opening the "Sweethearts Hour" with "Summer Serenade" (based on Herbert's piano piece, "Badinage"). She is now wearing a brown crêpe dress and turban trimmed in orange monkey fur

Sweethearts

They decide to seek peace and quiet in Hollywood, but first a farewell radio broadcast that brings out the police. Note the wonderful 1938 microphone.

Packing and singing. One of the most charming interludes in the film. *Courtesy Anna Michalik.*

(*not* PC!), with a matching fur muff. At RCA, Ernest is recording "On Parade," a stirring martial tune. The band is dressed in bright red uniforms for an exciting visual-aural combination. In the control room, we get a fascinating glimpse of contemporary recording equipment.

A heart-stopping ride up Park Avenue follows, with Kay and Ernest urging the taxi driver on while police sirens wail behind them. The police are not an escort, however. They pursue Ernest into Radio City, and he races onstage singing the first note of "Every Lover Must Meet His Fate." Gwen sings with him, shaking her head chidingly and straightening his tie. As the chorus joins them in "Sweethearts," the New York constabulary battle determined ushers for admittance a few yards away, and Kay sinks wearily onto a step, burying her head in her hands.

Despair reigns in Felix's office. Leo and Oscar may even have to go to work! But the crafty Leo formulates a plan to keep Gwen and Ernest on stage in *Sweethearts*. Together, they are dynamite, but separately—separately would Hollywood want them? Trumpett phones to gloat a bit and ask Felix if he wants to sell the movie rights to *Sweethearts*. "Doucement, doucement," he croons over Felix's splutters of rage. Felix is now mad enough to agree to Leo's plan. They will separate Gwen and Ernest.

The pair are preparing for their departure amidst dog kennels, trunks, and family chaos. The dogs, Brunhilde and Falstaff, are reluctant to travel, and Gwen's mother sits tearfully surveying the activities. Gwen is carefully packing everything Ernest is trying to put on. He just as carefully unpacks it, undoing all her work. As they circle each other, they merrily join in a tune Junior is playing downstairs, "Little Grey Home in the West." Ernest sings the last bars of the song as he starts downstairs to meet Kay for some last-minute errands. In a charming mock-dramatic moment, Nelson and Jeanette repeat the staircase sequence from the end of *Naughty Marietta*.

Gwen's packing is interrupted by Leo Kronk, who has come to read her his latest play. Gwen couldn't be less interested, but Leo insists. The action takes place in the drawing room of a country house on Long Island. "One of *those*, is it?" sighs Gwen. She putters about with her packing until she is struck by the dialogue. Exact quotes from her love letters!

Leo explains that he has gotten the charming epigrams from a lady who receives them in notes every day—from her married lover. He only knows the lady in the case, of course, but he understands the wife knows nothing about it. In torment, Gwen sends Leo away and goes looking for Ernest. The background music growls "The William Tell Overture" as she storms through the house.

Ernest is not back, but his pipe is in Kay's room—the room next to theirs. On Kay's dresser

Sweethearts

is a picture of the smiling threesome, Kay with her arm around Ernest. Gwen is interrupted in her detective work by the tailor's assistant (Forrester Harvey) delivering Ernest's new suit. Not the loud plaid one Gwen ordered. Kay has changed the order to a more conservative one. Furiously, Gwen hurls the suit into the fireplace, where it burns fiercely.

Gwen is in a most peculiar mood when Ernest returns with good news: Kay is going to Hollywood with them. To his astonishment, Gwen rushes out of the room. She retreats to Kay's office, where a note comes sliding under the door in Ernest's handwriting. With shaking fingers she opens it. "When you look in the mirror, you will see my favorite person." Her suspicions are confirmed. She runs out of the office, fighting her tears.

A few more bars of "William Tell," and Kay enters to find the note on the floor. Ernest comes in, not for a big love scene, but to be sure that Kay got the inscription for his anniversary present to Gwen, a vanity case. He pauses,

Leo suggests the inconceivable. Gwen is stunned. *Courtesy Anna Michalik.*

sniffing. Is something on fire? We see the remnants of the suit smoldering in the fireplace. "Something in this house is certainly burning up..."

A billow of smoke seems to confirm his statement, but it is only Gwen in a storm of talcum powder. She has locked herself in her dressing room, refusing to see Ernest or accept his love notes. When Trumpett arrives with the lawyers (two sets of twins) to sign the contract, she tells him ar*chly that Ernest can go to Hollywood alone. She is staying in New York.*

Ernest takes advantage of the open door to confront her. He is astonished at her decision. In the hallway, the conspirators watch the departure of Trumpett and the lawyers with glee. Felix, however, has some second thoughts. Oscar and Leo have to restrain him bodily.

The callboy announces "two minutes" as Gwen and Ernest square off. She should have known about Kay all along. Earnest has never heard of anything so ridiculous. The orchestra is playing their cue for the second time when Kay rushes in. Ernest won't let Gwen leave the room until she apologizes to Kay. Very well, Gwen replies, and flops down on the floor in her hoop skirt. She will sit there all night if necessary. Then Ernest isn't leaving either. There they sit until they recognize their cue music in its fifth repeat. They scramble for the door in a tangle of tulle and stage managers, as Kay again sinks wearily into a chair, shaking her head.

Leo and Oscar are now the best of friends. Their brilliant plan has resulted in the cancellation of the Hollywood contract. It only remains for Felix to use his two gold mines in separate touring companies. Harvey Horton and Una Wilson, the understudies, are ushered in, not to be fired as they expect, but to be offered the leads opposite Gwen and Ernest on the road.

In a Slavko Vorkapich montage, we see the *Sweethearts* poster depicting Ernest and Gwen torn in half. Then each star in turn appears on a split screen that rolls back to show that their actual partner is Una or Harvey. In between

Gwen mugs with red and white striped gardening gloves that remind her of candy canes.

In the fashion show sequence and throughout the film, costumer Adrian dresses Jeanette gorgeously in colors traditionally considered wrong for redheads—yellow, lavender, fire-engine red, and pink. *All photos courtesy Anna Michalik.*

stage sequences, we see the couple staring desolately out of train windows at the grim outskirts of small towns. A few scattered bars of "St. Louis Blues" and "Missouri Waltz" indicate their routes. The montage closes with a shot of a shabby hotel, late at night. One window still has a light on.

Ernest is saying goodnight to his valet, Harry (Gerald Hamer), who has brought him the latest *Variety*. Far away, Gwen is also poring over a copy of the show business paper, obtained by flagging down the mail train. She just wants to see what the other company is doing, she tells her mother. "Yes, where *is* Ernest?" asks her mother. Outside their window the whole town is asleep. "So unresourceful of them," mutters Mrs. Marlowe. She picks up *Variety* and clucks over the scathing review of Leo's new play. In *Variety*-ese, it describes the plot about a dopey wife who believes her husband is two-timing her because someone has stolen her love letters. "Believe it or not, wife is crazy enough to fall for this tripe. Audience is not, however..."

Gwen gives a cry and dives for the phone, just as Ernest, far away, is making the same discovery. For a few agonizing minutes they cannot get through to each other because each line is busy. Then, as they give up, the phones ring and they are connected. "Oh, *sweetheart...*"

Another surge of "The William Tell Overture" accompanies their march on Felix Lehman's office, Gwen in a bright blue suit with red trim. They storm in, brandishing their Hollywood

Eddy's striking "blond" hair was actually red hair that had turned prematurely silver. (His eyes were gray.) He appeared in only two more color films, *Bitter Sweet* and *Phantom of the Opera*.

Jeanette's name in *Sweethearts* was supposed to be "Gwen Arden," but she asked that it be changed to "Marlowe." After the success of *Naughty Marietta*, she felt that names beginning with N or M were lucky.

Sweethearts

It takes *Variety* to get Gwen and Ernest back together again. (Florence Rice, MacDonald, Eddy, and Frank Morgan.)

contract. Porters bearing their luggage troop along behind them. They're not even waiting for a train. They're going to *fly*!

Felix does what any Broadway producer would do. He collapses in tears. As the orchestra sobs "Hearts and Flowers," he reworks all the old stories until Gwen and Ernest are sitting beside him on the couch with their arms around him. "You awful old crook, you!" scolds Gwen, and they laughingly resign themselves to another six years of *Sweethearts*. Kay walks in, and they are all reconciled. There is nothing left but to show their gala return to Broadway, singing "Sweethearts" with full chorus as their audience cheers.

Sweethearts was a superb maiden effort in three-strip Technicolor on the part of the studio whose name would become almost synonymous with color musicals. The film plays on our emotions with color as carefully as it does with music, tastefully blending neutral tones and bright highlights. Photographer Oliver Marsh won a special Academy Award for his work in the new category of color photography.

MGM was the last major studio to "go Technicolor" in the new three-strip process.

Real-life husband and wife Douglas McPhail and Betty Jaynes played the understudies. *Courtesy Anna Michalik.*

Previously, they had used it only for inserts such as the finale of *The Cat and The Fiddle. Becky Sharp* (RKO-Radio, 1935) qualifies as the first three-strip Technicolor feature. In 1936, Walter Wanger produced *Trail of the Lonesome Pine,* the first outdoor color film, Twentieth Century- Fox issued *Ramona,* and Selznick International did *The Garden of Allah.* In 1937, Paramount debuted with *Ebb Tide,* Disney did *Snow White and the Seven Dwarfs,* and the British filmed *Wings of the Morning,* released through Twentieth Century-Fox. Even Warner Bros. beat MGM with three films, including their 1938 version of *The Adventures of Robin Hood.* In the fifties and sixties, Technicolor was slowly supplanted by more economical if less aesthetic one-negative processes—which proved to have a life expectancy of only ten years. Since Technicolor uses separate black and white negatives for each color, it is possible to reprint them indefinitely in their original splendor.

There is one tragic footnote to *Sweethearts.* Young baritone Douglas McPhail had sung in the choruses of *San Francisco* and *Maytime* when Jeanette met him and took an interest in his career. He plays Nelson Eddy's understudy in *Sweethearts* and in real life he married singer Betty Jaynes, who plays Jeanette's understudy. Miss Jaynes had made a successful appearance in 1936 as Mimi in *La Bohème* with the Chicago Civic Opera opposite Giovanni Martinelli. It was the only opera the fifteen-year-old high school junior knew!

McPhail's good looks and big baritone brought him leading rôles in *Babes in Arms,* with Judy Garland and Miss Jaynes, and in *Broadway Melody of 1940,* but demand for his kind of singing dwindled. His career slipped, and he began drinking. In 1944, after an earlier unsuccessful suicide attempt, he died of poison.

A happier *Sweethearts* story concerns a columnist who visited the set and found the two stars screaming abuse at each other. The item was quickly circulated that the screen lovers were off-screen enemies. Not at all, Eddy telegraphed the man, they had merely been rehearsing a scene. He invited the columnist to see the film as proof. When the picture was released, Eddy learned to his dismay that the scene had been left on the cutting-room floor.

Reviews:

The primary critical complaint, that the film was too long, was resolved with some judicious cuts before the film went into general release. *Variety* had said, "It will disappoint because of length—two hours flat—and general lethargy." This sentiment was echoed by the *New York World-Telegram* and by Archer Winsten in the *New York Post.* Therefore, it's fascinating that cutting just six minutes, probably the complete "Angelus" number, at an early point in the film, makes the currently available version of *Sweethearts* move rapidly and seem considerably shorter than it is.

Time magazine, a forerunner in the "clever dismissal" style of reviewing, gave *Sweethearts* a one line comment: "Jeanette MacDonald and Nelson Eddy unchanged by modern clothes and Technicolor."

Sweethearts

Before reproducing color photography in print became routine, many magazine covers and movie posters featured color paintings of the stars by talented commercial artists.

Mitch Woodbury wrote in *On the Movies*: "Sweethearts, the latest in the series of Nelson Eddy-Jeanette MacDonald screen operettas, is a "sweetheart" of a picture...the production cost a pretty penny (yeah, even the pennies come that way in H-wood). The gold has been wisely spent, however, for the finished product possesses everything movie audiences delight in."

The vast majority of the nation's newspapers found *Sweethearts* good entertainment. However, the more sophisticated seemed a bit embarrassed at enjoying such a lighthearted film and tried to qualify their comments. B.K. Crisler in the *New York Times* wrote, "Sweethearts is such a dream of ribbons, tinsel, Technicolor, and sweet theatrical sentiment, that it suggests a collaboration of all the leading steamer-basket architects between Fifth and Lexington Avenues. Although in the long run Sweethearts must be classified as a superlatively elaborate example of cinematic pastry-cookery, the MacDonald-Eddy bloc—the only one left in the metropolitan area which bursts into applause at the mere sound of a beloved voice—must likewise be conciliated with the admission that Jeanette and Nelson have never sung or acted with more fire or abandon."

Recordings (See Discography for further information)

Eddy recorded nothing from *Sweethearts*. Ten years later. Miss MacDonald recorded "Sweethearts Waltz" ["Sweethearts"] and "Summer Serenade" ["Badinage"].

Music in the Film

All music is by Victor Herbert unless otherwise indicated. In listing performers after each title, "and" denotes a genuine duet, while commas between names indicate a sequence of singers.

Overture: "Sweethearts," "Wooden Shoes," "On Parade"
"Wooden Shoes" (song and dance, Ray Bolger and MacDonald) [originally "Jeanette and her Wooden Shoes" in stage version, lyric changed to "Nanette and her Wooden Shoes"] - new lyrics by Bob Wright and Chet Forrest
"Wooden Shoes" reprise (MacDonald)
"Angelus" (MacDonald) [cut from general release print] - Stage lyrics by Robert B. Smith
"Every Lover Must Meet His Fate" (Eddy, male chorus, and MacDonald) - new lyrics by Wright and Forrest.
"Happy Day" (chorus) - bridge by Stothart, Wright and Forrest
"Sweethearts" (MacDonald and Eddy with chorus) - new lyrics by Wright and Forrest
"Sweethearts" reprise with "Auld Lang Syne" (MacDonald and Eddy with chorus)

"Pretty as a Picture" (MacDonald and Eddy with girls' chorus) - new lyrics by Wright and Forrest

"Mademoiselle" fragment heard over radio (MacDonald and Eddy) - source uncertain. Introduced by radio commentator as "Game of Love," but not the song of that title in stage version. New melody copyrighted as "Mademoiselle" in 1938 with music by Herbert, lyrics by Wright and Forrest.

"Sweethearts" reprise (MacDonald and Eddy)

"The Message of the Violets" ["My Heart's True Blue"] (Gene Lockhart, MacDonald, and Eddy) - from *The Prince of Pilsen*, music by Gustav Luders, lyrics by Frank Pixley

"Keep it Dark" (Gene Lockhart, Kathleen Lockhart, Lucile Watson, Berton Churchill, MacDonald, and Eddy) - also from *The Prince of Pilsen*, credits as above

"Badinage" ["Summer Serenade"] (MacDonald, Dalies Frantz on piano) - based on a Herbert piano piece with new lyrics by Wright and Forrest

"On Parade" (Eddy and male chorus) - with new lyrics by Wright and Forrest

"Every Lover Must Meet His Fate" reprise (Eddy, MacDonald)

"Sweethearts" reprise (MacDonald and Eddy with chorus)

"Little Grey Home in the West" (MacDonald and Eddy) - music by Hermann Lohr, lyrics by D. Eardley-Wilmot

ON TOUR MONTAGE, fragments of:
    "Give My Regards to Broadway" (orchestral) - George M. Cohan
    "Sidewalks of New York" (orchestral) - Charles B. Lawlor
    "Sweethearts" reprise (MacDonald, Eddy, Douglas McPhail, Betty Jaynes)
    "Angelus" (MacDonald)
    "Wooden Shoes" reprise (MacDonald, Jaynes)
    "St. Louis Blues" orchestral - W.C. Handy
    "Pretty as a Picture" reprise (McPhail, Eddy)

The preview for *Sweethearts* usually causes a ripple of laughter with modern audiences when the announcer extols the first appearance of Jeanette and Nelson in "modern dress." Here, a publicity still of the two in their cutting edge 1938 fashions.

"Sweethearts" reprise (MacDonald, McPhail, Eddy, Jaynes)

"In the Convent They Never Taught Me That" (Jaynes, MacDonald) - stage lyrics by Robert B. Smith

"On Parade" reprise (Eddy)

"Mademoiselle" (MacDonald, Eddy, McPhail, Jaynes, chorus)

"Missouri Waltz" (orchestral) - by Frederick Knight Logan and James Royce Shannon

"Sweethearts" (MacDonald and Eddy with chorus) with fragment inserted of "Home, Sweet Home" (chorus) - by Sir Henry Bishop and John Howard Payne, INTO:

"On Parade" (orchestral)

Songs from the stage production featured in the film were "Sweethearts," "Wooden Shoes" (originally "Jeanette and Her Wooden Shoes"), "Every Lover Must Meet His Fate," "Pretty as a Picture," and "On Parade," all with new lyrics by Bob Wright and Chet Forrest. In addition, fragments of "Angelus" and "In the Convent They Never Taught Me That" were heard, and Herbert's piano piece "Badinage" became "Summer Serenade." *Variety* praised the production values on "There Is Magic in a Smile," a song from the stage score, but either the number was cut from the final release prints, or, more likely, the reviewer was confused. The source of "Mademoiselle" has eluded me.

Script History
Contributed by Mary Truesdell

An earlier script (1/6/38) by the famous humorist S.J. Perelman, reports researcher Mary Truesdell, presented almost the same plot and characters as in the final Parker/Campbell script, except that Kay was not the cause of stars' separation. Instead, they quarreled over the adulation of their respective fans, a theme that would later be used in *The Chocolate Soldier*.

Perelman's draft used real names—Nelson and Jeanette, Jake Shubert (Felix Lehman), Sam Goldwyn (Mr. Silverman), and Arthur Hornblow (Trumpet). He also had a packing-to-move scene, although it occurred in the couple's Long Island mansion, and he made it hilariously clear that their desire for the "simple life" was never more than a dream, given their retinue of maids, footmen, family, dogs, and trunks. The scene as written is even more hilarious than that in the final screen version.

It is also obvious that Perelman adored Jeanette and Nelson, describing their screen characters thus: "generosity & charm being their virtues and their bêtes noir." Parker and Campbell did the final script, but Perelman was the uncredited architect.

Trivia

Child actor Terry Kilburn, who plays Jeanette's little brother, also appeared as Tiny Tim in *A Christmas Carol*, which opened the same week.

Movie Goofs

Movie magic sometimes comes about because scenes are routinely shot out of sequence and then rearranged in the editing process or parts of the same scene are shot on different days. Costumes may change within the same scene, props appear and disappear. The continuity person (called a "script girl" in the old days) tried desperately to prevent these mistakes, but sometimes they slipped in. Here are some favorites spotted by sharp-eyed fans.

When Jeanette leaves her dressing room wearing the navy suit, she is carrying nothing. Outside, she has gloves and a purse in her hand. (Joan Woolley)

During "Little Grey Home in the West," Nelson's suit jacket magically buttons itself as he steps from bedroom to hall. (Stephanie Loyd and Joan Woolley)

Nelson is portrayed as a true New Yorker, yet no self-respecting native would ever take a cab from 56th & Madison (the recording studio) to 50th between Fifth and Sixth Avenues (the radio station), a ten-minute walk tops, much less if he was in a hurry and forgot money and had to wait for someone to arrive with cab fare. This is a surprising error, considering Dorothy Parker was a New Yorker. Then, to top it off, when Nelson and Florence Rice are racing in that cab, it is shown driving north on Park Avenue in the 1940s, *toward* the recording studio, not away from it. No wonder Nelson was so late! (Tricia Lutz)

7
Celluloid Sweethearts: Their Offscreen Loves and Marriages

"Why didn't you marry Jeanette MacDonald?" Nelson Eddy was often asked. "I did," he would reply, "...eight times." He referred to their eight costarring pictures.

In many minds, the perfect union of Jeanette MacDonald and Nelson Eddy on screen did not allow for any separation in real life. This was a constant source of amusement to them both, for, while they were friendlier than most teams, they each had a very separate private life.

With Jeanette, career came first. According to *Hollywood Diva* biographer Edward Baron Turk, her first great love was Jack Ohmeis, tall and fair-haired, a wealthy architecture student at New York University. They shared an interest in horses and riding, and his family supported the union, but Jack insisted she give up her career for the rôle of a socially prominent wife. She could not, and they parted.

Soon she was officially engaged to her agent, Bob Ritchie, also tall and fair-haired, who accompanied her to Hollywood in 1929. Though such an engagement was an ideal situation for a proper young lady in a city famous for its casting couches, the romance was genuine. They were so close and engaged for so long that many suspected they were actually already married. Jeanette's costar Maurice Chevalier swore they *must* be because only married people could quarrel so bitterly. This time, the clash was not over career vs. marriage. Ritchie was all for her career, but he was rather casual about responsibilities and unable to keep his frequent vows of fidelity for more than a nanosecond. Jeanette was thoroughly miserable. She decided privately to end the relationship as soon as Ritchie acquired enough other clients to make him independent of her and a success in his own right.

In 1934, she attended a party given by Rosie Dolly, one of the Dolly Sisters. As Jeanette arrived, another guest—tall and fair-haired—joined her on the doorstep. The door opened and Rosie Dolly surveyed the pair. "How nice of you *both* to come!"

The young man was actor Gene Raymond, who had come to Hollywood in 1931 after a successful stint on Broadway. His blond

Celluloid Sweethearts

Just as fans had once been sure that Jeanette was romantically involved with her first screen partner, Chevalier, they were now certain she and her new partner, Nelson Eddy, were destined to wed.

Jeanette and Gene Raymond after their marriage on June 16, 1937. The bride wore pale pink. (The pink satin prayer book in her hand was buried with her when she died.) *Courtesy Anna Michalik.*

Actually, Jeanette was engaged to her agent, Robert Ritchie, who had accompanied her to Hollywood in 1929. Then she met Gene Raymond. *Courtesy Ken Richards.*

The "MacRaymonds" at home at Twin Gables after returning from their honeymoon.

The bride and groom with her attendants. Left to right, Helen Ferguson, Jeanette's sister Blossom (Mrs. Warren Rock), Jeanette, Gene, Fay Wray, Ginger Rogers, and Mrs. Johnny Mack Brown. *Courtesy Anna Michalik.*

good looks had typed him as a "leading juvenile" and he had done some fine film work, especially in Fox's *Zoo in Budapest* (1933) with Loretta Young. Robert Ritchie faded quietly from the scene, and, on August 21, 1936, Mrs. Anna MacDonald announced her daughter Jeanette's engagement to Raymond.

Having put off this important step for so long, Miss MacDonald determined to have a proper wedding and honeymoon, the kind every woman dreams about. She didn't go along with the new breed of Hollywood stars who preferred secret weddings and elopements. She arranged for three months off between *The Firefly* and *The Girl of the Golden West* and began planning.

On Wednesday, June 16, 1937, Jeanette MacDonald and Gene Raymond were married at Wilshire Methodist Church in Los Angeles. The police estimated that 15,000 spectators turned out to catch a glimpse of the couple. The crowds blocked traffic, delaying the arrival of the wedding party, and the wedding began twenty-five minutes late. Nelson Eddy sang "I Love You Truly," and then the bride walked down the aisle to *Lohengrin*.

Jeanette wore a shell-pink gown with a long train and carried a pink satin prayer book. Their attendants included many Hollywood notables: Fay Wray, Ginger Rogers, Blossom Rock (Jeanette's sister), Harold Lloyd, Allan Jones, Johnny Mack Brown, and Basil Rathbone. The church was banked with roses and lit with candles. The couple repeated their vows firmly and clearly, then dashed for their car amidst the traditional rain of rice. It took six motorcycle policemen to clear a path for them.

Life magazine reported that the wedding had cost $15,000. The new Mrs. Raymond tartly denied this extravagance in a letter to the editor, stating that the entire wedding plus her trousseau had not exceeded $5,000. That week, *Time* magazine's cover story was about the "Wedding of the Year"—no, not Jeanette and Gene. *Time* was referring to Franklin D. Roosevelt Jr and Ethel DuPont, a union that would end in divorce twelve years later.

Jeanette had to return for one more week of shooting on *The Firefly*, and then the "Mac-Raymonds" honeymooned in Hawaii with newlyweds Buddy Rogers and Mary Pickford.

They returned to Twin Gables, a Tudor-style home that Gene had secretly bought in Bel Air. Here they would live most of their married life, entertaining small groups of close friends for dinner and cards and music. Visiting celebrities of the music world were also frequent guests, but the couple never went in for "Hollywood parties." Their annual Christmas get-together became a holiday tradition for their friends and friends' children.

The MacDonald-Raymond marriage was frequently a "working partnership." They appeared together in both a film and a play, their careers complementing each other. Raymond was also a composer, and Jeanette frequently sang his songs at her concerts. She recorded one especially lovely one, "Let Me Always Sing."

In later years, Gene became philosophical about autograph seekers who stopped his wife and then mistook the blond Raymond for the blond Eddy. He would graciously inscribe Eddy's name without comment, and the fan would depart happy.

(If MacDonald-Eddy fans in America were stunned to learn in 1937 that their beloved stars weren't married to each other, a similar blow was delivered in Europe that same year. The continent's most popular musical team, Lilian Harvey and Willy Fritsch, had starred in fifteen films together, and fans and the press had long been sure they must be secretly married. The bubble burst in 1937 when Fritsch married revue star Dinah Grace.)

A rare photo of Eddy courting Ann Franklin at a baseball game. The fan magazines were still trying to link him with a dozen starlets. *Courtesy Diane Goodrich.*

The wedding party outside the judge's chambers in Las Vegas. Left to right, his mother Isabel Eddy, Nelson, Ann, and actress Doris Kenyon.

A wedding portrait of Nelson and Ann Eddy following their marriage on January 19, 1939. Powerful gossip columnist Louella Parsons maintained she was not surprised when the couple eloped, but everyone else was.

Ann's honeymoon included accompanying Nelson on a concert tour, an intense experience. *Courtesy Anna Michalik.*

If Jeanette had the wedding every woman dreams about, Nelson Eddy's courtship and marriage were the kind that every man in the public eye longs for. Gossip columnists and reporters had long sought to pair him with every eligible star and starlet on the lot. As nature abhors a vacuum, so every female heart abhors an unclaimed bachelor, and the media were constantly reciting the name of his latest "love." He recalled later that when he denied a story of his "living in sin" with a young lady, the reporter responded by questioning his masculinity.

Eddy could never accept the idea that his personal life was the business of anyone with the price of a newspaper. Essentially a very private person, he was always dismayed at the hunger of his "public" for stories, real or imaginary. It was probably with great satisfaction that he kept his courtship of pretty Ann Denitz Franklin in the background until they decided to marry. His bride was the former wife of director Sidney Franklin and had a fourteen-year-old son, Sidney Jr.

As newspapers across the country were announcing that the next MacDonald-Eddy film would be Friml's *Katinka*, Eddy quietly made the arrangements. Then, as the same papers heralded *Sweethearts* as the picture of the month, he drove to Las Vegas with his prospective bride. They were married on Thursday, January 19, 1939 in the chambers of District Judge William E. Orr. Present were Eddy's mother and his business manager, E. J. Osborne, as well as silent film star Doris Kenyon, who had introduced the couple five years earlier.

Their honeymoon was not as tranquil as that of his singing costar. The new Mrs. Eddy accompanied her husband on his concert tour, witnessing firsthand the enthusiastic mobs that occasionally lifted the strapping Eddy off his feet in the crush. It was truly a baptism by fire.

Generally the wives of singers have a reputation in show business second only to that of stage mothers for fierceness and aggressiveness in promoting their darling's career. Ann Eddy was a shining exception to that rule. Her time was spent in making a serene retreat for Eddy in the home he had longed for all his life. He was dedicated to his work, she said, and she was dedicated to him.

Both Jeanette MacDonald and Nelson Eddy married only once. Both were still happily united to their respective spouses when they died after twenty-seven years of marriage.

Let Freedom Ring

MGM.
Released February 24, 1939.
Directed by Jack Conway.
Produced by Harry Rapf.
87 minutes.
Issued in "Sepia Platinum."

A Danish poster. *Courtesy Anna Michalik.*

Prerelease titles: *The Dusty Road, Song of the West*
Spanish title: *¡Paso a la Libertad!* (Make way for liberty)
French title: *Le Flambeau de la Liberté* (Flame of liberty)
Danish title: *Frihedens Sång* (Freedom's song)
German title: *Rivalen* (Rivals)

Original story and screenplay by Ben Hecht. Camera: Sidney Wagner. Montage: John Hoffman. Musical Director: Arthur Lange. Editor: Frederick Y. Smith. Art Director: Cedric Gibbons. Art Associate: Daniel B. Cathcart. Set Decoration: Edwin B. Willis. Orchestrations: Leonid Raab. Sound: Douglas Shearer. Makeup: Jack Dawn. Women's Costumes: Dolly Tree. Men's Costumes: Vales. Second Unit Director: John Waters. Assistant Director: Horace Hough.

Nelson Eddy (Steve Logan)
Virginia Bruce (Maggie Adams)
Victor McLaglen (Chris Mulligan)
Edward Arnold (Jim Knox)
Lionel Barrymore (Tom Logan)
Charles Butterworth (The Mackerel)
Guy Kibbee (Judge David Bronson)
Raymond Walburn (Editor Underwood)
H. B. Warner (Ned Rutledge)
George F. ("Gabby") Hayes (Jerry "Pop" Wilkie)
Dick Rich (Bumper Jackson)
Trevor Bardette (Gagan)
Louis Jean Heydt (Ned Wilkie)
Eddie Dunn (Curley, the bartender)
Sarah Padden (Ma Logan)
Captain C.E. Anderson (Sheriff Hicks)
Philo McCullough, Ralph Bushman [Francis X. Bushman, Jr], Harry Fleischmann (Gagan henchmen)
Maude Allen (Hilda, the cook)
Adia Kuznetzoff (Pole)
Luis Alberni (Tony)
Emory Parnell (Axel, the Swede)
Tenen Holtz (Hunky [sic])
Mitchell Lewis (Joe)
Victor Potel (Second Swede, Ole Swenson)
Constantine Romanoff, Akim Dobrynin (Russians)
Lionel Royce (German)
Billy Bevan (Cockney)
Syd Saylor, Ted Thompson (Surveyors)
Hank Bell (Stage driver)

Bruce Mitchell, Cyril Ring, Heinie Conklin, Jimmy Aubrey (Ranchers)
Harry Wilson, Jack Lowe (Workmen)
Art Mix, Harry Tenbrook, James Mason [not the British actor] (Barflies)
Tim Stark, Henry Korn, Norman Nielsen, Ralph DeAngeles, J. Delos Jewkes, Abe Dinovitch (Railroad workers, "Where Else but Here.")

Nelson Eddy in a Western? Actually, Eddy, whose costumes so frequently sported gold braid or lace, saw himself as a rugged cowboy. His final film, *Northwest Outpost*, was written around that premise, but at this early stage in his career, *Let Freedom Ring* probably came his way through chance.

The unlikely title replaced two earlier and even duller ones, *Song of the West* and *The Dusty Road*. The film turns out to be a brightly paced Western with all the necessary bad guys and barn burners, but with a new gimmick. Not

Eddy goes over some Russian lyrics with actors Adia Kuznetzoff and Akim Dobrynin.

singing cowboys, for Gene Autry and Roy Rogers were already hot stuff. The new element was patriotism through brotherhood, a theme that Hollywood usually only hinted at with quick shots of minority types saluting the flag from a respectful distance while the "Americans" marched by.

Let Freedom Ring is probably the least known and seen of all Eddy's films. It turns out to be a minor delight, hokey as all get out and so full of MGM's finest character actors acting their heads off that there isn't a dull moment. If the music is singularly thin (definitely not Stothart), we are still treated to Eddy riding a horse, playing a convincing drunk scene, beating up Victor McLaglen, and finally stirring a sullen mob of immigrants with an impassioned speech that sends them off singing "America."

A French poster. *Courtesy Anna Michalik.*

Eddy's leading lady, Virginia Bruce, started with bit parts (including Jeanette's lady-in-waiting in *The Love Parade*) and worked up to leads in B's and supporting roles in A's, mostly wronged wives or secretaries. Here she shows the low-keyed charm that won her a devoted following. Eddy's father is played by veteran Lionel Barrymore, the eldest of the three remarkable Barrymore children. Like Ethel and John (*Maytime*), he began with an illustrious stage career and went into films, making over one hundred silent features and many silent shorts. He made an unforgettable impression in more than thirty talkies, including *Grand Hotel, Dinner at Eight,* and *Treasure Island,* until he was crippled by a combination of a broken hip and arthritis in 1938. Rather than slowing down, he continued to act from a wheelchair or crutches in major films like *You Can't Take It with You* and *Duel in the Sun,* as well as the *Dr. Kildare* series in which he played Dr. Gillespie. His handicap is not apparent in *Let Freedom Ring*, however. Director Jack Conway framed his scenes so that Barrymore always appeared seated or lying down.

Chief among the "character actors" in the film is Victor McLaglen. After starting out in British films, mainly in romantic roles, he came to America and played Flagg in the film version of *What Price Glory?* (Louis Wolheim created the stage rôle.) McLaglen's film character was generally the Irish plug-ugly with a heart of gold (e.g., *Annabelle's Affairs* and the Flagg-Quirt talkie spin-offs), but he is best remembered as the haunted Gypo in John Ford's *The Informer* (RKO 1935), for which he won an Oscar.

Other notables in the cast are H.B. Warner (*Girl of the Golden West, New Moon*), "Gabby" Hayes (Roy Rogers' sidekick), Edward Arnold (*Three Daring Daughters*), and of course the inimitable Charles Butterworth (*Love Me Tonight, The Cat and the Fiddle*), already fighting a losing battle with alcoholism.

Director Jack Conway had been in Hollywood since the early silent days. He had directed Grace Moore in *New Moon* (1930) and made some fine if not flashy films: *A Tale of Two Cities, Viva Villa!, Tarzan and His Mate,* and *Saratoga* (during which Jean Harlow died and some scenes had to be shot using a double). Some of the camera work for the crowd scenes in both *Viva Villa!* and *Let Freedom Ring* seems strongly influenced by Sergei Eisenstein's *Que Viva Mexico* (1933). Conway was not a Western director, but then *Let Freedom Ring* was no ordinary Western picture.

Its theme was tolerance, religious and ethnic. (Racial tolerance wasn't discovered in Hollywood, or in America for that matter, for another fifteen years.) Religious persecution was very real to many in the film community. Some actors, directors, writers, and technicians were in Hollywood as a direct result of fleeing the growing menace in Nazi Germany, and Hollywood was richer for it. Others who had

A German program. *Courtesy Anna Michalik.*

Director Jack Conway (right) gives instructions to Lionel Barrymore (seated) and Nelson. The film cleverly works around Barrymore's inability to stand. (Capt. C.E. Anderson as the Sheriff.) *Courtesy Anna Michalik.*

migrated years earlier still had families in Europe. While Corn Belt America could still sit snugly and smugly in their living rooms, dismissing events in Europe as unrelated to them, much of Hollywood knew better. As early as 1935, Jewish studio executives found they could no longer travel freely throughout Europe in search of talent, new markets, and relaxation as they had been used to doing. *Let Freedom Ring* became a message picture of the most obvious sort, not only against anti-Semitism (which would have limited its relevancy to the larger cities) but against all forms of discrimination. It sought to sugar-coat its purpose with standard action-picture devices and didn't quite succeed, but it is a fascinating glimpse into a very real and terrifying era in American history.

The film opens with a title informing us that the greatest battles for civil rights are not fought on battlefields, but in the hearts of a nation's people. Explosions follow, but it is only blasting to lay railroad track. In a nice montage of beautiful outdoor photography, we see a railroad line pushing through the West. A road sign announces that it is nearing Clover City.

Two surveyors on the project (Syd Saylor and Ted Thompson) have their minds on the civilization ahead and their telescopes on a beautiful blonde lady on a nearby hill. It is Maggie Adams (Virginia Bruce), in animated conversation with her horse, Sitting Bull. She doubts that the iron horse will be as much fun to ride. (Miss Bruce wears a snood and elbow length gloves, two new 1939 fashions.)

Her thoughts are interrupted by a passing buckboard. Rancher Tom Logan (Lionel Barrymore) tells her that a New York fella, Jim Knox, has offered to buy his land. He doesn't reckon he'll sell though, at least not until his son, Steve, gets back from Harvard. Maggie already knows of Steve's imminent arrival. He has written her, telling her to reserve a table at her restaurant and to have fresh doughnuts ready. Her smile indicates she'll be very glad to see him.

Other ranchers come by and report that Jim railroad-magnate Knox is trying to buy them out too. They all ride on, leaving Maggie alone on the hill. She gazes out over the valley and wonders if she is going to like the railroad. Well, she'll know in about six weeks.

The screen fills with flames and a title announces that "hooligans" have poured in from the desert to "wrest power" from the people in the name of progress. A number of hooligans find their way to Maggie's "restaurant," a saloon where the Mackerel (the delightful Charles Butterworth) plays the piano when he isn't picking up change by challenging strangers to knock him down for a count of ten.

Into this den of gambling and liquor come an infuriated landowner, Ned Wilkie (Louis Jean

Let Freedom Ring

Steve Logan (Eddy) returns home from Harvard and finds his childhood sweetheart, Maggie Adams (Virginia Bruce), waiting.

Heydt), and his father (George "Gabby" Hayes). They tell the local newspaper editor, Underwood (Raymond Walburn), that Jim Knox's men have burned their house down. Wilkie challenges two of the arsonists, Bumper (Dick Rich) and Cagan (Trevor Bardette). A gunfight is narrowly averted by the croupier, an elderly man named Rutledge (H.B. Warner). Clearly this is a case for the law.

The law in the form of Judge Bronson (Guy Kibbee, veteran of the Powell-Keeler musicals), takes its course. Wilkie not only fails to make a case against a fine man like Jim Knox, but the judge rules that, as a squatter with no roof over his head, his land is forfeit. Tom Logan and Maggie hear the Judge order the land sold to the highest bidder—or the best bidder in the eyes of the court. There is no doubt in anybody's mind that he means Jim Knox, the railroad boss.

We first see Jim Knox (Edward Arnold) in the midst of preparations for a gourmet repast. He is also preparing for "progress." Newspaper editor Underwood tells him happily that the *Clover City Bugle* will run a series of articles for the "foreign element," urging them to vote for Judge Bronson. Tom Logan has decided to

Steve's father (Lionel Barrymore, seated) thinks his son has come home a drunken sissy who won't stand up to the evil railroad boss (Edward Arnold, second from right). Others: C.E. Anderson, left; H.B. Warner, right, with gun.

oppose the Judge in the coming election, but Knox isn't worried. "My hunkies will vote for Judge Bronson, even if he were a giraffe."

Knox suggests that the Judge would be better served by articles on sunsets and scenery. He gives Underwood a large payment for "advertising." He also dispenses wages to his men, Bumper and Cagan, and tells them they will all be calling on Tom Logan that night. While Knox chats with Logan in the parlor, something just might happen in the barn.

Knox descends the stairs and, amazingly, is in Maggie's restaurant. He has brought his own dinner, a Welsh rarebit, but wants a chance to eat Maggie's biscuits and court her. She spiritedly calls him a thief. On Wall Street, he replies cordially, the term is "financier." She tells him that honest folks only need someone to show them how to fight and then no one can lick them. That someone is Steve Logan and he'll be home tomorrow. Steve will know what to do.

At that moment, the railroad arrives. Flat wagons full of scruffy workmen pour into town. A few bars of "Funiculi, Funicula" indicate their place of national origin, but the loudest

Let Freedom Ring

and largest of them is a big Irishman named Chris Mulligan (Victor McLaglen). He reports to Knox, who orders him to take the men over to the courthouse and register them. He'll need their votes. But, protests Mulligan, most of them have names you can't spell. Just call them all "Murphy," Knox replies cheerfully.

At Logan's ranch that night, Knox's hoodlum, Bumper, enters the barn with a kerosene can, but is interrupted. A mysterious figure appears in the darkness and knocks Bumper out cold. Knox keeps glancing out the parlor window, expecting to see flames, while he exhorts Tom Logan on the necessity of progress. Instead, there is a knock at the door, and Steve Logan (Nelson) stands before them.

Ma Logan (Sarah Padden) falls joyfully on her son, then steps back in concern. Steve is drunk. He fetches a bottle of whiskey and cordially invites Knox to stay for a drink. Since everyone has been waiting for him to come back and take care of things, he says, he will. They've all got to stop standing in the way of progress like a lot of Indians. Imagine calling an important man like Jim Knox a firebug! Tom Logan is astonished and dismayed. He orders his son from the house. As Steve and Knox leave, they find Bumper tied over the saddle of his horse. Crudely painted on the kerosene can at his side is: "Dear Mr. Knox—I lost my matches."

Steve's reputation for hard drinking continues through the bars of Clover City, with Mulligan as a companion. In one bar, Steve stops long enough to sing "Home, Sweet Home." The song reduces the big Irishman to tears, and we begin to suspect that he will turn out all right in the end.

Maggie's first joyous meeting with Steve shows us an entirely different man. The "drunkenness" vanishes, and he joins Hilda, the cook (Maude Allen), in a few bars of "Love Serenade," a new lyric to a nineteenth century ballet melody. (It proved so popular that it was taken up as the theme song of the radio soap opera "When a Girl Marries" several months after the film's release.) Steve had sung that song to Maggie the day he rode away to Boston four years earlier.

Steve is about to tell Maggie the "truth" when Knox walks in. Instantly, he reverts to his former line. Wouldn't she be proud if he got in with the railroads and became the biggest lawyer in these parts? Maggie is horrified.

Knox admires Steve's singing ("Dead Broke") and offers to hire him as his personal troubadour. Steve agrees, to Maggie's further disgust. And would Maggie request a song? Maggie replies bitterly that Steve knows her favorite.

The Mackerel plays "Love Serenade" on the old piano, and Steve sings. The song is so stirring that Maggie's icy manner softens. The Mackerel's attitude toward Steve also changes, for he spots the wound that Steve got fighting in the darkened barn.

Steve has been banished from his home and so takes up quarters with the Mackerel. The little man begs Steve to confide in Maggie too, but Steve refuses. There must be no slip-up in his plan to catch Knox. He is, of course, a government agent sent to gather evidence against

Steve's singing of a sentimental ballad reduces the inebriated Chris Mulligan (Victor McLaglen) to tears. Charles Butterworth, left, is the Mackerel.

the tyrant Knox. While he's at it, he manages quite a few patriotic homilies like: "If we could only get the truth to them, we might turn them into Americans," and "A man's as good as he thinks he is. All he's got to do is think." If only he had a newspaper, Steve says, he could reach the railroad workers. The Mackerel points out that there's one across the street.

"How do you feel about stealing?" Steve asks. "Oh, I'm indifferent," replies the Mackerel amiably.

The presses and editor of the *Daily Bugle* are soon packed for removal to a more secluded spot. Steve steps out to see if the coast is clear and meets first Maggie and then Mulligan, who is on his way into the newspaper office. Steve has just refused a romantic interlude with Maggie on the grounds that he is sick, but when Mulligan tries to pass, he insists they all go to Maggie's for a musical evening. Maggie is furious and leaves them in her parlor. There Steve regales Mulligan with "When Irish Eyes Are Smiling," while frantically signaling to the Mackerel to depart with their wagonload of equipment and the reluctant Editor Underwood.

Wistful comedian Charles Butterworth plays the Mackerel, a philosophical barfly who is easily persuaded to help Steve hold up the stage. Here they make their bumpy getaway with their precious booty—a printing press.

Editor Underwood (Raymond Walburn) also joins them—at pistol point—to help with their "underground" newspaper. (Eddy, who had been a real-life newspaper reporter, also ran a newspaper in *Knickerbocker Holiday*.)

The Mackerel is oblivious and settles down outside the window to enjoy the concert. Finally, in desperation, Steve invents a phony song ("Pat, Sez He") with a constant reprise of "Off to the mountains, off to the cave—giddyup, giddyup, giddyup!" The Mackerel gets the message on the fifth repeat and drives away.

A montage of whirling printing presses and headlines follows: "Vote for Thomas Logan and Human Rights"—"Knox Brand of Tyranny Stronger than American Ideals?" The papers are delivered in the night, tacked on doors and tucked in horses' harnesses. One man finds a copy in the seat of his long johns on the clothes line. Another reaches for a towel and gets a *Bugle*. The attacks are signed "The Wasp." Knox is in a rage, and Mulligan is especially incensed at a reference to himself as a "half-human hyena."

Steve is among the volunteers who go to search for "The Wasp," and Maggie follows him into the hills, thinking he means to betray

Let Freedom Ring

Eddy's outdoor rôle relieved him of the standard juvenile makeup with lipstick that afflicted film actors into the 1940s.

Victor McLaglen, who played Jeanette's husband in *Annabelle's Affairs* (1931), is a bully who gets his comeuppance from Steve in a fierce fist fight.

he replies. (Some self-esteem issues here!) Steve walks in at this moment, and, to spite him, Maggie agrees to Knox's proposal. Knox joyfully orders Steve to sing. The Mackerel doesn't want him to sing with a broken heart ("This is worse than *East Lynne*"), but Steve insists and delivers the robust "Dusty Road," the one-time title song of the film, which bears no relation to anything happening at the moment. "Much worse than *East Lynne*," the Mackerel decides.

Steve's purpose in coming to town is to persuade Knox to fight "The Wasp" by sending for another printing press so he can put out his own paper. In a beautiful long shot, we see the stagecoach bearing the new press crossing the prairie. Unfortunately the coach is waylaid by a masked cowboy and an odd-looking Indian, and the new press is soon turning out anti-Knox papers.

Steve sets out to deliver the latest *Bugles* surreptitiously to the railroad camp and ends up

her idol. She finds Steve just outside the cave that houses his press and steals his horse to stop his supposed treachery. Mulligan also turns up near the cave, and the Mackerel tries to lead him away. In a comical sequence, the printing ink on the Mackerel's hands ends up all over Mulligan's face while the Irishman bemoans the lack of a trail.

Steve and the Mackerel rush back to their precious press and find that Editor Underwood has managed to smash it to pieces in their absence. Steve returns to town and notes a $500 reward poster for "The Wasp." Mulligan is at the bar, denouncing the effects of "The Wasp" on the railroad workers. "Creatures you could scarcely distinguish from cattle calling themselves Americans," he snorts.

Knox is a very congenial villain. He is still trying to convince Maggie to marry him. Why does he want a woman who doesn't love him? she asks. "Maybe because the woman who *did* want him wouldn't be worth marrying,"

Eddy and McLaglen clowning between fight scenes.

Let Freedom Ring

Eddy and Bruce. While RKO was commissioning brilliant original scores from George Gershwin, Irving Berlin, and Jerome Kern, MGM tried to economize. *Let Freedom Ring* was an early prototype of the MGM musical made up of old favorites and songs in the public domain.

delivering a boisterous patriotic song, "Where Else but Here," appealing to each ethnic group. When he drops off another load of papers at his father's ranch, old Tom Logan learns the truth about his son. If they can just get the workers to "vote right," Knox will be finished. A trap has been set by Knox, however, and Steve escapes in a hail of bullets. Unknown to him, his father is wounded.

Steve eludes his pursuers in the mountains, but Mulligan finds him. He thinks Steve is chasing "The Wasp" too, until Steve enlightens him. Mulligan decides to beat him to a pulp. Steve takes him on, telling him in purple Ben Hecht prose that, as soon as he's had a good thrashing, he will see things right and become a good American. They fight in the eerie half-light, the action speeded somewhat comically, until Steve wins. Maggie has witnessed their fight and learned the truth.

Steve's triumph is short-lived. He looks up and sees his father's barn on fire. "What is it?" asks Mulligan. "It's America burning!" cries Steve.

Badly wounded, Steve's father has been taken to Maggie's restaurant, where Knox orders him to reveal the name of "The Wasp." Steve enters and calmly confronts Knox. He is "The Wasp," he announces.

Knox orders father and son hanged, but Rutledge, the old croupier, draws his gun. Steve turns to the crowd of surly railroad workers and makes an impassioned speech about tyrants and freedom. The men murmur among themselves. Knox senses rebellion and orders them out of the bar-room. The men mill about and begin moving reluctantly toward the door as Knox's men seize Steve.

Maggie steps forward and quietly begins singing "America." Steve takes up the song, and the crowd pauses. Knox screams at them to get out if they know what's good for them. The singing continues. Chris Mulligan turns and joins them, bellowing the song. The grizzled men stop, and, one by one, they begin singing until the whole room vibrates. Even editor Underwood joins them. Slowly Maggie walks through the crowd to meet Steve. They embrace as the crowd sings the second verse of "America," a truly remarkable feat for any American.

Reviews

"Let Freedom Ring is momentous," wrote *Variety*. "It's the first in the cycle of [proposed] film offerings to stress the American type of democracy and freedom for the classes and masses. Sweeping along with powerful, patriotic spine tingling, picture climaxes with Nelson Eddy leading a gang of railroad workers singing 'America.' In handing the lead assignment to Eddy, Metro apparently decided to provide him with a rôle that calls for a square jaw and a pair of handy fists. He takes full advantage of the opportunity, displaying a vigorous characterization of the western youth who battles all comers when necessary. Battle in the cave between Eddy and McLaglen is excitingly staged."

On the other end of the spectrum, William Boehnel of the *New York World-Telegram* deplored the story: "Leave it to Hollywood to spoil a good thing when it gets it." He had his usual knocks for Eddy: "The young Harvard lawyer is played by Nelson Eddy, which certainly makes it appear as if it took Steve a lot longer than the customary four to six years to get his degree."

Frank Nugent in the *New York Times* took a middle course: "It is sound dramatic stuff, as sure-fire now as it has always been. We don't dare criticize it adversely under penalty of being summoned before the Dies committee and we shouldn't, if we dare, for the piece has vigor, good characterization and, fortunately, Mr. Eddy's good singing."

Recordings (See Discography for further information)

Eddy recorded:
   "America"
   "The Dusty Road"

"They call you riffraff. I call you *Americans*!" Steve rallies the votes for his father. Left to right, H.B. Warner, Edward Arnold, Eddy, Guy Kibbee, C.E. Anderson. Lionel Barrymore, seated.

Steve leads the triumphant immigrants in song with remarkable results.

"Love Serenade" [also called "Drigo's Serenade"]

Music in the Film

In listing performers after each title, "and" denotes a genuine duet, while commas between names indicate a sequence of singers.

Overture: "The Dusty Road" with fragment of "Oh! Susanna" by Stephen Foster, "Nellie Gray" by B.R. Hanby, "Over the Waves" by J. Rosas (orchestral)
"I've Been Working on the Railroad" (male chorus) - traditional, with fragments of "Funiculi, Funicula" interpolated
"Home, Sweet Home" (Eddy) - by Sir Henry Bishop, lyrics by John Howard Payne
"Love Serenade" ["Drigo's Serenade"] (Maude Allen, Eddy, Bruce) - by Riccardo Drigo from his nineteenth-century ballet, "Les Millions d'Arlequin," new lyrics by Bob Wright and Chet Forrest
"Dead Broke" ["Ten Thousand Cattle Straying"] (Eddy) - music and lyrics by Owen Wister, written for his 1904 production of *The Virginian*, also used in the 1929 Paramount film with Gary Cooper
"Love Serenade" reprise (Eddy)
"When Irish Eyes Are Smiling" (Eddy) - by Ernest R. Ball, Chauncey Olcott and George Graff Jr.
"Pat, Sez He" (Eddy and Butterworth) - music by Phil Ohman, lyrics by Foster Carling and Marty Symes
"The Dusty Road" (Eddy) - by Otis and Leon René. Original title song of the film.
"Where Else but Here" (Eddy and male chorus, with spoken lines by several railroad workers) - music by Sigmund Romberg, lyrics by Edward Heyman. (Pay records for male chorus list Tim Stark, Henry Korn, Norman Nielsen, Ralph DeAngeles, J. Delos Jewkes, Abe Dinovitch.)
"America" ["My Country, 'Tis of Thee"] (Bruce, Eddy, Victor McLaglen, Lionel Barrymore, Raymond Walburn, chorus) - by Henry Carey and Samuel Francis Smith
Finale: "America" (orchestral)

Broadway Serenade
MGM.
Released April 7, 1939.
Produced and directed by Robert Z. Leonard.
113 minutes.
Issued in Sepia.

German title: Irrwege der Liebe (Confusions of Love)
Spanish title: La Serenata de Broadway

Original Story: Lew Lipton, John Taintor Foote, and Hans Kraly. Screenplay: Charles Lederer. Musical Director: Herbert Stothart. Dances: Seymour Felix.

A German program for *Broadway Serenade*. The title refers to the tribulations or confusions of love. As World War II loomed and then broke, most European markets were closed to Hollywood films. *Courtesy Anna Michalik.*

Musical Presentation: Merrill Pye. Camera: Oliver T. Marsh. Montage: John Hoffman. Editor: Harold F. Kress. Recording Director: Douglas Shearer. Art Director: Cedric Gibbons. Art Associate: Joseph Wright. Set Decoration: Edwin B. Willis. Gowns: Adrian. Men's Costumes: Valles. Makeup: Jack Dawn. Finale created and directed by Busby Berkeley. Assistant Director: Marvin Stuart. Vocal and Orchestral Collaboration: Léo Arnaud, Leonid Raab.

Jeanette MacDonald (Mary Hale)
Lew Ayres (Jimmy Seymour)
Ian Hunter (Larry Bryant)
Frank Morgan (Cornelius Collier Jr)
Rita Johnson (Judith "Judy" Tyrrell)
Virginia Grey (Pearl)
Al Shean (Herman)
Wally Vernon (Joey the Jinx)
William Gargan (Bob, a press agent)
Katharine Alexander (Miss Harriet Ingalls)
Franklin Pangborn (Gene, the choreographer)
Esther Dale (Mrs. Olsen)
Ray Mayer (Mr. Woods)
Kenneth Stevens ("No Time to Argue" baritone)
Edward Hearn (Frank)
Kitty McHugh (Kitty, the maid)
Ray Walker (Madison)
E. Alyn Warren (Everett)
Lawrence Wheat (Accountant)
William E. "Babe" Lawrence (Burke)
Paul Hurst (Reynolds, a drunk)
William Tannen (Asst. stage manager)
Morgan Wallace (Parks)
Arthur "Pop" Byron (Pat)
Arthur Housman (Jonathan)
Ted Oliver (Spike)
Al Hill (Chuck)
Frank Orth (Mr. Fellowes)
Esther Howard (Mrs. Fellowes)
Leon Belasco (The Squeaker)
Barbara Bedford (Secretary)
Hobart Cavanaugh (Mr. Ingalls)
Don Brodie, Jack Luden (Reporters)
Jack Carlton [Clayton Moore, later the "Lone Ranger"] (Cameraman)
Mary Beth Hughes (Girl at party)
Tom Hanlon (Announcer)
Hans Joby (Hans)
Bernard Siegal (Otto)
Estelle Etterre, Patricia West (Girls with Bryant)
Lionel Royce (Mr. Bachspiegal)
Bert Moorhouse, Charles Sherlock, Allen Fox (Reporters)
Ernie Alexander (Photographer)
Jack Hutchinson (Bryant's chauffeur)
Olaf Hytten (Hotel manager)
Mary MacLaren (Costumer)
Claude King (Mr. Gato)
Norman Willis (Process server)
Jack Raymond (Joey's companion)
Bruce Mitchell (Pullman conductor)
Paul Newlan (Big man)
Sidney Jarvis (Santa Claus)
Jane Barnes, Gertrude Short, Marjorie "Babe" Kane, Jill Dennett (Salesgirls, 5 & 10)
Mary Gordon (Annie)
Arthur Q. Bryan (Process server)
J. Delos Jewkes (Music maker)

Broadway Serenade

Broadway Serenade was styled to serve as a bridge between Jeanette MacDonald's operetta image and the lighter, less expensive, and more marketable modern-dress "swing" musicals that were becoming popular. She had "swung" a Victor Herbert number in *Sweethearts* with great success, and *Broadway Serenade* gave her several contemporary show songs plus an opera aria. The purpose of the film was worthy, but the resulting film was not.

The plot hinged on the simultaneous career success of a wife and career failure of her husband, a theme becoming hackneyed even in the late 1930s when men were acutely sensitive about the changing status of women. It might have served for the bare bones of a good film if it had been filled in with warm, believable characters and bright songs. Instead the characters are barely two dimensional, and the songs only pleasant at best. The major love theme of the film is Tchaikovsky's "None but the Lonely Heart," which is "dressed up for 1939."

The relationship between the heroine and her movie husband, Lew Ayres, is another source of concern. Ayres is obviously supposed to bring breezy, boyish charm to the film, but the rôle as written seems merely immature with paranoid touches. He does not have the material to enable him to bring off such an acting coup, even assuming that such a character belongs in a light musical. The wife's endless protective and placating gestures seem more maternal than anything else.

Ayres had made a strong impact as Greta Garbo's young admirer in the silent *The Kiss* in 1929. After scoring again in *All Quiet on the Western Front* (1930), he went from studio to studio, always working, but rarely finding parts worthy of him. He was quite fine as Katharine Hepburn's alcoholic brother in *Holiday* (1938) and then settled down at MGM. With one Dr. Kildare movie under his belt, he was put into *Broadway Serenade*. (His other films that year included *These Glamour Girls* and *Ice Follies of 1939*, an indication of how MGM regarded his talent.) It wasn't until his superb portrayal of the doctor in *Johnny Belinda* (1948) that he found another memorable rôle.

Director Robert Z. Leonard did five MacDonald/Eddy films and was one of their favorite directors. His early work as a singer (in a barbershop quartet) before going into films made him sympathetic to the problems of singers. He was also the master of the "scene." His films unreel with one beautifully played "scene" after another, but unfortunately, unless a tight script (*Maytime*, *Pride and Prejudice*) keeps things spinning along, they tend to bog down in atmosphere. *Broadway Serenade* is a prime example, each bit of "business" (the tossed hats, the smiling mask in the finale) making a point, but not contributing to the overall pattern or rhythm.

The film is historically interesting as Busby Berkeley's first MGM film after his brilliant years at Warner Bros. His work at Warners had declined somewhat—after all, what could Michelangelo have done to "top" the Sistine Chapel? Berkeley was expected to surpass himself with each new picture. He took to all-dramatic films, a genre at which he was as dismal as he was brilliant with musical numbers. At MGM, Berkeley started over in the musical field, working now in the MGM style, long on quality and gloss, short on gut originality and innovativeness. His bizarre finale to *Broadway Serenade* marked a halfway point between two styles, with the worst of both and the best of neither.

Broadway Serenade also made a slight bow of obeisance to the alcohol culture that was reflected in many films of the 1930s (*The Thin Man*, *The Philadelphia Story*) in which the "good guys" spend much of their time drunk without apparent physical or moral damage. Although Jeanette herself is never seen with a glass in her hand, she has lines like "It ought to be very drunk out tonight," and several verses of "High Flyin'" refer to an alcoholic high.

The lack of imagination in *Broadway Serenade* is evident from the beginning with flat show-card titles. The film opens in the Naughty Nineties Club in Greenwich Village, where a new act, Hale and Seymour, is entertaining the elite who have come slumming. Jimmy Seymour (Lew Ayres) is at the piano in derby and false moustache while Mary Hale (Jeanette) prances alluringly in a shorter, fancier version of her dance-hall dress in *San Francisco*.

As the formally dressed patrons arrive, they are handed derbies and can-can bonnets and seated at small tables where they can drink, watch the show, join in the old time songs—and drink. One patron (Paul Hurst) has overindulged and becomes boisterous, irritating Jimmy no end. Mary makes little soothing gestures, but when the drunk aims a champagne cork and hits Mary in the face, Jimmy leaps up and slugs him. The scene has been followed with interest by a distinguished gentleman at a back table.

The manager, Mr. Parks (Morgan Wallace), tells Jimmy that three knockouts in one week are enough and fires him. Mary can stay on, he says, but she chooses to depart. In their dressing room, Jimmy pitches his hat across the room onto the hat rack, a gesture he

Jimmy learns he that has gotten a scholarship to study composition in Italy. (Al Shean, left.)

will repeat throughout the film. Mary gives Jimmy a cigarette ("Same thing as counting ten, only easier"!) and consoles him. After all, he is a musical genius. All this will just make copy for his press agents when he is famous. Jimmy hugs her and tells her he's beginning to like having her for a wife.

At their colorful boardinghouse, full of colorful characters, a Christmas surprise is being planned by "the gang," Mrs. Olsen (Esther Dale), Herman (Al Shean, the "Professor" of *San Francisco*), and the rest. Although they are obviously supposed to be a unique and lovable group of individuals, neither the script nor the director gives them any background, so they are a faceless bunch. A small feast is laid out and a present, a water jug that plays "Auld Lang Syne," is being wrapped. When the couple arrives, Jimmy finds a letter announcing that he has won a scholarship for a year's study in Italy. If he and Mary can raise just one thousand dollars, they can spend a glorious year together on a belated honeymoon.

Old Herman starts a melody on his cello and ends up playing "The Blue Danube." It's that restaurant he works in, he complains. He has played "The Blue Danube" until he is blue in the

Jimmy Seymour (Lew Ayres) has a number of talents, among them getting fired. His wife, Mary Hale (Jeanette), still finds him lovable. (Morgan Wallace, left.) *Courtesy Anna Michalik.*

face. "It's a good thing for you the 'Black Bottom' is out of date," comments Mrs. Olsen.

Jimmy is sure he can sell his new song for the thousand dollars they need. The trouble with people today, he says, is that they are too busy to learn new songs. As an example he plays "A Tisket, a Tasket," then enjoying current popularity in an Ella Fitzgerald recording. He, too, will give them an old one: Tchaikovsky's "None but the Lonely Heart." He pulls out his version and Mary sings "For Ev'ry Lonely Heart." Then they rush off to sell it to the biggest producer in New York, Cornelius Collier.

Mr. Collier (Frank Morgan) is busy, his secretary tells a group of costumed chorines. His business turns out to be another chorus girl, Pearl (Virginia Grey), who is protesting the concealing costume that has been assigned her. Now, if she had one more like this: she strips off the ruffled gown and is clad in a bathing suit.

Judith (Rita Johnson) walks in on this attempted takeover of her man, and the two square off. Judith seizes Collier's cigar and, as Pearl bends to retrieve her costume, the cigar follows her out of the picture. A loud yell from Pearl, and Judith comments that now she'll be known as "Lady Scarface." Pearl protests volubly. It will show in the bathing suit number. Judith coolly remarks that if that spot shows, the police will close the show. "I'll get the police after *you*!" cries Pearl. "For defacing public property?" sneers Judith.

The show's backer, Larry Bryant (Ian Hunter), interrupts the fun, followed by a mass of technical people wanting decisions. Larry is the same distinguished man who witnessed Mary's departure from the Naughty Nineties Club, and he now spots her and Jimmy trying to get past the receptionist outside. He invites her in to audition Jimmy's song, but in the hubbub she ends up interpreting one of the show's tempo songs when the star will only sing it "straight." She lands a job with *Collier's Revue of 1939*. The train for Atlantic City will leave at 4:00 that afternoon. It is obvious that both Collier and Larry Bryant have taken a proprietary interest in Mary, for in a final shot, the press agent, Bob (William Gargan), rolls his eyes from one to the other and then heavenward in amusement.

Jimmy cheerfully refuses to tag along and sees Mary off at Penn Station. The show's star, Harriet Ingalls (Katharine Alexander), makes a grand entrance, and Pearl turns up in scanty practice clothes under her fur coat, causing Judith to reach for the cigar again.

The happy little family departs for Atlantic City, where Mary has one number in the show with a pleasant tenor (Kenneth Stevens). The production is a pallid reference to the Busby Berkeley style of raising a curtain and then escaping into a limitless fantasy land.

Mary's song opens with a train painted on a "traveler" curtain that then glides offstage, revealing a ski lodge in the Alps. Mary, in jaunty cap, white fur coat, and boots, sings "High Flyin,'" then dances down the mammoth steps of the lodge with lads in lederhosen. The lodge in turn slides offstage to reveal the bar

Mary and Jimmy go to sell one of his songs to raise money for their trip, but producer Larry Bryant (Ian Hunter, second from left) is more interested in Mary. (Left: Frank Morgan. Rear: William Gargan.) *Courtesy Anna Michalik.*

The "High Flyin'" production number has several costume changes for Jeanette, including a stylish ski outfit. *Courtesy Anna Michalik.*

inside. Mary dances in wearing slacks and plaid jacket, then four bartenders reprise the song while drunken patrons do a tired juggling act with oranges and bottles.

The bar is then whisked away, and we are on the snow that we have seen through the bar window. The tenor arrives on skis and sings "One Look at You," and Mary joins him in white snowsuit with fur-trimmed hood. They take off together on their skis with a rear projection whizzing by. The camera neither pulls back to show them on a treadmill set, nor opens up the action to Berkeley-style fantasy. They are quickly dumped, literally, back onto the ski-lodge set, comically flailing broken skis, for a final verse of "One Look at You."

On opening night, Jimmy phones Mary and finally reaches her in Larry Bryant's hotel room where she is being interviewed. The seed of suspicion is planted. The press agent is giving the reporters a fantastic version of discovering Mary on the top deck of a Fifth Avenue bus. (Actor William Gargan uses a rapid-fire delivery intended to lend tempo to the film.)

Larry slips Mary out on the balcony overlooking the moonlit Atlantic and tries to "make love to her" (1930s term for sweet talk), but she confesses that she is happily married. Busy little Pearl spots them through a window and gets reporters to photograph Larry giving Mary a brotherly hug. The next day's newspapers confirm Jimmy's jealous suspicions. Does he phone her, write her, or fly to her side to straighten things out? Oh, no, dear viewer, there are six more reels to go.

In a pseudo-Vorkapich montage, we see Mary slowly take over the show from its star, Harriet Ingalls, as Jimmy walks the streets alone, a failure. Working at a German café, he reads in *Variety* that *Collier's Revue* returns that week to New York. Simultaneously, he is picking out his oom-pah chords on the piano, accompanying Herman and a violinist. A bored

Larry Bryant (Ian Hunter) proposes in the moonlight. Offered a choice between a real gentleman and an erratic cad, Mary makes the traditional choice. *Courtesy Anna Michalik.*

Fashions were again in transition in 1939, and Jeanette's Adrian wardrobe was generally awkward, but she herself was lovely.

patron rudely turns on the radio, and Jimmy hears a gossip reporter mentioning Larry and Mary in romantic terms. Jimmy defends his wife's honor by slugging the patron, and he and Herman are back on the streets.

Herman tells Jimmy to stop believing the gossip and go greet Mary at the train. "With a smile that big," Jimmy gestures grandly, "and a bouquet that big." He makes a small circle with his hands and we dissolve to a matching bunch of violets. Mary appears at the train door, surrounded by reporters and admirers, her eyes searching the platform for Jimmy.

He manages to get the violets to her, and their ardent hugs are explained to reporters by the press agent: "That's her brother, just out of the hospital."

The violets are handed back to Jimmy and replaced by a splendid spray of roses for photographs. Then Mary, accompanied by her new maid, is swept off to a swank hotel for fittings and interviews, Jimmy in tow.

Mary ends up in Larry's revue, singing "Un Bel Di" from *Madame Butterfly* on top of an improbable bridge. Diva Grace Moore had a strong opinion about the number.

Jimmy protests that "the gang" is waiting with a banquet in her honor, but there is nothing she can do. She will see them after the show. She gives him opening night tickets for them all and also a check for $1,000. Now they can go to Italy. The music director (comedian Franklin Pangborn, who specialized in agitated, prissy rôles) bursts into the hotel room with a new number (the show is due to open in a few hours) and describes the lead-in—taste is changing, the world is restless, "and then, boom, we'll sock 'em in the puss with *Butterfly*."

Jimmy tries to catch Mary up on what he's been doing, but she misunderstands everything he says in the confusion. Larry arrives and breezes past Jimmy into the bedroom where Mary is being fitted. Jimmy's doubts return, and he accepts a stiff drink. By the time Mary emerges from the bedroom, draped in a splendid collection of jewels given her by Larry for the opening night, Jimmy is decidedly ugly.

Harriet Ingalls chooses this moment to charge in with a process server. She is suing Larry for throwing her out of the show because of his relationship with Mary. Mary starts crying, and Jimmy starts swinging, knocking Larry down. Jimmy runs, out and Mary starts to follow him just as the music director swoops through the door and drags her bodily to the piano to learn the new number.

We dissolve to the number on stage, "Time Changes Everything," with eight grand pianos (a shadow of Berkeley's multi-pianoed splendor in *Gold Diggers of 1935*). The song evolves into "Un Bel Di" from *Madame Butterfly*. Mary appears at the top of a forty-foot arched bridge in a Japanese kimono covered with bugle beads. She gracefully descends the steep stairs of the bridge (a fantastic accomplishment) and, ignoring some dreary plaster swans beneath it, sings the beautiful aria in a youthful, lyrical interpretation. It is a shame that her touching performance is engulfed in *Folies Bérgère* trappings. As she hits the high note, the stage is deluged in flower petals drifting from the flies. (The same aria was the finale for Grace Moore's film *One Night of Love* in 1934, and Miss Moore commented cattily that the height of the bridge did not reflect the level of performance.)

Back at the rooming house, "the gang" sit dejectedly waiting for Mary. She rushes in and learns that Jimmy has only just gotten home. He never gave them the tickets. Jeanette is wearing her first screen "strapless" costume, a vogue just beginning to cause a stir.

Mary finds Jimmy packing and makes him an emotional speech about believing. When she was a little girl she saw *Peter Pan*. Peter had told the audience that unless they believed someone would die, and so she believed with all her heart. Now, she believes in Jimmy with all her heart. "Won't you believe in *me*?" she begs.

"No," he replies.

Despite this, Mary tells Jimmy she forgives him. He leaves her anyway and heaves the musical water jug through the window, an unsuccessful attempt on the director's part at pathos.

Another montage begins imaginatively with a large poster of Mary Hale dripping rain (tears). It then offers a pale imitation of the Slavko Vorkapich montages in *Maytime* and *Sweethearts*. We see Mary doing a recital ("The Italian Street Song" from *Naughty Marietta*), a broadcast ("Les Filles de Cadix" from *Maytime*), and a film (Musetta's aria "Quando M'en Vo" from *La Bohème*). The last fades into "Jingle Bells."

It is Christmas, and Mary, Larry, Mr. Collier, and Judith are shopping. Collier stops to propose to Judith, who accepts and comments on the irony: Mary started divorce proceedings that morning.

The gum-chewing showgirls recognize Mary and beg her for a song. The pianist, hidden in an alcove of the sheet music section, is Jimmy. Mary sings "One Look at You" as the salesgirls and customers stand silent. She is dripping with jewels and furs while Jimmy is threadbare, so it is obviously supposed to be an important emotional moment.

Jimmy returns to the dreary hole where he and Herman now live and finds the announcement of divorce proceedings. He tosses his hat at the hat rack and this time he misses. In a fit of despondency, he throws his music into the stove, and old Herman burns his hands rescuing it. Herman makes an impassioned speech about suffering and creating and success and Jimmy sees the light.

The next scene finds Mary on closing night of her show, two years later. (The show opened in 1938, so that makes it 1940, a year after the film was released.) Her divorce has just come through, but Larry's proposal cheers her up. She accepts and announces to the entire cast that she is retiring from show business.

After two years of writing, Jimmy finally sells the song that he wrote way back in reel one, now a "concerto." He and Herman musically celebrate, singing of the "Scandinavian rights" and "television rights" that will make Jimmy rich.

Mary is packing to leave for England and her wedding. The decor of her apartment is truly astounding, with sequined Moorish columns, merry-go-round horses, and silken swags everywhere. Larry is just leaving when he runs into Jimmy and Herman in the hallway.

Mary decides to marry Larry. The show's director (Frank Morgan) has already found wedded bliss with one of the showgirls (Rita Johnson, right).

Jimmy knows nothing of Mary's engagement. He is in excellent spirits and offers to let Larry return the blow he gave him at their last meeting, just to show there are no hard feelings. Larry declines. The elevator man asks Larry if he is going down. "Yes," he answers thoughtfully, watching Jimmy go toward Mary's door. "I *guess* it will be all right."

Jimmy tells the startled Mary that he is a success now, and they can start all over. He has buried his inferiority complex "under a million notes." Mary tells him tearfully that she is marrying someone else. Collier arrives to persuade Mary to stay in the show. He has just bought a fabulous song, and only she can sing it in his new show. Of course it is Jimmy's song, and if Mary won't stay, Collier won't use it. By some incongruous logic, this puts Jimmy's success on Mary's shoulders, and, of course, she can't let Jimmy fail again.

Opening night of the new show. Backstage, Mary is heartbroken that Jimmy is nowhere to be found. Her fiancé Larry comes to her dressing room drunk and tells her that he recognizes her for a woman who loves with all her heart. That's why he wanted her, and that's why he can't have her. Mary tries to prove she is happy by holding up a smiling mask similar to those of the chorus girls, but Larry isn't fooled. (Poor Ian Hunter, playing respectable, intelligent, and considerate gentlemen, was invariably passed up by the heroine for a more dashing, less trustworthy hero.) Mary is called on stage, and Jimmy arrives moments later. This time Larry takes him up on his offer and socks him in the jaw.

The curtains rise on Busby Berkeley's first MGM film number. A close-up shot of a shepherd's pipe expands to reveal a shepherd and sheep (perched uncomfortably on rocky shelves) outside a composer's window. The composer takes up the melody and, in a pinpoint spot, Mary appears in white wig and Grecian gown, running through a set of crushed black plastic shapes. The camera arches and sweeps, picking out ranks of masked musicians and singers. All is dark, glittering, and ominous.

To a wild jungle beat, the squads are joined by jitterbugging African-masked dancers. The number becomes chaotic, a nightmare of sound and sight, finally resolved by a cymbal crash. Mary is standing in a white dress with sequin "wing" collar on a fifty-foot pedestal. About seventy-five feet away, in a darkened corner of the orchestra, she spots Jimmy playing the piano. She jumps as if stuck by a pin, then she beams and finishes the song triumphantly. The End.

Perhaps it is fortunate that the film wasn't a success, for if it had been, Miss MacDonald might never have returned to the operettas that her fans love so well.

Reviews

"The biggest bad show of the year" said the *New York Times*.

Recordings (See Discography for further information)

Jeanette recorded "Un Bel Di.

Broadway Serenade

Despite a mammoth and mind-boggling finale created by Busby Berkeley, the film didn't click. It was Jeanette's least favorite of all her films. *Courtesy Anna Michalik.*

Music in the Film

In listing performers after each title, "and" denotes a genuine duet, while commas between names indicate a sequence of singers.

Overture: "High Flyin'" fragment, "One Look at You" fragment, "For Ev'ry Lonely Heart"
GAY NINETIES MEDLEY:
    "Yip-I-Addy-I-Ay" (MacDonald and male quartet) - John H. Flynn and Will D. Cobb
    "Rufus Rastus Johnson Brown" ["What Ya Gonna Do When the Rent Comes 'Round?"] (MacDonald, Gus Reed Singers with Charles Bennett, Thad Harvey, and Abe Dinovitch) - music by Harry von Tilzer, lyrics by Andrew B. Sterling
    "Hearts Win, You Lose" (MacDonald) - music and words by Andrew B. Sterling
    "Love's Old Sweet Song" ["Just a Song at Twilight"] (MacDonald) - music by J.L. Molloy, lyrics by G. Clifton Bingham
NURSERY SONG MEDLEY:
    "A Tisket, a Tasket" (MacDonald)
    "Here We Go 'Round the Mulberry Bush" (MacDonald)
    "The Farmer in the Dell" (Al Shean)

"For Ev'ry Lonely Heart" (MacDonald) - based on "None but the Lonely Heart" ("Nür Wer die Sehnsucht Kennt") by Peter Ilich Tchaikovsky, arranged by Edward Ward and Herbert Stothart, new lyrics by Gus Kahn
"For Ev'ry Lonely Heart" reprise (MacDonald)
"High Flyin'" (Mary Kent dubbing for Katharine Alexander, Franklin Pangborn) - music by Herbert Stothart and Edward Ward, lyrics by Bob Wright and Chet Forrest
"High Flyin'" reprise (MacDonald and male quartet, chorus) INTO:
"One Look at You" (MacDonald) - music by Stothart and Ward, lyrics by Wright and Forrest
FIRST CAREER MONTAGE:
   "For Ev'ry Lonely Heart" (orchestra)
   "No Time to Argue" fragment (MacDonald and Stevens) - music by Sigmund Romberg, lyrics by Gus Kahn
   "Time Changes Everything" (MacDonald and chorus) - see credits below
   "For Ev'ry Lonely Heart (orchestral)
   "Time Changes Everything" reprise (MacDonald and chorus)
   "High Flyin'" (MacDonald and chorus)
"Time Changes Everything" reprise (Pangborn, male octet) - music by Walter Donaldson, lyrics by Gus Kahn
"Un Bel Di" (MacDonald) from *Madame Butterfly* - music by Giacomo Puccini, lyrics by Luigi Illica and Giuseppe Giacosa
SECOND CAREER MONTAGE:
   "Italian Street Song" (MacDonald) - music by Victor Herbert, lyrics by Rida Johnson Young
   "Les Filles de Cadix" (MacDonald) - music by Leo Delibes, lyrics by Alfred deMusset
   "Quando M'En Vo" ["Musetta's aria"] (MacDonald) - from the opera *La Bohème*, music by Giacomo Puccini, lyrics by Luigi Illica and Giuseppe Giacosa
"Jingle Bells" (orchestral) - traditional
"One Look at You" reprise (MacDonald)
"Musical contract" patter song (Al Shean and Lew Ayres) - Stothart and Ward (Copyrighted as such, no lyricist given.)
"For Ev'ry Lonely Heart" reprise (MacDonald and chorus)

Pay records indicate song fragments were recorded by Ken Darby's Octet, Six Hits and a Miss, and the King's Men Octet. Helen Seamon and Roy Lester performed a jitterbug number.

NOTE: "For Ev'ry Lonely Heart" was also copyrighted under the title "Broadway Serenade."

Trivia

Jeanette is wearing her white *Broadway Serenade* parka with fur-trimmed hood when she and Tyrone Power accept their "crowns" as "King and Queen of Hollywood" from columnist Ed Sullivan in a 1939 newsreel. Both stars make charming acceptance speeches thanking their fans.

Balalaika
MGM.
Released December 29, 1939.
Directed by Reinhold Schunzel.
Produced by Lawrence Weingarten.
102 minutes.

Spanish title: *En el Balalaika* (At the Balalaika)

Based on the London operetta that had music by George Posford and Bernard Grün, with book and lyrics by Eric Maschwitz. Screenplay: Leon Gordon, Charles Bennett, and Jacques Deval. Photography: Joseph Ruttenberg and Karl Freund. Music Adaptation and Score: Herbert Stothart. Orchestrations: Murray Cutter, Paul Marquardt, and Wally Heglin. Conductor: Dr. William Axt. Choreography: Ernst Matray. Russian Cossack Choir conducted by Anatol

Nelson as Prince Karagin. He sang flawless Russian. *Courtesy Anna Michalik.*

Frikin. Recording Director: Douglas Shearer. Art Director: Cedric Gibbons. Art Associate: Eddie Imazu. Set Decoration: Edwin B. Willis. Gowns: Adrian. Men's Costumes: Valles. Makeup: Jack Dawn. Editor: George Boemler. Assistant Director: Dolph Zimmer. Screenplay Contributions: Vincent Lawrence, Richard Connell. Ballet Choreography: Albertina Rasch, assisted by Florence Nelson. Technical Adviser: Count Andrey Tolstoy.

The stage musical *Balalaika* opened at the Adelphi Theatre in London on December 22, 1936 after several postponements. It starred Muriel Angelus, Roger Treville, Clifford Mollison, and Betty Warren, and ran more than 446 performances.

Nelson Eddy (Prince Peter Karagin, AKA Peter Fedorovitch Taranda)
Ilona Massey (Lydia Pavlovna Marakova)
Charlie Ruggles (Private Nicki Popoff)
Frank Morgan (Ivan Danchenoff)
Lionel Atwill (Professor Marakov)
C. Aubrey Smith (General Karagin)
Joyce Compton (Masha, Lydia's maid)
Walter Woolf King (Captain Sibirsky)
Dalies Frantz (Dimitri Marakov)
Frederick Worlock (Dr. Ramensky)
Abner Biberman (Leo)
Charles Judels (Batoff, the café owner)
Phillip Terry (Lieutenant Smirnoff)
Arthur W. Cernitz (Captain Pavloff)
Roland Varno (Lieutenant Nikitin)
George Tobias (Slaski, the counterman)
Paul Sutton (Anton)
William "Willy" Costello (Captain Testoff)
Marla Shelton (Olga)
Kay Sutton (Nina)
Erno "Ernst" Verebes (Danchenoff's secretary)
Eddy Conrad (Peasant)
Monte Vandergrift (Corporal)
Al Ferguson, George Volk, Bob Stevenson, Earl Seaman, Feodor Chaliapin, Charles Brokaw, Rand Brooks (Soldiers)
John Bleifer (Sailor)
Andrew Tombes (Wilbur Allison)
Florence Shirley (Mrs. Allison)
Lee Phelps (Doorman)
Jack Luden, John Gubbins, Rex Post, Dirk Thane (Imperial Guard officers)
Boris Glagolin (Customer in Slaski's)

Nelson's leading lady, Ilona Massey, won rave reviews from critics, who compared her with Dietrich. *Courtesy Anna Michalik.*

William Royle (Police detective)
Ellinore Vanderveer, Constantine Romanoff (Café extras)
Jac George (Violinist)
John Holland (Musician)
Harry Semels (Man in square)
Hector V. Sarno, Michael Mark, Demetrius Alexis, Harry Lamont (Workmen)
Dorothy Ates, Irene Colman, Linda Brent (Women in café)
Zeffie Tilbury (Princess Morodin)
Mildred Shay (Jenette Sibirsky)
Alma Kruger (Mrs. Danchenoff)
Harry Worth (Karagin's aide)
Opera sequence:
    Sigurd Nilssen (Sultan)
    Irra Petina (Nadine)
    Douglas Beattie (Markov)
    David Laughlin (Prince Igor)
Tiny [Paul] Newland (Policeman)
Frank Puglia (Orchestra conductor / Ivan, the café proprietor)

Balalaika

Maurice Cass (Prompter)
Alexis Davidoff (Man)
Eddie Hart, Edward Payson, Art Miles (Sailors)
Paul Irving (Prince Morodin)
Russian Cossack Choir

Cut from Release Print:
Albert d'Arno (Austrian aviator)
Harold Hoff (Austrian observer)
George Meeker (Sugar daddy)
Judith Allen (Blonde)
Rafael Storm (The Argentinean)

Oscar nomination for Best Sound Recording:
   Douglas Shearer

There is no rarer blossom than a British operetta successfully transplanted to American soil. With the exception of the Gilbert and Sullivan works of the 1880s, they could be counted on one hand: Edward German's *Tom Jones*; *Florodora* and *The Geisha*, both by Sidney Jones; and *The Quaker Girl* by Monckton; all making the journey before World War I.

Noël Coward's 1929 *Bitter Sweet*, a borderline operetta, was the last to cross the Atlantic. America had begun breeding its own unique hybrid, the combination of operetta, revue, minstrel show, vaudeville, and jazz that would become the American musical.

The British still clung to their beloved operetta, and the 1930s saw long successful West End runs of confections by Ivor Novello and Walter Leigh that would have emptied a Broadway theatre. In shows like *Glamorous Night*, *Pride of the Regiment*, and *Careless Rapture*, princes loved ravishing commoners in mythical European kingdoms surrounded by gypsies, secret love children, enormous choruses, and exotic stage effects (such as sinking an ocean liner on the stage of the Drury Lane every night).

A rather conservative example of this was *Balalaika*, a 1936 success in London that went straight to Hollywood without stopping in New York. The operetta was shorn of all but its title song (but unfortunately not of its plot) to make a vehicle for Eddy and Ilona Massey.

Miss Massey was one of Louis B. Mayer's European finds. On that same 1937 tour, he signed actresses Greer Garson and Hedy Lamarr and directors Victor Saville (who produced *Bitter Sweet*, *The Chocolate Soldier*, and *Smilin' Through*), Julien Duvivier (*The Great Waltz*), and Reinhold Schunzel (*Balalaika*), among others.

MGM publicity maintained that Hungarian-born Ilona Hajmassy had gotten her first break when a noted singer, Maria Nemeth, became ill and Ilona substituted. Her performance brought her to the attention of the head of the Vienna Staatsoper. In Hollywood her name, which means "garlic," was shortened to "Massey," and she was featured in *Rosalie*. Despite her superb reviews, it was two years before film audiences got another look at her. It was a charming look, although the studio might better have emphasized her Dietrich-like sexiness than her smoky but occasionally drifting soprano. She was also done a disservice by the photographer. In an apparent attempt to emphasize her blonde beauty, he so overlit her close-ups that most emotions as well as imperfections were washed from her face.

Balalaika reflected the new interest of Hollywood in non-czarist Russia, already our potential ally against the rising threat of Nazi Germany. Films like *Tovarich* (1937), *Ninotchka* (1939)—both dealing with Czarist expatriates meeting party members in Paris—and *Comrade X* (1940) showed our somewhat schizophrenic attitude toward pre- and post-revolutionary life in that exotic country. Czarist and Communist were lauded, ridiculed, and ultimately made to blend in a tidy Hollywood ending. *Balalaika*, as a musical, refrains from commenting on the struggle between the nobility and the revolutionaries despite making it the center of the action. And, although the irony and nostalgia of royal expatriates working as waiters and tailors is beautifully handled, the conflict of the drama is never realized. We do not thrill when the heroine wanders back into the hero's arms, just wonder why it took so long.

This is not to say that *Balalaika* is dull. It is richly mounted, excitingly photographed, and full of tender and funny moments. Eddy is in especially good voice and delivers some outstanding numbers. But the departures from the stage plot don't seem to add anything to the story. The action jumps from St. Petersburg to the wartime trenches to postwar Paris with no sense of dramatic thrust. No musical piece binds the separated lovers together or helps them to find each other. The crucial bit of hokum necessary to a successful operetta is missing.

The stage *Balalaika* made the two fathers protagonists, their children innocent victims of the passions of the time. This dramatic confrontation between the two opposing old men, the old order and new, is missing from the film. The stage Lydia was a ballerina, her "Count" Peter a bodyguard to the Czar. When her father tosses a bomb at the Czar, Peter saves his life. The "Stille Nacht" sequence ends Act II. In the film, we must assume that the heroine's father is executed, but in the play he becomes the Russian ambassador to France after the war, and his daughter is quite well off.

The play opens in 1924 in Paris, and then does a flashback to Russia before the revolution. The film, however, begins in 1914 in a village near St. Petersburg. The peaceful scene is disrupted by Cossacks, who gallop through the town, doing acrobatics on their charging horses while pretty girls thrill as their irate husbands and fathers drag them indoors. The leader of the two hundred or so uniformed men is Prince Peter Karagin (Nelson), looking splendid in his Cossack uniform and leading his men in the spirited "Ride, Cossack, Ride." Unlike the rear-projection Mounties that Eddy had to lead in *Rose Marie*, these are flesh and blood men who actually appear to be singing with him. The exciting camera work on the sequence gets the film off to a fast start.

Their destination is the Café Balalaika in the heart of gay St. Petersburg, a nitery that makes Maxim's look shabby. The Cossacks are soon getting their fill of wine and obliging women. Only one thing is missing, and that is provided by a new songstress, Lydia Pavlovna Marakova (Ilona Massey). Her dark, brooding brother, Dimitri (Dalies Frantz), is a pianist in the café orchestra, and her father, Professor Marakov (Lionel Atwill), is the conductor. Dimitri is disgusted that they must perform for these drunken saber rattlers, but the Professor points out that they must eat. There are no other jobs.

Lydia, in a black sequined gown split to the thigh, delivers a high-powered number, "Tanya," with most of the Cossacks joining in.

A Dutch poster. Note the prominence given European star Massey. *Courtesy Anna Michalik.*

Balalaika

A sultry café singer, Lydia Marakova (Ilona Massey), earns her living entertaining the nobility. *Courtesy Anna Michalik.*

Prince Peter watches from an upstairs dining room. He is fascinated and sends his orderly, Nicki Popoff (Charlie Ruggles), to summon the lady to the officers' private party.

Unfortunately, Nicki has been too busy with two Balalaika belles to notice what Lydia looks like. He goes to her dressing room and mistakes the maid, Masha (Joyce Compton), for the mistress. She disillusions him, giggling at his flowery compliments. He pleads for a date. Can he dance? she asks. He points proudly to the medals on his chest. "Only one is for bravery. The rest are for dancing."

Masha delivers the Cossacks' invitation, but Lydia has no intention of putting herself at their mercies. The café owner (Charles Judels) orders her to go. She refuses. Very well, he says. She and her family think they are too good to perform in a café? Well, they can all get out. Lydia quickly relents.

In a modest gown, she enters the crowded room and finds herself clutched and pawed by the revelers. The officers insist that she choose a "favored one" by drinking from one of their glasses. They close in, eagerly thrusting their glasses at her until there is no escape. Suddenly she sees a single glass on the table. The owner of that glass will be her favorite she says, pushing out of the circle. It belongs to the absent Prince Karagin, and the men fall back.

Lydia sings "At the Balalaika," a haunting tango, and tells them that her father was a Cossack too. He died fighting. Where did he fall? they ask. "In the streets of Kiev, battling against factory workers...a glorious death!" Peter has entered just in time to catch this bit of sarcasm.

One dashing officer, Sibirsky (Walter Woolf King, star of early film musicals and the singing villain of *A Night at the Opera*), decides to claim her for himself. She has an inspiration and turns on him in horror. Has he forgotten what he did to her sister? How the poor girl died of a broken heart? She rushes out the door, sobbing bitterly. Peter grins broadly at her successful deception.

He questions the café owner about her and learns that her father is a live conductor, not a dead Cossack. She is a talented performer, the owner concedes, but unfortunately she is an intellectual. She can actually read and write. She puts on airs, ignoring the officers and befriending the scruffy students who hang about the café.

Peter decides his uniform might be a hindrance in pursuit of the lady. He offers one of the students fifty rubles to change clothes with him and follows Lydia to a modest restaurant, where he sits beside her and tries to strike up a conversation. He is a poor voice student, "Peter Fedorovitch Taranda," just arrived in the city, he tells her. Reluctantly she smiles at his flamboyant attentions. He tells her his dear aunt has sent him some money for his birthday, and for one hour he is a millionaire. Lydia must join him in caviar and champagne.

The skeptical counterman (George Tobias) brings his order and demands payment. Unfortunately, Peter has left his money in his

Prince Peter Karagin of the Imperial Cossack Guard (Nelson) thinks that Lydia (Ilona) is spending too much time with suspected revolutionaries. He poses as a poor singing student to check her out. (George Tobias, left.) *Courtesy Anna Michalik.*

uniform. Lydia coldly pays the check and heads for the door. He must be careful when he picks his next victim, she tells him. That girl might need a new coat more than champagne. Peter wants to know where he can find her to pay her back. "I can't afford to meet you again," she says stonily and slams the door. "What a woman!" he cries.

At the Karagin house, Nicki the orderly is on the phone ordering roses for the many ladies who have been pining for Prince Peter while he was away on maneuvers. Nicki adds a bouquet of his own to the order: "From Masha's Nicki to Nicki's Masha." He reminds the florist of his usual kickback. Peter overhears and orders Nicki confined to barracks for thirty days—"and thirty nights!"

Peter's father, old General Karagin (C. Aubrey Smith), welcomes his son home. He wonders if Peter's men have been acting unusual in any way. One of them has been caught with revolutionary pamphlets. The General holds one out: "Rise against Karagin, the butcher." They must find out who is printing them. Dissolve from pamphlet to a shabby sign: "Professor Marakov, Vocal and Instrumental Lessons, Terms Moderate." Inside, Lydia's brother, Dimitri, plays Chopin on one grand piano while the Professor and Leo (Abner Biberman) operate a hand printing press hidden inside a second piano. The room is full of shabby, somber men. The maid Masha (for even revolutionaries must have maids, it seems) sweeps in with tea, and the piano lid drops into place, hiding the press. Just in time, for Nicki follows Masha, carrying a tray of biscuits. The Professor wants to know why she has a uniformed Cossack in the kitchen and she explains that he is her cousin. "Another cousin?" asks Lydia smiling. "Since last night I'm the only cousin," Nicki replies happily.

The Professor tells Nicki that they all love soldiers and want to help them. The only help Nicki can imagine is enough rubles to open a restaurant. That isn't quite what the revolutionaries had in mind, and they lecture him on freedom and brotherhood.

Outside, Peter asks directions of a passing constable (Paul Newland). There are no numbers on the houses. The officer explains that the new numbers are on brass plates.

Lydia's musician father and brother (Lionel Atwill, second from left, and Dalies Frantz, right) are indeed revolutionaries. They insist Peter sing for them to prove he is a music student. "The Volga Boatman" allays their fears. (At rear, John Holland, Abner Biberman.)

Balalaika

"That's progress. The janitors sell the brass plates for vodka. That's Russia."

Lydia opens the door to Peter. He tells her it is his duty to call the police. High treason is being committed in her apartment. Her face grows pale. "Against Beethoven," he continues happily, indicating the hastily organized rehearsal in the next room. He returns half of her money and asks to pay the rest in daily installments. "Mail it," she snaps and tries to ease him out the door. Professor Marakov stops her and boldly invites Peter to join them. They will soon be able to tell if he is a music student or a member of the secret police. The unsuspecting Peter sits down at the piano housing the printing press and picks up some sheet music into which they have stuffed revolutionary pamphlets. Lydia quickly pulls him to the middle of the room, and the men close around him. He must audition.

"What will you sing?" demands the Professor. Without accompaniment Peter begins "The Volga Boatman" in Russian. Slowly the men in the room join in, embellishing the chant with voice and instrument into a driving rhythm. Then, one by one, they drop out until Peter is singing alone, still facing Lydia in the center of the room.

Everyone relaxes. He is obviously one of them. Masha enters with more tea, and Peter turns to find his orderly, Nicki, passing out biscuits. Their mutual double take is so obvious that Peter hastily explains that Nicki is from his hometown. They were boys together. Nicki stutters his agreement, then warms to the task. He elaborates on their boyhood pranks and Peter's many romances. Peter grimly promises that they will get together later for a good long talk.

Lydia tells Peter she loves his voice. He ought to sing at the opera. No, he replies, she is the one who should be in the opera. The Professor explains that Lydia doesn't have a chance. Only girls who have the favor of a count or prince are hired.

Opera Director Danchenoff (Frank Morgan) has a good reason not to employ the Prince's current sweetie, but Peter has a persuasive argument. (Left, Erno Verebes.) *Courtesy Anna Michalik.*

Dissolve to the Imperial Opera House where a harried, elaborately mustachioed little man named Danchenoff (Frank Morgan) is on the phone. It is absolutely impossible! They cannot hire another singer! They have sixty too many already, all feminine and all protégées of prominent men. "Make it sixty-one," orders Prince Peter.

Still posing as a student, Peter drags Lydia bodily into Danchenoff's office and demands an audition. Danchenoff decides to let the supposed nightingale humiliate herself publicly. He leads her to the center of the opera stage, where a rehearsal is in progress. "Play something from *Carmen* and make it fast," he instructs the orchestra. In the kind of scene that reduces opera devotees to tears, the conductor instructs his men to play "the second act from the beginning." There follows a quick set of highlights from Acts II and IV, sung very well by Eddy and Miss Massey.

Lydia is hired. To celebrate, Peter makes reservations for a private room at his favorite country inn. He and Lydia drive there in a troika, through exquisitely-photographed sunlit woods, reminiscent of the "Vienna Woods"

An impromptu audition at the Imperial Opera House includes a synopsis of *Carmen*. *Courtesy Anna Michalik.*

sequence in *The Great Waltz*, also photographed by Joseph Ruttenberg.

Lydia asks to stop at a roadside church. There she sits beside her mother's grave and tells her that their dream has come true. She will sing at the opera, and it is Peter who has made it all possible.

Overhearing, Peter regrets his plans for their evening and tries to take her back to St. Petersburg. Her curiosity is aroused, and she insists they go on to the inn. Peter tries to get them a table on the terrace, but the proprietor (Frank Puglia) assures him their private room is ready. Over Peter's protests, Lydia sweeps up the stairs.

Everything is perfect, she tells him, surveying the flowers, the food, and the enormous cushioned couch. Peter must be a very rich student. It is certainly the equal of any other private dining room she has been taken to. Peter's mortification changes to pained anger. He didn't know he had to equal his predecessors. If she has had so much experience, then his efforts haven't been wasted after all. He grabs her and kisses her arrogantly. "How did that measure up?"

She struggles to leave. "All the others let me go," she explains, "as soon as I made it clear I didn't appreciate private dining rooms." Peter apologizes, and so does Lydia. (A few bars of

"Magic of Your Love" are heard teasingly in the background. The song's use as the finale love theme would have been much more effective if the lovers had enjoyed a reconciliation waltz and sung its lilting strains at this point.)

Lydia tells Peter she was more hurt than angry. She knew he loved her when she saw the room and realized he had changed his mind and tried to take her back to St. Petersburg. Their kiss dissolves to a "bridal bouquet" of lilies-of-the-valley.

Lydia is arranging the vase of flowers sent by Peter. She wears a bolero with padded shoulders, a popular 1939 fashion. In fact, costumer Adrian's only concession to the 1914 setting was to lengthen the skirts of the otherwise very 1939 styles.

One of the revolutionaries, Leo, bursts in drunk and tells the Professor that his son, Dimitri, is making a speech to the factory workers in the square. Father and daughter rush to the square to stop Dmitri just as the Cossacks arrive with the same idea. From a doorway, Lydia sees Peter leading them. In a beautifully edited sequence, the crowd scatters frantically, falling under the hooves of the charging horses.

Dimitri knocks a soldier from his horse with a well-aimed rock. Another Cossack turns his horse and runs Lydia's brother down, sword swinging. Dimitri crumbles to the cobblestones.

In her horror at the death of her brother, Lydia agrees to lure both Peter and his father, General Karagin, to the opera to hear her sing. There they will be assassinated. Peter comes to tell her how sorry he is about her brother. He has further news. He has submitted his resignation from the army so they can be married. She is torn between grief and happiness. She cannot tell him why, but he must not come to hear her debut at the opera. His father too must be kept away. She pretends she would be too nervous and Peter promises.

The opera is an Arabian Nights tale contrived from Rimsky-Korsakov's *Scheherazade*. Miss Massey's jeweled gown with midriff cutouts is in Adrian's most exotic Mata Hari vein.

To Lydia's dismay, the General appears in his box. He has come despite his son's objections. Unexpectedly, Peter appears beside him with a dispatch. Leo and the Professor are waiting in the balcony. Slowly the Professor raises the pistol concealed by his program. Suddenly the General raps for silence. Germany has declared war on Mother Russia, he tells the stunned audience. There is a pause, then the orchestra strikes up the national anthem. Professor Marakov lowers his gun. Russia will need soldiers now more than she needs revolutionaries. This infuriates Leo, who seizes the gun and fires madly at the box. The General falls and, in one of the many beautiful crowd scenes in the film, the audience flees in terror.

Peter finds Lydia trembling in her dressing room. There is nothing to be afraid of, he says, putting his arms around her. His father will recover and the assassins will be caught. When he returns from the war, they can be married. They are interrupted by soldiers. The gunmen

A romantic day in the country. Lydia stops to pray at her mother's grave, telling of her success and her love for Peter. Then Peter's cossacks kill her brother. *Courtesy Anna Michalik.*

Knowing that Peter's father (C. Aubrey Smith) is to be assassinated, Lydia begs Peter not to attend her debut at the Imperial Opera. But Peter is adamant. (Left: Harry Worth.)

have been arrested. One of them is Lydia's father. Peter is to arrest her at once. He is stunned and refuses to believe she is part of the plot, but she proudly declares her guilt. She believes as they do. "Including murder?" asks Peter. For an answer she wraps a cape over her costume and marches toward the door.

Dissolve to snow falling softly on the trenches. In a singularly clumsy bit of exposition, Nicki informs us that Lydia has gotten out of prison and is roaming the countryside "from café to café." He and Sibirsky decide not to tell the Prince.

The officers gather in an earthen dugout for an improvised Christmas dinner and reminisce about the old days. Sibirsky produces a balalaika and softly sings "At the Balalaika." Outside, Peter, in a dashing fur-collared coat and officer's cap, scolds a sentry who has complained his wife and children are going hungry. This is war, Peter says sharply. He enters the dugout and finds his fellow officers exulting over their only remaining bottle of vodka. Peter seizes it and takes it outside to the sentry. "Merry Christmas," he says and returns to the party. The sentry stares sullenly at the bottle, then smashes it, his face twisted with hatred.

The officers are protesting that Peter has taken their only bottle. "That's what makes it a Christmas gift," he tells them cheerfully. Their feast of borscht with "almost beef" is interrupted by distant voices. The Germans are saluting the Russian Christmas by singing "Stille Nacht" ("Silent Night"). The men stand in the softly falling snow and listen to the carol coming across the stretch of barbed wire and shell holes. Peter takes up the song, and the distant voices sing with him, a very nice scene indeed.

Biplanes fly over, and everyone dives for cover. They are Russian planes, dropping leaflets telling the soldiers to go home and join the revolution. When orders come to attack, many of the men won't move. Lt. Nikitin (Roland Varno) pulls a gun to make his troops go. He falls in a burst of gunfire that may be from the enemy—or his own men. A soundstage battle follows with lots of explosions, smoke, and falling bodies.

Dissolve to a smoky café where Lydia is entertaining in a gypsy costume, singing "Otchi Chornia." Someone bursts in to announce the end of the war. The men are shooting their officers, he shouts happily. A close-up of Lydia's horrified face dissolves to the Eiffel Tower in the rain.

A very American couple in evening clothes (Andrew Tombes and Florence Shirley) is discovered arguing about where to go next. A cab pulls up, and its driver, our old friend Captain Sibirsky, suggests the Café Balalaika. Its doorman turns out to be Danchenoff of the opera. The venerable old General Karagin is the one-armed wine steward, a greying Peter is the strolling singer who accepts tips from the customers, and the owner is none other than the lowly orderly, Nicki Popoff. Tonight is Russian New Year, and Nicki's wife, Masha, is happily totaling the receipts. Nicki is pleased, but somehow it isn't as he always imagined it. He always expected to serve the nobility, but now they are serving for him. Prince Peter, in full uniform, is singing "At the Balalaika" for the patrons, including the insulting Americans. At the request of some Russians, he sings wistfully of their past glories.

At 11:30, the club closes for a private Russian New Year party. The battered nobility gather in full court dress, discussing their tailor shops and flower stands. (Eddy smokes his only screen cigarette in this scene.) Everyone grows nostalgic, reminiscing about the old days, and Danchenoff, the former opera impresario, sings wistfully of their past glories.

A face appears at the rain-spattered kitchen window. Masha turns to find Lydia, dressed in a shabby trench coat and felt hat. Their tearful reunion is interrupted by the General. Lydia and Masha stand fearfully before him until he goes to Lydia and kisses her. Peter's voice comes from the next room in a happy drinking song.

In a touching scene in the trenches, the opposing German and Russian troops sing carols to each other on Christmas day. (Roland Varno, left.) *Courtesy Anna Michalik.*

After the Revolution, Peter and his refugee father work in a Paris café run by Peter's former orderly. (Ilona Massey, left, is wearing Jeanette's *Czaritza* gown. See page 263.)

The General tells Lydia there has been no joy in Peter's heart.

A traditional game begins before the restaurant mirrors. The players hold candles in each hand and chant a rhyme, asking the mirror to disclose their true love. When it is Peter's turn, Lydia appears behind him. (She is wearing Jeanette's *Czaritza* dress from *Maytime* with new sleeves.) "The Magic of Your Love" waltz booms excitedly, and Peter takes Lydia in his arms for a chorus and a kiss.

Reviews

Generally reviewers dismissed the plot, but praised Ilona Massey. "Miss Massey is a dream to see and hear," said William Boehnel in the *New York World-Telegram*. He added that "Eddy is first rate. [The film] says something nice about the workers and it also says something nice about the Holy Russians. That it says nothing of any consequence on behalf of either or both, may, perhaps, be excused on the ground that it is an operetta, and no one expects much from an operetta."

Variety called it "a sumptuously produced operetta in the opulent Metro-Goldwyn-Mayer tradition. With Nelson Eddy and a new personality looker topping the cast, it has enough marquee value...to carry it nicely for strong business. Miss Massey, the Magyar import, is as heady as tokay for the b.o. Eddy is hemannish and dashing, well suited to his rôle."

Frank S. Nugent said in the *New York Times* that, "In these propaganda-searching days, we know the comrades are going to howl bloody Metro-Goldwyn-Mayer. The picture is long on formula and short on originality. Listening to Mr. Eddy's baritone enriching 'Song of the Volga Boatman' and 'Holy Night, Silent Night' [sic] is our idea of killing time so pleasantly that it dies with a smile on its face."

The *New York Post* reported: "Consider and then reserve a niche in your dreams for the blonde Hungarian, Miss Massey."

Recordings (See Discography for further information)

Eddy recorded four of the songs on two ten-inch 78 RPM records in 1939:
"At the Balalaika"
"The Magic of Your Love"
"Ride, Cossack, Ride"
"Song of the Volga Boatman"

"Silent Night" (backed by "Adeste Fideles") and "Chanson du Toreador" (backed by "Vision fugitive") were recorded in 1940.

Music in the Film

In listing performers after each title, "and" denotes a genuine duet, while commas between names indicate a sequence of singers. Some or all of the "male chorus" listings are the Russian Cossack Choir, conducted by Anatol Frikin.

Overture: "At the Balalaika" verse, "Tanya," "At the Balalaika" (chorus) INTO:
Russian religious chant copyrighted as "After Service" (chorus) - arranged by Herbert Stothart, INTO:

Nelson sings "At the Balalaika." MGM was one of the chief consumers of American and European stage productions. They insisted on a clause permitting them to interpolate other songs, which occasionally caused vigorous opposition from the original composer and resulted in films that contained *none* of the music of their stage ancestors. Courtesy Anna Michalik.

"A Life for the Czar" fragment (male chorus) - Mikhail Glinka, *A Life for the Czar*, Act III, INTO:
"Ride, Cossack, Ride" (male chorus, Eddy, Walter Woolf King, male soloists, whistling by Sergei Protzenko) - music by Herbert Stothart, lyrics by Bob Wright and Chet Forrest, INTO:
"A Life for the Czar" reprise (Eddy and male chorus)
"Tanya" (Massey, male chorus) - music by Herbert Stothart, lyrics by Bob Wright and Chet Forrest

Balalaika

"Gorko" (male chorus, Massey) - Russian drinking song adapted by Stothart

"At the Balalaika" (Massey, male chorus) from the original London production - music by George Posford, lyrics by Eric Maschwitz, with new lyrics by Wright and Forrest

Chopin's Polonaise in A Flat, Opus 53 (Dalies Frantz at the piano)

"El Ukhnem" ["Song of the Volga Boatman"] (Eddy, male chorus) - traditional, arranged by Feodor Chaliapin and Feodor Feodorovich Koenemann

"Chanson Bohème" from *Carmen*, Act II (Massey) - music by Georges Bizet, libretto by Henri Meilhac and Ludovic Halevy

"Chanson du Toreador" ["The Toreador Song"] from *Carmen*, Act II (Eddy) - music as above

"Si Tu M'Aime" from *Carmen*, Act IV (Eddy and Massey) - music as above

"Tanya" (a very exciting orchestral reprise)

"Scheherazade" (Massey, Sigurd Nilssen, Irra Petina, Douglas Beattie, David Laughlin) - by Nickolas Rimsky-Korsakov, arranged as an opera by Bob Wright and Chet Forrest. Miss Massey's solo copyrighted as "Shadows on the Sand."

"God Save the Czar" ["Boze Carja Chrani," Russian National Anthem] (chorus, Eddy, C. Aubrey Smith, and Massey) - music by Alexei Fedorovich Lvov, lyrics by Vasili Andreevitch Zhukovsky

"At the Balalaika" reprise (King)

"Stille Nacht" ["Silent Night"] (Eddy and male chorus) - music by Franz Gruber, lyrics by Joseph Mohr

"Otchi Chornia" ["Dark Eyes"] (Massey) - traditional Russian gypsy cabaret song

"At the Balalaika" reprise (Eddy)

"Flow, Flow, White Wine" [lyric: "Bubbles in the Wine"] (King, Frank Morgan) - arranged by Stothart, lyrics by Kahn

"Wishing Episode" [lyric: "Mirror, Mirror"] (Alma Kruger, Mildred Shay, Eddy) - arranged by Stothart, lyrics by Wright and Forrest

"Magic of Your Love" (chorus, Eddy and Massey) - music by Franz Lehár, new lyrics by Gus Kahn and Clifford Grey. The song was originally "The Melody of Love" from Lehár's *Gypsy Love*. With new lyrics it was sung as "The White Dove" in MGM's 1930 musical *The Rogue Song* with Lawrence Tibbett.

Finale: "Song of the Volga Boatman" (orchestral)

The only song definitely used from the London production was "At the Balalaika." In addition, a number of songs were copyrighted for the film but apparently not used:

"My Heart Is a Gypsy" - Bronislau Kaper and Gus Kahn

"You and I" - Stothart, Wright, and Forrest

"How Many Miles to Go" - M. Glinka, Stothart, and Kahn

"Lovelight in Your Eyes" - Franz Lehár theme with lyrics by Gus Kahn

"Soldier of the Czar" - Romberg, Kahn (This does not appear to be "A Life for the Czar")

"Your Heart and My Heart" - words and music by Gus Kahn

"In a Heart as Brave as Your Own" - Tchaikovsky theme arranged by Romberg, words by Gus Kahn

Script History
Contributed by Mary Truesdell

Unfortunately, there are precious few production notes for *Balalaika* at the Fairbanks Center for Motion Picture Study in Los Angeles. The script for the original London operetta begins with the Imperial Cossacks doing a naked bathing scene by a river after their battles and before their leave. Their dialogue indicates they are far from honorable about women. The stage hero, Peter, is definitely a playboy.

The files do contain many rewrites of the troika and inn scenes, indicating that the writers were struggling to portray the encounter between Peter and Lydia as romantic and with a degree of integrity, rather than a one-night stand. Peter's character must be adapted to show that "true love changes man to faithful lover." His film dialogue should be "bantering, but an underlying seriousness and softness... charming eroticism, not glittering glinting."

Fanny Brice was the original choice for Masha!

Movie Goofs

As Lydia's father opens the door to his vestibule, he tucks his violin under his right arm and reaches for the doorknob with his left hand. When the door opens a split second later, he has the violin dangling in his left hand. (Joan Woolley)

New Moon

MGM.
Released June 28, 1940.
Produced and directed by Robert Z. Leonard.
Uncredited direction by W.S. Van Dyke II
104 minutes.

Prerelease title: *Lover, Come Back*
Swedish title: *Nymånen* (New Moon)
French title: *L'Isle des Amours* (Island of Love)
Spanish title: *Luna Llena* (Full Moon)
Portuguese title: *Lua Nova* (New Moon)

Based on the stage operetta with music by Sigmund Romberg, book and lyrics by Oscar Hammerstein II, Frank Mandel, and Laurence Schwab. Screenplay: Jacques Deval, Robert Arthur. Cameramen: William Daniels, Oliver Marsh. Music Director: Herbert Stothart. Editor: Harold F. Kress. Recording Director: Douglas Shearer. Art Director: Cedric Gibbons. Art Assoc. Eddie Imazu. Set Decoration: Edwin B. Willis. Gowns: Adrian. Men's Costumes: Gile Steele. Makeup: Jack Dawn. Dances: Val Raset. Assistant Directors: Marvin Stuart, Hugh Boswell. Boat scenes photography: Clyde de Vinna.

Swedish poster for *New Moon. Courtesy Anna Michalik.*

The stage version of *New Moon*, called *The New Moon*, opened in Philadelphia on December 22, 1927, and was closed for revamping. It reached Broadway on September 19, 1928, where it reigned at the Imperial Theatre for 509 performances. It starred Evelyn Herbert and Robert Halliday.

MGM's 1930 musical film *New Moon* starred Grace Moore and Lawrence Tibbett, and was directed by Jack Conway (*Let Freedom Ring*). It abandoned the stage plot entirely for a Russian setting in which a haughty aristocrat (Moore) must choose between a rich lover (Adolphe Menjou) and a dashing Russian officer (Tibbett). Since Menjou doesn't sing, her decision is easy. The 1919 Select silent, *The New Moon*, which starred Norma Talmadge, was also a Russian story, but totally unrelated to the operetta.

Jeanette MacDonald (Marianne de Beaumanoir)
Nelson Eddy (Charles Mission, Duc de Vidiers) *
Mary Boland (Valerie de Rossac)

New Moon

George Zucco (Vicomte de Ribaud)
H.B. Warner (Father Michel)
Richard [Dick] Purcell (Alexander)
Stanley Fields (Tambour)
Bunty Cutler (Julie, the maid)
Grant Mitchell (Governor of New Orleans)
Ray Walker (Coco)
John Miljan (Pierre Brugnon)
Ivan Simpson (Guizot)
George Irving (Ship Captain)
Edwin Maxwell (Captain de Jean)
Paul E. Burns (Guard on ship)
Trevor Bardette (Foulette)
LeRoy Mason (Grant)
William Tannen (Pierre)
Cecil Cunningham (Governor's wife)
Claude King (Dubois)

Rafael Storm (de Piron)
Winifred Harris (Lady)
Buster Keaton ("Lulu"- cut from print)
Robert Warwick (Commissar)
Sarah Edwards (Marquise della Rosa)
George Lloyd (Quartermaster)
Gayne Whitman (Mate)
Jean Fenwick (Woman)
George Magrill (Guard)
Christian J. Frank, Arthur Belasco, Edward Hearn, Nick Copeland, Gino Corrado, Fred Graham (Bondsmen)
Frank Remsden (Man)
Ed O'Neill (Lookout)
Warren Rock [Jeanette's real-life brother-in-law] (Mate)
Jewell Jordan (Woman)
Joe Yule [Mickey Rooney's father] (Maurice)
Max Marx (Officer)
[Stephen] Alden Chase (Citizen)
Jack Perrin (Officer)
Claire Rochelle (Drunken girl)
Frank Elliott, Kenneth Gibson, Victor Kendall, Gerald Fielding, Bea Nigro, Hillary Brooke (Guests)
Dorothy Granger (Fat bridesmaid)
June Gittelson (Madeline)
David Alison (Troubadour)
Ralph Dunn, Harry Strang, Ray Teal, Ted Oliver (Bondsmen)
Joe Dominguez (Wounded bondsman)
Florence Shirley (Guest)
Forbes Murray (Commandant)
Abe Dinovitch, Sally Mueller, Austin Grant ("Stout Hearted Men" soloists)
Nat Pendleton (Bondsman, Lulu's pal)
The Jericho Choir with Eddie Jones, Ben Carter, Lois Hodnett, Billy Mitchell (Negro spiritual singers)

* The stage hero is named *Robert* Mission.

Spanish poster. The title means full moon rather than new moon. *Courtesy Anna Michalik.*

For those who delight in *Naughty Marietta*, *New Moon* presents a problem. So many plot turns, scenes, even lines are identical that the mind boggles. Is it an attempt to invoke nostalgia for an already-distant moment of glory? Or a hack attempt to cash in on a former

Jeanette's mother, Anna MacDonald, visits the set of *New Moon*.

success? Or an intended parody? Or just an accident? We never find out.

Again we have the shipload of Casquette girls captured by pirates. Again, a leering pirate leader comes down the stairs into the hold to survey the cowering maidens. Again the matriarch of the group cries out in quivering outrage that they are not to lay one finger on the girls. Again we are in Louisiana amidst powdered wigs, panniers, and shoe buckles. Again Jeanette is a lady of rank with an unfinished song and a maid named Julie. Again we have a pompous governor, nobility incognito, a grand ball, and a curving staircase begging for a song.

A second problem in seeing the film today is that it thrusts naggingly into our social consciousness with its casual acceptance and treatment of the black slaves while vigorously denouncing the servitude of the white bond servants. And it is nearly impossible, without a wrench of the heart, to see Buster Keaton, only ten years earlier regarded as one of the world's greatest comedians, in a walk-on rôle.

Assuming that we can put these factors aside, *New Moon* is a pleasant film, heavily laden with "production value" and rich in well-known songs. Robert Z. Leonard again directs with his artful eye for getting the most out of each scene and his overall lack of structure and pacing. Having discovered that Jeanette shared with Carole Lombard the delightful ability to mug outrageously while being utterly feminine, he makes heavy use of her talent in every single scene. Thus, her emoting as the haughty Marianne de Beaumanoir offers no contrast to her later indignation when she finds herself reduced to taking orders and milking goats with the rest of the Casquette girls. MacDonald mannerisms are allowed to occur so frequently that they lose their effect.

Eddy, too, is not quite as we want to remember him. He hated the constant nagging by the studio about his weight. He was after all, a baritone and not a bathing beauty. In the days before the vogue for slender opera singers, Eddy was a sylph among singers. Nearly every prominent singer, male and female, outdid him for girth and tonnage and he couldn't understand the studio's preoccupation with starving him. Thus, in *New Moon*, he is perhaps

Nelson was a talented artist. Here he sculpts a bust of director "Woody" Van Dyke between takes on the set of *New Moon*.

In *Naughty Marietta*, Jeanette had a total of five costumes, two quite humble. For *New Moon*, designer Adrian outdid himself with lavish gowns. *Courtesy Anna Michalik.*

just a trifle heavy for his dashing revolutionary rôle. However, he leads his men with rousing fervor, and his rugged character freed him of the still traditional juvenile makeup with lipstick that continued to afflict even actors like Humphrey Bogart into the forties. (Eddy had frequently suffered at the hands of the makeup people, especially in *The Girl of the Golden West*.)

New Moon had been bought by MGM in the first days of sound after its 1928 Broadway success as *The New Moon*, referring to the name of a ship. Eighteen years had separated the stage versions of *Naughty Marietta* and *The New Moon*, so audiences didn't notice the similarities. The 1930 *New Moon* became a film vehicle for Grace Moore and Lawrence Tibbett. The Moore-Tibbett story concerned a dashing Russian officer and a haughty aristocrat who sings "Lover, Come Back to Me" from the battlements of an isolated fort as her man rides out to fight the Cossacks. The 1940 *New Moon* returns to the stage plot, more or less, eliminating the characters of Marianne's father and fiancé. Alexander, the comic servant of Marianne and partner of soubrette Julie, becomes a non-singing sidekick of the hero.

In the ship's surprisingly spacious salon, Marianne de Beaumanoir (Jeanette) is dazzling an audience with the latest Parisian song. *Courtesy Anna Michalik.*

Below decks on a ship bound for New Orleans, Charles Mission (Nelson) is caged with other prisoners, all destined to be sold as bond servants in the New World. *Courtesy Anna Michalik.*

Appearing only five years after *Naughty Marietta* and with the same stars, *New Moon* couldn't help calling attention to the similar plots. To be perfectly fair, the bride-ship device used in the film *Naughty Marietta* was not in the stage version and had been "borrowed" from the stage *The New Moon* originally. Still, we might wish for a fresh way to get all the men and maidens together on the island.

Behind the credits, we see the silhouette of an eighteenth-century ship slowly crossing a moonlit tropical ocean. Our opening scene takes place on board the luxurious vessel, the *Joie des Anges*. A dance is in progress, and the celebrants could not be dressed more grandly if they were at Versailles. Indeed, they are fresh from Paris and on their way to New Orleans.

The toast of the evening is Marianne de Beaumanoir (Jeanette), who has quite dazzled the handsome Monsieur Dubois (Claude King). Marianne's garrulous old aunt, Mme de Rossac (Mary Boland), gloatingly informs a cluster of gossiping biddies that Dubois can mean nothing to Marianne. Why, it is barely a month since "we" refused an offer of marriage from a prince. And Marianne has sung for the queen!

As the dance music dies, an ugly sound is heard in the distance. Only the cattle in the hold, the Captain (George Irving) assures Marianne.

New Moon

If Mademoiselle will sing for them, her music would make them all deaf even to the roar of lions. She gaily sings the flirtatious "Stranger in Paris." As she launches into an encore of "The Way They Do It in Paris," she is slowly drowned out by the singing of the "cattle" in the hold.

They are bond servants being shipped to the colonies as penalty for various crimes, and their lyrics are as bitter as Mademoiselle's are innocent. The Captain sends several officers to silence the miscreants and their leader, an especially outspoken but not outsung villain named Charles Mission (Nelson).

Charles demands that the Captain fulfill his promise to the King and deliver live bondsmen to New Orleans, not skeletons for medical students. The prisoners need food and air. The officer tells Charles ominously that he can see the Captain in the morning and deliver the request in person.

The bondsmen are all elated—all except Charles's three friends, Pierre (William Tannen), Alexander (Dick Purcell), and Tambour (Stanley Fields). The Captain may recognize him, and, if Charles Mission is

When the "officer" turns up in her boudoir in servants' livery, Marianne is first amused, then scandalized by his romantic daring.

As Charles (Eddy) awaits punishment, Marianne (Jeanette) mistakes him for a ship's officer and delivers her complaint about the howling prisoners in the hold.

guillotined, the noble Duke Charles de Vidiers will also be headless. Charles is indeed the revolutionary Duke. He has escaped the King's police by getting himself arrested for drunkenly singing seditious ditties and deported under an assumed name. But he has not escaped death to spend his life as a bond servant, he tells them. A month behind them on the high seas is the ship New Moon, loaded to capacity with guns and provisions. His brother officer, Captain Mondieux, is leading the rescue. The plan must be kept quiet until the time is right.

The sea is a bit rough the next morning when Marianne makes her way to the Captain's quarters to register a complaint. There she finds a handsome young man in shirt sleeves, also waiting for the Captain. In his embarrassment at being so discovered by a lady, he grabs the only coat in sight, an officer's jacket hanging on a peg. Instantly the rough-looking Charles

Charles has been bought by Marianne's overseer. Her loquacious aunt (Mary Boland) instructs him in his duties. *Courtesy Anna Michalik.*

Mission takes on the appearance of an officer and a gentleman. Marianne certainly thinks so, for she does not object too strenuously when he is mildly flirtatious or the pitching ship throws her into his arms.

She has come to tell the Captain of her aunt's problem, but perhaps she can tell his officer instead. Her aunt has been kept awake by the howling of the men in the hold and would like something done—not anything *unpleasant* of course. Charles apologizes elaborately for her aunt's distress. The men were merely clamoring for food and air. In New Orleans, they will be sold like cattle. Perhaps her aunt will consider the years of starvation and whips facing these men as atonement for her sleepless night.

Marianne is horrified and withdraws her complaint. Charles kisses her hand "on behalf of those abandoned men," but he must decline her invitation to one of the ship's dances. His duties keep him busy day and night. She asks his name but he will tell her only his given names, Charles Henri, since "they are the only ones a woman remembers."

This brief meeting apparently makes a tremendous impression on Marianne. When the ship reaches New Orleans, she decides to give a ball for all the ship's officers at her plantation. The plantation itself is complete with white-pillared mansion and smiling slaves waving at the gate.

Marianne has just completed an extremely modest bath (compared to Miss MacDonald's Lubitsch days) and is discussing the subject of love with her servant, Julie (Bunty Cutler), when Charles walks into the room bearing flowers. The amused and romantically inclined Marianne decides that he has boldly disguised himself in servant's livery for the escapade. She sends for her overseer, Brugnon, to chide him for permitting the charade. Meanwhile Charles returns with Mademoiselle's breakfast tray.

Flowers are one thing, but Charles' continued presence in her bedroom borders on impropriety. She spars verbally with him as he serves her hot chocolate, getting his gloved fingers caught in the sugar tongs. When Brugnon (John Miljan) arrives, Marianne upbraids him for going along with the deception. Brugnon disillusions her. Charles was bought at auction yesterday. He has a receipt. Charles belongs to her for life.

Of course, Charles comes highly recommended. He was the personal valet of the Duke de Vidiers. Angry and embarrassed, Marianne sends Charles off to his duties. They include polishing the shoes of the household, which he does musically under the trees. As he sings of "shoes that do not choose to run" (a reference to the 1940 presidential election), he tosses each finished shoe up into the air. Magically they vanish. The camera tracks up to reveal a tiny black boy in the tree who is catching the shoes and hanging them on the branches to dry. Charles's sprightly song continues until he reaches one particular shoe, her shoe. From her window, Marianne hears his singing turn to romance as he sings "Softly, as in a Morning Sunrise."

Marianne summons him to the library and reproaches him, not only for his singing but for his irritating attitude as well. He is actually assuming the manners of a nobleman. "Many noblemen have learned their good manners from their servants," he tells her. "That is a revolutionary remark!" she replies. "Many a truth is, Mademoiselle," he says.

She tells Charles that things are quite different from Paris here in the Colonies. The one who commands is merely a matter of circumstance, but someone must command. Charles eloquently and truthfully replies that even a Duke would be proud to serve her. Marianne sends Charles off to assist her Major Domo, Guizot, with the arrangements for the ball. Charles is to obey Guizot in every detail.

The reception is splendid beyond belief. Even Marianne is astonished at the elegance around her. Her delight turns to dismay when she learns that Charles, not Guizot, has directed everything. Angrily she tells Guizot (Ivan Simpson) that he is not to take orders from

New Moon was *Naughty Marietta,* only more so.

When a stage musical was converted to a MacDonald-Eddy vehicle, it was the custom to take songs originally sung by as many as a half-dozen people and assign them to the two principals. "Softly, as in a Morning Sunrise" was originally an anguished tenor aria expressing the grief of betrayal. For Eddy, it became a baritone tribute to his beloved. *Courtesy Anna Michalik.*

footmen! However, the guests, including the Governor (Grant Mitchell), are suitably dazzled.

Dancing and gossip are the main activities of the evening. Marianne's aunt holds forth with the latest tales of the scandalous Duke de Vidiers, which end with the Duke spending the night in the bed-chamber of the Princess de Caravye.

A loud chord of music summons Marianne to sing for her guests. Guizot, Charles tells her, has made it the feature of the party. And, asks Marianne tartly, has Guizot decided what she should sing? "Guizot is for 'One Kiss,' Mademoiselle," Charles murmurs.

"One Kiss" is delivered to the rapt guests, although several are not too rapt to notice Charles's adoring looks during the song. The regal Governor's wife (Cecil Cunningham, the laundress of *Love Me Tonight*) rolls her eyes toward her husband, her tongue making a knowing circuit inside her cheek. Another guest, the middle-aged Marquise della Rosa (Sarah Edwards), takes notice of Charles. As he summons her coach for the long journey to Baton

Rouge, she suggests that Marianne sell Charles to her. People's tongues are so uncharitable in New Orleans, she smirks. "I wouldn't trust them even in Baton Rouge," Marianne replies archly. Nevertheless, the Marquise urges, if Marianne should return to her guests and find the whispering too overwhelming, she can send Charles along to Baton Rouge on her fastest horse. The Marquise departs in a flurry of ruffles and innuendo.

Marianne fears that the elaborateness of her party will make her a laughingstock, and she rebukes Charles. He assures her that the party is an exact duplicate of one given years before by a lady of New Orleans who thereby gained her reputation for taste and grandeur. The lady was Marianne's mother, and the party celebrated Marianne's first birthday. The memory of the party was her mother's last joy on this earth. He knows all this, he says, from diaries kept in the library where he has been dusting. Even the song, "One Kiss," was sung that night. Moved and ashamed, Marianne dismisses him.

A whistled call of "La Marseillaise" summons Charles outside. Alexander reports that the New Moon is anchored three miles out. Everyone awaits Charles's orders. He tells Alexander to have everyone prepare to board just before dawn. He will join them soon.

As the party ends, the chanting of slaves is heard in the distance, singing "Troubles of the World." A guest explains to Marianne's aunt that they are "celebrating." "Are they eating someone?" she giggles.

Marianne is drawn to the garden by the music. Charles follows her, and they watch a ceremony in which the slaves stroke the trunk of a giant magnolia tree as they tell it of their troubles. We see the tree, an art director's masterpiece, in silhouette against a sound-stage moon while self-conscious extras mill around its massive roots. Suddenly we long for a director like Van Dyke who would have used a more realistic tree and sent the camera in close, searching the faces of the extras for real pathos, instead of opting for just a standard production number.

Marianne tells Charles about the time when her nurse took her to the trouble tree. She was desperately lonely after the death of her mother and somehow talking to the tree took away her sorrow.

The slaves switch to a melody in a minor key, and Marianne tells Charles how she has often tried to fit words to it: "The sky was blue. The moon was new." She trails off. Charles too, has a song: "Wanting You." Marianne is moved to join him and to let him kiss her. Then, alarmed at what is happening, she rushes back to the house alone.

There, the Governor and the Vicomte de Ribaud of the secret police are waiting. The Vicomte (George Zucco) has just arrived from France, searching for a traitor among the bondsmen. The man is the Duke de Vidiers. A

"One Kiss" is the highlight of Marianne's party.

Naughty Marietta, *Rose Marie*, and *Maytime* each had a key song that establishes the love relationship early in the film and then brings the lovers together again at the end. In *New Moon,* Charles and Marianne confess their love in the stirring "Wanting You," but a different melody will reunite them. *Courtesy Anna Michalik.*

foolish, misguided woman has aided him in his escape and suffered exile for her trouble. Now Ribaud is closing the net. He is warning all the plantation owners tonight and in the morning they will inspect the bondsmen and capture their man. Already they have discovered the Duke's plot to free all the bondsmen in the Colonies and have taken steps against it. The New Moon, lying in the harbor, which was to have been their escape vessel, is manned by the King's soldiers. By sunset tomorrow, the plotters will be on their way back to France for a date with Madame la Guillotine.

Marianne assures them of her full cooperation. After they have left, she summons Charles, who arrives ready for romance. Instead he is told that he has been sold to the Marquise. Nearly hysterical, Marianne orders him to pack and leave within the hour. He assumes that this is his punishment for having dared to kiss her and leaves in a fury. Outside, he joins his friends and rides, not to the Marquise in Baton Rouge but to the ocean and the New Moon. From the window, Marianne watches him go. At last, she finds the words of her song: "Lover, Come Back to Me."

Charles and his friends gallop full speed through the murky bayous to meet the others. Alexander cuts them off and tells them that "the marines have landed." Ribaud must have discovered their plan. Alexander has seen him and the Governor riding toward Marianne's plantation. "So *that's* why she sent me away," Charles exclaims. "Mercifully and insultingly. I'll remember both." Charles is urged to escape alone but he refuses. They will escape together or not at all.

First, they must reach the stockade before the marines and release the imprisoned bondsmen. This they do, and, as the camera tracks through the prison, clamoring prisoners spew forth through the unlocked doors.

Standing on the whipping block in the center of the torch-lit yard, Charles tells them that their only chance is to take the New Moon and pilot

Charles exhorts the white bond servants (but not the black slaves) to rebellion by singing "Stout Hearted Men." (Left to right, William Tanner, Nelson, Stanley Fields.) *Courtesy Anna Michalik.*

her to freedom. The grizzled faces stare at him sullenly. Piracy is a hanging offense. It's their only chance, Charles cries. If no one will come with him, he is going alone. "Wait!" cries Alexander. That's one. Tambour makes two. Then Pierre, Jacques, another, eight, nine, *ten*! With his ten men, Charles marches off for the New Moon to the rousing rhythms of "Stout Hearted Men."

The music and his courage are too much for the stragglers and, a few at a time, they begin following him until there is a solid wall of men racing after the briskly marching Charles. The camera tracks along just in front of Charles and his little band (shades of *Naughty Marietta*) as the crowd literally runs to catch up. They unite and march on through the swamp, joining Charles's fellow conspirators at the rendezvous. Falling into step, they surge on through the darkness, their torches blazing and the music pounding for one of the most exciting sequences in the film.

Silence falls. The New Moon is riding peacefully at anchor, the sailors lounging on the deck. Suddenly the conspirators pour over the side. The battle is brief and fierce, but within

One of the greatest film comedians of the twentieth century, Buster Keaton, wrote gags for *New Moon* and had a small role—but his scenes, like this one, were cut. *Courtesy Anna Michalik.*

minutes the New Moon is heading out to sea with a new crew and a new captain at the helm. (Buster Keaton is clearly visible in the right background of the captain's cabin, helping a fellow conspirator try on naval uniforms.)

Without the New Moon, Ribaud is forced to wait two weeks until another ship reaches New Orleans that can take him in pursuit. The Fleur de Lys arrives and is ordered by the Governor to transport Ribaud to Martinique, where he can call out the whole fleet. Marianne, too, demands passage. She is sick of New Orleans and wants to go back to France. Impossible, cries the Governor. The ship has no facilities for ladies. It is carrying a load of non-aristocratic brides for the colonists in Martinique. Marianne's aunt also demands passage. She'd take the boat if it had a cargo of baboons. "Ah, Paree!" she exclaims.

Marianne is on the deck of the boat as it pulls out to sea, surrounded by some of the same Casquette girls as in *Naughty Marietta*. Shades of *Naughty Marietta*, she sings a lovely hymn, this one fashioned from "Ombra Mai Fú" from Handel's *Xerxes*.

We have a strong premonition that pirates must be nearby and, sure enough, they appear in the moonlight and capture the ship, losing theirs in the process.

The shrieking girls have taken refuge in the hold and, in an exact duplicate of the sequence in *Naughty Marietta*, a scarred brigand lounges down the stairs to leer at them. He boasts the same scars but not the same bare chest, and fortunately his intentions are more or less honorable for he laughs at Auntie's warning instead of shooting her.

On deck, Charles has taken over the ship. He assures the Captain that they had only wanted supplies, but now that the New Moon has been sunk, they must use the Fleur de Lys. Its crew and passengers will be put ashore safely at the first opportunity.

Charles's duties as the new captain are interrupted by a lady passenger who insists on seeing him. He finds himself face to face again with Marianne. He meets her demand to be returned to New Orleans with quiet laughter and suggests that she join the courageous and

Charles and his followers commandeer a ship, but end up shipwrecked on a tropical isle, fortunately with Marianne and a load of colonial brides. (Left to right: Nelson, Dick Purcell, Stanley Fields, Mary Boland, Jeanette.) *Courtesy Anna Michalik.*

amiable ladies below to learn from their example. A tropical storm soon sinks the ship. In a superb sequence, we see the sailors trying to lash down tables and luggage in the hold as the ship pitches, tossing the girls around like dice. Auntie is hurled into the arms of the burly, uncouth Tambour where she finds a few moments for coquetry before another tilt of the ship separates them. On deck, Charles clings to the wheel as waves completely cover the deck. Below, the girls pray and sob, several hurt by the violent buffeting. The men are plainly protective of their charges, and, when the ship founders on a reef, nearly everyone makes it into the boats and onto a nearby island.

The island is happily deserted and well furnished with food and water. Marianne, her elaborate coiffure untouched by the storm, demands that they light signal fires. Charles tells her they are miles from the nearest shipping lane and have better uses for their timber. In another rallying speech, he organizes the new inhabitants of the island into working groups to create a new home. The padre responsible for the girls (H.B. Warner repeating his *The Girl of the Golden West* rôle and costume) fears for the virtue of his charges, but Charles assures him there will be no "disorder" on the island.

Marianne haughtily inquires whether he wants her to cook or milk goats. "Try cooking, Mademoiselle. Men are more lenient than goats." To her splutters of rage, he replies calmly that the one who commands is merely a matter of circumstance.

In a montage, we see the island community growing, trees felled, huts being built. Marianne is discovered trying to peel a potato that looks like a candidate for a first-aid class. Auntie is dismayed that she must bend down to milk the goats rather than having the goats rise to her. All this domesticity is interrupted by shouts.

A fight is in progress between two men over the affections of a "girl." Plainly a little orderly "disorder" is called for, and so again Charles

Charles takes command of building a community on the island. Nelson, left. At table, Dick Purcell ("Captain America") as Alexander.

makes a speech. Their crops have been good. Water is plentiful. Now they must have greater ambitions. In the past they have counted by heads. In the future they will count by families.

His plan is greeted with enthusiasm by all. As he tries to return to his cabin, he is surrounded by eager girls. Over their heads, he gets a glimpse of Marianne as she is engulfed in ardent suitors. Charles's maidens want to cook for him, but Marianne's wooers insist on singing, day and night. Outside her window, they sing chorus after chorus of "Marianne" until she flees to Charles's cabin and begs him to make them stop.

He can offer only one solution. If he permits her to marry him, they will leave her alone. He is, of course, suggesting a marriage of harmonious indifference. "You don't expect me to trust you?" she retorts. "Not if you overrate the temptation," he replies.

Marianne marches haughtily back to her cabin. The dignity of her passage is marred by a gaggle of caroling lovers who dog her footsteps. It is too much! We dissolve from her irate face to the benevolent face of the padre, his hand raised in blessing. It is her wedding day. The grim-faced lady is coiffed with flowers and surrounded by laughing, singing islanders, Charles at her side.

As with all wedding days, darkness eventually falls, and the lovers find themselves alone in their love nest. Marianne archly demands a lock for her bedroom. She does not wish to suffer the fate of the Princess de Caravye. Charles presents her with a massive log to bar her door. He intends to bar his door also. As for the Princess, what Marianne's aunt had failed to discover in her haste was that the lady was not only eighty years old—but also his grandmother.

He leaves and Marianne tries to follow, but the log in her arms blocks her passage through the door. She drops this "key" on her foot, and Charles returns to massage it. After all, he is a specialist, he tells her. "A doctor?" "No, a footman."

Marianne makes a shocking discovery.

To save Marianne from her ardent island suitors, Charles consents to marry her himself. Their honeymoon doesn't go smoothly. *Courtesy Anna Michalik.*

The proud lady is now thoroughly humbled. Charles tucks her into bed, and they are near reconciling. As he leans forward to kiss her, an explosion rocks the hut. French battleships are off the north side of the island.

Charles orders the women to the chapel, and the men to the barricades. As pirates, they have no choice but to fight. He asks Marianne to forgive him for any grief he has caused and rushes off. Marianne stands calling after him, "Lover, Come Back to Me," recalling the almost identical scene in *Rose Marie*. Though the island is under attack, Charles stops at the ocean's edge just long enough to join her in a verse and chorus before he dashes on to lead his men.

The sounds of the battle reverberate in Marianne's ears as she watches through the bamboo slats of her hut, the torch light making a dramatic pattern on her face. "You *will* come back," she murmurs fiercely. A bugle is heard. The French have won.

New Moon

Jeanette sings "Lover, Come Back to Me"—and Charles does.

Then shouts, confusion. The men are marching back, Charles at their lead. Behind him, the French officers carry a strange new flag, the *tricolore*. France is now a republic. The friendly salute of the French battleship was mistaken for an attack. Fortunately, Charles spotted their flag of truce and stopped the battle in time.

Charles and Marianne are now Citizen and Citizeness Vidiers. They can resume their honeymoon in earnest. As the islanders march off to their homes singing "Stout Hearted Men," Charles and Marianne embrace and sing a contrapuntal chorus of "Wanting You" under a lush, tropical *full* moon—not a new moon.

Reviews

"Not even Nelson Eddy's robust baritone and Jeanette MacDonald's dulcet soprano can overcome the handicaps of a stilted, ponderous, oft times silly narrative," wrote William Boehnel in the *New York World-Telegram*. Other reviewers blamed the stars. *Time* magazine commented that "Eddy's figure is becoming almost as operatic as his acting." *Variety* said, "Miss MacDonald overemphasizes the coyness in her characterization," but noted, "there's no question of the excellence and quality of the vocal numbers, especially the delivery and sound recording of Miss MacDonald and Eddy." Bosley Crowther in the *New York Times* chose to be facetious: "With tears welling in our eyes (sniff, sniff), we rather sadly suspect that this sort of sugar-coated musical fiction has seen its better days."

Such sarcasm also crept into the usually thoughtful commentary of Dilys Powell, film reviewer for the London *Sunday Times* for more than fifty years:

> *New Moon*, *mes enfants*, and the *pacquebot* is on its way from *la belle France* of, roughly, June, 1793, to New Orleans; and aboard her Mademoiselle Jeanette de MacDonald, all bimsy in wig and hoops trilling her way out to the old plantation. *Mille tonnerres*, who is this in the hold, shirt-sleeved, *parbleu*, and hair in a chignon? Why, 'tis Nelson, duc de Eddy, pretending to be a bondsman. *Sapristi*, he is discovered by an agent "straight from Paree," he waits only to bawl a duet with Mademoiselle before marching his fellow-bondsmen off to *fraternité* and piracy; and now Mademoiselle it is who, together with 100 brides bound for Martinique, is led to the hold ("Spare your minions! I know my way"). And now the storm, unabated by the choral rendering of Handel's "Largo," and the desert island, *sacrebleu;* and colonization, and courtship, and marriage, and—*tiens*, the French Fleet! But what is that they are singing? 'Tis the *Marseillaise*, harmonized with "Lover, Come Back to Me," 'tis the Revolution; 'tis the duc de Eddy for President. And what signifies "bimsy"? Bunk and whimsy, *mes gosses*.

The writing was clearly on the wall (and review pages). The operetta form, with its many delights and artificialities, was about to suffer one of its periodic declines.

Recordings (See Discography for further information)

"Lover, Come Back to Me" (MacDonald and Eddy made separate recordings.)
"One Kiss" (MacDonald)
"Softly, as in a Morning Sunrise" (Eddy)
"Stout Hearted Men" (Eddy)
"Marianne" (Eddy and Steber, also Steber) *
"Wanting You" (Eddy; also Eddy and Steber; also Eddy and MacDonald in their 1957 reunion album)
"Gorgeous Alexander" (Eddy) *
"The Girl on the Prow" (Eddy and Steber) *

* Eddy also recorded a *New Moon* album with Eleanor Steber that included the standards.

New Moon

The MacDonald/Eddy duet recordings ended in 1938, when Eddy signed with Columbia while Miss MacDonald continued at RCA Victor. They would not record together again until a reunion album at RCA in 1957.

Music in the Film

All songs have music by Sigmund Romberg and lyrics by Oscar Hammerstein II unless otherwise indicated. In listing performers after each title, "and" denotes a genuine duet, while commas between names indicate a sequence of singers.

Overture: "Stout Hearted Men" fragment, "Wanting You" (MacDonald and Eddy), "Softly, as in a Morning Sunrise" fragment, "Lover, Come Back to Me" (MacDonald and Eddy)
"Dance Your Cares Away" (chorus) - based on "Funny Little Sailor Man" from stage version, music by Romberg, lyricist uncertain
"Stranger in Paris" (MacDonald) - based on "Take a Flower" melody from the stage tavern sequence, Act I, Scene 2. Music by Romberg, lyricist uncertain. The song has an obvious cut in the middle.
"The Way They Do It in Paris" (MacDonald, drowned out by Eddy and male chorus shouting) - based on verse of "Gorgeous Alexander," music by Romberg, lyricist uncertain
"Shoes" (Eddy) - based on refrain melody of "Gorgeous Alexander," music by Romberg, lyricist uncertain, INTO:
"Softly, as in a Morning Sunrise" (Eddy)
"One Kiss" (MacDonald)
Spirituals: "Troubles of the World" ["Soon I Will Be Done"], "No More Weeping and Wailing" (The Jericho Choir with Eddie Jones, Ben Carter, Lois Hodnett, and Billy Mitchell)
"Wanting You" (Eddy, MacDonald)
"Lover, Come Back to Me" (MacDonald)
"Stout Hearted Men" (Eddy and male chorus)
"Ombra Mai Fú" [Handel's "Largo"] (MacDonald) from the opera *Xerxes* - music by George Frederic Handel, Latin lyricist uncertain
"Marianne" (male chorus)
"Marianne" reprise (chorus)
"Dance Your Cares Away" reprise (chorus)
"Marianne" reprise (chorus)
"Lover, Come Back to Me" reprise (MacDonald and Eddy), INTO:
"The Marseillaise" [French national anthem] (chorus) - words and music by Claude Rouget de Lisle, INTO:
"The Way They Do It in Paris" reprise (chorus), INTO:
"Stout Hearted Men" reprise (male chorus)
Finale: "Wanting You" reprise (MacDonald and Eddy) sung contrapuntally with "Stout Hearted Men" reprise (male chorus)
"Lover, Come Back to Me" (orchestral)

Songs from the stage operetta used in the film are "Marianne," "Softly, as in a Morning Sunrise," "Wanting You," "Stout Hearted Men," "One Kiss," and "Lover, Come Back to Me." Also used with new lyrics are "Take a Flower," "Gorgeous Alexander," and "Funny Little Sailor Man."

In *Deep in My Heart*, MGM's 1954 biography of Sigmund Romberg, Tony Martin sang "Lover, Come Back" accompanied by Joan Weldon for the last few bars; Helen Traubel sang "Softly" and "Stout Hearted Men." Ballerina Tamara Toumanova sang (dubbed) and danced to a lavishly staged "send-up" of "Softly," played very quickly in an audition sequence to demonstrate that the producers didn't understand Romberg's music.

Goofs

Jeanette loses the feathers in her hair when she steps from her party into the garden to sing "Wanting You." (Tricia Lutz)

The lace tablecloth, when Nelson serves Jeanette breakfast, is alternately crooked and straight. Then, when Nelson leads his ten Stout Hearted Men from the stockade, his collar is alternately in and out. (Joan Woolley)

When they land on the island, Nelson has what appears to be a sextant while one of his men looks through a telescope. Nelson says that they are 62.7 by 14.9. Latitude was easy to find from the position of the sun, but a method to compute longitude had not yet been discovered. Nelson was scientifically ahead of his time. (Trudy Gallagher)

Bitter Sweet

MGM.
Released November 8, 1940.
Directed by W. S. Van Dyke II.
Produced by Victor Saville.
94 minutes.
Technicolor.

Italian *and* Portuguese title: *Divino Tormento* (Divine torment)
French title: *Emporte Mon Coeur* (Take my heart)

Based on the stage production by Noël Coward. Screenplay: Lesser Samuels. Music Director: Herbert Stothart. Camera: Oliver Marsh with Allen Davey. Art Director: Cedric Gibbons. Gibbons Associate: John S. Detlie. Set Decorations: Edwin B. Willis. Recording Director: Douglas Shearer. Musical Presentation: Merrill Pye. Technicolor Director: Natalie Kalmus. Kalmus Associate: Henri Jaffa. Gowns: Adrian. Men's Costumes: Gile Steele. Hairstyles for Miss MacDonald: Sydney Guilaroff. Makeup: Jack Dawn. Editor: Harold F. Kress. Dance Director: Ernst Matray. Assistant Director: Hugh Boswell. Technicolor Photography: Allen Davey. Miss MacDonald's French Instructor: Ann Harriette Lee.

Noël Coward's masterpiece opened in London at His Majesty's Theatre on July 18, 1929. It starred George Metaxa (*Swing Time*) as "Carl" and American Peggy Wood as "Sari." English Evelyn Laye (whom MGM later tried to lure to America as a backup for Jeanette) starred in the New York premiere, which opened at the Ziegfeld Theatre on November 5, 1929, with Gerald Nodin as "Carl." The 1933 British film, released in the United States through United Artists, was directed by Herbert Wilcox and starred Anna Neagle, Fernand Gravey, and Ivy St. Helier, who recreated the stage rôle of "Manon."

Jeanette subsequently toured in a summer stock production of *Bitter Sweet* that played in Louisville, Pittsburgh, and St. Charles, Illinois in 1954, Dallas in 1955, and Warren, Ohio and Detroit in 1959.

Jeanette MacDonald (Sarah Millick / "Sari")
Nelson Eddy (Carl Linden)
Ian Hunter (Lord Shayne)
George Sanders (Captain von Tranisch)
Felix Bressart (Max)
Curt Bois (Ernst)
Edward Ashley (Harry Daventry)
Fay Holden (Mrs. Millick)
Diana Lewis (Jane)
Charles Judels (Herr Wyler)
Lynne Carver (Dolly)
Sig Rumann (Herr Schlick)
Janet Beecher (Lady Daventry)
Veda Ann Borg (Manon)
Herman Bing (Market keeper)
Greta Meyer (Mama Luden)
Philip Winter (Edgar)
Dalies Frantz (Roger)
Armand Kaliz (Headwaiter)
Alexander Pollard (Butler)
Colin Campbell (Sir Arthur Fenchurch)
Art Berry Sr (Cabby)
General Sam Savitsky (Bearded man in station)
Howard Lang (Pawnbroker)
Lester Scharff [Sharpe], Hans Joby, Jeff Corey (Men on Carl's stairs)
Paul E. Burns (Lathered man)
Hans Conreid, John Hendrick (Men at Mama Luden's) *
Ruth Tobey (Market keeper's child)
Warren Rock (Wyler's secretary)
William Tannen (Secretary at employment agency)
Davison Clark (Attendant)
Pamela Randall, Muriel Goodspeed (Singers at Schlick's) *
Erno "Ernst" Verebes (Orderly)
Earl Wallace (Wine waiter)
Louis Natheaux (Officer)
Margaret Bert (Woman on stairs)
Julius Tannen (Schlick's companion)

Bitter Sweet

Bitter Sweet, 1940.

Armand Cortes (Second croupier)
Irene Colman, June Wilkins (Women in casino)
Jack Chefe, Gino Corrado (Waiters)
Max Barwyn (Bartender)
Eugene Beday (Civilian)
Paul Oman (Gypsy violinist, "Ziegeuner")
Kay Williams (Entertainer extra)
Major Sam Harris (Dining officer extra)
Jean De Briac (Croupier)
Rosemarie Brancato, Jack Powell, Mauricette Melbourne, Katharine Harns, Neal Kennedy, Andrew Grieve (Stage performers)
J. Delos Jewkes (Bass singer at Mama Luden's)
Leni Lynn (Singer)
Charles Prescott, Tim Stark (Bits)
Music Hall Rockettes, Corps de Ballet, and Glee Club
Ann Harriette Lee ("Tokay" singing double for MacDonald)**
Lorraine Bridges (MacDonald's vocal stand-in)**
Earl Covert (Eddy's vocal stand-in)**

* Although these characters have no names in the film, they are listed in the American Film Institute index as "Rudolph" (Conried), "Fritz" (Hendrick), "Hansi" (Randall), and "Freda" (Goodspeed).

** These credits appear in *The American Film Institute Catalog: Feature Films, 1931-1940*, p. 170. A footnote states: "Some of the lyrics in the 'Tokay' number were dubbed for JMacD by Ann Harriette Lee, who also instructed MacDonald in French accents and pronunciation for the number." This highly unlikely information comes from misunderstanding payroll records. Jeanette does *not* sing "Tokay"! Nor does any song require Jeanette to sing in French, something she had already done in several films. (She made complete French-language versions of at least two films, *The Merry Widow* and *One Hour with You*.) Vocal doubles were used for orchestra rehearsals only.

Oscar nomination for Color Cinematography - Oliver T. Marsh and Allen Davey
Oscar nomination for Color Interior Decoration - Cedric Gibbons and John S. Detlie

Bitter Sweet was presented on the Railroad Hour (radio), 1/17/49, with Jeanette and Gordon MacRae.

Nöel Coward's romantic masterpiece, *Bitter Sweet*, had burst on the London and New York stages in 1929. The twenty-nine-year-old Coward was already a noted playwright, actor, and songwriter when he set out to be a twentieth-century Renaissance man, creating the book, lyrics, and music for an operetta.

A costume piece that covered fifty years of love's suffering, *Bitter Sweet* avoided the cloying trivialities of operetta, especially English operetta, with a story of razor-sharp irony. Using the operetta form, Coward created characters with definite character flaws and turned them loose in a milieu that might have inspired Brecht. It was a "realism" that would not be repeated until *Pal Joey* eleven years later. The story was indeed "bittersweet."

The final lesson before her society marriage. Sarah Millick (Jeanette) joins her Viennese singing teacher, Carl Linden (Nelson), in a poignant duet of "I'll See You Again," one of Noël Coward's all-time classics. *Courtesy Anna Michalik.*

When Jeanette went to England in 1932, one of the plums held out by producer Herbert Wilcox was *Bitter Sweet*. However, she returned to Paramount, and *Bitter Sweet* reached the screen in 1933 with Anna Neagle and Fernand Gravey (spelling changed to Gravet for American audiences) in the leads and Ivy St. Helier recreating her stage rôle of "Manon." MGM later used the skeleton of Coward's story and many of his unforgettable songs to fashion a vehicle for MacDonald and Eddy.

Even the most devout Cowardite might have forgiven the liberties taken with the source materials if a new entity had emerged, but this didn't quite happen. The audiences were uncritical if not wildly enthusiastic, but the critics were harsh and Coward himself wept when he saw the MGM film.

This was perhaps overreaction, for *Bitter Sweet* is not an unpleasant film if one forgets the exquisitely subtle source material. The MGM *Bitter Sweet* is not subtle. It attempts to recapture

Bitter Sweet

the hearty jocularity and good fellowship of *Sweethearts* and frequently succeeds, but the efforts of its stars show too clearly.

The stage *Bitter Sweet* concerned a stiff, repressed little English girl who runs off to Vienna with her dashing music teacher. There she discovers "life" in all its beauty and ugliness. A major character is Manon, the hero's discarded mistress, who sings the "Vissi d'Arte" of the musical comedy world, "If Love Were All." In Vienna, the girl arouses the interest of a lecherous officer who casually kills her husband. She then spends the rest of her years and the operetta seeking security and remembering love.

Our film heroine is not followed much past the loss of her husband, so we know nothing of her later activities. (It is a curious phenomenon that, barring simultaneous expiration, the heroine invariably dies in opera—(*La Bohème, La Traviata, Carmen*—while in operetta or musical comedy it is always the hero who succumbs—*Bitter Sweet, Carousel, The King and I, West Side Story.*) Our film hero is also relieved of his former mistress, which makes the film much more wholesome and much less touching.

Sarah's fiancé, Harry (Edward Ashley, left), thinks that music gets Sarah too excited. In the future, she will have no time for lessons. (Fay Holden, second from right.) *Courtesy Anna Michalik.*

The best musical numbers from the stage version were understandably divided up between the two principals, which gave Eddy a chance to sing the robust "Tokay" and let Miss MacDonald frolic through the naughty "Ladies of the Town." Two Coward characters were combined into one villain rôle for George Sanders, and the stage format of an old woman advising a young girl through a flashback to her own youth, though filmed, was wisely abandoned, since it had already been borrowed for use in *Maytime*.

Eddy has his two now-mandatory sidekicks played by veteran Felix Bressart and by little Curt Bois, who could convey more with a look than many actors with a page of dialogue. Herman Bing provides a pleasant comedy sequence. However, all the hair bows in the world can't convince us that Jeanette is eighteen or English or repressed, and Eddy makes no attempt at depicting a romantic Viennese rake. They are simply Jeanette MacDonald and Nelson Eddy singing the exquisite Coward songs and not presuming to anything else. If we wonder at the sight of them starving in a garret when just one of Miss MacDonald's many Adrian gowns would bring enough at a pawnshop to keep them for a month, it is not their fault. The music is just too beautiful and the stars too earnest for us to quibble.

We first see Sarah Millick (Jeanette) at her singing lesson with her Viennese teacher, Carl Linden (Nelson). It is spring in London, but Carl is homesick. He tells Sarah of the spring festivals in his country, where everything is so much gayer. He has enjoyed teaching her, singing with her, but now that she is getting married, he is going away. This is the last time he will see her, except in the crowd at the party tonight. He leads her in her scales which evolve into the haunting "I'll See You Again."

Sarah's mother (Fay Holden, perhaps best remembered as Andy Hardy's mother) and Sarah's stodgy fiancé, Harry Daventry (Edward Ashley) interrupt them. Harry's icy snobbery is laid on with a musical comedy trowel, somewhat

At her engagement party, Sarah (Jeanette) exchanges pleasantries with Jane (Diana Lewis, left), who apparently has designs on Sarah's fiancé, Harry Daventry (Edward Ashley, second from left). Sarah's friend Dolly (Lynne Carver, right) enjoys the little drama.

blunting the subtlety of his insults to this "foreigner." There can be no doubt in anyone's mind as to Sarah's course.

At the party that night, Sarah's high spirits disconcert Harry and her future mother-in-law (Janet Beecher). Sweet little baby-talking Jane (Diana Lewis) twines herself around Harry's arm, sympathizing with his distress. Sarah's friend, Dolly (Lynne Carver of *Maytime*), matches Sarah's mood and cheers when Sarah dumps claret on an elderly gentleman who has been too free in patting the girls.

Carl is present as a paid entertainer. He sings "If You Could Only Come with Me," and it is obvious it is meant for one person. Sarah can no longer mask her feelings with vivacity. Fighting tears, she ridicules his song in front of everyone and orders him to play something gay. He launches into the exciting, off-beat waltz "What is Love?" and she takes up the song, circling the dance floor alone.

Harry is horrified at this exhibition, but Sarah is oblivious. She follows Carl into the garden, and he tells her of Vienna. Everything is so warm and haphazard there. Even her name would be different. She would be called "Sari" (pronounced "Shari"). Of course, she could never go there with him. He has nothing to offer

Bitter Sweet

Sarah realizes she loves Carl. They decide to elope during the engagement party, much to Dolly's delight. (Carver, Eddy, MacDonald.) *Courtesy Anna Michalik.*

her. Her wedding is all arranged. He can't support her. Her new house is waiting for her. How long will it take her to pack?

They recruit the excited Dolly to get Sarah's trunks ready and send them to the station. Sarah returns to the party, kisses her bewildered mother, and slips off to join Carl in a cab. "Where to?" asks the driver. "Vienna," Carl sighs happily.

Sarah, now "Sari," gets her first glimpse of St. Stephen's Cathedral from the train window. The sight of Vienna's traditional sign of good luck is cut short by a cinder in her eye. Oh, well, Carl tells her, she'll see plenty of it in the future. She will also see plenty of the Imperial Hussars, especially one Captain von Tranisch (George Sanders), who attempts a conquest while Sari waits for Carl to collect their luggage. Von Tranisch returns her handkerchief amidst clicking heels and compliments, much to Carl's amusement.

In the crowded station, Sari is startled by a little man who leaps out at them uttering wild whoops. It is Carl's friend, Ernst (Curt Bois). A tall, long-legged man with a drooping moustache comes galloping toward them like a drunken gazelle and takes Sari in his arms. It is Carl's friend, Max (Felix Bressart). A third man with enormous chin whiskers strides toward her, beaming, and Sari offers her cheek expectantly. *He* is a perfect stranger.

Carl and Sari are anxious to get home, but first Max and Ernst insist they all dine together. At dinner, the newlyweds learn that their apartment is not quite as Carl left it. Their wedding has been so popular with Carl's friends, that, piece by piece, all his furniture has been pawned to pay for refreshments. Carl sends Max and Ernst to retrieve his possessions, and Sari comments that it would have been very romantic to be carried over the threshold of a pawnshop. Carl carries his bride over his own threshold and up the endless stairs, resorting to the fireman's carry for the last flight. His apartment is empty except for Max and Ernst's wedding present: a gilt-framed portrait of Max and Ernst.

At Mama Luden's café, Sari is introduced to Carl's friends. Mama Luden (Greta Meyer) brings out a barrel of tokay that she has been saving, and Carl sings the exuberant hymn to wine, "Tokay." Sari, in turn, is asked for a sample of her singing prowess and responds

In Vienna, the couple is greeted by Karl's exuberant friend Ernst (Curt Bois). He and Max have a surprise for them. *Courtesy Anna Michalik.*

At Mama Luden's beer garden, Sarah, now "Sari," sings for Carl's friends, Ernst (Curt Bois, center) and Max (Felix Bressart, right).

with a lively cabaret song, "Love in Any Language," sung in a heavy French accent, a charming number but certainly an unusual "introduction."

In their garret, Carl is working on his operetta, repeating one refrain over and over in a major key. Suddenly he switches to a minor key, and we recognize "Zigeuner." Sari has sung it "wrong" and given him the idea. The operetta is now finished: *Zigeuner* by Carl Linden.

He goes off to sell his masterpiece to Herr Wyler, the great impresario, and Sari goes off to shop for dinner. Max and Ernst are coming for Chicken Paprika. (She walks down "Quality Street," a set built for the Marion Davies film of that name in 1927.) She is examining a scrawny chicken far beyond her means when a terrible sound greets her ears. Upstairs in the grocer's apartment, a young girl (Ruth Tobey) is mutilating Rosina's aria, "Una Voce Poco Fa," from Rossini's *The Barber of Seville*.

Quickly, Sari persuades the grocer (Herman Bing) that his child's voice is in danger. Now, if he were to hire a professional singing teacher!

A few minutes later, Carl also passes the grocery and hears the yowling. When he learns that the grocer has traded a chicken for a singing lesson, he sees his duty. He convinces the now thoroughly confused little man that the hideous noises issuing from upstairs mean that the new teacher is ruining his daughter's voice. The grocer mounts the stairs in a rage, followed by Carl. He throws open the door, and Sari and Carl confront each other. A plot, the grocer decides. Sari and Carl unite to convince him of their skill. Singing at the top of their lungs, they are slowly forced out the door by the shrieking grocer. The door slams. The grocer sighs. The door bursts open and the pair sings the last high note full blast, as the little man quivers.

Back home chickenless, Sari and Carl sing of their hopes and plans to own a "Dear Little Café." What will they tell Max and Ernst? Carl wonders. "As the evening wears on, they're sure to find out." Max and Ernst arrive bearing enormous baskets of food. Carl and Sari look suspiciously around the apartment. The sofa is gone.

Max has a plan to alleviate their mutual poverty. They will all go to Baden and sing for the millionaires who take the baths. Degrading, Carl replies. Not at all, says Max. If you can sing

In search of a chicken, Carl and Sari encounter an apoplectic butcher (Herman Bing).

Bitter Sweet

Carl has written an operetta that will make them rich—if only he can get the famous impresario Herr Wyler to hear it. *Courtesy Anna Michalik.*

Though they sing hopefully of the "Dear Little Café" they hope to own one day, they are hungry and discouraged. *Courtesy Anna Michalik.*

in your own bath, why not sing in someone else's?

Above the plop-plop of the mud springs and swish of steam, we hear their voices drifting into the luxurious spa from the street. Their singing also carries to the nearby gambling casino where our old friend, Captain von Tranisch, is playing banco with the English Lord Shayne (Ian Hunter). Suddenly, Lord Shayne realizes that the music has stopped, and so has his luck. He sends a waiter with a five-hundred-gulden note and a request to continue. The song resumes. Von Tranisch loses.

Perhaps the lady at the Captain's elbow is causing his misfortune. She is Manon (Veda Ann Borg, just recovered from facial surgery following an auto accident), a cabaret singer at the Captain's favorite café.

Two men who will play significant rôles in the lives of Sari and Carl: Captain von Tranisch (George Sanders, center) and Lord Shayne (Ian Hunter) are visited by Manon (Veda Ann Borg).

Von Tranisch stalks to the window and recognizes the street singer as the lady he met on the train. He sends an anonymous note out to her. If she and her friends prefer singing indoors, they are to go to Herr Schlick's café.

The little troupe happily accept employment at Schlick's Café, thinking that Lord Shayne is their benefactor. Actually, Herr Schlick (Sig Rumann) is only interested in keeping von Tranisch happy and the Imperial Hussars as customers. Von Tranisch's happiness depends on ready access to Sari, but unfortunately he is called away on maneuvers. Sari is baffled at being kept on salary with nothing to do. After

Max (Felix Bressart, left) and Ernst (Curt Bois, right) arrive with a feast—but the sofa is gone.

Bitter Sweet

Sari doesn't realize she has been hired by Herr Schlick solely to entertain the lecherous Captain von Tranisch. Here she sings and dances the lively "Ladies of the Town" with Muriel Goodspeed, left, and Pamela Randall, right.

two weeks she confronts Herr Schlick, who leeringly tells her that at last she will have something to do. The Imperial Hussars have returned.

It is a gala night at the café, whose decor resembles a Victorian Versailles. Sari encounters both von Tranisch and Lord Shayne. Lord Shayne tells her that it isn't often a lady sings under a gentleman's window. It gives him all sorts of chivalrous ideas, he says sharply, glaring at von Tranisch. Sari is at last called on to sing. She joins two of the other girls (Pamela Randall, Muriel Goodspeed) in the lively "Ladies of the Town." Sari's duties also include dancing with the customers, and von Tranisch claims a waltz. He claims a number of other things too, and Sari laughs until she realizes that she and Carl owe their livelihood to him. Her dismay is doubled when her former fiancé, Harry, and lisping little Jane find her in von Tranisch's arms. Harry, who so detests foreigners, has been sent to Vienna by the Foreign Office with his new bride. He is appalled to find Sarah in this condition of degradation and tells Carl so.

Sari tells Carl nothing, but refuses ever to go back to the café. Von Tranisch arrives the next night at Herr Schlick's for his rendezvous. Schlick is frantic when he learns that Sari has quit. He tries to explain to von Tranisch that she is married *and* English, but von Tranisch will not make allowances. It is clear that the Hussars will take their business elsewhere if Sari does not appear. (At this point we hear Manon's wistful "If Love Were All" used as a bouncy dance tune.)

Desperate conditions require desperate measures. Schlick tells Max and Ernst, now dishwashers, that the great impresario, Herr Wyler, is expected that night. What a shame that Sari couldn't sing Carl's operetta for him. Sari arrives within minutes, dressed in an exquisite apricot brocade gown.

Carl smells a rat and demands to know where Herr Wyler is. Schlick splutters and starts making excuses. (Actor Sig Rumann was a master interpreter of Germanic slyness and

Harry and Jane, now married, offer their sympathy to the widow Linden. *Courtesy Anna Michalik.*

bombast and had been the Marx Brothers' principal target in *A Night at the Opera* and *A Day at the Races*.) A passing waiter informs the astonished Schlick that Wyler is indeed there, accompanied by Lord Shayne. With Carl at the piano, Sari waltzes around the room, singing "What Is Love?"

Von Tranisch watches her throughout the number, obviously drunk. As she dances past his table, he seizes her. "You look lonely, dancing by yourself." Carl starts toward them as von Tranisch kisses her. Without thinking, Carl knocks him to the floor.

The crowd stands frozen. The honor of the Hussars is at stake. Carl is handed a sword to defend himself. Sari is frantic with fear, but Carl thrusts her aside toward Lord Shayne. "Will you take care of my wife, please?" It is sheer bravado on Carl's part, for he has never dueled. Von Tranisch finishes him with one thrust, and Sari sinks weeping beside him. Fade out.

Harry and Jane mount the stairs to Sari's flat to offer condolences. It's outrageous, says Jane, that the neighbors should be playing music under such circumstances. The music is coming from behind the Linden door, and they find Sari standing beside the piano, singing Carl's songs

Von Tranisch (George Sanders) returns from maneuvers and tries to claim his prize.

Bitter Sweet

The beautiful "Zigeuner" ballet from Carl's operetta is richly costumed in cream and sepia. (Adrian's costume for Jeanette includes another of his favorite "skullcap with fan" headdresses, similar to those in *Maytime* and *Sweethearts*.)

for Herr Wyler and Lord Shayne. Sari won't go back to England with Harry and Jane, she says. This is her home now, here with everything Carl loved. Herr Wyler is going to produce Carl's operetta. Sari begins singing "Zigeuner" for him, but can't get through it. Sobbing, she puts her head against Carl's picture, as Harry and Jane smirkingly take their leave.

The "Zigeuner" music is taken up by a full orchestra. It is opening night, and Lord Shayne wishes Sari well. (In the original version, he is Sari's second husband.) On stage, we are treated to a stunning visual treatment of the "Zigeuner" ballet, the sets and costumes all in sepia and white. Sari, as the gypsy princess is presented with a single rose by her handmaidens. She hears the strains of a gypsy ("zigeuner") violin and follows it. The rest of the ballet is a superb "gypsy" dance, interrupted midway by Carl's voice singing "I'll See You Again."

Especially charming is the performance of Paul Oman as the Zigeuner of the title. Though he hasn't a line, he draws the eye whenever he is on camera. The lush perfection of this number makes the deficiencies of the rest of the film all the more regrettable.

Still in her stage costume, Sari runs up the stairs to her apartment, the audience's ovations ringing in her ears. She stands at the window looking out over moonlit Vienna. "Carl...they heard your music tonight. The things we dreamed came true."

She begins singing "I'll See You Again" very slowly. Carl's face appears in the clouds and joins her. The effect is just a bit too startling for genuine pathos. For all but the most innocent heart, the film ends with a synthetic tug at the heartstrings.

Coward himself vowed that no more of his works would ever be done in Hollywood, and he kept that promise. (The rights to *We Were Dancing* had already been acquired, and it was filmed after *Bitter Sweet*.) His plays were thereafter filmed in England where, he felt, his integrity as the creating artist was preserved.

A word should be said about "corn." There is nothing so basic to satisfying film- or theatre-going as total emotional response to a situation. It doesn't matter how much of a cliché the situation is if it works. Whether it's *Love Story* or *Lassie, Come Home*, the most sophisticated audience loves to be moved. This very willingness to be "taken" has an equal and opposite reaction: anger and derision when the given stimuli—the pink-nosed puppy or the dying child—is handled clumsily and does not produce the desired effect. Much of *Bitter Sweet* is overwritten and overplayed. We would gladly forgive this if it worked. It doesn't.

Reviews

Reviewers were undecided whether it was the source material that was dated or the film itself. The *New York Daily News* gave it three stars but said, "[it] drips with Technicolor and sentimentality... Miss MacDonald and Mr. Eddy, both in fine voice, recall memories of another day."

The *New York Post* used adjectives like "Technicolor," "elaborate," and "expensive," but not in an entirely favorable sense. They rated the film only fair to good on their dial: "Miss MacDonald is a red-haired, blue-eyed perfect Technicolor subject. Her wardrobe is stunningly picturesque (ladies will adore it), her voice lovely.

Mr. Eddy, who gives over the bulk of camera footage and song to his pretty partner, doesn't get much of a break even when he's under lens focus."

The *New York Times*'s Bosley Crowther was most concerned about the original: "...Metro's battered screen version...patched together out of Mr. Coward's fragile and tender work. Miss MacDonald and Mr. Eddy play it all with such an embarrassing lack of ease—she with self-conscious high spirits and he with painful pomposity."

Recordings (See Discography for further information)

"Dear Little Café" (Eddy)
"If You Could Only Come with Me" (Eddy)
"I'll See You Again" (recorded separately by both MacDonald and Eddy)
"Tokay" (Eddy)
"Zigeuner" (MacDonald)

Eddy also recorded "Call of Life" from the original score.

Music in the Film

All music by Noël Coward except where indicated. In listing performers after each title, "and" denotes a genuine duet, while commas between names indicate a sequence of singers.

Overture: "I'll See You Again," "Tokay,"
"I'll See You Again" (MacDonald and Eddy)
Polka (orchestral) - credited to Coward, source uncertain
"If You Could Only Come with Me" (Eddy)
"What Is Love?" (Eddy, MacDonald)
"Tokay" (Eddy and male chorus)
"Love in Any Language" (MacDonald with Eddy, Curt Bois, Felix Bressart, male chorus) - based on "Bonne Nuit, Merci!" from stage version, new lyrics by Gus Kahn
"Una Voce Poco Fa" from *The Barber of Seville* (Georgia Stark dubbing for Ruth Tobey) -

Bitter Sweet

Adrian outdid himself costuming red-haired Jeanette in Technicolor, choosing colors that few redheads had previously dared to wear. For "Ladies of the Town," top left, she wears purple and fuchsia. For "Dear Little Café", lower left, she is in dove blue. Apricot brocade sets off her red hair in "Tell Me, What Is Love?", top right. And a vivid jade-green taffeta with matching velvet trim and bonnet, lower right, sets off her beauty as she sings "If Love Were All."

music by Gioacchino Rossini, libretto by Cesare Sterbini
"What Is Love?" reprise (MacDonald, Eddy)
"Dear Little Café" (MacDonald and Eddy) - with additional lyrics by Gus Kahn
"If You Could Only Come with Me" reprise (MacDonald and Eddy)
"Kiss Me" ["before you go away"] (MacDonald)
Rehearsal fragment: "Kiss Me" (MacDonald), "Ladies of the Town" (orchestral)
"The Last Dance" (orchestra at Schlick's Café)
"Ladies of the Town" (Trio: MacDonald, Pamela Randall, and Muriel Goodspeed) - new lyrics by Gus Kahn
"What Is Love?" reprise (MacDonald and Eddy)
"Dear Little Café" reprise (MacDonald)
"Zigeuner" (MacDonald sings, orchestral dance number) - containing fragments of Bartok's Rhapsody #1, Kodaly's "Hary Janos Suite," and Fritz Kriesler's "Caprice Viennois;" Eddy sings fragment of "I'll See You Again"
"I'll See You Again" reprise (Eddy and MacDonald)
Finale: "I'll See You Again" (orchestral)

Songs from the stage production used in the film are "I'll See You Again," "If You Could Only Come with Me," "What is Love?," "Tokay," "Dear Little Café," "Kiss Me," "The Last Dance," "Ladies of the Town" (with new lyrics), and "Zigeuner." "Bonne Nuit, Merci!" became "Love in Any Language." "Call of Life" and "If Love Were All" are background music.

Trivia

Behind-the-scenes footage is used in an 11-minute 1940 short, *The Miracle of Sound*. Directed and narrated by MGM's sound genius Douglas Shearer, the "infomercial" ostensibly shows how sound is recorded, serving as a free plug for the forthcoming film in the guise of an entertainment short. Nelson and Jeanette, with director W.S. Van Dyke, can be seen shooting the "Dear Little Café" scene.

Movie Goofs

During the song "Tokay," Carl picks up a glass of wine for Sari, but then hands her his own glass, which is almost completely empty! A moment later, however, it is completely full. Then Carl hands both their glasses to a friend to hold while they bounce exuberantly on the wooden table, but when they are handed their glasses back, apparently someone has been sipping from Sari's glass for the wine level is significantly lower. (Minami Pennington)

Smilin' Through

MGM.
Released October 1941.
Directed by Frank Borzage.
Produced by Victor Saville, Frank Borzage.
100 minutes.
Technicolor.

French title: *Chagrin d'Amour* (The Grief of Love)
Italian title: *Cantene del Passato* (Chains of the Past)
Dutch title: *Liefdesmart* (Heartache)
Portuguese: O Amor que Não Morreu (The Love that Didn't Die)

From the play by Jane Cowl and Jane Murfin. Screenplay: Donald Ogden Stewart and John Balderston. Director of Photography: Leonard Smith. Technicolor Director: Natalie Kalmus. Technicolor Associate: Henri Jaffa. Music Director: Herbert Stothart. Recording Director: Douglas Shearer. Art Director: Cedric Gibbons. Art Associate: Daniel B. Cathcart. Set Decorations: Edwin B. Willis. Special Effects: Warren Newcombe. Montage Effects: Peter Ballbusch. Gowns: Adrian. Men's Costumes: Gile Steele. Makeup: Jack Dawn. Editor: Frank Sullivan.

Smilin' Through, written under a pseudonym (Allan Langdon Martin) by its star, Jane Cowl, opened at the Broadhurst on December 30, 1919, and featured Orme Caldara as Kathleen with Henry Stephenson as John. It ran for 175 performances, and was a tremendous hit on the road. First National filmed it in 1922 with Norma Talmadge, Wyndham Standing, and Harrison Ford (not related to the *Star Wars* Harrison Ford). Sidney Franklin was the director. Franklin was again at the helm of the first sound version in 1932 for MGM, starring Norma Shearer as

Smilin' Through

Jeanette poses on the set with Jackie Horner, who plays her as a child. *Courtesy Anna Michalik.*

Moonyean / Kathleen, Fredric March as Jeremy Wayne/ Kenneth Wayne, and Leslie Howard as Sir John.

Vincent Youmans wrote an operetta based on the stage play, calling it *Through the Years*. It starred Natalie Hall, Charles Winninger, Reginald Owen, and Michael Bartlett, and its book was by Brian Hooker (*The Vagabond King*) and lyrics by Edward Heyman. However, it ran only 20 performances after opening January 28, 1932.

Jeanette MacDonald (Kathleen / Moonyean Clare)
Brian Aherne (Sir John Carteret)
Gene Raymond (Kenneth Wayne / Jeremy Wayne)
Ian Hunter (Rev. Owen Harding)
Jackie Horner (Kathleen as a child)
Frances Robinson (Ellen, the maid)
Patrick O'Moore (Willie)
Eric Lonsdale (Charles, the batman)
Frances Carson (Dowager)
Ruth Rickaby (Woman)
David Clyde (Sexton)
Emily West [later Jeanette's real-life secretary]
   (Chorus singer in "Land of Hope and Glory")
Wyndham Standing (Doctor) [Wyndham Standing played Sir John in the 1922 film version]

Smilin' Through was presented on Cecil B. DeMille's Lux Radio Theatre, 1/5/42, with Jeanette, Gene Raymond, and Brian Aherne.

In 1941, the world was at war. Some Americans were still convinced that it was not *our* war, but the majority were clinging to the last bright days before darkness fell. Just after World War I, actress-author Jane Cowl had fashioned a sentimental tale of lovers in wartime, mixed with the popular theatrical device of their ghostly counterparts from a bygone age. MGM had successfully filmed this play in 1932 with Norma Shearer, Fredric March, and Leslie Howard. Now it seemed the ideal vehicle for the real-life team, Mr. and Mrs. Gene Raymond.

Sidney Franklin had directed both the 1922 Norma Talmadge silent for First National and the 1932 MGM talkie. Now Frank Borzage directed the musical remake. Although his few musicals were minor efforts, he was an expert at tales of bittersweet love (*Man's Castle*, *Seventh Heaven*). The 1932 MGM script was reused almost scene for scene and line for line, allowing for song insertions (just as MGM would do in Eddy's *The Chocolate Soldier*, a remake of its earlier *The Guardsman*). The music was culled from the ballads of Scotland and Ireland, with a few classical numbers and hymns thrown in. The MacDonald-Raymond combination seemed perfect for a story of lovers separated by war. In real life they would soon be parted.

With so many pluses and the tremendous emotional appeal that a strong film on men and women in wartime would have had, it is almost heartbreaking that the film registers as a standard competent musical, no more. Mr. Raymond gives a surprisingly wooden performance, considering his fine work in other films. (Both Gene and Jeanette said later that their love scenes together were among the hardest they ever had to do.) Jeanette is also a bit too elegant to be convincing as the teenaged Kathleen. The mannerisms in her performances were beginning to

A French-Flemish poster printed in Brussels.

intrude: the delicate gripping of the bridge of the nose in moments of stress, the slight intake of breath and lifting of chin before delivering an important line, the thrust of the open palm in dramatic confrontations. Many fine performers have based their careers on mannerisms, to the delight of their impersonators, but in this case they get in the way of the character.

The valentine mood of the film is set by titles decorated with highly romantic eighteenth century tapestry figures. In a slightly ponderous piece of exposition, we join the elderly Sir John (Brian Aherne) and his equally aged friend Owen, the town vicar (Ian Hunter), on Queen Victoria's sixtieth jubilee. A service of celebration takes place at the vicar's church, but Sir John is in a somber mood as he leaves through the tiny cemetery behind the chapel.

He walks home sadly, pausing in his garden to remember. There the ghost of his dead sweetheart, Moonyean, comes to him, telling him they will soon be together again.

Owen interrupts Sir John's reverie. He has come for a game of chess and to urge Sir John to join the villagers for the speeches and fireworks that night. Sir John mustn't live so much in the past. Owen has also brought bad news. Moonyean's sister and her husband have died in Ireland, leaving their little daughter completely alone. What would John say to bringing the little girl to live with him? Impossible, John answers. But, Owen urges, a little girl would give him someone else to think about. John offers money for her care, but that is all he can do.

Owen leaves, and John finds a little girl (Jackie Horner) standing quietly at his elbow. Her name is Kathleen, she tells him, and she will be five in August. Awkwardly, John tries to make friends and finally invites her to sing for him. Accompanying herself on the piano, she sings "The Kerry Dance" in a childish trill. A montage begins of a child romping through flowered fields, and the voice is joined by that of the grown Kathleen. The camera tracks from the trees outside the window to Kathleen (Jeanette) at the piano.

It is Kathleen's birthday and "Uncle" John presents her with Moonyean's pearl ring. Kathleen is growing more like her aunt every day, Owen tells her. John tries to slip the ring on her finger, but can't bring himself to do it. She must do it herself. The distant sound of cannons across the channel in France throws a further pall on their celebration. World War II—"the Great War"—has begun.

Kathleen's current suitor, Willie (Patrick O'Moore), calls to take her out, and they get caught in a thunderstorm. Willie keeps trying to propose, but the practical Kathleen is more concerned with getting away from the rain and lightning. At her instigation, they break into a deserted house nearby. It is the old Wayne house, and its dusty interior indicates no one has been there in decades. As Willie makes a fire, Kathleen contemplates the strange chaos of the

American Kenneth Wayne (Gene Raymond) comes to England to enlist in World War I and falls in love with Kathleen (Jeanette). This was Raymond's only film with his wife, and he confessed to being unusually nervous during the love scenes. *Courtesy Anna Michalik.*

Young Sir John (Brian Aherne) loves Moonyean (Jeanette). *Courtesy Anna Michalik.*

But Jeremy Wayne (Gene Raymond) loves her too. *Courtesy Anna Michalik.*

Jeremy appears in the choir loft, brandishing a gun. The shot intended for Sir John kills Moonyean, and Jeremy escapes. Frances Robinson and Ian Hunter (in ministerial robes) at left. *Courtesy Anna Michalik.*

room. A newspaper dated 1864, the remains of a half-finished drink, a chair overturned, a riding crop on the floor. She is fascinated by the untold story. Something terrible happened in this room. Someone shut the doors and never came back.

Ominous footsteps are heard in the hallway and, in spite of themselves, the two shrink back in fear. A shadowy figure emerges into the firelight. It is a handsome blond American who acts as if he owns the place. In actual fact, he does, for he is Kenneth Wayne (Gene Raymond), son of the owner, Jeremy Wayne. Willie is all for getting out, but Kathleen is taken with the young man. Kenneth brings out a bottle of ancient port, and they exchange toasts. They discuss the difference in their accents, and, since Kathleen has not a trace of a brogue, this is somewhat puzzling. Kathleen plays an old spinet (in tune after 30 years!) and sings "Drink to Me Only with Thine Eyes," as Kenneth raises his glass to her in the flickering firelight.

They meet a few days later for a picnic beside a lake. The thunder of cannons is heard in the distance, and Kenneth tells her he has come over to England to join up. Their meal is interrupted by a passing goat with a loud bell. (A human hand is clearly visible on its shoulder at one point, keeping it from wandering off.) It is a charming scene, although they again discuss the difference in their accents, with Kenneth launching into a mock brogue that makes her lack of one even more apparent. As the sun sets, they canoe on the lake, and she sings "A Little Love, a Little Kiss" against a shimmering pink and orange sky.

Kathleen cheerfully reports their unusual first meeting to her "uncle" and is astonished at his rage. He orders her never to see the son of Jeremy Wayne again! John rushes from the room, and Kathleen begs Owen to tell her what is wrong. He refuses, and she follows John into the garden.

Reluctantly, he tells her of a night fifty years past, the night before his wedding. The house was full of people. The garden dissolves back to that night, and young John is walking with his beautiful Moonyean (a brown-haired Jeanette). Moonyean goes off to her guests, and a dashing Owen takes John aside to warn him. Jeremy Wayne is at the tavern drinking heavily and making threats against John. But John dismisses it as too much brandy. From the next room, Moonyean is heard singing "Ouvre ton coeur."

Ellen, the maid (Frances Robinson), tells Moonyean that Jeremy Wayne is in the garden acting very strangely. She had best get Sir John. No, Moonyean tells her, she will handle it. She finds Jeremy (also played Gene Raymond) and tells him how glad she is that he has come to wish her well on her wedding eve. The tormented Jeremy insists that she marry him, that he won't let another man have her. He kisses her wildly and rushes off as John enters the garden. Shuddering, Moonyean clings to John. He is unaware of Jeremy's visit and thinks she is having an attack of nerves before their wedding. He slips her pearl ring on and off, practicing for the ring ceremony the next day, and they waltz around the garden to "Smilin' Through."

At the Wayne house, Jeremy acts out the sequence that created the confusion discovered

Moonyean's niece, Kathleen (Jeanette in a dual rôle), meets the son of Jeremy Wayne (also played by Gene Raymond). *Courtesy Anna Michalik.*

Young Sir John in the garden with Moonyean. *Courtesy Anna Michalik.*

by Kathleen. He sees the wedding announcement in the paper. It is too much. He pushes aside his drink, hurls down his riding crop, and knocks over a chair as he rushes off to the church.

In the churchyard, the villagers are gathered as Moonyean arrives in a garland-draped carriage. The ceremony is proceeding, with the bride in a lovely white gown and flowered snood (a popular 1941 fashion). John has only to slip the ring on Moonyean's finger when Jeremy Wayne appears, waving a pistol. "You shall never have her!" he cries. Moonyean flings herself in front of John as the gun goes off. She sinks slowly to the floor and Jeremy flees. As she hangs suspended between life and death, she asks John to put the ring on her finger. "If you ever need me, I'll find a way to come to you," she whispers and she dies. (Jeanette said she knew they had done a successful "take" when she looked up to see most of the crew in tears.)

We are back in the garden with Kathleen and Uncle John. She weeps for him and accepts his will that she never see Kenneth again. Later at the canteen, she sings for the troops, a dreamy rendition of "There's a Long, Long Trail Awinding." (Considering the many stirring songs that came out of World War I, it is a pity that more didn't find their way into the film.)

Ken waits for her outside and insists on walking her home. He has to know more than what she told him in her letter. Of course, he can understand her feelings since he is going away to war. It would be wrong to tie her down.

Smilin' Through

The ghost of Moonyean comes to the elderly Sir John in the garden. *Courtesy Anna Michalik.*

Kathleen breaks down in tears. What are they going to do?

They have one last picnic together, with the distant cannons sounding ominously in the background. Ken tells her that he is leaving for France tomorrow. She begs him to marry her that night. They go to tell Sir John, who bitterly denounces them. If Kenneth takes Kathleen away, she need never come back.

In a tearful scene, Ken decides that he can't deprive Kathleen of her security and leave her with nothing. Kathleen returns home, alone and devastated. Ken has refused to marry her, she tells Sir John. Now she may never see him again. If God is just, John tells her, she never will. Kathleen flees in horror, and Owen denounces John for his curse. Their friendship is over. Alone, John is visited by Moonyean, who tells him that his hate has come between them.

Four years later, Owen's church is the scene of a victory celebration. Kathleen, in choir robe and smart Adrian cap, leads the choir in "Land of Hope and Glory." Outside, Kenneth Wayne approaches the church and enters in time to hear her finish the song. He has been sent to the church from the city hall to find his father's birth certificate. Owen greets him joyously, but Kenneth tells Owen he has only come to settle his father's estate. Then he is leaving for America. He won't be seeing Kathleen. Does Owen think she would want him now? He gestures to his crutches.

As a captain, Kenneth has been assigned an aide, Charles (Eric Lonsdale), who helps him

In *Smilin' Through*, Gene Raymond plays a World War I American soldier in the British army. Soon he would be wearing a real American uniform as a pilot in World War II. *Courtesy Anna Michalik.*

pack up things at the old house. Kenneth sits in the room where he first met Kathleen, brooding and sipping port. As he stares into the glass, he hears Kathleen's voice singing "Drink to Me Only with Thine Eyes."

Kathleen herself rushes in, crying "Ken! Ken!" He barely has time to hide his crutches under the couch. At first she is too busy laughing and crying and talking to notice his silence. Why, oh, why did he stop writing? She thought he'd been wounded, but he's all right. She can see that. How long is his leave?

He tells her he doesn't have to go back. As an American, he can't be kept in the service if he doesn't want to stay. Kathleen happily concludes that he has come to fetch her before returning to America, but again he disillusions her. He is going home alone.

Owen visits John for the first time in four years. He tells him about Kenneth and begs him to stop opposing the marriage. Kenneth has lied to Kathleen. John must tell her the truth.

John refuses. Using John's own words, Owen tells him that "if God is just," he and Moonyean will never be together if he keeps Kenneth and Kathleen apart.

Kathleen arrives home, completely shattered. John tells her that she will get over it. "*You* didn't," she replies. John has always had the memory of someone who loved him, but she has nothing. John relents and tells her what has happened, that Kenneth is crippled and doesn't want to burden her. His train is leaving soon. She must hurry and bring him back with her.

In a joyful rush, she drives off in her car, passing Owen in the road. "Go to Uncle John," she cries. John and Owen gruffly shake hands and settle down to a game of chess. Someone else, Owen tells him, will be very glad at what he has done. "Yes...she *is* glad," says John. Concentrating on his move, Owen looks up to find John dozing and smilingly leaves.

John's sleep is deeper than Owen knows. Moonyean comes to him for the last time, and the ghost of the young John rises to greet her. "Moonyean, at last you've come to me." "No, John," she says, "*you've* come to *me*."

Sir John, now an old man, forbids Kathleen to marry the son of the man he hates. *Courtesy Anna Michalik.*

Kathleen begs Ken to marry her. He refuses. *Courtesy Anna Michalik.*

To the strains of "Smilin' Through," they walk out through the garden to their wedding carriage, surrounded by happy neighbors. On the road, they pass the young lovers happily driving back to the house. Kenneth has his arm around Kathleen. The flower-covered wedding carriage continues down the road, and Moonyean's voice is heard in the last verse of "Smilin' Through."

Reviews

The reviewers were nearly unanimous in a qualified thumbs-down on *Smilin' Through*, but remarkably diverse in placing the blame. The word "tearjerker" appeared in almost every review, followed by descriptive phrases like "indescribably dull" (*Cue*), a "museum piece" (*New York World-Telegram*), "satisfactory but not exciting" (*Variety*), "lachrymose, sticky, super-sentimental" (*Time*), and "mawkish" (*New York Times*).

The performers got mixed reviews. "Miss MacDonald has a fine voice and makes you listen every time she sings...but she is not an emotional actress," reported Bosley Crowther in the *New York Times*. *Variety* disagreed: "On the credit side...is the fine acting by Miss MacDonald and, of course, her voice." They regretted the lack of "production" numbers and liked Gene Raymond's performance, but not Brian Aherne's.

The *New York World-Telegram* took an opposite view, calling Aherne "fine" and Raymond "monotonous." Archer Winsten in the *New York Post* gave the film a fair to good rating on their movie dial, thought Aherne "a perfectly splendid old man" and rated Raymond's performance "good enough," noting that Jeanette sang "with her customary polish."

Recordings (See Discography for further information)

Jeanette recorded a 78 RPM album called "Smilin' Through" with the following songs:

Adrian's versions of World War I fashions were far closer to 1941, the year the film was made, than to 1914, having padded shoulders and fitted waists.

A birthday celebration on the set of *Smilin' Through*. Louis B. Mayer (second from left) thought of himself as the benevolent father of a happy studio family, but after Jeanette stood her ground in several disputes, she felt he wasn't backing her up anymore. (Left to right: Greer Garson, Mayer, MacDonald, Raymond, and director Frank Borzage.)

"Drink to Me Only With Thine Eyes"
"The Kerry Dance"
"Land of Hope and Glory"
"A Little Love, A Little Kiss"
"Ouvre ton coeur"
"Smilin' Through"

Music in the Film

In listing performers after each title, "and" denotes a genuine duet, while commas between names indicate a sequence of singers.

Overture: "Smilin' Through"
"Recessional" (Douglas Beattie, Nan Merriman, and chorus) - music by Reginald de Koven, lyrics by Rudyard Kipling, written for Queen Victoria's Jubilee
"The Kerry Dance" (Jackie Horner, MacDonald) - by James Lyman Molloy
"Drink to Me Only with Thine Eyes" (MacDonald) - music anonymous, lyrics by Ben Jonson
"A Little Love, A Little Kiss" ["Un Peu d'Amour"] (MacDonald) - music by Leo Silesu, English lyrics by Adrian Ross
"Rose of Tralee" (orchestral waltz at ball) - music by Charles W. Glover
"Ouvre ton coeur" ["Open Your Heart"] (MacDonald) - music by Georges Bizet, lyrics by S. Louis Delatre

"Smilin' Through" (MacDonald) - music and words by Arthur Penn, written in conjunction with the 1919 stage production
"There's a Long, Long Trail Awinding" (MacDonald and male chorus) - music by Alonzo Elliott, words by Stoddard King
"Smiles" (male chorus) - music by Lee S. Roberts, lyrics by J. Will Callahan
"Land of Hope and Glory" (MacDonald and chorus) - based on "Pomp and Circumstance" by Sir Edward Elgar, lyrics by A.C. Benson
"Drink to Me Only with Thine Eyes" reprise (MacDonald)
Finale: "Smilin' Through" reprise (MacDonald)

Trivia

For people who care about such things, the dates of the various flashbacks are inconsistent. If Jeremy Wayne was about twenty-five when he killed Moonyean in 1864, and his son Kenneth was old enough to fight in World War I (1914-1918), then Jeremy was over fifty before he sired a son. Not impossible. However, Moonyean's niece, Kathleen, came to John on Victoria's Diamond Jubilee, 1897, at the age of five, putting her birth in 1892, fifty years after Moonyean's birth. Therefore, Moonyean's sister (Kathleen's mother) would need to be about thirty years younger than Moonyean!

Movie Goofs

When the young Kathleen sits down to play the piano, Uncle John sets her little purse and gloves on top of the piano twice—first in a long shot and then again a split second later in a medium shot. Then the purse and gloves change position during the scene. (Claudia J. Sysock)

During the picnic scene, the hand of the goat wrangler is clearly visible on the goat's shoulder, keeping him from fleeing into the nether regions of the soundstage. (Tricia Lutz)

In the picnic scene, Kenneth says, "You'd make someone a good wife," without ever moving his mouth. He just sits with it wide open, half stuffed with sandwich. (Kayla Sturm)

When the ghost of Sir John rises, his chair creaks. I thought ghosts went right through their surroundings. (Julie Illescas)

The Chocolate Soldier

MGM.
Released November 1941.
Directed by Roy Del Ruth.
Produced by Victor Saville.
102 minutes.

Based on Ferenc Molnár's play *The Guardsman*, and incorporating songs from Oscar Straus's operetta, *The Chocolate Soldier*. Screenplay: Leonard Lee, Keith Winter, Ernest Vajda, and Claudine West. Music Adaptation and Direction: Herbert Stothart and Bronislau Kaper. Dances: Ernst Matray. Editor: James E. Newcom. Director of Photography: Karl Freund with Ray June and Harold Rosson. Sound Recording: Douglas Shearer. Art Director: Cedric Gibbons. Musical Arrangements: Merrill Pye. Set Decorations: Edwin B. Willis. Costumes: Adrian.

The Chocolate Soldier (*Der Tapfere Soldat*), with music by Oscar Straus (composer of the 1903 *The Waltz Dream*, then the greatest musical hit until eclipsed by Lehar's *The Merry Widow* in 1905) and lyrics by Rudolph Bernauer and Leopold Jacobson, was based on George Bernard Shaw's 1903 play, *Arms and the Man*. Shaw had sold the rights for a German operetta version of his play, certain that such an unlikely project was doomed to failure. However, he learned his lesson. When the show became an international hit, he vowed never again to sign away rights to any of his work.

The militant Germans found Shaw's pacifist plot a little hard to take, but the popularity of the music led to runs in England and the U.S. The German book and lyrics were by Leopold Jacobson and Rudolph Bernauer. The show reached New York's Lyric Theatre on September 13, 1909, where it ran for 296 performances with Ida Brooks Hunt and Flavio Arcaro in the leads. The following year, it was an even bigger success in London, running 500 performances. Like most plays of its time, its

A charming publicity shot of Nelson with his new costar, Risë Stevens. Eddy worked with many young singers during the 1940s, such as Nadine Conner, Dorothy Kirsten, and Eleanor Steber.

comparatively short Broadway run was no indication of its success, for it went on the road and has enjoyed popularity ever since.

When MGM decided to film the operetta in 1940, they had the music rights, but not the rights to George Bernard Shaw's source play. Instead, they looked around for a cheaper property and settled on Ferenc Molnár's delightful play *Testör*, for which they already owned the rights. This play was first performed in Hungary in 1911. Molnár's play opened in New York on September 3, 1913 as *Ignorance is Bliss,* with William Courtleigh and Rita Jolivet. This production survived only eight performances and did not reach popularity until the Theatre Guild produced it with the legendary stage couple, Alfred Lunt and Lynn Fontanne, in a considerably revised version. Retitled *The Guardsman*, it opened on October 13, 1924 at the Garrick, and ran 248 performances. The Lunts also appeared in MGM's 1931 film version, the only film in which the exquisite Miss Fontanne starred.

Jeanette MacDonald and her husband, Gene Raymond, toured in a stage version of *The Guardsman* in 1951, with Herbert Berghof playing the Critic. Jeanette's rôle became that of a singer rather than straight actress so that songs could be added.

In February 2001, a new musical version, *Enter the Guardsman*, was presented at the Oregon Shakespeare Festival, with music by Craig Bohmier, lyrics by Marion Adler, and book by Scott Wentworth, based on the Molnár play. It starred Michael Elich, Suzanne Irving, and Richard Farrell.

Nelson Eddy (Karl Lang / Vassily Vassilievitch Varonofsky)
Risë Stevens (Maria Lanyi) [screen debut]
Nigel Bruce (Bernard Fischer, the Critic)
Florence Bates (Madame Helene, called "Pugsy")
Dorothy Gilmore [Virginia Lowell] (Magda, a soubrette)
Nydia Westman (Liesel, the maid)
Max Barwyn (Anton, the valet)
Charles Judels (Klementov, the café proprietor)
Sig Arno (Voice coach, Emile)
Dave Willock (Delivery boy)
Leon Belasco (Waiter)
Betty Jane Graham, Vondell Darr, Ellen Hall, Grace Grant, Virginia Haroldson (Autograph seekers)
Yvette Duguay (Child who presents flower)
Maurice Cass (Flutist)
George Bookasta (Attendant)
James B. Carson (Stage manager)
Louis Adlon (Thin man)
Jack "Tiny" Lipson (Masaroff in "Seek the Spy")
Bess Flowers (Bit, regal type)

Oscar nominations:
Best Black and White Cinematography - Karl Freund
Best Sound Recording - Douglas Shearer
Best Scoring of a Musical Picture - Herbert Stothart and Bronislau Kaper

Considering that *The Chocolate Soldier* was a simple, small-cast, low-budget vehicle for Nelson Eddy, it is a surprising and satisfying delight. MGM did not make B musicals in the late 1930s as Universal, Republic, and, to some extent, Fox did, but they *did* put considerably less money into some

The Chocolate Soldier

musicals than others. While Miss MacDonald was working on the Technicolor *Smilin' Through* with crowd scenes, period costumes, and elaborate sets, Nelson Eddy was working on a black-and-white musical remake of Molnár's *The Guardsman* with simple stock sets and only four other principal actors.

It is a curious little film that finds Eddy playing a dual rôle, harking back to Mozart's *Cosi Fan Tutte*. As the jealous husband, poor Nelson is directed in a whining, nail-biting imitation of Alfred Lunt, who created the rôle both on Broadway and in the 1931 film. Since Lunt was one of the few actors who could carry on like an hysterical old maid and still be convincingly masculine, Eddy fails miserably.

However, in his dual rôle as the Russian suitor (the husband in disguise), Eddy turns the tables. With an accent and a beard to hide behind and some genuine scenery-chewing to do, Eddy fills the screen in a burst of glory. While it would have been impossible to write a string of such roles for him, especially as the vogue for non-swing musical films was waning, it is still a shame that more such parts didn't come his way. A definitive character piece such as Frank Morgan finally got in *The Wizard of Oz* or Clifton Webb in *Sitting Pretty* was certainly Eddy's due.

Opposite Eddy, in the Lynn Fontanne rôle, is young Risë ("Rhymes with 'Pisa,'" *Time* magazine noted) Stevens of the Metropolitan Opera. While she was well received in the film, she didn't make another until *Going My Way* in 1944, in which she played priest Bing Crosby's former girlfriend.

Third in the central trio is Nigel Bruce, the British character actor already synonymous with Dr. Watson in Basil Rathbone's *Sherlock Holmes* series. Two wonderful character actresses, Nydia Westman and Florence Bates, complete the household (and the cast) as the vague maid and the domineering duenna-companion.

Director Roy Del Ruth had started in the first days of sound at Warner Bros. where he directed the now mostly lost *Gold Diggers of Broadway* and a stage-bound version of *The Desert Song* in 1929-30. In the mid 1930s, he directed the much brighter *Broadway Melody of 1936* and *On the Avenue*. In between, he did melodramas and some of Cagney's best early films. He was one of the best all-purpose directors in early Hollywood.

MGM had bought the music rights to Oscar Straus's *The Chocolate Soldier*, and Louis B. Mayer visited George Bernard Shaw to secure the rights to its script, based on Shaw's *Arms and the Man*. Shaw was still smarting at his lack of business sense thirty years earlier when he had sold the rights for peanuts. He set terms too steep for the practical Mayer. So, MGM used the Straus songs in a "musical within a musical" as they had done with *Sweethearts*, plus a few opera arias for good measure. The script of the

Newlywed Karl Lang (Eddy) is already jealous of his bride, Maria Lanyi (Risë Stevens).

Their nightly performance in *The Chocolate Soldier* gives Maria a chance to ogle the officers in the audience. Karl, too, has his adoring fans.

1931 film *The Guardsman* is used almost scene for scene and line for line. (Ferenc Molnár is one of the most adapted and least acclaimed playwrights in film history.)

We open on a stage in "Balkany." Our leads are near the end of the evening's performance, singing "My Hero." The rapturous duet gives way to biting sarcasm as they wait in the wings for their final cue. In the six months since their marriage, they have rarely had a kind word for each other. Even their curtain calls are an occasion for bickering. Maria Lanyi (Risë Stevens) flirts outrageously with an officer, while her irate husband, Karl Lang (Nelson), threatens to drag the gentleman out of his box by his beard.

The battle continues into Maria's dressing room. Maria's middle-aged companion, Pugsy (Florence Bates), is an active participant in this enjoyable pastime. She snidely implies that Maria gave up more than an operatic career when she left all those broken-hearted officers in Vienna to marry Karl. The argument grows hotter and hotter until Pugsy tearfully dares

Karl to hit her. "I never hit women bigger than myself!" he storms.

Bernard (Nigel Bruce), their best friend and severest (newspaper) critic, drops in to see them. He is promptly dragged off to Karl's dressing room to hear the tales of Maria's infidelity. Night after night, Karl finds her sitting in the dark, playing "Evening Star" from *Tannhäuser*. She is in love with romance. Soon she will be leaving him as she left all the others, and he will be merely number nine in her string of amours. "Ten," corrects Bernard. "Nine," insists Karl. "I cannot allow anyone to cast aspersions on my wife!" Bernard sighs. Whatever the number, he was not one of them. "Sorry, old man," consoles Karl.

Karl himself is inconsolable. He can hear the heavy footsteps of his successor, coming closer and closer. Although he was the only one she ever married, he might as well not have bothered. Only six months and already her eyes stray about the theatre each night, lighting up at the sight of a uniform. Karl's sad story is interrupted by a half-dozen adoring girls who crash his dressing room begging for autographs. "Rather touching, don't you think?" he comments happily, as Maria stares daggers at him through the open doorway.

For further evidence of Maria's cruelty, Karl invites Bernard home with him. They enter and are greeted with applause. The applause is for Maria, who is entertaining a group of society people with "Mon coeur s'ouvre à ta voix" from *Samson et Dalila*. First *Tannhäuser* in the bedroom and now Samson in the drawing room!

Bernard's solution is simple. Karl loves Maria. He should go to her and tell her so, passionately, romantically, heroically. No woman can resist that.

Karl prepares carefully for the big moment, shaving, putting on his most handsome dressing gown. He strides expectantly into their bedroom, only to find her sobbing over *Tannhäuser*. The music is not meant for him, and he angrily retreats to the couch for the night.

Their friend Bernard (Nigel Bruce, right) tries to reassure Karl that Maria loves him, but Karl plans a test of his own.

On a subsequent evening, we see a good bit of Straus's *The Chocolate Soldier* on stage, much of it incredibly dull. To recover, Karl, Maria, and Bernard retire to a little Russian café for a late dinner. Maria sarcastically remarks that the decor reminds her of a production of *Scheherazade* she once saw in Omsk. The owner, Klementov (Charles Judels), appears at her elbow. "What a charming place," she coos. "May heaven forgive you," whispers Karl.

A mysterious telegram comes for Karl, and he excuses himself to go "bail out a friend." Maria is sure that any bailing Karl does will be with the show's soubrette. Karl's mysterious scheme doesn't involve the soubrette, however. The café owner announces the surprise appearance of the famous singer, Vassily Vassilievitch Varonofsky. It is Karl in a magnificent disguise, all whiskers and uniform.

He dazzles the assemblage and especially Maria with Moussorgsky's "Song of the Flea." Afterward, in an accent dripping with borscht, he tells Maria that she "cannot deny to permit to introduce" himself. He has seen her in the

Karl woos his wife disguised as a dashing guardsman, Vassily Vassilievitch. She responds warmly at first, then seems to flee his advances.

"Soldier of Chocolates," and, even though she is married, the "jah-lousy of the husband" will not keep him from seeing her again. Vassily exits to music and applause.

Bernard is unimpressed. This zoo-escapee is beneath contempt. Maria is not so negatively inclined. Karl bustles in, complaining about the slowness of the law. "That shouldn't worry a fast worker like *you*, dear," Maria murmurs sweetly.

Flowers begin arriving at their home, flowers that Maria swears are not accompanied by any card. Bernard and Pugsy know this is a lie. Karl throws a temper tantrum that includes screaming at the pasty-faced maid, Liesel (the delightful Nydia Westman). Lunt could carry off this type of scene humorously and sympathetically, but it is too much to ask of Eddy. Bernard tries to calm his friend. He suggests that Karl simply call the florist and ask who sent the flowers. Karl shrugs. He knows who sent the flowers. "Who?" "I did." Karl drops into the heavy Russian accent he used at the restaurant: "You cannot deny to permit me to introduce myself."

Pugsy and Maria are in an ecstasy of conspiracy. The note with the flowers has informed Maria that if she will stand at the window at 5 PM, the Russian will see her and join her a half-hour later. She can barely conceal her pleasure when Karl announces that he has been called away for an emergency concert. Bernard and Karl take their leave of Maria at just 5 PM. Karl apologizes elaborately for his tantrum. Maria is strolling casually around the room, touching tables, lamps, vases. She reaches the window as Karl and Bernard stand in breathless suspense. Slowly she draws back the curtain and peers out. "Don't miss your train, darling," she says.

Pugsy is atwitter with vicarious excitement. Maria will add this Russian to her long list of conquests. Maria confesses that she has had many *admirers*, but they were just that. Only because Karl was always surrounded by doting women did she let him believe that she, too, has had many amours. Pugsy is disappointed—or would be if she believed her.

Maria is nearly as excited as Pugsy over the Russian, but, unlike her stage counterpart, she reveals that she definitely knows her own husband when she sees him. Vassily is admitted and soon has the lady in his arms. His lovemaking is so high-powered that Maria desperately suggests that he slow down long enough to express himself in song. Not "The Volga Boatman," of course. That would be too stimulating. Reluctantly, Vassily untangles himself to sing his favorite song: "Evening Star" from *Tannhäuser*.

Back on the sofa, Vassily-Karl is torn between the obviously obtainable success of his conquest and his reluctance to cuckold himself. It is a magnificent scene as Maria goads Vassily to the limit, only to leap up at the last moment, insulted. She orders him from the house. Triumphantly, Vassily-Karl slinks from the room. She is faithful to him. "Wait!" She calls him back—to tell him how much she loves her husband. In a frenzy of joy, Vassily prepares to leave again. Again he is called back. "My husband," Maria whispers, "will be out this evening."

There is only one thing for Vassily to do. Karl returns to catch Maria dressing for her assignation. He has missed his train. Besides, he hates to leave her. He doesn't *have* to leave her, Maria assures him. She will come with him to the station to see that he catches the next train.

Darkness brings moonlight and the Russian serenading in the garden: "While My Lady Sleeps." Vassily escorts the lady, not to heaven as the lyric proposes, but to a romantic little Russian restaurant overlooking the Danube. As they waltz, she strokes his beard and croons the tune the orchestra is playing, "Ti-ra-la-la." The waltz over, the orchestra bursts into a fiery Russian *gopak*. The dance that follows should be a highlight of the film, but is dulled considerably by over-arty cutting.

A little girl presents Maria with a flower that Vassily has selected for her. Maria is touched and responds with a soft, romantic version of "My Hero." Again Maria leads Vassily on, then rebuffs him at the last minute. She rushes off in tears. She never wants to see him again! Bernard

Maria seems elated when Karl tells her he has been called out of town. Shortly after he leaves, her new lover is knocking at her door. (Florence Bates as Pugsy, center.) *Courtesy Anna Michalik.*

The Chocolate Soldier

PHOTO LEFT: Vassily serenades Maria with "While My Lady Sleeps," a sensuous Bronislau Kaper song written for the film. *Courtesy Anna Michalik.*

hails Karl from behind a trellis, where he has been watching the performance. "Karl, follow her! She expects it!"

A cab brings Vassily to Maria's door at the same time as the lady, who has not been fleeing too quickly. Again, she confirms that Vassily can be nothing to her. It is over. She shuts the door behind her, and Karl hugs himself with glee. He has won. The window of the upstairs bedroom opens and a slender white hand reaches out. Something shiny drops at his feet. It is the door key.

When Karl "returns" the next day, he finds Maria and Pugsy humming with self-satisfaction. His trip was ghastly, he tells them. How he must have suffered, Maria sympathizes. Yes, he mutters darkly, she'll never know how he suffered.

All during the performance that night, Maria giggles. In the midst of some of the dowdiest choreography ever perpetrated, she finds a secret source of amusement. Karl storms into his dressing room and locks the door. The frantic Bernard fears that he will do away with himself, but Karl quickly reappears—as Vassily. He leaps on stage for the "accusation scene" of the operetta in full Vassily regalia. Maria does not flutter an eyelash. Gently stroking his beard, she croons "My Hero" as she did that moonlit night by the Danube.

Backstage, Karl furiously rips the disguise from his face as Maria laughs. He refuses to believe that she knew all along. Why, she counters, did he think he could play a difficult part well enough to fool her but she couldn't do the same? Besides, does he know what really gave him away? His kiss.

Poor Karl's face drains. All his fears about his deficiencies are true. Maria moves toward him and places her hands on his face. "No man on earth can kiss like you." Back on stage, they

In Risë Stevens, Eddy had a beautiful, world-class opera diva for a singing partner, but the magic just wasn't there.

embrace for the "reconciliation scene" and, of course, a final chorus of "My Hero."

The Chocolate Soldier was a nice, lightweight film for an ongoing star, but Eddy's pull at the box office was leveling off. Wartime prosperity would give box-office control to younger audiences and their passion for "hepcats" who were "on the beam." A young crooner named Frank Sinatra began attracting some attention, and the big bands were about to take over the movie musical.

It wasn't entirely that operetta was old-fashioned. It had been that in 1935 when *Naughty Marietta* exploded on the scene. It was just that in attempting to cash in on a sure-fire box-office gimmick, the quality of the "product" was slowly diminishing. It is rare that a work in any form gains mass recognition without someone somewhere putting a little love into it. With the exceptions of *Cabin in the Sky* (1943),

Meet Me in St. Louis (1944), and *Anchors Aweigh* (1945), three inspired exceptions, there would not be another musical redolent with love until *On the Town* in 1949.

Reviews

Bosley Crowther of the *New York Times*, definitely not an Eddy fan, called the film "tidy and musical. Mr. Eddy is an utter revelation in the character and costume of a mad Cossack." He then went on to suggest snidely that Eddy continue playing Russians. *Time* magazine made its usual reference to Eddy's dimples and felt it necessary to compare Eddy's appearance to that of a "midwest swimming coach." William Boehnel of the *New York World-Telegram* gave high praise to Miss Stevens and admitted, "It must be said that [Eddy] plays the Cossack with considerable gusto," the closest Eddy ever got to a compliment from Mr. Boehnel.

Archer Winsten of the *New York Post* gave the film a good rating on the Post Movie Meter and said, "Nelson Eddy still has it. His voice rings out strong and clear and virile. Opposite him, Risë Stevens, the pride of Queens [a borough of New York City] and a genuine member of the Metropolitan Opera, is equally clear and strong. Not only has she taken the spot ordinarily reserved for Jeanette MacDonald, but also she looks like Jeanette from several angles. A man sitting directly behind this department actually thought she was. But she is bigger, younger, less dental, sings as well or better, and is not so cute."

Recordings (See Discography for further information)

Eddy and Risë Stevens recorded a 78 RPM album of songs from the film:
    "The Chocolate Soldier" (Eddy and Stevens)
    "Forgive" (Eddy and Stevens)
    "My Hero" (Eddy and Stevens)
    "Sympathy" (Eddy and Stevens)
    "Ti-ra-la-la" (Stevens)
    "While My Lady Sleeps" (Eddy)
Eddy recorded "Evening Star" in 1941 and "Song of the Flea" in 1942.

Music in the Film

All music is by Oscar Straus with American lyrics by Stanislaus Stange unless otherwise indicated. Because the "standard" Stange translation was used, source titles will be given in English, not German. (This was one place where MGM really missed a bet by not updating the lyrics. Stange's convoluted poesy included gems like "naught can efface you.") In listing performers after each title, "and" denotes a genuine duet, while commas between names indicate a sequence of singers.

Overture: fragments of "My Hero," "Seek the Spy," "The Chocolate Soldier Man," "Ti-ra-la-la" (Dorothy Gilmore, Jimmy Alexander, Robert Bradford, Thomas Clarke, Paul Keast, Bob Priester, Harry Stanton, and Jack (Tiny) Lipson; dubbing for dancers: Roy Loomis, Lee Murray, Buddy Ray, Alan Speer, Foy Van Dolsen, and Cas Twid), INTO:
"My Hero" (Stevens, Eddy)
"Thank the Lord the War Is Over" (Eddy, Stevens, with Lorraine Bridges, Robert Bradford, chorus) - original opening of Act III, stage version
"Mon coeur s'ouvre à ta voix" ["My heart opens to your voice"] (Stevens) - from the opera *Samson et Dalila*, with music by Charles Camille Saint-Saëns and libretto by Ferdinand Lemaire
"Evening Star" fragment ["O, Du Mein Holder Abendstern"] (Stevens) - from the opera *Tannhäuser*, music by Richard Wagner, English lyrics by Gus Kahn
Section of Act I of *The Chocolate Soldier*, including "Sympathy" (Stevens, Eddy) and "Seek the Spy" (bass, male chorus) with flamenco, middle-eastern, and conga variations -lyrics by Stange and Kahn

The Chocolate Soldier

Karl appears unexpectedly on stage, dressed as the Russian. He thinks he will astonish Maria, but she has a surprise of her own.

"Song of the Flea" ["Mephistopheles' Song of The Flea"] (Eddy) - music by Modeste Moussorgsky, Russian lyrics by Strugovshchikov from Goethe. English lyrics by Gus Kahn.
"Evening Star" reprise (Eddy)
"Thank the Lord the War is Over" reprise fragment (Stevens and Florence Bates)
"While My Lady Sleeps" (Eddy) - music by Bronislaw Kaper, lyrics by Gus Kahn
"Ti-ra-la-la" (Stevens) based on Aurelia's melodic line in finale of Act I of the stage version, English lyricist uncertain, probably Gus Kahn
Dance sequence (gypsy orchestra, dancers: Deena Newell, Joyce Coles, Paul Godkin, Lee Brent, Jack Vlaskin, William Sabbot, Leo Galitzine, Gabriel Solodihin, Zara Lee) - based on Russian folk melodies arranged by Herbert Stothart
Flower presentation (Yvette Duguay, chorus, Stevens, Eddy) - based on "The Letter Song," Act III, new lyrics probably by Gus Kahn, INTO:
"My Hero" reprise (Stevens)
"The Chocolate Soldier" reprise (Eddy and Stevens)
Accusation scene (Eddy) - not in stage version, probably arranged by Stothart with lyrics by Gus Kahn, INTO:
"My Hero" reprise (Stevens)
"Forgive, Forgive, Forgive" (Eddy) - part of finale of Act II, INTO:
"My Hero" reprise (Stevens and Eddy)
Finale: "Seek the Spy" reprise (orchestral)

Trivia

An interesting footnote to the film is that the 1931 film of *The Guardsman* on which it was based was directed by the first husband of the new Mrs. Eddy, Sidney Franklin. He also directed the silent version of *Smilin' Through*, starring Norma Talmadge, remade as a musical with Jeanette MacDonald. And in a further example of *la plus ça change*, in 1951 Jeanette MacDonald toured with her husband, Gene Raymond, in *The Guardsman*.

The 11-minute 1942 promotional short *We Must Have Music* includes a sequence in which composer-conductor Herbert Stothart conducts a recording session for *The Chocolate Soldier*, followed by a clip from the film of Risë Stevens singing "My Hero." Other scenes show Bronislau Kaper, Judy Garland, and Busby Berkeley.

Movie Goofs

When Nelson rips off his disguise backstage at the end of the movie, he is wearing Hussar's boots and pants, yet when he returns to the stage moments later to confront Risë Stevens, he is wearing street shoes. (Stephanie Loyd)

I Married an Angel

MGM.
Released June 1942.
Directed by Maj. W.S. Van Dyke II
Produced by Hunt Stromberg.
98 minutes. (Now 84 minutes.)

French title: *Ma Femme est un Ange* (My Wife is an Angel)
Portuguese title: *Casei-me com um anjo* (I Married an Angel)

From the Dwight Deere Wiman production of a Broadway musical by Richard Rodgers and Lorenz Hart. Screenplay: Anita Loos. Some sequences directed by Roy Del Ruth. Assistant Director: Marvin Stuart. Director of Photography: Ray June with Leonard Smith and Harold Marzorati. Recording Director: Douglas Shearer. Art Director: Cedric Gibbons. Art Associates: John S. Detlie and Motley Associates. Set Decorations: Edwin B. Willis. Special Effects: Arnold Gillespie and Warren Newcombe. Dance Director: Ernst Matray. Costumes: Motley. Gowns: Kalloch. Hair Styles: Sydney Guilaroff. Makeup: Jack Dawn. Editor: Conrad A. Nervig.

I Married an Angel was based on *Angyalt Vettem Feleségül* (I Married an Angel), a 1932 Budapest hit by János Vaszary. After being adapted as a Rodgers and Hart musical for a proposed but never produced film at MGM, *I Married an Angel* debuted on Broadway on

I Married an Angel

May 11, 1938 at the Shubert Theatre, starring Dennis King (*The Vagabond King*), Vivienne Segal (*The Cat and the Fiddle*), Audrey Christie, Walter Slezak, and the angel herself, ballerina Vera Zorina. It ran 338 performances.

Jeanette MacDonald (Anna Zador / Brigitta, the angel)
Nelson Eddy (Count Willie Palaffi)
Binnie Barnes (Peggy)
Edward Everett Horton (Peter)
Reginald Owen (Herman Rothbart, "Whiskers")
Mona Maris (Marika Szabo)
Janice [later Janis] Carter (Sufi)
Inez Cooper (Iren)
Douglass Dumbrille (Baron Szigetti)
Leonid Kinsky (Zinski)
Marion Rosamond (Dolly)
Anne Jeffreys (Polly)
Marek Windheim (Marcel)
Georges Renavent (Pierre)
Max Willenz (Assistant manager)
Francine Bordeaux (First maid)
Mildred Shay (Second maid)
Odette Myrtil * (Modiste)
Tyler Brooke (Lucien)
Jacques Vanaire (Max)
Luis Alberni (Jean Frederique)
Micheline Cheirel (Annette)
Rafaela Ottiano (Madelon)
Margaret Moffat (Mother Zador)
Vaughan Glaser (Father Andreas)
Gino Corrado (Valet)
Sid D'Albrook, Mitchell Lewis (Porters)
Sig Arno (Waiter)
Jacqueline Dalya (Olga)
George Humbert (Taxi driver)
Ben Hall (Delivery boy)
Ferdinand Munier (Rich man)
George Davis (Pushcart vendor)
Jack Vlaskin (Milk wagon driver)
Veda Ann Borg, Carol Hughes (Willie's morning ladies)
Ludwig Stössel (Janitor – also Customs Agent, cut from film)
Robert Greig (Major domo)
Maxine Leslie, Lillian Eggers (Willie's evening ladies)
Maude Eburne (Juli)
Bodil Rosing (Customs Agent's wife – cut from film)

I Married an Angel, 1942. *Courtesy Anna Michalik.*

I Married an Angel, 1942.

Frederik Vogeding, Charles Judels (Customs officers)
Anthony Blair, Joel Friedkin, Maj, James McNamara, Earle S. Dewey, Bert Roach (Board members)
Suzanne Kaaren (Simone, a maid)
Lisl Valetti (Maid)
Leonard Carey, Guy Bellis (Servants)
Esther Dale (Mrs. Gherkin)
Grace Hayle (Mrs. Gabby)
Gertrude W. Hoffman (Lady Gimcrack)
Maude Allen, Eva Dennison, Winifred Harris (Women)
Florence Auer (Mrs. Roquefort)
Walter Soderling (Mr. Kipper)
Dick Elliott (Mr. Scallion)
Oliver B. Prickett [Blake] (Mr. Gherkin)
Almira Sessions (Mrs. Scallion)
Lon Poff (Mr. Dodder)
Charles Brabin (Mr. Fairmind)
Otto Hoffmann (Mr. Flit)
Beryl Wallace (Fifi)
Anita Bolster [Sharp-Bolster] (Mrs. Kipper)
Frank Reicher (Driver)
Rafael Storm (Berti)
Cecil Cunningham (Mrs. Fairmind)
Jack (Tiny) Lipson (Mr. Roquefort)
Harry Worth, James B. Carson (Waiters)
Alphonse Martell (Headwaiter)
Arthur Dulac, Harry Horwitz (French news vendors)
General Sam Savitsky (Doorman)
Evelyn Atchison (Marie Antoinette)
Charles Bancroft (Chimney sweep)
Muriel Barr (Mermaid)
Edwina Coolidge (Queen Elizabeth)
Ruth Alder (Night #1)
Leda Nicova (Night #2)
Vivian DuBois (Night #3)
Betty Hayward (Night #4)
George Ford (Neptune)
Guy Gabriel, Dorothy Haas, Aileen Haley (Infantas)
Joe Harman (Marc Antony)
John Marlowe (Louis XIV)
Paul Power (Scottish highlander)
Robert Spencer (Peacock)

* Odette Myrtil played the "cat" in the original Broadway production of *The Cat and the Fiddle*.

I Married an Angel was presented on Screen Guild Theatre (radio), 6/1/42, with Jeanette and Nelson.

I Married an Angel was the last film Jeanette MacDonald and Nelson Eddy made together. In an interview done during shooting, Nelson was quoted as saying, "This is either going to be the best film we've ever made or the worst."

For about twenty minutes, *Angel does* promise to be the most entrancing MacDonald-Eddy film ever made, with style and wit equal to that of the Dorothy Parker/Alan Campbell *Sweethearts*. Then the censors get out their shears, leaving an incoherent shambles, but one that still yields occasional moments of delight.

The score contains two hits that became standards, the title song and "Spring is Here." Rodgers and Hart had originally written the musical as a follow-up to their 1932 Paramount film, *Love Me Tonight*, which starred MacDonald and Chevalier. *Angel* was proposed as Jeanette's first film when she moved to MGM in 1933. However, the cyclical rise of Puritanism was just taking effect, and the story of an angel who loses her wings and her virginity simultaneously was considered too risqué.

Rodgers and Hart reclaimed their work and took it to Broadway, where, in 1938, it was a sensation. Jeanette's *Vagabond King* costar, Dennis King, played Willie, and Vera Zorina was a dancing Angel.

Since contemporary critics were fond of proclaiming the superiority of the stage *Angel* over the film version, it is important to note that the brightness of the original was based more on style than substance. Once the concept of the angel who becomes charmingly and embarrassingly mortal after her wedding night is established, the story falls into more conventional musical comedy lines with a plot involving getting money for Willie's bank from a wealthy widow.

The 1942 film made a number of changes. On Broadway, the Angel appeared after the hero denounced his wayward girlfriend and vowed to marry no one but an angel. His angel was a dancer (Zorina) who didn't sing a note. MGM merged the two parts of Willie's girlfriend,

I Married an Angel

Behind the cameras on *I Married an Angel*. The most intimate love scenes were conducted with several dozen crew members looking on. *Courtesy Anna Michalik.*

MGM head Louis B. Mayer (right) visits the set of *I Married an Angel*, destined to be the last MacDonald-Eddy film. *Courtesy Anna Michalik.*

W.S. Van Dyke (right) had directed five previous team films. *Angel* would be the last time the three worked together. *Courtesy Anna Michalik.*

The film originally opened with a big production number, "Little Work-a-Day World," as Count Willie Palaffi (Nelson) arrives for work at his family's bank after a night of revelry with two lady friends, Veda Ann Borg, left, and Carol Hughes, right. Eddy recorded the song, but the scene was cut from the final film. (Jack Vlaskin as wagon driver.) *Courtesy Anna Michalik.*

Anna Murphy, and his angel-wife, Brigitta, into a single singing rôle for Jeanette. The MGM Anna is demoted from girlfriend to secretary, while Willie's sister, Peggy, a major stage rôle that starred Vivienne Segal, is transformed into his ex-girlfriend. (That, at least, is an innovation—usually Hollywood turned mistresses into sisters.) Willie's valet, Peter, an important character in the stage version, becomes a glorified walk-on for Edward Everett Horton, probably due to censorship cuts. With Willie's assertive sister gone, a new character is added to the film, that of an older man who berates Willie for his profligacy. Finally, to avoid religious and moral censure, the audience is continually reminded that the angel sequences are just a dream.

Ever since the success of *Naughty Marietta*, Jeanette had insisted that her character names begin with N or M, a good luck superstition. Therefore, it is intriguing that the script writers replaced the stage character's name, Murphy, with Zador. Actually, it would have taken more than luck to save *I Married an Angel*, for almost no one involved seems to have cared terribly about it. Scriptwriter Anita Loos didn't have time to be incensed at the revisions in her script. She was doing three films and a Broadway show simultaneously and mostly remembered long coast-to-coast flights. She recalled only that

I Married an Angel

Marika (Mona Maris) is Willie's very private secretary. Early in production, Jeanette played his other secretary, Anna Zador, as distinctly dowdy (above), but in the final version she is glamorous, if unworldly and unnoticed. *Courtesy Anna Michalik.*

Jeanette and Nelson stopped speaking to each other for a time when not in front of the cameras. Rodgers and Hart were in Hollywood, but generally "unavailable." (Hart died the following year.) Bob Wright and Chet Forrest were so incensed at having to do a wholesale rewrite of Hart's classic lyrics that they quit MGM and went to New York, where they achieved fame with *Song of Norway* and *Kismet*. And obviously someone wasn't listening to director W.S. Van Dyke. His efforts at screwball comedy were so thoroughly undermined that parts of the story are incomprehensible.

The film starts off as a tale of a mousy secretary unnoticed by her playboy boss, an old but serviceable plot device. However, footage of Jeanette in horn rim glasses and dowdy dress was scrapped, and now she first appears as a creature so ravishing that only a blind man could pass her by. Our wonder at the hero's lack of perception is fleeting, for we are quickly whisked into the dream sequence. Since there are repeated shots of Eddy tossing in his sleep, any dramatic tension that the body of the picture might establish is lost. Whenever we are in danger of getting involved in the improbable events, a superimposed shot of Eddy on his couch reminds us that it is just a dream.

Behind the opening credits of the film, Jeanette is seen bicycling across the countryside, humming—not a Richard Rodgers tune but Fritz Kreisler's "Caprice Viennois." A title tells us we are in "Budapest in the gay days not so long ago," a sad reminder that the Nazis had invaded Hungary. Anna Zador (Jeanette) arrives for work at the Palaffi Bank and formally greets the series of portraits of the founding fathers that line the oak-paneled hall: Great Great Grandpa Palaffi, Great Grandpa Palaffi, Grandpa Palaffi, Papa Palaffi. Finally, she pauses at the last painting. "Good morning, Count Palaffi," she murmurs softly. She slips into the Count's office to place her little bouquet of flowers in a vase on his desk. Marika Zabo (Mona Maris), the Count's senior secretary, catches her. Marika belittles Anna's "country posies," but says it is all right

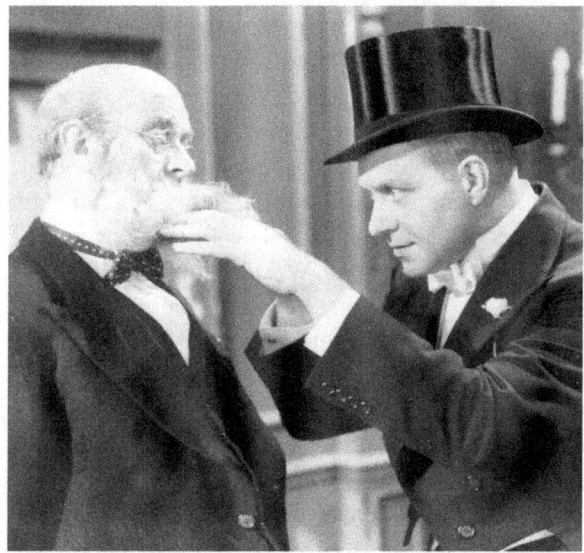

Bank Director Rothbart (Reginald Owen) lectures Willie on his responsibilities, but the irrepressible playboy is more concerned with discovering whether "Whiskers" is wearing a tie. *Courtesy Anna Michalik.*

Forced by Rothbart to invite "the other secretary," Marika tricks innocent Anna (Jeanette) into wearing a homemade angel costume to Willie's lavish birthday party. *Courtesy Anna Michalik.*

to leave them. The Count never notices them anyway.

Eight AM. Anna is hard at work at her typewriter when Willie (Nelson) arrives in evening clothes, accompanied by two evening ladies (Veda Ann Borg and Carol Hughes). The final moments of the "Little Work-a-Day World" number, cut from the film, are visible just before he enters the bank. Willie effusively greets the staff, even Anna, and charges into his office to do his day's work. Marika welcomes him with one of Anna's flowers for his buttonhole. She has grown them just for him, she purrs.

Willie's first task is to send a memo to the Chairman of the Board: "Dear Whiskers." He respectfully informs the venerable old man that he has once again reached his desk on time in imitation of his ancestors. The depositors can relax.

His second duty is to order some jewelry for his two female companions, and, just to be sure his secretary Marika isn't jealous, she is added to the list. Whiskers, otherwise known as Mr. Rothbart (Reginald Owen), finds her thanking Willie with a kiss.

Whiskers brings bad news. Their biggest depositor, the Baron Szigetti, is threatening to remove his account unless Willie stops neglecting business. If the Baron goes, there will be a run on the bank. But, Willie counters, why should he stop having fun with a great man like Whiskers in charge? His work completed, Willie retraces his steps through the outer office at precisely 8:05.

Whiskers asks Marika about several matters, including Willie's birthday, and learns that she has planned an elaborate costume party. She will be taking the afternoon off to have her costume fitted, she tells him imperiously. Whiskers reasons that if the Count can invite one secretary, he should be thoughtful enough to invite the other one. "Anna?" Marika asks incredulously. Why, Willie doesn't even know her! "It might be very good for him if he did," Whiskers declares.

Marika delivers the invitation to Anna as if she herself had thought of it. Dear Anna must come dressed as something very good, someone very angelic. Marika will help her.

We dissolve in a roar of music to the wildest costume party since DeMille's *Madame Satan* (1930). Each guest is more exquisitely costumed than the last, and the sets are lavishly complex, no doubt to make up for the film not being in Technicolor. Each lady greets Willie with a kiss that indicates he is not a casual acquaintance. Peter (Edward Everett Horton) stands at Willie's elbow with a handkerchief to remove the lipstick from each encounter.

Miss Peggy (Binnie Barnes) is announced as "Mimi from Montmartre." The elegant lady pauses at the top of the stairs, then races raucously into Willie's arms. They are hugging and reminiscing as the liveried major domo

I Married an Angel

Willie must marry for the good of the family bank, and his potential brides line up to serenade him at his birthday party. Left to right, Janis Carter, Marion Rosamond, Mona Maris, Anne Jeffreys, Binnie Barnes, Inez Cooper.

(Robert Greig of *Love Me Tonight* and *Rose Marie*) announces, "Miss Anna Zador as an angel." The doorway remains empty. Anna lingers in the hall, debating whether to go in. Does everyone have to kiss the Count? she asks Peter. "Yes. Now take off!" His shove sends her into view and the whole room bursts into laughter as one of her cardboard wings falls off.

Her costume is a bed sheet, and her halo hits Willie in the nose when she tries to kiss him. In one of Miss MacDonald's funniest visual sequences, she must make three passes before she connects with his cheek. The guests are convulsed. To save the party, Peter leaps forward and announces the purpose of the occasion in a charming evocation of the sung dialogue of the early 1930s, pioneered by Rodgers and Hart, but composed here by Stothart with lyrics by Wright and Forrest. Peter tells the crowd that it is time for the Count to

Willie's sophisticated friends ridicule the innocence of Anna's artless bed-sheet angel costume. Then, to Willie's astonishment, a real angel joins him. Brigitta (also Jeanette) tells him that she has come from heaven to marry him. (The body harness necessary to support Jeanette's 60-lb. wings was incredibly uncomfortable.)

select a wife, and some unattached ladies are about to present themselves.

To the melody of "At the Roxy Music Hall," the girls (Mona Maris, Janice Carter, Inez Cooper, Marion Rosamond, and Anne Jeffreys) parade in white "wedding gowns" of beads and feathers and sing of their qualifications in a delightful number dubbed "Tira Lira La." The girls' ideas of marriage are as exotic as their costumes, and Willie rejects their offers, also in song. They are all beautiful and charming, but the girl he marries would have to be—he spies Anna—"an angel!"

Anna is mortified and flees. Willie rushes after her to apologize as his friends roar with laughter. To evade the "brides," Willie asks Anna to dance. So she works in his bank? he inquires politely. He doesn't know the new employees very well. "I've been there six years," she tells him. Their conversation exhausted, he fetches her some birthday cake and slips off upstairs.

Whiskers follows him and scolds him for his rudeness. Willie must settle down. No Palaffi has ever passed his thirty-fifth birthday without marrying. Willie must marry a good woman, virtuous and loyal. "Virtuous and loyal," scoffs Willie as he stretches out on a couch. Well, Whiskers can just reach up to heaven and pull one down for him. There *are* angels, Whiskers replies, but they aren't found in nightclubs. Willie doesn't hear him. He is asleep.

Into his dream comes the voice of an angel. In an exquisite bit of film magic, the Angel, with dazzling wings, floats into his room as she sings to him. "Don't be frightened," she tells him. "I'm an angel." He is skeptical. "That's what they *all* say."

It is at this point that an incredibly light hand is needed, but is sadly lacking. As the angel moves about the room, the flowers and statues bow to her. Speaking in an elaborate monotone, the angel Brigitta (also played by Jeanette) tells Willie that she has come to be his wife and give him children. (Their offspring were excised from an early script when church censors protested they were "sacrilegious.")

Willie is intrigued, but tells her that marriage is an earthly as well as a spiritual institution. She replies that she will be a woman if he will teach her how. She loves him and knows all about him. "You do?" Willie chokes. Only the *nice* things, she assures him. In heaven they only hear the nice things like "little children's laughter and their prayers." Willie tries to embrace her, but an invisible wall is between them. She steps through it and kisses him. "So *that's* what kisses are like?" she murmurs. "Only *mine*," he tells her quickly.

The guests burst through the bedroom door, and Brigitta hides Willie by stepping in front of him. To Willie's astonishment, his friends find a note on his desk saying that he has run away to marry Brigitta. "A fly-by-night!" wails Peter. They decide it is a joke and go back downstairs to search for him. Willie and Brigitta make their escape by running out the window into the night sky. A flurry of accordions indicates that their destination is the city of love, Paris.

Spotlights pick out individual singers in a black void as tinkers, tailors, and sailors herald Willie's news: "I Married an Angel." Then the lights come up on a crowded Paris street scene. Willie's favorite hotel is in a fever of preparation as the angel's shadow is seen approaching along the hall. Champagne is brought by a hissing waiter, one of many unexplained sequences. Night falls, and Brigitta prepares to return to her fleecy cloud. Willie, however, has other ideas. He asks for a good-night kiss. With the bed prominently in the background, she obliges. Fade out.

Fade in on the bed, where a wingless, smiling Brigitta is still sleeping. She awakes with consternation, but Willie assures her it is all for the best. Now he can put his arms all the way around her. He prepares to finish dressing, but Brigitta sits and pouts. She hasn't anything to wear. That is an old, familiar phrase, Willie says, but they are in the right city to remedy it.

The morning after their wedding night, the Angel discovers she has lost her wings, thus shocking the censors. *Courtesy Anna Michalik.*

a fantastic cut-glass dome, she joins the harpists in song. Back on his dream couch, the sleeping Willie begins tossing fretfully.

Brigitta is such a success that she is invited to sing with the group during their two-week engagement. She agrees happily, much to Willie's dismay. He faints and is caught by Peter, who has just arrived to fetch him back to Budapest. The bank is being investigated, and Willie must present his new bride as evidence of his stability. Quickly, Peter checks Brigitta's teeth and tongue, feels her muscles, and whips out a stethoscope to listen to her heart. Yes, she will do. Willie reports by phone to Whiskers and his board of directors, all bearded, that he is bringing home an angel.

Peter is nervously setting out place cards for the party to introduce Willie's bride to the society of Budapest. Seating is of the utmost importance, since nearly everybody hates nearly everybody else. Of course, the Baron Szigetti, the bank's chief depositor, will sit next to Countess Palaffi. There is only one major

They go on a whirlwind shopping tour in which the best of Paris fashion is paraded before her. Brigitta gets off on the wrong foot by refusing to wear the feathers and furs of dead animals. "That's a Schiaparelli!" cries a horrified vendeur (Luis Alberni). "Poor little Schiaparelli!" she moans, stroking the fur trim on the dress. The couturiers of Paris threaten to revolt, but Willie challenges them. His wife needs angelic clothes and they have failed. They rush off to try again.

Suitably costumed in an outfit with flowered peplum and muff, Brigitta joins Willie in one of the most lilting songs ever written, "Spring is Here." At precisely the moment when the screen should open up and show us the lovers touring Paris or the nearby countryside in a hymn to spring and love, they are confined to a hotel terrace. Brigitta beckons to a bush that bursts into flower, and a songbird alights on her outstretched finger. Willie repeats her gestures, but no flowers and no bird.

Willie wants to take his wife to the races (stills exist of a race sequence), but she prefers a harp concert at the Académie de Musique. Under

Jeanette rehearses for the "Spring Is Here" scene. The bird trainer's arm can be seen at right. *Courtesy Robert Friess.*

I Married an Angel

A major scene in the original script, the harp concert is drastically cut in the final release print. Censorship cuts make much of the film incomprehensible. Courtesy Anna Michalik.

problem: the Count's five house guests. It seems that Marika has tried to make trouble by telling Brigitta of Willie's affection for the ladies. Brigitta, of course, has invited them to move in. The five "house cats...er...house guests" must not be seated next to married men.

Peggy, who has politely refused Brigitta's invitation to move in, has come to help her prepare and put on makeup for the big occasion. She is baffled that Brigitta doesn't seem to need any. Feeling very protective toward this innocent surrounded by scheming felines, Peggy cautions Willie on the propriety of the arrangement. Willie thinks it is just fine. They wanted him to marry innocence, didn't they? Well, he has.

Peter introduces Brigitta in a musical monologue, and then Brigitta makes a spectacular entrance, singing while sliding down the banister. She greets each guest with a perfectly true remark that insults them terribly. She tells one dowager that her gown doesn't make her look fat as the lady's husband claims. She *is* fat. She disputes the musical ability of the leading music critic, who is wearing opaque glasses. Willie lounges uneasily against a dress dummy that turns into the Baron Szigetti (Douglass Dumbrille). Brigitta greets an elderly gentleman and his youthful companion, begging the girl to bring her father more often. Willie grows frantic. He explains that in society one doesn't tell the truth. So Brigitta greets the next pretty girl by telling her she is old and ugly. The party begins to pall.

A footman blows the racing call to colors on a trumpet, and the major domo, standing on a chair, announces dinner. Peter discovers a wooden leg under the table and begins checking each lady present for its owner. Brigitta decides that the guests are unhappy because they are not sitting next to the person they are fond of and begins rearranging them. Baron Szigetti thinks this is a delightful idea and urges her on. Brandishing a giant monkey wrench, Brigitta unites each elderly gentleman with his young mistress in an elaborate game of musical chairs, accompanied by "Turkey in the Straw." A servant is seen vacuuming up the straw on the floor. The wives finally rebel and drag their errant spouses away. Peggy and Willie rush off to apologize to everyone while the Baron consoles Brigitta.

He thinks the whole thing is tremendously funny. Why didn't he see her before Willie did, he wonders. "What difference does *that* make?" asks Brigitta innocently. He assumes she is flirting with him and kisses her just as Willie

Cameraman Ray June checks the light level during the zany banquet scene. He photographed Jeanette's last four films at MGM. Douglass Dumbrille as Baron Szigetti at right.

Peter (Edward Everett Horton) arrives to inspect Willie's new wife and is delighted to find her so angelic. (Peter's identity is never established, probably due to all the censors' cuts.) *Courtesy Anna Michalik.*

and the entire party return. Willie furiously takes a punch at the Baron in slow motion. The Baron storms off, threatening to close Willie's bank. Willie rages at Brigitta with Peggy echoing his every word, making mechanical doll motions. This sequence makes no sense whatsoever and may be explained in some of the missing footage.

Willie is through. He is sick of the truth. He wants nothing but lies. He leaves Brigitta, and Peggy tries to help her. First she suggests that Brigitta go home to mother, but Brigitta tells her she can't do that until Judgment Day. In the meantime, Brigitta will do anything to save Willie's bank. If she really means that, Peggy replies, she may *not* get home on Judgment Day. Of course, if Brigitta is really willing to sacrifice herself for Willie, then she only needs "A Twinkle in Your Eye." Brigitta joins Peggy in the song and a jitterbug. ("Burn the air, Jeanette," director Van Dyke shouted to her as she writhed to the prerecorded number.)

Willie finds his lies and consolation in the company of his lady friends in the nightclubs of

I Married an Angel

In contrast to his beautiful former girlfriends, Willie must now entertain the highly respectable wives of his bank's clients. (Back row: Almira Sessions, Esther Dale, Cecil Cunningham. Front row: Anita Bolster, Jeanette, Florence Auer.) *Courtesy Jack Tillmany*.

Budapest. One night, to his astonishment, Brigitta sweeps in, swathed in a fabulous zebra coat and black sequined gown. By coincidence, the people she insulted are also present, and she manages to apologize musically with untruthful appeals to their vanity.

She is soon joined by the Baron Szigetti, who obviously has been seeing quite a bit of her. Now Willie understands why his bank hasn't been closed. Brigitta tells him she is the Baron's "business advisor." She is a "working girl" now, just like Marika. Willie can't stand to see his Angel like this. She replies that she isn't his angel anymore. He didn't take up her option. She slinks off on the Baron's arm to see the world, and Willie rushes after her.

He chases their car on a fantasy street reminiscent of the geometrics of *The Cabinet of Dr. Caligari*. Back on the bedroom couch, the dreaming Willie is kicking violently. Brigitta is first discovered singing *Carmen* to the Baron in a smoky Spanish café. Willie pursues her, and she appears on an opera stage singing in the final trio from *Faust* with a tiny pug dog in her arms. The curtain falls, revolves, and we are on the beach at Waikiki with the surf rolling on a

Angels must always tell the truth. Brigitta refers to Lady Gimcrack (Gertrude W. Hoffman) as a "sweet old lady," to the outrage of the Lady's young protegé (Rafael Storm). *Courtesy Anna Michalik.*

rear projection screen. Brigitta, in a black cellophane skirt, is doing a hula to "Aloha Oe" as the Baron leers approvingly. One of her fellow dancers rips off the skirt and whirls her into the Baron's arms. He kisses her, and the film "revolves" to Brigitta and the Baron on water skis coming straight at Willie. This is done via rear projection with Willie swaying in front of it, his back to the camera. A giant wave hits Willie, and he wakes up.

He is back in his own bedroom at his own birthday party. Rushing downstairs to Anna Zador, he tells her he is in love. He wants to be like his ancestors, and he proposes to the astonished secretary. He mustn't lose her again. "But you don't *know* me," she gasps. "Oh, yes, I do," he answers. "You're crazy about harp concerts." They will go to the next one and hold hands. The lady happily joins him in a final chorus of "I Married an Angel."

As the last "team" film, *Angel* is frequently cited as the cause of their demise as major film stars, just as *Two Faced Woman* is blamed for Garbo's exit. On re-viewing, one finds *Two Faced Woman* is a delightful if minor George Cukor comedy, far from Garbo's worst. Likewise, if *I Married an Angel* is a weak film, its flaws would have passed unnoticed if other factors hadn't entered in.

The film is torn internally between conflicting points of view. It is neither a sophisticated sex romp nor a "kiddie" film, and lovers of either operetta or swing could not have found it their kind of picture. Van Dyke, with his hearty good humor, may have been the wrong director, but given a free hand he might have reshaped it into a new and consistent entity if he had not been ill. Obviously a lot of behind-the-scene changes went on, for Edward Everett Horton appears out of nowhere, and Binnie Barnes's echo scene exists like a dinosaur footprint. The static "Spring Is Here" number may have been filmed inexpensively after the picture was finished to replace footage containing the deleted children. In any event, we can only regret that the film wasn't made in 1934 with a young MacDonald and Eddy plus a Lubitsch or a Mamoulian at the helm!

I Married an Angel bombed, and the critics, glorying in their new power, were quick in getting out their most acid quips. The musical film was entering a new phase and *Angel* had tried—disastrously—to meet the change.

Reviews

Memories of an enchanting evening at the Broadway show four years earlier loomed large in most New York City reviews. *Variety* said: "The click Broadway musical emerges on the screen as a slow moving, poorly acted, expensive production." Bosley Crowther in the *New York Times* wrote, "A more painful and clumsy desecration of a lovely fiction has not been perpetrated in years." *Time* magazine thought that it "vigorously rubs the bloom from the wings of the brisk, fresh, imaginative musical that ran on Broadway."

Archer Winsten began his *New York Post* review: "Fortunately this reviewer did not see the stage production of *I Married an Angel*, so

I Married an Angel

Willie's former girlfriend, Peggy (Binnie Barnes), takes the earthbound angel under her wing.

you will be spared odious comparisons..." His newspaper rated it fair on its movie dial.

The stars took the brunt of the attack from the ladies and gentlemen of the press, although *Variety* also blasted the producer and director. The *New York Times'* comments are perhaps the most typical, if not as sarcastic as some: "Mr. Eddy and Miss MacDonald are just not geared to toss a gossamer fable like this one about in the air. Granted they can sing—and they do so in voices loud enough to wake the dead. Their heavy and unaesthetic mooning is just too much for the sensibilities to take." MacDonald and Eddy, having reached the status of a national institution, were now considered fair game for the wittiest abuse the media could muster.

Recordings (See Discography for further information)

Eddy recorded the following:

"I Married an Angel"
"I'll Tell the Man in the Street"
"Little Work-a-Day World" (cut from film)
"Spring is Here"

Music in the Film

All music is by Richard Rodgers and all lyrics by Lorenz Hart unless otherwise indicated. (Bob Wright and Chet Forrest were dismayed at being asked to rewrite lyrics by the master, Lorenz Hart, and said later that this was the reason they left MGM after completing this film.) In listing performers after each title, "and" denotes a genuine duet, while commas between names indicate a sequence of singers.

Overture: "I Married an Angel" (with female chorus); "Angel without Wings"; "Caprice Viennois" by Fritz Kreisler (MacDonald humming and singing into opening of film)
"How to Win Friends and Influence People" fragment (orchestra)
Talk Song: "There comes a time..." (Edward Everett Horton) – music by Herbert Stothart, lyrics by Bob Wright and Chet Forrest

Brigitta tells Willie she is no longer his angel. He didn't take up her option. She goes off with Baron Szigetti (Douglass Dumbrille, center). *Courtesy Anna Michalik..*

"Tira Lira La" (Dubbing for some brides were Marjorie Briggs, Betty Noyes, and Dorothy Compton; Burgren Sisters Children's Quartet dubbing three black children) – based on "At the Roxy Music Hall" from the stage version, with new lyrics by Wright and Forrest

"I Married an Angel" (Eddy and chorus)

"I'll Tell the Man in the Street" (Eddy), INTO:

"I Married an Angel" reprise (Eddy, four speaking parts, MacDonald), with "Hey, Butcher" bridge interpolation (Eddy) – music by Stothart, lyrics by Wright and Forrest *

"Spring is Here" (MacDonald and Eddy)

Talk Song: "To Count Palaffi..." (Horton) – music by Stothart, lyrics by Wright and Forrest

"Hey, Butcher" reprise

"I Married an Angel" reprise (MacDonald and Eddy)

Harp concert: "Villanelle" (MacDonald vocalizing) – by Eva dell'Acqua

"May I Present the Girl" (Horton) – music by Stothart, lyrics by Wright and Forrest

"Now You've Met the Angel" (Eddy) – music by Stothart, lyrics by Wright and Forrest

Willie is relieved to discover that it has all been a dream! (Left to right: Nelson, Reginald Owen, Edward Everett Horton, and Binnie Barnes.) *Courtesy Anna Michalik.*

The bizarre, psychedelic dream sequence includes opera with a pug dog, waterskiing, and Jeanette doing a wild and sexy hula. *Courtesy Anna Michalik.*

"May I Present the Girl" reprise (Eddy), INTO:

"Tira Lira La" reprise (five girls, chorus), sung contrapuntally with:

"I Married an Angel" reprise (MacDonald and Eddy)

"But What of Truth" (MacDonald) – two-line fragment, music by Stothart, lyrics by Wright and Forrest, INTO:

"A Twinkle in Your Eye" (Binnie Barnes and MacDonald)

"A Twinkle in Your Eye" reprise (MacDonald with Grace Hayle, Charles Brabin) – additional lyrics by Wright and Forrest

DREAM MONTAGE: (Eddy sings comments throughout the number)

"Chanson Bohème" from *Carmen* by Georges Bizet (MacDonald with Eddy) – additional English lyrics by Wright and Forrest

"I Married an Angel" reprise fragment (MacDonald and Eddy)

"Anges Purs" (MacDonald, tenor, bass) final trio from *Faust* by Charles Gounod

"Aloha Oe" (MacDonald and male chorus) – music by Princess Liliuokalani

I Married an Angel

"I'll Tell the Man in the Street" reprise (Eddy),
  INTO:
"I Married an Angel" reprise (MacDonald and Eddy)
Orchestral finale: "Spring is Here," "I Married an Angel"

Singers who recorded small bits throughout the film were Elinore Davenport, Muriel Good- speed, Pamela Randall, Patti Brilhante, Virginia Rees, Sally Mueller, Georgia Stark, Robert Bradford, Gene Ramey, Earl Covert, Abe Dinovitch, J. Delos Jewkes, Tudor Williams, Betty Rome, Clarence Badger Jr, Austin Grout, Margot Morgan, and Marshall Sohl.

Original stage songs used in the film were the lovely "Angel without Wings" (used without words behind credits), "I Married an Angel," "I'll Tell the Man in the Street," and "How to Win Friends and Influence People." The melody of "At the Roxy Music Hall" became "Tira Lira La." "Did You Ever Get Stung" was reworked as "Little Work-a-Day World," but then was cut from the film.

* For his biography of Jeanette, *Hollywood Diva*, M.I.T. professor Edward Baron Turk asked lyricists Bob Wright and Chet Forrest about a hard-to-understand line sung by a woman brandishing a wrench during the first rendition of "I Married an Angel." The woman asks Eddy: "Can she run a range?" MacDonald replies in song, "When I cook an omelet, I'll cook it like an ange-el."

Script History
Contributed by Ginny Sayre

The files of the Motion Picture Academy Library have more than a dozen scripts and treatments for a film version, starting in 1931.

An initial 7/11/32 treatment by Alexander G. Kenedi starts with Willie trying to propose to the wealthy and socially prominent Anna as he flies her about in his plane. He can't bring himself to do so, perhaps because singing angels appear in the sky and follow the plane. Back on the ground, he must justify his failure to his godmother, the redoubtable Countess. We have flashbacks of Willy's childhood showing why he distrusts women. Then Anna is revealed to be definitely unangelic, and the rest of the script unfolds more or less as in final version.

In a 1933 treatment by Moss Hart, Larry Hart, and Richard Rodgers, a young man swears he will only marry an angel. He then marries a young aviatrix who has parachuted into his garden. Her deviltry wins back his ancestral estate and convinces him that she's an angel. Following the Rodgers and Hart custom of the time, much of the film was to be in charming sung dialogue.

Another 1933 treatment was by Vicki Baum (*Grand Hotel*). She has Willie eager to become a diplomat, but he's told he must first give up chasing women and settle down. He then gets drunk and marries the Angel, with the rest of the plot following the final version.

Lenore Coffee, in an August 14, 1935 treatment, sets the story in the Swiss Alps. The hero is appearing in an operetta called *I Dream of an Angel*. His best friend's wife, Anna, is in love with him. He, in turn, falls for a girl at the local orphanage. She wants to be a dancer. After some very bizarre plot twists, an angel arrives to save the hero's new show, now called *I Married an Angel*, and to sort out the tangled marriages.

Vienna is the scene of Walter Wise's 1935 screenplay. Willie is a Viennese playwright, engaged to Anna, but he dumps her in search of a pure woman. He meets up with Louise (the Angel of the story), an impoverished but honest young lady who has found and returned a large sum of money. He sees her as "an angel of the slums," falls in love with her, and proposes a marriage in name only so he can care for her two young brothers. Louise accepts and they marry secretly.

Then Willie loses his money through bad business decisions. He alienates Louise, and at

A scene cut from the film. On their flight from Budapest, Brigitta and Willie are stranded overnight at a border customs house. Sleeping arrangements bothered the censors. (Bodil Rosing in cap, left. Ludwig Stössel at telephone, right.) *Courtesy Anna Michalik.*

first she seeks revenge by insulting his party guests. Then she repents and works behind the scenes to make him successful again. His mother reveals the source of his success and all ends happily.

Starting in 1940, Anita Loos became the principal writer. Her 7/31/40 version, with changes dated 8/26/40, opens with taxi drivers speculating about the ennui of the world-weary Budapest playboy, Prince Palaffi, and also about the brilliant showers of golden shooting stars which always coincide with his appearance. On this night, one of the meteorites swoops right past Willie and falls with a sizzle into the Danube. Unperturbed, Willie tosses the carnation from his buttonhole after it and continues on his way, singing a melancholy song of spring: "Spring is Here."

Back at his palace, all is dark. He stumbles about, taking off his clothes. Suddenly the lights go on. It's a big surprise party, and he is in his B.V.D.s. He withdraws and Peggy, an old flame, follows. She urges him to consider marriage as a cure for his depression, perhaps with the virtuous Lola. He glances out the window and sees Lola misbehaving. All women are alike!

Peggy leaves and Brigitta flies in the window. Brigitta and Willy soon go off to be married, her wings only partially covered by a coat. On their honeymoon trip, Brigitta gets Willie in trouble with a customs agent, but they are soon having an idyllic time in a picturesque village, singing and dancing. (Willie must teach the Angel how to dance.)

When they return to Budapest, they find there is a run on Willie's bank. Willie throws a party to head off trouble, but Brigitta's truth-telling soon infuriates the guests. Heartbroken, Brigitta calls upon her angel sisters to take her back to heaven, but they can't. She has become mortal. They sing the beautiful "Angel without Wings," used only as background music in the release print.

Peggy then teaches Brigitta how to avoid lying by insinuation: "A Twinkle in Your Eye." Brigitta persuades Baron Szigetti to save Willie's bank, but Willie tears up the check and punches the Baron in the nose. Somehow Willy will pay off his creditors and live an angelic life with Brigitta. As the two walk home together, they cross a bridge over the Danube. A golden glow comes from the riverbed. It is one of the golden stars that Brigitta had tossed down to Willie before they met, worth at least ten million pengoes. Willie's bank is saved!

A year later, 10/10/41 through 12/20/41, the Loos script had undergone some major changes. The film now opens with Anna praying at a country shrine outside Budapest. She happily departs for her bank job in the city, carrying a bouquet of fresh flowers. Her mother senses a secret and confides her concern to a visiting priest.

At the bank, Anna is arranging the flowers when she hears a noise outside the window. She smiles as Willie arrives amidst much commotion, having commandeered a milk wagon after a night of dissipation. He is causing a traffic jam, thus beginning the sung dialogue of the "Little Work-a-Day World" number, cut from the finished film:

> MAN: (angrily) Come on, Mister! Move that crate!
> I'm already minutes late!
> WILLIE: Wait!

Later, when Willie takes the Angel to Paris for clothes, she also refuses to wear snake-skin gloves and a pearl necklace stolen from poor little oysters.

The harp concert scene is much longer, with the Angel singing "Clair de Lune" using lyrics by Hart. She promises the conductor she will attend his next concert, but Willie lies, saying they must go to his aunt's funeral. Instead, he sweeps her off to Venice. On the train, he reveals his lie. Brigitta is horrified at his deception, but eventually accepts his kisses and then happily tells the customs agent about the cigarettes Willie is trying to smuggle.

A major scene at the customs house follows, where their midnight arrival awakens the customs agent's wife (Bodil Rosing), children, and dog. All are astonished that someone *wants* to pay duty. During the hubbub, the train leaves without the honeymooners, and they are forced to spend the night bunking with the children. Willie sits up reading a newspaper and learns that all Budapest thinks he has eloped with a chorus girl. He immediately phones Whiskers and learns there is a run on his bank.

When Willie eventually awakens from his dream, Whiskers says the Baron Szigetti has just called an emergency meeting of the bank's Board of Directors after seeing the bill for the party still in progress downstairs. However, Willie seems confident that his marriage to the angelic Anna will mollify everyone and save the day.

Willie returns to his birthday party to claim his previously unnoticed secretary, Anna Zador, as his angelic bride. *Courtesy Anna Michalik.*

Hollywood version: The angel has a dangling foil-covered cardboard wing and a tinsel halo.

British-censored version of the same scene. The angel has no wings or halo.

The files are full of lengthy memos demanding censorship cuts from the Breen Office. These include deleting all references to oysters, naming a dog "Fifi," and the line "I've lost my wings!"

Angel without Wings: British Censorship

During the chaotic production of *I Married an Angel*, censorship was a constant issue. *Variety* soon reported that many changes were being made in the script of the U.S. version and also that a separate version was being prepared for distribution in Great Britain which had quite different censorship requirements. (For example, nudity, sexual situations, and rough language were not entirely frowned on in the U.K.; however, children were not allowed to witness violence or death of any kind—thus, the usual Saturday matinee westerns, so popular here, were forbidden in Britain.)

In preparation for viewing the British-censored print at the British Film Institute, the author "logged" the American version scene by scene. One of my greatest hopes was that, somehow, the British version might still contain Nelson's lavish "Work-a-Day World" production number, which originally opened the film. The scene was cut from the American release version, though the conclusion with its dozens of extras can still be seen just before Nelson runs into the bank with his two pretty friends.

Sadly, "Work-a-Day World" is not in the U.K. version. The British film goes along identically to the U.S. version, and I was beginning to think *Variety*'s report about censorship was just another example of the MGM publicity department's constant efforts to keep the names of its films and stars in the press. (About a third of the "information" sent out in studio press releases to newspapers and fan magazines was speculation or pure fantasy, churned out by the stables of on-staff, $25-a-week writers whose mandate was to supply the studio with free publicity via newspaper space and to stimulate the insatiable American public with endless "news.")

I had just about decided that the report of a different U.K. version was erroneous. Then suddenly I shouted, "Whoa!" and backed up the film. In the U.S. version, Jeanette's rival, Mona Maris, deceitfully offers to help her create a costume for Nelson's birthday party, an elaborate costume ball. Jeanette arrives wearing a simple but fetching bed-sheet gown and foil-covered cardboard wings. A tinsel-wire halo bobs about over her head. The major domo announces her entrance to the assembled crowd: "Miss Anna Zador as an angel."

Yet, in the U.K. version—obviously shot simultaneously because MGM couldn't or wouldn't have gone back to recreate and reshoot the crowds of elaborately costumed extras on lavish sets—Jeanette comes down the stair wearing only the sheet. The humorous bits of her halo bobbing about and hitting Nelson in the face throughout the scene are thus missing. Yet, vestiges remain of the winged version. We still see "Cleopatra" in the crowd laughing uproariously as she mimes the bobbing halo encircling Jeanette's head. In the U.S. version, one of the angel's cardboard wings falls off on the stair, and an extra cries, "The angel's molting." The line is cut, of course, but when Edward Everett Horton begins his song, he is still holding the lost wing!

In the U.S. version, Jeanette is unaware that her bobbing halo bumps Nelson in the face several times while they are waltzing. With no halo, it is just a dance, and his sudden breaking off of the dance is less motivated and more brusque. And when the Angel blocks Nelson from the view of his friends, her attempt to hide the six-foot Nelson without the aid of wings seems rather odd.

The changes for the U.K. market go beyond shooting some scenes twice, with and without wings and halo. When Nelson falls asleep and dreams an angel flies in the window, and later when they run out the window together, separate special effects had to be created showing an angel without wings. Then, when Willie and Brigitta arrive in Paris, another special U.S. effect of the angel's winged shadow coming down a hotel hallway changes in the U.K. version to a shadow of a lady in a long dress—no wings—yet everyone is still astonished.

The wedding night is entirely reshot with a wingless Jeanette. When she awakes the next morning, wingless, and stretches happily in bed, the identical U.S. footage is used. However, it is cut as her fingers give the little twitch when she realizes her wings are gone. We hear her anguished cry of "Willie!" as we watch Nelson

When the wingless Angel flies in the window of the British-censored version, she appears to be a lady in a chiffon peignoir. U.K. audiences and critics were understandably puzzled when everyone began exclaiming, "It's an angel!"

Willie finds his true angel, and everyone sings "I Married an Angel" for a huge, happy, black and white musical finale. While "Technicolor musical" was becoming the industry adage, MGM still hoped to do lavish musicals in the much cheaper black and white format. *Courtesy Anna Michalik.*

in dressing gown in next room. Subsequent dialogue—about what happened to her wings and how he can now put his arms all the way around his wife and she can't fly away—is all cut. He embraces her as in the U.S. version, and the remainder of the U.K. film is identical. Amusingly, this includes a long shot of the angel removing her halo as Willie, awakened from his dream, returns to the ballroom at the end of the film!

Great Britain at that time had no standard censorship codes as Hollywood did. Decisions were made on a totally subjective and apparently capricious basis by whoever was doing the censoring. This led to rebellion in many parts of the U.K. Local jurisdictions set up their own censorship authorities and ignored the dictates of London.

The most common censorship targets of the London office were anything that might inspire rebellion against the established political order. It was, after all, a time of great social and political unrest. Communism and Fascism were fighting for supremacy in much of Europe. Britain was also sensitive about presenting anything that might offend either Catholics or the various Protestant sects. (Several now-classic films that looked at religious issues were banned from being shown in the U.K.) BFI library files cite many examples of British censorship during this time, but the only officially stated religious restriction I could find was against mentioning birth control. Nothing about feathers—or birth control with feathers. Deleting wings and halos was an astounding and utterly incomprehensible example of censorship gone mad, probably on the say-so of one overly nervous bureaucrat. (Considering the slang meaning of "Willie" in U.K. culture, it is amazing this overly sensitive censor didn't also require Nelson's character to change his name!)

Three contemporary newspaper reviews of the film were equally amusing. *Today's Cinema*, 8/14/42, and *Motion Picture Herald*, 5/23/42, both state that the Angel loses her wings on her wedding night, indicating the reviewers saw the Hollywood version. However, the third reviewer, reporting in *Kinematograph Weekly*, 8/20/42, obviously saw the British-censored version. He reports that the Angel sacrifices her innocence to aid her husband's failing bank and thus is corrupted by modern business practices!

Sadly, we may never know the full story of this eccentric exercise in censorship. The London censors' office was bombed the year following *Angel*'s release, and all related correspondence is presumed lost.

A final ironic note: the music played behind the film credits is a haunting song from the stage version that is never sung in the film—"Angel without Wings."

Trivia

What would the team do next? A Louella Parsons column, 5/22/42, says that Nelson would next play dual roles in an untitled film about a man pretending to be a famous baritone. In a small town, young Kathryn Grayson competes to act as the hostess of the visiting singer, actually the imposter. Robert Z. Leonard and O.O. Dull would coproduce and Eddie Buzzell was to direct. Perhaps proposals for such trite programmers as this speeded Nelson in his decision to buy out his contract and leave MGM.

Movie Goofs

Nelson enters the Palaffi Bank (one "l") at the opening of the film, but the birthday party invitation reads Pallaffi (two "l's"). (John Cocchi)

When viewing a 35mm print, it is possible to see the tiny thread that guides the bird to Jeanette's finger in the "Spring is Here" number. (Author)

8
Music to Make War By

The recent interest of scholars and historians in the musical film has created an interesting puzzle: exactly what is a musical? What distinction do we draw between a film that depends utterly on music for its shape and form and a film in which "numbers" are inserted like raisins in rice pudding? If we take the purist view, there were only three notable musicals made during World War II: *Cabin in the Sky*, *State Fair*, and *Anchors Aweigh*. The best-remembered musical films of the period, *Going My Way*, *Meet Me in St. Louis*, and *Yankee Doodle Dandy*, could all have existed independently, if not happily, without their songs.

When America went to war at the end of 1941, Hollywood went with it. The country needed its morale boosted, and the film industry undertook the job, patriotically if not entirely philanthropically. The number of musical films more than doubled during the war years, from approximately thirty in 1939 to more than seventy in 1944. (This is not even counting the dozens and dozens of "films with music," the "Road" pictures, the Esther Williams and Abbott and Costello vehicles, or the horse-opera and bobbysoxer epics ground out at Monogram and Republic Studios.) With all this activity, one looks expectantly for the corresponding ratio of classic musicals. Sadly, they are not there.

The music, of course, was fine, and some of the nation's best balladeers were turning out the "standards" of the decade, to be popped into some of the blandest and most banal films ever to hit the screen.

Of course, much of the propaganda was useful and necessary, for we didn't *know* that we were going to win the war. There was always the dark uncertainty flickering in the back of everyone's mind that the horrors of Europe could soon be happening on our soil. A buoyant, tuneful interlude at the local cinema, complete with wisecracking GIs, bathing beauties, and patriotic slogans could push back the fear for a little while. Anyone who tries to draw parallels between "escapism" and the dark days of the Depression should take a good look at the candy-coated Hollywood tranquilizers of the early 1940s.

Much of the straight propaganda looks pretty transparent today. *Stage Door Canteen*, one of the Ten Best Pictures of 1943, includes a scene

Miss MacDonald worked tirelessly as part of the "war effort." When she and her husband were not away, they held open house for military personnel on Sundays.

in which the heroine reads a letter from her boyfriend overseas. With tears of joy streaming down her face, she quotes: "They can talk all they want abot the Japs' jujitsu, but a marine will tell you that it doesn't work against a round-house right to the jaw."

Much of Hollywood's manpower was siphoned off by the war effort, and so we can "blame" the second decline of the American film musical on Hitler, Mussolini, and Tojo. The actors, directors, technicians, writers, musicians, and laborers who weren't actually in the services were busy turning out training and morale films. Some of the top talent of the day worked extensively and creatively in this form. (See *Agee on Film*.)

The MacDonald/Eddy wartime films included their last joint effort, *I Married an Angel*, released in mid-1942, Jeanette's *Cairo* later in 1942, Eddy's Technicolor prestige film *Phantom of the Opera* for Universal in 1943, his *Knickerbocker Holiday* in 1944, Jeanette's patriotic guest shot in the all-star *Follow the Boys* in 1944.

During the war years both Jeanette and Nelson participated wholeheartedly in the "war effort." Eddy, in fact, had done his first war benefit on October 19, 1939, when he appeared with Leopold Stokowski at a Polish war relief concert in Los Angeles. It was the first in his long line of benefits, USO and camp shows. In 1942, he became an air raid warden and also put in long hours at the Hollywood Canteen. In 1943 he went on a two-month, 35,000 mile tour, giving concerts in Belem, Brazil; Natal; Accra, Gold Coast; Central Africa; Aden; Asmara, Eritrea; Cairo (where he met King Farouk); Teheran, Persia (now Teheran, Iran); Casablanca; and the Azores.

Christmas of that year found him singing on Ascension Island for the GIs. The island occupied thirty-five square miles in the south Atlantic, and the soldiers stationed there had a motto: "Miss Ascension, your wife collects the pension." Eddy and Ted Paxson made it to the island, and, after some much-needed sleep, toured the wards. The soldiers were so glad to see someone from "home" that they carried the startled pair through the hospital on their shoulders. Eddy and Paxson talked for hours with the men, played ping-pong with them, ate in their mess. When concert time came, no piano could be found, so Paxson improvised on a tiny organ. The night ended with everyone singing Christmas carols. On Christmas day, Eddy did four concerts, singing everything from Gershwin to Handel with the little organ pumping along. He returned to the United States six weeks later, not for a rest but a concert tour.

Jeanette was one of the founders of the Women's Voluntary Services and was active with the Army Emergency Relief. She raised over $100,000 for them with benefits throughout the country in the fall of 1943. After each regular concert, she would auction off encores for additional donations. Her husband, Gene Raymond, enlisted in the Air Force and served during most of the war in England, rising to the rank of colonel. Jeanette wanted to join him there, but he felt it was too dangerous. Instead, she threw herself into a heavy concert and camp show schedule, proudly wearing Gene's pilot wings on her lapel. When she was in Hollywood, she held open house at her home, Twin Gables, on Sunday afternoons for G.I.s.

Her camp shows provided a surprise for the "boys," many of them still teenagers, who expected a "prima donna of the cinema." Instead, they found a vivacious performer who worked uncomplainingly through heat, cold, and exhaustion wherever she was wanted. At the end of a performance, she would invite the soldiers or sailors up on stage to whistle the flute portion of "The Donkey Serenade" with her or would dedicate a song to the nurses in the audience. She was surprised to find that the song she was most often asked to sing was "Ave Maria."

The reviews of her concerts at this time were so uniformly warm and glowing that even if we

Jeanette with her husband, Gene Raymond, on a Stage Door Canteen broadcast, 11/12/42. During much of the war, he was stationed in Britain. She wore his pilot's wings on her gown during concerts. *Courtesy Anna Michalik.*

Music to Make War By

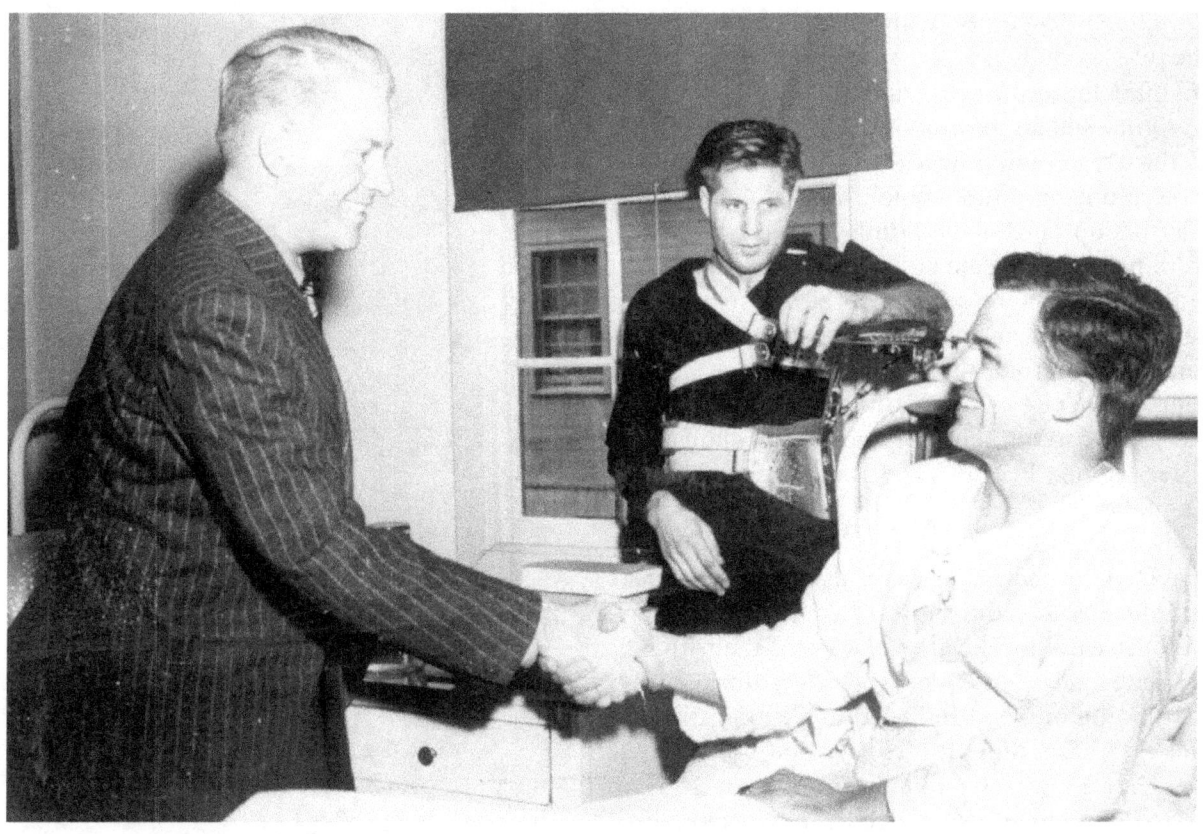

Both stars frequently sang for the wounded and toured the wards afterwards, greeting the recuperating military personnel. *Courtesy Anna Michalik.*

discount the patriotic enthusiasm of a wartime audience, we know that Jeanette was a smash wherever she went. Although she moaned that she rarely had time to do more than run a comb through her hair, her spectacular appearance and assured manner frequently rated as much newspaper copy as her songs. In Boston, she drew a decidedly untypical but revealing review by Warren Storey Smith: "At times Miss MacDonald's voice seemed tired. The wonder is she has any voice at all left. Between her singing and her exhortations to the audience and her frequent descriptions of the songs she was about to sing, she did the work of a dozen singers and managed to look and seem fresh throughout. This is not the proper occasion to weigh Miss MacDonald's merits as an artist—her concert came close to being a charity affair. Yet, it must be said that those who would belittle her vocal accomplishments are taking quite a lot on their shoulders. For all her faults, she was no vocal piker."

Jeanette was ingenious at improvising before an audience. At one concert she was "auctioning off" encores when a man bid ten dollars for "One Dozen Roses." She looked puzzled for a moment, then stepped off stage. She returned with a bouquet from her dressing room. "I don't know the song, but I'll sell you the real thing for twenty dollars." He bought them.

Lt. Ronald Reagan was stationed at Fort Mason in San Francisco in the early days of the war. The USO (United Services Organization) was not yet operating, and he was asked if he could find a fellow performer to sing the National Anthem on "I Am an American Day." He called

Jeanette, who agreed without hesitation. Since she was coming so far, she added, was there anything more she could do?

On a Sunday afternoon she stood in a box at the Dog Racing Track and sang to twenty-thousand men in the infield. Most of them were due to ship out for the South Pacific where we were fighting on Bataan. She sang request after request until there seemed to be no song they had forgotten, and still they asked for more. Finally, she told them there was one more song, a special favorite of hers. As she sang, the men rose to their feet and twenty-thousand voices joined hers in "The Battle Hymn of the Republic."

Between their war work and films, both MacDonald and Eddy were also doing dozens and dozens of radio shows. Especially popular were Lux Radio Theatre versions of their films. Jeanette had done *Irene* (2/15/36) during the first month of Cecil B. DeMille's extraordinary weekly radio plug for Hollywood. She took the Gloria Swanson role in *Tonight or Never* (1/25/37), which also starred Melvyn Douglas and the venerable opera star, Mary Garden. During the war, Jeanette did *Smilin' Through* (1/5/42) with her husband and Brian Aherne. Eddy starred in *Phantom of the Opera* (9/13/43) with Susanna Foster and Basil Rathbone. They both appeared in *Naughty Marietta* (6/12/44) and *Maytime* (9/4/44). If their careers were "finished" as is commonly thought today, they were both much too busy to notice.

Jeanette at this time made a daring decision. At forty, she resolved to become an opera singer. It was a brave if dangerous step, although not without precedent. Grace Moore had already made the transition "backward" from the popular musical stage to true eminence in grand opera.

Once Jeanette's mind was made up, she approached it as she had every major step in her life, with absolute determination and exhaustive effort. She trained like a soldier until she had total technical command of her voice. Leon

Jeanette was one of the founders of the Army Emergency Relief and tirelessly raised funds on concert tours. She would auction off encores. *Courtesy Diane Goodrich.*

Rothier and the great diva Lotte Lehmann were among her teachers.

As described by Edward Baron Turk in *Hollywood Diva*, "the Met's Board of Directors had little wish to compromise their institution's elitism through association with an icon of mass culture." Yet, Jeanette had many supporters and fans among the opera aristocracy, including Kirsten Flagstad, Lauritz Melchior, and André Kostalanetz, husband of Lily Pons. Metropolitan Opera director Edward Johnson began delicate negotiations with Jeanette, urging her to learn the rôle of Juliette in Gounod's *Roméo et Juliette* for a possible Met engagement. It was hinted that she might make a guest appearance at the

Metropolitan if she enrolled in the Julliard School and were presented as an outstanding student! In addition, a sizable donation wouldn't hurt. Jeanette, however, was determined to be engaged as a mature artist on ability alone. "Buying my debut is the one way I couldn't accept," she wrote in her autobiography.

In February of 1943, her concert manager, Charles L. Wagner, sent out a press release saying she was studying the rôle of Juliette for a Metropolitan debut. Whatever the motivation behind the announcement, the move backfired. Johnson issued an icy statement that he had no contract with Miss MacDonald, but was "always interested in a potential box-office draw."

Undaunted, Jeanette appeared as Juliette at His Majesty's Theatre in Montreal on May 8, 1943. Music critic Thomas Archer wrote: "[She] undertook the role of Juliette with a determination and vocal ability that called for more and more admiration as the evening's proceedings went on." Ezio Pinza sang Friar Lawrence and Armand Tokatyan was Roméo. Jeanette repeated the rôle there 5/10/33; at the Capitol Theater, Quebec City 5/12/43; Auditorium, Ottawa 5/20 and 5/22/43; Arena, Windsor 5/24/43; and in the U.S. at the Cincinnati Zoological Gardens Pavilion 7/10/43.

During the fall of 1943 she toured for Army Emergency Relief, and it was more than a year later, on November 4, 1944, when she made her American debut as Juliette with the Chicago Civic Opera. Michael Bartlett, who had sung the *La Bohème* sequences with Grace Moore in *Love Me Forever*, was her Roméo. Claudia Cassidy, Chicago's high priestess of criticism, wrote in the *Chicago Tribune*: "Her Juliet [sic] is breathtakingly beautiful to the eye and dulcet to the ear. Her voice is slender, a little reedy, but sweet and she uses it delicately with a sensitivity that accents the drama of the music."

Eleven days later, on November 14, 1944, she debuted as Marguerite in Gounod's *Faust* with the Chicago Civic Opera. Ezio Pinza sang Mephistopheles, and Raoul Jobin was Faust. She repeated the role the following year at the Cleveland Zoological Gardens Pavilion on 7/15 and 25/45 with Armand Tokatyan and Nicola Moscona, Fausto Cleva conducting, and at the Chicago Civic Opera 10/27 and 11/3/45. Faust was Nino Martini (star of Rouben Mamoulian's *The Gay Desperado* and with whom she had dueted in *Paramount on Parade* before her footage was cut), and Nicola Moscona sang Mephistopheles. Claudia Cassidy again noted her "purity of line and tone." Jeanette repeated the rôle with the Philadelphia Civic Grand Opera 12/12/51 with David Poleri and Raffaele Arie, Giuseppe Bamboschek conducting.

What prompted a successful movie star with a safe niche in the entertainment world to lay herself open to criticism and even ridicule at the hands of the frequently caustic music critics?

A soldier's snapshot of Eddy in Africa on a USO tour. *Courtesy Anna Michalik.*

Why should a middle-aged film actress imagine she could penetrate the insular world of opera? Well, why *not*? We are at once appalled by her foolishness and thrilled by her guts.

She didn't make it. Critics felt her voice was too small to carry without amplification in the enormous auditoriums necessary to make opera profitable. Despite the adoration of her fans and the warm response of both fans and critics alike to her acting, she was still a musical curiosity, not a recognized opera singer. Her failure was in part the failure of anyone who has challenged the "impossible dream."

"When Jeanette MacDonald approached me for coaching lessons," Lotte Lehmann wrote, "I was really curious how a glamorous movie star, certainly spoiled by the adoration of a limitless world, would be able to devote herself to another, a higher level of art. I had the surprise of my life. There couldn't have been a more diligent, a more serious, a more pliable person than Jeanette. The lessons which I had started with a kind of suspicious curiosity, turned out to be sheer delight for me. She studied Marguerite with me—and lieder. These were the ones which astounded me most. I am quite sure that Jeanette would have developed into a serious and successful lieder singer if time would have allowed it."

On December 1, 1943, the *Motion Picture Herald* announced: "Script for SHOW BOAT into work January 3, 1944. Property [originally] acquired from Universal for Jeanette MacDonald and Nelson Eddy, now recast. Kathryn Grayson likely choice for Magnolia, Judy Garland as Julie. Arthur Freed to produce." Grayson, almost twenty years younger, was already being groomed for the forthcoming Technicolor operetta cycle of the 1950s. Also in 1944, Deanna Durbin was quoted as saying she wanted to film *The Life of Jeanette MacDonald* at Universal, but, according to the trade publications, she was the only one who was crazy about the idea.

Time, the enemy of all performers, of all mankind, was stalking softly behind Jeanette MacDonald and Nelson Eddy.

Cairo

MGM.
Released September-November 1942.
Premiere: September 16, 1942, Richmond, VA
Directed by Major W.S. Van Dyke II.
A Metro-Goldwyn-Mayer Production.
101 minutes.

Original title: *Shadow of a Lady*

Based on an idea by Ladislas Fodor. Screenplay: John McClain. Assistant Director: Marvin Stuart. Musical Director: Herbert Stothart. Conductor: Georgie Stoll. Director of Photography: Ray June. Dance Director: Sammy Lee. Recording Director: Douglas Shearer. Art Director: Cedric Gibbons. Associate: Lyle Wheeler. Set Decoration: Edwin B. Willis. Associate: Richard Pefferle. Gowns: Kalloch. Editor: James E. Newcom.

This 1942 film is unrelated to the 1963 *Cairo*, also made by MGM, which was a remake of *The Asphalt Jungle* (1950) and starred George Sanders.

Jeanette MacDonald (Marcia Warren)
Robert Young (Homer Smith)
Ethel Waters (Cleona "Cleo" Jones)
Reginald Owen (Philo Cobson)
Mona Barrie (Mrs. Morrison)
Lionel Atwill ("Teutonic Gentleman") [so listed]
Edward [Eduardo] Ciannelli (Ahmed Ben Hassan)
Dennis Hoey (Colonel Woodhue)
Dooley Wilson (Hector)
Harry Worth (Bartender)
Mitchell Lewis (Ludwig)
Frank Richards (Alfred)
Rhys Williams ("Strange man")
Grant Mitchell (O.H.P. Banks, editor)
Bert Roach (Sleepy man in movie)
Larry Nunn (Bernie)
Jack Daley (Man in newspaper office)
Demetrius Emanuel, Jay Novello (Italian officers)
Pat O'Malley (Junior officer)
Selmer Jackson (Ship captain)
Cecil Cunningham (Madame Laruga)

Cairo

Jacqueline Dalya (Female attendant)
Dan Seymour (Doorman)
Lorin Raker (Worried man)
Alan Schute (Soldier)
Guy Kingsford (Squadron leader)
William Tannen, Michael Butler (Soldiers on boat)
Sidney Melton (Private Schwartz)
James [Jim] Davis (Sergeant)
Lee Murray (Messenger)
Cecil Stewart (Pianist)
Buck Woods (Negro)
Louise Bates (Mrs. Woodhue)
Kanza Omar (Theatre cashier)
Petra R. de Silva (Fat woman)
Ray Cooper (Waiter)
George London * (Chorus)

* Young Mr. London, later the famous Metropolitan Opera baritone, can be seen standing behind Jeanette in the finale. He starts to sing just a bit sooner than the others. (Thanks to Ken Richards for spotting this.)

Cairo had the misfortune to be issued shortly after a major war conference in Cairo, so audiences weren't expecting a musical comedy.

Cairo is an unjustly overlooked film, full of the same hearty, undemanding pleasures as a well-crafted sitcom. Except for the unfortunate coincidence of its title and release date, it would probably have won critical approval. In the middle of World War II, *Cairo* was just what the public needed—a tongue-in-cheek spy spoof that poked good-natured fun at Nazi spies in the best wartime tradition. (If you can't dehumanize your opponents, at least make them absurd.)

Director W.S. Van Dyke was in his milieu, the breezy action film with comedy touches. *Cairo* featured bubbly songs by E.Y. Harburg and Arthur Schwartz, both *Hit Parade* veterans, and Jeanette was rarely more lovely with her tailor-made rôle as a former operetta screen queen turned sophisticated nightclub singer. The film's finale, in which the diva opens a pharaoh's tomb by singing high C, is obviously intended as the broadest of spoofs, but most critics and audiences missed the point.

Their perceptions were understandably blunted by current events. Just before *Cairo* was released, Churchill and Roosevelt met in Cairo for a major war conference with Turkish and Chinese leaders. So audiences came expecting a serious war film and found a light entertainment instead. It was a little like issuing a frivolous musical called *Pearl Harbor* in late 1941. A title change might have helped, but the film was considered too unimportant to warrant the heavy expense of a new publicity campaign. It was Jeanette's check-out picture from MGM after nine years as its top musical star.

Her costar was Robert Young, whose quality of amiable earnestness would see him through more than eighty films in the first twenty-five years of sound films before television claimed him for "Father Knows Best" and "Marcus Welby, M.D."

Ethel Waters was a box-office question mark, and promotion for *Cairo* carefully captioned her

Their ship torpedoed, reporter Homer Smith (Robert Young) shares a raft with Englishman Philo Cobson (Reginald Owen), who entrusts Homer with a secret. *Courtesy Anna Michalik.*

photo "Broadway musical comedy star." Black performers were still either servants or nightclub performers who could easily be snipped out of prints for Dixie distribution. A year later, Miss Waters would give a superb performance, recreating her stage role in Vincente Minnelli's all-black film, *Cabin in the Sky*. In the 1950s, she appeared in the stage and film versions of Carson McCullers' unforgettable *Member of the Wedding* with Julie Harris and Brandon de Wilde. With her zest, sparkling good humor, and ultimate dignity, she comes close to stealing *Cairo* from its nominal stars, despite her brief footage.

Behind cleverly cartooned opening credits, we hear Jeanette's voice singing "Les Filles de Cadix" from *Maytime*. A caption "irreverently" dedicates the film to "the authors of impossible spy dramas, without whose inspiration international spies could not be as clever as they are." We find ourselves in a small town movie theatre where *Maytime* is playing. No one in the crowded audience is more rapt than Homer Smith (Robert Young). An urgent message from his boss at the newspaper almost fails to move him, although he has seen the film eight times. After all, he says, this is the last picture Marcia Warren made in the United States.

Homer is dragged to the newspaper office and greeted by his boss (Grant Mitchell) and a cheering crowd. The Small-Town Newspaper Association is sending Homer to the Near East to do a series of dispatches called "The Small Town Looks at the War." Homer leaps on a desk and humbly accepts the assignment. He states his credo: "Get the story first, get all of it, and get it right." He is drowned out by a brass band and exuberant cheers.

The cheers are in turn drowned by ominous woodwinds as headlines flash on the screen: "Homer Smith in Convoy Disaster"—"Homer Feared Lost in Mediterranean"—"WHERE IS HOMER?" They dissolve in turn to a tiny life raft floating in an empty ocean.

On it are Homer and a dapper Englishman, Philo Cobson (Reginald Owen). Homer is holding up his coat for a sail. Apparently he is successful, for another dissolve brings us to a campfire on dry land. Our intrepid adventurers are in the Libyan desert, somewhere west of Cairo.

Cobson is cleaning his gun. When Homer accidentally fires it, they find themselves surrounded by Italian troops. Mussolini's finest haven't come to capture them, however. They are fleeing the oncoming Germans and want to surrender. (The comforting myth of the Italian soldier proclaiming "I'm a lover, not a fighter" was apparently already popular in the U.S.) Gunfire is heard a few yards away, and the Italians vanish into the darkness.

Homer and Cobson decide they'd better follow. They will separate to give themselves a better chance. Homer asks Cobson to report his demise to the Cavity Rock *Times-Leader* if he doesn't make it. Cobson in turn gives Homer a mysterious message to deliver if Homer reaches

Cairo

Cairo. He is to go to the Viceroy Hotel bar at 5 PM. A lady named Mrs. Morrison will be drinking a rainbow cocktail with two cherries. (An in-joke: Jeanette's name in *Maytime* was Morrison.) Homer is to say, "Every precaution must be taken. We cannot afford to fail."

Cobson confides to Homer that he is with British Intelligence. They are seeking a ring of espionage agents, the "Big Six," headed by a woman. Homer must keep the whole thing a secret, of course, until the right time. Just then, gunfire moves closer, and Cobson slinks off into the darkness. Homer finds Cobson's pipe, shrugs, and pockets it before heading off toward Cairo.

At the Viceroy Hotel, Homer locates the mysterious Mrs. Morrison (Mona Barrie), whose manner makes it apparent to all but the innocent Homer that she is not what she seems. Homer begs her for the name of the leader of the "Big Six" for his story. She replies by rolling her eyes toward the next room, where a familiar voice is heard.

Marcia Warren (Jeanette), former film queen, is singing "The Waltz Is Over." Homer can't believe it. What better cover for a woman who wants to meet influential people? coos Mrs. Morrison. And Marcia hasn't made a film in three years!

Homer decides the song must be a code and begins making frantic notations of Marcia's vocalese. Triumphantly, he looks at the finished product and finds he has inscribed "C-A-V-I-T-Y-R-O-C-K" on his napkin.

A distinguished man at a nearby table begins staring suspiciously at Homer. He follows Homer to the stage door, where they overhear Cleo (Ethel Waters) telling Marcia she must interview butlers the next morning. The distinguished man frowns as Homer beams from his hiding place.

Morning finds Marcia vocalizing in an enormous bathtub with Cleo joining the song. Marcia remembers her more conventional Beverly Hills bathroom and wishes heartily that she had never left it. Cleo seconds the motion. They are both thoroughly homesick.

Marcia prepares to interview the waiting butlers. One catches her eye and her fancy: "He looks like 'Goodbye, Mr. Chips.'" Cleo summons Homer, who is complete with bowler hat, umbrella, and thick British accent. Marcia asks him who his former employer was, and he blurts out that it was "Lord Philo Cobson," the only English name he knows. She quickly sees through his disguise. "If there's anything you learn from making musical pictures, it's how to recognize bad acting."

She does believe his second story, that he is an American down on his luck and far from home, so she hires him. He tells her his name is

Homer (Robert Young) suspects Marcia Warren (Jeanette) of being a Nazi spy. She is equally suspicious of the obviously phony English butler, but hires him anyway. Soon they are quarreling about geography. *Courtesy Anna Michalik.*

To tease Homer, Marcia acts suspiciously with a visitor, actually Colonel Woodhue of British Intelligence (Dennis Hoey). *Courtesy Anna Michalik.*

Juniper Jones. "You might as well have said 'Smith,'" she says skeptically.

He's from California, he continues. Her delight turns to disdain when she learns he is from *northern* California. She thinks the fog and rain in San Francisco ruin the brain, and he thinks the unending sunshine in Beverly Hills has the same effect. "Have you ever *been* to San Francisco?" he challenges. "Yes, once with Gable and Tracy and the joint fell apart," she declares.

The heated argument is overheard by a sinister little man (Rhys Williams) seated among the prospective butlers outside. He reports to the distinguished man from the nightclub who turns out to be Colonel Woodhue (Dennis Hoey), head of British Intelligence. Why, the Colonel wants to know, is the top Nazi agent, Philo Cobson, decoding Marcia Warren's songs, and why does she quarrel loudly with a man she supposedly doesn't know as soon as he is in the room with her?

Marcia, oblivious to the plots and counterplots swirling around her, goes shopping. Homer skulks after her through the exotic alleys of the bazaar. When she pauses to admire some trinkets in one shop, the shopkeeper's pet mouse escapes and darts across her foot. Her scream startles the shopkeeper, Ahmed Ben Hassan (Edward Ciannelli—formerly "Eduardo" before our altercation with Italy), in more ways than one. As the astonished Homer watches from hiding, a wall panel glides open behind her. "Are you in the habit of screaming a perfect high C?" Ahmed asks sharply. She never screams flat, she tells him and departs hurriedly.

Homer turns and runs into Mrs. Morrison. He tells her happily that he is tracking the leader of the "Big Six" and shows her the sliding panel. Their conversation is heard by a sinister group clustered around a radio receiver in the back room of the shop. Prominent among them is a "Teutonic gentleman" (Lionel Atwill). Mrs. Morrison assures Homer that he will get the whole story soon enough. Homer rushes off after

Dancing to "Waiting for the Robert E. Lee." *Courtesy Anna Michalik.*

Cairo

Cleo (Ethel Waters) encounters a strange-looking Arab named Hector (Dooley Wilson, before *Casablanca* fame) who hails from Central Avenue, Los Angeles. How he acquired his Bedouin identity is a droll but logical tale, and they find that they can make beautiful music together.

Marcia, and Mrs. Morrison joins the spies behind the shop. She is indeed a Nazi and tomorrow, after they dispose of Homer, they will send a robot plane to destroy a United States transport. If it works, the same secret explosive device will be used on the Suez Canal—and then on the Allied powers.

This fervent Nazi patriotism is drowned by a chorus of male voices singing "We Did It Before and We Can Do It Again." We move to Marcia's living room. Homer arrives and finds her exhorting a group of five men on the importance of getting their message across at the festival. "Six," he notes, counting heads. The men are musicians, and Marcia is rehearsing a medley of songs designed to recall the charming homesick sequence in *Maytime*. At one point in the number, Cleo goes into a tray-carrying shuffle to "Waiting for the Robert E. Lee," and Marcia takes up the song and shuffle, swing style. The medley continues and Homer is so moved he joins in the final bars of "Avalon." Then they all sing "Home, Sweet Home" and conclude with a patriotic ditty composed for the film, "Keep the Light Burning Bright in the Harbor."

Despite the overwhelming "evidence," Homer is now sure that Marcia couldn't be a Nazi. He is about to confess his silly suspicion when a call comes from Madame Laruga (Cecil Cunningham). Marcia says she must receive the prints by the following night, and Homer is again convinced of her guilt.

His behavior becomes even more erratic. At dinner, he learns that the prints have arrived, and he tries to persuade Marcia to go for a long walk with Cleo, leaving him alone in the house. At that moment, Cleo ushers in Marcia's old friend, Colonel Woodhue, and Homer drops his tray. "You can tell he don't know nothing about the movies or he'd'a' landed smack in them mashed potatoes," Cleo comments. Homer trips and lands smack in the mashed potatoes.

Homer acts so strangely during the Colonel's visit that Woodhue confides to Marcia he has come to check up on this strange butler. Juniper Jones is actually Philo Cobson, a Nazi agent. Marcia is stunned and uncertain how to proceed. She hasn't played in many spy movies. Now she realizes that Juniper was trying to get her out of the house. She must get *him* out instead and search his room.

She and Cleo try to take Juniper to a show (where a large poster of Nelson Eddy can be seen in the background). He chivalrously offers to pay for the tickets, but finds he has only hundred-dollar bills left in his money belt. "C-notes," Cleo calls them. "*C-notes?*" intones Marcia.

When Homer pays for their movie tickets with a C-note, Marcia and Cleo suspect that *he* may be a Nazi spy. *Courtesy Anna Michalik.*

Marcia's maid is played by Broadway star Ethel Waters. "Sweet Mama Stringbean," as Miss Waters was called in her early days, was starting to fill out a bit, but her sparkle steals every scene she is in. *Courtesy Anna Michalik.*

Inside the theatre, the ladies separate from Homer and all three make their respective ways back to Marcia's. A lengthy and moderately amusing "old dark house" sequence follows, ending with Marcia and a dripping wet Homer reconciling under a grand piano. She explains that the "message" she is delivering at the music festival the next night is the same one Homer got when they sang: love of America. The "prints" are two print dresses from her dressmaker. Besides, the Screen Actors' Guild would never hear of her being a spy. Homer claims a kiss and then knocks himself out trying to jump for joy under the piano.

At the festival, Cleo, in black evening gown and lamé jacket, swings a hot number, "Buds Won't Bud." In the audience is an unusual Arab who turns out to be Hector (Dooley Wilson) from Central Avenue, Los Angeles. He tells Cleo that he played so many "A-rabs" in movies

Marcia Warren performs the film's title song at an outdoor music festival. *Courtesy Anna Michalik.*

that he thought he'd try being one. Now he's as homesick as Cleo. They do a rousing reprise of "Buds Won't Bud," the high point of the film. (Dooley Wilson achieved film immortality the next year as "Sam" in *Casablanca*. His rendition of "As Time Goes By" and the expression "Play it again, Sam," never actually used in the film, have passed into American folk culture.)

The festival stage is a giant Egyptian tomb, and Marcia now descends its stony steps, her chiffon gown billowing in an artificial breeze. She sings the film's title song, "Cairo," a very pleasant minor-key melody that deserved popularity despite its untimely title.

Outside in the garden, Homer finds Ahmed retrieving one of his ubiquitous white mice. Homer tells him pointedly that he and some friends plan to call at the shop. Marcia, too, makes her way to the moonlit garden, where she discovers Homer's pipe on the grass, but no Homer. The garden is a busy place, for the sinister group from the radio room are also gathered there, discussing their plans before driving to one of the pyramids. Mrs. Morrison recommends that Ahmed teach his mice to sing high C. That would save them the trouble of bringing a tuning fork to the tomb. When they return, they will dispose of Homer.

The bad guys drive off with Homer crouched on their rear bumper. He has a festival program in his pocket and by judicious tearing he manages to create a message: "Marcia-Smith-the Pyramids," which he tosses to a passerby. Fortunately, it is one of Colonel Woodhue's men. Ahmed spots Homer in the rear view mirror and smiles to himself.

Marcia can't find Homer and returns home. She slams down her purse, then realizes Homer's pipe is in it. Rolled up in the broken stem are a German map and the real Cobson's ID papers. British Intelligence must be notified.

At the pyramids (Hollywood soundstage variety), the conspirators admire the camouflaged robot plane. Loaded with bombs, it will be dispatched shortly to crash into a United States troop ship in the Mediterranean that has five thousand men on board. The spy's "hideout" is inside the tomb behind a panel that can be opened only by a perfect high C. With the aid of a tuning fork, the wall opens, and they drive their car inside.

This business completed, they turn to where Homer has hidden behind a rock. As he is led away at gunpoint, Homer surreptitiously drops his C-notes behind him. The Teutonic gentleman hints loudly that Homer is too stupid to make his escape in the waiting plane, so Homer decides to prove him wrong. He sprints to where the plane is sitting, motors running, and takes off. Homer quickly finds he has no control over the plane. The spies merrily throw it into a loop-the-loop pattern and send it off to its date with the troop ship.

Marcia and a group of British Intelligence men arrive at the tomb and find tire tracks leading up to a solid stone wall. Simultaneously Cleo and Hector find the C-notes nearby. "C-notes!" cries Marcia. She takes her cue and tries singing various C's. Low and middle C have no effect. She tries high C. Nothing.

"Ordinarily I wouldn't admit this," she says, "but I was a little flat that time." She tries again, and the tomb wall slides open. The spies are

Outside the pyramid, Marcia shows Colonel Woodhue (Dennis Hoey, left) a C-note that Homer has left as a clue. Rhys Williams, right. *Courtesy Anna Michalik.*

discovered in their control room and captured. When Mrs. Morrison makes a disparaging remark about Homer, she faces Marcia's rage and fingernails.

Far away, Homer has donned a convenient parachute and inspected the bomb cargo. Although the Nazis have hinted at a super explosive, possibly even a nuclear device, the bombs are numerous and ordinary looking. British planes pursue Homer, machine-gunning his plane. He ties the controls with his necktie and bails out before the plane explodes harmlessly. Homer's parachute descent terminates in the smokestack of the troop ship.

Back in Cairo, Homer and Marcia entertain the sailors they have saved. Homer learns that he has been offered a movie contract. Marcia, as his new wife, offers to teach him the tricks of the trade. Of course, when they kiss, her face will be closer to the camera. The sailors crowd around as she demonstrates, and then they all sing a final chorus of "Keep the Light Burning Bright in the Harbor."

Director W.S. Van Dyke and Robert Young teamed once more, on Van Dyke's next and last film, *Journey for Margaret*. It was a genuinely touching tale of war orphans, the second film of five-year-old Margaret O'Brien. The film was in the can two weeks when W.S. Van Dyke II died of a heart attack. His wartime films listed him proudly as "Major," and, despite illness, he spent his last year awaiting assignment to active duty. Toward the end, he began sleeping in his Marine uniform, refusing to believe he was too sick to be called. In the years since *Naughty Marietta*, he had captained five more MacDonald/Eddy films. With his death and the departure of Jeanette and Nelson from MGM, an era was truly ended.

Reviews

The critics were nearly all unkind to this very pleasant little film: "For the first 10 minutes, it makes good nonsense," reported the *Christian Science Monitor*. *Variety* said, "the producers still have not done right by Jeanette MacDonald....While a step in the right direction, trouble is that the farcical tale goes completely haywire....What might have been a wacky kidding of spy melodramas turns out an undistinguishable hybrid. Cairo is about the third straight weaky for Miss MacDonald.... She sings well and is delightful in those lighter romantic moments....[the] fact that most scenes are supposed to be near Libya or in the city of Cairo calls for costly production background. But the use of too many miniatures and newsreel clips in action scenes do [sic] not enhance the picture."

Archer Winsten in the *New York Post* touched on a hard truth in his "witty" comments: "Today's problem is what to do with Jeanette MacDonald. She does not crack, wither or blow away. She stays pretty much the same, the same limpid soprano voice, the same archly wooden O-how-surprising operetta technique of acting. Only the popularity is different."

Bosley Crowther in the *New York Times* thought the film "a silly and obviously labored attempt to lampoon the spy dramas. Every so often, Miss MacDonald tosses off a full-voiced song. Major W.S. Van Dyke II has directed as though he were laying bricks. In the musical line, however, Miss MacDonald does much better....in a medley of old time favorites she leans rather heavily on sentiment and manages not to fall."

Recordings (See Discography for further information)

Miss MacDonald recorded "From the Land of the Sky Blue Waters" as part of a medley.

Music in the Film

Harold Arlen and E.Y. Harburg composed the score for an anti-war musical called *Hooray for What!* which opened on Broadway on December 1, 1937, starring Ed Wynn. The show closed after a rocky six-months run. MGM then bought the rights to the show (whose score included the popular "God's Country"), but never filmed it. Instead, they used its songs in other films, including *Cairo* and *Babes in Arms*. "Buds Won't Bud," sung in *Cairo* by Ethel Waters and Dooley Wilson, was introduced by Hannah Williams in the pre-Broadway tryout of *Hooray*

Two loyal Americans. *Courtesy Anna Michalik.*

A happy, patriotic finale. Robert Young and Jeanette, center. Note future Metropolitan Opera star George London, immediately above Jeanette's clasped hands. *Courtesy Anna Michalik.*

for What!, but cut from the show. Judy Garland sang it in *Andy Hardy Meets Debutante*, but again the song was cut.

In listing performers after each title, "and" denotes a genuine duet, while commas between names indicate a sequence of singers.

Overture: "Cairo," evolves into "Les Filles de Cadix" ("The Maids of Cadiz") from *Maytime* (MacDonald) - music by Leo Delibes, French lyrics by Alfred deMusset

"The Waltz is Over" ("but my heart goes dancing on") (MacDonald) - music by Arthur Schwartz, lyrics by E.Y. Harburg

OPERATIC BATHTUB ARIAS, fragments from:
  "A Heart That's Free" (MacDonald) - music R.J. Robyn and T. Railey
  "Il Bacio" (MacDonald and Waters) - by Luigi Arditi
  Sextet from *Lucia di Lammermoor* (MacDonald and Waters) - by Gaetano Donizetti

"We Did It Before and We Can Do It Again" (The King's Men) - music by Cliff Friend, lyrics by Charles Tobin

REHEARSAL MEDLEY:
  "To a Wild Rose" (MacDonald and King's Men) - from "Woodland Sketches" by Edward MacDowell
  "From the Land of the Sky Blue Waters" (MacDonald and the King's Men) - music by Charles Wakefield Cadman, lyrics by Nelle Richmond Eberhart
  "Beautiful Ohio" (MacDonald and the King's Men) - music by "Mary Earl," a

MEDLEY - continued
- pseudonym for Robert A. King-Keiser, lyrics by Ballard MacDonald
- "Waiting for the Robert E. Lee" (Waters, MacDonald) - music by Lewis F. Muir, lyrics by L. Wolfe Gilbert
- "Avalon" (MacDonald and King's Men with Robert Young) - music based on theme in third act of *Tosca* by Giacomo Puccini, rewritten by Al Jolson and Vincent Rose, lyrics by B.G. DeSylva
- "Home, Sweet Home" (MacDonald, Waters, Young, King's Men) – music by Sir Henry Bishop, lyrics by Howard Payne
- "Keep the Lights Burning Bright in the Harbor" (all) - music by Arthur Schwartz, lyrics by Howard Dietz and E.Y. Harburg
- "Buds Won't Bud" (Waters) - music by Harold Arlen, lyrics by E.Y. Harburg
- "Buds Won't Bud" reprise (Waters and Wilson)
- "Cairo" (MacDonald and male chorus) - music by Arthur Schwartz, lyrics by E. Y. Harburg
- "Keep the Lights Burning Bright in the Harbor" reprise (male chorus, MacDonald, Young)

Copyrighted for the film but not used were "In Times Like These" (Schwartz, Harburg) and "A Woman with a Man" (Schwartz, Harburg). The latter was mentioned in pre-release publicity as a number for Miss Waters, but may not have been filmed.

Trivia

Sharp eyes will note that the film clip from *Maytime* is not composed entirely of the original 1937 footage. To cover the spots in the original where the camera cut away to show the court of Louis Napoleon, MGM shot new footage of Jeanette alone. apparently in the same dress and hairstyle, to fill in the gaps. However, her dress and hair are both obviously different.

Note the huge poster of Nelson Eddy in the lobby of the movie theatre visited by Jeanette, Ethel Waters, and Robert Young.

Phantom of the Opera

Universal.
Released August 27, 1943.
Directed by Arthur Lubin.
Produced by George Waggner.
92 minutes.
Technicolor.

Swedish release title: *Fantomen På Stora Operan* (Phantom of the Great Opera House)
Danish title: *Spøgelset i Operaen* (Specter of the Opera)
French title: *Le Fantôme de l'Opéra*
Portuguese title: *O Fantâsma* (The Apparition)

Based on the novella "Le Fantôme de l'Opéra" by Gaston Leroux, published in Paris in 1910. Screenplay: Eric Taylor and Samuel Hoffenstein. Adaptation: John Jacoby. Executive Producer: Jack Gross. Photography: Hal Mohr and W. Howard Greene. Technicolor Director: Natalie Kalmus. Art Directors: John B. Goodman and Alexander Golitzen. Sound Director: Bernard B. Brown. Sound Technician: Joe Lapis. Set Direction: R. A. Gausman, Ira S. Webb. Dialogue Director: Joan Hathaway. Costumes: Vera West. Hair Stylist: Emily Moore. Makeup Artist: Jack Pierce. Musical Score and Direction: Edward Ward. Opera Sequences: William von Wymetal, Lester Horton. Choral Direction: William Tyroler. Orchestrations: Harold Zweifel, Arthur Schutt. Editor: Russell Schoengarth. Assistant Director: Charles Gould. Western Electric Recording.

Other Phantoms: The Leroux work has inspired a number of film and stage versions:

1925 – Lon Chaney made an indelible impression as the Phantom in Universal's silent screen classic, produced and directed by Rupert Julian. Mary Philbin and Norman Kerry played the lovers. The film featured Gibson Gowland (star of *Greed*) and William Tyroler, who would be choral director of the 1943 version. Disributed in hand-colored prints and, in 1930, with a musical score.

1930 – Universal reissued their earlier film with music and sound effects and new sequences. Chaney had died, but those actors still living dubbed their voices to the silent footage.

1957 – James Cagney played the Phantom in one sequence of his Lon Chaney biography, *The Man of a Thousand Faces,* for Universal.

Danish poster for *Phantom of the Opera*, 1943. *Courtesy Anna Michalik.*

1962 – Herbert Lom starred and Terence Fisher directed in Technicolor for Universal. Heather Sears played the ingenue.

1974 – *Phantom of Hollywood*, starring Jack Cassidy as a John Barrymore-ish actor, his face scarred by an explosion, who now lurks around old, unused movie sets.

1974 – Brian DePalma directed a rock adaptation, *Phantom of the Paradise*, which starred William Farley as the Phantom, plus Paul Williams and Jessica Harper.

1983 – A TV movie was made with Maximilian Schell as the Phantom, and Jane Seymour and Michael York as the lovers. Robert Markowitz directed. Filmed in Budapest.

1983 – A stage version by Arthur Kopit.

1986 – Andrew Lloyd Webber's hit musical version premiered at Her Majesty's Theatre, London, on 10/9/86, with libretto by Charles Hart and additional lyrics by Richard Stilgoe. Michael Crawford and Sarah Brightman (the second Mrs. Webber) starred as the Phantom and Christine when the show opened in New York at the Majestic on 1/26/88.

1989 – Producers capitalized on Robert Englund's fame as Freddy Krueger in the *Nightmare on Elm Street* series to cast him as the *Phantom*. Directed by Dwight H. Little. Also filmed in Budapest.

1990 – Another TV movie, shown originally in two parts. Burt Lancaster starred as the Phantom's father (!), a character absent from all other versions. Charles Dance was the Phantom, and Teri Polo was Christine. Ian Richardson also starred. Directed by Tony Richardson.

1998 – A surreal slasher version called *Il Fantasma dell'opera*, directed by Dario Argento, produced in Italy and Hungary and filmed in French and English. A maskless phantom seeks to protect the rats of Paris under the Opera House. Starring Julian Sands as the Phantom and Asia Argento (the director's daughter) as Christine Daae.

2004 – Film version of Andrew Lloyd Webber's stage musical, directed by Joel Schumacher and starring Gerard Butler as the Phantom and Emmy Rossum as Christine.

Nelson Eddy (Anatole Garron)
Susanna Foster (Christine DuBois)
Claude Rains (Erique Claudin)
Edgar Barrier (Inspector Raoul Daubert)
Leo Carrillo (Signor Ferretti)
Jane Farrar (Biancarolli)
J. Edward Bromberg (Amiot)
Fritz Feld (Lecours)
Frank Puglia (Villeneuve)
Steven Geray (Vercheres)
Barbara Everest (Aunt)
Hume Cronyn (Gerard)
Fritz Leiber (Franz Liszt)
Nicki Andre (Lorenzi, diva playing Russian Princess)
Gladys Blake (Jeanne, lady-in-waiting in *Martha*)
Elvira Curci (Biancarolli's maid, Yvette)
Hans Herbert (Marcel, Anatole's valet)
Kate [Drain] Lawson (Marie, the landlady)
Miles Mander (Pleyel)
Rosina Galli (Christine's maid, Celeste)
Walter Stahl (Doctor Lefours)
Paul Marion (Desjardines)
Tudor Williams, Anthony Marlow (Singers in *Martha*)
Beatrice Roberts (Nurse)

Phantom of the Opera

Marek Windheim (Renfrit, the secretary)
Muni Seroff (Reporter)
Belle Mitchell (Feretti's maid)
Ernest Golm (Office manager)
Renee Carson (Georgette, girlfriend of Pleyel)
Lane Chandler, Stan Blystone (Officers)
Cyril Delevanti (Bookkeeper, Pleyel & Desjardines)
John Walsh (Office boy)
Dick Bartell, James Mitchell * (Reporters)
Alphonse Martell (Policeman)
Wheaton Chambers (Reporter)
Edward Clark (Usher)
Hank Mann (Stagehand)
William Desmond (Stagehand / theatre extra)
Hal Varney (Claude Rains's double)
Eric Mayne, Manuel Paris (Christine's admirers - extras at end)
Edmund Mortimer (Opera patron, extra)
Francis White (Opera singer)

* The dancer/actor.

French poster. *Courtesy Anna Michalik.*

Swedish sheet music cover for "Lullaby of the Bells." *Courtesy of Anna Michalik.*

Oscars:
Best Color Cinematography: Hal Mohr and W. Howard Greene.
Best Color Interior Decoration: Alexander Golitzen, John B. Goodman, Russell A. Gausman, and Ira S. Webb.

Oscar Nominations:
Best Sound Recording: Bernard B. Brown.
Best Scoring for a Musical Picture: Edward Ward.

Phantom of the Opera was presented on Cecil B. DeMille's Lux Radio Theatre, 9/13/43, with Nelson, Susanna Foster, and Basil Rathbone as the Phantom.

In July of 1942, Eddy obtained a release from his MGM contract to freelance. He didn't make another film for six months, but this hardly meant he was "at liberty." His heavy schedule of concerts, radio appearances, and recordings was now supplemented by his wartime volunteer work—as air raid warden (a serious job for anyone living on one of our nation's coastlines) and as entertainer at the Hollywood Canteen and abroad.

In 1943, he signed with Universal for a lavish Technicolor remake of Universal's silent classic, *Phantom of the Opera*. The original had starred Lon Chaney as the "Phantom" who terrorizes the Paris Opera, plus Norman Kerry and Mary Philbin as the love interest. The 1943 version employed the glories of three-strip Technicolor as well as the obvious addition of opera. (The sound rerelease of the Chaney silent in 1930 had used two-strip Technicolor inserts and dubbed music and dialogue.)

In the novella on which both films were based, "Erik" is born deformed. A genius, he designs the Paris Opera House and builds himself an underground retreat. The silent film version has Lon Chaney playing a maniac escaped from Devil's Island who is secreted in the opera cellar as the film opens. He guides Christine to stardom, then unleashes a reign of terror to get her better roles. Finally he kidnaps her and brings her to his lair where she unmasks him. Her sweetheart, Raoul, rescues her, and a

In his first actual opera sequence in a film (*Maytime* used an invented opera, *Balalaika* a rehearsal montage), Eddy as opera star Anatole Garron sings "Plunkett's Aria" from *Martha*.

mob chases the Phantom to a watery death in the Seine. *Faust* served as the key opera in both the book and the silent film.

The 1943 sound version reputedly cost $1,500,000 and uses the original Universal Opera House set. Eddy plays "Anatole," the romantic lead and now the star of the opera company. Claude Rains, who had started out in horror films at Universal in 1933 and then "gone straight," completed *Casablanca* at Warners and returned to Universal for the role of the Phantom. Leading lady Susanna Foster was very well received although her career was to be short lived. She was Universal's backup to their own Deanna Durbin, but she never transmitted the Durbin spontaneity and warmth. Her unique ability to hit F above high C gets full play in the film.

Claude Rains as the misunderstood Claudin who turns into the Phantom. *Courtesy Ginny Sayre*.

Eddy tired of his "blond" image and reverted to the dark hair he had used once before as the bandit in *The Girl of the Golden West. Courtesy Anna Michalik.*

Ambitious chorus singer Christine Dubois (Susanna Foster) is torn between two equally ardent suitors, baritone Anatole Garron (Nelson, left) and Police Inspector Raoul Daubert (Edgar Barrier, second from right). Hume Cronyn, far right, plays fellow officer Gerard. *Courtesy Anna Michalik.*

Producer George Waggner (who wrote the lyrics for the film's "folk song") had a bunch of horror films to his credit (*The Wolf Man, Ghost of Frankenstein, Frankenstein Meets the Wolf Man, Man Made Monster*), and he selected a director, Arthur Lubin, who had dealt mostly in gangster Bs and Abbott and Costello movies. Given this background, it is surprising that, as one critic put it, there is "too much opera and not enough phantom" for the film to rate as a horror classic. And the manufactured opera sequences are too thin for the film to rate high as a musical. The chance to make a first-rate picture on both counts was lost, despite the obvious efforts of the participants.

The titles set the high visual standard with gilt lettering against a red velvet curtain. The film opens in the magnificent Paris Opera House, circa 1880, with Anatole Garron (Nelson) singing "The Porterlied" ("Plunkett's Aria") from *Martha* just as magnificently. He is very dashing in a brown leather jacket, boots, and a wide-brimmed hat. To break his "blond" image, Eddy dyed his hair black and sported a moustache for this role, perhaps seeking some of the dramatic quality that his *The Chocolate*

Soldier makeup had given him. Unfortunately, his romantic rival in the film, Edgar Barrier, also has black hair and a pencil moustache.

The "Porterlied" opera sequence is delightful, although Eddy said later that when the film was assembled, it was obvious the scene should have been played faster. "Anyone can tell you things like that after the film is completed," he noted. "What you need is someone who can tell you while you're filming."

During his song, there is a superb tracking shot up past the massive chandelier. The opera is nearly over when the Inspector of Police, Raoul Daubert (Edgar Barrier), appears backstage. It is not a police matter that has brought him, but the shining eyes of a singer, Christine DuBois (Susanna Foster). It becomes obvious that she is being courted by both Raoul and Anatole, but that her heart is currently pledged to her music.

Someone else in the Opera House also has strong feelings about Christine—Monsieur Claudin, a violinist in the orchestra. Raoul's exuberant greeting has caused her to miss a curtain call, and she is ordered to the director's office for a scolding. Little Claudin (Claude Rains) waits outside the office, also summoned by director Villeneuve (Frank Puglia). As Christine passes Claudin in the waiting room, he summons his courage to ask if she is all right. He is being presumptuous, of course, but he has worked there so long. As she smilingly turns to go, he calls her back: "*Christine*." The gaucherie of addressing a strange lady by her Christian name in the 1880s is evident from the discordant notes of background music. Christine frowns and departs.

The little man's problems are further compounded in his interview with the director. Villeneuve has long been aware that someone in the string section is not playing well. He suspects Claudin and asks him to play something. Claudin nervously takes up his violin and begins a haunting little tune, a folk melody. It is perfect. Still Villeneuve wonders. He'd like to hear the opening movement of the third act of *Martha*.

Claudin must confess. His hand is partially paralyzed. He could only play the lullaby because it required no fingering. Reluctantly, Villeneuve discharges Claudin, despite his twenty years of service. No doubt Claudin has saved a tidy little nest egg from his earnings, Villeneuve says cheerfully, and the opera will issue him a season ticket.

Shattered, Claudin quietly leaves and makes his way to his hovel of a room. There is a superb shot of him walking over wet cobblestones glittering under the gas streetlights. His landlady (Kate Lawson) is waiting to demand her rent. He may choose to hoard his money and starve to death, but she must be paid. Alone, he strokes the piano keys with his stiffening fingers, playing the concerto he has written around the little folk tune.

The next day, he pays an important call on the studio of Signore Feretti (Leo Carrillo), where Christine is having her singing lesson. Christine is not in good voice, and the Signore scolds her. If there is some man upsetting her, she must get him out of her life. Christine murmurs obediently that she understands. "Women *never* understand," the Signore says. "But," he adds happily, "they are docile." She departs without seeing Claudin.

Signore Feretti is delighted to receive Christine's patron and discuss her progress. Claudin has come, however, to beg Feretti to continue the lessons without payment until he can find another position. It means everything to him. But, Feretti replies, it means *nothing* to him. His expenses are high, and there are paying pupils waiting for an opening. However, out of consideration for the business Claudin has given him, he will teach Christine a few more times for nothing, and then tell her she no longer needs him.

Such a pity, Feretti says, because she was just ready to be launched on a career—if only she had the money. Claudin is desperate. He will

Claudin (Claude Rains, right) mistakenly thinks that music publisher Pleyel (Miles Mander on floor) has stolen his concerto. Pleyel's lady friend (Renee Carson) defends him by hurling etching acid in Claudin's face. *Courtesy Anna Michalik.*

pay. He has written a concerto and is sure that Pleyel & Desjardines Music Publishers will buy it and give him a large advance. Feretti chuckles at his optimism as the little man hurries off.

At Pleyel & Desjardines, Claudin sits hopefully, hour after hour, while M. Pleyel (Miles Mander) is amusing himself with his two hobbies, women (Renee Carson) and etchings. Finally Claudin asks for his manuscript back. A vague secretary and an officious clerk are unable to find it, and, when Claudin becomes irate, Pleyel appears and insultingly orders him out. Claudin is frantic, for it is his only copy. He stands outside the door, not knowing which way to go. Suddenly he hears a piano playing his concerto. Unknown to him, Desjardines (Paul Marion) is showing the manuscript to Franz Liszt (Fritz Leiber), who is delighted with the work. Claudin runs back into the office, crying that they have stolen his music.

He rushes at Pleyel, seizing him by the throat. As Pleyel crumples to the floor, his pretty companion seizes a tray of etching acid and flings it in Claudin's face. Claudin's cries are horrible, and he flees into the night like a wounded animal as the woman screams for the police. In another exquisite color sequence, Claudin lowers himself into a slimy sewer while the gendarmes comb the lamplit streets for him.

Mysterious things begin happening around the Opera House. Vercheres, the stage manager (Steven Geray), suspects ghosts. Costumes and masks have disappeared, as well as food. Then the master key to the entire Opera House is stolen.

Unaware of all this, Christine is entertaining Anatole with "Lullaby of the Bells," a charming Provençal song of her childhood. It is the same theme Claudin used for his concerto. They are interrupted by Raoul. Although no one has seen Claudin since the murder, the police have concluded that he is now a "homicidal maniac" and very dangerous. In searching his room, they have found a statuette of Christine (carved in real life by Eddy). Anatole steps forward and identifies the piece as one he had sculpted for Christine's birthday. Claudin must have stolen it. Raoul and Anatole take their leave, each murmuring "after you, Monsieur," until they start through the doorway simultaneously and get stuck.

A big night at the opera. Madame Biancarolli (Jane Farrar, niece of diva Geraldine Farrar) is gaily vocalizing in her dressing room. Christine, too, is making up in her private dressing room (a unique understudy, indeed!) when a mysterious voice is heard: "Christine, you're going to be a great and famous singer. I'll help you."

The opera, called *Amour et Gloire*, begins with the chorus in Empire court attire singing Chopin's "Polonaise." The effect is a bit startling, and we feel ungracious at not accepting it, since a similar "manufactured" opera was so successful in *Maytime*. However, the *Maytime* "Czaritza" sequence can keep a casual opera buff guessing for hours at the identity of what, he is sure, is a real opera. The Chopin themes fool no one. (Perhaps this is because Tchaikovsky wrote extensively for the voice and Chopin did not.) Von Wymetal, who created the "Czaritza" sequence, here tries a similar feat but without the stunning success.

Madame Biancarolli is dazzling the audience while Christine watches from the wings. Anatole slips up behind Christine and repeats the words she heard in her dressing room. A coincidence, but she is extremely puzzled.

Anatole joins Madame Biancarolli on stage for a duet. Madame drinks from a prop goblet of wine—a goblet we have seen manipulated by a mysterious hand—and she exits. Backstage, she predictably passes out, and Christine is recruited to perform in her place. The audience roars its approval for Christine, and, far below the Opera House, the masked Phantom sits in the ghastly green light listening to their applause.

Raoul, in his official capacity, is quite interested in Madame's charges that Anatole has drugged her. He summons the parties to the incident and challenges Anatole, who had motive and opportunity. "Certainly, Inspector," Anatole replies coolly. The camera records each face in the room in quick succession. "We *all* did." Madame, however, will have her revenge. During the two years remaining to her contract, Christine must return to the chorus—and stay there. Otherwise, Madame will charge Christine and Anatole with attempted murder.

The Phantom has overheard and comes to threaten Madame Biancarolli. Bravely, she reaches for his mask. Her screams of horror are heard from the hall. Rushing into her dressing room, her maid (Elvira Curci) encounters the departing Phantom and she, too, falls at his hands. A horrified crowd finds them both murdered.

The Phantom flees into the rigging, pursued by Anatole, who is wearing an identical opera cape. Raoul spots Anatole climbing into the flies and mistakes him for the Phantom. In the eerie half-light over the stage, the chase goes on. Anatole pauses on a narrow scaffold to listen for his quarry. Silently, the Phantom swings a rope weighted with a heavy metal pulley straight at Anatole's back. Anatole is knocked into space. He grabs at the rope and clings precariously as he is carried out over the stage. There he thuds against the curtain and loses his grip. Clawing frantically at the velvet drapery, he grabs a rope and plummets to the stage where he lands in the middle of a freshly painted canvas flat.

The Inspector confronts Anatole, who protests that he has been chasing the murderer. Surely the Inspector saw the man? "No, Monsieur," replies Raoul, "I was chasing *you*."

The Opera House is closed, and Paris talks of nothing but the murders. Raoul proposes a plan that will stop the talk and draw the murderer into the open. The Phantom has sent a note

Amour et Gloire, an opera sequence created from Chopin melodies. Eddy had rarely been trimmer and in better physical shape. *Courtesy Anna Michalik.*

Dangling high above the stage.

demanding that Christine replace Madame Biancarolli. They will end the speculation in the press by reopening the opera, but Christine will not sing. A substitute singer will go on—a substitute who will lure the irate Phantom out of hiding.

The opera is reopened. Again the camera moves from the expectant audience up past the ominous chandelier that will play an important part in the coming scenes. Police are posted throughout the theatre and on stage. The plucky Madame Lorenzi (Nicki Andre) has agreed to be the bait, and the "fish" is rising. Another threatening note is found, but, Raoul declares, Madame Lorenzi can be in no danger. A police matron is in her dressing room, and a detective is waiting to escort her to the stage. We see the stalwart detective being sliently garrotted with a rope, and begin to suspect that Madame Lorenzi will not be doing much singing.

Anatole also has a plan to bring the Phantom out of hiding, but first the opera. The curtain rises on a picturesque scene in a Tartar camp. Anatole enters in a Mongol chariot drawn by four horses. He is wearing an Oriental half-mask covering the upper part of his face, and the chorus is similarly masked. In excellent Russian, Anatole delivers an aria based on Tchaikovsky's Fourth Symphony, and then, with a crack of his whip, he snatches a vivacious dancing girl into his chariot. The audience is rapt, too rapt to notice a movement high in the vaulted roof over their heads. A masked figure is sawing the massive chain that holds the chandelier.

We cut back and forth between the exciting action on stage and the patient labor of the little man above. Madame Lorenzi appears and begins her aria. She throws back her head to hit a high note, and her eyes fill with horror. The note turns into a scream.

The chandelier is just tearing loose. It trembles, lurches, and crashes into the orchestra. In the midst of the pandemonium, a masked chorus member takes Christine's arm. She knows that Raoul has disguised dozens of his men as singers and assumes this is an officer.

An unseen figure saws away at the chain supporting the chandelier. *Courtesy Anna Michalik.*

A spectacular opera sequence, *Le Prince de Caucasie*, manufactured from Tchaikovsky's Fourth Symphony. Eddy and Nicki Andre on platform at right. *Courtesy Anna Michalik.*

She follows him blindly as he promises to look after her. He has always looked after her, he says. Suddenly she realizes who he is. She tries to run, but his strength is too much for her. Petrified with fear, she is half carried, half dragged, into his subterranean realm. As she shivers in terror, he tells her of the peace and beauty of his underground home. Here he has everything, even the music from the stage of the opera above. The subdued green lighting is superb, reflecting on the slimy walls and mysterious lake.

On the opera stage, Anatole's plan goes into effect. As he and Raoul enter the underground caverns in search of Christine, Franz Liszt and full orchestra begin playing Claudin's concerto. (Presumably, there are still dead bodies pinned under the fallen chandelier.)

The Phantom's world is not as secure as he imagines. The walls are giving way with age and water damage. Raoul and Anatole just miss being struck by crumbling rocks in the ghostly passageways. The music vibrates downward, increasing in resonance with its distance. "Sing," orders the Phantom, and Christine takes up the melody. Anatole and Raoul follow her voice in search of the Phantom.

Like Madame Biancarolli, Christine wants to see the Phantom's face. She snatches off his mask, and we see the hideously scarred face of Claudin. We are half horrified and half fascinated by the superb makeup job. Claudin

The Phantom takes Christine to his mysterious underground world of shimmering Technicolor. Universal specialized in horror films with elaborate Gothic sets. *Courtesy Anna Michalik.*

takes up a sword from the theatrical props around his cave, and Raoul fires his pistol. The reverberations grow and grow as Anatole and Raoul grab Christine and run for safety. In a cataclysm of tumbling rock, rushing water, and Technicolor, the entire subterranean world collapses. All that is left of Claudin is a violin, bow, and mask amidst the rubble.

The music changes to a brighter motif, and we find Christine in her dressing room after a triumphant performance. Anatole has come with a bouquet to take her to dinner. Raoul arrives with an identical bouquet and request. Why, suggests the lady, don't they dine together? Raoul declines. He does not take baritones to dinner. Anatole declines. He does not wish to be seen with a policeman.

Christine's public swarms in the door, and, oblivious to both gentlemen, she is borne away in the crush of their enthusiasm. Raoul relents. Will Anatole join him for dinner? If only they can fight their way through the crowd. But after all, who would notice a mere baritone and a lowly detective. "After you, Monsieur," they both cry, and then, arm in arm, they go off to enjoy their dinner.

A nice, off-beat ending for a picture that generally could have used more subtlety. Historically, it is interesting as the only Eddy vehicle in which he didn't get the girl.

Reviews

The newly influential "family" magazine reviewers lauded *Phantom*, and the National

Phantom of the Opera

Legion of Decency found it morally unobjectionable for adults: "[Eddy and Foster] both give performances under Lubin's direction that surpass anything they have ever done. Miss Foster definitely bids for stardom..." *Variety* called it "vivid, elaborate, and, within its original story limitations, an effective production geared for substantial grosses."

Film Daily thought that "the studio has also been wise in building up the musical aspects of the story and cutting down the Phantom role," but the *New York Times* disagreed: "the richness of the decor and the music is precisely what gets in the way of the tale. Who is afraid of a Phantom that is billed beneath Mr. Eddy in the cast?" Some felt the film implied that Christine was Claudin's daughter. Apparently a scene was filmed stating this, but it was later cut.

No Recording.

Music from the Film

In listing performers after each title, "and" denotes a genuine duet, while commas between names indicate a sequence of singers.

Eddy looked especially dashing as a Cossack in the opera designed to lure the Phantom from hiding.

Christine is rescued by both Anatole and Raoul who prepare to duel with the Phantom. How can she choose between them? Left to right, Rains, Eddy, Barrier, Foster. *Courtesy Anna Michalik.*

Overture: trumpet fanfare, "Lullaby of the Bells" INTO:
"The Porterlied" ("Lasst Mich Euch Fragen"- Plunkett's aria) (Eddy and male chorus) - from the opera *Martha*, music by Friedrich von Flotow, special libretto by George Waggner, translated into French by William von Wymetal INTO
Third act finale of *Martha* ("Mag der Himmel Euch Vergeben") (Tudor Williams, male chorus) - credits as above
"Lullaby of the Bells" (violin solo) - music by Edward Ward, lyrics by George Waggner
"Lullaby of the Bells" reprise as piano concerto
"Lullaby of the Bells" reprise (Susanna Foster and Eddy)
Amour et Gloire, an opera contrived from Frédéric Chopin themes with French lyrics by William von Wymetal

"Grand Polonaise" (chorus)
"Nocturne in E Flat" and "Waltz in C Minor" (Eddy and Jane Farrar, possibly dubbed by Francia White, with chorus)
Le Prince de Caucasie, an opera contrived from the Fourth Symphony of Peter Ilich Tchaikovsky, English libretto by George Waggner, Russian translation by Max Rabinowitz.
    Opening chorus (chorus, tenor, and bass-baritone, possibly Tudor Williams)
    Solo (Eddy)
    Solo, interrupted by the falling chandelier (Nicki André)
"Lullaby of the Bells" reprise (Foster with piano)
Finale: "Lullaby of the Bells" (orchestral)

Eddy would have loved recording some arias, but the famed Petrillo/Musicians' Union Strike barred orchestras from recording until late 1944.

Knickerbocker Holiday

United Artists.
Released March 17, 1944.
Produced and Directed by Harry Joe Brown.
A Producers Corporation of America Production.
85 minutes.

Danish title: *Den syngende Oprører* (The Singing Rabble-rouser)
Spanish title: *La Chica y el Gobernador* (The Girl and the Governor)

Based on the Broadway musical with music by Kurt Weill and book and lyrics by Maxwell Anderson. Screenplay: David Boehm, Rowland Leigh, and Harold Goldman. Adaptation: Thomas Lennon. Musical Score: Werner R. Heymann. Musical Director: Jacques Samossoud. Photography: Philip Tannura. Editor: John F. Link.

Best remembered for its immortal "September Song," *Knickerbocker Holiday* opened at the Ethel Barrymore Theatre on October 19, 1938. Walter Huston played the one-legged "Pieter Stuyvesant," Ray Middleton was "Washington Irving" (who doesn't appear in the film version), and Jeanne Madden and Richard Kollmar were the young lovers. It ran a modest 168 performances.

Nelson Eddy (Brom Broeck)
Charles Coburn (Pieter Stuyvesant)
Constance Dowling (Tina Tienhoven)
Ernest Cossart (Tienhoven)
Johnnie "Scat" Davis (Ten Pin)
Richard Hale (Tammany)
Shelley Winter [Winters] (Ulda Tienhoven)
Glenn Strange (Big Muscle)
Fritz Feld (Poffenburgh)
Otto Kruger (Roosevelt)
Percival Vivian (De Vries)
Charles Judels (Renssaler)
Ferdinand Munier (De Pyster)
Percy Kilbride (Schermerhorn, the jailer)
Chester Conklin (Town crier)
Richard Baldwin (First pal)
Lang Page (Second pal)
Connie Conrad, Freda Stoll, Veta Lehman, May Cloy, Harriet Dean (Councilmen's wives)
Herbert Corthell (Captain)
Phil Green (Sailor)
Gerald Oliver Smith (English colonist)
John Sheehan (Irish colonist)
Sven Hugo Borg (Swedish colonist)
Dorothy Granger (Barmaid)
Patti Sheldon, Ruth Tobey (Giggling girls)
Fern Emmett (Critical woman)
Bruce Cameron, Irving Fulton, Walter Pietela, Paul Allen Spears, Tony Shaller (Tumblers)
Harold De Garro (Stilt walker)
Harry Johnson, Fred Johnson, Johnny Johnson (Jugglers)
Lou Manley (Punch and Judy show)
Casey MacGregor (Fire eater)
Harry Bayfield, Buster Brodie, Bobbie Hale (Clowns)
The Carmen Amaya Troupe (Gypsy dancers)
Sabicas (Guitarist)
Irving Bacon (Peter Van Stoon)

Cut from the release print were:
Ralph Dunn (Guard)
Edward Earle (Barker)
Harry C. Bradley, George Bunny (Old men)

Oscar nomination:
Best Scoring of a Musical Picture (Werner R. Heymann and Kurt Weill)

Knickerbocker Holiday

Knickerbocker Holiday demonstrates some of the tribulations that can befall a stage production in transition to the screen. The stage *Knickerbocker* had music by the master, Kurt Weill, but only three of his songs survived the trip. The haunting "It Never Was You" got lost along the way. The stage *Knickerbocker* (which admittedly enjoyed only a modest success) concerned the gut issues of patriotism, political corruption, man's inhumanity to man, and the rights of the individual to dissent. In the strongly pacifistic times before World War II, it depicted war as a condition brought about by greedy politicians. The film *Knickerbocker*, coming in the midst of the worldwide conflict, tiptoed delicately over anything resembling an issue and came up with a curious tangle of operetta love story and patriotic homilies. Villainy was of the black-and-white horse opera variety.

Maxwell Anderson's stage libretto concerned the search by author Washington Irving for the roots of the American spirit. He finally discovers it in the person of Brom Broeck, "the first American." Irving and Brom explore the elusive American quality in "How Can You Tell an American?" Their description of this highly unorthodox individual seems mild by today's standards, but in 1944, anyone with "a really fantastic and inexcusable aversion to taking orders" would have been regarded as dangerous, possibly even traitorous.

Eddy's leading lady is lovely Constance Dowling, who came to Hollywood from Broadway, where she appeared in *Panama Hattie*. She was pretty and pleasant with a clear voice, but her film career never quite clicked. Charles Coburn undertook the Pieter Stuyvesant rôle created so memorably by Walter Huston and did a nice job.

The film opens on the streets of New Amsterdam, where the town crier (silent comedian Chester Conklin) is announcing the imminent arrival of Pieter Stuyvesant. The townspeople discuss their new Governor in sung dialogue. He is, it seems, "hard as steel" with

Eddy plays colorful freedom-fighter Brom Broeck, in love with pretty Tina Tienhoven (Broadway's Constance Dowling). *Courtesy Anna Michalik.*

"love appeal." The remarkable Governor Stuyvesant (Charles Coburn) is at that moment at sea, smelling out the land well before his little valet, Poffenburgh (Fritz Feld), can spy it through a telescope. Due to the Governor's superior navigation, their ship has crossed the Atlantic in ninety days, shaving six days off the Mayflower's record. Stuyvesant is indeed a most remarkable man! He will rule New Amsterdam with an iron fist, albeit a silver-plated leg.

The City Council of "Nieuw Amsterdam" eagerly awaits his arrival. It is a festive day, and there is nothing like a good hanging to make a reception go with a swing. The council's chief nominee for the honor is the troublemaker, Brom Broeck. Brom thinks, and he makes others think. (We are told this throughout the film, but it is never demonstrated.) If too many people begin thinking, it may reduce the council's illegal profits. Only one distinguished gentleman does not go along with their logic, a silver-

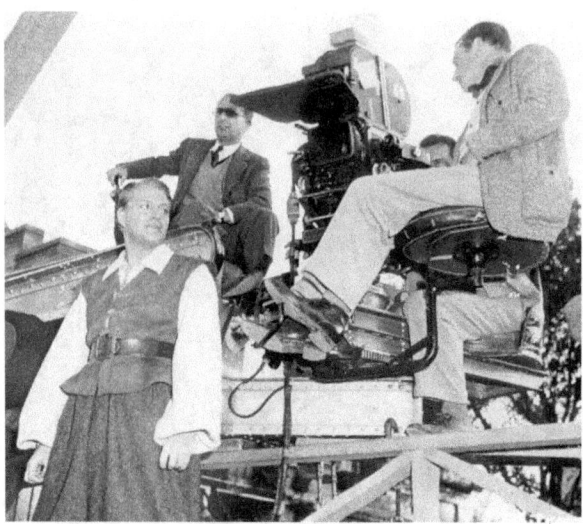

On the set of *Knickerbocker Holiday*, 1944. *Courtesy Anna Michalik.*

haired elder named Roosevelt (Otto Kruger), who looks oddly familiar.

The council summons the clerk, Schermerhorn (Percy Kilbride, before the "Ma and Pa Kettle" series). Schermerhorn is a veritable monument to wishy-washiness. His dour countenance is a visual delight throughout the film. He reads the list of hanging offenses to the eager councilmen, and, though several of them squirm in their seats when a particular one is called out, they can find nothing for which to hang Brom. They must content themselves with putting him in the stocks.

At his printing shop, Brom (Nelson) is happily operating the hand press, printing new attacks against the dishonest councilmen. Being a fighter for liberty is not always profitable or easy, but Brom isn't discouraged and delivers a fine, breezy rendition of "There's Nowhere to Go But Up," one of the three remaining Weill songs. Tina Tienhoven (Constance Dowling) dashes in, completely out of breath. "Don't talk," Brom orders. "Stand just where you are, there, with the sun on you." Tina's young sister, Ulda (Shelley Winter, later Winters), has come with her to see Brom's sidekick, Ten Pin (Johnnie "Scat" Davis). She is slightly more forward than Tina. "Don't talk!" she orders Ten Pin and repeats Brom's romantic command.

Tina has come to warn Brom about the council and to suggest that if he were a little less of an independent fighter, she might not have to remain a spinster. Her arguments, punctuated by tears and loving looks, finally do the trick, and Brom agrees to go to work for the Dutch Trading Company and make her a good home. (This scene has an especially nice musical background, as does the whole film.)

Tina's father, Councilman Tienhoven (Ernest Cossart), and Schermerhorn come to arrest Brom and find the two couples oblivious to interruption. Papa Tienhoven admits that arresting Brom isn't fair—"but it's legal," and Brom is marched off to the stocks.

Tina orders Ten Pin to round up the whole town, which he does musically to "Holiday." (Written by Nelson Eddy and Ted Paxson, it is a nice, offbeat tune, but delivered to bear a maximum resemblance to "Hooray for Hollywood," which Johnnie Davis introduced in *Hollywood Hotel*, Warners, 1937. It even juxtaposes the words hooray and holiday.)

When Stuyvesant arrives, he finds only a group of dowagers, the councilmen's wives,

Brom learns from Tammany (Richard Hale, left) that the government is selling guns and liquor to the Indians. Big Muscle (Glenn Strange, later the bartender on *Gunsmoke*) and Ten Pin (Johnny "Scat" Davis, right) watch.

Knickerbocker Holiday

Governor Peter Stuyvesant (Charles Coburn) arrives to put Brom in his place. He also has a place in mind for Tina.

waiting to greet him. The townspeople are all over in the square, listening to Brom sing in the stocks, another upbeat song called "Let's Make Tomorrow Today."

Papa Tienhoven tells the Governor that *this* is why he has been summoned. To take care of dangerous men who think. "I thought I smelled a thinker," Stuyvesant mutters. Stuyvesant understands that when you make a martyr out of a nuisance, he becomes a hero. Brom is not only released, but given a job as "Secretary of Printing." Now he and Tina can be married. In one of the clumsiest exits since "Tennis, anyone?" Brom grabs Tina's hand, saying, "Com'on Tina, we've got things to do."

Brom is soon so busy that he has no time to think, except, of course, about Tina: "Love Has Made This Such a Lovely Day." The Indian, Tammany (Richard Hale), notes that while the white man runs the country, the white woman runs him. His squaw mutters that if they don't like it, they can go back where they came from.

The councilmen soon discover that the new Governor has not only failed to make their thieving easier, he has taken over their rackets. Papa Tienhoven is especially unhappy, because

Much of Kurt Weill's Broadway score was discarded, and the film added songs by other composers, including one by Eddy and his accompanist, Ted Paxson. *Courtesy Anna Michalik.*

Brom's salary from the state permits him to marry Tina. Stuyvesant has the perfect solution to this problem. He will marry her himself.

Brom's revolutionary plan to unite the Colonies is Stuyvesant's bait. Brom is appointed his emissary and must leave immediately for Long Island, Albany, Hartford, Boston, and other distant points. There, he will organize free trade and a united front against outside aggression. "It *can* happen here," Brom warns (a reference to the isolationists' motto, "It can't happen here"). Of course, the purpose of the trip must be kept a secret, even from Tina.

Brom returns from this successful tour to find that Tina won't speak to him. She seems to have eyes only for Governor Stuyvesant. At an elegant ball, Stuyvesant entertains her with a group of Spanish dancers led by Carmen Amaya, who just happens to be on the lot—er, in New Amsterdam that day. Brom slips into the party and manages to get Tina into the garden. There they are stormily reconciling when Tienhoven's voice is heard inside announcing Tina's betrothal to Stuyvesant. Brom and Tina part in a mutual huff.

Brom thinks that Stuyvesant has been more successful in affairs at home than Brom has been in the affairs of the Colonies. Stuyvesant tells Brom he has a cure for thinking. Brom is ordered to write a book with chapters and footnotes and references and indices. Don't think. Write a book.

Stuyvesant wastes no time with his "affairs." He suggests that Tina marry him within twelve hours. Tina was thinking more in terms of years. "Years!" he cries. He protests any delay in the classic "September Song." His rendition is perhaps a bit jauntier than Walter Huston's familiar recording, but no less touching.

Brom turns from thinking to action and tries to elope with the somewhat reluctant Tina. The Governor discovers them and stylishly arrests, tries, convicts, and sentences Brom to five years in jail, all in one minute. Schermerhorn barges in at the wrong moment as usual, but this time it is the right moment, for he can escort Brom to jail.

Tina follows Brom and breaks into jail. Breaking out was what Brom had in mind, and so they use her petticoat, torn into strips, to make a rope. They tie one end to the window grill and the other to Tammany's horse. The window follows the horse, and they are free, to Schermerhorn's horror and Ten Pin's delight. Poor Schermerhorn tries to summon help by firing the cannon, but it revolves and blows the jail to pieces.

Brom and Tina resolve to part temporarily, but first—Ten Pin, trying to get Brom to safety, fears that he is going to sing. Both lovers do, dueting "One More Smile," a pathetic substitute for the classic "It Never Was You," which

The scene with Tina in her pantalets is also a key piece of comedy business in the stage version. *Courtesy Anna Michalik.*

Dancer-choreographer Carmen Amaya poses between Nelson and Constance Dowling, surrounded by her troupe. (What Spanish dancers are doing in old Nieuw Amsterdam is never explained, but it is a great opportunity to see this talented artist.) Director Harry Joe Brown is second from right. *Courtesy Anna Michalik.*

lurks enticingly in the background music throughout the film.

The Governor and Tienhoven find the skirtless Tina kissing Brom in the middle of the moonlit woods. Stuyvesant is not persuaded by this scandal to cancel his marriage plans. On the contrary, he murmurs, eyeing Tina's bare limbs, he is more eager than ever.

Papa Tienhoven is beginning to have doubts about forcing his daughter's marriage, but Stuyvesant is very persuasive. He points out that when the government takes over selling liquor and guns to the Indians, they will need an agent—who will make ten percent. "Only ten percent," objects Tienhoven. However, they seal the agreement by singing "The One Indispensable Man" (the third Weill song remaining in the film) and doing a sprightly soft-shoe.

Brom and his mighty printing press hide out in the last place anyone will look for them, the ruined jail. His blistering pamphlets begin circulating just as the representatives from the other Colonies begin arriving for the conference that Brom has arranged. Stuyvesant orders a fair to honor the delegates, a fair that will also draw Brom out of hiding to meet with his friends. With a ten-thousand-guilder reward on his head, Brom will soon know who his real friends are.

Brom appears, but not as Stuyvesant had foreseen. He and Ten Pin circulate through the fair in disguise, handing out leaflets while Tina manages to steal the Governor's leg. Brom

Knickerbocker Holiday

Brom in disguise fools jailer Schermerhorn (Percy Kilbride, later Pa Kettle). *Courtesy Anna Michalik.*

diverts the delegates to the nearby tavern, where Ten Pin is to buy them drinks, using the proceeds from pawning the Governor's leg. Stuyvesant senses that a plot is afoot and summons Tina so that they can be married immediately. The action stops dead for several delightful minutes while the Spanish gypsies again entertain, and then we return to the square where the Governor is preparing to wed Tina.

Brom decides to do just what the Governor wants, make an appearance. The townspeople arrive for the wedding and find Brom sitting in the stocks and singing "Sing Out," the third and weakest of Eddy's "up songs" in the film.

In another sung dialogue sequence, Brom exhorts them to reject the religious and economic tyranny of Stuyvesant (the first time we've heard of the religious aspect, although the stage version had the City Council happily hanging Quakers).

The crowd joins him in "Sing Out" as a sign of their agreement. Stuyvesant, a consummate politician, realizes which way the wind is blowing. Brom is not so knowledgeable and is dismayed when the crowd he has gathered so patriotically becomes a mob completely out of control. Brom and Stuyvesant strike a bargain. Brom will stop the mob from hanging Stuyvesant if he will agree to a democracy. "What's that?" the Governor asks. "That's when you're governed by amateurs," Brom tells him.

Stuyvesant agrees, and Brom convinces the mob that Stuyvesant is a good guy. Stuyvesant, in turn, reforms in time to unite the lovers, become a great Governor, and join in the final chorus of "Let's Make Tomorrow Today."

Knickerbocker Holiday can be regarded as a thoughtfully created film that missed. Producer-director Harry Joe Brown (*Alexander's Ragtime Band*, *Hollywood Cavalcade*, *Down Argentine Way*) obviously put a lot of "love" into the film, but critics and audiences alike agreed that it just didn't click. The time was ripe for a reaffirmation of the "American spirit," the complex national emotions that are represented in political jargon by "apple pie" and "mother." *Mrs. Miniver*, despite its British locale,

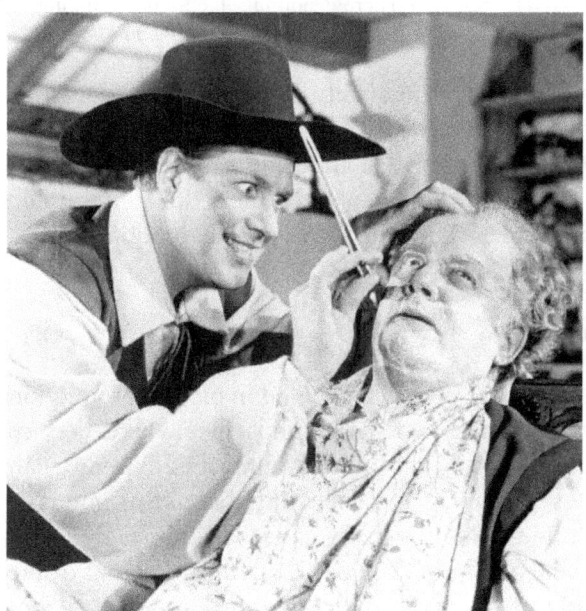

So, you won't let me marry your daughter! Nelson and Ernest Cossart. *Courtesy Anna Michalik.*

There is nothing like a good hanging to help the Governor's wedding festivities go with a swing. *Courtesy Anna Michalik.*

had done it dramatically. It remained for *Meet Me in St. Louis* to do it musically. If *Knickerbocker Holiday* had had a little more thought, a little more insight, and a little more luck, it might have been become a classic incarnation of the American spirit.

Review

"When the persons involved in picture production fail to make up their minds just where they're going with the show, almost anything can develop, up to and including a certain amount of dullness. Nelson Eddy carries his musical chores as he always does, but his attempted acting of the rôle of the harem-scarem young firebrand, Brom Broeck, is too much of a drain on his vitality." (*New York Times*)

No recordings

Music in the Film

In listing performers after each title, "and" denotes a genuine duet, while commas between names indicate a sequence of singers.

Overture: "Dutch March" by Werner Richard Heymann; "September Song"
"Hear Ye" (Chester Conklin, chorus) - music by Jule Styne, lyrics by Sammy Cahn
"There's Nowhere to Go But Up" (Eddy and male chorus) - music by Kurt Weill, lyrics by Maxwell Anderson
"Holiday" (Johnnie "Scat" Davis and chorus) - music by Theodore Paxson, lyrics by Nelson Eddy

Knickerbocker Holiday

"Let's Make Tomorrow Today" (Eddy and chorus) - music by Werner Richard Heymann, lyrics by Furman Brown

"Love Has Made This Such a Lovely Day" (Eddy, Dowling, with Shelley Winter) - music by Jule Styne, lyrics by Sammy Cahn

Spanish dance (Carmen Amaya dancers) - probably traditional

"Zuyder Zee" (male quartet) - music by Jule Styne, lyrics by Sammy Cahn

"September Song" (Charles Coburn) - music by Kurt Weill, lyrics by Maxwell Anderson

"Jail Song" (Eddy) - music by Kurt Weill, lyrics by Furman Brown and Nelson Eddy

"One More Smile" (Eddy and Dowling, possibly dubbed by Sally Sweetland) - music by Jule Styne, lyrics by Sammy Cahn

"The One Indispensable Man" (Coburn and Ernest Cossart) - music by Kurt Weill, lyrics by Maxwell Anderson

Spanish dance (Carmen Amaya dancers) - probably traditional

"Sing Out" (Eddy and chorus) - music by Franz Steininger, lyrics by Furman Brown

"Let's Make Tomorrow Today" reprise (Eddy and chorus)

Stuyvesant and Brom find that democracy needs both ideals and executive ability. After some maneuvering, Brom and Tina are free to marry.

Songs from the stage version that were used in the film were "September Song," "The One Indispensable Man," and "There's Nowhere to Go But Up," plus "It Never Was You," used only as background music. A Weill melody was used for "The Jail Song" with new lyrics by Furman Brown and Nelson Eddy.

Movie Goofs

In "One More Kiss," the part in Nelson's hair keeps switching from right to left. (Joan Woolley)

Follow the Boys
Universal.
Released May 5, 1944.
Directed by Eddie Sutherland.
A Charles K. Feldman Group Production.
122 minutes.

Prerelease titles: *Three Cheers for the Boys, Hip Hip Hooray, On with the Show, Cheers for the Boys, Three Cheers, Happy Day.*
French title: *Hollywood Parade.*

Original screenplay by Lou Breslow and Gertrude Purcell. Musical Director: Leigh Harline. Dances: George Hale. Photographer: David Abel. Associate Producer: Albert L. Rockett. Assistant Directors: Howard Christie, William Holland, and Willard Sheldon. Editor: Fred R. Feitshans Jr. Special Effects: John Fulton.

George Raft (Tony West)
Vera Zorina (Gloria Vance West, née Bertha Lindquist)
Charley Grapewin (Nick West)
Grace McDonald (Kitty West)
Charles Butterworth (Louie Fairweather)
George Macready (Walter Bruce)
Elizabeth Patterson (Annie)
Theodor von Eltz (William Barrett)
Regis Toomey (Dr. Jim Henderson)
Ramsay Ames (Laura)
Spooks (Junior, a dog)
Mack Gray (Lt. Reynolds)
Molly Lamont (Miss Hartford, secretary)

Reel life: Jeanette sings "I'll See You in My Dreams" to a wounded soldier in one of the studio sequences of *Follow the Boys*. Courtesy Jack Tillmany.

John Meredith (Blind soldier, "I'll See You in My Dreams")
John Estes (Patient in MacDonald hospital sequence)
Ralph Gardner (Patient wearing leg cast in MacDonald hospital sequence)
Doris Lloyd (Nurse)
Charles D. Brown (Col. Starrett)
Nelson Leigh (Bull fiddler)
Lane Chandler (Ship's officer)
Cyril Ring (Laughton, *Life* photographer)
Emmett Vogan (Harkness, *Life* reporter)
Addison Richards (MacDermott, *Life* editor)
Frank LaRue (Mailman)
Tony Marsh (First officer)
Stanley Andrews (Australian officer)
Leslie Denison (Reporter)
Leyland Hodgson (Australian reporter)
Bill Healy (Ship's officer)
Frank Jenks (Chick Doyle)
Ralph Dunn (Loomis)

Follow the Boys

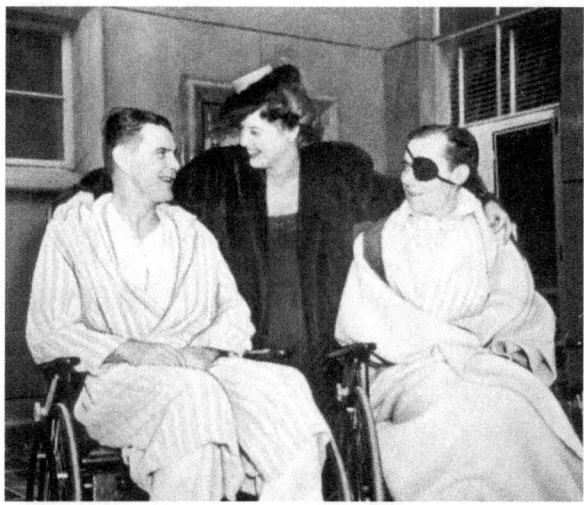

Real life: Jeanette visiting a military hospital. Many actual USO performances by stars like Sophie Tucker, the Andrews Sisters, and Donald O'Connor were filmed and intercut with studio footage for the film. *Courtesy Anna Michalik.*

Billy Benedict (Joe, a soldier)
Grandon Rhodes (George Grayson, guild member)
Howard Hickman (Dr. Wood)
Edwin Stanley (Taylor, Film director / Room clerk)
Roy Darmour (Eddie, assistant director)
Carl Vernell (Terry Dennis, dance director)
Tony [J. Anthony] Hughes (Man)
Wallis Clark (Victory committeeman)
Richard Crane (Marine officer)
Frank Wilcox (Captain Williams, Army doctor)
Jimmy Carpenter, Bernard Thomas (Soldiers)
Carey Harrison (Colonel)
George Riley (Jimmy)
Steve Brodie (Australian pilot)
Jack Wegman (Mayor)
Billy Wayne (Columnist)
Clyde Cook (Stooge)
Bobby Barber (Stooge soldier in W.C. Fields routine)
Dick Nelson (Sergeant)
John Whitney, Walter Tetley, Joel Allen, Carlyle Blackwell Jr., Michael Kirk, Mel Schubert, Stephen Wayne, Charles King (Soldiers)
Anthony Warde (Captain)
William Forrest (Colonel)
Tom Hanlon (Announcer)
Don McGill, Franklin Parker (Men in office)
Dennis Moore (H.V.C. officer)
Odessa Lauren, Nancy Brinckman, Janet Shaw, Jan Wiley (Telephone operators)
Martin Ashe (Man in office)
Duke York (M.P.)
Lennie Smith, Bob Ashley (Jitterbugs)
Jackie Lou Harding (Girl in montage)
Genevieve Bell (Mother in montage)
Don Kramer, Allan Cooke, Luis Torres, Nicholai, John Duane, Ed Browne, Clair Freeman, Bill Meader, Eddie Kover (Dancers)
Lee Bennett (Acrobat)
Daisy (Fifi, a dog)
John Cason (Soldier at radio)
George Eldredge (Submarine officer)
[Baby] Marie Osborne (Nurse)
Nicodemus Stewart (Lt. Reynolds, USAF)
George "Shorty" Chirello (Orson Welles's assistant)
Janice Gay, Jane Smith, Marjorie Fectean, Doris Brenn, Rosemary Battle, Lolita Leighter, Mary Rowland, Eleanor Counts, Linda Brent (Magic Maids)
Bill Wolfe (Zoot-suiter in W.C. Fields routine)
Bill Dyer (Messenger boy)
Cappell and Patricia (Dance team)

Guest Stars (alphabetically)
Louise Allbritton
Carmen Amaya and Her Company
The Andrews Sisters
Evelyn Ankers
Louise Beavers
Noah Beery Jr.
Turhan Bey
Nigel Bruce
Lon Chaney Jr.
Peter Coe
Lois Collier
Alan Curtis
Delta Rhythm Boys
Andy Devine
Marlene Dietrich
W.C. Fields
Susanna Foster
Leonard Gautier's Bricklayers
Thomas Gomez
Samuel S. Hinds
Gloria Jean
Louis Jordan and His Orchestra
Elyse Knox

Ted Lewis and His Band
Jeanette MacDonald
Philo McCullough
Maria Montez
Clarence Muse
Donald O'Connor
Martha O'Driscoll
Robert Paige
Maxie Rosenbloom
Artur Rubinstein
Peggy Ryan
Augustin Castellon Sabicas
Randolph Scott
Dinah Shore
Freddie Slack and His Orchestra
Gale Sondergaard
Charlie Spivak and His Orchestra
Sophie Tucker
Orson Welles and His Mercury Wonder Show

Plus film clips of Joan Bennett, Hedy Lamarr, Martha Scott, and Irene Dunne.

Oscar nomination: Best Song - "I'll Walk Alone," music by Jule Styne, lyrics by Sammy Cahn.

While 1944 gave us *Meet Me in St. Louis*, it also gave us a surfeit of assembly line wartime musicals designed to sell popcorn and boost the spirits without leaving any real impression. *Follow the Boys* is a perfect example. Using footage of many top stars doing USO appearances, it intercuts studio shots of the same performers plus about seven minutes of plot to tie the whole star-studded package together.

The story concerns egocentric hoofer George Raft, who has no time for his wife, Vera Zorina (who played the original Broadway "Angel"), due to his dedication to his career and the war effort. Zorina leaves him and has a baby. He finds out he is a father just before his ship sinks, for a weepy, patriotic finale. In between we are treated to Orson Welles sawing Marlene Dietrich in half, W.C. Fields wielding a crooked pool cue, and actual outdoor camp show performances by Sophie Tucker, Donald O'Connor and Peggy Ryan, the Andrews Sisters, and, of course, Jeanette MacDonald. Considering the excitement and charm of seeing many of these performers before a live audience, it is slightly uncharitable to notice the jarring transitions to studio close-ups within the same numbers.

Follow the Boys is a musical film only in the sense that it contains music, and it might even have difficulty qualifying as a film, but it is certainly a fascinating record of the way

Jeanette played herself and sang "Beyond the Blue Horizon." The lyric was changed to "shining sun" because the Japanese flag depicted a "rising sun." *Courtesy Anna Michalik.*

America felt about itself and its "boys" during World War II.

Jeanette MacDonald appears in three sequences. In the first, which must have been fun to shoot, most of the guest stars of the film are seated on folding chairs listening to a pep talk by George Raft. Jeanette offers to leave on a camp-show tour in a week when her picture is finished. She will cancel her concert tour. One by one, each performer offers their services. Dietrich will go anywhere for soldiers, sailors, and marines. Dinah Shore says she can sing over shortwave for the GIs. And black actress Louise Beavers, not to disrupt any unfortunate stereotypes, offers to cook for the boys.

Jeanette's first number is a rousing rendition of "Beyond the Blue Horizon," ostensibly sung outdoors before thousands of GIs. Studio close-ups are intercut with long shots of a real performance. Jeanette, in a short, black crepe dress, sings the song she introduced fourteen years earlier in *Monte Carlo*. The "rising sun" of the original lyric becomes a "shining sun" to avoid any reference to the design of the Japanese flag.

Her second song is done entirely on a soundstage representing a hospital ward. She jokes with the wounded GIs and then sings a throaty "I'll See You in My Dreams" for a homesick blinded soldier (John Meredith). It is pure corn, but tremendously touching, and it must have been dynamite in 1944 when nearly everyone had someone overseas.

Reviews

Time Magazine called it a "glorification of the service which cinemice and men are rendering the Armed Forces." Howard Barnes in the *New York Herald Tribune* thought that "it piles up entertainment too indiscriminately....[it] is a fine tribute to Hollywood's victory committee activities. While it is a helter-skelter picture, it should prove beguiling for civilians." *Variety* said it "show[s] that a good thing can be overdone....a real tug is Miss MacDonald's 'I'll See You in My Dreams' with a blinded young soldier in a hospital bed as the vis-à-vis."

Recordings (See Discography for further information)

"Beyond the Blue Horizon" (Jeanette MacDonald)

Music from the Film

Jeanette sang "Beyond the Blue Horizon" by Richard A. Whiting, W. Franke Harling, and

Leo Robin and "I'll See You in My Dreams" by Isham Jones and Gus Kahn. Other musical highlights of the film were Sophie Tucker singing "The Bigger the Army and the Navy" (Jack Yellen) and "Some of These Days" (Shelton Brooks), Dinah Shore singing "I'll Get By" (Roy Turk and Fred E. Ahlert), "I'll Walk Alone" (Jule Styne and Sammy Cahn), and "Mad About Him Blues" (Larry Markes and Dick Charles). The Andrews Sisters did a medley of their current hits: "Bei Mir Bist Du Schön," "Apple Blossom Time," "Beer Barrel Polka," and "Shoo, Shoo Baby." Artur Rubinstein played Chopin's "Polonaise in A-Flat" and the Delta Rhythm Boys got especially nice reviews for their performance of "The House I Live In" (Earl Robinson and Lewis Allan).

Make Mine Music

A Walt Disney Production.
An RKO Radio Pictures Release.
Released August 15, 1946.
75 minutes.
Technicolor.

Production title: *Swing Street*
Swedish title: *Spela för mej* (Play for Me)

Eddy's voice is used in "The Whale Who Wanted to Sing at the Met" sequence of this animated collection of stories and musical numbers. Original story by Erwin Graham. Directors: Hamilton Luske, Clyde Geronimi. Story Adaptation: T. Hee, Richmond Kelsey. Layout: A. Kendall O'Connor, Hugh Hennesy, Al Zinnen, and John Hench. Backgrounds: Ralph Hulett, Thelma Witmer, Ray Huffine, and Art Riley. Animation: Ward Kimball, John Lounsbery, Hal King, Hugh Fraser, John Sibley, and Fred Moore. Effects Animation: Joshua Meador and George Rowley. Production Supervisor: Joe Grant.

Eddy's segment was rereleased as a short, *Willie, the Operatic Whale*, by RKO in 1954.

Perhaps the most heartbreaking cartoon character ever created was Willie, the operatic whale, sung by Nelson Eddy. He appeared in one of ten episodes in Walt Disney's first postwar feature, *Make Mine Music*. The Disney organization had gone to war with the rest of the nation, and, aside from *The Three Caballeros* (1944), their wartime output consisted of short cartoons and training and morale films for the armed forces, including one feature, *Victory through Air Power* (1943).

Disney, of course, had created Jeanette's biggest musical rival of 1937-38, the diminutive heroine of *Snow White and the Seven Dwarfs*, the first feature-length cartoon. The charming Florida-produced *Gulliver's Travels* by the Fleischer brothers (creators of Betty Boop, Koko the Clown, and Popeye) followed it in 1939, but by then "Disney cartoon" had become almost one word.

In 1940, Disney laid permanent claim to the feature cartoon market with *Pinocchio* and the classic *Fantasia*. *Make Mine Music* followed the *Fantasia* format with a series of unrelated sequences, each growing out of a particular musical idea. However, it created no chilling moments of horror, no bizarre bits of Freudian

Eddy provides all three voices of the remarkable Willie, the trio-singing whale who wanted to sing at the Met. His narration of the touching story is especially moving. *Copyright MCMXLVI by Walt Disney Productions.*

Make Mine Music

Walt Disney (right) shows Jerry Colonna and Nelson Eddy the story boards for Nelson's episode in the multi-part *Make Mine Music*. Colonna narrated the "Casey at the Bat" segment. *Copyright MCMXLVI by Walt Disney Productions.*

imagery, and thus has never had the appeal of its predecessor, *Fantasia*. The film is remembered mainly for the "Willie" sequence, whose tragic story is still guaranteed to have the children (and adults) sobbing into their popcorn. It can occasionally be seen on the Disney Channel and is well worth watching for.

Musically, the sequence is fascinating, for Eddy not only narrates but sings all the voices—bass, baritone, tenor, soprano, and hundred-voiced choir. With the tremendous advancements in home recording equipment, any audio buff today could approximate this achievement, but in 1946 it represented the summit of technical artistry. Electronically distorted voices in cartoons had frequently been done before that time, and the speeding up of normal voices for comic effect was familiar (e.g., the Munchkins' voices in *The Wizard of Oz*). But to take one single voice and alter its pitch to create separate voices singing together was an accomplishment. Eddy must have been fascinated by the project after his long sessions in his home recording studio. He later recorded a multiple-track record album.

The different sequences of *Make Mine Music* are divided by title pages turning in a "program," and so we first read of "The Whale Who Wanted to Sing at the Metropolitan." [sic] The next page tells us: "Any similarity between voices in this story are [sic] easily explainable because they are all Nelson Eddy."

A baritone voice is heard holding a high note, and the page begins to flutter, then is blown away in a great gust of wind that also contains hats, curtains, flowers, and newspapers. One newspaper settles down in camera range, and we read the headline about a singing sea monster. The camera pulls back, and the paper is now in the hand of a newsboy who is hawking his papers on a crowded city street. The passersby sing of their disbelief.

A group of eminent voice authorities also don't believe it, until one of them, Professor Tetti Tatti, gets an inspiration. The whale has swallowed an opera singer! What marvelous publicity, what fame, what fortune if he should rescue the singer. The professor departs with a harpoon to find the modern Jonah.

But out in the ocean there really is a singing cetacean. His name is Willie and he is happily entertaining the seals and pelicans with "Shortnin' Bread" (Eddy's classic concert song), while the seals clap their flippers in unison. Whitey the seagull, flies in at top speed with a newspaper announcing that the famous impresario Tetti Tatti of the Metropolitan Opera has gone looking for Willie. This is what Willie has been waiting for! To sing at the Metropolitan! "After all these years of casting his shortnin' bread upon the waters...."

Willie finds the Professor's boat and begins to audition. First he dazzles him with "Figaro" (actually "Largo al Factotum" from *The Barber of Seville*—Hollywood never discovered there is no song called "Figaro"), his rapid arpeggios delivered through a cascade of bubbles. The crew of the tiny ship are enchanted, and Tetti Tatti leaps up and down with delight.

Next, Willie launches into the beginning of the sextet from *Lucia di Lammermoor*, singing all three male voices. "He's a swallowed *three* h'opera singers!" cries Tetti Tatti.

Willie imagines himself dominating the stage of the Metropolitan Opera House in appropriate costume, his gigantic voice dislodging the hairdos of the ladies in the balconies. Tetti Tatti

A Swedish advertisement for *Make Mine Music*. The title translates as "Play for Me." Nelson's segment was one of the most popular in the film. *Courtesy Anna Michalik.*

races for the harpoon gun, but the frantic crew cling to him, trying to spare this wondrous creature.

In Willie's fantasy, he is performing in *I Pagliacci, Tristan und Isolde* (both voices), and *Mefistofele* to ever increasing waves of applause. The sailors are transfixed and relax their hold. Tetti Tatti leaps for the harpoon gun and pulls the trigger. The light glints on the murderous spear as it hurtles toward its target. There is a terrible thrashing and a last toss of the mighty tail. Then quiet.

Whitey the seagull sits alone as Eddy's voice tells us: "Now Willie will never sing at the Met. But don't be too harsh on Tetti Tatti. He just didn't understand. You see, Willie's singing was a miracle and people aren't used to miracles...but miracles never die. And somewhere, in whatever heaven is reserved for creatures of the deep, Willie is still singing...."

The three voices of Willie are heard, and we see him singing happily on a celestial cloud bank. The Pearly Gates of heaven close softly, revealing a small sign: "Sold Out."

All dialogue copyright MCMXLVI Walt Disney Productions, used with permission.

Make Mine Music

Sequences in Film

"The Martins and the Coys" (The King's Men) - song by Ted Weems and Al Cameron, arranged by Oliver Wallace. NOTE: This sequence has been censored from some prints and a black bar placed across the name of the King's Men in the opening credits. Political correctness gone amuck? Or a threatened lawsuit by surviving McCoys of the famous Hatfield-McCoy feud?

"Blue Bayou" (Ken Darby Chorus) - song by Ray Gilbert and Bobby Worth, with Debussy's "Clair de Lune"

"All the Cats Join In" (played by Benny Goodman and his orchestra, sung by the Pied Pipers) - music by Eddie Sauter, words by Alec Wilder and Ray Gilbert

"Without You" ["Tres Palabras"] (sung by Andy Russell) - Spanish lyric and music by Osvaldo Farres, English lyric by Ray Gilbert

"Casey at the Bat" (a poem by Ernest Lawrence Thayer, recited by Jerry Colonna) - the song "Casey, the Pride of Them All" by Ray Gilbert, Ken Darby and Eliot Daniel

"Two Silhouettes" (Dinah Shore) - music by Charles Wolcott, lyrics by Ray Gilbert; ballet silhouettes of Tatiana Riabouchinska and David Lichine

"Peter and the Wolf" (narrated by Sterling Holloway) - music by Serge Prokofieff

"After You're Gone" (played by the Benny Goodman Quartet, with Cozy Cole, Sid Weiss and Teddy Wilson) - song by Henry Creamer and Turner Layton

"Johnny Fedora and Alice Blue Bonnet" (The Andrews Sisters) - music by Allie Wrubel, lyrics by Allie Wrubel and Ray Gilbert

"The Whale Who Wanted to Sing at the Met" (Nelson Eddy) - credits below

Reviews

"And the finale, 'The Whale Who Wanted to Sing at the Met,' is as imaginative a conceit as Disney ever essayed. Audiences are set on their ears as Willie (yclept Nelson Eddy, who sings all three voices, tenor, baritone and bass, and through scientific alchemy is made to sing a trio with himself) truly wows the musical world. Willie the Whale will crowd Sonia the Duck [heroine of 'Peter and the Wolf' segment] for popularity in the Disney stable." (*Variety*)

"[It] tells of a fabulous cetacean with a triple gaited voice. No less a star than Nelson Eddy provides the sound track for this event which presents a temptation for a wise crack that we will quietly avoid." (Bosley Crowther in the *New York Times*)

Recordings (See Discography for further information)

Eddy recorded a 78 RPM album, "The Whale Who Wanted to Sing at the Met," containing the music listed below.

Music from the "Willie" Sequence

Nelson's segment is almost entirely music, a true "singspiel," combined with the following songs, all sung by Eddy:

"Shortnin' Bread" - See page 162.
"Largo al Factotum" from *The Barber of Seville* - music by Gioacchino Rossini, libretto Cesare Sterbini
"Chi Me Frena?" ["The Sextet"] from the opera *Lucia di Lammermoor* - music by Gaetano Donizetti, libretto by Salvatore Cammarano
MONTAGE with fragments from the following operas:
    Pseudo *I Pagliacci* passage by Nelson Eddy (Eddy as tenor); see Addenda, page 590
    Tristan und Isolde by Richard Wagner (Eddy as tenor and soprano)
    Mefistofele by Arrigo Boito (Eddy as bass)
    "Mag der Himmel Euch Vergeben" from *Martha* (Eddy as tenor and two baritones) - music by Friedrich von Flotow, libretto by Friedrich W. Riese

Northwest Outpost

Republic.
Released June 25, 1947.
Director and Associate Producer: Allan Dwan.
91 minutes.

Prerelease titles: *One Exciting Kiss, End of the Rainbow,* and *Will Tomorrow Ever Come*
Danish title: *Hvor Regnbuen Ender* (Where the Rainbow Stops)

Original Story: Angela Stuart. Screenplay: Elizabeth Meehan, and Richard Sale. Adaptation: Laird Doyle. Assistant Director: Johnny Grubles. Musical Director: Robert Armbruster. Director of Photography: Reggie Lanning. Second Unit Director: Yakima Canutt. Sound: Earl Crain Sr, and Howard Wilson. Art Director: Hilyard Brown. Associate Art Director: Fred Ritter. Orchestrations: Ned Freeman. Costume Supervision: Adele Palmer. Set Decorations: John McCarthy Jr, and James Redd. Special Effects: Howard and Theodore Lydecker. Makeup Supervision: Bob Mark. Hair Stylist: Peggy Gray. Technical Advisor: Alexis Davidoff. Editor: Harry Keller.

Miles Kreuger of the Institute of the American Musical states that "*Northwest Outpost* is the film version of an unproduced stage musical called *Russian River* which Rudolf Friml had composed with Angela Stuart. Apparently the plot was similar to the film. An agent named Spitzer brought the project to Herbert Yates, studio head of Republic, which purchased Friml's 16-inch transcription disks of the score for $65,000. Friml did not work on the film."

Nelson Eddy (Captain Jim Laurence)
Ilona Massey (Natalia Alanova Savinova)
Joseph Schildkraut (Count Igor Savin)
Hugo Haas (Prince Nickolai Balinin, the Governor)
Elsa Lanchester (Princess Tatiana (Tanya) Balinova)
Lenore Ulric (Baroness Kruposny, "Katushka")
Peter Whitney (Volkoff, prison overseer)
Tamara Shayne (Olga, the maid)
Erno [Ernst] Verebes (Kyril)
George Sorel (Baron Kruposny)
Rick Vallin (Dovkin)
Countess Rosanska, Dina Smirnova, Antonina Barnett, Lola De Tolly, Myra Sokolskaya (Noble ladies)
Michael Visaroff (Capt. Tikhonoff)
George Blagoi, Gen. Sam Savitsky, Igor Dolgoruki, Nestor Eristoff (Noblemen)
The American G.I. Chorus (Chorus of prisoners)
Muni Seroff (Sentry)
Max Willenz (Peasant)
Nina Hansen (Princess Tanya's maid)
Eugene Sigaloff (Priest)
Henry Brandon (Chinese junk captain)
Michael Mark (Small convict)
Dick Alexander (Large convict)
George Paris (Ship's officer)
Ray Teal (Wounded trapper)
Zoia Karabanova, Inna Gest (Bit women)
John Bleifer (Groom)
Molio Sheron (Naval officer)
Gene Gary (Second sentry)
Gregory Golubeff (Bit man)
Nicco Romoff, Henry Kulky (Peasants)
Peter Seal (Bit man)
John Peters (Officer)
Jay Silverheels (Indian scout)
Constantine Romanoff (Convict)
Peter Gurs (Trumpeter)
Marvin Press (Young man)
Abe Dinovitch (Rough man)
Nicholas Kobliansky (Deacon)
Glenn Strange (Tall man)

Nelson Eddy and Ilona Massey with Allan Dwan. Ilona is jokingly presenting the director with the Cross of St. George which figures so prominently in the plot. *Courtesy Anna Michalik.*

Northwest Outpost

On location at Fort Ross. Nelson is on horseback at left. *Courtesy Anna Michalik.*

Northwest Outpost was at one point entitled *End of the Rainbow*, and that would have been a fitting title indeed, for it was destined to be Nelson Eddy's final film. In the three years since *Knickerbocker Holiday*, he had been approached on numerous occasions with proposals for a new film. "It was always the same," he said. "They had the producer, the director, and a list of talent available for the cast. A name composer would agree to furnish the score, but always one thing was missing. The story. Without that, it was all worthless."

This film *did* have the germ of a good story. The hero was in love with a married woman. This intriguing premise was then padded with plot devices from four or five past Eddy vehicles, including a title suggestive of the Northwest Mounties, and furnished with the least memorable Friml score since *The Lottery Bride*.

Friml was always an erratic composer. Melodies poured out of him, but it took a strong collaborator to select and shape the great ones. Eddy recalled that Republic Studio (one rung above Monogram on the studio status ladder) was delighted to get a "name" like Friml, but couldn't seem to get any finished songs out of him. They finally sent a recording crew to the home of the sixty-eight-year-old composer and made tapes of his endless improvisations at the

Captain Jim Laurence (Nelson) is welcomed back to the Russian settlement, Fort Ross, after a tour of the countryside. *Courtesy Anna Michalik.*

keyboard. When they finished, they had tapes of—endless improvisations at the keyboard. Of the songs constructed from these bits, the only one that stayed with the viewer past the popcorn stand was the oft-repeated "W-e-a-r-y." It was not exactly the tone to set for the picture.

In *Northwest Outpost*, Eddy is reteamed with his *Balalaika* costar, Ilona Massey. Her career never really developed after her brilliant reception in *Balalaika*, and so she is the surprise of the film, giving a fine performance, warm and womanly. Her fruity soprano had developed an unfortunate edge, but she succeeds in lighting up the dimmer moments of the film.

Hugo Haas as the Prince gives a droll performance, but Elsa Lanchester, as usual, is pretty much left to her own devices and pieces her performance out of past comic endeavors. Only in her compassionate scenes is she able to endow her role with her unique blend of humor and pathos.

Director Allan Dwan was a Hollywood veteran. He started with Gloria Swanson vehicles in the late teens, went on to Douglas Fairbanks epics in the 1920s, Shirley Temple films in the 1930s, and Dennis O'Keefe comedies in the 1940s. He worked chiefly at Republic after that, turning out action and comedy films, always competent and with occasional bright touches. His *The Sands of Iwo Jima* in 1949 brought John Wayne an Oscar nomination, certainly a testament to Dwan's directorial skills. Dwan obviously regarded *Northwest Outpost* as nothing more than a few weeks' work, but there are still some nice moments.

Our story begins in 1838 at Fort Ross, a Russian settlement on the coast of what would later become California. The Governor, Prince Nikolai Balinin (Hugo Haas), is awakened by his aide Kyril (Erno Verebes) at daybreak. Since the Princer apparently fell asleep fully dressed, we presume he has been out quite late and is unhappy at being aroused. His displeasure dissipates when he learns that a ship is in the harbor, a Russian ship with a lady on board, a real lady.

The ship needs official permission to put its passengers ashore. Kyril can assure the governor that the lady is neither old nor plain, but he can furnish no information on whether or not she has knobby knees. The governor's wife, Princess Tatiana (Elsa Lanchester), is suitably surprised to see him up at this hour, but assumes it is because he is interested in meeting the ship—especially since *she* is traveling with only a maid. Not a husband in sight.

How can his wife think him so foolish? the Prince sputters. It is not his foolishness she objects to, she coos, but his remorse afterward. It seems the Prince's peccadilloes in the past have caused him to be assigned to this wilderness outpost instead of Paris.

On board the ship, the beautiful Natalia Alanova (Ilona Massey), daughter of General Alanov, is greeted by an enthusiastic governor and his overly cordial wife. Princess Tatiana invites Natalia to stay with them and inquires why a beautiful woman would prefer the wilderness. "A matter of health, your highness," Natalia replies coolly.

In her quarters at the governor's house, Natalia prepares to dress for dinner. Her maid, Olga (Tamara Shayne), suggests one of her most devastating gowns. "It will arouse the men to thoughts of valor." "And the ladies to thoughts of murder," Natalia decides and chooses a plainer gown. Outside the window, a perfectly trained male chorus is heard singing in four-part harmony. It is the convicts, trudging past in their shackles. Natalia searches their faces for the one she has come to find. He is not there, though he had sailed before she did. Perhaps, Olga suggests, the convict ship is slower and has not arrived yet. In the meantime, the Prince may be persuaded to help. Already there is a gleam in his eye.

To keep it there, Natalia changes to the devastating gown and dazzles the after-dinner gathering with "Tell Me with Your Eyes," getting the Prince to join her. The men of the outpost gather around the piano as the ladies gather around the Princess to discuss the intruder. Perhaps her "reasons of health" had something to do with a court scandal. Perhaps the Czarina asked her to leave.

In any event, the Prince is soon escorting Natalia to the garden. "It was your *fifth* tea, before you meandered among the camellias," the Princess chides one of her husband's former lady friends who has been casting aspersions on Natalia.

In the moonlit garden, Natalia thanks the governor for taking her in, especially since they know so little about her. Oh, the Prince assures her, he doesn't like to know too much about anybody. Besides, his very efficient Captain Laurence will find out all that is necessary. Captain Laurence is an American who led the first wagon train west to Monterey and is now in the employ of the fort. Of course, his real employer is probably the American government, which has territorial eyes on the west when Russia leaves. In the meantime, the local Mexicans love and trust the Captain, which is fortunate since they don't trust the Russians. (Written during the period of disillusionment with our wartime comrades and just before the McCarthy hearings.) Captain Laurence does all the work, leaving the Prince time for play.

However, the Prince warns when he sees the expectant gleam in Natalia's eye, the Captain could decorate the walls of his quarters with frustrated female hearts. "A man who collects hearts usually hasn't got a heart of his own," Natalia comments. Not at all, the Prince assures her. Laurence *has* got a heart—for his horse.

This is the cue for the entrance of Captain Jim Laurence (Nelson), leading his men on horseback while singing "One More Mile to Go." There are some effective if arty shots of the crowd surging toward the fort gate to welcome their hero. Captain Jim is handsomely weather-beaten in fringed leather jacket (*Naughty Marietta*) and black cowboy hat (*The*

The jovial Governor of the fort, Prince Nikolai Balinin (Hugo Haas), has a roving eye and must constantly placate his jealous wife, Tatiana (Elsa Lanchester). *Courtesy Anna Michalik.*

A mysterious Russian beauty, Natalia Alanova, arrives by ship. While Princess Tatiana admires Jim's new Cross of St. George decoration, "the only one in North America," her husband admires the pretty newcomer. (Left to right, Nelson, Elsa Lanchester, Hugo Haas, Ilona Massey.)

Girl of the Golden West). He is greeted by an ineptly blown bugle call and the ceremonious presentation of a variety of scrolls and trophies. One of them is a handsome court sword from the Czar himself. The Prince leans toward the light, trying to read the exact title on the sword. "Damocles?" suggests Jim. "That will do," smiles the relieved Prince.

The formalities over, the Prince affectionately welcomes his old friend and catches him up on the new arrival. He can't praise Natalia enough. Her voice is like a silver bell, her eyes are like twin sapphires, her hair is like spun gold. "She is a woman you'd take to paradise!" "From your description, I'd rather take her to a pawn shop," Jim replies.

Natalia's laughter interrupts them. The Princess tactfully calls her husband away, and Jim and Natalia are left to make conversation. Champagne is sent in. Jim inspects Natalia's papers and then toasts the official who signed Mademoiselle's passport—so unfortunate that this official had died six months before the date on the papers. He returns her papers without further comment and they drink.

One of Jim's first duties at the fort is to check up on the convicts. He comes upon the overseer, Volkoff (Peter Whitney), whipping an elderly prisoner who cannot lift a heavy stone. Snatching the whip from him, Jim orders Volkoff to lift the stone himself. Natalia rides up just in time to witness the scene. Volkoff strains at the rock while Jim lashes him as Volkoff had lashed the old man. "Don't order a man to do something you can't do yourself," Jim tells him and hurls the forbidden whip into the bushes.

The movement startles Natalia's horse. The beast rears and darts away over the stony terrain with the lady clinging frantically to its neck. Jim gallops after her and manages to stop her horse just at the edge of a cliff. He apologizes and seats her on a rock so that she can admire the view—"if you can forget you nearly became part of it." Natalia thanks him.

She is now doubly in his debt, first for the passport business and now this. They discuss her reasons for forging a passport—her father, General Alanov, has enemies—and Jim's reasons for working for the Russians—when American settlers come west, he wants to be sure the Russians have left things in "good order." He is referring to the prisoners. "Don't they ever escape?" she asks. Not often, he tells her. If they do, they usually succumb to the Indians, the wild animals, or the sea. If they evade all these, he brings them back "tamer and more philosophical." Natalia shudders as the prisoner's song is heard. She tells Jim that the Prince has referred to California as a ripe plum. Jim must not want any worms in it when America picks it. "When a plum is ripe, you don't have to pick it," Jim tells her, helping her onto her horse. She slides back into his arms for a long kiss. "I deserved that," she murmurs. "You got it," he replies.

After dinner that night, Natalia is still pensive. Jim invites her to see something from the stockade. Princess Tatiana takes advantage of their absence to speculate on Natalia's past and future. What will happen if Jim falls in love with Natalia but she departs? Even more tragic, the Prince comments, what if Jim gets tired of her and she stays?

Jim rescues Natalia when her horse bolts. *Courtesy Anna Michalik.*

Jim helps Natalia up the ladder to the stockade lookout tower and points to the prisoner ship that has just arrived in the harbor. On it are six peasants and, oh, yes, a Captain Igor Savin of the Imperial Guards. In a duel of words, Jim implies that she might have some romantic interest in the Captain, but she assures him she has sentimental ties to no man. Besides, she thought he was immune to women. Not immune, he replies, just cautious. Caution may make him a lonely man, she warns, and sings him the film's love song, "Raindrops on a Drum," a pleasant tune with an impossible lyric.

Jim is certain, despite Natalia's carefully worded denial, that she has come to Fort Ross to find Captain Savin. He seeks out the only one who can understand both his official and personal problems—the Princess. She is in the garden, embroidering on a lace cloth stretched on a vertical frame. Much of the scene is filmed through the lace, giving a nice if slightly pretentious sense of intimacy to the scene. The

Natalia's husband, the convict, Igor Savin (Joseph Schildkraut, right), bribes a guard (Peter Whitney) with his Cross of St. George to help him escape. *Courtesy Anna Michalik.*

Princess's advice is to ignore the rules and make it possible for Natalia to speak to Captain Savin. That is the only way Jim will ever know for sure.

Alarm bells interrupt their conversation. Indians have attacked in the north, and Jim must ride immediately. He summons Natalia and tells her there is a visitor for her in his office. If, after speaking with him, she still has no sentimental ties to Igor Savin, she is to take the next ship for Russia. "This is goodbye, Natalia Alanova. God bless you." He rides off.

Natalia enters the dim office to face Captain Igor Savin—her husband. Igor (Joseph Schildkraut) is pleased to see that she has kept her word and followed him. Now, if she will help him escape, he will not betray her father, the only undiscovered conspirator in their aborted coup. To save her father, Natalia has bought Igor's silence by marrying him. To save her "husband" Igor suggests that she offer herself to Captain Laurence. With a bitter smile, Natalia informs him that Jim has gone to fight the Indians. Igor answers that he can wait.

The warm-hearted Princess finds Natalia crying and extracts the whole story from her. The Princess suggests that the easiest way to be rid of Igor would be to help him escape. Under the circumstances, it would be quite correct to trick Jim. When a man breaks the law for a woman, the Princess says, he generally feels very noble about it. The Princess is sure Jim will take care of the uprising and be home in time for Easter.

Igor is making plans of his own. The detestable guard Volkoff also wants to leave the fort and proposes that he and Igor go together. Volkoff takes the only valuable Igor has left, the jeweled Cross of St. George, to sell for food and horses. "Sic Transit Gloria Mundi," comments Igor philosophically as he hands over his precious cross—and then obligingly translates for the peasants in the audience.

The fort gloomily prepares for an Easter without its men. Providentially, music is heard in the distance, and the men come riding home to great celebration. Now it will really be a happy Easter. Natalia runs out to greet Jim, but he deliberately ignores her. The Princess pats Natalia consolingly. She will be able to see him that night at the Easter service.

In a tiny chapel, the rich and poor of the fort stand holding the traditional candles of Russian Easter and sing the ancient music. Somewhat surprisingly, the American Jim sings the solo portions. Even the prisoners are present in their shackles. Igor takes this opportunity to pass a note to Natalia reminding her of the fate that awaits her father if she fails him. The bells ring to the announcement "Christ is risen," and the congregation kiss each other in the traditional joyous celebration. Natalia turns expectantly to Jim, but again he avoids her.

Natalia's maid, Olga, suggests that she send Jim a note asking to meet him at the Easter feast. Natalia sits, pen in hand, and imagines first the voice of Igor threatening her father and then that of the Princess suggesting that she trick Jim to be rid of Igor. She hesitates, then writes.

Northwest Outpost

Russian Easter at this remote outpost of Russia. The whole village is present, including the convicts. Igor manages to slip a note to Natalia, reminding her that her father will die if she betrays him. *Courtesy Anna Michalik.*

Jim's duties are going to keep him from the feast, that is, until he gets Natalia's provocative note. In her room, Natalia selects her most seductive gown and takes a shot of brandy. Tonight, she must be foolishly wise.

At the ball, she swirls through the dancing couples by herself, singing "Love Is the Time." Jim follows her and she turns to find herself in his embrace. They waltz.

The Prince is romancing his new amour, Katushka (the great stage actress Lenore Ulric), behind a bush in the garden when the Princess and two gentlemen appear on the terrace. One of the men is Katushka's husband, Baron Kruposny (George Sorel). Urged on by the Princess, he has bet a fellow guest that he can shoot down two Easter eggs in a row. The Princess tosses them into the air, directly over the heads of the cowering couple. Bang. Bang. Perfect! Covered with eggshells, the Prince gets the message. He follows the Princess and begs her to help him retrieve some love letters. *This* husband can read…

It is a night for rendez-vous. Jim and Natalia meet on top of the stockade overlooking the ocean, where the full moon seems never to set. They make up, and Jim gives her an Easter present, his Cross of St. George, awarded him by the Czar. As far as he knows, it is the only one in California. He takes up the song from the feast, "Nearer and Dearer," and she joins him.

Natalia cannot bring herself to deceive him, so instead she slips into the jail and gives Igor her jewels to aid his escape. She even strips the

Tanya and Jim learn that Igor plans to escape on the same Chinese junk that is transporting the banished Natalia. (Henry Brandon, right.) *Courtesy Anna Michalik.*

Jim swings on a rope and crashes through the window. *Courtesy Anna Michalik.*

rings from her fingers. For a moment she considers Jim's cross on a ribbon around her neck, but decides she cannot bear to part with that. When she has gone, Igor passes the jewels to Volkoff, who adds Igor's Cross of St. George to the collection.

The next morning, the Prince finds that his beloved Princess has been able to recover the love letters he foolishly wrote the lady with the marksman husband. How did she do it? he inquires delightedly.

Simple, she replies. She has circulated a rumor that the full moon brings out the Prince's homicidal as well as amorous nature. The Prince is horrified. What if the rumor gets back to St. Petersburg? "Then half of Her Majesty's ladies-in-waiting will boast that they have looked death in the face—time and time again."

All during the day, Natalia and Olga await word that Igor has escaped. Everything is ominously quiet. At last Natalia decides to go to Jim's office. She must know. She will tell him the truth and then return to Russia. "There is only one truth, Madame," says Olga. "You love him."
Natalia arrives at headquarters just as word reaches Jim that Igor has escaped. Jim leaps on his adjutant's horse and orders two men to follow him, fanning out to prevent the escapees's doubling back. Igor and Volkoff have a good start, but Volkoff's horse falls, and he is forced to double-mount with Igor.

Soon their horse tires, and Volkoff sends Igor ahead while he waits to ambush Jim. A shot and Jim falls. Leaving him for dead, Volkoff takes Jim's horse and sets off after Igor. Meanwhile, one of Jim's soldiers finds some of the jewels that fell from Volkoff's pocket when his horse threw him.

Republic's familiarity with the western genre is all too evident here, for the chase sequence continues for quite a while, with the orchestra rising in ominous harmonics more suited to a Saturday afternoon serial.

Jim regains consciousness and returns to the fort. He confronts Natalia with the recovered

Northwest Outpost

jewels. She has betrayed her country and, worst of all, she has betrayed him. Among the jewels is a Cross of St. George. He ignores her protests. She must leave immediately for Russia. A Chinese junk is waiting to take her.

Igor, of course, has arranged his escape with the sinister Captain of the junk (Henry Brandon, the Fu Manchu of serials, who looks only slightly Chinese). When Natalia boards the ship, she finds Igor waiting happy to renew her acquaintance on the long sea voyage ahead. The weeping Olga takes her leave from Kyril, the Prince's valet, on the dock. Their romantic interlude comes to an end when Kyril spots Igor through a porthole and rushes off to tell Jim.

He learns that Jim Laurence has resigned, so he must convey this news to the Prince. The startled Princess finds the Prince loading his pistol to go after Igor. If he is successful, he says, he will be able to unite a married woman with someone other than himself. The delighted Princess sends a messenger to find Captain Laurence.

On the Chinese junk, the Prince is soon overpowered by Igor. The Princess and Jim gallop up, and Jim performs a daring leap (obviously performed by a stunt man), swinging from the deck of the ship, out over the water, and back in the window of the cabin, where Igor is about to blow out the brains of the Prince. The Saturday matinee "shoot-out" syndrome again takes over midst crashing, crushing orchestration.

Of course, Captain Laurence manages to save Natalia and the Prince. Igor is conveniently shot dead in the scuffle, and Jim can now escort the beautiful widow back to the fort. The Prince and Princess too are happily reunited. They follow the mounted Jim and Natalia in a carriage, surrounded by singing chorus. Natalia shows Jim his Cross of St. George still on the ribbon around her neck. "The Czar is entirely too free with those things," Jim comments, and they sing a chorus of "Love Is the Time," trotting along toward the camera in a *Naughty Marietta* finish.

In the shoot-out that follows, Igor meets his fate, and the craven Volkoff tries to use Natalia as a shield. (Left to right: Peter Whitney, Ilona Massey, Tamara Shayne, Nelson.) *Courtesy Anna Michalik.*

The inconvenient husband properly disposed of, the lovers are united in an equestrian musical finale. *Courtesy Anna Michalik.*

Northwest Outpost is a pleasant film, but a distinctly minor note on which to end Eddy's film career. As a "swan song" it was something of a personal triumph, for he looked good and sang better. But, like Garbo, he knew when to quit. He was forty-six. Europe and England have always had a definite veneration and place for their older performers, but America is consumer-oriented. Old products and old stars alike are generally cast aside in favor of the newer models. Each generation seeks its own unique self-image by discarding the favorites of its elders.

Thus, in the late 1940s, Nelson Eddy recognized that he might not make another movie. Radio, which had made such good use of his talents, was about to be replaced by television and the "Top Forty." The extensive concert circuits of fifteen years earlier had already succumbed to radio and the phonograph, which made music a part of everyday life. Nelson Eddy had to make a basic decision. Was he going to continue as a performer, and if so, what was he going to do?

Reviews

"Apart from a strangely disturbing feeling that *Northwest Outpost* belonged to a distant, languid and more ingenuous past, this romantic musical seemed designed to neither stimulate nor greatly depress an interested viewer," wrote A.H. Weiler in the *New York Times*. "It has been a proverbial month of Sundays since Mr. Eddy has raised his resonant baritone for the sound cameras."

And director Peter Bogdanovich describes an interview with *Northwest Outpost* director Allan Dwan in his book *Allan Dwan, The Last Pioneer*, published by Praeger, 1971:

PB: I felt you were definitely making fun of the material in the film, and of the stars, particularly Nelson Eddy.
AD: Yes, of course. Nelson Eddy was the ham of hams—a nice guy, but he wanted to play a cowboy above all things. So he got as near to a cowboy as he could in this. But the whole subject matter was peculiar—Russian atmosphere up in California—which did exist—but we had an Englishwoman playing a Russian Princess and a German playing a Russian—all kinds of dialects playing Russians. And a lot of White Russians. The best thing in the picture was the Easter episode in the church which was authentic because I just turned the Russians loose and said, "I want a real Russian Easter" and they put it on. Even provided all the food and conducted the church services the way they should be. We got a hold of a good Orthodox priest of theirs who was hiding somewhere behind his beard. We had fun with that. But Nelson Eddy riding down the street into town with a lot of Cossacks singing "hullabaloo"—that's for the birds.
PB: So you made fun of it?
AD: Why not? Why suffer?

Recordings (See Discography for further information)

Eddy recorded a 78 RPM album, "Northwest Outpost," which contained six songs:
    "Love Is the Time"
    "Nearer and Dearer"
    "One More Mile to Go"
    "Raindrops on a Drum"
    "Russian Easter Hymn"
    "Tell Me with Your Eyes"

Music in the Film

All music is by Rudolf Friml, all lyrics by Edward Heyman. In listing performers after each title, "and" denotes a genuine duet, while commas between names indicate a sequence of singers.

Overture: "Raindrops on a Drum" (The American G.I. Chorus)
"Weary" (The American G.I. Chorus)

"Tell Me with Your Eyes" (Ilona Massey, reprised by Hugo Haas)
"One More Mile to Go" (Eddy with The American G.I. Chorus)
"Weary" reprise (American G.I. Chorus)
"Raindrops on a Drum" (Massey, Eddy)
Russian Easter Hymn (Eddy and chorus) - traditional, including "Slava" (Praise) and "Paskha Nova" (New Easter)
"Love is the Time" (Massey)
"Nearer and Dearer" (chorus, Eddy, Massey)
"Weary" reprise (bass, American G.I. Chorus)
Finale: "Love is the Time" reprise (Eddy and Massey with chorus)

Three Daring Daughters
MGM.
Released March 5, 1948.
Directed by Fred Wilcox.
Produced by Joseph Pasternak.
116 minutes.
Technicolor.

Prerelease titles: *The Birds and the Bees*, *Keep Young with Music*
French title: *Cupidon Mène la Danse* (Cupid Leads the Dance)
Danish title: *Mors Ferie Flirt* (Mother's Flirtatious Vacation)
Portuguese title: Três filhas queridas (Three Darling Daughters)

Screenplay: Albert Mannheimer, Frederick Kohner, Sonya Levien, and John Meehan. Photography: Ray June. Technicolor Director: Natalie Kalmus. Associate: Henri Jaffa. Assistant Director: Dolph Zimmer. Art Directors: Cedric Gibbons, Preston Ames. Music Direction: Georgie Stoll. Recording Director: Douglas Shearer. Set Decorations: Edwin B. Willis. Associate: Arthur Krams. Costume Supervision: Irene. Associate: Shirley Barker. Makeup: Jack Dawn. Editor: Adrienne Fazan.

Based on the play *The Bees and the Flowers* by Frederick Kohner and Albert Mannheimer, which opened September 26, 1946 at the Cort Theatre for a run of 28 performances. Barbara Robbins played "Louise Morgan," and the daughters were Sybil Stocking, Rosemary Rice, and Joyce Van Patten.

With *Three Daring Daughters* in 1948, the 45-year-old Jeanette graduated to playing mother roles. Rather sexy mothers, of course. *Courtesy Anna Michalik.*

Jeanette MacDonald (Louise Rayton Morgan)
José Iturbi (José Iturbi)
Jane Powell (Tess Morgan)
Ann E. Todd (Ilka Morgan)
Mary Eleanor Donahue (Alix Morgan)
Edward Arnold (Robert Nelson)
Harry Davenport (Dr. Cannon)
Moyna Macgill (Mrs. Smith)
Larry Adler (Himself)
Kathryn Card (Jonesy, housekeeper)
Richard [Dick] Simmons (Harlow)
Amparo Iturbi (Specialty pianist)
Tom Helmore (Mike Pemberton)
Dorothy Porter (Specialty singer)
Thurston Hall (Mr. Howard)
Nan Bennett (Toney Tiger)
Charles Coleman, Ian Wolfe (Butlers)
Stephen Hero (Ribs)
Leon Belasco (Ship's orchestra leader)
Virginia Brissac (Miss Drake)
William Forrest (Ship's captain)

Frank Pershing, Bill Lewin, Thomas E. Breen (Stewards)
Joanee Wayne (Telephone operator)
Don Avalier (Headwaiter)
Diane Lee Stewart, Dorita Pallais, Nina Bara, Phyllis Graffeo, Conchita Lamus (Singers)
Jack Lipson (Fat man on street)
Anita Aros, Estellita Zarco, Connie Montoya, Aldana Rios (Telephone operators)
Wheaton Chambers (Stage manager)
Ed Peil Sr. (Waiter)
Joan Valerie (Hostess)
Brick Sullivan (Taxi driver)
Amparo Ballester (Cigarette girl)
David Cota (Cuban bellboy)

In 1947, Joe Pasternak persuaded Miss MacDonald to return to MGM for *Three Daring Daughters,* and she made the transition to "mother" roles with style and charm. Even the most illustrious career must have a "last film," and it is almost a shame that this wasn't it, for it is the perfect MGM mélange of music, comedy, pathos, and cute kids with Mozart, boogie woogie, and Jeanette singing "Sweethearts." She was again a feast for the eyes (in Technicolor) and the ears, and the songs she sang were perfect for her richer, lower voice.

Comparisons of *Three Daring Daughters* with Pasternak's first producing venture, the 1936 *Three Smart Girls* (the film that introduced Deanna Durbin), were inevitable. However, the differences are quite revealing. Miss Durbin dominated a film that required a gray-haired mother to remarry her errant and divorced spouse. Miss MacDonald, on the other hand, performed a near miracle by outshining her bubbling offspring, and she looked more at home in a slinky evening gown than a housedress. She was, of course, the sophisticated editor of a smart fashion magazine, and, although women executives were still not permitted their success without a concomitant nervous breakdown (e,g., *Lady in the Dark*), they certainly were not required to remain celibate divorcées. The heavy postwar divorce rate made that idea as outdated as rumble seats. (However, the Catholic Legion of Decency rated the film "morally objectionable in part for all" since it "tends to justify as well as reflect the acceptability of divorce.")

Director Fred Wilcox is perhaps best remembered for *Lassie Come Home*. The three daughters of the title were portrayed by Jane Powell, already a movie veteran at eighteen, Mary Eleanor Donahue, later of "Father Knows Best" on television, and Ann E. Todd (not to be confused with British actress Ann Todd). The cast also included the personable pianist José Iturbi who, somewhat disconcertingly, plays a fictional personable pianist named "José Iturbi."

A Danish cinema program uses a caricature of four of the principals. The title, *Mors Ferie Flirt*, means "Mother's Flirtatious Vacation."

Three Daring Daughters

Jeanette rehearses with her three film daughters, left to right, Mary Eleanor Donahue, Ann E. Todd, and Jane Powell. During the weeks of filming, Ann E. Todd had a growth spurt and became taller than her "older" sister Powell. *Courtesy Anna Michalik.*

(A name change would have been an excellent idea.)

Edward Arnold, who had so much fun being mean to Nelson Eddy in *Let Freedom Ring*, is permitted here to be jocularly mean to the daring and exasperating daughters, although the twinkle in his eye belies any real malice.

The film is a hodgepodge that by all logic and precedent shouldn't work at all, but it comes together beautifully, thanks to light, sure direction, fine performances, and a comedy situation with just enough roots in real human drama to keep everything going.

Our story opens in the garden of a posh girls' school. A chorus of voices is heard in the "Alma Mater," and we find the oldest of the daughters, Tess (Jane Powell), about to graduate. Tess and her sisters Ilka at the piano and little Alix in the audience are oblivious to the joyful aspects of the occasion. Their attention is riveted on the empty chair next to Alix. Finally Tess and Ilka (Ann E. Todd) slip from the platform for a conference with Alix (Mary Eleanor Donahue). Something must have happened to mother. Alix is dispatched with a nickel to phone her office.

Miles away in the offices of Modern Design Publications, editor Louise Morgan (Jeanette) is out cold. As her manager, Mr. Howard (Thurston Hall), and Dr. Cannon (Harry Davenport) hover over her, she comes to and

Three worried daughters. Tess (Jane Powell, center) is about to sing at her graduation, but their mother hasn't arrived. Alix (Mary Eleanor Donahue, left) and Ilka (Ann E. Todd, right) are sure something bad has happened to her. *Courtesy Anna Michalik.*

to support him. Louise will get no rest if they go along.

The girls pile into Louise's room and snuggle around her on the bed. They explain that her disobeying doctor's orders is as naughty as their disobeying her. Their indomitable servant, Jonesy (Kathryn Card), can run the house, and Mr. Howard can edit the magazine himself. Louise laughingly consents, and then asks Ilka to repeat the piano solo that she had missed that afternoon. Ilka begins Mozart's "Turkish Sonata," which slides into the jaunty "Dickey Bird Song" with everyone joining in.

The girls see their mother off on the boat. Louise promises to have a perfect time. Of course, to be really perfect, Alix adds, Daddy should be going with her. Louise stutters an agreement. But, she explains, divorced people don't take trips together, and besides, they've all been perfectly happy, haven't they? The false jolliness in her voice indicates a sore spot has been touched.

Dr. Cannon lingers to warn Louise. She's made a big mistake not telling the girls the truth about their father. How could she? she asks. Tell them that he left her without a penny and doesn't care enough about them to send them a

apologizes. It must have been the excitement, and, besides, she forgot to eat breakfast. Alix's call has her on her feet and out the door over her doctor's protest. She reaches the school just in time to hear a lovely solo, "Fleurette," sung by Tess.

Back home in a stunning and enormous duplex overlooking Central Park, the girls await the doctor's verdict. As he examines their mother upstairs, they arrive at their own diagnosis. Mother is pining away for their father, whom she divorced years ago—only because his foreign correspondent job kept him away all the time.

Dr. Cannon's prescription is somewhat different. He recommends a boat trip alone for complete relaxation and gets the girls to agree

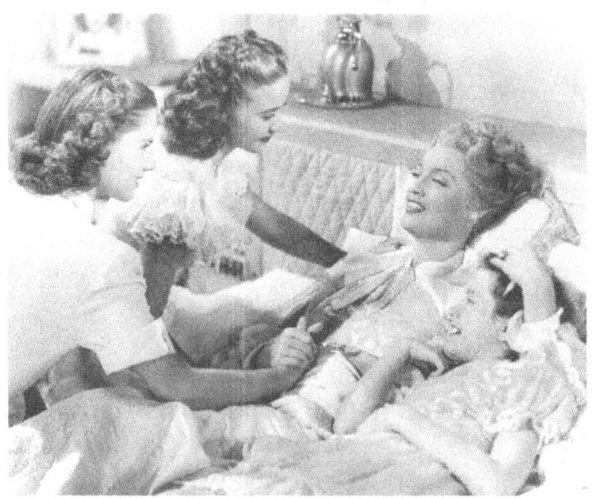

The doctor has one diagnosis for what ails Louise (Jeanette), but the daughters have another.

Three Daring Daughters

Ilka, Tess, and Alix are sure their mother is sick because she is pining for her ex-husband, their highly idealized newspaper correspondent father. As they see Louise off on a nice, relaxing cruise, they are already plotting how to reunite their parents. Left to right, Ann E. Todd, Jane Powell, Mary Eleanor Donahue, Jeanette.

postcard? It would break their hearts. Nevertheless, Dr. Cannon thinks her fairy stories about him may lead to trouble. The most important thing now, though, is the cruise. Louise is to get plenty of rest, and, if an eligible man should turn up, she shouldn't turn him down. Romance is the doctor's prescription.

The girls have romantic ideas of their own. They march on the home of their father's boss, Mr. Nelson, the thirteenth richest man in the world. "Gee, we start with an unlucky number," Alix notes. Mr. Nelson (Edward Arnold) is dining when three young ladies are announced. He sends his secretary, Mr. Harlow (Dick Simmons, television's Sergeant Preston of the Yukon), to get rid of them. While Tess and Ilka "explain" their problem volubly in each of Mr. Harlow's ears, Alix slips past him into the dining room.

Mr. Nelson asks his butler for the sugar and finds it handed to him by little Alix. She pours out a garbled version of their family history, ending in a request that her daddy come home. Mr. Nelson is distracted from this tale by a voice

A fellow passenger, pianist José Iturbi, finds Louise captivating—and a good singer and dancer. *Courtesy Patrick Kuster.*

in the next room. Tess is keeping Mr. Harlow busy by singing "Passepied."

Harlow is able to throw more light on the situation. Their father, Charlie Morgan, is a foreign correspondent for one of Mr. Nelson's newspapers. His constant absence has caused a divorce. "Only temporarily," Tess hastens to assure them. The girls would be so grateful if Mr. Nelson would make them a happy family again. Abandoning his meal, Mr. Nelson sets the wheels in motion to bring Charlie Morgan back. He is a sucker for kids, he confides to the astonished Harlow.

Far away on the high seas, Louise is happily unaware of this development. Her garrulous dinner companion, Mrs. Smith (Moyna Macgill, mother of Angela Lansbury), boasts that now she has successfully tracked down every important person on the boat, including Louise. All, that is, except José Iturbi. She nods toward the musician, who is just taking a seat at a nearby table.

Mrs. Smith decides to send him a note reminding him that they once met in Newport and asking him to play. Louise tries to deter her. A man of his stature shouldn't be asked to play in restaurants. Mrs. Smith is determined and gushingly inscribes a menu, which is dispatched with a reluctant waiter.

Iturbi is predictably unenthusiastic. He asks the waiter to point out the lady in question. The waiter tells him that he can see her in the mirror by his table. The waiter is slightly to one side of Iturbi, and when the pianist glances in the mirror, it is Louise Morgan he sees. Iturbi decides to play for the lady, to the dismay of his manager, Mike Pemberton (Tom Helmore). He launches into "Liebestraum," casting long

Three Daring Daughters

glances at Louise while Mrs. Smith squirms happily.

When Iturbi comes to their table to renew acquaintance, he is disillusioned and introduced to the real Mrs. Smith. Retreating in horror, he lapses into voluble Spanish. The astonished Mrs. Smith accepts his "apology."

Iturbi is not finished with Louise. He tracks her down on the deck and determines in a few moments that she would not mind his sitting next to her or smoking his pipe and that she is divorced—but "not unattached." Mrs. Smith hadn't told him anything about that, he says. He just happened to run across Mrs. Smith. Louise tells him that no celebrity ever "ran across" Mrs. Smith. The lady herself is spotted bearing down on them, and they flee together.

They find a quiet spot and discuss his music and his constant sense of not reaching perfection. She tries to assure him. She has been to his concerts, and the crowds love him. Crowds can be very lonely, he tells her. It takes only one person—they are interrupted by a steward with a cablegram for Louise. She takes advantage of this distraction to escape. Iturbi catches her. Won't she dine with him the next night? Perhaps.

In her cabin, she opens the cablegram. It is from the girls, sending their love. They in turn receive a cable several days later telling them what an interesting voyage Louise is having. "Trips are always interesting," Alix assures her sisters.

The phone rings. Mr. Nelson's secretary is calling to inform them that their father is on his way home. Tess is just conveying this news to Ilka and Alix when their housekeeper, Jonesy, comes out on the terrace with their breakfast. Instantly Tess lapses into double talk. Jonesy is unimpressed. She wouldn't dream of eavesdropping, and, besides, she's going to cardarp fenabish their paracarkus.

On shipboard, the romance is progressing. Louise joins Iturbi in "Where There's Love," the waltz from *Der Rosenkavalier*, at an evening concert. Perhaps things are progressing too fast. When the ship docks in Havana, where Iturbi is giving a concert, Louise decides to go on with the cruise. Iturbi comes to her cabin and begs her to stay with him in Havana. The concert is really just for her. He won't take no for an answer.

The highlight of the concert is the "Ritual Fire Dance," which Iturbi performs in an outdoor arena with his real life sister, Amparo, on twin grand pianos. The stirring music and the starlight combine to make quite a romantic evening.

Later, in the Café Allegra, Louise manages a chat with Iturbi's manager, Mike Pemberton, while Iturbi dances with the ubiquitous Mrs. Smith. Mike tells her that, as Iturbi's business manager, he's traveled with him day in and day out and never tired of his company. "He wears well, does he?" Louise asks. Mike has never seen Iturbi play so well as he did tonight. Louise is certainly serious business to him.

Louise is not sure she wants to be serious business. Pleading a headache, she flees to her hotel room. Iturbi is concerned and sends roses, for which she politely thanks him on the phone. The romance seems stopped before it has really started, but fortunately Iturbi has the room just across the air well. From her darkened room,

Romance blossoms. (José Iturbi, left.)

The girls burst in on their father's boss, Mr. Nelson, and beg him to bring their father back from his foreign assignment. It is only the long separations that have caused the divorce. (Left to right: Ann E. Todd, Jane Powell, Edward Arnold.)

Louise can see him, but he can't see her. He begins playing "You Made Me Love You," and Louise slowly circles the room in the dark watching him. She first hums, then croons the song softly, stretching sensuously on the couch. Yes, Louise is ready for romance.

The phone rings. It is not Iturbi, but her daughters wishing her happy birthday. The conversation is not entirely honest on either side, for the girls don't tell her about Charles Morgan and she doesn't tell them about José Iturbi. They each are going to have their little surprise.

As Louise and Iturbi dine the next evening, a cake magically appears, borne by lovely Spanish señoritas who sing happy birthday in Spanish. Sometimes Mrs. Smith conveys useful information, Iturbi comments. He wants to marry Louise. She says no. She has three daughters who still love their absentee father. They would never forgive her. Iturbi is undaunted. He loves children and they always love him. Everything will work out fine.

And so Mr. and Mrs. Iturbi return to New York City, to an apartment building on a Hollywood side street that has no resemblance to any known New York thoroughfare. Louise will tell the children of their marriage, and then Iturbi will arrive an hour later with presents for a family get-together. Her announcement goes undelivered, for the girls surprise her first. Daddy is coming home. Mr. Nelson has arranged it all. Horrified, Louise rushes off to try to undo the damage.

Mr. Nelson is in the middle of breakfast, when a lady by the name of Morgan is announced. "The little one?" he inquires. "I should say it is the *big* one," the butler murmurs. "Oh, Tess—I'd better stop her before she starts singing." He goes to greet the daughter and finds the mother, who faints when he confirms the news.

Mr. Nelson is understandably disconcerted. Louise explains that she has remarried. Here she is with a new husband whom she adores, and an old one she doesn't want is about to walk in. Mr. Nelson agrees to ship Charlie Morgan back to China.

Iturbi arrives at the Morgan apartment, his arms full of presents, for a grand meeting with his new family. The girls think he has come to rent the apartment. When they discover he is the famous pianist, they decide he has come to audition Tess.

Obviously, Louise has not told them about their marriage and so he gingerly feels his way through the audition, wondering what has happened. Louise arrives home and, in turn, is unsure what has been said in her absence. She and Iturbi manage to exchange stories and decide he will go to a hotel until things are straightened out.

Of course, the family is invited to his concert that night. The children begin to suspect something is fishy, and, when Louise sits starry-eyed all through the "Roumanian Rhapsody" (with harmonica solo by Larry Adler), they are sure.

Back home, Ilka comes to her mother's room after everyone is asleep. She wants to know the truth about Daddy. Ilka is sure that if she ever

Louise returns from her cruise with a surprise for her daughters—a new husband. They also have a surprise for her—an old husband. Left to right: Mary Eleanor Donahue, Ann E. Todd, Jane Powell, Jeanette, José Iturbi. *Courtesy Anna Michalik.*

loved anyone, it would be forever. When that happens, Louise tells Ilke, she will be very happy—or very unhappy. Ilka returns to her room, and her sobs awaken the other girls. They decide to show Iturbi that if he tries to disrupt their little family, they'll make his life miserable.

Louise arrives in the middle of a rehearsal, and Iturbi introduces her to the orchestra as his "soloist." He begs her to sing for them. "But what shall I sing?" she asks. The piano begins and a violin picks up the melody: "Sweethearts." It is a moment dripping with nostalgia and completely effective. Ten years fall away, and we are back with "Gwen Marlowe" in *Sweethearts*, swaying to the lilting strains of the romantic waltz.

Louise feels that they should tell the children right away, but now it is Iturbi who hesitates. He would like one more visit so that they can get to know him. Louise is out shopping and the children are upstairs when he arrives. He "announces" himself by sitting down at the piano. The girls hear the music, square their shoulders, and go downstairs to demolish the interloper. They hate classical music, they tell him. Well, he concedes, they are honest. What do they like?

Tess and Ilka launch into a delightful swing version of "Route 66." They conclude and face Iturbi triumphantly. He likes it very much, he confesses, but their version is not quite in the groove. He reprises the song, boogie-woogie style. The girls are reluctantly impressed but

The way to a singer's heart? Try praising her voice. Iturbi pretends he has come to "audition" Tess. Unable to acknowledge that he is their new father, he proves to them that he is in the groove. Left to right: Powell, Donahue, Todd, Iturbi.

stick to their guns. They admit their purpose has been to make him as unwelcome as possible.

"Mummy belongs to us," Alix blurts out. Iturbi sadly agrees. It is clear that he is leaving not only the apartment but their lives. He pauses at the door and turns to them. "I wish I was so sure about *anything* as you are about *everything*."

Tess and Ilka dispatch Alix to follow him. She is to phone them if he goes near mother. And so a monumentally conspicuous little Alix, complete with dark glasses and a bobbing feather on her hat, "tails" Iturbi. She slouches along behind a fat man (Jack "Tiny" Lipson), trying not to be seen, as Iturbi pauses to light his pipe and contemplate his "shadow."

The fat man turns into a liquor store, and Alix finds herself facing Iturbi. "Young lady," he announces firmly, "you and I are going to have a little talk."

Lunch is just being served when the butler announces that José Iturbi is waiting to see Mr. Nelson. Iturbi demands that Mr. Nelson snatch Charlie Morgan from the China-bound tramp steamer he is currently inhabiting and return him by the first plane to face his children. Otherwise, they will go on thinking he is Hercules, Apollo, and General MacArthur rolled into one. Mr. Nelson

Three Daring Daughters

agrees. He also has a suggestion. If he were Iturbi, he'd get his hat and his cane and his wife and tell the kids that he is married. Iturbi enthusiastically agrees.

Tess and Ilka catch Alix sneaking home with a large stuffed rabbit. She has been to the zoo with Iturbi. "Traitor!" they cry. Louise and Iturbi interrupt them and, as carefully as possible, explain to the girls that they are married. Tess and Ilka are horrified and storm out of the house, leaving Louise to console the sobbing Alix. As Iturbi gets his hat and heads for the door, he hears Louise murmuring to Alix that nothing in the world will ever come between them. He puts on his hat and closes the door with finality.

Dinner is just being served in the Nelson residence when Tess and Ilka are announced. This is the last straw! Mr. Nelson gives them a royal tongue lashing. They should mind their own business! Their father refused to come home until ordered to do so. Now their mother has a fine new husband. She's a young and beautiful woman and has a right to her own life. If they don't know what he's talking about, they should go find a couple of birds and bees! (The film's original title was *The Birds and the Bees*.) The girls want him to help them out? Well, he cries, pointing to the door, "Out!"

They depart thoroughly chastened and he begins chuckling. He'd give anything to have a couple of kids like that. Mr. Nelson orders that Morgan be dispatched to Tibet with a long-term contract. Oh, yes, he adds. Cable and get a complete report on his activities for the last five years.

Tess and Ilka return home to complete chaos. Iturbi is gone, Alix is desolate, and Louise is on the phone asking for another leave of absence so that she can take the girls away for a rest. After dinner, Tess tries to tell her mother how wrong they were. Louise doesn't want to discuss it any further. Instead, she plays an old favorite on the piano, and the two voices mingle exquisitely in a vocal version of Grieg's "Springtide" ("An den Frühling"). Louise is resigned to devoting her life to her children.

The three young plotters again swing into action. When their mother works late at the office, they slip out. Iturbi is conducting a vigorous interpretation of the fourth movement of Tchaikovsky's "Fourth Symphony" when three familiar faces appear in the box just right of the stage. Angrily, he speeds up, and the orchestra races at breakneck speed to the finish. He turns and the girls are gone.

Backstage, Tess is waiting for him. It was all her fault, she says. He spurns her truce offer and marches on down the hallway. Ilka steps from behind a door and begs for another chance. It is all her fault, she insists. He tells her it is not a game to be started over and over. He slams his dressing room door in her face. Alix is sitting on the couch. "Hullo," she says in a small voice. And is it all her fault? he asks. No, she assures him, it's all Tess and Ilka's fault. She liked him from the beginning.

Alix asks him to return home. They are all so unhappy. Iturbi pulls open the dressing room

A telegram brings news of her husband—but which husband? Edward Arnold, left, with Jeanette.

door, and Tess and Ilka, obviously listening at the keyhole, tumble in. He orders them to take Alix home to bed. He won't change his mind. The girls regroup on the sidewalk. What can they do now?

Louise is going over some work with Mr. Howard at the office when a phone call summons her to Mr. Nelson's house. Her ex-husband has arrived. Mr. Nelson greets her at the door. Before she goes in, she should read a cablegram he has just received. It reports that Charlie Morgan married his secretary three years earlier. She looks in amazement from the cablegram to Mr. Nelson as a familiar song comes from the next room.

"All I said," Mr. Nelson chuckles, "is that your ex-husband is here." The girls and Iturbi are gathered around the piano, happily waiting for her. As Mr. Nelson returns to his late-night snack with great gusto, the family sings a final joyous chorus of "The Dickey Bird Song."

Reviews

Variety called the film "a typical Metro-Joe Pasternak songfest" and predicted rightly "that means it probably won't be appreciated by the so-called sophisticates, but will do well at the box office." They added, "Miss MacDonald's soprano comes over as bell-like and clear-toned as ever and she's lost none of her appealing beauty." The *New York Times* called the film "a silly little tale," and the *New York Herald Tribune* elaborated that it was "a thin, crawling story of mother love and second romance which leaves one bleary-eyed and exhausted from bright colors and dull girlish talk."

So much for the baddies. West of the Hudson, just about every review contained the words "charming" and "delightful," with "gay" and "heartwarming" tied for third place. *Film Daily* subheaded its review with, "Lovely to Look At, Delightful to Hear, and Almost Certain to Please." It noted that "Jeanette MacDonald parades through this in an assortment of beautiful creations, casting an aura of charm. Technicolorfully speaking, she photographs superbly and, although absent from celluloid for several years, sings as well as ever."

Recordings (See Discography for further information)

"Springtide" (Jeanette MacDonald)
"Sweethearts Waltz" (Jeanette MacDonald)
"Where There's Love" [Waltz from *Der Rosenkavalier*] (Jeanette MacDonald)

Although "The Dickey Bird Song" was on the Hit Parade before the film was released, Jeanette never recorded it. Recordings include one by Freddy Martin with vocal by Glen Hughes (RCA Victor), and one by Larry Clinton with vocal by Helen Lee and the Dipsy Doodlers (Decca).

Music in the Film

In listing performers after each title, "and" denotes a genuine duet, while commas between names indicate a sequence of singers.

Overture: "The Dickey Bird Song" (orchestral)
"Alma Mater" (Jane Powell with girls' chorus) - music by Georgie Stoll, lyrics by Billy Katz
"Fleurette" (Jane Powell) - music by Victor Herbert, lyrics by Ralph Freed
"Turkish March" by Mozart (Ann E. Todd at piano), INTO:
"The Dickey Bird Song" (Todd dubbed by Pat Hyatt, Powell, Mary Eleanor Donahue dubbed by Beverly Jean Garbo, MacDonald) - music by Sammy Fain, lyrics by Howard Dietz
"Passepied" (Powell) - music by Leo Delibes, lyrics by Princess Anna Eristoff
"Liebestraum" (José Iturbi at the piano with orchestra) - by Franz Liszt
"Where There's Love" (MacDonald singing, Iturbi playing) - based on a waltz aria from the opera *Der Rosenkavalier*, "Ohne Mich

Jeder Tag dir zu lang," music by Richard Strauss, English lyrics by Earl Brent
"Ritual Fire Dance" from "El Amor Brujo" (José and Amparo Iturbi at twin pianos with orchestra) - by Manuel deFalla
"You Made Me Love You" (MacDonald singing, Iturbi playing) - music by Jimmy Monaco, lyrics by Joe McCarthy
"Happy Birthday" evolving into "The Dickey Bird Song" reprise (Powell, Todd dubbed by Pat Hyatt, Donahue dubbed by Beverly Jean Garbo)
"Feliz Cumpleanos" ["Happy Birthday" in Spanish] (Dorothy Porter, Diane Lee Stewart, Dorita Pallais, Nina Bara, Phyllis Graffeo, Conchita Lamus)
"Je Veux Vivre dans ce Rêve" ["Juliet's Waltz"] (Powell singing, Iturbi at piano) - from the opera *Roméo et Juliette*, music by Charles Gounod, libretto by Jules Barbier and Michel Carré
"Roumanian Rhapsody No. 1" (José and Amparo Iturbi at twin pianos, Larry Adler on the harmonica, orchestra) by Georges Enesco
"Hungarian Fantasy" (Iturbi at the piano, orchestra) - music by Franz Liszt
"Sweethearts" (MacDonald, Iturbi at piano, orchestra) - music by Victor Herbert, lyrics by Bob Wright and Chet Forrest
"Allegro Appasionato" (Iturbi at piano) - by Camille Saint-Saëns
"Route 66" (Powell with Todd who sings, dubbed by Pat Hyatt, and plays piano) - by Bobby Troup
"Route 66" reprise (Iturbi at piano)
"Springtide" ("An den Frühling") (MacDonald and Powell) - music by Edvard Grieg, English lyrics by Earl Brent, additional lyrics by Nathan Haskell Dole
Tchaikovsky's "Fourth Symphony," 4th movement coda (Iturbi conducts orchestra)
"The Dickey Bird Song" reprise (Powell, Todd dubbed by Pat Hyatt, Donahue dubbed by Beverly Jean Garbo, MacDonald, with Iturbi at the piano)

Movie Goofs

When Jeanette gets roses from José Iturbi, they go from buds to full blown flowers in ten seconds. (Julie Illescas)

The Sun Comes Up

MGM.
Released February 1949.
Directed by Richard Thorpe.
Produced by Robert Sisk.
94 minutes.
Technicolor.

Prerelease titles: *Sun in the Morning, A Family for Jack*
French title: *Lassie Perd...et Gagne* (Lassie Loses ... and Wins)
Dutch/Flemish title: *Lassie verliest, Lassie wint* (Lassie Loses, Lassie Wins)

French poster for *The Sun Comes Up*. The title translates as "Lassie Loses...and Wins." *Courtesy Anna Michalik.*

Based on the Marjorie Kinnan Rawlings short story, "A Mother in Mannville," in the *Saturday Evening Post*, December 12, 1936 and her six-part serial, "Mountain Prelude," in the *Saturday Evening Post*, April 26 through May 31, 1947. Screenplay: William Ludwig and Margaret Fitts. Musical Score: André Previn. Director of Photography: Ray June. Art Directors: Cedric Gibbons and Randall Duell. Set Decorations: Edwin B. Willis, Hugh Hunt. Sound: Douglas Shearer. Gowns: Irene. Editor: Irvine Warburton.

Jeanette MacDonald (Helen Lorfield Winter)
Lloyd Nolan (Thomas Chandler)
Claude Jarman Jr. (Jerry)
Percy Kilbride (Mr. Willie B. Williegoode)
Lewis Stone (Arthur Norton)
Nicholas Joy (Victor Alvord)
Margaret Hamilton (Mrs. Golightly)
Ida Moore (Sally)
Esther Somers (Susan, the Maid)
Dwayne Hickman (Hank Winter)
Hope Landin (Mrs. Pope, orphanage matron)
Teddy Infuhr (Junebug)
Barbara Billingsley (Nurse)
Charles Trowbridge (Dr. Gage)
John A. Butler (Doorman)
Peter Roman (Love)
Mickey McGuire (Cleaver)
Cameron Grant, John Sheffield, Douglas Carter, Wilson Wood, Barry Norton (Music lovers)
Paul E. Burns (Dr. Sample)
Guy Wilkerson (Man)
Lassie (Lassie)
Timmy Hawkins, Alan Dinehart III, Michael Dill, Charles Bates Perry, Jimmy Crane, Bobby Beyers (Orphans)
Henry Sylvester, John Beck, Ed Peil Sr., Frank Pharr (Ad lib bits)
Cy Stevens, Cosmo Sardo, Stuart Holmes, George Calliga, Albert Pollet, Ed Agresti (Musicians)
Cecil Stewart (Accompanist)
Jessie Arnold (Woman)

Jeanette's last film found her competing for close-ups with another lady who had fallen into disfavor at MGM: Lassie. The success of *Lassie Come Home* in 1943 had started a string of *Lassie* films, but the studio was taking less and less interest in the vehicles of their canine star. Lassie made only one more film after *The Sun Comes Up*, a 1951 cheapie. Then her trainer, Rudd Weatherwax, bought the TV rights from MGM and made television history.

The Sun Comes Up is a pointless title for a story about a war widow who loses her only son and withdraws from the world, full of bitterness and self-pity. Eventually she recovers from her loss by mothering an orphan boy, played effectively by Claude Jarman Jr.

Jarman had made a stunning debut in *The Yearling* (MGM 1946), a Marjorie Kinnan Rawlings novel about a boy and a deer. *The Sun Comes Up* was taken from two Rawlings stories. In 1936, the *Saturday Evening Post* printed her moving first-person account of meeting the orphan, Jerry ("A Mother in Mannville"). She expanded the simple story into a six-part fictional serial, "Mountain Prelude," for the same magazine in 1947, padding her usually tart and tight narrative with all kinds of continued-next-week devices, most of which found their way into the film.

While many incidents and much dialogue are identical, there are some interesting differences. In the magazine serial, Helen Jackson is a pianist-composer who fashions a "Mountain Prelude" from one of the folk melodies that Jerry plays on his harmonica. Jerry is the hero, not the victim, of the orphanage fire, rescuing the matron and catching the infants that Helen tosses to him from a second-story window. Bill Chandler, the romantic interest, is a badly crippled war vet who adopts Jerry, hoping that Helen will marry him to complete the family.

MGM obviously hoped for the success of *The Yearling* to rub off on the venture, but the basic humanity of the tale is ignored for a Lassie-rescue finish. The genuinely touching moments between the woman and the boy are crushed beneath monumental crescendos of the "important" style of orchestration so popular at the time. (It was one of twenty-year-old André

The Sun Comes Up

Widow Helen Winter comes out of retirement for a triumphant concert, unaware that tragedy awaits. Left to right: Lewis Stone, Jeanette, Nicholas Joy, Dwayne Hickman (later TV's Dobie Gillis).

Previn's first scoring efforts.) With Jeanette singing opera, Lassie performing ridiculous feats, and Claude Jarman Jr. grown well beyond his child image but not permitted to act it, the film could not have entirely pleased any segment of the audience.

Director Richard Thorpe was a workmanlike craftsman who turned out an average of two films a year, year after year, featuring Lassie or Tarzan along with a sprinkling of comedies. His output included *Night Must Fall* (1937) and *The Crowd Roars* (1938) with Robert Taylor. He later directed *The Great Caruso* (1951) with Mario Lanza and *Ivanhoe* (1952) with Elizabeth Taylor and Robert Taylor.

Our story opens with singer Helen Winter (Jeanette) rehearsing "Tes Yeux" in her spacious country home while her son, Hank (Dwayne Hickman, later television's Dobie Gillis), romps on the lawn with Lassie. Hank calls his mother to watch a trick he has taught the dog. He runs and Lassie trips him. "Please be careful," Helen murmurs as she smiles gallantly.

Her business manager, Arthur Norton (the brilliant character actor Lewis Stone, nearing the end of his career), arrives and tells her that the concert, her first in three years, is a sellout. Still, she is nervous and concerned whether she has made the right decision. After her husband was killed, she realized how much time her music had taken that she might have spent with him. Hank is all she has now and she doesn't want to waste a minute.

Arthur tells her that she can't live in the boy, that he must have some freedom to grow up. She admits Arthur may be right, but she will quit her singing if it ever comes between them.

The concert is a great success with "Un Bel Di" from *Madame Butterfly* as the final selection. Helen and Hank are gaily leaving the concert hall on their way to a party when Lassie arrives in a chauffeured car. She spots Hank and dashes toward him across a busy thoroughfare. Amidst a blare of horns, orchestral and auto, we hear a car accelerating as they only do in Hollywood, then cries of "Lassie, get back," and Hank runs into the street to save the dog. Naturally, he is killed by a speeding truck.

Helen takes to her bed for weeks, avoiding the sight of neighborhood children and, most of all, of Lassie. When spring makes the children's shouts unbearable, she decides to go away, as far as she can from her memories. As she prepares to drive off, she instructs her maid, Susan (Esther Somers), to give Lassie away.

But Lassie has other ideas and follows the car. Susan begs Helen to take the dog. Lassie has suffered as much as Helen has, Susan tells her. What would Hank think? Lassie gives Helen a long, brown-eyed look, and Helen relents.

They drive south, on and on through pine forests and farmland and mountains, with the Santa Cruz mountains doubling for the Blue Ridge variety in the story. Finally, Helen comes to a nice-looking house with a "For Rent" sign. The property is being leased by Mr. Williegoode of the general store. The owner is Tom Chandler, a nice fella from the city who writes books. Mr. Williegoode (Percy Kilbride of "Pa Kettle" fame) is a character and extracts a good

Helen and Lassie retreat to an isolated community where she rents a house. Here, she buys supplies from the local storekeeper (Percy Kilbride of Pa Kettle fame).

bit of business from depositing her rent payment in his ancient cash register.

He then requests her "poke" to pack up some supplies she will need. She discovers that he refers to a sack and, when it is full, she can't lift it. Mr. Williegoode reckons it won't kill him to carry it to her car this once (especially since he has gotten an exorbitant rent from her). Helen finds a group of children gathered around the car, petting Lassie. Angrily, she orders them away and drives off.

The next morning, she finds a harmonica-playing orphan named Jerry (Claude Jarman Jr.) waiting on her doorstep. Mr. Williegoode has sent him to do her chores. "All of us here are obliged to be handy for folks hereabout." She dismisses him and tells him she will send a dollar to Mr. Williegoode for the work he has already done. Best not, he replies. He's had his fun out of it. "Fare you well, Miss Lady," he mutters and shuffles off.

Lassie follows him and encounters her first rattlesnake, which Jerry dispatches with a stick. Jerry wonders at a dog so dumb that she tries to chase a rattler. He reckons he could teach her a lot of things. Helen reckons he could too and gratefully tells him he can be her "handy boy."

She decides to stay on in Brushy Gap, as the place is called, and goes down to the general store to send a telegram to Arthur. He is her manager, she explains to the curious Mr. Williegoode. She used to sing. At last his face lights up. He tells her that her landlord, Tom Chandler, sings too. Almost as good as the radio. Mr. Williegoode is still astonished by the extravagance of a telegram and even more surprised when Helen asks him where she can find a maid. He looked around after his wife died, he tells her, but there was nary a maiden in the whole valley.

Miz Sally (Ida Moore) and Miz Golightly (Margaret Hamilton) enter, vigorously ignoring Helen. They are miffed that she has "run off their youngin's," Mr. Williegoode tells Helen. The ladies are eager to learn all about the telegram as soon as Helen has left. A relative? they ask. Her *manager*, Mr. Williegoode tells them. "She comes right out with it, don't she?" gasps Miz Golightly.

Twilight is descending over the quaint old house, and we can hear Helen singing "Songs My Mother Taught Me," as Jerry listens outside. He finally knocks. She is delighted to see him because oil lamps are a mystery to her. The boy happily shows her where Mr. Tom keeps the oil and how to light them. Mr. Tom was a great one for music too, he says. Jerry tells her about the feeling he gets from music, like you get from "the sun in the morning" (the original film title).

Helen offers to play any piece he fancies, and he asks for the one she was just singing. She sings for him in the lamplight, a lovely moment indeed. When she reaches the line about "children," she breaks down and cries. She had a boy once, she tells Jerry, and now she doesn't have him anymore. Jerry is standing there with such eyes and such funny big-boy's feet—she turns sharply and asks him to leave. She had no right to say those things. He tells her he's proud to hear anything she feels like saying. He's not so young he doesn't know what losing means.

Jerry comes to Mr. Williegoode's store the next morning, proudly clutching the dollar Helen has given him. He is followed by a large group of curious youngsters. He selects a mouth-organ, much to their disgust. Mr. Williegoode suggests he "put the dollar by" and just borrow the mouth-organ, as he has always done. It blows the same either way, he says, but Jerry reckons it blows sweeter when it belongs to you.

A local orphan, Jerry (Claude Jarman Jr.), is sent to do Helen's chores. Jeanette's wardrobe by Irene was in the fussy tailored style so popular in the late 1940s.

Helen is afraid to love another child, but Jerry and Lassie begin to wear down her resistance.

The children then pour along the road and discover Helen's convertible. Jerry hops in and gives the wheel a few turns. Helen appears, and the children back off in alarm. Instead of scolding, she offers them a ride. The car is too full for Jerry and his friend, Junebug (Teddy Infuhr). Jerry yanks one of the older boys from the back seat and thrusts Junebug into his place as the car pulls away.

The jaunt gives the boys a chance to sing a tedious, pseudo-folk song, "Cousin Ebenezer." Helen offers to drop the boys at their homes and learns they all live together. Their home is the county orphanage.

They question Helen closely, wondering if she thinks eating too much is bad and if she approves of chores on Sunday. Her negative answers please them, and they nod happily. They want to be sure she isn't adopting Jerry to have an extra farmhand. Helen starts to protest, but they run off across the fields toward the grim orphanage.

Helen returns to Mr. Williegoode's store and telephones Arthur. He is to reinstate her canceled concert tour. She will meet him in Atlanta in a few days. Jerry comes to the store after she has left and has a philosophical chat with Mr. Williegoode about wanting people.

The Sun Comes Up

Jerry agrees that one person wanting just ain't enough.

Helen sees Jerry walking past her house and joins him. She is going away, she tells him cheerfully, but she will write him. Does he like letters? He's not sure, he replies. He never got any. She's not to worry about him, though, since he is going away soon himself. He's going to live with his mother in Mannville. Helen is so surprised that she doesn't see he is obviously lying. She leaves Lassie with him while she goes to Atlanta and Jerry sobs his grief into the dog's soft fur. This is no time for chores, he decides, and together he and Lassie go off for a romp that lands Jerry in an icy creek. He returns to the orphanage thoroughly chilled. By dinner time he is looking poorly, but he assures kindly matron Mrs. Pope (Hope Landin) that he will be all right.

Lassie whines outside the window during the meal, and Jerry tries to send her away. She won't go, so Jerry waits until bedtime, then sets out to take her back to Helen's house. They are caught in a storm reminiscent of the finale of *Moby Dick*. Lightning flashes, cymbals crash, and Jerry sinks unconscious on Helen's doorstep.

Helen returns home the next day to find Jerry bedded down with pneumonia. Her landlord, Tom Chandler (Lloyd Nolan), had decided to pay her a visit and found the boy. A doctor has been called, and Helen is told that Jerry can't be moved. The doctor (Paul E. Burns) says the boy needs a nurse, and Helen decides to go for his mother. Jerry becomes hysterical. She mustn't bother anyone, he cries. The orchestra underlines each word so ostentatiously that the scene loses any real drama.

With the care of Helen and Tom, Jerry slowly returns to health. (In the magazine version, Chandler owned another house down the road, but the film never makes it clear where he is staying.) Miz Golightly, who had snooted Helen, becomes downright friendly when she sees the care the boy is getting. She grudgingly

The local ladies are slow to be friendly until they see how kind Helen is to Jerry. Jeanette's snuff scene with Margaret Hamilton is a comic delight.

acknowledges that Helen is not as peculiar as she had thought and offers some posies for the boy. Helen wants to return the favor and asks Mr. Williegoode what would be an appropriate gift.

"Snuff," he replies. Of course, she mustn't present it as a gift. He explains the local etiquette. She must tell the lady that she has somehow gotten more snuff than she can use, and she'd be obliged if the lady would take it off her hands while it is still fresh. He outlines the dialogue that will ensue, and it does, word for word.

Unfortunately Miz Golightly insists that Helen join her in partaking of the snuff. Helen tries bravely to imitate her but swallows it. "I always eat it," she chokes. Miz Golightly is rightfully impressed with the hardiness of city women. (Again the background music intrudes, cutting the effectiveness of the simple scene.)

Jerry and "Mr. Tom" sit outside the house, listening as Helen sings "Romance." Jerry wonders when Mr. Tom is going to sing for Miss Lady, but Tom says he can't compete with singing like that. (With the constant references to Tom's singing, we are all set for a charming, impromptu duet, but, alas, it never happens.) Mr.

Tom Chandler (Lloyd Nolan) turns up. He owns the house that Helen has rented. After numerous tribulations, we are sure that the four of them—Helen, Tom, Jerry, and Lassie—will form a happy family.

Williegoode comes by to bring Helen her train ticket. Jerry and Tom are both hurt and surprised. Jerry reckons he's well enough to ride along with Mr. Williegoode to the orphanage. They are short-handed for the harvest. He's not sure he'll even have time to come back for goodbyes. Helen is very upset at his departure. She defends herself to Tom, saying that what she is doing is right. She can't take Jerry away from his real mother. "You already have," Tom says.

On her way to the train station, Helen stops at the orphanage to say goodbye to Jerry. Then she drives off amidst shattering violin harmonics, and Jerry rushes upstairs to hide in a storeroom. A lamp is tipped over, and flames begin licking the wooden walls.

From the depot, Helen and Tom hear the fire bell. They rush back to find Jerry. He, of course, is stuck in the store room. A flimsy wooden catch has dropped into place that any healthy five-year-

The Sun Comes Up

old could dislodge, but the six-foot boy must summon Lassie with his cries. The dog unlocks the door and rescues Jerry.

The now-homeless children of the orphanage are divided up among the townsfolk, and Helen takes Jerry back to Mr. Tom's place. She decides to drive to Mannville to give Jerry's mother whatever she needs to have Jerry come home.

After she leaves, Tom learns that Jerry has lied about having a mother. Lassie scratches at the door, and a car is heard coming down the road. Helen is returning. She didn't try to find Jerry's mother, she tells Tom. She changed her mind. Why should she give Jerry back to her when she needs him more?

They go to find Jerry, but he has fled across the fields. "Trip him, Lassie," Helen cries, and the dog tackles the boy. They are all reunited amidst tears and violins, and we assume they will form a family. The final shot is of Lassie yipping her delight into Jerry's ear, a wistful ending to Jeanette MacDonald's last film and to a career that spanned the first two decades of the film musical.

Reviews

"Eminently suitable for the family trade.... Miss MacDonald maintains her high standard of singing," said *Film Daily*. *Time* Magazine, at the other end of the spectrum, said the film "is as unnatural as a purple zebra."

A.H. Weiler in the *New York Times* took a middle course: "Wholesome, inoffensive, sometimes banal, always standard. While the new film arrival sheds plenty of Technicolored light, it sheds little warmth. Jeanette MacDonald never looked lovelier. And she proves she has kept at her vocal exercises by neatly rendering several lieder and an aria from *Madame Butterfly*. The proceedings are all very sweet and simple, perhaps too sweet,"

Recordings (See Discography for further information)

Jeanette recorded:
    "Romance" ("If You Were Mine")
    "Songs My Mother Taught Me"
    "Un Bel Di"

Music in the Film

In listing performers after each title, "and" denotes a genuine duet, while commas between names indicate a sequence of singers.

Overture: theme by André Previn, used throughout the film
"Tes Yeux" ["Thine Eyes"] fragment (MacDonald) - music by René Alphonse Rabey
"Un Bel Di" from the opera *Madame Butterfly* (MacDonald) - music by Giacomo Puccini, libretto by Luigi Illica and Guiseppe Giacosa
"Als die Alte Mutter" ["Songs My Mother Taught Me"] (MacDonald) - music by Antonin Dvorak (Opus 55, #4), German lyrics by Adolf Heyduck
"Songs My Mother Taught Me" reprise (MacDonald) - music as above, English lyrics by Natalie MacFarren
"Cousin Ebenezer" (MacDonald and boys) - music by André Previn, lyrics by William Katz
"Romance" ["If You Were Mine"] (MacDonald) - music by Anton Rubinstein, lyrics by Paul Bourget
Finale: Previn theme

Prerelease publicity stills show Jeanette and Armand Tokatyan, her stage *Roméo et Juliette* costar, in what is described as a scene from *La Traviata*. She and Tokatyan are in street clothes on an opera set. Pay records indicate Tokatyan sang and acted in a sequence, "Oh, Gran Dio." However, this sequence does not appear in the completed film.

9
The Finale That Never Was

In the years after film stardom, Jeanette MacDonald and Nelson Eddy had to work out new identities. Jeanette, with the privilege accorded her sex, became a "great lady of song," a happily married woman who could step out on stage or before the television camera when she wished for the pleasure of her still-loyal fans. Fortunately she wished to frequently—the trouper instinct was still strong—but she would have suffered no disgrace if she had chosen to remain a wife and homemaker.

The great shame was that she was not permitted to go on to the sophisticated, funny roles she could have done so well, the kind of parts that added so much luster to the careers of Claudette Colbert, Rosalind Russell, and even Doris Day. But the film machine is basically inefficient, and she joined long-time greats like Irene Dunne, Myrna Loy, and Greer Garson in the ranks of "star emeritus."

Eddy's situation was distinctly different. He had risen to public acclaim in a very specialized type of film. The genre had passed from popularity, and when the new cycle began in the early 1950s, there were younger, thinner baritones fighting for the roles.

Radio was going Top Forty. Television was a voracious medium that could be casually cruel to older performers. The concert circuits were fewer and no longer highly lucrative. The doors were closing all around him, and he needed to work, financially and spiritually.

He also recognized that in the eyes of many he had become an amusing anachronism. When the life's work of a man of talent and integrity is held up to ridicule, it is a personal tragedy. When the man accepts this without losing his sense of humor, dignity, and zest for living, it is his own personal triumph. Nelson Eddy was such a man.

Eddy might have "retired" at this point to become a figurehead for a commercial product (as many astronauts, ball players, and movie stars have done). He might have gone back to writing or sold his sculpture to adoring fans or opened a chain of music schools. He chose to do none of these things. He was a performer.

In the years following *I Married an Angel* in 1942, numerous film projects were suggested, proposed, and even announced that would reunite the Nelson and Jeanette team. *East Wind* by Romberg was one and *Emissary to Brazil*

The Finale That Never Was

another. The *Hollywood Reporter* (8/1/46) reported, "Deal is on the fire between Hunt Stromberg and Warner Bros. to purchase MISSISSIPPI BELLE complete with musical score by Cole Porter, and screenplay is expected to be completed today or tomorrow with Stromberg intending as a Jeanette MacDonald musical. Price in $200,000 range." It never happened.

Lubitsch was also eager to film Richard Strauss's *Der Rosenkavalier* with Jeanette as the Marschallin, but he never solved the problem of the leading man, a vocal part written for a woman, and the project was still pending when he died in 1947.

Another film suggested for the pair was *The Thrill of It All*, a 1963 Doris Day vehicle in which they were asked to play a couple who find themselves "expecting" after thirty years of marriage. They turned it down, thinking it would conflict with their public image, and the parts were played stylishly by Arlene Francis and Edward Andrews. The columns regularly announced their "return," but, as with more than a dozen projects announced during their prime years at MGM, nothing came of it.

In the late forties, the two were kept busy by radio and concerts. Miss MacDonald appeared with Gordon MacRae on the "Railroad Hour" doing condensed versions of favorite operettas (*Bitter Sweet*, *The Merry Widow*, *Naughty Marietta*, *Apple Blossoms*). Eddy hosted the "Kraft Music Hall" during the summers of 1947, '48, and '49, as well as making numerous guest appearances, but the days of radio concerts and theatre were drawing to a close.

Television antennas were springing up across the nation. Both entertainers made their television debuts in 1951. Jeanette appeared on Ed Sullivan's "Toast of the Town" and "The Ken Murray Show" and Eddy guested on "The Alan Young Show." Miss MacDonald always seemed to enjoy herself in front of the camera, but Eddy found it "nerve wracking—compared to TV, radio is child's play."

Nelson was the mystery guest several times on TV's "What's My Line?" hosted by John Daly. *Courtesy Ginny Sayre.*

Jeanette on "This Is Your Life." Left to right: Nelson Eddy, Jeanette's sisters Blossom Rock and Elsie Scheiter, Grace Adele Newell, Miss Edna Clear, and the Rev. Willsie Martin, who married Jeanette and Gene. Seated, Jeanette and husband Gene Raymond. *Courtesy Anna Michalik.*

Many of Nelson's fans thought he should return to opera. He soon ended their hopes and told them why. In early 1949, he had attended a concert by Leonard Warren, one of his favorite singers (who, like Eddy, would die while performing). Warren sang seven very difficult arias in a row. "I couldn't match that," Eddy acknowledged, "so I'll leave it to him. I like

Nelson rehearsing with Gale Sherwood, who would be his nightclub singing partner for the next fourteen years. She is wearing an Indian costume for their satirical *Rose Marie* sketch.

whatever is first class—Crosby, good jazz, bebop. But no second class opera singing for me!"

Eddy decided to try the nightclub circuit. In 1952, he began gathering material and interviewing girls for a "partner" to sing duets and do dialogue with him. Gale Sherwood was one of the girls. She recalled that several hours after her audition, the phone rang, and a man asked when she could rehearse. It was Eddy. "Didn't they tell you you got the part?" he asked. While Gale was getting ready, he made his first club appearance as a solo act at "The Tops" in San Diego. He was warmly received, and Gale joined him several weeks later in Las Vegas. It would be the first of thousands of appearances that would take them across the United States, through Canada, Mexico, and on four tours of Australia.

Eddy may have been as surprised as everyone else at the success of his new venture. *Billboard* headlined their review: "NELSON EDDY BACK ON RISING BOUNCE WITH CLICK NITERY TURN" (6/20/53). Louis Sobol wrote: "Over to the Copa later...not without misgivings about Nelson Eddy, the starring attraction, for he was not a chap I could see in a nightclub diversion. Let me report I was unnecessarily apprehensive. He came through like the master he is—and they stormed for him to come back for encore after encore."

Gale Sherwood brought blonde good looks, bubbling good humor, and an excellent soprano to Eddy's act. She also brought loyalty and friendship that would last through fourteen years of touring together. She, too, had a film background. She had appeared as a child, billed as Jacqueline Nash, with Jascha Heifetz in *They Shall Have Music* (1939) and later in several adult roles including Tchaikovsky's wife in *Song of My Heart* (1947).

Eddy wrote most of their material, sketches, lyrics, and parodies. Together with Eddy's longtime accompanist and co-manager, Ted Paxson, Eddy and Gale spent ten months of every year on the road. During "vacation" time, Eddy returned to his home—"my most precious possession"—for a rest and a chance to do some gardening. In his spare time, he also made changes in the act, arranged and orchestrated new numbers, settled wardrobe, and rehearsed for the coming season. Interestingly, in his published songs—"The Laughing Song," "Out of the Night," and "My Magic You"—he contributed the lyrics, not the music.

Both Nelson and Jeanette appeared regularly on television during the 1950s. Eddy starred in a ninety-minute color special of *The Desert Song*, produced by Max Liebman (5/7/55). His costar was his new partner, Gale Sherwood. His other television appearances included guest spots on

The Finale That Never Was

Gale Sherwood and Nelson in *The Desert Song*, a live telecast in 1955, also starring Earl William, Salvatore Baccalone and Otto Kruger.

"The Bob Hope Show" (2/15/54), where he imitated Ezio Pinza and Mario Lanza, with Spike Jones (4/30/57), "The Dinah Shore Show" (12/l/61), and, with Miss Sherwood, "The Hollywood Palace" (3/27/65).

Eddy was always willing to laugh at a joke at his own expense, but he took his music seriously. Thus he was not always the loose "anything-goes" type of guest so desirable on a talk show. His banter was relaxed, friendly, and frequently quite funny in a bluff, good-humored sort of way, but he was not a master of the rapier slash or sly innuendo. And when his carefully prepared musical numbers were turned into interludes for slapstick, he was not amused.

Nelson Eddy on TV

The following list was compiled by Christine Souter.

May 22, 1951 CBS The Alan Young Show
Oct. 28, 1952 NBC Nelson Eddy's Back Yard (TV pilot)
Nov. 1952 NBC This Is Your Life, Jeanette MacDonald
Nov. 30, 1952 CBS Ed Sullivan Show
Feb. 11, 1953 CBS Colgate Comedy Hour (no documentation found)
May 17, 1953 CBS Colgate Comedy Hour
Feb. 16, 1954 NBC Bob Hope Show
Feb. 21, 1954 NBC Edgar Bergen Show
May 7, 1955 NBC The Desert Song
Sept. 8, 1956 CBS Ed Sullivan Show
Sept. 20, 1956 CBS Lux Video Theatre (Nelson and Jeanette)
Jan. 3, 1957 Tennessee Ernie Ford show
April 30, 1957 CBS Spike Jones Show
Sept. 25, 1957 CBS The Big Record (Patti Page, hostess, with Jeanette). Two other possible dates could not be documented.
March 13, 1958 NBC Rosemary Clooney Show
March 2, 1959 NBC Jack Paar Show (Tonight Show)
June 12, 1959 Juke Box Jury in LA
Oct. 20, 1959 NBC Jack Paar (with Gale Sherwood)
Jan. 31, 1960 NBC Jack Paar (with Gale Sherwood)
May 22, 1960 CBS Ed Sullivan Show (with Gale Sherwood)
Dec. 1, 1960 NBC Dinah Shore Chevy Show
April 25, 1963 NBC Today Show, Hugh Downs as host (with Gale Sherwood)
March 27, 1965 ABC Hollywood Palace (with Gale Sherwood)
July 15, 1965 Dialing For Dollars
March 30, 1966 Merv Griffin (with Gale Sherwood)
Oct. 26, 1966 Mike Douglas Show (with Gale Sherwood)
Dec. 31, 1966 Guy Lombardo New Year's Eve Show (with Gale Sherwood)

Constantly on tour: Ted Paxson, Gale Sherwood, and Nelson. *Courtesy Anna Michalik.*

Once, during a "Jack Paar Show," he sang "Hello, Young Lovers!" while being pummeled and buffeted by Kaye Ballard and Cliff (Charlie Weaver) Arquette. He didn't miss a note, but his polite coolness afterward spoke volumes. Another performer might have unbent enough to clown through the number. Another host might have recognized that Eddy took nothing in life seriously except his music.

This was not to say that he couldn't joke about it. His nightclub act included imitations of popular entertainers—Arthur Godfrey, Frankie Laine, Ted Lewis—doing imitations of him. And in a comedy sketch on "The Hollywood Palace," he and Gale reminisced:

> EDDY: Gale and I have been together twelve years.
> GALE: Ever since I was three.
> EDDY: In that time, we've sung 100,000 songs together.
> GALE: Yes.
> EDDY: Before that I sang 50,000 songs...
> GALE: All in one picture.

He could laugh at himself, too, recounting the story of the lady who rushed up to him and asked: "Weren't you Nelson Eddy?"

Jeanette also appeared on early TV, most frequently as a singing guest star. On "Playhouse 90" (3/28/57) she played Charley's real aunt to Art Carney's impersonation in *Charley's Aunt*. Her dazzling *tour-de-force* appearance on "The Voice of Firestone" (11/13/50) has recently been released on video. Her husband, Gene Raymond, wrote and produced a sprightly sitcom pilot for her, "Prima Donna" (2/1/56), which failed to find a network slot.

On 11/12/52, Jeanette was the subject of Ralph Edwards's "This Is Your Life." Nelson appeared as a voice from her past, singing the song he sang at her wedding to Gene Raymond. She also appeared with Jackie Gleason (12/53), as hostess for the Tournament of Roses (1/1/56), with Eddy on "The Lux Video Theatre" (1956 and 1957) and "The Big Record" (9/25/57), and on numerous celebrity guest shows.

Jeanette did a pilot for a sitcom with songs called "Prima Donna." Script was by her husband, Gene Raymond. Alfred Caiazza (left) played a singing newsboy. *Courtesy Ken Norton.*

She also made occasional club appearances, although she did not enjoy them as much as Eddy. She sang at the Sands and the Sahara in Las Vegas in 1953, the Coconut Grove in Los Angeles in 1954, and the Sahara again in 1957, but she much preferred the concert or musical comedy stage.

In March and April of 1951, she and her husband toured in *The Guardsman*, playing the roles originated by the Lunts. (Molnár's play had provided the plot for Eddy's *The Chocolate Soldier* in 1941.) Four songs were interpolated for Jeanette, and the role of "The Actress" became that of "The Singer," an easy transition. Herbert Berghof played "The Critic." Jeanette asked Alfred Lunt to direct, but he was only able to offer advice. The show played the Forrest Theatre in Philadelphia, the American Theatre in St. Louis, and the Gaiety Theatre in Washington, D. C. There, President Truman forgot the threats of impeachment for firing General MacArthur and, unannounced, slipped off to the theatre with his wife and General Omar Bradley. Miss MacDonald was not yet an outspoken Republican, but even if she had been, it would not have deterred the doughty Democrat. Later, she was a favorite of President Eisenhower, attending his inaugural ball in 1956 and doing "command performances" at the White House.

Her concerts continued to be warmly emotional occasions for her many fans. They went to experience a performance and they always got their money's worth. When a recital was announced, every ticket would sell immediately. This enthusiasm was ultimately detrimental because it forced her to perform in auditoriums much too large for a lyric soprano voice. The following from the *New York Times* is typical of the criticism she began encountering when she sang in big concert halls:

> Jeanette MacDonald, the Hollywood soprano, whose face and voice are familiar to movie goers all over the world, made her second [Carnegie Hall] recital last night

Jeanette at Twin Gables, seated beneath the beautiful "Pink Lady" portrait by Portuguese artist Enrique Medina. *Courtesy Velma Menét.*

[1/16/53]. Visually it was a spectacular event as such things go in Carnegie Hall. Miss MacDonald made her appearance before a specially constructed acoustical shell wearing a green evening gown that complimented beautifully her coppery red hair.

It was a charming picture that brought back pleasant memories of Miss MacDonald in *Naughty Marietta*, in *Rose Marie*, in *Maytime*, in this and that and the other thing. Unhappily the spell was broken when Miss MacDonald began to sing.

The plain fact is that, off screen, Miss MacDonald's is not much of a voice. It is used in the main with taste and intelligence; it shows the results of study and careful preparation; but it is inclined to be shrill

Jeanette as Mrs. Anna in *The King and I*. Dancing in 100 degree heat in the huge hoop skirts the costumes required took its toll on her health.

and tremulous in the loud passages and trailing off into near inaudibility when used pianissimo.

Altogether, the evening was not very rewarding musically. But Miss MacDonald looked lovely and the capacity audience greeted her with enthusiasm.

In the mid 1950s, she toured in summer stock productions of her old favorite, *Bitter Sweet*, plus *The King and I* (both originally written for Gertrude Lawrence, although the former turned out to be too musically demanding for her). Jeanette's sensitive and warm portrayals of the two roles brought the MacDonald magic to new audiences.

While performing in *The King and I* at the Starlight Theatre, Kansas City, Missouri in August of 1956, she collapsed. Officially it was heat prostration, brought on by the ninety-degree heat, vigorous dancing, and the elaborate corseted costumes that the role required. Actually it was a heart seizure. She began limiting her appearances.

Two landmark events occurred in 1957, one happy, one sad. That summer she and her husband celebrated their twentieth wedding anniversary with a party for their friends. After dinner, Jeanette stood for more than an hour, radiant in a lavender gown, singing the songs requested by their guests. October saw the funeral of Louis B. Mayer. The old man, once monarch of MGM, had died of leukemia at seventy-five. The stars he had pasted up in the MGM firmament were scattered by death, alienation, and the erosion of the studio itself. Yet many returned to pay their respects, and Jeanette MacDonald was one. She sang Mayer's old favorite, "Ah, Sweet Mystery of Life."

Jeanette and Gene were interviewed by Edward R. Murrow on his popular *Person to Person* TV show, 10/3/58. Between Gene's more and more frequent television appearances, the couple took time to travel. In the summer of 1959, they toured throughout Europe, and her old fans turned out to greet them. She used her new

The Guardsman, 1951, which also starred her husband, Gene Raymond. (Molnár's plot was borrowed for Eddy's film, *The Chocolate Soldier*.)

The Finale That Never Was

A major difference between Nelson and Jeanette was that he cherished his privacy while she believed that publicity meet-and-greet photo sessions were part of her job description. Here she presents Roy Rogers with a safety award. Left to right: Gabby Hayes, Jeanette, Dr. Wayne Hughes, Margaret O'Brien, Lloyd Nolan (partially obscured), Roy Rogers, and Maureen O'Sullivan. *Courtesy Ken Norton.*

"spare time" for the many projects for which she had always been too busy. She taught Sunday school at the First Presbyterian Church in Los Angeles and became an active supporter of Barry Goldwater in his 1964 presidential campaign. She worked extensively on her autobiography and suggested calling it *The Iron Butterfly*, a sly acknowledgment of the sobriquet some people used behind her back. In an era of "confession" books dripping with sordid details, her ladylike reminiscences did not excite the publishers. And so her personal story went untold until Gene Raymond gave biographer Edward Baron Turk access to the manuscript for use in his 1998 biography, *Hollywood Diva*.

In 1962, MGM reissued eight MacDonald/Eddy films as part of a "Golden Age of Hollywood" series, and the pair were discovered by a whole new audience. Television's showings of their films also brought them many new fans, most of them born after MacDonald and Eddy made their last film together. In 1986, the Turner Broadcasting System's Ted Turner bought the remnants of MGM and sold off everything but the film library, which he used to start the Turner Classic Movie channel. MacDonald/Eddy films make frequent appearances on Turner's TCM and TNT, and MGM/UA Home Entertainment Group has issued videos of all their MGM films except *Broadway to Hollywood* and *Student Tour.* (The American Movie Classics channel also airs Jeanette's early Paramount films.)

At sixty, Eddy was still going strong. While baritones usually have longer careers than

Jeanette and her husband Gene in old-age makeup for a party in the late 1930s. *Courtesy Diane Goodrich.*

Jeanette and Gene in 1959. *Photo by Nat Dallinger, © King Features Syndicate.*

The Finale That Never Was

Eddy in old-age makeup for the unreleased first version of *Maytime* in 1936. *Courtesy MGM.*

tenors, the fact that Eddy still sang extremely well is a tribute to his vocal technique. At an age when most men are slowing down, he undertook four tours of Australia (1962, '63, '64, and '67). He loved the country there and found that his Australian fans were, if possible, more devoted than his American fans. On one of his tours he became ill, and more than one thousand letters from all over Australia poured in to the hospital. He planned to take his wife, Ann, with him on the 1967 tour, but family business detained her at the last minute. He had wanted her to see the beautiful land, still relatively free of the encroachment of mankind, the kind of place where, as Eddy had said humorously in *Sweethearts*, a man could "put on overalls and get out and chop down his own fruit trees."

Over the years, the legend grew about his occasionally "blowing" lyrics that he had sung a hundred times. Once, he laughingly acknowledged, he had started "Shortnin' Bread" three times and finally had to give up. There was also a recurring rumor, vigorously denied, that he was going blind. It started in the mid-1930s when his eye became badly infected after a makeup man accidentally slashed it with a pair of scissors. The story followed him the rest of his life, and, in later years, it was probably encouraged by the fact that performers exiting a darkened stage are frequently "led off" because their eyes have not had time to adjust from spotlight to darkness.

Eddy's one regret in later years was that he had not completed his education, although he was probably better educated at that point than most college graduates. When Temple University in Philadelphia awarded him an honorary degree in 1950, he told the crowd that he much preferred it to an Oscar.

Eddy at an RCA recording session in 1957. *Courtesy RCA Records.*

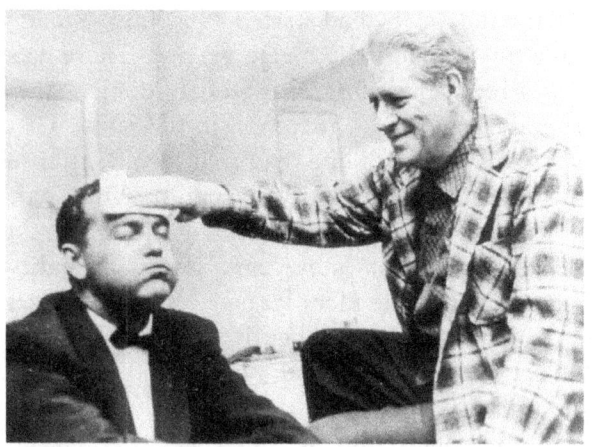

Accompanist Ted Paxson and Nelson clown during a rehearsal. *Courtesy Anna Michalik.*

Nelson Eddy was basically a very private person, but, despite the weirdoes and psychotics who sometimes haunt people in public life, he tried to maintain an open graciousness toward everyone with whom he came in contact. When he succumbed to rudeness, no matter how justified, he was generally filled with remorse. Once a man who had been giving him loud encouragement during a show at the Royal York in Toronto came back to ask for his autograph. Eddy was always upset by people who were noisy when he sang, and he brushed the man off coldly. A few minutes later he regretted his action and had the house manager page the man to come up on stage for an autograph and an apology.

"He was always on time, a stickler for details, embarrassed by noisy fans," recalled his friend Russ Byrd. "He was a trouper who could not afford to retire." He summarized Eddy succinctly in three words: "A delightful square."

Eddy was indeed a delightful square. He admired Leonard Bernstein and Andy Williams and added many contemporary songs to his repertoire. His philosophy on popular music was, "If you can't lick 'em, join 'em." However, he also felt that there was such a thing as "dirty music...designed to excite the meaner parts of our nature." For all his years in nightclubs, he rarely drank. His only vices remained his pipe and his perfectionism. A delightful square, indeed.

His concert manager, George Brown, summed up Eddy thus: "He was never temperamental like some of the famous stars I've been associated with. In my twenty years of close association with him, he has never used a harsh word or an unkind one. I made dozens of mistakes, and he had very good reason to bawl me out, but there was never criticism of any kind. I'd sometimes book a town that looked good a year in advance, and, when he got there, it didn't pan out, but he always went through it with a smile. He always gave one hundred percent of his very best efforts, no matter what the conditions of the auditorium, hotel, or audience were. I never knew a harder worker or a more honest and conscientious student than Nelson Eddy. While traveling on trains and planes or in hotel rooms, he never wasted a minute. He was always studying languages, looking over a new song for future programs, or reading good books. He was generous almost to a fault in many cases. He had many pet charities the public never heard about."

The parallels in the lives of Jeanette MacDonald and Nelson Eddy, two very different performers, are intriguing. Both were born to middle-class, conservative, religious families of British origin. Both spent part of their youth in Philadelphia. Both had many years of stage experience and hard knocks before becoming "overnight successes." Both married late and successfully. Neither had children. Both maintained warm relationships with their mothers after it was no longer fashionable to do so. Both were perfectionists, constantly driving themselves. Both died after twenty-seven years of marriage to their one and only spouse.

PHOTOS RIGHT: Nelson was a talented sculptor and painter, often capturing the people he worked with. He found it was a good way to relax on the set between takes. *Photos courtesy Helen Crawford, Leah Campion, and Anna Michalik.*

The Finale That Never Was

A bronze bust of his music teacher, Dr. Lippé

Working on a bust of Jeanette between takes

A horse sculpture by Nelson Eddy

Anna May Wong

10
As They Had Lived

The Clan-MacDonald and the Family-Eddy were a remarkably hardy bunch. Jeanette's mother lived to the age of seventy-six (dying 5/17/47), her sister Edith Blossom to eighty-two (1/14/78) and her eldest sister, Elsie, to seventy-eight (10/2/70). Eddy's mother was going strong in her mid-seventies when she died (12/19/57) and his father was a whopping ninety-two (11/4/68).

Despite their exhausting schedules, both singers took care of themselves and Jeanette had been especially careful in later years because of her heart trouble. She worsened somewhat in 1963 and underwent an arterial transplant at Methodist Hospital in Houston, Texas. After the operation she developed pleurisy and was hospitalized for two and a half months. Her friends kept the news from the press until just before her release. She went home to a newly acquired apartment that would not require so much of her energies.

She was again stricken in 1964, and on Christmas Eve she was operated on for abdominal adhesions. She was able to go home for New Year's, but in mid-January she was flown back to Methodist Hospital. It was hoped that Dr. Michael DeBakey, who had recently operated successfully on the Duke of Windsor, could perform the same miracle for her. She checked in on January 12 and a program of intravenous feedings was begun to build her up for possible surgery.

On Thursday, January 14, she seemed to be responding to treatment. That afternoon she awoke to find her husband beside her. "My feet are cold," she said and he began rubbing them as a nurse prepared an intravenous feeding. "I love you," she whispered. "I love you too," he replied. She died a few minutes later at 4:32 PM.

Eddy was the only healthy member of the Eddy-Paxson-Sherwood trio during the winter of 1966-67. First Gale Sherwood underwent surgery and then Ted Paxson came down with bronchitis that kept him from going on their Australian tour. It was the first time since 1928 that Eddy had played an engagement without him.

On New Year's Eve 1967, Eddy and Gale helped Guy Lombardo ring in the New Year and then they set out on a series of club dates in Florida. "I'll continue working until I drop because I love it," he told an interviewer in late February.

On Sunday night, March 5, he was singing at the Sans Souci Hotel in Palm Beach. The first of

As They Had Lived

Troupers to the last. Nelson was performing with his nightclub partners Ted Paxson and Gale Sherwood when he had a stroke. Like his hero, opera baritone Leonard Warren, he literally died while performing. *Courtesy Anna Michalik.*

two scheduled shows was proceeding well, with an enthusiastic audience of four hundred. Gale Sherwood had just left the stage to make her second costume change when Eddy began having trouble speaking.

He said he couldn't seem to get the words out and would the audience bear with him. They chuckled, knowing he was famous for forgetting the lyrics. He stepped toward the orchestra pit where Ted Paxson was and asked him to play "Dardanella," saying that maybe the words would come back to him.

"Is there a doctor in the house?" he asked and again the audience tittered. All this time he was holding the left side of his face, which was getting numb.

The audience was still convinced that it was part of the show, but Ted Paxson leaped up and helped him off stage. A doctor from the audience administered first aid, and Eddy was rushed to Mount Sinai Hospital in Miami. He had suffered a stroke. All through the night, the reports were favorable and it looked as if he would pull through. Then, at 7:50 AM on Monday, March 6, 1967, he died without regaining consciousness.

The "singing sweethearts"—the "iron butterfly" and the "delightful square"—were gone, but they left us a heritage of some of the finest musical films ever made.

And did they have great voices? In the sense of technical perfection, perhaps not. But in the

1971—The Jeanette MacDonald International Fan Club annual convention in Los Angeles.

2000—The Nelson Eddy Appreciation Society's annual convention in Cambridge Springs, PA.

sense of a performer who can move an audience to laughter or tears, who can "sell" a song and create a moment of great beauty and total, sublime theatrical catharsis, then they were indeed great *singers*.

So Jeanette MacDonald and Nelson Eddy, separately and together, created their own rare kind of magic. An editorial in the *San Diego Evening Tribune* perhaps said it best:

> Songs like 'Rose Marie' and 'Indian Love Call' espoused no great causes. There was no profound social, economic or political significance to be extracted from *Maytime* or *Sweethearts*. That was part of their appeal. They simply hinted that love and beauty and honor, however ethereal, had value and meaning...and that anyone could, for a moment at least, taste something of the 'Sweet Mystery of Life.'

More than any other performers of this century, Jeanette and Nelson were responsible for introducing millions of people to the excitement of "classical" music, the concert and opera repertoires. It would be interesting to know exactly how many who subsequently became musicians felt the first stirrings of future ambition as they sat in a darkened movie theatre watching MacDonald and Eddy. Certainly hundreds, and probably thousands.

The team left us another heritage too, less tangible perhaps, but far more valuable. They touched us to the heart as only great performers can and gave us their special gift of music, laughter, and love. As long as their films and recordings survive, each new generation will know the joy that was Jeanette MacDonald and Nelson Eddy.

Epilogue

Jeanette MacDonald was buried on January 18, 1965 at Forest Lawn Memorial Park in Glendale, California. The pallbearers included Senator Barry Goldwater, tenor Lauritz Melchior, actors Leon Ames and Jack Oakie, composer Meredith Willson, and General Lauris S. Norstad. Lloyd Nolan, who had appeared with Miss MacDonald in her final film, *The Sun Comes Up*, delivered the eulogy.

Nelson Eddy was buried at Hollywood Cemetery on March 9, 1967 beside his mother's grave. The cemetery is located between the Paramount and RKO studios. Ted Paxson, Eddy's friend and accompanist for thirty-seven years, played one of Eddy's special favorites on the organ. It was Paxson's own composition, "Der Tod das ist die Kuhle Nacht"–"Death Is the Cool Night." (Ted died a dozen years later on September 16, 1979 at age seventy-one.)

Jeanette's sister Blossom died January 14, 1978 in Los Angeles at the age of eighty-three.

A decade after Jeanette's death, her widower Gene Raymond remarried in 1975. His second wife's first name was, coincidentally, Nelson—the former Mrs. Bentley Hees. "Nels," as she was called, died in 1995. Gene followed her on May 3, 1998 at age 87. He was laid beside Jeanette at Forest Lawn, with Nels' family among the mourners. Gene left $1 million to the University of Southern California Thornton School of Music to establish scholarships for aspiring vocalists in Jeanette's name.

Other Notable Film Appearances

Nelson and Jeanette: America's Singing Sweethearts

Turner Entertainment.
Distributed by PBS and WTTW-TV, Chicago.
First televised February 14, 1992.
Written and produced by Elayne Goldstein.
Director: Michael Lorentz.
57 minutes.

An excellent overview of the film careers of the two stars, capturing much of the charm and excitement that the original audiences must have felt. Jane Powell (*Three Daring Daughters*) narrates. Jeanette's husband, Gene Raymond, offers commentary.

***Romeo and Juliet* trailer**, 1936. Clark Gable and Nelson Eddy are shown praising the film that stars Norma Shearer and Leslie Howard. Gable says, "I'm proud to be part of the movie family that produced *Romeo and Juliet*." Nelson, looking incredibly young and handsome, says, "Tonight I heard a remarkable music—like a symphony or a glorious tone poem. It was the dialogue in Shakespeare's *Romeo and Juliet*." Apparently, MGM hoped to use the popularity of these two "he-man" stars to attract middle-American audiences to Shakespeare.

Hollywood Goes to Town, MGM, released July 1938. Director: Herman Hoffman. 9 minutes. More than three-dozen top Hollywood stars are shown attending the lavish world premiere of *Marie Antoinette,* which starred Norma Shearer and Tyrone Power. A self-promoting short. Jeanette is among the guests.

The Love Goddesses

Janus Film.
Released: March 3, 1965.
Directed by Saul J. Turell.
87 minutes.

At a time when CBS television was censoring the doctor scene from showings of *Love Me Tonight* as too racy for the easily shocked American public (thus making the plot incomprehensible), this documentary offered most of the scene as an example of preCode naughtiness. Such deletions are absurd by today's standards.

That's Entertainment

In the mid 1970s, someone came up with the idea of putting out an anthology of musical and comedy scenes from the MGM vault as a reminder of the studio's past glory and a possible boost for television screenings. (Video was yet to come.) *That's Entertainment!* and its two sequels present film clips, concentrating mainly on the Technicolor extravaganzas of the forties and fifties (rendered, regrettably, in one-strip Metrocolor.) Sadly, these three films treat most black and white sequences as quaint curiosities, often ridiculed by a narrator. Even the brilliance of silver nitrate images that inspired the soubriquet "Silver Screen" are profaned, presented in washed-out tints of tan, green, and blue. Happily, this device was abandoned in the two subsequent compilations.

While film lovers are thrilled by several of the rarities trotted out of the vault, many squirm

Other Notable Film Appearances

Dorothy Kirsten poses with Eddy during rehearsals for the "Kraft Music Hall" in 1948. Eddy hosted the show from 1947 to 1949. From the earliest days of his career, he constantly boosted the careers of up and coming singers.

at the inaccuracies and misrepresentations of the narration, which even manages to imply that MGM was responsible for the Astaire-Rogers RKO classics, the Bing Crosby Paramount musicals, and the Twentieth-Century-Fox Carmen Miranda gems!

That's Entertainment!
MGM
Released: May 23, 1974.
Directed, written, produced by Jack Haley Jr.
Executive Producer: Daniel Melnick.
Metrocolor / black and white.
134 minutes.

Host/narrators: Fred Astaire & Gene Kelly with commentary by Bing Crosby, Peter Lawford, Liza Minnelli, Donald O'Connor, Debbie Reynolds, Mickey Rooney, Frank Sinatra, James Stewart, and Elizabeth Taylor.

Bits of *Rose Marie* and *Rosalie* comprise the film's total obeisance to the operetta form. The mountain-top rendition of "Indian Love Call" from *Rose Marie* starts with Eddy singing the first two lines and then cleverly cuts to the duet finale, unfortunately presented in mushy sepia. *San Francisco* is represented with a quick shot of Clark Gable and Spencer Tracy, and Eddy is glimpsed viewing Eleanor Powell dancing the title number from *Rosalie*, happily in crisp black and white.

Review

"Ceva" on the IMDb wrote: "For serious students of the MGM musical, however, this film is not beyond criticism. The great singing stars tend to receive only cursory recognition. Jeanette MacDonald and Nelson Eddy, whose series of musicals were the most popular in the studio's history, are seen in only one clip—"Indian Love Call" from *Rose Marie*. As Haley was sure to know, this number with Eddy bedecked as a Canadian Mountie invariably draws laughs and snickers from modern audiences. Mario Lanza, Vera-Ellen, and Jane Powell are also poorly represented."

That's Entertainment, Part II*
MGM
Released May 17, 1976.
Directed by Gene Kelly.
Produced by Saul Chaplin and Daniel Melnick.
Metrocolor / black and white.
133 minutes.
* Also listed as *That's Entertainment, Part 2*.

Host/narrators: Fred Astaire, Gene Kelly. (One of two films in which they dance together. The other is *Ziegfeld Follies*, 1946.)

With this sequel, it becomes painfully obvious that whoever is making the selections either has neither love for nor knowledge of the MacDonald/Eddy films. With dozens of highly excerptable scenes to choose from, scenes that

Jeanette became an active Republican in the 1950s. Here she and husband Gene pose with presidential candidate Barry Goldwater (left). *Courtesy Anna Michalik.*

are as fresh and lively today as when they were made, the film instead focuses on moments that were questionable at the time and even more embarrassing when seen out of context.

Jeanette's and Nelson's names in the credits are spelled out by the drifting blossoms that open *Maytime*. Later, Astaire intones, "Nelson Eddy and Jeanette MacDonald were the King and Queen of operetta, and *New Moon* was one of their most popular." All true. Then Nelson delivers his spirited "Stout Hearted Men," followed by Jeanette's dramatic reprise of "Lover, Come Back to Me"—acceptable within the context of the film, but unfortunately hammy and mirth-provoking as presented.

Broadway Serenade provides another giggle-producing sequence in which Lew Ayres composes while Al Shean cheers him on. Chevalier is shown singing a snatch of "Girls, Girls, Girls" which takes him from hotel room to Maxim's in *The Merry Widow*. This allows Gene Kelly to talk about movies set in Paris, which leads to his classic *An American in Paris*. Later, "The Merry Widow" waltz is shown, chorus only. To cover the cuts in the scene to eliminate MacDonald and Chevalier, music from the 1952 Lana Turner remake was dubbed over part of the dancing!

That's Entertainment! III
MGM
Released June 16, 1994.
Directed and produced by Bud Friedgen & Michael J. Sheridan.
Executive producers: Peter Fitzgerald & George Feltenstein.
Metrocolor / black and white.
113 minutes.

Commentary by Gene Kelly, assisted by June Allyson, Cyd Charisse, Lena Horne, Howard Keel, Ann Miller, Debbie Reynolds, and Esther Williams.

To emphasize their continuing disdain for their former top stars, MGM used only three seconds of material from MacDonald/Eddy films in this third compilation. There is a one-second shot of Eleanor Powell raising a window shade in *Rosalie*, and two-second shot of Jeanette in the swing in *Maytime*. (To be fair, the film *does* offer some fascinating outtakes and behind-the-scenes footage of later musicals with other stars.)

Jeanette and her long-time secretary Emily West. *Courtesy Anna Michalik.*

Books about Both Stars

Castanza, Philip, *The Films of Jeanette MacDonald and Nelson Eddy*, Citadel Press, 1978. 220 pages, 400 photos. Reprinted 1991 as a paperback, unfortunately without allowing corrections of some erroneous cast listings.

Goodrich, Diane and Rich, Sharon, *Farewell to Dreams*, privately printed 1979 hardcover, 1986 paperback. A sex fantasy in English. 292 pages, plus 32 pages of photos. Reissued in paperback several times.

Hamann, G.D. (Ed.), Collections of contemporary newspaper and magazine references.
Jeanette MacDonald in the 30's. (141 pp.)
Jeanette MacDonald in the 40's (100 pp.)
Nelson Eddy in the 30's and 40's (128 pp.)
Hollywood, CA, Filming Today Press, 2005 (www.GDHamann.com)

Kiner, Larry, *Nelson Eddy: A Bio-Discography*, Scarecrow Press, Metuchen, NJ, 1992. 683-page compendium with exhaustive statistics on Eddy's opera and radio performances, recordings, film costars, and videos, plus 156 photos.

Lulay, Gail, *Nelson Eddy: America's Favorite Baritone,* Goldfleet Publishing, Wheeling, IL, 1992. 240 pages including 16 pages of photos. Features exclusive interviews with Eddy's surviving relatives and his nightclub singing partner for fourteen years, Gale Sherwood.

Parish, James Robert, *The Jeanette MacDonald Story*, Mason/Charter, New York, 1976. Hardcover, 182 pages including 32 pages of photos.

Privat, Maurice, *Jeanette MacDonald? Les Documents Secrets*, Impr. E. Ramlot et Cie, 52 Av. du Maine, Paris, 1931. 60 pages. A sex fantasy paperback in French. No photos.

Rich, Sharon, *Jeanette MacDonald: A Pictorial History*, privately printed by Tom Hartzog, 1973. Handsome 252 slick pages with 300 photos.

Rich, Sharon, *Jeanette MacDonald Autobiography: The Lost Manuscript*, Bell Harbour Press, NY, 2004. 455 pages. Reproduction of one of the drafts of Jeanette's unpublished autobiography.

Rich, Sharon, *Jeanette MacDonald: The Irving Stone Letters*, Bell Harbour Press, NY, 2002. 217 pages. Correspondence during her Broadway and early film career.

Rich, Sharon, *Nelson Eddy: The Opera Years*, Bell Harbour Press, NY, 2001. 194 pages. Index of his extensive opera performances plus reviews and photos.

Rich, Sharon, *Sweethearts*, Donald I. Fine, 1994. 432 pages with photos. An expansion of the fictional *Farewell to Dream,* with Goodrich..

Stern, Lee Edward, *Jeanette MacDonald*, Harvest/HBJ Book, Jove Publications, New York, 1977. Part of the Illustrated History of the Movies series. A small 160-page, 5" x 8" paperback with 150 photos.

Truesdell, Mary, selections from her unpublished monographs delivered at annual meetings of the Nelson Eddy Appreciation Society convention in Cambridge Springs, PA, 2001-2004. (She drew on production meeting notes held at the Fairbanks Center for Motion Picture Study in Los Angeles.)

Turk, Edward Baron, *Hollywood Diva: A Biography of Jeanette MacDonald*, University of California Press, 1998. 450 pages, 60 photos. An excellent scholarly social-biography by M.I.T. professor Turk (who previously was knighted by the French government for his highly acclaimed biography of film director Marcel Carné).

Stars in the Hollywood Walk of Fame

Nelson has three stars in the Hollywood Walk of Fame. They are located in front of:

- 6512 Hollywood Boulevard – for radio
- 6311 Hollywood Boulevard – for film
- 1639 Vine Street – for recordings

The center bronze medallion of the star in this photo shows a film camera, indicating it was awarded for his achievements in film.

Nelson is also honored by a star in front of the Philadelphia Academy of Music.

Jeanette has two stars in the Hollywood Walk of Fame. They are located in front of:

- 6157 Hollywood Boulevard – for film
- 1628 Vine Street – for recordings

The center bronze medallion in the above photo shows this one is for achievement in the recording industry. It depicts a 78rpm disk with playing arm. Jeanette's husband, **Gene Raymond**, also has a star for film, located in front of 1798 Vine Street.

Footprints in cement

Both stars placed their footprints in the cement in the forecourt of Graumann's Chinese Theatre, she on 12/4/34, he on 12/28/39.

Cowboy star Tom Mix is to the left of Nelson at top, Maurice Chevalier to the left of Jeanette.

Discography

by J. Peter Bergman

Since 1976 when J. Peter Bergman originally prepared a discography for this book, technology has brought us new methods of reproducing music, and (rather disconcertingly) even more are promised in the near future. Many of these songs have since been issued on audio tape and CD, and almost weekly, new compilations are appearing on CDs—almost too many to keep up with. To chronicle them all would require another book. The best way to locate currently available commercial recordings is to do an internet search.

Jeanette and Nelson: "Ah, Sweet Mystery of Life." Jeanette and Nelson: "Indian Love Call." Jeanette and Nelson: "Will You Remember?" And how we remember.

Their singing together, on screen or on record, signaled the height of the erotic power of vocal music and just their names, coupled, spelled magic to millions of Americans during the dark, somber 1930s. Separately and together, their careers spanned five decades and so, coincidentally, did their recordings. From Jeanette MacDonald's 1929 recording of "Dream Lover" and "March of the Grenadiers" to Nelson's albums in the mid 1960s, they sent a very personal kind of magic into homes of countless fans.

Whether singing the sophisticated, brittle, and edgy songs from her Paramount films with Chevalier or the romantic exercises from her MGM operettas, Jeanette could always be relied upon to provide a mini-masterpiece. There was no need to see her to be aware of her facial expressions. They were present in her voice. You can still see them now, listening to her recordings. Even if you've never seen a filmed moment, her smile can be heard. Likewise her frown. When she rolls her eyes it is there in her voice. Her expressive vocal gestures are far more French and much more seductive than her Philadelphia upbringing would lead us to expect.

Nelson, on the other hand, brings power to his recordings and, only occasionally, subtlety. He knows how, in his very well-trained way, to make his songs important. What stands out in his solo recordings is his voice, not his interpretive skills. For that, you must *see* him sing, watching his mouth, his eyes, his hands and chest. He is a *visual* soloist, more than an interpretive vocalist.

Together on record, Jeanette MacDonald and Nelson Eddy are perfection. His splendid diction makes up for her technique and her emotional range improves his limitations. They manage, in each of their songs together, to create a complete and utterly realized rendition. No other singing twosome has ever matched this accomplishment.

In addition to the songs they recorded from their films and the musical plays that had given birth to these films, both recorded extensively, with Nelson Eddy far outstripping his soprano partner. Jeanette MacDonald recorded only fifty-five additional titles while Nelson Eddy recorded 216 additional titles. Most of their recordings are detailed in the discography that follows. In addition to his commercial recordings, Nelson made dozens of 16" transcription recordings intended for rebroadcast. While I have not listed these, some have now made their way onto privately issued CDs. (See Larry Kiner's *Nelson Eddy: A Bio-Discography* for more details.)

The musical tastes of the two stars varied greatly, but both seem to have enjoyed singing religious music. There is even an overlap. Both recorded "Panis Angelicus," "Agnus Dei," "Abide With Me," and two different "Ave Maria's."

Both recorded musical shows in which they hadn't appeared: Nelson in *Oklahoma!* and Jeanette in *Up in Central Park*. Nelson also recorded *The Desert Song*, which he starred in on TV.

Both singers had a taste for foreign languages: Jeanette's "Parlez Moi d'Amour," "Tes Yeux," and operatic arias; Nelson's foreign love songs in French, Italian, Russian, and other languages.

Both recorded "I Love You Truly," "The Old Refrain," and "The Holy City," while Eddy recorded two songs that Jeanette had sung in films, "Isn't It Romantic" from *Love Me Tonight* and "Smilin' Through" from *Smilin' Through*.

While Eddy made many solo recordings, he also recorded with Risë Stevens, Nadine Conner, Eleanor Steber, Dorothy Kirsten, Gale Sherwood, Doretta Morrow, Jo Stafford, and others, besides his sessions with Jeanette. Jeanette, on the other hand, recorded only a few duets with Robert Merrill for the *Up in Central Park* album.

Recording History

Jeanette recorded for RCA-Victor throughout her career. Eddy started at Victor, but switched to Columbia in 1938, which made duets of songs from their films impossible until they were reunited at RCA in 1957.

The *Victor Record Review* in January of 1944 ran an article about Jeanette that expressed the world's unvoiced opinion of their favorite soprano:

> For hearing the recorded voice of Jeanette MacDonald is much more than hearing a song projected with virtuosity and taste, with rich color and deep feeling. With every playing, there emerges the figure of an incredibly beautiful woman, vividly recalled.

Eddy's recordings also drew rave reviews during the thirties and forties, but it is a special tribute to his vocal technique that he continued to rate them into the 1960s. The *Los Angeles Herald Examiner* of 10/4/64 noted:

> Nelson Eddy continues to roll along, physically and vocally indestructible. Proof is his newest recording on the Everest label, 'Of Girls I Sing.' At the age of 63 and after 42 years of professional singing, Eddy demonstrates there has not been much change in his romantic and robust baritone—the baritone that made him America's most popular singer in the early '30s.

Other Recordings of Interest

Many people who find the operettas and musical comedies enjoyable also like to listen to full recordings of them in their own comfortable living rooms. For these people, I will also include a partial list of recordings by other artists of the full or near-full scores of the shows which MGM brought to the screen for Jeanette and Nelson.

A *Reader's Digest* record issue of some years ago, which may still be available, included the following: *The Merry Widow, Naughty Marietta, Rose-Marie, The New Moon, The Vagabond King,* and also *Die Fledermaus, Mlle. Modiste, A Waltz Dream, A Night in Venice, Babes in Toyland, The Desert Song, Blossom Time, The Student Prince, The Red Mill, Show Boat,* and *Porgy and Bess*. Appearing on these recordings are Anna Moffo, Rosalind Elias, Jeanette Scovotti, Mary Ellen Pracht, William Lewis, Peter Palmer, Richard Fredricks, Sara Endich, and Valentine Pringle.

Joan Sutherland has recorded "Indian Love Call" from *Rose-Marie*, "Vilja" from *The Merry Widow*, "My Hero" from *The Chocolate Soldier*, and "At the Balalaika" from *Balalaika*, as well as other songs from other works, on London OSA 1268 (The Golden Age of Operetta).

Risë Stevens has recorded the entire score of *The Chocolate Soldier* with Robert Merrill, Peter Palmer, Jo Sullivan, and others on RCA Victor LOP 6005 or LSO 6005.

Discography

Bitter Sweet with an English cast has been put on disc by Angel records. The number is S35814.

There is a very good recording of *The Merry Widow* on RCA Victor LOC 1094 and LSO 1094. This one features the 1964 Lincoln Center revival cast. Mario Lanza made a recording of *The Vagabond King* for RCA Victor, LM 2509 or LSC 2509. After a Broadway revival of *Sweethearts* in 1947, a recoreded version was made by Al Goodman with an entirely different cast that included Earl Wrightson, Frances Greer, Christina Lind, and Jimmy Carroll. The number is RCA Victor LK 1015.

In addition, fans of Jeanette's Paramount films will be fascinated by an LP release of the contemporary recordings of Australia's Gladys Moncrieff (known as "Our Glad"). On Australian Columbia 330SX-7626, Miss Moncrieff sang "One Hour with You," "Dream Lover," "March of the Grenadiers," and "The Merry Widow Waltz," plus non-Jeanette songs. On Australian Columbia OEK-9535 she renders "Vilia" and on 330SX-7776 she sings "Love Me Tonight," "We Will Always Be Sweethearts," and "Isn't It Romantic." In the last she duplicates Jeanette's trick of talking one line of the lyric rather than singing it.

With the advent of the CD, many more stage and film musicals have been released, including selections recorded by Jeanette and Nelson. They are not included here, but can be easily found in catalogues, on the disc display shelves in stores, and, in many cases, on line.

I hope this list will inspire you to search for recordings of your favorite shows and possibly even prompt the recording companies to reissue some of the all-time favorites, including more Jeanette MacDonald and Nelson Eddy recordings. There are still many more exciting items waiting to be let loose on a whole new generation of adoring fans.

How to Use This Guide

This discography is divided into three sections:

- Songs from Their Films*
- Jeanette MacDonald's Non-film Recordings
- Nelson Eddy's Non-film Recordings

*The first section lists all recorded songs from their films, along with the source stage works, and includes recordings by other artists such as Maurice Chevalier, Risë Stevens, and Allan Jones, who sing these songs in their roles in the MacDonald/Eddy films. Others, like Misses Steber, Kirsten, and Conner, recorded with Nelson Eddy and sing songs from the original stage scores.

Abbreviations

F–French	L–Latin
G–German	P–Polish
I–Italian	R–Russian
H–Hungarian	pf.–piano

Full names of Conductors

Robert Armbruster
Léo Arnaud
Guiseppe Bamboschek
Robert Russell Bennett
Russ Case
Ken Darby
Lehman Engel
Nathaniel Finston
Skitch Henderson
Theodore Paxson (Eddy's accompanist)
Maximillian Pilzer
David Rose
Nathaniel Shilkret
Harry Sosnick
Frieder Weissmann
Paul Weston
Hugo Winterhalter

Dates are given in American sequence: month/day/year.

Soundtrack selections are often available now on CD.

SONGS FROM THEIR FILMS

	Performer	Rec. date	Company	Conductor

AH, SWEET MYSTERY OF LIFE (*Naughty Marietta*)
    Nelson Eddy   3/11/35   RCA   Shilkret
    Jeanette MacDonald   3/20/35   RCA   Stothart
    MacDonald & Eddy   9/17/36   RCA   Shilkret
    Eddy & Nadine Conner   9/20/49   Columbia   Armbruster
    Jeanette MacDonald   11/16/50   RCA   Bennett
    MacDonald & Eddy   9/27/57   RCA   Engel

AIR DES BIJOUX – "The Jewel Song" (*San Francisco*)
  F   Jeanette MacDonald   9/15/39   RCA   Bamboschek

ALWAYS IN ALL WAYS (*Monte Carlo*) with The Rounders male quartet
    Jeanette MacDonald   8/4/30   RCA   Leroy Shield

AMERICA – "My Country, 'Tis of Thee" (*Let Freedom Ring*)
    Nelson Eddy   7/21/40   Columbia   Armbruster

AT THE BALALAIKA (*Balalaika*)
    Nelson Eddy   10/3/39   Columbia   Finston

BADINAGE – See SUMMER SERENADE

BATTLE HYMN OF'THE REPUBLILIC (*San Francisco*)
    Jeanette MacDonald   1/29/45   RCA   Pilzer

BEYOND THE BLUE HORIZON (*Monte Carlo, Follow the Boys*)
    Jeanette MacDonald   8/5/30   RCA   Leroy Shields
        with The Rounders male quartet
    Jeanette MacDonald   8/4/50   RCA   Bennett
    Jeanette MacDonald   6/5/58   RCA   Rose

CALL OF LIFE, THE / IF YOU COULD ONLY COME WITH ME (*Bitter Sweet* medley)
    Nelson Eddy   10/4/40   Columbia   Armbruster

CHANSON DU TOREADOR – "The Toreador Song" (*Balalaika*)
  F   Nelson Eddy   7/28/40   Columbia   Armbruster

CHANSON DE VILYA – See VILIA

CHANTE ITALIENNE – "Italian Street Song" (*Naughty Marietta, Broadway Serenade*)
  F   Jeanette MacDonald   3/20/35   RCA–unreleased

CHOCOLATE SOLDIER, THE (*The Chocolate Soldier*)
    Eddy & Risë Stevens   10/5/41   Columbia   Armbruster

Songs From Their Films

	Performer	Rec. date	Company	Conductor

COEUR CONTRE COEUR – "We Will Always Be Sweethearts" (*One Hour with You*)
    F   Jeanette MacDonald   4/24/32   RCA   Finston

DEAR LITTLE CAFÉ (*Bitter Sweet*)
    Nelson Eddy   10/4/40   Columbia   Armbruster

DONKEY SERENADE (*The Firefly*)
    Allan Jones   RCA   unknown
    Jeanette MacDonald   4/18/46   RCA   Case
    Allan Jones   1966   ANX 118   unknown

DOOR OF MY DREAMS (from stage version of *Rose Marie*)
    Nelson Eddy   2/1/51   Columbia   Armbruster

DREAM LOVER (*The Love Parade*)
    Jeanette MacDonald   12/11/29   RCA   Shilkret

DRIGO'S SERENADE – See LOVE SERENADE

DRINK TO ME ONLY WITH THINE EYES (*Smilin' Through*)
    Jeanette MacDonald   9/22/41   RCA   Stothart

THE DUSTY ROAD (*Let Freedom Ring*)
    Nelson Eddy   12/31/35   RCA   Shilkret

ESSAYONS D'OUBLIER – "Try to Forget" (*The Cat and the Fiddle*)
    F   Jeanette MacDonald   8/30/34   RCA   Stothart

EVENING STAR (*The Chocolate Soldier*)
    Nelson Eddy   11/1/40   Columbia   Armbruster

FAREWELL TO DREAMS (cut from *Maytime*)
    MacDonald & Eddy   9/21/36   RCA   Shilkret

FILLES DE CADIX, LES – "Maids of Cadiz" (*Maytime, Broadway Serenade, Cairo*)
    F   Jeanette MacDonald   9/13/39   RCA   Bamboschek
    F   Jeanette MacDonald   8/4/50   RCA   Bennett

FORGIVE (*The Chocolate Soldier*)
    Eddy & Risë Stevens   10/5/41   Columbia   Armbruster

GIANNINA MIA (*The Firefly*)
    Allan Jones   RCA   unknown
    Jeanette MacDonald   4/16/46   RCA   Case

GIRL ON THE PROW, THE (stage version of *New Moon*)
    Eleanor Steber   9/?/50   Columbia   Arnaud

Performer	Rec. date	Company	Conductor

GORGEOUS ALEXANDER (stage version of *New Moon*)
    Nelson Eddy — 9/7/50 — Columbia — Arnaud

HOLY CITY, THE (*San Francisco*)
    Jeanette MacDonald — 1/29/45 — RCA — Pilzer
    Nelson Eddy — 8/10/50 — Columbia — Arnaud

I LOVE HIM (stage version of *Rose Marie*)
    Eddy/Dorothy Kirsten — 2/1/51 — Columbia — Arnaud

I LOVE YOU SO – "Merry Widow Waltz" (*The Merry Widow*)
  F Jeanette MacDonald — 2/27/33 — Disque Gramophone — M. Vervily

I MARRIED AN ANGEL (*I Married an Angel*)
    Nelson Eddy — 2/1/42 — Columbia — Armbruster

IF I WERE KING (*The Vagabond King*)
    Dennis King — 1930 — RCA

IF YOU COULD ONLY COME WITH ME – See CALL OF LIFE (*Bitter Sweet*)

IF YOU WERE MINE ALONE – "Romance" by Rubinstein (*The Sun Comes Up*)
    Jeanette MacDonald — 5/18/49 — RCA — Armbruster

IL ÉTAIT UN R01 DE THULE – from *Faust* (*San Francisco*)
  F Jeanette MacDonald — 9/15/39 — RCA — Bamboschek

I'LL SEE YOU AGAIN (*Bitter Sweet*)
    Nelson Eddy — 10/14/40 — Columbia — Armbruster
    Jeanette MacDonald — 12/17/47 — RCA — Armbruster

I'LL TELL THE MAN IN THE STREET (*I Married an Angel*)
    Nelson Eddy — 2/1/42 — Columbia — Armbruster

I'M AN APACHE – See POOR APACHE

I'M FALLING IN LOVE WITH SOMEONE (*Naughty Marietta*)
    Nelson Eddy — 3/11/35 — RCA — Shilkret
    Nelson Eddy — 9/20/49 — Columbia — Armbruster

IN THE STILL OF THE NIGHT (*Rosalie*)
    Nelson Eddy — 12/16/57 — Columbia — Rose

INDIAN LOVE CALL (*Rose Marie*)
    MacDonald & Eddy — 9/17/36 — RCA — Shilkret
    Jeanette MacDonald — 8/4/50 — RCA Vic — Bennett
    Eddy & Dorothy Kirsten — 2/5/51 — Columbia — Arnaud
    MacDonald & Eddy — 9/27/57 — RCA — Engel

Songs From Their Films

	Performer	Rec. date	Company	Conductor

ISN'T IT ROMANTIC (*Love Me Tonight*) – See also N'EST-CE PAS POETIQUE
    Jeanette MacDonald   7/5/32   RCA   Finston
    Eddy & Gale Sherwood   1964?   Everest   unknown

IT NEVER, NEVER CAN BE LOVE (from stage version of *Naughty Marietta*)
    Eddy & Nadine Conner   9/20/49   Columbia   Armbruster

ITALIAN STREET SONG (*Naughty Marietta, Broadway Serenade*)
    Jeanette MacDonald   3/20/35   RCA   Stothart
    Jeanette MacDonald   1/31/45   RCA   Pilzer
    Nadine Conner   9/20/49   Columbia   Armbruster
    Jeanette MacDonald   6/5/58   RCA   Rose

J'AIME D'AMOUR ("Merry Widow Waltz") – See also I LOVE YOU SO
  F   Jeanette MacDonald   2/27/33   Disque Gramophone   M. Bervily

JE SUIS UN MECHANT – "Poor Apache" (*Love Me Tonight*)
  F   Maurice Chevalier   6/29/32   RCA

JE VEUX VIVRE DANS CE REVE – "Juliet's Waltz" (*Rose Marie*)
  F   Jeanette MacDonald   9/15/39   RCA   Bamboschek

JERUSALEM – See HOLY CITY (*San Francisco*)

JEWEL SONG – See AIR DES BIJOUX (*San Francisco*)

JULIET'S WALTZ – See JE VEUX VIVRE DANS CE REVE (*Rose Marie*)

KERRY DANCE, THE (*Smilin' Through*)
    Jeanette MacDonald   9/22/41   RCA   Stothart

LAND OF HOPE AND GLORY (*Smilin' Through*)
    Jeanette MacDonald   9/22/41   RCA   Stothart

LAND OF SKY BLUE WATERS (*Cairo*)
    Jeanette MacDonald   9/11/39   RCA   Bamboschek

LES FILLES DE CADIX – See FILLES DE CADIX, LES (*Maytime*)

LITTLE LOVE, A LITTLE KISS, A (*Smilin' Through*)
    Jeanette MacDonald   9/22/41   RCA   Stothart

LITTLE WORK-A-DAY WORLD (cut from *I Married an Angel*)
    Nelson Eddy   2/1/42   Columbia   Armbruster

LIVE FOR TODAY (stage version of *Naughty Marietta*)
    Eddy & Nadine Conner   9/13/49   Columbia   Armbruster

Performer	Rec. date	Company	Conductor

LOVE IS THE TIME *(Northwest Outpost)*
    Nelson Eddy   4/27/44   Columbia   Armbruster

LOVE ME TONIGHT *(Love Me Tonight)*
    Jeanette MacDonald   7/5/34   RCA   Finston

LOVE SERENADE – *"Drigo's Serenade" (Let Freedom Ring)*
    Nelson Eddy   8/1960   Everest   Henderson

LOVER, COME BACK TO ME *(New Moon)*
    Jeanette MacDonald   9/16/39   RCA   Bamboschek
    Nelson Eddy   7/14/40   Columbia   Finston
    Eddy & Eleanor Steber   9/9/50   Columbia   Arnaud

MAGIC OF YOUR LOVE *(Balalaika)*
    Nelson Eddy   10/19/39   Columbia   Finston

MARCH OF THE GRENADIERS *(The Love Parade)*
    Jeanette MacDonald   12/11/29   RCA   Shilkret

MARIACHE *(The Girl of the Golden West)*
    Nelson Eddy   3/14/38   RCA   Stothart

MARIANNE *(New Moon)*
    Eddy & Eleanor Steber   9/7/50   Columbia   Arnaud

MERRY WIDOW WALTZ – See I LOVE YOU SO

MIMI *(Love Me Tonight)*
    Maurice Chevalier   6/29/32   RCA

MON COCKTAIL D'AMOUR – "My Love Parade" *(The Love Parade)*
    Maurice Chevalier   1929?   World Record Club, SH 156

MOUNTIES, THE *(Rose Marie)*
    Nelson Eddy   12/31/35   RCA   Shilkret
    Nelson Eddy   2/12/51   Columbia   Arnaud

MY HERO *(The Chocolate Soldier)*
    Eddy & Risë Stevens   10/6/41   Columbia   Armbruster

MY LOVE PARADE *(The Love Parade)* – See also MON COCKTAIL D'AMOUR
    Maurice Chevalier   1930   RCA   unknown

NAUGHTY MARIETTA (stage version of *Naughty Marietta*)
    Nadine Conner   9/20/49   Columbia   Armbruster

N'EST-CE PAS POETIQUE – "Isn't It Romantic" *(Love Me Tonight)*
    F   Jeanette MacDonald   7/5/32   RCA   Finston

Songs From Their Films

Performer	Rec. date	Company	Conductor

NEARER AND DEARER (*Northwest Outpost*)
    Nelson Eddy   4/26/47   Columbia   Armbruster

NEARER MY GOD TO THEE (*San Francisco*)
    Jeanette MacDonald   1/29/45   RCA   Pilzer
    Nelson Eddy   4/2/46   Columbia   Pilzer

'NEATH THE SOUTHERN MOON (*Naughty Marietta*)
    Nelson Eddy   3/11/35   RCA   Shilkret
    Nelson Eddy   9/20/49   Columbia   Armbruster

NOBODY'S USING IT NOW (*The Love Parade*) – See also PERSONNE NE S'EN SERT MAINTENANT
    Maurice Chevalier   1930   RCA   unknown

NONE BUT THE LONELY HEART (*Broadway Serenade*)
    Nelson Eddy   8/31/39   Columbia   Finston

OBEY YOUR HEART – See WHO ARE WE TO SAY?

OH, CETTE MITZI – "Oh! That Mitzi!" (*One Hour with You*)
  F   Maurice Chevalier   World Record Club, SH 156

OH, EVENING STAR – See EVENING STAR

OH! THAT MITZI! (*One Hour with You*)
    Maurice Chevalier   2/24/32   RCA   unknown

ONE HOUR WITH YOU (*One Hour with You*)
    Jeanette MacDonald   4/24/32   RCA   Finston
    Donald Novis and the   1932   Victor   Grier
      Jimmie Grier Orchestra

ONE KISS (*New Moon*)
    Jeanette MacDonald   9/16/39   RCA   Bamboschek
    Eleanor Steber   9/7/50   Columbia   Arnaud

ONE MORE MILE TO GO (*Northwest Outpost*)
    Nelson Eddy   4/17/47   Columbia   Armbruster

ONLY A ROSE (*The Vagabond King*)
    Jeanette MacDonald   8/2/50   RCA   Bennett

OUVRE TON COEUR (*Smilin' Through*)
  F   Jeanette MacDonald   9/22/41   RCA   Stothart

PARIS, JE T'AIME D'AMOUR – "Paris, Stay the Same" (*The Love Parade*)
  F   Maurice Chevalier   4/10/30   RCA   unknown

Performer	Rec. date	Company	Conductor

PARIS, STAY THE SAME (*The Love Parade*)
    Maurice Chevalier   1930   RCA   unknown

PERSONNE NE S'EN SERT MAINTENANT – "Nobody's Using It Now" (*The Love Parade*)
  F   Maurice Chevalier   1930   RCA   unknown

POOR APACHE (*Love Me Tonight*) – See also JE SUIS UN MECHANT
    Maurice Chevalier   1933   RCA   unknown

PRETTY THINGS (Stage version of *Rose Marie*)
    Dorothy Kirsten   2/5/51   Columbia   Arnaud

QU'AURIEZ VOUS FAIT – "What Would You Do?" (*One Hour with You*)
  F   Maurice Chevalier   World Record Club, SH 156

RAINDROPS ON A DRUM (*Northwest Outpost*)
    Nelson Eddy   3/26/47   Columbia   Armbruster

RIDE, COSSACK, RIDE (*Balalaika*)
    Nelson Eddy   9/27/47   Columbia   Finston

ROMANCE by Rubinstein – See IF YOU WERE MINE

ROSALIE (*Rosalie*)
    Nelson Eddy   12/14/57   RCA   Rose

ROSE MARIE (*Rose Marie*)
    Nelson Eddy   12/31/35   RCA   Shilkret
    Nelson Eddy   2/12/51   Columbia   Arnaud
    Nelson Eddy   12/16/57   RCA   Rose

RUSSIAN EASTER HYMN (*Northwest Outpost*)
    Nelson Eddy   4/2/47   Columbia   Armbruster

SAN FRANCISCO (*San Francisco*)
    Jeanette MacDonald   11/16/50   RCA   Bennett

SENORITA (*The Girl of the Golden West*)
    Nelson Eddy   3/22/38   RCA   Stothart

SERENADE by Drigo – See LOVE SERENADE

SHADOWS ON THE MOON (*The Girl of the Golden West*)
    Nelson Eddy   3/14/38   RCA   Stothart

SHORT'NIN' BREAD (*Make Mine Music*)
    Nelson Eddy   2/1/42   Columbia   Armbruster

Songs From Their Films

Performer	Rec. date	Company	Conductor

SILENT NIGHT (*Balalaika*)
    Nelson Eddy   11/1/40   Columbia   Armbruster
    Nelson Eddy   7/21/51   Columbia   Weston

SMILIN' THROUGH (*Smilin' Through*)
    Jeanette MacDonald   9/22/41   RCA   Stothart
    Nelson Eddy   6/24/37   RCA   Stothart

SOFTLY, AS IN A MORNING SUNRISE (*New Moon*)
    Nelson Eddy   7/14/40   Columbia   Finston
    Nelson Eddy   9/15/50   Columbia   Arnaud

SOLDIERS OF FORTUNE (*The Girl of the Golden West*)
    Eddy & quartet   3/22/38   RCA   Stothart

SONG OF LOVE (Stage production of *Blossom Time*)
    MacDonald & Eddy   9/21/36   RCA   Shilkret

SONG OF THE FLEA (*The Chocolate Soldier*)
    Nelson Eddy   1/18/42   Columbia   Armbruster

SONG OF THE MOUNTIES – See MOUNTIES, THE (*Rose Marie*)

SONG OF THE VAGABONDS (*The Vagabond King*)
    Dennis King   1927   RCA   unknown

SONG OF THE VOLGA BOATMAN (*Balalaika*)
    Nelson Eddy   10/13/39   Columbia   Finston

SONGS MY MOTHER TAUGHT ME (*The Sun Comes Up*)
    Jeanette MacDonald   5/18/49   RCA   Armbruster

SPRING IS HERE (*I Married an Angel*)
    Nelson Eddy   2/1/42   Columbia   Armbruster

SPRINGTIDE – Grieg (*Three Daring Daughters*)
    Jeanette MacDonald   12/18/47   RCA   Armbruster

STOUT HEARTED MEN (*New Moon*)
    Nelson Eddy   7/14/40   Columbia   Finston
    Nelson Eddy   9/15/50   Columbia   Arnaud
    Nelson Eddy   12/16/57   RCA   Rose

SUMMER SERENADE – "Badinage" (*Sweethearts*)
    Jeanette MacDonald   1/31/45   RCA   Pilzer

Performer	Rec. date	Company	Conductor

SUN-UP TO SUNDOWN (*The Girl of the Golden West*)
Eddy & male quartet	3/22/38	RCA	Stothart

SWEETHEARTS WALTZ (*Sweethearts, Three Daring Daughters*)
Jeanette MacDonald	4/18/46	RCA	Case

SYMPATHY (Strauss) (*The Chocolate Soldier*)
Eddy & Risë Stevens	10/5/41	Columbia	Armbruster

TELL ME WITH YOUR EYES (*Northwest Outpost*)
Nelson Eddy	4/26/47	Columbia	Armbruster

TES YEUX (*Rose Marie, The Sun Comes Up*)
Jeanette MacDonald	5/18/49	RCA	Armbruster

TI–RA–LA–LA (*The Chocolate Soldier*)
Risë Stevens	10/5/41	Columbia	Armbruster

TOKAY (*Bitter Sweet*)
Nelson Eddy	10/4/40	Columbia	Armbruster

TONIGHT WILL TEACH ME TO FORGET – "The Diary Song" (*The Merry Widow*)
	Jeanette MacDonald	8/30/34	RCA	Stothart
F	Jeanette MacDonald	8/30/34	RCA	Stothart

TOREADOR SONG – See CHANSON DU TOREADOR

TOTEM TOM TOM (*Rose Marie*)
Eddy/Dorothy Kirsten	2/5/51	Columbia	Arnaud

TRAMP, TRAMP, TRAMP (*Naughty Marietta*)
Nelson Eddy	3/11/35	RCA	Shilkret
Nelson Eddy	9/13/49	Columbia	Armbruster

TRY TO FORGET (*The Cat and the Fiddle*) – See also ESSAYONS D'OUBLIER
	Jeanette MacDonald	9/20/34	RCA	Stothart
F	Jeanette MacDonald	9/20/34	RCA	Stothart

UN BEL DI VEDREMO (*Broadway Serenade, The Sun Comes Up*)
I	Jeanette MacDonald	9/11/46	RCA	Weissmann

UNE HEURE PRÈS DE TOI – "One Hour with You" (*One Hour with You*)
F	Jeanette MacDonald	4/24/32	RCA	Finston

VEUX–TU M'AIMER – "Love Me Tonight" (*Love Me Tonight*)
F	Jeanette MacDonald	7/5/32	RCA	Finston

Songs From Their Films

	Performer	Rec. date	Company	Conductor

VILIA (*The Merry Widow*)
	F	Jeanette MacDonald	2/27/33	Disque Gramophone	M. Bervily
		Jeanette MacDonald	8/14/34	RCA	Stothart
		Jeanette MacDonald	5/18/49	RCA	Armbruster

WALTZ HUGUETTE (*The Vagabond King*)
Susan Hayward	1955	MGM	Charles Henderson

WALTZ SONG – See JE VEUX VIVRE DANS CE REVE (*Rose Marie*)

WALTZ from *Der Rosenkavalier* – See WHERE THERE'S LOVE (*Three Daring Daughters*)

WANTING YOU (*New Moon*)
Nelson Eddy	7/14/40	Columbia	Finston
Eddy & Eleanor Steber	9/9/50	Columbia	Arnaud
MacDonald & Eddy	9/27/57	RCA	Engel

WE WILL ALWAYS BE SWEETHEARTS (*One Hour with You*)
Jeanette MacDonald	4/24/32	RCA	Finston

WHALE WHO WANTED TO SING AT THE MET, THE (*Make Mine Music*)
Nelson Eddy	6/5/46	Columbia	Armbruster & Ken Darby

WHAT WOULD YOU DO? (*One Hour with You*)
Maurice Chevalier	1932	RCA	unknown

WHERE THERE'S LOVE – "Der Rosenkavalier Waltz" (*Three Daring Daughters*)
Jeanette MacDonald	12/18/47	RCA	Armbruster

WHILE MY LADY SLEEPS (*The Chocolate Soldier*)
Nelson Eddy	10/6/41	Columbia	Armbruster
Nelson Eddy	12/14/57	RCA	Rose

WHO ARE WE TO SAY? – "Obey Your Heart" (*The Girl of the Golden West*)
Nelson Eddy	3/22/38	RCA	Stothart

WHY SHOULDN'T WE? (stage version of *Rose Marie*)
Eddy/Dorothy Kirsten	2/5/51	Columbia	Arnaud

WILL YOU REMEMBER? (*Maytime*)
MacDonald & Eddy	9/21/36	RCA	Shilkret
Jeanette MacDonald	11/16/50	RCA	Bennett
MacDonald & Eddy	9/27/57	RCA	Engel

ZIGEUNER (*Bitter Sweet*)
Jeanette MacDonald	12/18/47	RCA	Armbruster

JEANETTE MACDONALD'S NON-FILM RECORDINGS

Performer	Rec. date	Company	Conductor
ABIDE WITH ME (with Victor Chorus)			
Jeanette MacDonald	1/29/45	RCA	Pilzer
AGNUS DEI (with Victor Chorus)			
Jeanette MacDonald	1/31/45	RCA	Pilzer
ANNIE LAURIE / COMIN' THROUGH THE RYE			
Jeanette MacDonald	9/11/39	RCA	Bamboschek
AVE MARIA (Bach/Gounod)			
L Jeanette MacDonald	9/13/39	RCA	Bamboschek
BEAU SOIR (Debussy)			
F Jeanette MacDonald	12/17/47	RCA	Armbruster
BIG BACKYARD OF THE CITY, THE (from *Up in Central Park* with Robert Merrill)			
MacDonald/Merrill	2/3/45	RCA	Bennett
BREEZE AND I, THE			
Jeanette MacDonald	9/28/57	RCA	Engel
CAROUSEL IN THE PARK (from *Up in Central Park*)			
Jeanette MacDonald	2/3/45	RCA	Bennett
CINDERELLA (album with Verna Felton, others)			
Jeanette MacDonald	1946	RCA	Case
CIRIBIRIBIN			
Jeanette MacDonald	8/4/50	RCA	Bennett
CLOSE AS PAGES IN A BOOK (from *Up in Central Park* with Robert Merrill)			
MacDonald/Merrill	2/3/45	RCA	Bennett
COMIN' THROUGH THE RYE / ANNIE LAURIE			
Jeanette MacDonald	9/11/39	RCA	Bamboschek
DEAR WHEN I MET YOU (from *Viktoria and Her Hussars*)			
Jeanette MacDonald	9/25/31	HMV	Ray Noble
DEPUIS LE JOUR (from *Louise* by Charpentier)			
F Jeanette MacDonald	9/13/39	RCA	Bamboschek
DO NOT GO MY LOVE			
Jeanette MacDonald	9/11/39	RCA	Bamboschek, pf.

Jeanette MacDonald's Non-Film Recordings

Performer	Rec. date	Company	Conductor
FIREMAN'S BRIDE, THE (from *Up in Central Park*)			
Jeanette MacDonald	2/3/45	RCA	Bennett
GOOD NIGHT (from *Viktoria and Her Hussars*)			
Jeanette MacDonald	9/25/31	HMV	Ray Noble
I LOVE YOU TRULY			
Jeanette MacDonald	12/17/47	RCA	Armbruster
IT DOESN'T COST YOU ANYTHING TO DREAM (from *Up in Central Park*)			
Jeanette MacDonald	2/3/45	RCA	Bennett
LET ME ALWAYS SING / LAND OF SKY BLUE WATERS			
Jeanette MacDonald	9/11/39	RCA	Bamboschek
MAN I LOVE, THE (cut from both *Strike up the Band* and *Lady Be Good*)			
Jeanette MacDonald	12/18/47	RCA	Armbruster
MI CHIAMANO MIMI (from *La Bohème* by Puccini)			
I Jeanette MacDonald	10/11/46	RCA	Weissmann
OH, LORD, MOST HOLY – "Panis Angelicus"			
Jeanette MacDonald	1/29/45	RCA	Pilzer
OLD REFRAIN, THE			
Jeanette MacDonald	8/2/50	RCA	Bennett
ONE ALONE (from *The Desert Song*)			
Jeanette MacDonald	11/9/50	RCA	Bennett
ONE NIGHT OF LOVE (from the film *One Night of Love*)			
Jeanette MacDonald	8/4/50	RCA	Bennett
PANIS ANGELICUS – See OH, LORD, MOST HOLY			
PARDON MADAME (from *Viktoria and Her Hussars*)			
Jeanette MacDonald	9/25/31	HMV	Ray Noble
PARLEZ MOI D'AMOUR			
F Jeanette MacDonald	11/9/50	RCA	Bennett
PERFECT DAY, A			
Jeanette MacDonald	12/17/47	RCA	Armbruster
REVIENS			
F Jeanette MacDonald	9/25/31	HMV	Ray Noble
ROMANCE by Debussy			
F Jeanette MacDonald	12/17/47	RCA	Armbruster

Performer	Rec. date	Company	Conductor

ROMANY LIFE (from *The Fortune Teller*)
    Jeanette MacDonald   4/18/46   RCA   Case

SMOKE GETS IN YOUR EYES (from *Roberta*)
    Jeanette MacDonald   4/18/46   RCA   Case

SUMMERTIME (from *Porgy and Bess*)
    Jeanette MacDonald   12/18/47   RCA   Armbruster

THEY DIDN'T BELIEVE ME (from *The Girl from Utah*)
    Jeanette MacDonald   4/16/46   RCA   Case

WHEN I HAVE SUNG MY SONGS
    Jeanette MacDonald   9/11/39   RCA   Bamboschek, pf.

WHEN YOU WALK IN THE ROOM – (from *Up in Central Park* with Robert Merrill)
    Jeanette MacDonald   2/3/45   RCA   Bennett

WHEN YOU'RE AWAY (from *The Only Girl*)
    Jeanette MacDonald   11/9/50   RCA   Bennett

NELSON EDDY'S NON-FILM RECORDINGS

	Performer	Rec. date	Company	Conductor

ABIDE WITH ME
    Nelson Eddy   4/2/46   Columbia   Paxson

ADESTE FIDELES
    Nelson Eddy   11/1/40   Columbia   Armbruster

ADESTE FIDELES / O LITTLE TOWN OF BETHLEHEM – Medley
    Nelson Eddy   8/2/51   Columbia   Weston

AGNUS DEI
    Nelson Eddy   8/10/50   Columbia   Arnaud

ALL SOULS DAY (Richard Strauss' Allerseelen)
  G   Nelson Eddy   10/19/39   Columbia   Finston

ALONE TOGETHER
    Eddy, Gale Sherwood   c. 1964   Everest   unknown

AMERICA – "My Country, Tis of Thee"
    Nelson Eddy   7/21/40   Columbia   Armbruster

AND THIS IS MY BELOVED (from *Kismet*)
    Eddy, Gale Sherwood   8/1960   Everest   Sosnick

ANGELINA BAKER – See OLD FOLKS AT HOME

AS YEARS GO BY
    Nelson Eddy   12/1960   Everest   Henderson

AT DAWNING
    Nelson Eddy   6/29/37   RCA   Shilkret
    Nelson Eddy   7/24/50   Columbia   Arnaud

AUF WEIDERSEHEN (from *The Blue Paradise*)
    Nelson Eddy   6/12/35   RCA   Shilkret

AVE MARIA (Schubert)
  L   Nelson Eddy   2/5/45   Columbia   Armbruster
      (Eddy had recorded this song 2 months earlier on 12/10/44 with Armbruster. It is presumed the issued recording is the second version.)

AWAY IN A MANGER (Murray) / GOD REST YE MERRY GENTLEMEN – Medley
    Nelson Eddy   8/2/51   Columbia   Weston

BEAUTIFUL DREAMER / DON'T BET YOUR MONEY ON DE SHANGHAI – Stephen Foster Medley
    Nelson Eddy   9/22/47   Columbia   Armbruster

Performer	Rec. date	Company	Conductor
BECAUSE			
Nelson Eddy	12/3/44	Columbia	Armbruster
Nelson Eddy	8/10/50	Columbia	Arnaud
BERCEUSE (from *Jocelyn*)			
Nelson Eddy	8/10/50	Columbia	Arnaud
BIANCA			
Nelson Eddy	12/?//60	Everest	Henderson
BLACK-EYED SUSIE – See PRETTY BLACK-EYED SUSIE			
BLIND PLOUGHMAN, THE			
Nelson Eddy	11/7/40	Columbia	Armbruster
BLUE TANGO			
Eddy, Gale Sherwood	c. 1964	Everest	unknown
BOOTS			
Nelson Eddy	1/19/42	Columbia	Armbruster
BY THE WATERS OF THE MINNETONKA			
Nelson Eddy	6/21/37	RCA	Paxson
CAMPTOWN RACES, DE – See OH BOYS, CARRY ME ALONG – Stephen Foster Medley			
CAPTAIN STRATTON'S FANCY			
Nelson Eddy	8/29/49	Columbia	Armbruster
CHARMAINE			
Nelson Eddy	12/?/60	Everest	Henderson
CHILD'S EVENING PRAYER			
Nelson Eddy	1/18/42	Columbia	Armbruster
CHRIST HAD A GARDEN			
Nelson Eddy	1/18/42	Columbia	Armbruster
COME WHERE MY LOVE LIES DREAMING / THE MERRY, MERRY MONTH OF MAY – Stephen Foster Medley			
Nelson Eddy	7/14/47	Columbia	Armbruster
COMRADES FILL NO GLASS FOR ME – See SWEET EMERALD ISLE – Stephen Foster Medley			
CORK LEG, THE			
Nelson Eddy	8/29/49	Columbia	Armbruster
DANNY BOY			
Nelson Eddy	12/3/45	Columbia	Armbruster

	Performer	Rec. date	Company	Conductor

DANSANDO O SAMBA
Nelson Eddy — 9/17/49 — Columbia — Armbruster

DANSE MACABRE
Nelson Eddy — 7/28/40 — Columbia — Armbruster

DE CAMPTOWN RACES – See OH BOYS, CARRY ME ALONG – Stephen Foster Medley

DECK THE HALLS
Nelson Eddy — 7/21/51 — Columbia — Weston

DEDICATION (Richard Strauss' Zueignung)
G Nelson Eddy — 10/19/39 — Columbia — Finston

DEEP IN MY HEART, DEAR (from *The Student Prince*)
Eddy, Risë Stevens — 8/18/42 — Columbia — Armbruster

DEEP RIVER
Nelson Eddy — 6/29/37 — RCA — Shilkret

DELILAH
Nelson Eddy — 12/60 — Everest — Henderson

DESERT SONG, THE (from *The Desert Song*)
Eddy, Doretta Morrow — 5/8/58 — Columbia — Engel

DOLLY DAY – See MY OLD KENTUCKY HOME – Stephen Foster Medley

DOLORES
Nelson Eddy — 12/1960 — Everest — unknown

DON JUAN'S SERENADE by Tchaikovsky
F Nelson Eddy — 7/28/40 — Columbia — Armbruster

DON'T BET YOUR MONEY ON DE SHANGHAI – See BEAUTIFUL DREAMER – Stephen Foster Medley

DREAM, A
Nelson Eddy — 6/29/37 — RCA — Shilkret
Nelson Eddy — 7/20/50 — Columbia — Arnaud

DRINKING SONG (from *The Student Prince*)
Nelson Eddy — 8/18/47 — Columbia — Armbruster

EASTERN AND WESTERN LOVE (from *The Desert Song*) – See also FINALE – Medley
Eddy, Wesley Dalton, Lee Cass — 5/8/52 — Columbia — Engel

FAIRY BELLE – See OPEN THY LATTICE, LOVE – Stephen Foster Medley

Performer	Rec. date	Company	Conductor

FARMER AND THE COWMAN, THE (from *Oklahoma!*)
    Nelson Eddy   5/12/52   Columbia   Engel

FINALE (from *The Desert Song*) – See also EASTERN AND WESTERN LOVE – Medley
    Eddy, Doretta Morrow   5/8/52   Columbia   Engel

FIRST NOWELL, THE – See HARK THE HERALD ANGELS SING

FLING OUT THE BANNER / NOW THE DAY IS OVER – Medley
    Nelson Eddy   4/30/46   Columbia   Paxson

FROG WENT A-COURTIN'
    Nelson Eddy   12/3/44   Columbia   Armbruster

FULL MOON AND EMPTY ARMS
    Nelson Eddy   12/60   Everest   Henderson

GENTLE ANNIE / GIVE US THIS DAY OUR DAILY BREAD – Stephen Foster Medley
    Nelson Eddy   9/22/47   Columbia   Armbruster

GHOST RIDERS IN THE SKY – See RIDERS IN THE SKY

GIVE US THIS DAY OUR DAILY BREAD – See GENTLE ANNIE – Stephen Foster Medley

GOD REST YE MERRY GENTLEMEN – See AWAY IN THE MANGER

GOLDEN DAYS (from *The Student Prince*)
    Nelson Eddy   8/11/47   Columbia   Armbruster

GOOD KING WENCESLAS
    Nelson Eddy   7/16/51   Columbia   Weston

GOPAK (Mussorgsky)
  R   Nelson Eddy   1/18/42   Columbia   Armbruster

GREAT DAY
    Nelson Eddy   11/19/44   Columbia   Armbruster

HARK, HARK, MY SOUL
    Nelson Eddy   3/19/46   Columbia   Paxson

HARK THE HERALD ANGELS SING / THE FIRST NOWELL – Medley
    Nelson Eddy   8/2/51   Columbia   Weston

HILLS OF HOME, THE
    Nelson Eddy   6/29/37   RCA   Shilkret

HOLY ART THOU (Handel)
    Nelson Eddy   9/10/50   Columbia   Arnaud

Nelson Eddy's Non-Film Recordings

Performer	Rec. date	Company	Conductor

HOPAK – See GOPAK

I AM AS BRAVE AS JOHN – "Sailormen"
    Nelson Eddy   8/22/49   Columbia   Armbruster

I AM THE MONARCH OF THE SEA (from *H.M.S. Pinafore*)
    Nelson Eddy   11/29/40   Columbia   Armbruster

I CONCENTRATE ON YOU (from the film *Broadway Melody of 1940*)
    Eddy, Gale Sherwood   c. 1964   Everest   unknown

I LOVE YOU (Grieg, from *Song of Norway*)
    Nelson Eddy   11/19/44   Columbia   Armbruster

I LOVE YOU (Porter)
    Eddy, Gale Sherwood   8/60   Everest   Sosnick

I LOVE YOU TRULY
    Nelson Eddy   5/28/37   Unissued   unknown
    Nelson Eddy   7/24/50   Columbia   Arnaud
    Eddy, Jo Stafford   2/12/51   Columbia   Weston

I ONLY HAVE EYES FOR YOU (from the film *Dames*)
    Eddy, Gale Sherwood   c. 1964   Everest   unknown

I WANT A KISS (from *The Desert Song*)
    Eddy, Doretta Morrow   5/8/58   Columbia   Engel

I WILL BE TRUE TO THEE by Stephen Foster
    Nelson Eddy   8/4/47   Columbia   Armbruster

IF I LOVED YOU (from *Carousel*)
    Eddy, Gale Sherwood   8/1960   Everest   Sosnick

IF YOU ARE BUT A DREAM
    Nelson Eddy   12/1960   Everest   Henderson

IF YOU GIVE ME YOUR ATTENTION / WHENE'ER I SPOKE (from *Princess Ida*)
    Nelson Eddy   4/16/46   Columbia   Armbruster

IF YOU'RE ANXIOUS FOR TO SHINE (from *Patience*)
    Nelson Eddy   12/10/44   Columbia   Armbruster

IF YOU'VE ONLY GOT A MOUSTACHE – See SWEET EMERALD ISLE – Medley

ISN'T THIS A NIGHT FOR LOVE
    Nelson Eddy   12/16/57   RCA   David Rose

Performer	Rec. date	Company	Conductor

IT'S LOVE, LOVE, LOVE
Nelson Eddy — 12/60 — Everest — Henderson

JEANNIE WITH THE LIGHT BROWN HAIR (Stephen Foster)
Nelson Eddy — 8/4/47 — Columbia — Armbruster

JENNY JUNE (Stephen Foster)
Nelson Eddy — 8/4/47 — Columbia — Armbruster

JERUM! JERUM! (from *Die Meistersinger*)
Nelson Eddy — 11/7/40 — Columbia — Armbruster

JINGLE BELLS – See JOY TO THE WORLD

JOY TO THE WORLD / JINGLE BELLS Medley
Nelson Eddy — 7/16/51 — Columbia — Weston

JUST A-WEARYIN' FOR YOU
Nelson Eddy — 8/2/51 — Columbia — Arnaud

JUST FOR TONIGHT
Eddy, Gale Sherwood — 8/1960 — Everest — Sosnick

JUST WE TWO (from *The Student Prince*)
Eddy, Risë Stevens — 8/11/47 — Columbia — Arnaud

KASHMIRI SONG (from *Indian Love Lyrics*)
Nelson Eddy — 8/16/39 — Columbia — Finston

KIT KENE ELVENNI – "Which Girl Should I Marry?"
H Nelson Eddy — 9/10/49 — Columbia — Armbruster

KUSS, DER
G Nelson Eddy — 9/10/49 — Columbia — Armbruster

LAMP IS LOW, THE
Nelson Eddy — 12/1960 — Everest — unknown

LAUGHING SONG, THE
Nelson Eddy — 8/29/49 — Columbia — Armbruster

LAURA
Nelson Eddy — 12/1960 — Everest — unknown

LEAD, KINDLY LIGHT
Nelson Eddy — 4/23/46 — Columbia — Paxson

LEGEND – See CHRIST HAD A GARDEN

Nelson Eddy's Non-Film Recordings

Performer	Rec. date	Company	Conductor

LESS THAN THE DUST (from *Indian Love Lyrics*)
    Nelson Eddy   8/16/39   Columbia   Finston

LET LOVE GO – See EASTER AND WESTERN LOVE (from *The Desert Song*)

LORD CHANCELOR'S NIGHTMARE SONG (from *Iolanthe*)
    Nelson Eddy   11/29/40   Columbia   Armbruster

LORD'S PRAYER, THE
    Nelson Eddy   7/31/40   Columbia   Armbruster
    Nelson Eddy   9/6/40   Columbia D   Armbruster

LOST CHORD, THE
    Nelson Eddy   4/21/40   Columbia   Armbruster

LOUISIANA BELLE – See OLD DOG TRAY – Stephen Foster Medley

LOVE AND MARRIAGE (from the TV Special *Our Town*)
    Eddy, Gale Sherwood   c.1964   Everest   Sosnick

LOVE'S OLD SWEET SONG
    Nelson Eddy   6/12/35   RCA   Shilkret

MAJOR GENERAL'S SONG (from *H.M.S. Pinafore*)
    Nelson Eddy   11/28/40   Columbia   Armbruster

MARIA (from *West Side Story*)
    Nelson Eddy   12/1960   Everest   Henderson

MARTA
    Nelson Eddy   12/1960   Everest   Henderson

MASSA'S IN DE COLD, COLD GROUND / NELLY BLY – Stephen Foster Medley
    Nelson Eddy   9/8/47   Columbia   Armbruster

MATUS MOYA MATUS
    P   Nelson Eddy   10/10/49   Columbia   Armbruster

MERRY, MERRY MONTH OF MAY, THE – See COME WHERE MY LOVE LIES DREAMING –
    Stephen Foster Medley

MOTHER CAREY
    Nelson Eddy   1/19/42   Columbia   Armbruster

MULE TRAIN
    Nelson Eddy   10/30/49   Columbia   Winterhalter

MY ALICE FAIR ("Sweetly She Sleeps") / **UNCLE NED** – Stephen Foster Medley
    Nelson Eddy   8/25/47   Columbia   Armbruster

Performer	Rec. date	Company	Conductor

MY BOY, YOU MAY TAKE IT FROM ME (from *Ruddigore*)
    Nelson Eddy   4/16/46   Columbia   Armbruster

MY BRUDDER GUM – See OLD BLACK JOE

MY MESSAGE – "I Sent You Red Roses"
    Nelson Eddy   12/3/44   Columbia   Armbruster

MY NAME IS JOHN WELLINGTON WELLS (from *The Sorcerer*)
    Nelson Eddy   11/28/40   Columbia   Armbruster

MY OBJECT ALL SUBLIME (from *The Mikado*)
    Nelson Eddy   11/28/40   Columbia   Armbruster

MY OLD KENTUCKY HOME / DOLLY DAY – Stephen Foster Medley
    Nelson Eddy   7/14/47   Columbia   Armbruster

MY REVERIE
    Nelson Eddy   12/1960   Everest   unknown

NELLY BLY – See MASSA'S IN DE COLD, COLD GROUND – Stephen Foster Medley

NELLY WAS A LADY / O LEMUEL – Stephen Foster Medley
    Nelson Eddy   9/15/47   Columbia   Armbruster

NIĚT, NIĚT, YA NIE KHOTOCHO – "No, No, I Don't Wish That"
  R Nelson Eddy   9/17/49   Columbia   Armbruster

NON PIU ANDRAI (from *The Marriage of Figaro*)
  I Nelson Eddy   1/22/42   Columbia   Armbruster

NOW HEAVEN IN FULLEST GLORY SHONE
    Nelson Eddy   1/22/42   Columbia   Armbruster

NOW THE DAY IS OVER – See FLING OUT THE BANNER

NYET, NYET, YA NIE KHOTOCHO – See NIĚT, NIĚT, YA NIE KHOTOCHO

O COME ALL YE FAITHFUL
    Nelson Eddy   7/16/51   Columbia   Weston

O HOLY NIGHT
    Nelson Eddy   7/16/51   Columbia   Weston

O LEMUEL – See NELLY WAS A LADY – Stephen Foster Medley

O LITTLE TOWN OF BETHLEHEM
    Nelson Eddy   7/16/51   Columbia   Weston

Nelson Eddy's Non-Film Recordings

Performer	Rec. date	Company	Conductor

OH! A PRIVATE BUFFOON (from *Yeoman of the Guard*)
    Nelson Eddy   11/29/40   Columbia   Armbruster

OH BOYS, CARRY ME ALONG / DE CAMPTOWN RACES – Stephen Foster Medley
    Nelson Eddy   7/14/47   Columbia   Armbruster

OH, PROMISE ME
    Nelson Eddy   6/24/37   RCA   Shilkret

OH! SUSANNA – See OPEN THY LATTICE, LOVE

OH! WHAT A BEAUTIFUL MORNING (from *Oklahoma!*)
    Nelson Eddy   11/26/44   Columbia   Armbruster
    Nelson Eddy   5/12/52   Columbia   Engel

OKLAHOMA! (from *Oklahoma!*)
    Nelson Eddy   5/12/52   Columbia   Engel

OLD BLACK JOE / MY BRUDDER GUM – Stephen Foster Medley
    Nelson Eddy   8/25/47   Columbia   Armbruster

OLD DOG TRAY / LOUISIANA BELLE – Stephen Foster Medley
    Nelson Eddy   9/22/47   Columbia   Armbruster

OLD FOLKS AT HOME / ANGELINA BAKER – Stephen Foster Medley
    Nelson Eddy   9/8/47   Columbia   Armbruster

OLD REFRAIN
    Nelson Eddy   12/3/44   Columbia   Armbruster

ONCE I LOVED THEE, MARY DEAR / SLUMBER MY DARLING / SOME FOLKS SAY – Stephen Foster Medley
    Nelson Eddy   9/22/47   Columbia   Armbruster

ONE ALONE (from *The Desert Song*)
    Nelson Eddy   5/8/58   Columbia   Engel
    Eddy, Gale Sherwood   8/1960   Everest   Sosnick

ONE NIGHT OF LOVE
    Eddy, Gale Sherwood   8/1960   Everest   Sosnick

ONWARD CHRISTIAN SOLDIERS
    Nelson Eddy   2/12/46   Columbia   Paxson

OPEN THY LATTICE, LOVE / FAIRY BELLE / OH! SUSANNA – Stephen Foster Medley
    Nelson Eddy   8/25/47   Columbia   Armbruster

OUR LOVE
    Eddy, Gale Sherwood   8/1960   Everest   Sosnick

Performer	Rec. date	Company	Conductor

OUT OF THE NIGHT
    Nelson Eddy   12/14/57   RCA   Rose

PALMS, THE
    Nelson Eddy   9/15/50   Columbia   Arnaud

PANIS ANGELICUS
    Nelson Eddy   9/21/50   Columbia   Arnaud

PEG O'MY HEART
    Nelson Eddy   8/1960   Everest   Sosnick

PEOPLE WILL SAY WE'RE IN LOVE (from *Oklahoma!*)
    Eddy, Virginia Haskins   5/12/52   Columbia   Engel

PERFECT DAY, A
    Nelson Eddy   6/29/37   RCA   Shilkret
    Nelson Eddy   7/20/50   Harmony   Arnaud

PLAY'S THE THING, THE, Parts 1 & 2 (from *Hamlet* by Skiles)
    Nelson Eddy   11/16/39   Columbia   Armbruster

POLICEMAN'S LOT IS NOT A HAPPY ONE, A / WHEN A FELON'S NOT ENGAGED IN HIS EMPLOYMENT / WHEN THE FOEMAN BARES HIS STEEL (from *Pirates of Penzance*) – Medley
    Nelson Eddy   3/21/45   Columbia   Armbruster

POR ESO TE QUIERO
  S   Nelson Eddy   9/17/49   Columbia   Armbruster

PORE JUD IS DAID (from *Oklahoma!*)
    Nelson Eddy   5/12/52   Columbia   Engel

PRAISE THE LORD AND PASS THE AMMUNITION
    Nelson Eddy   3/21/45   Columbia   Armbruster

PRETTY BLACK-EYED SUSIE
    Nelson Eddy   12/1960   Everest   Henderson

RACHEL
    Nelson Eddy   12/1960   Everest   Henderson

RED ROSEY BUSH
    Nelson Eddy   12/3/44   Columbia   Armbruster

REJOICE YE PURE IN HEART / SUN OF MY SOUL
    Nelson Eddy   2/12/46   Columbia   Paxson

RICCORDATI DI ME!
  I   Nelson Eddy   9/10/49   Columbia   Armbruster

Nelson Eddy's Non-Film Recordings 585

Performer	Rec. date	Company	Conductor

RIDERS IN THE SKY
Nelson Eddy — 8/22/49 — Columbia — Armbruster

RIFF SONG (from *The Desert Song*)
Eddy, Wesley Dalton — 5/8/58 — Columbia — Engel

RIO RITA (from *Rio Rita*)
Nelson Eddy — 12/1960 — Everest — Henderson

RISING EARLY IN THE MORNING (from *The Gondoliers*)
Nelson Eddy — 4/9/46 — Columbia — Armbruster

ROCK OF AGES
Nelson Eddy — 3/19/46 — Columbia — Paxson

RODGER YOUNG – "The Ballad of Roger Young"
Nelson Eddy — 3/21/45 — Columbia — Armbruster

ROLLING IN FOAMING BILLOWS (from *The Creation*)
Nelson Eddy — 1/22/42 — Columbia — Armbruster

ROSARY, THE
Nelson Eddy — 6/24/37 — RCA 4370 — Shilkret
Nelson Eddy — 7/27/50 — Columbia — Arnaud

ROUTE MARCHIN'
Nelson Eddy — 1/19/42 — Columbia — Armbruster

SABRE SONG, THE (from *The Desert Song*)
Eddy, Doretta Morrow — 5/8/52 — Columbia — Engel

SAILORMEN – See I AM AS BRAVE AS JOHN

SE VUOL BALLARE (from *The Marriage of Figaro*)
I   Nelson Eddy — 1/22/42 — Columbia — Armbruster

SERENADE (from *The Student Prince* by Romberg)
Nelson Eddy — 8/11/47 — Columbia — Armbruster

SERENADE (Schubert)
Nelson Eddy — 12/10/44 — Columbia — Armbruster

SHADRACK, MESHACK AND ABEDNEGO
Nelson Eddy — 8/22/49 — Columbia — Armbruster

SHALL WE DANCE? (from *The King and I*)
Eddy, Gale Sherwood — 8/1960 — Everest — Sosnick

Performer	Rec. date	Company	Conductor

SI TU VEUX, MIGNONNE (Massenet art song)
   F   Nelson Eddy   9/17/49   Columbia   Armbruster

SLUMBER, MY DARLING – See ONCE I LOVED THEE, MARY DEAR

SMILIN' THROUGH – See film song listing

SOME FOLKS SAY – See ONCE I LOVED THEE, MARY DEAR

SOMEWHERE IN THE NIGHT
    Nelson Eddy   12/14/57   RCA   Rose

SONG IS YOU, THE (from *Music in the Air*)
    Eddy, Gale Sherwood   8/1960   Everest   Sosnick

SPEAK LOW (from *One Touch of Venus*)
    Eddy, Gale Sherwood   c. 1964   Everest   unknown

STAND UP, STAND UP FOR JESUS
    Nelson Eddy   4/23/46   Columbia   Paxson

STAR SPANGLED BANNER
    Nelson Eddy   7/21/40   Columbia   Armbruster

STELLA BY STARLIGHT
    Nelson Eddy   8/1960   Everett   Sosnick

STORY OF A STARRY NIGHT
    Nelson Eddy   8/1960   Everett   Sosnick

STRANGE MUSIC (from *Song of Norway*)
    Nelson Eddy   11/19/44   Columbia   Armbruster
    Nelson Eddy   12/1960   Everest   Henderson

STRANGER IN PARADISE   (from *Kismet*)
    Nelson Eddy   12/1960   Everest   Henderson

SUN OF MY SOUL – See REJOICE YE PURE IN HEART

SURREY WITH THE FRINGE ON TOP, THE (from *Oklahoma!*)
    Nelson Eddy   11/26/49   Columbia   Armbruster
    Nelson Eddy   5/12/52   Columbia   Engel

SWEET AND LOVELY
    Eddy, Gale Sherwood   c. 1964   Everest   Sosnick

SWEET EMERALD ISLE / COMRADES, FILL NO GLASS FOR ME / IF YOU'VE ONLY GOT A
    MOUSTACHE – Stephen Foster Medley
        Nelson Eddy   9/22/47   Columbia   Armbruster

Nelson Eddy's Non-Film Recordings

Performer	Rec. date	Company	Conductor

SWEETEST STORY EVER TOLD, THE – "Tell Me that You Love Me"
    Nelson Eddy — 6/23/50 — Columbia — Armbruster

SWEETLY SHE SLEEPS – See MY ALICE FAIR

SYLVIA
    Nelson Eddy — 7/2/37 — RCA — Paxson
    Nelson Eddy — 7/27/50 — Columbia — Arnaud

TANGO BLEU – See BLUE TANGO

TEMPLE BELLS (from *Indian Love Lyrics*)
    Nelson Eddy — 8/16/39 — Columbia — Finston

TEN THOUSAND TIMES TEN THOUSAND
    Nelson Eddy — 4/2/46 — Columbia — Paxson

THEN YOU WILL KNOW (from *The Desert Song*)
    Eddy, Doretta Morrow — 5/8/58 — Columbia — Engel

THERE IS A GREEN HILL FAR AWAY
    Nelson Eddy — 9/21/50 — Columbia — Arnaud

THERE'S NO SUCH GIRL AS MINE – Stephen Foster
    Nelson Eddy — 8/4/47 — Columbia — Armbruster

THROUGH THE YEARS
    Nelson Eddy — 12/31/35 — RCA — Shilkret

THY BEAMING EYES
    Nelson Eddy — 6/29/37 — RCA — Shilkret

TIL THE END OF TIME
    Nelson Eddy — 12/1960 — Everest — Henderson

TILL I WAKE (from *Indian Love Lyrics*)
    Nelson Eddy — 8/16/39 — Columbia — Finston

TILL WE MEET AGAIN
    Eddy, Jo Stafford — 2/23/51 — Columbia — Weston

TOMORROW
    Nelson Eddy — 11/7/40 — Columbia — Armbruster

TONIGHT WE LOVE
    Nelson Eddy — 12/1960 — Everest — Henderson

TOWER OF BABEL
    Nelson Eddy — 8/23/49 — Columbia — Armbruster

	Performer	Rec. date	Company	Conductor
TRADE WINDS				
	Nelson Eddy	1/21/42	Columbia	Armbruster
TREES				
	Nelson Eddy	6/29/37	RCA	Shilkret
	Nelson Eddy	7/20/50	Columbia	Arnaud

UNCLE NED – See MY ALICE FAIR

	Performer	Rec. date	Company	Conductor
VERY THOUGHT OF YOU, THE				
	Eddy, Gale Sherwood	c. 1964	Everest	unknown
VISION FUGITIVE (from *Herodiade*)				
F	Nelson Eddy	7/28/40	Columbia	Armbruster
WATER BOY				
	Nelson Eddy	1/21/42	Columbia	Armbruster
WHAT IS THIS THING CALLED LOVE?				
	Eddy, Gale Sherwood	c. 1964	Everest	unknown

WHEN A FELON'S NOT ENGAGED IN HIS EMPLOYMENT – See POLICEMAN'S LOT IS NOT A HAPPY ONE (*from Pirates of Penzance*) – Medley

	Performer	Rec. date	Company	Conductor
WHEN I, GOOD FRIENDS, WAS CALLED TO THE BAR (from *Trial by Jury*)				
	Nelson Eddy	4/9/46	Columbia	Armbruster
WHEN I GROW TOO OLD TO DREAM (from the film *The Night Is Young*)				
	Nelson Eddy	6/12/35	RCA	Shilkret
	Eddy, Jo Stafford	2/23/51	Columbia	Weston
WHEN I WAS A LAD (from *H.M.S. Pinafore*)				
	Nelson Eddy	11/28/40	Columbia	Armbruster

WHEN THE FOEMAN BARES HIS STEEL – See POLICEMAN'S LOT IS NOT A HAPPY ONE (from *Pirates of Penzance*) – Medley

WHENE'ER I SPOKE – See IF YOU GIVE ME YOUR ATTENTION

	Performer	Rec. date	Company	Conductor
WHITE CHRISTMAS (from the film *Holiday Inn*)				
	Nelson Eddy	7/21/51	Columbia	Weston
WHOOPEE–TI–YI–YO – "Get Along, Little Doggies"				
	Nelson Eddy	10/30/49	Columbia	Winterhalter
WITH THESE HANDS				
	Eddy, Jo Stafford	2/23/51	Columbia	Weston

Nelson Eddy's Non-Film Recordings

	Performer	Rec. date	Company	Conductor

WITHOUT A SONG (from *Great Day*)
    Nelson Eddy   11/19/44   Columbia   Armbruster

WRECK OF THE JULIE PLANTE, THE
    Nelson Eddy   8/23/49   Columbia   Armbruster

WUNDERBAR (from *Kiss Me, Kate*)
    Eddy, Gale Sherwood   8/1960   Everest   Sosnick

YOU AND THE NIGHT AND THE MUSIC
    Eddy, Gale Sherwood   8/1960   Everest   Sosnick

YOU ARE FREE – "Love Is Just a Game" (from *Apple Blossoms*)
    Nelson Eddy   6/12/35   RCA   Shilkret

YOU ARE LOVE (from *Show Boat*)
    Eddy, Gale Sherwood   8/1960   Everest   Sosnick

Addenda

by John Cocchi

The Merry Widow, 1934
Manuel Paris (Dance extra at Maxim's)
Louis Adlon (Admirer)
George Magrill (Court guard)

Naughty Marietta, 1935
Television version: Max Liebman Presents did a TV special of the stage version in 1955. It starred Alfred Drake (star of Broadway's *Oklahoma!*, *Kismet*, and *Kiss Me, Kate*) and Patrice Munsel (Metropolitan Opera star), with John Conte, Bambi Lynn and Rod Alexander, and Gale Sherwood, Nelson Eddy's blonde nightclub partner, in the rôle of the "quadroon" slave who sings (beautifully) "'Neath the Southern Moon."

Maytime, 1937
Douglas McPhail (Baritone in chorus)
General Sam Savitsky (*Czaritza* officer)
Gloria Talbot (Child)
Allan Watson (Success montage bass)

Cast of first, uncompleted version: MGM pay records indicate that the following performers were on salary between the beginning of shooting on August 21, 1936 and late September: Jeanette MacDonald, Nelson Eddy, Paul Lukas, Ted Healy, Stanley Morner (later Dennis Morgan), Anna Demetrio, John (Skins) Miller, William (Billy) Benedict, James B. Carson, Torben Meyer, Douglas Wood, George Meeker, Effie Ellsler, Sterling Holloway, John T. Murray, Paul Weigel, George Chandler, Genaro Spagnoli, Tyler Brooke, Ruth Renick. No character names are listed.

Rosalie, 1937
Camille Soray, Lois Clements, The Esquires – singers for "Who Knows?"

The Girl of the Golden West, 1938
Zari [Zarubi] Elmassion (MacDonald "vocal stand-in") – See page 399 for explanation of this term.

Broadway Serenade, 1939
Warren Lewis (Baritone)
Helen Seamon, Roy Lester (Jitterbugs)
Zarubi Elmassian (MacDonald's singing stand-in for auditioning vocal arrangements and for orchestra rehearsals – See page 399 for explanation of this term.
Dorothy Ward (MacDonald's dancing stand-in for choreographing dances and camera tests)

Balalaika, 1939
Lorraine Bridges (Massey "vocal stand-in") – See page 399 for explanation of this term.

New Moon, 1940
Lorraine Bridges (MacDonald's "vocal stand-in") – See page 399 for explanation of this term.

Bitter Sweet, 1940
Lorraine Bridges (MacDonald's "vocal stand-in")
Earl Covert (Eddy's "vocal stand-in") – See page 399 for explanation of this term.

Addenda

Smilin' Through, 1941
Assistant writers: Claudine West and Ernest Vajda
Lorraine Bridges (MacDonald "vocal double") – See page 399 for explanation of this term.

The Chocolate Soldier, 1941
Assistant Director: Marvin Stuart
Art Associate: John S. Detlie
Men's Costumer: Gile Steele
Music Conductor: Nat Finston
Makeup: Jack Dawn
Nan Merriman (Jeanette's "vocal stand-in") – See page 399 for explanation of this term.
Earl Covert (Eddy's "vocal stand-in").
Bob Mascagno (Eddy's double in Gypsy café) – See page 399 for explanation of this term.
Faith Kruger (Solo in Gypsy café sequence)
Jimmy Alexander (Singer in "Seek the Spy")

I Married an Angel, 1942
Dance coach for boogie-woogie number: Jeni LeGon
Thora Mathiason (MacDonald's "vocal stand-in") – See page 399 for explanation of this term.
Ludwig Stossel (Customs inspector, cut from film, but recast as janitor)
Burgren Sisters Quartet: Elinore Davenport, Pamela Randall, Virginia Rees, Betty Rome (specialties at Count's birthday party)
Muriel Goodspeed (Specialty at birthday party)
Max Lucke, Roland Varno, Frances Carson, Bess Flowers, Doris Day [not the famous singer] (Bits)
Jack Vlaskin (Milkwagon driver)

Cairo, 1942
Marine sequence Director of Photography: Jack Smith.
Orchestrations: Basil Adlam, Robert Van Eps, George Bassman.
Technical advisor: Major C.S. Ramsay Hill.
Lorraine Bridges (MacDonald's "vocal stand-in") – See page 399 for explanation of this term.

Phantom of the Opera, 1943
Phantom of Hollywood was made for TV, shot on MGM's back lot. It costarred Broderick Crawford whom Universal had originally picked in 1940 to costar opposite Deanna Durbin in their version of *Phantom*.

Knickerbocker Holiday, 1944
Assistant Editor: Walter Hannemann.
Associate Producer: Stanley Logan.
Assistant Director: Raoul Pagel.
Production Designer: Bernard Herzbrun.
Set Decorations: Julia Heron.
Costumes: Walter Plunkett.
Additional musical numbers by Ted (Theodore) Paxson.
Sound Recording: Ben Winkler.
Makeup: Steve Drum.
Hairstylist: Nina Roberts.

Follow the Boys, 1944
Art Directors: John B. Goodman and Harold H. MacArthur.
Set Decoration: R.A. Gausman and Ira S. Webb.
Gowns by Vera West.
Zorina's gowns by Howard Greer.
Dance Director: George Balanchine.
Sound Director: Bernard B. Brown.

Make Mine Music, 1946
Music Director: Charles Wolcott.
Music Associates: Ken Darby, Oliver Wallace, Edward Plumb.
Il Pagliacci – Although we see a marquee announcing that Willie is appearing in "Pagliacci," Disney couldn't get (or didn't want to pay for) the rights to use the Leoncavallo aria. According to the American Film Institute, Nelson Eddy "wrote a phony one himself"—actually composing a phrase of fifteen Pagliacci-ish notes—which he sang as Willie sobs in his clown costume.

Three Daring Daughters, 1948
Sam Ash (Graduation attendee)

The Sun Comes Up, 1949
Assistant Director: Al Jennings.
Special Effects: Warren Newcombe.
Technicolor Director: Natalie Kalmus.
Technicolor Associate: James Gooch.
Makeup: Jack Dawn.

Index

Numbers in **boldface** indicate:
- an entire section dealing with the film, *e.g. Bitter Sweet* 91, **398–412**, 544
- a page featuring a photo of the person, *e.g.* Beavers, Louise 82, **84**, 87

Film and book titles are in alics, song titles and adio/TV ograms in quotes.

42nd Street 91, 113
Aarons, Alex 10
42nd Street 91, 113
Aarons, Alex 10
42nd Street 91, 113
Aarons, Alex 10
Abel, David 498
"Abide with Me" 572, 575
Academy of Music, Philadelphia 4, 158, 203
Achard, Marcel 146, 152
Acker, Jean 229, 245
Ackerman, Belinda (Nelson's great-grandmother) 154, 155
Ackerman, Caroline (Nelson's grandmother) 154, 155, 271
Ackerman, Joseph (Nelson's great-grandfather) 154, 155
Adair, Robert 172
Adams, Frank 117
Adams, Sarah F. 247
Adams, Stephen 246
Adams, Victor 275
Adamson, Harold 171, 172
Adelphi Theatre, London 368
"Adeste Fideles" 575
Adlam, Basil 591
Adler, Larry 517, 524, 529
Adler, Marion 424
Adlon, Louis 424, 590
Adorée, Renée 207
Adrian 10, 117, 120, 125, 129, 136, 170, 174, 175, 206, 228, 247, 271, 274, 281, 286, 300, 315, 326, 330, 356, 361, 368, 375, 380, 383, 398, 409, **411**, 412, **421**, 423, 450
Affairs of Annabel, The 81
"After You're Gone" 505
AgaKhan, Yannek 166, 169

Agee on Film 459
"Agnus Dei" 572, 575
Agresti, Ed 530
"Ah, Sweet Mystery of Life" 177, 186, 187, 189, 189, 220, 544, 562
Aherne, Brian 413, 414, **416**, **418**, **419**, 420, 421, 462
Ahlert, Fred A. 170, 502
Aida 158, 163, 205
Aimez-moi ce soir! (*Love Me Tonight*) 101
"Air des bijoux"("Jewel Song") 247, 562
Akst, Harry 222
Al White's Song Birds 5
Alacorn, Rinaldo 207
"Alan Young Show" 539, 541
Alberni, Luis 343, 435, 444
Albertina Rasch Ballet / Dancers (See also Rasch, Albertina) 117, 146, 167, 170, 288, 289, 299
Alder, Ruth 436
Aldrich, Mariska 248, 270
Aldridge, Katharine (Kay) 288
Alexander, Dick 506
Alexander, Ernie 207, 356
Alexander, Jimmy 432, 590
Alexander, Katharine 356, 359, 366
Alexander, Rod 590
Alexander, Tad 167
Alexis, Demetrius 368
"Alice Blue Gown" 8
Alison, David 381
All Quiet on the Western Front 53
All Saints' Church, Providence, RI 155

"All the Cats Join In" 505
"All Souls Day" 575
"All Women Are Bad" 77
Allan, Maude 228
Allbritton, Louise 499
"Allegro Appasionato" (by Saint-Saëns) 529
Allen, Joel 499
Allen, Judith 369
Allen, Maude 343, 349, 355, 436
Allen, Ricca 288
Allen, Theresa 33
Allen, Wayne 174
Allister, Claud 51, 53, **57**
Allyson, June 556
"Alma Mater" 519, 528
"Aloha Oe" 450
"Alone Together" 575
"Als die Alte Mutter" – See "Songs My Mother Taught Me"
Alstock, Bernice 249, 270, 288
Alter, Lou 170
"Always in All Ways" 53, 57, 58, 59, 60, 201, 562
Always You 267
Amants (*Sweethearts*) 315
Amato, Pasquale 300
Amaya, Carmen 488, 493, **494**
Ambassador Theatre, NY 14
Amenabar, Franco 116
"America" 344, 354, 355, 562, 575
"America Calling" 201
America's Singing Sweethearts (documentary) 554
America's Sweetheart 114
American Film Institute Catalog: Feature Films, 1931–1940 399

Index

American Film Institute 51
American G.I. Chorus 506, 516, 517
American in Paris, An 432
American Magazine 133
American Movie Classics channel 545
American Theatre, Saint Louis 543
Americans Can Sing 176
Ames, Leon 553
Ames, Preston 517
Ames, Ramsay 498
Amour et Gloire 482, **483**, 487
"Anchors Aweigh" 292, 299
Anchors Aweigh 432, 458
"An den Frühling" ("Springtide" by Grieg) 527, 529
"And This Is My Beloved" 575
Anderson, Capt. C.E. 343, **346**, **348**, **354**
Anderson, Maxwell 488, 489, 496, 497
André, Lona 130
André, Monya 275
Andre, Nicki 476, 484, 485, 488
Andrews Sisters 499, 502, 505
Andrews, Edward 539
Andrews, Julie 195
Andrews, Stanley 498
Andriot, Lucien 77
Andy Hardy Meets Debutante 474
"Angel Without Wings" 449, 451, 453, 457
Angela 14, 69, 71
"Angelina Baker" 575, 583
"Angelus, The" **319**, 334, 335, 336, 337
Angelo, Nick 247, 270
Angelus, Muriel 368
"Anges Purs" 247, 450
Angyalt Vettem Feleségül (*I Married an Angel*) 434
Animal Crackers 50
Ankers, Evelyn 499
Annabelle's Affairs 81–88
Annie Dear 81
"Annie Laurie" 572
"Antoinette and Anatole" 181

"Anvil Chorus" (by Verdi) 269
Anything Goes 290
"Anything to Please the Queen" 32
Apfel, Oscar 228
Appel, Sam 275
Applause 88, 114
Apple Blossoms ("The Railroad Hour," radio) 539
Apple Blossoms 590
"Apple Blossom Time" 502
Arabeloff, Sergei 301
Aranson, Shirley 170
Arbuckle, Marie 288
Arcaro, Flavio 423
Arceri, Gene 219
Archer, Thomas 463
Arcos, Pilar 275
Ardell, Alice 146
Arden, Eve 170
Arditi, Luigi 474
Arena Theatre, Windsor 463
Ariadne auf Naxos 161
Arie, Raffaele 463
Arlen, Harold 473
Arlen, Joan 172
Armbruster, Robert 506, 561, 562, 563, 564, 565, 566, 567, 568, 569, 570, 571, 572, 573, 574, 575, 576, 577, 578, 579, 580, 581, 582, 583, 584, 585, 586, 587, 588, 589
Armenta, Phillip 301
Armetta, Henry 117, 130
Armont, Paul 101
Arms and the Man 423, 425
Army Emergency Relief 460, **462**, 463
Arnaud, Léo 247, 288, 300, 356, 561, 563, 564, 566, 567, 568, 569, 570, 571, 574, 575, 576, 577, 578, 579, 580, 584, 585, 587, 588
Arno, Sig 424, 435
Arnold, Edward 343, 345, 347, **348**, **354**, 517, 519, 521, **524**, **527**
Arnold, Jessie 530
Aros, Anita 518

Arquette, Cliff (Charlie Weaver) 542
Arthur, Robert 380
"As Years Go By" 575
Asch, Amy 128
Asgelo, Nick 249
Ash, Sam 146, 229, 591
Ashe, Martin 499
Ashley, Edward 398, **401**, **402**, **408**
Askam, Earl 43
Asphalt Jungle, The 464
Associated-First National 300
Astaire, Fred 113, 170, 171, 200, 202, 555, 556
Astor, Gertrude 228
Astra-Pathé 245
"At a Georgia Camp Meeting" 240, 247
"At Dawning" 575
"At the Balalaika" 371, 376, **378**, 379, 379, 379, 562
"At the Roxy Music Hall" 443, 450, 451
AT&T 2
Atchinson, Evelyn 436
Atchley, Hooper 275
Ates, Dorothy 368
Atkinson, Brooks 13, 14, 16
Atkinson, Doris 207
Atwill, Lionel 368, 370, **372**, 464, 468
Aubrey, Jimmy 344
Auditorium Theatre, Ottawa 463
Auer, Florence 436, **447**
Auer, Mischa 172, 315, 318, **326**, **329**
"Auf Weidersehen" 575
"Auld Lang Syne" 321, 335, 358
Austernprinzessin, Die (*The Oyster Princess*) 26
Austin, William 43, **45**, **47**, **50**, 51
Autry, Gene 344
Avalier, Don 518
"Avalon" 469, 475
"Ave Maria" (by Bach/Gounod) 307, 314, 460, 572
"Ave Maria" (by Schubert) 575

"Away in a Manger" (by Murray) 575
Axt, Dr. William 166, 366
Ayer, N.W. Advertising 156
Ayres, Lew 356, 357, **358**, **359**, 366, 556
Babes in Arms 247, 334, 473
Baccalone, Salvatore 541
Bach, Johann Sebastian 315
Bacon, Irving 316, 488
Badger, Clarence Jr. 451
"Badinage" ("Summer Serenade" by Herbert) 326, 335, 336, 337, 569
Baggott, King 229, 245
Bailey, Polly 117
Baird, Dolores 259
Baker, Josephine 232
Balalaika (1936 stage version) 366, 368, 369, 370
Balalaika 290, **366–380**, 561, 562, 566, 568, 569; Addenda, 590; Oscar nomination, Best Sound Recording, 369
Balanchine, George 591
Balderston, John 412
Baldwin, Richard 488
Balfé, Michael William 270
Ball, Ernest R. 170, 246, 355
Ball, Lucille 81
"Ballad of Rodger Young, The" 585
Ballard, Kaye 542
Ballard, Lucien 92
Ballbusch, Peter 412
Ballester, Amparo 518
Bamboschek, Giuseppe 463, 460, 561, 562, 563, 564, 565, 566, 567, 572, 573, 574
Bampton, Rose 205
Bancroft, Charles 436
Band Wagon, The 53
"Banjo Song" 128
Banky, Vilma 115
Banton, Travis 32, 92, 101
Bara, Nina 518, 529
Barber of Seville, The 269, 404, 410, 504, 505
Barber, Bobby 499

Barbier, George 92, 95, **138**, 130, 316, 324
Barbier, Jules 220, 247
Barclay, Don 316
Barclay, Joan 316
Barcroft, Roy 288
Bardette, Trevor 343, 347, 381
Bari, Lynn 170
Barker, Bonita 170
Barker, Shirley 517
Barkleys of Broadway, The 202
Barlow, Reginald 117
Barnes, Binnie 435, 440, **441**, 448, **449**, **450**
Barnes, Howard 501
Barnes, Jane 174, 228, 356
Barnes, Katharine 170
Barnett, Antonina 506
Barnett, Vince 228, 232
Barondess, Barbara 130, 141
Barr, Muriel 436
Barr, Stephanie Loyd 192, 434
Barrie, Elaine 266
Barrie, Mona 464, 467
Barrier, Edgar 249, 476, **480**, 481, **487**
Barry, Mrs. Minnie 4
Barrymore, John 18, 33, 248, 253, **254**, 262, **264**, 266, 274
Barrymore, Lionel 343, 345, **346**, **348**, **354**, 355
Bartell, Dick 477
Bartlett, Michael 413, 463
Bartok, Bela 412
Barwyn, Max 146, 399, 424
Basevi, James 228, 231
Bassman, George 591
Bates, Blanche 300
Bates, Florence 424, 425, 426, **429**, 434
Bates, Louise 465
Battle, Rosemary 499
"Battle Hymn of the Republic, The" 244, 246, 247, 462, 562
Baum, Vicki 451
Baumann, Sue 309
Baxley, Jack 170, 228
Baxter, George 131
Bayfield, Harry 488
Beard, Tony 207

Beattie, Douglas 368, 379, 422
"Beau Soir" (by Debussy) 572
"Beautiful Dreamer" 575
"Beautiful Ohio" 474
Beavers, Louise 77, 77, 79, 82, **84**, 87, 499, 501
"Because" 576
Beck, John 530
Becky Sharp 114
Beday, Eugene 146, 399
"Bedelia" 170
Bedford, Barbara 356
Beecher, Janet 288, 398, 402
Beecher, Sylvia 16
"Beer Barrel Polka" 502
Beery, Noah Jr. 499
Beery, Noah Sr. 301, **303**, 304, 314
Beery, Wallace 128
Bees and the Flowers, The 517
"Bei Mir Bist Du Schön" 502
"Bei mir daheim ist's nicht der Brauch" 145
Belasco Theatre, NYC 300
Belasco, Arthur 174, 381
Belasco, David 300, 301, 302, 315
Belasco, Leon 356, 424, 517
"Believe Me If All Those Endearing Young Charms" 72, 77
Bell Laboratories 2
Bell, Genevieve 499
Bell, Hank 301, 344
Bell, James 172
Bell, Monta 172
Bellah, James Warner 170
Belle Cabaretière, La (Girl of the Golden West) 300
Bellew, Cosmo Kyrle 131
Bellis, Guy 436
Belmore, Lionel 21, 51
Beloved Rogue, The 33, 35
Ben Hur 118, 127
Benchley, Robert 170
Benedict, Billy – see Benedict, Willaim (Billy)
Benedict, Brooks 316
Benedict, William (Billy) 499, 590

Index

Benge, Wilson 288, 316
Bennett, Bruce 172
Bennett, Charles 365, 366
Bennett, David 43
Bennett, Lee 499
Bennett, Nan 517
Bennett, Raphael (Ray) 275
Bennett, Robert Russell 561, 562, 563, 564, 567, 568, 571, 572, 573, 574
Benny Goodman Orchestra 505
Benny Goodman Quartet 505
Benny, Jack 18
Benson, A.C. 423
Beranger, George André 82
"Berceuse" 576
Berg, Alban 161
Bergen, Edgar 162, 541
Berger, Florence 172
Berger, Ludwig 32, 34, 35, 36, 40
Berghof, Herbert 424, 543, **544**
Bergman, J. Peter 559
Berkeley, Busby 171, 213, 356, 357, 359, 360, 364, **365**, 434
Berley, André 146
Berlin, Irving 21, 353
Bernard, Harry 43
Bernauer, Rudolph 423
Bernhardt, Curtis 129
Berolund, Chester, and B. 316
Berry, Art Sr. 398
Berry, Nyas 228
Berry, Ralph W. and Rollin 316
Bert, Margaret 398
Berton, Pierre 224
Bervily, M. 565, 571
Besoyan, Rick 195
Bettinson, Rob 247
Bevan, Billy 51, 301, **304**, 308, 343
Bey, Erik 51, 60
Bey, Turhan 499
Beyers, Bobby 530
"Beyond the Blue Horizon" 52, 53, 55, 59, 60, **501**, 562
"Bianca" 576
Biberman, Abner 368, **372**
"Bicycle Built for Two" 166

"Big Backyard of the City, The" 572
"Big Record, The" 541, 542
Big Tree, Chief 301
"Bigger the Army and the Navy, The" 502
Billboard 540
Billingsley, Barbara 530
Billy Mitchell Singers 381
Bing, Herman 117, 130, 207, 248, **257**, 257, 262, 267, 271, 316, 319, **326**, 398, **404**
Bingham, G. Clifford 269, 365
Birds and the Bees, The 517, 527
Bishop, Sir Henry 336, 355, 475
Bispham, David 157, 161
Bitter Sweet (1933 UK film) 115, 398, 400
Bitter Sweet ("The Railroad Hour," radio) 399, 539
Bitter Sweet (1929 stage version) 118, 250, 398, 399, 401, 409, 410, 412
Bitter Sweet (Summer stock production) 398
Bitter Sweet (1940 U.S. film) 91, 369, **398–412**, 544; Addenda, 591; Oscar nomination, Color Interior Decoration, 399; Oscar nomination, Color Cinematography, 399; Addenda, 590
Bizet, Georges 379, 422, 450
Bjorndahl, Joseph 271
"Black Eyed Susie" 575
Black Pirate, The 35
Black, Maurice 275, 280
Blackmer, Mrs. Sidney 316
Blackwell, Carlyle Jr. 172, 499
Blagoi, George 506
Blair, Anthony 436
Blake, Gladys 476
Blake, James 169
Blake, Marie – See MacDonald, Blossom
Bland, James 269
Blane, Sally 82, 83, **85**, **87**
Blaue Küste, *Die (The Blue Coast)* 51
Bleifer, John 368, 506

"Blind Ploughman, The" 576
Bloodgood, Margaret 175
Blore, Eric 14
Blossom Time 560, 569
"Blue Bayou" 505
Blue Coast, The 51
"Blue Danube, The" 358
Blue Paradise, The 575
"Blue Tango" 576, 586
Blue, Monte 172
Blystone, Stanley 170
Blyth, Ann 207, 208
Bob Grimes Sheet Music Collection 49
"Bob Hope Show" 541
Bodenheim, Maxwell 9
Boehm, David 488
Boehnel, William 126, 189, 246, 285, 354, 377, 396, 432
Boemler, George 368
Bogart, Humphrey 10, 270
Bogdanovich, Peter 516
Bohème, La – See *La Bohème*
Bohemian Girl, The 270
Bohmier, Craig 424
Bohrman, Lulu May 316
Bois, Curt 398, 401, **403**, **404**, **406**, 410
Boito, Arrigo 505
Boland, Mary 10, 380, 384, **386**, **392**
Boles, John 224
Bolger, Ray 288, 290, **292**, **294**, 299, 301, **304**, 315, **318**, 319, 335
Bolster, Anita 436, **447**
Bolton, Guy 8, 21, 287
Bond, Tommy 288, 292
Bond, Ward 82
Bonelli, Richard 204
"Bone of Contention," 128
Bonn, Walter 301
"Bonne Nuit, Merci!" 410, 412
Bookasta, George 424
Books, Shelton 502
Boom! Boom! 15
Booth, Margaret 170
"Boots" 576
Bordeaux, Francine 435
Borden, Eugène 117, 146, 275

Bordoni, Irene   53
Borg, Sven Hugo   488
Borg, Veda Ann   398, **406**, 435, **438**, 440
Borgato, Agostino   207, 248, 275
Borland, Barlowe   249
Born to Dance   290
Borodin, Alexander   289, 295, 299
Borzage, Frank   412, **422**
Boswell, Hugh   315, 380, 398
Bouillon, Jo   232
Boulton, Matthew   275, 284
Bourget, Paul   537
Bow, Clara   18, 41, 115, 248
Bowden, Charlotte   **163**
Bowes, Major Edward Bowes   7
Boyce, George   288
"Boze Carja Chrani"   379
Brabin, Charles   436
Bracey, Sidney   51, 54, 228, 275, 288
Bradford, Robert   432, 451
Bradley, Harry C.   170, 488
Brady, Alice   16, 166, 167, **168**, 170
Brady, Ed   174
Brancato, Rosemarie   399
Brandon, Henry   506, **514**, 515
Braun and Sharp Manufacturing Company   153
Breamer, Sylvia   300
Breen Office   141, 175, 454
Breen, Thomas E.   518
"Breeze and I, The"   572
"Breeze Kissed Your Hair, The"   127
Brenn, Doris   499
Brennan, J. Keirn   16, 60, 66
Brennan, William   206
Brent, Earl   529
Brent, Lee   434
Brent, Linda   368, 499
Breslaw, Joan   249
Breslow, Lou   498
Bressart, Felix   398, 401, 403, 404, **406**, 410
Brewster, James   228
Brewster's Millions   12
Brian, Donald   129, 132

Brice, Fanny   380
Bricklayers, The   499
"Bride 66"   60
Bridges, Lorraine   399, 432, 590, 591
Briggs, Harlan   248
Briggs, Marjorie   450
Brilhante, Patti   451
Brinckman, Nancy   499
Brissac, Virginia   517
British Dominion Films   115
British Film Institute   456
Brix, Herman [Bruce Bennett]   172
Broad Street Theatre, Phila.   158
Broadhurst Theatre, NYC   412
Broadway Melody, The   88
Broadway Melody of 1936   290, 313, 425
Broadway Melody of 1940   334, 578
Broadway Serenade   556, **355–366**; Addenda, 590.
"Broadway Serenade" (song)   366
Broadway to Hollywood   165, 166–170, 545
Brock, James   247, 300
Brodie, Buster   488
Brodie, Don   356
Brodie, Steve   499
Brodine, Norbert   166
Brokaw, Charles   368
"Broken Hearts"   10
Bromberg, J. Edward   476
Bromley, Sheila   92, 130
Brooke Hillary   381
Brooke, Tyler   51, 60, 102, 105, 114, 131, 435, 590
Brooks, Pauline   172
Brooks, Ralph   175, 316
Brooks, Rand   368
Brooks, Shelton   222
Brophy, Ed (Edward)   167, 184, **185**
Brown, Bernard B.   475, 591; Oscar nomination, *Phantom of the Opera*, 477
Brown, Charles D.   498
Brown, Furman   497, 498

Brown, George   161, 165, 548
Brown, Harry Joe   488, **494**, 495
Brown, Hilyard   506
Brown, Joe E.   60, 62, **64**, 67
Brown, Johnny Mack, Mr. & Mrs.   340
Brown, Lucille   316
Brown, Nacio Herb   173, 246
Brown, Tom   248, 252
Brown, Virginia Eddy (Nelson's half-sister)   156
Browne, Ed   499
Brownlee, Frank   60
Bruce, Nigel   424, 425, **427**, **428**, 499
Bruce, Virginia   22, **23**, 26, 32, 33, 43, 343, 345, 346, **347**, **353**, 355
Bruggeman, George   172
Bruin, Charles   175, 181, 207
Brunette, Fritzi   229, 245
Bruzlin, Al   81
Bryan, Arthur Q.   356
"Bubbles in the Wine"   379
Bubblin' Over   12
Buchanan, Jack   51, 53, **54**, **55**, **56**, **58**, **60**
Bucknall, Nathalie   230
Bud Murray Children   249
"Buds Won't Bud,"   471, 473, 475
Bunny, George   488
Bunny, John   245
Bupp, Moyer   229
Bupp, Tommy   229
Burgren Sisters Children's Quartet   450, 591
Burke, Billie   81
Burke, Katharine   131
Burke, Orrin   228
Burnett, Carol   195
Burns, Nica   247
Burns, Paul E.   381, 398, 530, 535
Burress, William   174
Bushman, Francis X. Jr.   343
Bushman, Ralph   343
"But What of Truth"   450
Butler, John A.   530
Butler, Michael   465

Index

Butterworth, Charles 101,**105, 110, 111,** 114, 117, **120, 122,** 172, 173, 173, 343, 345, 346, **349,** 498
Buzzell, Eddie 457
"By the Waters of the Minnetonka" 576
Byrd, Ralph 275
Byrd, Russ 548
Byron, Arthur "Pop" 131, 316
Byron, Jack 92
Byron, Marion "Peanuts" 102, 114

Cabin in the Sky 277, 431, 436
Caesar, Irving 13
Cahn, Sammy 496, 497, 502; Oscar nomination, *Follow the Boys,* 500
Caine, Georgia 175
"Cairo" **471,** 474, 475
Cairo 464–475; Addenda, 591
Cairo, 1963 film 464
"Caissons Go Rolling Along, The" 299
Caldara, Orme 412
Caldwell, Anne 8
"Call of Life, The" 410, 412, 562
Callahan, J. Will 423
Callas, Maria 271
Calliga, George 530
Calvert, E. H. 22, 25, 43
Cameron, Al 505
Cameron, Bruce
Cameron, Cecile 33
Cameron, Kate 189, 219
Cammarano, Salvatore 505
Campbell, Alan 315, 317, 337
Campbell, Colin 398
Campbell, Craig 274
Campeau, Frank 275
Campion, Leah 549
"Camptown Races" – See"De Camptown Races"
Canadian Mounted Police 195
Canepari, Alexander 288
Cantene del Passato (*Smilin' Through*) 412
Cantor, Eddie 18, 98

Canutt, Yakima 506
Capitol Theatre, NYC 3, 6, 7, 187, 189, 314
Capitol Theater, Quebec City 463
Cappell and Patricia 499
"Capriccio Espagñole" 284, 287
"Caprice Viennois" 412, 439, 449
"Captain Stratton's Fancy" 576
Card, Kathryn 517, 520
Careless Rapture 369
Carewe, Edwin 300
Carey, Henry 355
Carey, Leonard 207, 436
Carle, Richard 92, 96, 101, 131, 228
Carleton, Bob 247
Carling, Foster 355
Carlisle, Alice 117
"Carlo, The" 173
Carlyle, Aileen 207
Carmen 373, **374,** 378, 379, 447, 450
Carmen Amaya Dancers 488, **494,** 497,499; See also Amaya, Carmen
Carnegie Hall 163, 543
Carney, Art 542
"Caro Nome" 269
Carousel 579
"Carousel in the Park" 572
Carpenter, Jimmy 499
Carré, Michel 220, 247
Carrillo, Leo 300, 304, 476, 481
Carroll, Earl 89
Carroll, John 51
Carroll, Mildred 170, 172
Carroll, Nancy 18, 88
"Carry Me Back to Old Virginny" 269
Carson, Frances 275, 413, 424, 436, 591
Carson, Frances 591
Carson, James B. 590
Carson, Renee 477, **482**
Carter, Ben 381, 397
Carter, Douglas 530
Carter, Janice (Janis) 435, 443, **441, 453**

Caruso, Enrico 300, 302
Carver, Lynne 248, 249, 252, 273, 398, **402, 403**
Case, Russ 561, 563, 570, 572, 574
"Casey at the Bat" ("Casey, the Pride of Them All") 505
Casino Theatre, NY 16, 33
Cason, John 499
Cass, Lee 577
Cass, Maurice 248, 275, 369, 424
Cassidy, Claudia 463
Castiglioni, Iphigenie 248, 253
"Castle of Dreams" 8
Cat and the Fiddle, The (1931 stage version) 117
Cat and the Fiddle, The 116, **117–128**
Cathcart, Daniel B. 343, 412
Catholic Legion of Decency 518
"Catskills, Hello" 8
Cavan, Allan 249
Cavanaugh, Hobart 356
Cavens, Fred 146
Cawthorn, Joseph 102, 108, 114, 117, 123, 174, **179,** 180
Cecil, Nora 131
Cernitz, Arthur W. 368
"Ceva" 555
Chace, Raymond 314
Chadwick, Helene 229, 245
Chagrin d'Amour (*Smilin' Through*) 412, **414**
Chaliapin, Feodor 368, 378
Chambers, Shirley 130
Chambers, Wheaton 477, 518
"Champagne and Orchids" 128
Champagne and Orchids 128
"Champagne" 25, 32
Chan, Charlie 36, 69
Chan, Helen 172
Chancel, Jules 21
Chandler, George 590
Chandler, Howard 247
Chandler, Lane 131, 275, 288, 477, 498
Chaney, Lon Jr. 499
Chaney, Lon Sr. 477, 478

Channing, Ruth 130, 139, 167
"Chanson Bohème" 379, 450
"Chanson de Vilya" ("Vilia") 562
"Chanson du Toréador" 378, 562, 570
"Chanson" (Friml) 287
"Chansonette" (Friml) 180, 287
Chant du Printemps, Le (Maytime) 247, **248**
"Chante Italienne" 189, 562
Chaplin, Saul 555
Charell, Erik 114
Charig, Philip 13
Charisse, Cyd 556
Charles K. Feldman Group Production 498
Charles, Dick 502
Charles, Rosalind 22, **23**, 26, 32
Charley's Aunt 542
Charlie Chan 36, 69
Charlie Spivak and His Orchestra 500
Charlot's Revue 53
"Charmaine" 576
Charpentier, Gustave 572
Chase & Sanborn Hour 162
Chase, (Stephen) Alden 381
Chase, Newell 40, 41
Chat et le Canari, Le 117
Chat et le Violin, Le 128
Chatburn, Jean 174
Chatterton, Ruth 18, 41
Chauve Souris 9
Cheers for the Boys 498
Chefe, Jack 92, 117, 399
Cheirel, Micheline 435
Chemin du Paradis, Le 91
Cheron, André 22, 25, 68, 73, 101, 146
Chevalier, Maurice 16, 18, 21, **22**, **24**, **25**, **27**, **28**, **29**, 35, 41, **91**, **92**, **93**, **94**, 95, **98**, **99**, 100, 101, **107**, 110, 111, 112, 114, 115, **129**, 130, 134, 136, **139**, **140**, **141**, **144**, 146, **149**, 152, 195, 338, 556, 561, 561, 565, 566, 567, 568, 571, 558, 559, 561, 566, 567, 568, 571;

Career, 30; Oscar nomination, *The Love Parade*, 22
Chevret, Lita 92
"Chi Me Frena?" (Sextet from *Lucia di Lammermoor*) 269, 270, 505
Chica y el Gobernador, La (Knickerbocker Holiday) 488
Chicago Civic Opera 463
Chicago Tribune 463
Chierchetti, David 95, 252
Childers, Naomi 229, 245
"Child's Evening Prayer" 576
Chirello, George "Shorty" 499
Chisholm, Robert 60, 61, 63, **65**, 67, 68
"Chocolate Soldier, The" 432, 434, 562
Chocolate Soldier, The (1909 stage version) 423, 424
Chocolate Soldier, The 337, 369, **423–434**; Oscar nomination, Best Black and White Cinematography, 424; Oscar nomination, Best Scoring of a Musical Picture, 424; Oscar nomination, Best Sound Recording, 424; Addenda, 590
Chopin, Frédéric 269, 379, 482, 487, 502
Chopin's "Polonaise in A-Flat" 502
Chorrie, Joseph 207
"Christ Had a Garden" 576
Christian Science Monitor 473
Christie, Audrey 435
Christie, Howard 498
Christy, Dorothy 316
Chu Chin Chow 61
Church of the Transfiguration, Providence 153
Churchill, Berton 14, 316, 320–321, **322**, 336
Cianci, Vincent 154
Ciannelli, Eduardo (Edward) 464, 468
Cincinnati Zoological Gardens Pavilion 463
Cinderella (recording) 572
Cinéma Madeleine, Paris 152

"Ciribiribin" 572
Clair, René 95
"Clair de Lune" 505
Claire, Bernice 313
Clancy, Margaret 81
Clark, Davison 398
Clark, Edward 477
Clark, Neville 172
Clark, Richard 499
Clark, Wallis 288, 499
Clarke, Betty Ross 316
Clarke, Charles 68, 81, 117
Clarke, Thomas 432
Claypoole, Ocean 288
Clear, Edna **539**
Clemant, Dora 172
Clement, Clay 288
Clements, Lois 591
Cleva, Fausto 463
Cline, Maggie 167
Clinton, Larry 528
Clooney, Rosemary 541
"Close" (by Porter) 299, 300
"Close as Pages in a Book" 572
Cloy, May 488
Clyde, David 207, 413
CNN, *Inside Politics* 273
Cobb, Edmund 174
Cobb, Will D. 365
Coburn, Charles 488, 489, **491**, **497**
Coca, Imogene 13
Cocchi, John 272, 457, 591
Cocoanut Grove Orchestra 100
Cocoanut Grove, L.A. 543
Cocoanuts, The 88
Code, The 118
Cody, Bill 207
Cody, Bill Jr. 301, **303**, 304, 314
Cody, Iron Eyes 207
Coe, Peter 499
"Coeur contre coeur" ("We Will Always Be Sweethearts") 100, 101, 563
Coffee, Lenore 451
Cohan Theatre, NYC 117
Cohan, George M. 113, 336
Colbert, Claudette 13, 35
Colcord, Mabel 275
Cole, Cozy 505

Index

Colega, George 146
Coleman, Charles 92, 97, 517
Coleman, Claudia 131
Coles, Joyce 434
Coleson, Elinor 288
"Colgate Comedy Hour" 541
Collier, Constance 128
Collier, Lois 499
Collier, William Sr. 81, 166
Collins, Cora Sue 174
Collins, G. Pat 228
Colman, Irene 368, 399
Colman, Ronald 31, 33
Colonial Dames of the Art Alliance 157
Colonna, Jerry 288, 294, 503, 505
Columbia Concerts 161; Nelson's contract with, 159
Columbia Records 397, 560, 561, 562, 563, 564, 565, 566, 567, 568, 569, 570, 571, 574, 575, 576, 577, 578, 579, 580, 581, 582, 583, 584, 585, 586, 581
"Columbia, the Gem of the Ocean" 270
"Come Back to Sorrento" 41, 42
"Come Down, Ma Evenin' Star" 167, 170
"Come Drink to the Girl of My Dreams" 41
"Come Drink to the Girl That You Love" 62, 66
"Come to the Moon" 7
"Come Where My Love Lies Dreaming" 576, 581
Comedia 152
"Comin' Through the Rye" 572
Compton, Dorothy 450
Compton, Joyce 83, **85**, **87**, 368, 371
"Comrades, Fill No Glass For Me" 586
Congress Dances 114
Conklin, Chester 488, 489, 496
Conklin, Gene 288
Conklin, Heinie 344
Conlin, Jimmy (James) 207, 210, 211, 316, 320

Connell, Richard 368
Conner, Nadine 189, 424, 562, 565, 566
Conrad, Connie 488
Conrad, Eddy 368
Conreid, Hans 398
Conroy, Frank 117, 124
Considine, John W. Jr. 60, 77, 170
Conte, John 590
Conti, Albert 51, 68, 72, **74**
Converse, Roger 316
Conway, Jack 343, 345, **346**, 380
Coogan, Gene 301
Coogan, Jill 178
Cook, Clyde 499
Cooke, Allan 499
Cooke, Hal 316
Coolidge, Edwina 436
Cooper, Gary 41, 355
Cooper, George 316
Cooper, Inez 435, **441**, 443
Cooper, Jackie 167
Cooper, Ray 465
Copeland, Nick 172, 381
Cording, Harry 174
Corey, Jeff 398
"Cork Leg, The" 576
Coronado 51
Corrado, Gino 68, 131, 146, 381, 399, 435
Cort Theatre, NYC 517
Cortes, Armand 399
Corthell, Herbert 488
Cosgrave, Luke 249
Coslow, Sam 40
Cossart, Ernest 488, 490, **495**, 497
Costello, Dolores 266
Costello, William "Willy" 368
Cota, David 518
Counts, Eleanor 499
Couple Ideal, Le (*Sweethearts*) **317**
Courtleigh, William 424
"Cousin Ebenezer" 534, 537
Covert, Earl 222, 223, 249, 270, 399, 451, 590
Cowan, Jerome **542**

Cowan, Lynn 172
Coward, Noël 70, 369, 398, 399, 400, 410
Cowl, Jane 412
Cox, Judith Mary 159
Cradle Snatchers, The 10
Crain, Earl Sr. 506
Cramer, Duncan 81
Crane, Richard 499
Crawford, Broderick 591
Crawford, Helen 156, 549
Crawford, Joan 170, 171, 172, 207, 224, 249, 315
Creamer, Harry 505
Creation, The 585
Creelman, Eileen 189
Cremonesi, Paul 249
Crewe, Regina 189
Crisler, B.K. 335
Crockett, Charles 117
Cronyn, Hume 476, **480**
Crosby, Bing 18, 113, 555
Crowell, William 275
Crowther, Bosley 115, 396, 410, 421, 432, 448, 473, 505
"Crystal Candelabra, The" 128
Cuban Love Song 176
Cue Magazine 421
Cukor, George 91, 92
Cunningham, Cecil 102, 112, 114, 381, 388, 436, **447**, 464, 470
Cupidon Mène la Danse (*Three Daring Daughters*) 517
Curci, Elvira 476, 483
Curtis, Alan 275, 499
Cutler, Bunty 381, 387
Cutter, Murray 288, 300, 366
Czaritza **263**, 270, 377

D'Albrook, Sid 435
d'Ambricourt, Adrienne 117, 146, 228, 237, **240**
d'Arno, Albert 369
d'Avril, Yola 22, 25, 117
D'Ennery, Guy 249, 275
D'Orsay, Fifi 150
"Da geh' ich zu" 145
Daas, Eddie 172
Dacre, Harry 166

"Daisy Bell" 166
Dale, Esther 356, 358, 436, **447**
Daley, Jack 464
Dallinger, Nat 546
Dalton, Wesley 577, 584
Daly, John 539
Dalya, Jacqueline 435, 465
Damita, Lili **95**, 101
Damone, Vic 270
"Dance Like a Fool" 128
Dance of Life, The 88
"Dance Your Cares Away" 397
Dancing Lady 113, 125, **170–172**, 200
Dane, Olga 207, 223
Daniel, Eliot 505
Daniell, Henry 274, 277
Daniels, William 166, 174, 206, 380
Danilo, Prince 132–133
"Danny Boy" 576
"Dansando O Samba" 577
"Danse Jeanette" 287
"Danse Macabre" 577
Darby, Ken 366, 505, 561, 571, 591
"Dardanella" 551
"Dark Eyes" – See "Otchi Chornia"
Darmour, Roy 499
Darr, Vondell 424
Darro, Frankie 102
"Das hat Rrrrass!" 145
Daumery, Carrie 102, **105**, 146
Davenport, Elinore 451, 592
Davenport, Harry 248, 517, 519
Davey, Allen 315, 398; Oscar nomination, *Bitter Sweet*, 399; Special Oscar citation, *Sweethearts*, 317
David, James (Jim) 465
Davidoff, Alexis 369, 506
Davidson, Lawford 33, 37
Davidson, Max 60, 62, 117, 288
Davidson, William B. 68, 72
Davies, Blair 248
Davies, Georges 146, 151
Davies, Marion 177, 192, 289
Davis, Dorothy 33

Davis, George (Georges) 92, 102, 107, 117, 248, 258, 435
Davis, Johnnie "Scat" 488, **490**, 496
Dawn, Isabel 300
Dawn, Jack 248, 343, 356, 368, 380, 398, 412, 434, 517, 590, 591
Dawn, Lyle 248
Dawson, Hal K. 316, 320
"Day after Day" 100
Day at the Races, A 408
Day, Doris 539
Day, Doris (not the singer) 591
Day, Dulcie 117, 316
De Briac, Jean 399
de Brulier, Nigel 228
"De Camptown Races" 314, 576, 582
de Cordoba, Pedro 275
de Falla, Manuel 529
de Fremery, James and Eileen 224–225
De Gaetano, Al 68
De Garro, Harold 488
De Gombert, Georges 146
de Koven, Reginald 192, 422
de Musset, Alfred 269, 474
De Neel, Germaine 117
de Ravenne, Arthur 146
de Schauensee, Max 158, 197
de Silva, Petra R. 465
De Spionne van Castillie (*The Firefly*) 274, **275**
De Tolly, Lola 506
de Vinna, Clyde 380
De Winton, Albert 22
"Dead Broke" 349, 355
Deagon, Arthur 207
Dean, Dalie 170
Dean, Diana 249
Dean, Dixie 172
Dean, Harriet 488
DeAngeles, Ralph 344, 355
"Dear Little Café" 404, 406, 410, **411**, 412, 563
"Dear When I Met You" 572
Dearing, Edgar 207
"Death Is the Cool Night 553
"Death March" 41

DeBakey, Dr. Michael 550
Debussy, Claude 505
"Deck the Halls" 577
"Dedication" 577
Dee, Frances 33, 51
Deep in My Heart 270, 397
"Deep in My Heart, Dear" 577
"Deep in Someone's Heart" 10
"Deep River" 577
Dees, Mary 172
DeGaw, Boyce 300
deGresac, Fred 315
Dehn, Dorothy 131
DeKoven, Reginald 300
Del Rio, Dolores 202
Del Ruth, Roy 423, 425, 434
Delatre, S. Louis 422
Delevanti, Cyril 477
Delibes, Leo 269, 366, 474, 528
Delicious 69
"Delilah" 577
Dell, Claudia 88, 313
dell'Acqua, Eva 450
Dellys, Emile 146
Delsarte, François 179
Delta Rhythm Boys 499, 502
Demarest, William 288, 292
Demetrio, Anna 248, 258, 590
DeMille, Cecil B. 70, 175, 249, 300, 413, 462, 477
Demi-Tasse Revue, The 6, 7, 8
Demorest, Drew 275
deMusset, Alfred 366
Den syngende Oprører (*Knickerbocker Holiday*) 488
Denison, Leslie 498
Denitz, Ann – See Eddy, Ann
Dennett, Jill 130, 356
Dennis, Dick 249, 270
Dennison, Eva 436
Denny, Reginald 68, **69**, **70**, **71**, 72, **73**, **75**, 76
Dent, Vernon 228, 245
Depp, Harry 117
"Depuis le Jour" 572
Der Kongress Tanzt 91
"Der Tod das ist die Kuhle Nacht" ("Death Is the Cool Night") 553
Deschamps, Émile 269

Index

Desert Song, The 224, 425, 540, **541**, 560, 573, 577, 579, 580, 583, 584, 585, 587
"Desert Song, The" 577
Desmond, William 477
Destinn, Emmy 300
DeSylva, B.G. 475
Det var i maj (*Maytime*) 247
Detlie, John S. 398, 434, 590; Oscar nomination, *Bitter Sweet*, 399
Deval, Jacques 366, 380
Devine, Andy 499
Devlin, Joe A. 316
Dewey, Earle S. 436
"Dialing for Dollars" 541
"Dickey Bird Song, The" 520, 528, 529
Dickinson, Dick 165
"Did You Ever Get Stung" 451
Dietrich, Marlene 499, 501
Dietz, Howard 475, 528
Digges, Mae 228
Dika, Juliet 146
Dill, Michael 530
Dillon, John Francis 300
Din för i kval (Yours for an Evening) 101
"Dinah" 222
"Dinah Shore Chevy Show" 541
Dinehart, Alan III 530
Dinovitch, Abe 344, 355, 365, 381, 451, 506
Dipsy Doodlers 528
Disney, Walt 502, **503**
Disque Gramophone 564, 565, 570
Divino Tormento (*Bitter Sweet*) 398
Dix, Richard 10, 16
Dixon, Mrs. George Dallas 158
"Do Not Go My Love" 572
Doblinger, Ludwig 132
Dobrynin, Akim 344
Doctor Kildare 357
Dodge, Beth and Betty (Dodge Sisters) 166
Dole, Nathan Haskell 529
Dolgoruki, Igor 506
"Dolly Day" 577, 581

Dolly Sisters 338
Dolly, Rosie 338
"Dolores" 577
Dominguez, Joe 301, 381
Dominion Theatre, London 90
Don Cossack Choir 254, 269, 249
"Don Juan's Serenade" (by Tchaikovsky) 577
"Don't Ask Me Not to Sing" 127
Don't Bet on Women 77–81
"Don't Bet Your Money on De Shanghai" 575, 577
"Don't I Do" 51
"Don't Tell Us Not to Sing" 127
Donahue, Mary Eleanor 517, 518, **519**, **520**, **521**, **525**, **526**
Donaldson, Walter 366
Donizetti, Gaetano 269, 270, 474, 505
"Donkey Serenade, The" 276, 279, 285, 287, 460, 563
Dooley, Billy 117, 174, 181
Door, W. Ripley 229
"Door of My Dreams" 220, 223, 563
Doran, Mary 102, 174
Dorr, Lester 275, 316
D'Orsa, Lonnie 60
D'Orsay, Fifi 146, **149**
Double Takes 47
Douglas, Jean 33
Douglas, Melvin 462
Douglas, Mike 541
Douglas, Milton 175
Dowling, Constance 488, **489**, 490, **491**, **493**, **494**, **497**
Downs, Hugh 541
Doyle, Laird 506
Doyle, Maxine 172, 173
Drake, Alfred 590
Drake, Roger 275
"Dream, A" 577
"Dream Lover" 26, 28, 29, 32, 563
"Dreams Never Die" 13
"Dream of Love" 314
Drei von der Tankstelle, Die 91

Dreier, Häns, 21, 32, 34, 51, 92; Oscar nomination, *The Love Parade,* 22
Dresden Opera 159
Dressler, Marie 166
Drigo, Riccardo 355
"Drigo's Serenade"– See "Love Serenade"
"Drink to Me Only with Thine Eyes" 417, 420, 422, 423, 563
"Drinking Song" (*The Student Prince*) 577
Driscoll, Tex 174
Drum, Steve 591
Du Frane, Frank 288
Duane, Nicholai John 499
DuBois, Vivian 436
DuBrey, Claire 167
Duck Soup 44, 113
Duell, Randall 530
Dugan, Tom 228, 424, 434
Dulac, Arthur 436
Dull, O.O. 60, 457
DuMaurier, George 13
Dumbrille, Douglass 174, **180**, **187**, 274, 277, **279**, 435, 445, **446**, **449**
Dunbar, Charles 174
Dunlap School, Philadelphia 5
Dunn, Bobby 61
Dunn, Eddie 343
Dunn, Josephine 92, 101
Dunn, Ralph 381, 488, 498
Dunne, Irene 8, 165, 277, 500
Dunne, Philip 172
Durante, Jimmy 167, 172, 173, 176,
Durbin, Deanna 313, 464, 478, 518, 591
DuRey, Peter 275
Dusty Road, The (Let Freedom Ring) 343, 344
"Dusty Road, The" 354, 355, 563
"Dutch March" 496
Duval, Odette 146
Duvivier, Julien 369
Dvorak, Antonin 537
Dvorak, Geraldine 51

Dwan, Allan **506**, 508, 516
Dyer, Bill 499

Earl, Mary 474
Earle, Edward 228, 288, 316, 488
Early, Margo 172
"Eastern and Western Love" 577
Eberhart, Nelle Richmond 474
Ebsen, Buddy 128, 290, 300, **305**, **306**, 313, 315
Ebsen, Vilma 128, 290
Eburne, Maude 435
"Ed Sullivan Show" 541
Eddy, Ann Denitz Franklin (wife of Nelson) 153, **341**, **342**, 434, 547
Eddy, Isaac N. (Nelson's grandfather) 156
Eddy, Isabel (Caroline Isabel Kendrick, Nelson's mother) 153, 154, 155, **195**, **341**; death, 550
Eddy, Marguerite E. (Nelson's stepmother) 156
Eddy, Martha Gardiner (Nelson's grandmother) 156

Eddy, Nelson
    ancestry 154–156;
    archive at Occidental College 205
    archive at University of Southern California 205
    art collection 204
    as composer 490, 492, 496, 497, 498, 505, 540
    as part of team 195–202
    as sculptor 382, 482, 549
    Australian tours 547, 550
    Balalaika 366–380
    birth 153
    Bitter Sweet 398–412
    Broadway to Hollywood 166–170
    childhood 153–155
    childhood homes 154
    Chocolate Soldier, The 423–434
    contract with MGM 165, 477
    contract with Universal 478
    Dancing Lady 170–172
    death 550–551
    early career 156, 157
    European voice training 159
    funeral 553
    Gilbert & Sullivan rôles 157
    Girl of the Golden West, The 300–315
    Handlebars 165–166
    home recording studio 205
    honorary degree 547
    I Married an Angel 434–458
    Knickerbocker Holiday 488–498
    Let Freedom Ring 343–355
    Make Mine Music 502–505
    marriage 341–342
    Maytime 247–274
    million-selling record 220
    multi-voice recording 503
    musical training 157, 159
    Naughty Marietta 174–193
    "Nelson's Eddy's Back Yard" 540
    New Moon 380–398
    newspaper work 156–157
    night club act 542, **540**, 548
    Northwest Outpost 506–517
    parents' divorce 156
    Phantom of the Opera 475–488
    radio career 162
    RCA recording session, 1957 547
    red hair 153, 154
    religious beliefs 155–156
    Rosalie 287–300
    Rose Marie 206–227
    screen personality 196–197
    Sweethearts 315–337
    television appearances 539, 540
    television pilot, "Nelson's Back Yard" 540
    war work 460, **463**

Eddy, William Darius (Nelson's father) 153, 154, 155, 156; death, 550

Edens, Roger 288
"Edgar Bergen Show" 541
Edwards, Cliff ("Ukulele Ike") 301, 303, **306**, 313
Edwards, Gus 169
Edwards, Sarah 249, 381, 388
Eggers, Lillian 435
Egner, Philip 299
Eisenhower, President Dwight D. 543
Eisenstein, Sergei 345
"El Amor Brujo" 529
"El Capitan" 299
El Desfile del Amor 21
"El Ukhnem"– See "Song of the Volga Boatman"
Eldredge, George 499
Elgar, Sir Edward 423
Elich, Michael 424
Elliott, John 43
Elliott, Alonzo 423
Elliott, Bill 92, 170
Elliott, Dick 436
Elliott, Frank 249, 381
Elliott, Gordon (Bill) 165, 166
Ellis, Jeanne 301, **303**, 314
Ellis, Mary 207
Ellis, Paul 131
Ellsler, Effie 590
Elmassian, Zarubi (Zari) 175, 247, 249, 590
Emanuel, Demetrius 464
Emerson, John 228, 245
Emmett, Fern 488
Empire Theatre, Paris 90
Empire Theatre, Syracuse 274
Emporte Mon Coeur (*Bitter Sweet*) 398
En el Balalaika (*Balalaika*) 366
Enamoradas (*Sweethearts*) 315, **316**
End of the Rainbow 506, 507
Enesco, Georges 529
Engång I Maj (*Maytime*) 247
Engel, Lehman 561, 562, 564, 571, 572, 577, 579, 583, 584, 585, 586, 587
English, Kay 174
"English March" 287
Enter the Guardsman 424

Index

Entwhistle, Harold 249
Episcopal Cathedral Church of the Saviour, Philadelphia 156
Eristoff, Nestor 506
Eristoff, Princess Anna 528
Ernest, George 316
"Es Waren Zwei Koenigskinder" 145
"Essayons D'Oublier" 126, 563
Esquires, The 591
Estes, John 498
Etchepare, Pierre 101
Ethel Barrymore Theatre, NYC 488
Etterre, Estelle 317, 356
Evans, Herbert 172
Evans, Madge 166, 167, 170
Evening Bulletin, Philadelphia 157
Evening Public Ledger, Philadelphia 156
"Evening Star" 269, 427, 429, 432, 434, 563, 567
Everest Records 560, 565, 566, 574, 575, 576, 577, 578, 579, 580, 581, 582, 583, 584, 585, 586, 587, 588, 589
Everest, Barbara 476
Everson, William K. 59
"Every Lover Must Meet His Fate" 319, **320**, 328, 335, 336, 337
"Everything I Have Is Yours" 171, 172

Fagan, Barney 166, 167
Fagan, Fred M. 228
Fain, Sammy 528
Fair of Sorochinsk, The 578
Fairbanks Center for Motion Picture Study 272, 379
"Fairy Belle" 577, 583
Faith, Gloria 33
Fallon, Charles 172
Family for Jack, A 529
Famous Music Corp. 99, 104, 105, 107, 108, 110, 112
Fanciulla del West, La (Girl of the Golden West) 300, 301, 302

Fantasia 502
Fantasio 90
Fantastic Fricassee 9
Fantôme de l'Opéra, Le 475, **477**
Fantomen På Stora Operan (Phantom of the Opera) 475, **477**
"Farewell to Dreams" 269, 271, 563
Farham, Dick 172
Farley, James (Jim) 228, 301
Farley, Pat 174
Farley, Patricia 130
"Farmer and the Cowman, The" 578
"Farmer in the Dell, The" 365
Farnum, William 33
Farrar, Jane 476, 482
Farrell, Charles 68
Farrell, M. 117
Farrell, Richard 424
Farrell, Vessie 175
Farres, Osvaldo 505
"Father Knows Best" 465
Father Lani's Choir 301, 314
Faust 158, 237, 247, 269, 270, 447, 450, 463, 564
Faye, Alice 313
Faylauer, Adolph 22
Fazan, Adrienne 146, 517
Fealey, Margaret 22, **23**, 26, 32
Fectean, Marjorie 499
Feist, Felix 192
Feist, Leo 304
Feitshans, Fred R. Jr. 498
Feld, Fritz 476, 488, 489
Feldman, Charles K. 498
Felix, Seymour 355
"Feliz Cumpleanos" ("Happy Birthday") 529
Feltenstein, George 556
Felton, Verna 572
"Femmes, Femmes, Femmes" 146
Fenwick, Jean 381
Ferguson, Al 368
Ferguson, Helen 340
Ferny, Ernst 101
Feuersnot 161
Fielding, Gerald 381

Fields, Stanley 381, 385, **391, 392**
Fields, W.C. 499
"Filles de Cadix, Les" 254, 269, 363, 366, 466, 474, 563
Film Daily 487, 528, 537
Film Daily's Ten Best Films list, San Francisco 229, 245
Film Fan Monthly 114
"Finaletto" (Friml) 222, 223
Finch, Flora 229, 245
Fine, Budd 61
Fine, Larry 170
Finston, Nathaniel (Nat) 101, 102, 114, 561, 562, 563, 564, 565, 566, 567, 568, 569, 570, 571, 574, 575, 577, 580, 581, 587, 590
Firefly, The, (1912 stage version) 274, 276
Firefly, The 177, **274–287**, 341
"Fireman's Bride, The" 573
First National Studios 412
"First Nowell, The" 578
First Presbyterian Church, Los Angeles 545
First Regimental Band of the Rhode Island National Guard 156
Fischer, Robert C. 248
Fisher, Marjory M. 204, 205
Fitts, Margaret 530
Fitz, Abbe 170
Fitzgerald, Peter 556
Five O'Clock Girl, The 289
Flagstad, Kirsten 462
Flaherty, Diane 9, 61, 175, 181
Flaherty, Pat 175
Flaherty, Robert 176
Flambeau de la Liberté, Le (Let Freedom Ring) 343, **344**
Flavin, James 316, 318
Fleischer brothers 502
Fleischmann, Harry 343
"Fleurette" 520, 528
Flickan från gyllene västern (Girl of the Golden West) 300, **302**
"Fling Out the Banner" 578
Flint, Sam 172

Florence and Alvarez 172
Florodora Girls 7
Florodora 369
Flotow, Friedrich von – See Von Flowtow, Friedrich
"Flow, Flow, White Wine" 379
Flowers, Bess 92, 317, 424, 591
Floyd, Frank 288
Flying Down to Rio 113, 200
Flynn, John H. 365
Fodor, Ladislas 464
Follow the Boys , **498–502**; Addenda, 591; Oscar nomination, Best Song , 500
Foltz, Paul 248
Fontanne, Lynn 424
Foote, John Taintor, 355
"For Ev'ry Lonely Heart" 359, 365, 366
Ford, Francis 301
Ford, Freddie 117
Ford, George 436
Ford, Harrison 248, 412
Ford, James 92
Ford, Tennessee Ernie 541
Forest Lawn Memorial Park, Glendale, CA 177, 553
"Forgive, Forgive, Forgive" 434
"Forgive" 432, 563
Forrest Theater, Philadelphia 543
Forrest, Chet 248, 267, 269, 270, 287, 315, 335, 336, 337, 355, 366, 378, 379, 439, 441, 449, 450, 529
Forrest, William 499, 517
42nd Street 91, 113
Fortune Teller, The 574
42nd Street 91, 113
Foster, Ed 167
Foster, Stephen 314, 355, 575, 576, 577, 579, 580, 581, 582, 583, 586, 587
Foster, Susanna 462, 476, 477, 478, **480**, 481, **486**, **487**, 499
Four Cohans Theatre, Chicago 16
Fowley, Douglas 172
Fox Films 33, 68, 77, 81, 290

Fox Movietone Follies of 1930 69, 70
Fox, Allen 356
Foy, Eddie Jr. 117
Foy, Gloria 170
Foy, Mary 174, **181**
Fralay, James 316
Francis, Arlene 539
Francis, Kay 43, **45**, 47, 49, **50**, 51
Francis, Tom 131
Frank, Christian J. 33, 131, 248, 381
Frank, Jerry 172
Franke, Constant 146
Franklin, Ann – See Eddy, Ann
Franklin, Calvin 161
Franklin, Irene 117, 125
Franklin, Sidney 133, 342, 412, 413, 434
Frantz, Dalies 316, 336, 368, 370, **372**, 379, 398
Fraser, Hugh 502
Frazee, H.H. 13
Freddie Slack and His Orchestra 500
Frederici, Blanche 102, **105**, **111**, 114
Freed, Arthur 173, 246, 464
Freed, Ralph 528
Freedley, Vinton 10
Freeman, Clair 499
Freeman, Ned 506
French, Charles K. 61
French, Dick 317
French, Park 60
Freudeman, A.E. 92, 101
Freund, Karl 60, 366, 423; Oscar nomination, *The Chocolate Soldier*, 424
Fried, Captain George 16
Friedgen, Bud 556
Friedkin, Joel 436
Friend, Cliff 474
Friend, Helene 22, 26, 32
Fries, Otto 117, 131
Friess, Bob 444
Frihedens Sång (*Let Freedom Ring*) 343
Frikin, Anatol 366–368, 378

Friml, Rudolf 32, 35, 40, 60, 61, 66, 206, 219, 220, 274, 287, 506, 507, 516
Frisco, Otto 172
Fritsch, Willy 341
"Frog Went A-Courtin'" 578
From Broadway to Heaven 166
"From the Land of the Sky Blue Waters" 473, 474
Fugue de Mariette, Le 174, **178**
Fuller, Marlyse 226
"Full Moon and Empty Arms" 578
Fulton, Irving 488
Fulton, John 498
"Funiculi, Funicula" 355
"Funny Little Sailor Man" 397

Gable, Clark 170, 171, 228, 229, **230**, 231, **233**, **234**, **237**, 554, 555
Gabriel, Guy 436
Gaiety Theater, Wash. D.C. 543
Galas de la Paramount 41
Gale, Joan 131
Galitzine, Leo 434
Gallagher and Shean 234, 245
Gallagher, Richard "Skeets" 43, **48**, 49, **50**
Gallagher, Trudy 398
Galli, Rosina 476
Galli-Curci, Amelita **201**
"Game of Love" 336
Gan, Chester 228
Garbo, Beverly Jean 528, 529
Garbo, Greta 357
Garcia, Capt. Fernando 275
Garden, Helen 51, 58, 60
Garden, Mary 273, 462
Gardiner, Reginald 316, 318, **324**
Gardner, Jack 316
Gardner, Ralph 498
Gargan, William 356, **359**, 360
Garland, Judy 290, 313, 334, 434, 464,
Garon, Pauline 146
Garrick Theatre, NYC 424
Garrick, John 60, 61, 62, **63**, 66, 67

Index

Garson, Greer 369, **422**
Gary, Gene 506
Gasnier, Louis 248
"Gaudeamus Igitur" 300
Gausman, Russell A. 475, 591; Oscar, *Phantom of the Opera*, 477
Gautier, Leonard 499
Gay Desperado, The 463
Gay Divorce, The 290
Gay, Janice 499
Gaynor, Janet 68, 69
Geary, Bud 229
Geisha, The 369
Geldert, Clarence 61
"Gentle Annie" 578
George Edwards Agency 156
George White's Scandals of 1935 290
George, Jac (Jacques) 275, 281, 316, 368
George, John 207
Geray, Steven 476, 482
German, Edward 369
Geronimi, Clyde 502
Gerrard, Henry 32
Gershwin, George 10, 18, 21, 69, 267, 287, 288, 289, 290, 299, 353
Gershwin, Ira 10
Getchell, Sumner 117
"Ghost Riders in the Sky" 578, 585
Giacosa, Giuseppe 223, 366, 537
"Giannina Mia" 280, 284, **285**, 287, 563
Gibbons, Cedric 129, 135, 172, 174, 206, 228, 247, 274, 288, 300, 315, 343, 356, 368, 380, 398, 412, 423, 434, 464, 517, 530; Oscar for *The Merry Widow*, 131; Oscar nomination, *Bitter Sweet*, 399
Gibson, Kenneth 381
Giglio, Alesandro 207, 223
Gilbert and Sullivan 369
Gilbert, Billy 131, 248, 274, 288, 294
Gilbert, Boyd 275
Gilbert, John 18, 129, 132

Gilbert, L. Wolfe 475
Gilbert, Ray 505
Gillespie, Arnold 172, 174, 228, 434
Gilmore, Dorothy 424, 432
"Ginette" 14
"Girl, a Fan, and a Fella, A" 167
Girl from Utah, The 574
Girl of the Golden West, The (1905 stage version) 300, 302
Girl of the Golden West 277, **300–315**; Addenda, 590
"Girl of the Golden West" (song) 315
"Girl on the Prow, The" 396, 563
"Girls at Maxim's, The" 145
"Girls, Girls, Girls!" 135, 138, 145, 556
Gish, Dorothy 10
Giterman, Juan 116
Gittelson, June 172, 381
"Give Me a Moment, Please" 58, 60
"Give My Regards to Broadway" 336
"Give Us This Day Our Daily Bread" 578
Gladstone, Hazel 9
Glagolin, Boris 368
Glamorous Night 369
Glaser, Vaughan 435
Glass, Elsa Dik 154, 192, 223
Glasser, Samuel 228
Glazer, Benjamin 133
Gleason, Pat 316
Gleason, Jackie 542
Glinka, Mikhail 378, 379
Globe Theatre, NYC 117
Glover, Charles W. 422
"God Rest Ye Merry, Gentlemen" 575, 578
"God Save the Czar" 379
"God's Country" 473
Goddard, Ed 249
Godfrey, Arthur 542
Godkin, Paul 434
Goethe, Johann Wolfgang von 434

Goetz, Ray 89
Goetz, William 81
Going My Way 425
Gold Diggers of 1933 113
Gold Diggers of Broadway 425
Golden Dawn 88
Golden, Red 170
"Golden Age of Hollywood" film reissues 545
"Golden Days" 578
Golden, Robert A. 300
Goldman, Harold 488
Goldsmith (*New York Times* reviewer) 13
Goldstein, Elayne 554
Goldwater, Senator Barry 545, 553, **556**
Goldwyn, Sam 337
Golitzen, Alexander 474; Oscar, *Phantom of the Opera*, 477
Golm, Ernest 477
Golubeff, Gregory 506
Gombel, Minna 130, **139**
Gomez, Thomas 499
Gondoliers, The 584
Gonzales, Soledad 275
Gooch, James 591
Good Gracious Annabelle 81, 83
"Good King Wenceslas" 578
"Good Night Boat" 8
"Good Night" (*Viktoria and Her Hussars*) 573
"Goodbye Forever" 299
Goodhart, Al 170
Goodman, Benny 505
Goodman, John B. 475; 591; Oscar, *Phantom of the Opera*, 477
Goodrich, Diane 9, 157, 158, 164, 341, 462, 546
Goodrich, Frances 174, 206, 274
Goodspeed, Muriel 398, **407**, 412, 451, 591
Goosson, Stephen 68
"Gopak" 578
Gordon, Alex 69
Gordon, Bobby 172
Gordon, Leon 77, 81, 366
Gordon, Mary 68, 356

Gordon, Max 126
"Gorgeous Alexander" 396, 397, 564
"Gorko" 379
"Gotta Be Good" 51
Gottschalk, Ferdinand 170
Goul, George 228
Gould, Charles 475
Gould, Dave 288
Gouldeni, Gene 146
Goulding, Edmund **250**, 251, 271, 272
Gounod, Charles 220, 247, 269, 270, 315, 450, 462, 463
Gravey, Fernand – See Gravet, Fernand
Grable, Betty 172, 313
Grace Church, Providence 155
Grace, Dinah 341
Graff, George Jr. 355
Graffeo, Phyllis 518, 529
Graham, Betty Jane 424
Graham, Erwin 502
Graham, Fred 207, 220, 249, 381
Granger, Dorothy 130, 381, 488
Grant, Austin 381
Grant, Cameron 530
Grant, Cary 15, 16
Grant, Grace 424
Grant, Joe 502
Grant, Kirby 248
Grant, Lawrence 175
Grapewin, Charley 301, **303**, 498
Grauman's Chinese Theatre 206, 558
Graves, Robert 117, 175
Gravet, Fernand 398, 400
Gray, Dorothy 207, 316
Gray, Gilda 207, **211**, **212**, 222
Gray, Jenifer 316
Gray, Mack 498
Gray, Peggy 506
Gray, Roger 131, 175
Grayson, Kathryn 33, 457, 464
Great Caruso, The 134, 531
Great Day 589
"Great Day" 578
Great Man Votes, The 266
Great Victor Herbert, The 61
Great Waltz, The 369, 374

Great Ziegfeld, The 277
Greed 53
Green Grow the Lilacs 171
Green, Harry 41, 43
Green, Phil 488
Greene, W. Howard 475; Oscar, *Phantom of the Opera,* 477
Greenstreet, Sydney 10
Greenwich Village Theatre 9
Greer, Howard 591
Greig, Robert 102, 105, 114, 207, 211, **212**, 223, 435, 441
Grey, Clifford 14, 21, 32, 379
Grey, Virginia 288, 292, 356, 359
Gribbon, Harry 60, 64, 67
Grieg, Edvard 529
Grier, Jimmie 100, 567
Grieve, Andrew 399
Griffies, Ethel 102, **105**, **111**, 114
Griffin, Merv 541
Griffith, Catherine 174
Griffith, D.W. 31, 228, 245, 276
Grimes, Bob 49
Groesse, Paul 274
Gross, Jack 475
Grout, Austin 451
Grove Street School, Pawtucket 156
Gruber, Edmund L. 299
Gruber, Franz 379
Grubles, Johnny 506
Grün, Bernard 366
Guard, Kit 175
Guardsman, The (1911 stage version) 423
Guardsman, The (1924 stage version) 424
Guardsman, The (1931 film version) 424, 425, 426, 434
Guardsman, The (1951 stage tour) 424, 543, **544**
Guardsman, The (2001 stage version) 424
Gubbins, John 368
Guilaroff, Sydney 398, 434
Guilbert, Gilles 247, 248, 270
Guinle, Pierre 22, 71, 90, 101

Guion, Raymond – See Raymond, Gene
Gulliver's Travels 502
Gurs, Peter 506
Gus Reed Singers 365
Guy Lombardo New Year 541, 550
Gypsy Love 18, 379

H.M.S. Pinafore 578, 581, 588
Haas, Dorothy 436
Haas, Hugo 506, 508, **509**, **510**, 517
Hackett, Albert 174, 206, 272
Hackett, Karl 275
Hagney, Frank 170, 174
Hajmassy, Ilona – See Massey, Ilona
Hale, Chester 172, 206, 213
Hale, George 498
Hale, Richard 488, **490**, 491
Halevy, Ludovic 379
Haley, Aileen 436
Haley, Jack 313
Haley, Jack Jr. 555
Hall, Ben 175, 229, 435
Hall, Bettina 117
Hall, Charlie 43
Hall, Donald 68, 229, 245
Hall, Ellen 68, 424
Hall, Geneva 249
Hall, Homer 229, 247
Hall, James 43, **44**, **45**, **48**, **50**, 51
Hall, Josephine 22, **23**, 26, 32
Hall, Mordaunt 32, 40, 50, 66, 81, 113
Hall, Natalie 413
Hall, Sherry 172, 228
Hall, Thurston 517, 519
Hall, Winter 28, 131
Hallelujah, I'm a Bum 113
Halliday, Robert 380
Halsey, Mary Jane 130
"Ham and Eggs" 257, 269
Hamer, Gerald 316, 330
Hamilton, Chuck 61
Hamilton, Margaret 530, 533, **535**
Hamlet (by Skiles) 584

Index 607

Hammerstein, Arthur 60, 66, 68, 206
Hammerstein, Oscar II 128, 206, 220, 222, 267, 380, 397
Hanby, B.R. 355
Handel, George Frederic 392, 397
Handel's "Largo" 397
Handlebars 165–166
Handy, W.C. 220, 336
Hanley, James 87
Hanlon, Tom 356, 499
Hanna, Henry 229
Hannemann, Walter 591
Hansen, Franklin 21; Oscar nomination, Best Sound Recording, 22
Hansen, Nina 506
"Hansom Cab Drivers" 169
Hanson, Howard 204
"Happy Am I" 128
"Happy Birthday" 529
"Happy Day" 335
Happy Days 498
Happy Days Are Here Again 129
"Happy New Year" 246
Harbach, Otto A. 117, 126, 206, 220, 222, 274, 287
Harburg, E.Y. 465, 473, 474, 475
"Hard Boiled Herman" 220
Hardie, Russell 166, 169, 170
Harding, Ann 300
Harding, Jackie Lou 499
Hardy, Sam 81, 84, **86**
"Hark, Hark, My Soul" 578
"Hark the Herald Angels Sing" 577, 578
Harlan, Kenneth 228
Harline, Leigh 498
Harling, W. Frank (Frankie) 9, 59, 60, 501
Harlow, Jean 22
Harman, Joe 436
Harmon, Pat 43
Harns, Katharine 399
Haroldson, Virginia 424
Harris, Major Sam 102, 207, 399
Harris, Marilyn 229
Harris, Roy 275

Harris, Winifred 381, 436
Harrison, Carey 499
Harrold, Orville 174
Harrold, Patti 8
Hart, Eddie 172, 369
Hart, Jeanne 130
Hart, Lorenz 21, 101, 104, 113, 114, 116, 129, 145, 171, 172, 313, 434, 439, 441, 449, 451
Hart, Moss 116, 272, 451
Harvey, Forrester 316, 329
Harvey, Jolly Lee 249
Harvey, Lew 275
Harvey, Lilian 114, 341
Harvey, Thad 365
"Hary Janos Suite" 412
Haskins, Virginia 584
Hasson, Jamiel 172
Hathaway, John 475
Hawkins, Timmy 530
Hayden, Harry 248
Hayden, Joe 170, 246
Hayden, Julie 251, 273
Hayes, George F. (Gabby) 114, 192, 343, 345, 347, **545**
Hayes, W. Donn 300
Hayle, Grace 117, 248, 316, 436
Hays Office 118, 195
Hayward, Betty 436
Hayward, Susan 40, 570
"He Who Loves and Runs Away" 280, 287
Head, Edith 101
Healy, Bill 498
Healy, Ted 170, 228, **230**, 232, 246, 273, 590
"Hear Ye" 496
Hearn, Edward 174, 228, 356, 381
"Heart That's Free, A" 9, 234, 246, 474
"Hearts Win, You Lose" 365
Heath, Percy 43
Hebrew Actors' Union 43
Hecht, Ben 9, 343
Hee, T. 502
Hees, Nelson (Mrs. Bentley Hees, Gene Raymond's second wife) 553
Heggie, O.P. 33, **36**, 37

Heglin, Wally 366
Heifetz, Jascha 540
Held, Tom 228
Helmore, Tom 517, 522
"Hello, Young Lovers!" 542
Hemingway, Richard 175
Hench, John 502
Henderson, Charles 571
Henderson, Dell 301
Henderson, Skitch 561, 566, 575, 576, 577, 578, 579, 580, 581, 584, 585, 586, 587
Hendrick, John 398
Henie, Sonia 313
Henley, Althea 68
Hennesy, Hugh 502
Hensen, Franklin 32
Herbert, Evelyn 380
Herbert, Hans 476
Herbert, Tom 131
Herbert, Victor 174, 177, 315, 317, 335, 366, 528, 529
"Here We Go 'Round the Mulberry Bush" 365
Hero, Stephen 517
Herodiade 588
Heron, Julia 591
Hershmensky, Leon B. 132
Hersholt, Jean 117, **118**
Hervey, Irene 208
Herzbrun, Bernard 591
Het Was in de Mei (*Maytime*) 247
Hewlett, Bentley 275
Heydt, Louis Jean 343, 346–347
Heyduck, Adolf 537
Heyman, Edward 355, 413, 516
Heymann, Werner Richard 488, 496, 497; Oscar nomination, *Knickerbocker Holiday*, 488
"Hh! Cha Cha!" 124, 128
Hickman, Dwayne 530, **531**
Hickman, Howard 248, 499
Hicks, Rick 252
Hicks, Russell 207, 210, 248
"High and Low" 65, 67
"High Flyin'" 267, 357, 359, **360**, 365, 366
Highlanders, The 247
Hill, Al 356

Hill, C.S. Ramsay, Major 591
Hill, Dorothy 224
Hill, Ramsay 275
Hilliard, Robert 300
"Hills Of Home, The" 578
Hinds, Samuel S. 499
Hip Hip Hooray 498
Hirschhorn, Clive 133
His Majesty's Theatre, London 398
His Majesty's Theatre, Montreal 463
Hit Parade 528
Hoban, Stella 8
Hobbes, Halliwell 207
"Hobbies" 8
Hodgson, Leyland 498
Hodnett, Lois 381, 397
Hoey, Dennis 464, 468, **472**
Hoff, Harold 369
Hoffenstein, Samuel
Hoffman, Gertrude W. 436, **448**
Hoffman, John 228, 315, 343, 356
Hoffman, Otto 436
Hoffsenstein, Samuel 475
Hoheit tanzt inkognit (*Rosalie*) 287, **288**
Hold That Coed 266
Holden, Fay 316, 390, **401**
"Holiday" 490, 496
Holiner, Mann 14, 16
Holland, John 368, **372**
Holland, William 498
Holloway, Edith 207
Holloway, Sterling 117, 121, 130, 136, 170, 505, 590
Hollywood Canteen 460
Hollywood Cemetery 553
Hollywood Diva 338, 462, 545
Hollywood Goes to Town 554
Hollywood Hotel 490
Hollywood Musical, The 133
Hollywood on Parade, 102
"Hollywood Palace" 541, 542
Hollywood Parade 498
Hollywood Reporter 539
Hollywood Revue 18
Hollywood Walk of Fame 558
Hollywood's Canada 224

Holmes, Maynard 170
Holmes, Stuart 530
Holming, Fay 266
Holt, Jack 228, 234, **236**, **240**, 241
Holtz, Tenen 343
"Holy Art Thou" (by Handel) 578
"Holy City, The" 235, 246, 564
"Home, Sweet Home" 336, 349, 355, 469, 475
Homans, Robert E. 61
"Honeysuckle and the Bees, The" 170
Hooker, Brian 32, 33, 40, 413
Hoon, Kirby 248
"Hooray for Hollywood" 490
Hooray for What! 473–474
"Hopak" 579
Hope, Bob 231
Hope, Frederic 129; Oscar for *The Merry Widow*, 131
Hopkins, Robert 228, 229; Oscar nomination, *San Francisco*, 229
Hopper, DeWolf 166
Hornblow, Arthur 337
Horner, Jackie **413**, 414, 422
Hornez, André 101, 146
Horton, Edward Everett 130, 139, **141**, 435, 440, **446**, 448, 449, 450, **453**, 455
Horton, Lester 475
Horwitz, Harry 436
Hot Heiress, The 313
"Hot Time in the Old Town Tonight, A" 105
Hough, Horace 81, 343
"House I Live In, The" 502
Housman, Arthur 131, 356
"How Are You?" 114
How Green Was My Valley 313
"How Long Has This Been Going On?" 288
"How Many Miles to Go" 379
"How to Win Friends and Influence People" 449, 451
"How'd You Like To?" 13
Howard, William K. 117
Howard, Esther 356

Howard, Jean 167, 170
Howard, Leslie 31, 413, 554
Howard, Mary 316
Howard, Moe and Curley 167, 169, 170
Howard, William K. 77, 81, 118
Howe, Julia Ward 247
Howell, Virginia 301
Howland, Olin 175, 301, **306**, 316, 318, **326**
Hoyos, Rudolfo Sr. 301
Hoyt, Arthur 117, 172
Hubbard, Lucien 207
Huber, Harold 184, **185**, 228, 232
Hubert, Ali 129
Hudson, Mildred 153
Huffine, Ray 502
Hughes Kiddies, The 170
Hughes, Carol 435, **438**, 440
Hughes, Glen 528
Hughes, Mary Beth 356
Hughes, Rush 288
Hughes, Tony (J. Anthony) 499
Hughes, Wayne **545**
"Huguette's Waltz" 36, 38, 40, 41, 571
Huguenots, Les 258
Hulett, Ralph 502
Hull, Arthur Stuart 249
Hull, Frank 117, 172
Humbert, Crown Prince 89
Humbert, George 288, 435
"Hungarian Fantasy" (by Liszt) 529
"Hunt, The" 114
Hunt, Eleanor 130
Hunt, Hugh 530
Hunt, Ida Brooks 423
Hunter, Ian 356, **359**, **360**, **364**, 398, **406**, 413, 414, **416**
Hurst, Brandon 248, 275
Hurst, Paul 61, 356, 358
Huston, Walter 229, 488
Hutchinson, Jack 356
Hvor Regnbuen Ender (*Northwest Outpost*) 506
Hyatt, Pat 528, 529
Hyman, Bernard H. (Bernie) 117, 228, 245

Index

Hymer, Warren B. 68, **73**, 75, 228
Hytten, Olaf 356

"I Am as Brave as John" 579
"I Am the Monarch of the Sea" 579
"I Can't Believe It's True...Maybe So"14
"I Can't Sing" 128
"I Concentrate on You" 579
"I Dreamt I Dwelt in Marble Halls" 270
"I Love Him" (by Friml) 220, 564
"I Love You" (by Porter) 579
"I Love You" (by Grieg) 579
"I Love You So" 564, 565, 566
"I Love You Truly" 340, 573, 579
I Married an Angel (1933/1938 stage versions) 33, 116, 434–435, 436, 451
I Married an Angel (unproduced 1933 film) 116, 118, 176, 434
I Married an Angel (1942 film) 434–458, 564; Addenda, 591
I Married an Angel (Screen Guild Theatre, radio) 436
"I Married an Angel" 443, 448, 449, 450, 451, 456, 564
"I Only Have Eyes for You" 579
I Pagliacci 158, **160**, 504, 591
"I Remember Mama" 250
"I Say It With Music" 173
"I Want a Kiss" 579
"I Watch the Love Parade" 122, 123, 127, 128
"I Will Be True to Thee" 579
"I'll Bring You a Song in the Springtime" 125
I'll Cry Tomorrow 40
"I'll Follow the Trail" 67
"I'll Get By" 502
"I'll See You Again" 400, 401, 409, 410, 412, 564
"I'll See You in My Dreams" **498**, 501, 502
"I'll Tell the Man in the Street" 449, 450, 451, 564
"I'll Walk Alone" (Oscar nomination) 500, 502
"I'm a One Man Girl" 13
"I'm a Red Hot Cradle Snatcher" 13
"I'm an Apache" 564
"I'm Falling in Love with Someone" 184, 189, 564
"I'm Just Nuts About You" 76, 77
"I've a Strange New Rhythm in My Heart" 290, 293, 299
"I've Been Working on the Railroad" 355
"I've Gotta Yen for You." 49, 51
If I Had a Million 71
"If I Loved You" 579
If I Were King 32, 33
"If I Were King" 40, 564
"If Love Were All" 408, **411**, 412
"If Someone Should Kiss Me Tonight" 87
"If Widows Are Rich" 146
"If You Are But a Dream" 579
"If You Could Only Come with Me" 402, 410, 412, 562, 564
"If You Give Me Your Attention" 579, 588
"If You Were Mine Alone" – See "Romance"
"If You're Anxious for to Shine" 579
"If You've Only Got a Moustache" 586
Ignorance is Bliss 424
"Il Bacio" 474
"Il Balin" 271
"Il était un Roi de Thule" 246, 564
Il Est Charmant 91
"Il se fait tard" 247
Il Trovatore 269, 270, 271
Illescas, Julie 223, 423, 529
Illica, Luigi 223, 366, 537
Im Goldenen Westen (*Girl of the Golden West*) **300**
Imazu, Eddie 300, 368, 380

IMDb (Internet Movie Database) 555
Imhof, Roger 228
Imperial Theatre, NYC 13, 206
"Impressions in a Harlem Flat" 126, 127
"In a Heart as Brave as Your Own" 379
"In an Old Rose Garden" 13
"In the Convent They Never Taught Me That" 336, 337
"In the Garden of My Heart" 169, 170
"In the Night" ("Nocturne") 41
"In the Still of the Night" 290, 295, 299, 564
"In Times Like These" 475
Indian Love Call 206
"Indian Love Call, The" 214, 215, 219, 220, 222, 223, 555, 564
Indian Love Lyrics 581, 587
Infuhr, Teddy 530, 534
Innocents of Paris 16
Institute of the American Musical 247, 506
Internet Movie Database 555
Intolerance 245
Iolanthe 158, 580
Irene (costume designer) 517, 530, 533
Irene 8
Irene ("Lux Radio Theatre") 462
Iron Butterfly, The 545
Irrwege der Liebe (*Broadway Serenade*) 355, **356**
Irving, George 381, 384
Irving, Margaret 228, 231, 316
Irving, Mary Jane 172
Irving, Paul 369
Irving, Suzanne 424
"Isidore the Toreador" 41
"Isn't It Romantic" 104, 114, 565, 566
Isn't Life Wonderful 31
"Isn't This a Night for Love" 579
'It Doesn't Cost You Anything to Dream" 573

"It Never, Never Can Be Love" 565
"It Never Was You" 489, 493, 498
"It Seems to Be Spring" 47, 51
"It Was Only a Dream Kiss" 100
"It Wasn't Meant for Me" 300
"It's a Great Little World" 10
"It's All Over But the Shouting" 297, 299, 300
"It's Love, Love, Love" 580
"Italian Street Song, The" 183, 189, 363, 366, 565
Iturbi, Amparo 517, 523, 529
Iturbi, José 517, 518, 522, 523, **526**, 528, 529
Ivins, Perry 21, 131

"J'Aime d'Amour" 565
"Ja, das Studium der Weiber ist schwar" 145
"Jack Paar Show" ("Tonight Show") 541, 542
"Jackie Gleason Show" 542
Jackson, Ethel 129, 132
Jackson, George 146
Jackson, Horace 60
Jackson, Selmer 464
Jacobson, Leopold 423
Jacoby, John 475
Jaffa, Henri 398, 412, 517
"Jail Song, The" 497, 498
James, Dudley 172
Janus Film 554
Jarman, Claude Jr. 530, 531, 532, **533, 534, 536**
Jarrett, Art 170, 171
Jarvis, Sidney 249, 356
Jaynes, Betty 316, 321, **334**, 336
Jazz Singer, The 1
"Je m'en vais Chez Maxim's" 148
"Je Suis un Méchant" ("Poor Apache") 114, 565, 568
"Je Veux Vivre dans ce Rêve" – See "Juliet's Waltz"
Jean, Gloria 499
"Jeanette and her Wooden Shoes" 335, 337

Jeanette MacDonald International Fan Club 552
Jeanette MacDonald? Les Documents Secrets **90**
"Jeannie with the Light Brown Hair" 580
Jeffreys, Anne 435, 441, 443
Jenks, Frank 498
Jennings, Al 591
"Jenny June" 580
Jepson, Helen 161
Jericho Choir 381, 397
Jerome, Ben 13
Jerome, William 170
"Jerum! Jerum!" 580
"Jerusalem" 565
"Jewel Song, The" ("Air des bijoux," *Faust*) 247, 565
Jewkes, J. Delos 175, 207, 220, 229, 344, 355, 356, 399, 451
Jimmy Grier Orchestra 567
"Jingle Bells" 363, 366, 580
Jobin, Raoul 463
"Job With a Future, A" 60
Joby, Hans 249, 356, 398
Jocelyn 576
"Joe Jazz" 47, 48, 51
Johanneson, Bland 189
"Johnny Fedora and Alice Blue Bonnet" 505
Johnson, Edward 462
Johnson, Fred 488
Johnson, Harry 488
Johnson, Howard 169, 170
Johnson, Johnny 488
Johnson, Kay 70
Johnson, Rita 356, 359, 364, 424
Jolson, Al 2, 7, 113, 475
Jones, Allan 207, 208, 217, 218, 208, 220, 223, **276**, 277, **278**, **279**, **280**, **282**, **283**, 285, 287, 313, 340, 563; *The Firefly*, 274–287
Jones, Eddie 381, 397
Jones, Edna May 172
Jones, Isham 502
Jones, Marvin 316
Jones, Robert Edmond 161
Jones, Sidney 369
Jones, Spike 541

Jonson, Ben 422
Jordan, Jewell 381
Jordan, Louis 499
Joslyn, Allyn 316, 317, **326**
Journey for Margaret 471
Jowett, Arthur 131
Jowitt, Anthony 228
Joy, Nicholas 530, 531
"Joy to the World" 580
Judels, Charles 92, 228, 248, 254, **255**, 368, 371, 398, 424, 436, 488
Judson, Arthur 159
"Juke Box Jury" Los Angeles 541
Julia Richman High School, NY 8
"Juliet's Waltz" 208, 220, 529, 565, 571
Julliard School of Music 463
"Jump Jim Crow" 267, 271, 272
June, Ray 60, 423, 434, **446**, 464, 517, 530,
Jurman, Walter 246, 247
"Just a Song at Twilight" – See "Love's Old Sweet Song"
"Just A-Wearyin' for You" 580
"Just for Tonight" 580
"Just For You" 213, 222, 223
Just Imagine 70
"Just We Two" 580

Kaaren, Suzanne 316, 436
Kahn, Gus 21, 129, 145, 170, 220, 246, 247, 273, 287, 300, 314, 314, 366, 379, 379, 410, 412, 432, 434, 502
Kahn, Otto 133
Kalish, Mel 102, 114
Kaliz, Armand 117, 398
Kalloch 434
Kalmus, Natalie 32. 117, 315, 398, 475, 517, 591
Kandiba, Alexander 249, 270
Kane, Helen 14
Kane, Marjorie "Babe" 316, 356
Kaper, Bronislau 246, 247, 379, 423, 430, 434; Oscar nomination *The Chocolate Soldier*, 424

Index

Karabanova, Zoia   506
Karels, Harvey   248
"Kashmiri Song"   580
Katz, Billy (William)   528, 537
Kay, Arthur   68
Kaye, Claudelle   167
Keane, Ed (Edward)   175, 183, 275
Keast, Paul   432
Keaton, Buster   173, 245, 381, **392**
Keel, Howard   207, 208, 556
Keenan, Frank   300
"Keep It Dark"   324, 336
"Keep the Light Burning Bright in the Harbor"   469, 472, 475
Keep Young with Music   517
"Keepsakes"   10
Keller, Harry   506
Kelly, Gene   555, 556,
Kelly, John   228
Kelsey, Richmond   502
Kemper, Jimmy   9
Ken Darby Chorus   505
Ken Darby's Octet   366
"Ken Murray Show"   539
Kendall, Cy   228, 301
Kendall, Victor   381
Kendrick, Caroline Isabel (Nelson's mother) – See Eddy, Isabel Kendrick
Kendrick, Clark (Nelson's uncle)   155, 156
Kendrick, Daniel, Mrs. (Nelson's great-aunt)   154
Kendrick, Edward Jr. (Nelson's uncle)   155
Kendrick, Edward Stillman (Nelson's grandfather)   155
Kendrick, William (Nelson's great-uncle)   155
Kenedi, Alexander G.   451
Kennedy, Edgar   228, 237, 245
Kennedy, Jack   228
Kennedy, Neal   399
Kenny, Colin   275
Kent, Crauford   175
Kent, Mary   366
Kenyon, Doris   **341**, 342
Kerby, Paul   316

Kerman, David   316
Kern, Hal C.   60
Kern, Jerome   8, 21, 117, 118, 126, 128, 353,
Kern, Robert J.   60, 274, 315
Kernell, William   77
Kerrigan, J. M.   77, 78
Kerrigan, J. Warren   300
Kerry, Norman   477–478
"Kerry Dance, The"   414, 422, 565
Keystone Kops   245
Kibbee, Guy   343, 347, **354**
Kilbride, Percy   488, 490, **495**, 530, 532
Kilburn, Terry   316, **321**, **322**, 324, 337
Kilpatrick, Reid   316
Kimball, Ward   502
Kinemacolor   35
Kinematograph Weekly   457
Kiner, Larry   559
King and I (summer stock production)   **544**, 585
King Features Syndicate   546
"King Louie"   40, 41
King of Jazz   18
King, Carlotta   224
King, Charles   499
King, Claude   249, 356, 381, 384
King, Dennis   18, **33**, **34**, 36, **37**, **39**, 40, 41, 207, 208, 435, 435, 564, 569
King, George   288
King, Hal   502
King, Stoddard   423
King, Walter Woolf   88, 368, 371, 378, 379
King's Men   43, 51, 366, 474, 475, 505
King-Keiser, Robert A.   475
Kingsford, Guy   465
Kingsford, Walter   174, **180**, 248, 262
Kinsky, Leonid   117, 131, 248, 435
Kipling, Rudyard   422
Kirk, Michael   499
Kirsten, Dorothy   220, 424, **555**, 560, 561, 564, 568, 570, 571

Kismet   267, 439, 575, 586
Kiss in a Taxi, A   13
"Kiss Me" ("before you go away")   412
Kiss Me Again   313
Kiss Me Kate   589
"Kit Kene Elvenni"   580
Klein, Philip   68
"Knee Deep in Rhythm"   170
Knickerbocker Holiday (1938 stage version)   488, 489, 493, 495, 498
Knickerbocker Holiday   488–498; Addenda, 591; Oscar nomination, Best Scoring, 488
Knox, Elyse   499
Kobliansky, Nicholas   506
Kodaly, Zoltan   412
Koenemann, Feodor F.   379
Kohner, Frederick   517
Kolker, Henry   77, 79, 117
Kollmar, Richard   488
Kolloch   464
Korn, Henry   344, 355
Kostalanetz, André   462
Kover, Eddie   499
Koverman, Ida   165
"Kraft Music Hall"   539, 555
Kraly, Hans   355
Kramer, Don   499
Krams, Arthur   517
Kreisler, Fritz   439, 449
Kress, Harold F.   356, 380, 398
Kreuger, Miles   247, 506
Kriesler, Fritz   412
Kruger, Alma   368, 379
Kruger, Faith   590
Kruger, Otto   488, 490, 541
Kulky, Henry   506
Kummer, Clare   81, 83
"Kuss, Der"   580
Kuster, Patrick   68, 102, 107, 176, 522
Kuznetzoff, Adia   248, 263, 270, 343, **344**

L'Amant de Minuit   68, **71**
L'Amore dei Tre Re   158, **160**
L'Elisir d'Amore   158

L'Espionne de Castille (*The Firefly*) 274
L'Isle des Amours (*New Moon*) 380
La Bohème 158, 334, 363, 366, 463
"La Donna e Mobile" 269
La Lucciola (*The Firefly*) 274
La Traviata **238**, 240, 270, 537
La Veuve Joyeuse – See *Veuve Joyeuse, La*
"Ladies of the Town" 401, **407**, **411**, 412
Lady Dances, The 129
Lady Windermere's Fan 22
Lady, Be Good 10
Lady's Morals, A 18, 70, 33,134
LaGalle, Fay 135
Lahr, Bert 207
Laidlaw, Harriet 9
Laine, Frankie 542
Laird, Julie 207
Lamarr, Hedy 369, 500
Lamas, Fernando 129, 135, 207
Lamkoff, Paul 206, 228
Lamont, Connie 131
Lamont, Harry 146, 368
Lamont, Molly 498
"Lamp Is Low, The" 580
Lamus, Conchita 518, 529
Lancaster, Elsa 174, 182, **185**, **186**, **506**, 508, **509**, **510**, **514**
"Land of Hope and Glory" 413, 419, 422, 423, 565
"Land of Sky Blue Waters" 565, 573
Landin, Hope 530, 535
Lane, Al 166
Lane, Burton 171, 172
Lane, Lupino 21, 25, **27**, 31
Lane, Marjorie 299
Lang, Howard 398
Lange, Arthur 343
Langley, Noël 247, 251, 272
Lanning, Reggie 506
Lansbury, Angela 522
Lanza, Mario 134, 531, 541, 555
Lapis, Joe 475
"Largo al Factotum" 269, 504, 505

"Lasst Mich Euch Fragen" ("Plunkett's Aria") 487
LaRocque, Rod 115
Larson, Sara 224
LaRue, Frank 498
Lassie 530, **533**, **534**, **536**
Lassie Come Home 518, 530
Lassie Perd...et Gagne (*The Sun Comes Up*) **529**
Lassie verliest, Lassie wint.(*The Sun Comes Up*) 529
"Last Dance, The" 412
Last Pioneer, The 516
"Last Rose of Summer" 270, 271
"Laughing Song, The" 540, 580
Laughlin, David 368, 379
"Laura" 580
Laurel and Hardy 44
Lauren, Odessa 499
Lawford, Peter 555
Lawlor, Charles B. 270, 336
Lawrence, Gertrude 17, 53, 544
Lawrence, Vincent 51, 368
Lawrence, William E. "Babe" 356
Lawson, Kate [Drain] 476, 481
Lawson, Priscilla 301, 304
Laye, Evelyn 398
Layton, Turner 505
Le Guere, George 117
Le Prophête 270
Le Sueur, Joan 248
Leach, Archie [Cary Grant] 15, 16
"Lead, Kindly Light" 580
Lean, Cecil 12
Lebedeff, Ivan 248
LeBorg, Reginald 300
Lederer, Charles 355
Lee, Ann Harriette 398, 399
Lee, Helen 528
Lee, Leonard 423
Lee, Sammy 166, 170, 464
Lee, Zara 434
Lefert, Joe 129
"Left All Alone Again Blues" 8
LeGay, Sheila 92
"Legend" ("Christ Had A Garden") 560, 580
LeGon, Jeni 591

Lehár, Franz 18, 129, 131, 132, 145, 146, 379
Lehman, Lilli 471
Lehman, Veta 488
Lehmann, Lotte 162, **201**, 266, 462, 464
Leiber, Fritz 476
Leigh, Nelson 498
Leigh, Rowland 488
Leigh, Walter 369
Leighter, Lolita 499
Leipold, John 100
Lemaire, Ferdinand 432
Leo Feist Inc. 304, 307
Leon, Victor 129, 132
Leonard Gautier's Bricklayers 499
Leonard, Barbara 92, 99, 130, 146
Leonard, Gus 248
Leonard, Robert Z. 170, 250, 273, 274, 275, 280, 300,315, 355, 357, 380, 382, 457, 247
Leopold, Ethelreda 316
Leps, Wassil 4
Leroux, Gaston 475
LeRoy, Mervyn 207
"Les Filles de Cadix" – See "Filles de Cadix, Les"
Les Huguenot 269, 271
LeSaint, Edward 172
LeSeuer, Hal 301
Leslie, Maxine 435
"Less Than the Dust" 581
Lester, Roy 366, 590
Let Freedom Ring **343–355**
"Let Love Go" 580
"Let Me Always Sing" 341, 573
"Let's Be Common" 28, 32
"Let's Go Bavarian" 125
"Let's Go Native" 49, 51
Let's Go Native 16, **43–51**
"Let's Make Tomorrow Today" 491, 495, 497
Letsindige Marietta 174, **178**
"Letter Song," 434
Levey, Harold 10
Levien, Sonya 517
Lewin, Albert 133

Index

Lewin, Bill 518
Lewis, Allan 502
Lewis, Diana 398, **402**, **408**
Lewis, George 131
Lewis, Mitchell 343, 435, 464
Lewis, Ralph 228
Lewis, Sam 172, 222
Lewis, Sharon 316
Lewis, Ted 18, 500, 542
Lewis, Warren 590
"L'Heure exquise" ("Merry Widow Waltz") 145, 150, 152
Liberty Theater, NYC 8, 10
Library of Congress 128
Lichine, David 505
Lieber, Fritz 482
Liebesparade 21
"Liebestod" (by Wagner) 69, 71, 77, 270
"Liebestraum" 306, 312, 314, 522, 528
Liebman, Max 540, 590
Liefdesmart (*Smilin' Through*) 412
"Life for the Czar, A" 378
Life for the Czar, A 378
Life Magazine 340
Life of Jeanette MacDonald, The 464
Lightner, Winnie 18, 170, 171
Liliuokalani, Princess 450
Lillie, Bea 18, 53
Lincoln, Caryl 130
Lind, Herta 249
Lindley, Bert 207, 212, 214
Linehan, Tom 226
Link, John F. 488
Lion's Share, The 115
Lippé, Dr. Edouard 158, 161, 174, **183**, 205, 549
Lipson, Jack "Tiny" 424, 432, 436, 518, 526
Lipton, Lew 355
Liszt, Franz 314, 528
"Little Bit O' Scotch, A" 7
"Little Grey Home in The West" 328, 336, 337
Little Mary Sunshine 195

"Little Love, a Little Kiss, A" 417, 422, 565
"Little Work-a-Day World" 438, 440, 449, 451, 565
Littlefield, James H. and Caroline 4
Littlefield, Lucien 207, 211
"Live for Today" 565
Lloyd, Doris 498
Lloyd, George 381
Lloyd, Harold 115. 340
Lloyd, Stephanie 337
Loblov, Bella 131
Lockhart, Gene 316, 321, **322**, 336
Lockhart, Kathleen 316, 320, **322**, 336
"Lock Step" 167
Loeb, Philip 317
Logan, Frederick Knight 336
Logan, Stanley 591
Lohengrin 271, 340
Lohr, Hermann 336
Lombardo, Guy 541, 550
London *Sunday Times* 396
London Times 90
London, George 249, 465, **474**
Long Beach Boys Choir 228, 246
Long, Walter 174
Lonsdale, Eric 249, 413, 419
"Looking for a Boy (to Love)" 10
Loomis, Roy 432
Loos, Anita 228, 434, 438, 453
Loos, Mary Anita 172, 175, 207
"Lord Chancelor's Nightmare Song" (*Iolanthe*) 581
"Lord's Prayer, The" 581
Lorentz, Michael 554
Lory, Jacques 131, 146, 275, 249
Los Angeles Examiner 273
Los Angeles Opera 201
"Lost Chord, The" 580
Lottery Bride, The **60–68**, 88
Louis Jordan and His Orchestra 499
Louise 134, 572
"Louisiana Belle" 580, 583
Lounsbery, John 502
"Love and Marriage" 580

Love Goddesses, The 554
"Love Has Made This Such a Lovely Day" 491, 497
"Love in Any Language" 404, 410, 412
Love in the Afternoon 144
"Love is Like a Firefly" 287
"Love is Like That" 14
"Love Is the Time" 513, 515, 516, 517, 566
"Love Me and the World Is Mine" 232, 246
Love Me Forever 463
"Love Me Tonight" (by Friml) 39, 41
"Love Me Tonight" (by Rodgers) 102, 110, 114, 566
Love Me Tonight 16, **101–114**, 134, 554, 565
Love Parade, The **21–32**, 59, 88; Oscar nomination, Best Picture, 22; French version, 22
"Love Serenade" ("Drigo's Serenade") 349, 355, 563, 566, 568
"Love's Old Sweet Song" 269, 281, 365
"Lovelight in Your Eyes" 379, 391, 394, **395**, 396, 397, 566
"Lover" 104, 107, 114
Lover, Come Back 380
"Lover, Come Back to Me" 384, 391, 394, 395, 396, 397, 566
Lowe, Edmund **77**, **78**
Lowe, Jack 344
Lowell, Virginia 424
Loy, Myrna 102, 105, **110**, **111**, 114, 198
Luana 61, 65
Lubell, Jack 172
Lubin, Arthur 475, 479, 487
Lubitsch, Ernst 16, **20**, 21, 23, **27**, 31, 32, 35, 51, 52, 53, 91, 92, 100, 129, **129**, **135**, 195, 539; Oscar nomination, Best Director, *The Love Parade*, 22; "second acting," 94
Lucas, Paul 590
Lucas, Wilfred 175
Lucia di Lammermoor 270, 504

Lucke, Max 591
Luden, Jack 356, 368
Luders, Gustav 336
Ludwig, William 530
Lugosi, Bela 68, 72
Lukas, Paul 251, 590
"Lullaby of the Bells" 482, 487
Luna Llena (*New Moon*) 380, **381**
Lunt, Alfred 424, 425
Lupino, Ida 31
Luske, Hamilton 502
Lustige Witwe, Die 129
Lutz, Tricia 192, 224, 274, 337, 397, 423
"Lux Radio Theatre" 175, 249, 413, 462
"Lux Radio Theatre", *Maytime* 249
"Lux Radio Theatre", *Smilin' Through* 413
"Lux Radio Theatre", *Tonight or Never* 462
"Lux Video Theatre" 541, 542
Lvov, Alexei Fedorovich 379
Lydecker, Howard and Theodore 506
Lynn, Bambi 590
Lynn, Leni 399
Lyric Theatre, NYC 274, 423
Lys, Lya 146

"M'Appari" 271, 299
"Ma Blushin' Rosie" 169, 170
Ma Femme est un Ange (*I Married an Angel*) 434
Mac – See also Mc
MacArthur, Harold H. 591
Macaulay, Joseph 60, 62, **63**, 67, 68
Macauley, Amy Revere 12
MacDonald, Anna Wright (Jeanette's mother) 3, 4, **5**, 6, **89**, 340, **382**; death, 550
MacDonald, Ballard 475
MacDonald, Christie 315
MacDonald, Daniel (Jeanette's father) 3, 4, **5**, 6; death, 7
MacDonald, Edith Blossom [Blossom Rock] (Jeanette's sister) 4, 6, 7, 8, 90, 205, 340, **539**; death, 550, 553
MacDonald, Elsie (Mrs. Scheiter, Jeanette's sister) 4, 6, 206, **539**; death, 550

MacDonald, Jeanette Anna
20th anniversary 544
Angela 14
as part of team 195–202
autobiography 545
birth 3
Bitter Sweet 398–412
Boom! Boom! 15, 16
Broadway Serenade 355–366
Bubblin' Over 12
Cairo 464–475
changing screen personality 195
character names 438
Charley's Aunt (TV) 542
childhood 3, 4
death 550
Demi-Tasse Revue 6, 7, 8
early career 4, 6
engagement to Gene Raymond 276
engagement to Jack Ohmeis 338
engagement to Robert (Bob) Ritchie 338, 340
European contract offers 90
European tour 1931 90
European tour, 1933 115
European tour, 1959 544
Fantastic Fricassee 9
Firefly, The 274–287
Follow the Boys 498–502
French scandal book, 1931 89–90
funeral 553
Girl of the Golden West, The 300–315
heart seizure 544
I Married an Angel 434–458
Irene 8
Magic Ring, The 9, 10
Maytime 247–274
million-selling record 220
Naughty Marietta 174–193
New Moon 380–398
Night Boat, The 8
night club appearances 543
opera career 462–464
Prima Donna, TV pilot **542**
radio debut 90
Rose Marie 206–227
San Francisco 228–247
scholarship fund 553
Shubert contract 16
screen test 14, 16
Smilin' Through 412–423
Studio Girl, The 13
Sun Comes Up, The 529–537
Sunday school teaching 5
Sunny Days 13, 14
Sweethearts 315–337
Tangerine 8
television appearances 539, 542
television pilot, *Prima Donna* **542**
Three Daring Daughters 517–529
Tip Toes 10
war work **459–463**, 499
wedding **339–340**
Yes, Yes, Yvette 12, 13, 14

MacDowell, Edward 474
MacFadden, Hamilton 68, 69, 76
MacFarren, Natalie 537
Macgill, Moyna 517, 522
MacGregor, Casey 488
Maciste, Manuel Alvarez 275, 279, 287
Mack, James T. 77, 78
Mack, Wilbur 82, 166, 228
MacKaye, Frederic 275
MacKenzie, Tandy 228, 247
Macklin, James 228
MacLaren, Mary 229, 356
MacQuarrie, Murdock 61
MacRae, Gordon 131, 175, 399, 539
Macready, George 498
"Mad About Him Blues" 502
Madame Butterfly 302, **362**, 363, 366, 532, 537
Madame Satan 70

Index

Madden, Jeanne 488
"Mademoiselle" 336, 337
Mademoiselle Ma Mère 16
"Mag der Himmel Euch Verbegen" 487, 505
Magic Flute, The 179
"Magic of a Woman's Kiss" – See "Woman's Kiss, A"
"Magic of Your Love, The" 375, 377, 378, 379, 566
Magic Ring, The 9, 10
Magrill, George 229, 288, 381, 590
Maher, Frank 60
Mahin, John Lee 174
Mahoney, Tom 228, 301
"Maids of Cadiz, The" – See "Filles de Cadix"
Maienzeit (*Maytime*) 247, **249**
Main, Marjorie 207
"Major General's Song" (*H.M.S. Pinafore*) 581
Make Mine Music 162, 205, **502–505**; Addenda, 591
Malatesta, Fred 146, 172
Malin, Jean 170
Malone, Ralph 316
Mamoulian, Rouben 88, 101, 104, 114, 463
"Man for Me, The" 114
"Man I Love, The" 573
"Man Is the Lord of It All" 9
Mandel, Frank 380
Mander, Miles 476, **482**
Mankiewicz, Herman J. 32, 35
Manley, Lou 488
Mann, Hank 82, 477
Mann, Louis 166
Manners, Sheila 92
Mannheimer, Albert 517
Mannix, Ed 229
Mannors, Sheila 130
Manon Lescaut 158
Maple, Audrey 274
Maran, Francisco 249
"March of the Grenadiers" 29, 32, 90, 566
"March of Time, The" 166, 170
March of Time, The 66, 167, 169
March, Fredric 413

Marchand, Léopold 101
Marcus, Martin L. 247
"Marcus Welby, M.D." 465
"Maria" (*West Side Story*) 581
Maria Igiziaca (*Mary in Egypt*) 161, 163
"Mariachie" 308, 315
Maria-Curci, Gennaro 207
"Marianne" (*New Moon*) 393, 396, 397, 566
Marianne 289
Marie Antoinette 554
Marie-José, Princess 89
"Marine Hymn, The" 292
Marion, Frances 272
Marion, George Jr. 16, 43, 51, 101
Marion, George Sr. 16
Marion, Paul 476
Maris, Mona 435, **439**, **441**, 443
Mark, Bob 506
Mark, Michael 368, 506
Markes, Larry 502
Marks, Dave 229
Marks, Joe 288
Marlow, Anthony 476
Marlowe, John 436
Marquardt, Paul 129, 174, 300, 315, 316, 366
Marriage Circle, The 91, 94
Marriage of Figaro, The 582, 585
Marriage Tax, The 158
"Marseillaise, The" 397
Marsh, Frances 129
Marsh, Mae 129, 276
Marsh, Oliver T. 129, 170, 228, 247, 274, 276, 286, 288, 300, 315, 333, 356, 380, 398; Oscar nomination, *Bitter Sweet*, 399; Special Oscar citation, *Sweethearts*, 317
Marsh, Tony 498
Marshall, Boyd 10
Marshall, Captain Robert 14
Marshall, Herbert 31, **91**, 115
"Marta" 581
Martell, Alphonse 436, 477
Martha 270, 299, 478, 480, 487, 505

Martin, Allan Langdon 412
Martin, Freddy 528
Martin, John 70
Martin, Mary 250
Martin, Mildred 40, 50, 76, 87, 100, 113
Martin, Tony 397
Martin, Willsie (Reverend) **539**
Martinelli, Giovanni 205, 334
Martini, Nino 41, **42**, 463
"Martins and the Coys, The" 505
Marx Brothers 44, 50, 88, 113
Marx, Max 381
Marx, Samuel 172
"Mary, Queen of Heaven" 40
Marzorati, Harold 434
Mascagno, Bob 590
Maschwitz, Eric 366, 379
Mason, James (American silent actor) 207, 344
Mason, LeRoy 381
Mason, Lowell 247
"Massaa's in De Cold, Cold Ground" 581
Massenet, Jules 586
Massey, Ilona 288, 290, 290, 292, 299, 313, **368**, 369, 370, 371, **372**, 373, **375**, 377, **377**, 378, 379, 379, 506, **506**, 508, 509, **510**, **511**, **515**, 517; 591; *Balalaika*, 366–380; *Northwest Outpost*, 506–517
Masters, Harry 288
Mathiason, Thora 591
Matray, Ernst 366, 398, 423, 434
"Matus Moya Matus" 581
Max Liebman Presents 590
Maxwell, Charles 129, 174
Maxwell, Edwin 167, 381
"Maxim's" 138, 145, 148, 150
"May I Present the Girl" 450
Mayer, Louis B. 165, 177, 229, 290, 369, **422**, 425, 437; funeral, 544
Mayer, Ray 356
Mayfield, Cleo 12, 13
Maynard, Ken 102
Mayne, Eric 249, 477
Mayo, Frank 228
Mayo, Walter 60

Maytime 158, 202, 229, **247–274**, 357, 363, 466, 474, 556, 556; Addenda, 590; first uncompleted film version, 250, 547, 590; Oscar nomination, Best Score, 249
Maytime (1917 stage version) 247, 248, 250–251
Maytime ("Lux Radio Theatre") 249, 462
Mazzeo, Gary 287
McAfee, Harry 228
McAvoy, Charles 167
McCarey, Leo 43, 44, 51
McCarthy, Charlie 162
McCarthy, Joe 529
McCarthy, John Jr. 506
McCarthy, Joseph M. 8
McCarthy, Justin Huntly 32
McClain, John 464
McCormack, John 18
McCoy, Tim 176
McCullough, Philo 229, 343, 500
McDonald, Grace 498
McGill, Don 499
McGlynn, Frank 301
McGuire, Mickey 530
McGuire, Tom 228
McGuire, William Anthony 77, 287, 289, 300
McHugh, Kitty 356
McHugh, Matt 170
McIntyre, Frank 13, 16
McKenzie, Fay 172
McKenzie, Robert (Bob) 175, 228
McKenney, Florine 92, 131, 170, 172, 173
McKinney, Mira 316
McLaglan, Victor 77. 81, **82**, **83**, **86**, 343, 344, 345, **349**, **352**, 354, 355
McLaughlin, Mike 247, 274, 288, 300
McLennan, Oliver 288
McNamera, Maj. James 436
McPhail, *Douglas* 229, 247, 271, 313, 316, 321, **334**, 336, 590
"Me voilà toute seule" 247

Meader, Bill 499
Meador, Joshua 502
Medina, Enrique 543
Meehan, Elizabeth 506
Meehan, John 517
Meek, Donald 128, 130, 138
Meeker, George 369, 590
Meet Me in St. Louis 432, 500
Mefistofele 504, 505
Meglin Kiddies 249
Meilhac, Henri 379
Meistersinger, Die 580
Melbourne, Mauricette 399
Melchior, Lauritz 462, 553
Mellor, William 92, 101
Melnick, Daniel 555
"Melody in F" 170
Melody of the Heart 52
"Melody of Laughter" (by Lehár, from *The Merry Widow*) 145, 146, 148
"Melody of Love" (by Lehár from *Gypsy Love*) 379
Melton, Sidney 465
Mendelssohn Club, Albany 161
Mendelssohn, Felix 299
Menét, Vilma 543
Menjou, Adolphe 380
Menzies, William Cameron 60, 61, 67
Mercer, Jane 174
Mercier, Louis 175, 207
Meredith, John 498, 501
Merkel, Una 77, 77, 78, **80**, 81, 129, 130, **138**, 147, 167
Merkyl, John 131
Merlo, Tony 102, 107
Merman, Ethel 18
Merrill, Robert 560, 561, 572, 574
Merriman, Nan 422, 590
"Merry, Merry Month of May, The" 576, 581
Merry Mount 204
Merry Widow, The (1905 & 1907 stage versions) 129, 131–132
Merry Widow, The 72, 90, 94, **129–152**, 165, 556; Addenda, 590; American rights, 115; Censorship cuts, 129; French

version, 129, 146–152; Trailer, 129
Merry Widow, The (radio) 131, 539
Merry Widow, The ("The Railroad Hour," radio) 131
"Merry Widow Waltz, The" 131, 141, 142, 143, 145, 146, 150, 152; 566; Addenda, 591
Merton, John 275
Merv Griffin Show 541
"Message of the Violets, The" 336
Messager, André 60
"Messin' Around" 16
Metaxa, Georges 117, 118, 398
Methodist Hospital, Houston 550
Metrocolor 554–555
Metro-Goldwyn-Mayer – See also MGM 115, 117, 129, 133, 166, 170, 171, 172, 174,189, 194, 206, 228, 230, 247, 267, 274, 287, 300, 302, 313, 315, 317, 333, 343, 355, 366, 377, 380, 398, 400, 412, 423, 432, 434, 449, 457, 464, 517, 529; 547, 555, 556
Metropolitan Opera, NYC 18, 133, 161, 161, 300, 302, 425, 432, 462–463, 465, 474
Metz, Theodore A. 170, 246
Meyer, Greta **179**, 398, 403
Meyer, Torben 61, 590
Meyerbeer, Giacomo 269, 270
MGM film library 545
MGM/UA Home Entertainment Group 545
"Mi Chiamano Mimi" 573
"Mi velimo dase dase velisimo" 146
Michalik, Anna 67, 84, 85, 94, 95, 97, 122, 150, 151, 152, 154, 155, 159, 163, 165, 171, 186, 192, 195, 211, 214, 217, 223, 231, 232, 236, 248, 249, 251, 252, 271, 274, 275, 279, 280, 288, 289, 290, 293, 294, 295, 296, 300, 301, 302, 303, 306, 310, 311, 312, 313, 316, 317, 324, 325, 328, 329, 330,

Index

334, 339, 340, 343, 344, 345, 346, 356, 358, 359, 368, 370, 371, 372, 373, 374, 375, 377, 378, 380, 384, 386, 388, 391, 392, 392, 394, 400, 401, 403, 405, 406, 408, 413, 415, 416, 417, 418, 419, 420, 421, 429, 430, 437, 438, 439, 440, 444, 445, 446, 448, 449, 450, 450, 452, 453, 456, 460, 461, 463, 466, 467, 468, 470, 471, 472, 473, 474, 480, 482, 483, 484, 485, 486, 489, 493, 494, 495, 496, 496, 499, 501, 504, 506, 507, 508, 509, 512, 513, 514, 515, 517, 519, 520, 525, 526, 529, 539, 542, 548, 549, 551, 556
Middleton, Ray 488
Mikado, The 581
"Mike Douglas Show" 541
"Milaiya" 10
Miles, Art 369
Miles, Capt. Alfred H. 299
Miljan, John 381, 387
Millard, Helene 77, 78
Miller, Alice Duer 206, 274
Miller, Ann 556
Miller, Johnny "Skins" 131, 228, 590
Miller, Marilyn 17, 288
"Millions d'Arlequin, Les" 355
Million Dollar Legs (1932) 98
Million, Le 91, 95
Mills, Frank 316
Mills, Harry D. 43, 51
Mills, Kerry 247
Milner, Victor 21, 43, 51, 92, 101; Oscar nomination, *The Love Parade,* 22
"Mimi" 104, 107, 109, 114, 566
Minjir, Harold 117
Minnelli, Liza 555
Minnelli, Vincent 466
Minnie and Me 9
Minor's Bronx Theatre, New York 5
¡Mio Sera! 68, 75
Miracle of Sound, The 412
Mirriman, Nan 249

"Mirror, Mirror" 379
"Miserere" (*Il Trovatore*) 39, 270
Mississippi Belle 539
"Missouri Waltz" 330, 336
Mitchell Boys' Choir 229
Mitchell, Belle 228, **240**, 249, 274, **277**, 278, **279**, 477
Mitchell, Billy 381, 397
Mitchell, Bruce 228, 316, 344, 356
Mitchell, Grant 170, 381, 388, 464, 466
Mitchell, Rhea 229, 245
Mitzi 9, 10
Mix, Art 344
Mix, Tom 558
Moffat, Margaret 435
Mogelever, Lou 156
Mohr, Hal 475; Oscar, *Phantom of the Opera,* 477
Mohr, Joseph 379
Mollison, Clifford 368
Molloy, James Lyman "J.L." 269, 365, 422
Molnár, Ferenc 423, 424, 425, 426, 544
"Mon Cocktail d'Amour" ("My Love Parade") 32, 566
"Mon coeur s'ouvre à ta voix" 427, 432
Monaco, Jimmy 529
Moncrieff, Gladys 561
Monkton, Lionel 369
Monsieur Beaucaire 51, 58, 60
"Monte Carlo" 54
Monte Carlo 13, **51–60**, 98, 501
Montez, Maria 500
"Montezuma" 13
Montoya, Connie 518
Moore, Dennis 499
Moore, Emily 475
Moore, Fred 502
Moore, Grace 18, 70, 133–134, 189, 208, 223, 267, 272, 345, 362, 363, 380, 384, 462, 463
Moore, Ida 530, 533
Moore, Thomas 77
Moore, William 175
Moorhouse, Bert 356
Moran, Richard 248

More Than a Kiss 77
Morgan, Dennis [Stanley Morner] 273, 277, 590
Morgan, Frank 117, **118**, 120, **122**, **123**, 166, 167, 170, 174, 182, 288, 290, 293, **295**, 299, 315, 317, **326**, **333**, 356, **359**, 364, 368, **373**, 379
Morgan, Helen 88
Morgan, Margot 451
Morin, Alberto 248, 301
Morley, Thomas 269
Morner, Stanley [Dennis Morgan] 273, 277, 590
Morova, M. 248, 270
Morris, Corbett 275
Morrow, Doretta 560, 577, 578, 579, 585, 587
Morrow, Geoff 247
Mors Ferie Flirt (*Three Daring Daughters*) 517, **518**
Mortimer, Edmund 477
Morton, Bonnie 274
Morton, James C. 174
Moscona, Nicola 463
"Mother Carey" 581
"Mother in Mannville, A" 530
Motion Picture Academy Library 451
Motion Picture Code 192
Motion Picture Herald 464, 457
Motley 434
Mott Iron Works 155, 156
Mount Sinai Hospital, Miami 551
"Mountain Prelude" 530
"Mounties, The" 210, 220, 223, 566, 569
Moussorgsky, Modeste 427, 434
Movietone Recording 21, 32, 43, 51, 60, 68, 77
Mowbray, Alan 207, **209**
Mower, Jack 175
Mozart, Wolfgang Amadeus 528
"Mule Train" 581
Müller, Hans 51
Mueller, Sally 381, 451
Muir, Lewis F. 475
Mundin, Herbert 102
Muni, Paul **201**

Munier, Ferdinand   131, 435, 488
Munoz, Gabriel   275
Munsel, Patrice   590
Murfin, Jane   412
Murnau, F.W.   267
Murphy, Jack   248
Murphy, Jeanne   200
Murphy, Robert   301, **306**
Murray, Forbes   249, 301, 381
Murray, James   207
Murray, John T.   590
Murray, Lee   432, 465
Murray, Mae   129, 132, 135
Murray, Rae   33
Murrow, Edward R.   544
Muse, Clarence   500
"Musetta's Aria" – See "Quando M'en Vo"
Museum of Modern Art, NY   68, 77
Music Box Revue, The   133
Music Hall Rockettes, Corps de Ballet, and Glee Club   399
Music in the Air   128, 586
Musical Courier   165
musicals, unpopularity of   88–89
"My Alice Fair"   581, 587
"My Boy, You May Take It from Me"   582
"My Brudder Gum"   582, 583
"My Country, 'Tis of Thee" – See "America"
"My Heart Goes Dancing On"   467
"My Heart Is a Gypsy"   379
"My Heart's True Blue"   324
"My Hero"   426, 429, 431, 432, 434, 566
"My Lady"   13
"My Love Parade"   28, 30, 32, 566
"My Mad Moment"   45, 51
"My Magic You"   540
"My Message"   582
"My Name Is John Wellington Wells"   581
"My Northern Light"   63, 66, 67
"My Object All Sublime"   581
"My Old Kentucky Home"   577, 581

"My Reverie"   581
Myers, Harry C.   228, 245
Myers, Richard   13
Myril, Odette   117, 118, 435

"N'est-ce pas poetique?" ("Isn't It Romantic")   114, 566
"Napoli"   67
Nardelli, George   117, 146
Nash, Jacqueline – See Sherwood, Gale
Nash, Maxine   172
Nash, Ogden   274
Natheaux, Louis   398
National Legion of Decency   486–487
National Registry of Films   175
"Naughty Marietta"   566
Naughty Marietta (1910 stage version)   174, 178, 184
Naughty Marietta   161, **174–193**, 363; Addenda, 591; National Registry of Films – 2004, 175; New York Film Critics Ten Best list, 175; Oscar for Sound Recording, 175; Oscar nomination for Best Picture, 175; Photoplay Gold Medal Award, 175
Naughty Marietta ("Lux Radio Theatre)   175, 462
Naughty Marietta ("The Railroad Hour," radio)   539
Naughty Marietta (TV version)   590
Nawn, Tom and Company   167
Neagle, Anna   90, 398, 400
Neal, Paul   170
"Nearer and Dearer"   516, 517, 567
"Nearer My God to Thee"   244, 246, 247, 567
"'Neath the Southern Moon"   182, 189, 567, 590
Negri, Pola   16, 61
Neilson, Grace   288
"Nellie Gray"   355
"Nelly Bly"   581, 582

"Nelly Was a Lady"   582
Nelson and Jeanette: America's Singing Sweethearts (TV documentary)   554
Nelson Eddy Appreciation Society   165, 552
"Nelson Eddy's Backyard"   541
Nelson, Dick   499
Nelson, Eddie   16
Nelson, Florence   368
Nemeth, Maria   369
Nertsery Rhymes   167
Nervig, Conrad A.   247, 434
New Amsterdam Theatre, NYC   129, 288, 315
"New Love Is Old, A"   123, 127, 128
New Moon, The (1919 film)   380
New Moon, The (1927 stage version)   380, 384
New Moon (1930 film)   21, 134, 345, 384
New Moon   **380–398**, 556; Addenda, 590
New York American   189, 196
New York Daily Mirror   189
New York Daily News   187, 189, 196, 410
New York Film Critics "Ten Best" Award, *San Francisco*   229
New York Herald   115, 196
New York Herald Tribune   31, 66, 126, 189, 267, 314, 501, 528
New York Journal   189, 220
New York Post   9, 81, 87, 144, 285, 313, 314, 334, 378, 410, 421, 432, 448, 473
New York Sun   189
New York Theatre, NYC   174
New York Times   4, 10, 13, 14, 32, 40, 50, 66, 100, 113, 126, 144, 189, 220, 245, 246, 250, 266, 267, 285, 298, 301, 314, 335, 354, 364, 378, 396, 410, 421, 432, 448, 449, 473, 487, 496, 496, 505, 516, 528, 537, 543
New York Tribune   9
New York World   59

Index

New York World-Telegram 87, 126, 145, 189, 246, 285, 298, 298, 314, 314, 334, 354, 377, 396, 421, 421, 432
New Yorker, The 314
Newcom, James E. 423, 464
Newcombe, Warren 412, 434, 591
Newell, David **42**, 43, 46
Newell, Deena 434
Newell, Grace Adele **89**, 205, **539**
Newell, William (Billy) 228
Newlan, Paul "Tiny" 356, 368, 372
Newman, Joseph M. 129, 206, 228, 247
Newman, Joseph, Oscar nomination, *San Francisco* 229
"Nice Baby" 10
"Nichavo" 41
Nichols, Alberta 14
Nickolaus, John M. 300
Nicova, Leda 249, 436
Nielsen, Norman 344, 355
"Niĕt, Niĕt, Ya Nie Khotocho" 582
"Night and Day" 293, 299
Night at the Opera, A 277, 408
Night Boat, The 8
"Night Is Young, The" 588
"Night Was Made for Love, The" 121, 122, 127, 128
Nigro, Bea 381
Nilssen, Sigurd 368, 379
Niven[s], David 207, 208, 208
"No More Weeping and Wailing" 397
No, No, Nanette 12
"No Time to Argue" 366
Noble, Ray 572, 573
"Nobles Seigneurs, salut" 258, 269
"Nobody's Using It Now" 29, 32, 567
"Nocturne" ("In the Night") 41
Nodin, Gerald 398
Nolan, Lloyd 530, 535, **536**, **545**, 553
"Non Piu Andrai" 582

"None but the Lonely Heart" – See also "For Every Lonely Heart" 357, 366, 567
"Noontime" 246
Nordica, Lillian 271
Norris, Edward 175
Norstad, General Lauris S. 553
North Lake Tahoe Historical Society 224
North, Joe 275
Northwest Outpost 344, **506–517**
Norton, Barry 530
Norton, Edgar 21, 26, 51, 102, 114, 248
Norton, Ken 314, 545
Nothing But the Truth 14
Novarro, Ramon 117, 118, **118**, **121**, **123**, **125**, 127, **127**
Novello, Ivor 369
Novis, Donald 51, 59, 60, 92, 98, 100, 567
"Now Heaven in Fullest Glory Shone" 582
"Now I Believe" 114
"Now is the Month of Maying" 269
"Now the Day Is Over" 577, 582
"Now You've Met the Angel" 450
Nowell, Wedgewood 131
Noyes, Betty 450
Nugent, Frank S. 251, 301, 378
"Nuit il faut aimer, La" 122
Nunn, Larry 464
Nur ein Traum 91
"Nür Wer die Sehnsucht Kennt" ("None But the Lonely Heart") 366
Nye, Carroll 60, 62, **63**
"Nyet, Nyet, Ya Nie Khotocho" 582
Nymånen (New Moon) **380**

"O Come All Ye Faithful" 582
"O Holy Night" 582
"O Kommet doch, O kommt, Ihr Ballsirenen" 145
"O Lemuel" 582
"O Little Town Of Bethlehem" 575, 582

"O, Du Mein Holder Abendstern" – See "Evening Star"
O'Brien, Bill 229
O'Brien, David (Dave) 172
O'Brien, Margaret 473, **545**
O'Connor, A. Kendall 502
O'Connor, Donald 499, 500, 555
O'Connor, Frank 249, 301, **307**
O'Connor, Una 207, **208**, 209
O'Donnell, Spec 228
O'Driscoll, Martha 500
O'Keefe, Dennis 228, 275, 280
O'Malley, Charles 315
O'Malley, Pat 228, 464
O'Moore, Patrick 413, 414
O'Neill, Ed 381
O'Shea, Oscar 288, 294
O'Sullivan, Maureen **545**
Oakie, Jack 43, 44, **45**, 47, **50**, 51, 81, 98, 553
"Obey Your Heart" – See "Who Are We to Say"
Occidental College, LA 205
Oettinger, Malcolm H. 289
O'Farrell, Broderick 61
"Oh! A Private Buffoon" 583
"Oh Boys, Carry Me Along" 576, 583
"Oh, Cette Mitzi" 100, 567
"Oh, Evening Star" – See "Evening Star"
Oh, For a Man! 68–55, 209
"Oh, Gran Dio" 537
"¡Oh, Jeannette!" 116
"Oh, Lord, Most Holy" 573
Oh, Mama 16
"Oh, Promise Me" 299, 300, 583
"Oh! Susanna" 306, 355, 582, 583
"Oh! That Mitzi!" 100, 567
"Oh! What A Beautiful Morning" 583
Ohman, Phil 355
Ohmeis, Jack 338
"Ohne Mich Jeder Tag dir zu lang" – See "Rosenkavalier Waltz"
"Ojos Rojos" 287
"Oklahoma!" 583

Oklahoma! 560, 578, 582, 583, 584, 586
Oland, Warner 33, 35, 36, 37
Olcott, Chauncey 355
"Old Black Joe" 581, 583
"Old Dog Tray" 580, 583
"Old Folks at Home" 575, 583
"Old Refrain, The" 583
Oliver, Edna May 19, 288, 293, **295**
Oliver, Gerald 488
Oliver, Ted 356, 381
Olivet Presbyterian Church, Philadelphia 3
Oman, Paul 399, **409**
Omar, Kanza 465
"Ombra Mai Fú" 392, 397
"On a Summer Night" 75, 77
"On, Brave Old Army Team" 299
"On Parade" 328, 335, 336, 337
On the Avenue 425
On the Movies 335
On with the Show 167, 498
"Once I Loved Thee, Mary Dear" 583, 585
"One Alone" 573, 583
One Exciting Kiss 506
"One Hour with You" 97, 98, 100, 567
One Hour with You – See also *Une heure près de toi* 13, **91–101**; Oscar nomination, 92
"One Indispensable Man, The" 494, 497. 494
"One Kiss" 388, 389, 396, 397, 567
"One Look at You" 360, 363, 365, 366
"One Moment Alone" 118, 127, 128
"One More Kiss" 498
"One More Mile to Go" 509, 516, 517, 567
"One More Smile" 497
"One Night of Love" 573, 583
One Night of Love 134, 189, 363, 573
One Sunny Day 13
One Touch of Venus 586

O'Neill, Alice
"Only a Kiss" 220
"Only a Rose" 37, 40, 41, 567
Only Girl, The 574
"Onward Christian Soldiers" 583
"Open Thy Lattice, Love" 577, 582, 583
"Opera Wardrobe" 128
Oregon Shakespeare Festival 424
Oreste 33
Ormandy, Eugene 203
Orr, District Judge William E. 342
Orry-Kelly 16
Orson Welles's Mercury Wonder Show 500
Orth, Frank 356
Osborn, E.J. 342
Osborne, "Baby" Marie 499
Oscars (Academy Awards):
  Merry Widow The, Best Interior Decoration 131
  Naughty Marietta, Best Sound Recording 175
  Phantom of the Opera
    Best Color Cinematography 477
    Best Color Interior Decoration 477
  San Francisco, Best Sound Recording 229
Oscar nominations:
  Balalaika, Best Sound Recording 369
  Bitter Sweet
    Best Color Cinematography 399
    Best Color Interior Decoration 399
  Chocolate Soldier, The
    Best Black and White Cinematography 424
    Best Scoring of a Musical Picture 424
    Best Sound Recording 424
  Follow the Boys, Best Song 500

  Knickerbocker Holiday, Best Scoring 488
  Love Parade, The
    Best Actor: Maurice Chevalier 22
    Best Cinematography: Victor Milner 22
    Best Director: Ernst Lubitsch 22
    Best Interior Decoration: Häns Dreier 22
    Best Picture 22
    Best Sound Recording: Franklin Hansen 22
  Maytime, Best Score: Herbert Stothart 249
  Naughty Marietta, Best Picture 175, 177
  One Hour with You, Best Picture 92
  Phantom of the Opera
    Best Scoring for a Musical Picture 514
    Best Sound Recording 477
  San Francisco
    Best Original Story 229
    Best Score 317
    Best Sound Recording 317
Ottiano, Rafaela 248, 252, **258**, 435
"Otchi Chornia" ("Dark Eyes") 376, 379
Our Lady of the Angels Choir 275
"Our Love" 583
Our Town 580
"Out of the Night" 540, 584
Outlook Magazine 40, 59
"Ouvre ton coeur" 417, 422, 567
"Over the Waves" 355
Overman, Lynne 13
Owen, Milton 207
Owen, Reginald 207, 209, 288, 293, 413, 435. **439**, 440, **450**, 464, **466**
Owin, Rita 102, 112, 114
"Owl and the Bobcat, The" 182

Index

Oxford, Earl 117, 128, 131
Oyster Princess, The 26

Paar, Jack 541
Padden, Sarah 343, 349
Page, Lang 488
Page, Patti 541
Pagel, Raoul 591
Paggi, M.M. 92, 101
Pagliacci – See *I Pagliacci*
Paige, Robert 500
Palange, Inez 275
Pallais, Dorita 518, 529
Pallette, Eugene 22, 27, 43, **44**, 45, 61
Palmer, Adele 506
"Palms, The" 584
"Pampa Rose" 51
Pangborn, Franklin 356, 362, 366
"Panis Angelicus" 573, 584
"Para la Salud" 287
Parade d'Amour (*The Love Parade*) 21, 22
Paramount on Parade 18, **41–43**, 463
Paramount Orchestra 114
Paramount Pictures 3, 21, 32, 33. 41, 51, 68, 91, 133, 165, 300, 400
Paramount Publix 43, 101
Paramount Publix Hour 90
Paramount Studios, Joinville, France 115
Paramount Theatre, Paris 101
Paramount Theatre, San Francisco 245
"Pardon Madame" 573
"Pardon Me Madame" 209, 220, 267
Paris Daily Mirror 115
Paris, George 506
"Paris, Je T'aime d'Amour" ("Paris, Stay the Same") 32, 567
Paris, Manuel 477, 590
"Paris, Stay the Same" 26, 32, 567
Parish, James 237
Parker, Cecilia 174, 181, 182

Parker, Dorothy 315, 317, 337
Parker, Franklin 499
Parker, Linda 172, 174, 207
"Parlez Moi d'Amour" 573
Parnell, Emory 316, 343
Parola, Danièle 146, 147
Parrish, Helen 167, 249
Parrish, Robert **82**
Parsons, Louella 342, 457
¡Paso a la Libertad! (*Let Freedom Ring*) 343
"Passepied" 522, 528
Pasternak, Joe (Joseph) 129, 517, 518, 528
"Pat – Sez He" 350, 355
Patience 579
Patterson, Elizabeth 102, **105**, 111, 114, 128, 498
Patterson, Sue 33
Pawley, Anthony 275
Paxson, Helen 205
Paxson, Ted (Theodore) 153, 161, 205, 460, 490, 492, 496, 496, 540, **542**, 548, 550, 551, **551**, 561, 575, 576, 578, 580, 583, 584, 585, 586, 587, 591; death, 553
Payne, Howard 336, 475
Payne, John Howard 355
Payson, Edward 369
Pearson, John 228
Pefferle, Richard 464
"Peg O'My Heart" 584
Peil, Edward (Ed) Sr. 301, 518, 530,
Pelswick, Rose 220
Pendleton, Nat 381
Penn, Arthur 423
Penn, Leonard 274, **277**, 301
Penn, Max 170
Pennick, Jack 207
Pennington, Ann 4
Pennington, Minami 192
Pennsylvania Railroad Y.M.C.A. 4
"People Will Say We're in Love" 584
Pepper, Barbara 316
Percy, Donald 51. 60
Perelman, S.J. 315, 337
Perelman, Laura 315

"Perfect Day, A" 573, 584
Perrin, Jack 381
Perry, Charles Bates 530
Perry, Jean 146, 275
Pershing, Frank 518
Person to Person 544
"Personne Ne S'en Sert, Maintenant" ("Nobody's Using It Now") 32, 568
"Peter and the Wolf" 505
Peters, House 207
Peters, J.H. 117
Peters, John 506
Petina, Irra 368, 379
Petit, Albert 146
Phantom of Hollywood 591
Phantom of the Opera 158, **475–488**; Addenda, 591
Phantom of the Opera ("Lux Radio Theatre") 462, 477
Phantom President, The 113
Pharr, Frank 530
Phelps, Lee 207, 316, 368
Philadelphia Academy of Music 158, 558
Philadelphia Bulletin 158, 197
Philadelphia Civic Grand Opera 158, 161, 463
Philadelphia Inquirer 40, 50, 76, 83, 87, 100, 113, 169, 172
Philadelphia Opera Society 158, 263
Philadelphia Press 156
Philadelphia Record 158
Philadelphia Symphony Orchestra 158, 161, 203
Philbin, Mary 477–478
Philharmonic Auditorium, San Diego 162, 165
Philharmonic Society 161
"Philippine Dance, The" 240, 247
Philips, Mary 273
Phillips, Eddie 275
Photoplay Gold Medal Award, Best Picture, *Naughty Marietta* 175
Photoplay Gold Medal Award, Best Picture, *San Francisco* 229

Photoplay Gold Medal Award, Best Picture, *Sweethearts* 317
Photoplay Magazine 51
Piave, Frencesco Maria 247
Pickford, Mary 341
Picon, Molly 43
Picorri, John 275, 288
Picture Play magazine 266, 289
Pidgeon, Walter 88, 305, 300, 303, **306**, **313**
Pied Pipers, The 505
Piel, Ed 167
Pierce, Bob 301
Pierce, Edna 8
Pierce, Jack 475
Pietela, Walter 488
Pigen frå det gyldne Vesten (Girl of the Golden West) 300, **301**
Pike, Anita 146
Pilzer, Maximillian 561, 562, 564, 565, 566, 567, 569, 572, 573
"Pink Lady" portrait 543
Pinocchio 313
Pinza, Ezio 205, 463, 541
Pirates of Penzance 584, 588
Pitts, ZaSu 51, **52**, 53, 56, 60, 61, 62, **64**
Pixley, Frank 336
Planquette, Robert 269
"Plantons la vigne" 255, 269
"Play's the Thing, The" 584
Playboy of Paris 35
"Playhouse 90" 542
"Plays and Players" 158
Plaza Cinema, NYC 187
Plumb, Edward 591
Plunkett, Walter 591
"Plunkett's Aria" **478**, 480, 487
Poff, Lon 436
Poleri, David 463
Pollard, Alexander 398
Pollet, Albert 131, 139, 249, 530
"Policeman's Lot Is Not a Happy One, A" 584
"Polonaise in A Flat, Opus 53" (by Chopin) 379
"Polovetsian Dances" (by Borodin) 299

"Pomp and Circumstance" 423
"Poor Apache" 110, 114, 564, 565, 567
"Poor Little G String" 170
"Poor Pierrot" 118, 126, 127, 128
Pons, Lily **204**, 267, 462
Popkin, Joe 301
"Por Eso Te Quiero" 584
Porcasi, Paul 117. 207, **209**, 248, 254
"Pore Jud Is Daid" 584
Porgy and Bess 560, 574
Porgy 104
Porter, Cole 11, 287, 290, 299, 300, 539
Porter, Dorothy 517, 529
"Porterlied, The" – See "Plunkett's Aria"
Posford, George 366, 379
Post, Guy Bates 248, 253
Post, Rex 368
Post, William H. 32
Potel, Victor 301, 343
Potoker, O. 32
Potters, The 10
Powell, Dylys 396
Powell, Eleanor **289**, **290**, **291**, 292, **296**, **297**, **298**, **299**, 313, 555, 556; *Rosalie*, 287–300
Powell, Jack 399
Powell, Jane 270, 517, 518, 519, **520**, **521**, **524**, **525**, **526**, 528, 529, 529, 554, 555
Powell, Richard 175
Powell, Russell (Russ) 22, 28, 131, 167, 275
Power, Paul 436
Power, Tyrone **198**, 366, 554
Prager, Tim 247
"Praise the Lord and Pass the Ammunition" 584
Pratt, Purnell 288
Pray, Leonie 92, **93**
"Prayer" (by Victor Herbert) 181
Prescott, Charles 399
Press, Marvin 506
"Pretty as a Picture" **323**, 324, 336, 337
"Pretty Black-Eyed Susie" 584

"Pretty Girl Is Like a Melody, A" 277
"Pretty Things" 220, 568
Previn, André 530, 537
Price, Stanley 275, 283
Prickett, Oliver B. 436
Pride and Prejudice 357
Pride of the Regiment 369
Priester, Bob 432
Primavera (Maytime) 247
"Prima Donna" **542**
Prince Consort, The 21
Prince de Caucasie, Le 485, 488
Prince Igor 299
Prince of Pilsen, The 336
Princess Ida 579, 588
Prins Gemålen, I 21, **31**
Prinz, Eddie 170
Prior, Herbert 172
Prison Reform Association 9
Prisoner of Zenda, The 176
Prival, Lucien 130
Private Lives 70
Prizma Color 35
Producers Corporation of America 488
Prokofieff, Sergei 505
Prophête, Le – See *Le Prophête*
Protzenko, Sergei 378
Protzman, Albert 77
Prouty, Jed 82
Providence Opera House 153
Puccini, Giacomo 219, 223, 250, 271, 300, 302, 366, 366, 475, 537
Puglia, Frank 248, 263, 275, 368, 374, 476, 481
Purcell, Charles 248
Purcell, Dick (Richard) 381, 385, **392**, **393**
Purcell, Gertrude 498
Pye, Merrill 170, 288, 300, 315, 356, 398, 423

"Qu'auriez Vous Fait?" ("What Would You Do?") 100, 101, 568
Quaker Girl, The 369
Quality Street 404

Index

"Quando M'En Vo" ("Musetta's Aria") 363, 366
Queen, The 115
Queen's Affaire, The 90
"Queen is Always Right, The" 29, 32
Queen's Taste, The 14
Questel, Mae 92
Quillan, Eddie 167, 169, 170

Raab, Leonid 129, 174, 274, 300, 343, 356
Rabey, René Alphonse 220, 537
Rabinowitz, Max 488
"Rachel" 584
Raft, George 498, 500, 501
Railey, T. 246, 474
"Railroad Hour, The" (radio) *Apple Blossoms* 539
"Railroad Hour, The" (radio) *Bitter Sweet* 399, 539
"Railroad Hour, The" (radio) *Merry Widow, The* 131, 539
"Railroad Hour, The" (radio) *Naughty Marietta* 175, 539
"Raindrops on a Drum" 511, 516, 517, 568
Rains, Claude 476, **478**, 481, **482**, **484**, **486**, 487
Raker, Lorin 465
Ralph, Jessie 228, **240**, 451
Ramey, Gene 451
Rand, William 92
Randall, Pamela 398, **407**, 412, 451, 591
Rapf, Harry 166, 343
Raphaelson, Samson 92, 129
Rasch, Albertina – See also Albertina Rasch Dancers 12, 129, 166, 274, 275, 280, 288, 300, 308, 315, 319, 368
Raset, Val (Michael) 206, 228, 247, 380
Rasputin and the Empress 133
Rathbone, Basil 340, 462, 477
Raucourt, Jules 146
Rawlings, Marjorie Kinnan 530
Rawlinson, Herbert 81
Ray, Buddy 432

Raymond, Gene (Jeanette's husband) 10, 113, 202, **286**, 338, 413, 413, **415**, **416**, **417**, **420**, 421, **421**, **422**, 424, **514**, **539**, 542, **544**, 545, **546**, **556**, 558; as composer, 341; death, 553; marriage to Jeanette, **339**, **340**; second marriage, 553
Raymond, Jack 356
RCA recording session, 1957 547
RCA-Victor Records 397, 528, 547, 560, 561
Rebecca of Sunnybrook Farm 177
"Recessional" (by de Koven) 422
Red Hot Rhythm 44
Red Mill, The 177
"Red Rosey Bush" 584
Reed, David Jr. 246
Reed, Donald 275
Reed, Gus 365
Reed, J.T. 60
Rees, Virginia 451, 591
Reese, David 117
Regan, Phil 172, 173
Regas, George 207, **209**
Regas, Pedro 301
"Regiment de Sambre et Meuse, Le" 254, 269
Reicher, Frank 436
Reid, Virginia 249, 273
Reid, Vivian 172, 316
Reid, Wallace 129
Reiner, Fritz 158
Reisner, Charles F. 172
"Rejoice Ye Pure In Heart" 584, 586
Remsden, Frank 381
Renaud, André 117
Renault, George 146
Renavent, Georges 146, 435
René, Otis and Leon 355
Renick, Ruth 591
Rennahan, Ray 32, 117
Rennie, James 300
Republic Studios 506
Requa, Charles 131, 249
Resnick, Brooke 590

Respighi, Ottorino 161
Rethberg, Elisabeth 205
Revere, Amy (McCauley) **12**
"Reviens" 573
Reynolds, Debbie 555, 556
"Rhapsody in Blue" 18
Rhapsody No. 1 (by Bartok) 412
Rhodes, Georgette 146
Rhodes, Grandon 499
"Rhythm of the Day, The" 113, 170, 172
Riabouchinska, Tatiana 505
Ricardi, Enrico 117, 274
Ricciardi, William 228, 234, **236**
"Riccordati Di Me!" 584
Rice and Cady 167
Rice, Florence 315, 320, **322**, **333**
Rice, Rosemary 517
Rich, Dick 316, 343, 347
Richards, Addison 498
Richards, Frank 464
Richards, Ken 242, 339, 465
Richelavie, George 248, 274
Richetts, Thomas 37
Rickaby, Ruth 413
Ricketts, Thomas (Tom) 33, 102
"Ride, Cossack, Ride" 370, 378, 568
"Riders In The Sky" 577, 584
Ridges, Stanley 16
Riese, Friedrich W. 505
Riesenfeld, Hugo 60
"Riff Song" 584
Right Girl, The 14
Rigoletto 269
Riley, Art 502
Riley, Bill 166
Riley, George 499
Rimsky-Korsakov, Nickolas 284, 287, 375, 379
"Rintantou, Rintantirette" 145
Ring, Cyril 12, 77, **82**, 316, 344, 498
"Rio Rita" 585
Rio Rita 8, 584
Rios, Aldana 518
Rise and Shine 128
"Rising Early in the Morning" 585

Ritchie, Robert (Bob) 115, 338, **339**, 340
Ritter, Fred 506
"Ritual Fire Dance" 523, 529
Rivalen (*Let Freedom Ring*) 343, **345**
Rivkin, Allen 170
RKO Radio Pictures Release 502
RKO 165, 353
Roach, Bert 102, 104, 114, 228, 231, 436, 464
Roach, John 131
"Road to Paradise" 251, **259** 261, 269, 270, 271
Robards, Jason Sr. 131, 228, 245, 275
Robbins, Barbara 517
Robel, David 207
Roberta 127, 574
Roberts, Beatrice 175, 228, 476
Roberts, Florence 172
Roberts, Lee S. 423
Roberts, Nina 591
Robin Hood (by de Koven) 192, 226
Robin, Leo 13, 40, 41, 59, 60, 92, 502
Robinson, Dewey 117, 131, 172
Robinson, Earl 502
Robinson, Frances 413, **416**, 417
Robson, May 167, 169, 170
Robyn, A.J. 246, 474
Roccardi, Albert 22
Roche, John 51, 56, 60
Rochelle, Claire 381
"Rock and Blossom" 205
Rock, Blossom – See MacDonald, Edith Blossom
Rock, Mrs. Warren – See MacDonald, Edith Blossom
Rock, Warren (Clarence Warren) 205, 381, 398
"Rock of Ages" 585
Rockett, Albert L. 498
"Rodger Young" 585
Rodgers, Richard 21, 101, 113, 114, 116, 145, 171, 172, 313, 434, 439, 441, 449, 451
Roe, Guy 92, 101
Rogers, Buddy 18, 341

Rogers, Dr. Frank Sill 161
Rogers, Ginger 113, 200, 340
Rogers, Howard Emmett 60
Rogers, Roy 344, **545**
Rogers, Stanwood 166
Rogers, Will 10
Rogue Song, The 18, 33, 379
Roi des Vagabonds, Le 32, 33
"Rolling in Foaming Billows" 585
Roma, Caro 170
Roman, Peter 530
"Romance" ("If You Were Mine" by Rubinstein) 535, 537, 564, 568
"Romance" (by Debussy) 573
Romanoff, Constantine 174, 343, 506
"Romany Life" 574
Romberg, Sigmund 81, 247, 248, **250**, 269, 273, 287, 288, 289, 290, 299, 300, 302, 314, 355, 366, 379, 380, 397, 397
Rome, Betty 451, 591
Romeo and Juliet (1936 trailer) 554
Roméo et Juliette 158, 206, **207**, 208, 220, 462, 537
Romoff, Nicco 506
Rondell, Ronnie 301
Rooney, Mickey 167, 169, 555
Roquemore, Henry 174, 228, 248
"Rosalie" 290, 293, 295, 298, 299, 300, 568; Addenda, 590
Rosalie (1928 stage version) 288
Rosalie (Marion Davies version) 289, 295, 298
Rosalie 177, **287–300**, 369, 555, 556
Rosamond, Marion 435, **441**, 443
Rosanska, Countess 506
"Rosary, The" 585
Rosas, J. 355
"Rose Marie" 213, 222, 223, 568
Rose Marie – See also *Rose-Marie* 195, 200, 206–227, 305, 555
Rose Marie (1954 film) 207

"Rose of Tralee" 422
Rose, David 561, 562, 563, 564, 565, 566, 568, 569, 570, 571, 579, 584, 586
Rose, Vincent 475
Rose-Marie (1924 stage version) 33, 206–207, 208, 267
Rose-Marie (1928 silent film) 207
"Rosemary Clooney Show" 541
Rosenbloom, Maxie 500
"Rosenkavalier Waltz" 528, 570
Rosenkavalier, Der 135, 523, 539
Rosing, Bodil 68, 435, 452, 453
Rosley, Adrian 207
Ross, Adrian 422
Ross, Shirley 228, 231
Rossini, Gioacchino 269, 269, 404, 412, 505
Rosson, Harold 117, 423
Roth, Lillian 18, 21, 27, 31, 32, 33, 36, 37, **39**, 40
Roth, Sandy 172
Roubert, Matty 131, 170, 207
Rouget, Claude 397
"Roumanian Rhapsody No. 1" (by Enesco) 524, 529
"'Round She Whirls" 63, 67
Rounders, The (male quartet) 562
"Route 66" 525, 529
"Route Marchin'" 585
Rowan, Don 228
Rowland, Mary 499
Rowley, George 502
Royal Family, The 14
Royal York, Toronto 548
Royce, Lionel 343, 356
Royle, William 368
Rub, Christian 117, 126, 249
Ruben, Jose 117
Rubens, Alma 129
Rubini, Jan 131
Rubinstein, Anton 170, 537
Rubinstein, Artur 500, 502
Rubio, Jose 248
Ruddigore 582
Rudolph, Oscar 249
Ruffino, Carlos 275, 301, 315

Index

"Rufus Rastus Johnson Brown" 365
Ruggles, Charlie 92, 94, **97**, 100, 101, 104, **111**, 114, 368, 371
Rumann, Sig 248, 257, 398, 406, 408
Russell, Andy 505
Russian Cossack Choir 366, 369, 378
"Russian Easter Hymn" 512, **513**, 516, 517, 568
"Russian National Anthem" 379
Russian River 506
Rutherford, Ann 172
Rutherfurd, Tom 274, 277, 288, 293,
Ruttenberg, Joseph 366, 374
Ryan, Peggy 500

Sabbot, William 434
Sabel, Josephine 166, 167, 170
Sabicas, Augustin Castellon 488, 500
"Sabre Song" 585
Sadler, Donald 288, 301
Sahara, Las Vegas 543
"Sailormen" 585
Saint – See also St.
Saint-Saëns, Camille 432, 529
Sale, Richard 506
Sam Harris Theatre, NYC 13
Samo, Hector V. 229, 368
Samossoud, Jacques 488
Samson et Dalila 158, 427, 432
Samuels, Lesser 398
San Diego Evening Tribune 553
"San Francisco" 234, 240–242, 244, 246, 247, 568
San Francisco (planned stage version) 247
San Francisco **228–247**, 555; alternate endings, 244–245; Oscar, Best Sound Recording, 229; Oscar nomination, Best Actor: Spencer Tracy, 229; Oscar nomination, Best Assistant Director, 229; Oscar nomination, Best Director: W.S. Van Dyke II, 229; Oscar nomination, Best Original Story, 229; *Film Daily*'s Ten Best list, 229; *Photoplay's* Gold Medal Award, 229
San Francisco News 204
San Francisco Opera 163, 205
San Francisco, Stadt der Sünde 228
San Franzisko 228, 231
Sanders, George 398, 401, 403, **406**, **408**, 464
Sanderson, Julia 8
Sands, Las Vegas 543
Sanford, Ralph 316
Sans Souci Hotel, Palm Beach, Florida 550
"Santa Lucia" **259**, 261, 269
Santley, Fred 316
Sardo, Cosmo 530
Sargent, Brent 316
Sarno, Hector 131
Saturday Evening Post 68, 170, 530
Saunders, Blanche 33
Sauter, Eddie 505
Savage, Henry W. 9, 129, 132
Saville, Victor 369, 412, 423
Savitsky, General Sam 398, 436, 506, 590
Saylor, Syd 343, 346
"Say It with a Uke" 13
"Say It with Flowers" 7
Sayre, Ginny 39, 451, 478, 539, 542
Scharff, Lester 398
Scheherazade 375, 379
Scheiter, Bernard J. 206
Scheiter, Elsie – See MacDonald, Elsie
Schenck, Joseph M. 60
Schertzinger, Victor 21, 32
Schildkraut, Joseph 506, **512**
Schirmer & Co. 252, 261, 264, 319
Schlickenmeyer, Dutch 172
Schmidt, Lothar 91
Schoengarth, Russell 475
Schonberg, Alexander 248
Schubert, Mel 499
Schulz, Franz 271
Schunzel, Reinhold 366, 369
Schuster, Harold 77

Schute, Alan 465
Schutt, Arthur 475
Schwab and Mandel 89
Schwab, Laurence 380
Schwartz, Arthur 465, 474, 475
Schwartz, Häns 52
Schwartz, Jean 9, 14, 170
Scognamillo, Gabriel 129
Scott, Clement 300
Scott, Martha 500
Scott, Randolph 500
"Screen Guild Theatre" (radio) 204, 207, 317
Scribe, Eugène 269
Scully, William 288
"Se Vuol Ballare" 585
Seabury, Ynez 301, 305, **307**
Seal, Jean 172
Seal, Peter 506
Seaman, Earl 368
Seamon, Helen 366, 590
Sears, Zelda 9, 10
Seaton, George 172
Secrets of Suzanne 158
Sedan, Rolfe 51, 102, 105, 114, 117, 131, 207, 275
"Seek the Spy" 432, 434
Segal, Vivienne 88, 117, 118, **123**, 127, 128, 435, 438
Selander, Lesley 117
Selbie, Evelyn 131
Sellon, Charles 43, **47**, **48**
Selznick, David O. 170
Semels, Harry 275, 288, 301, 368
"Sempre Fidelis" 299
"Sempre Libera" (*La Traviata*) 240, 247, 270
Sennwald, Andre 189
"Señorita" 307, 314, 315, 568
Sepia-Platinum 274, 277, 300, 343, 355
"September Song" 488, 493, 497, 498
"Serenade" (by Drigo) – See "Love Serenade"
"Serenade" (by Romberg) 585
"Serenade" (by Schubert) 585
Seroff, Muni 477, 506
Sessions, Almira 436, **447**

Sewell, Blanche 174, 206, 288
"Sextet" (*Lucia di Lammermoor*) 269, 474, 504, 505
Seymour, Ann 16
Seymour, Dan 465
Shadow of a Lady 464
"Shadows on the Moon" 304, 314
"Shadows on the Sand" 379
"Shadrack, Meshack and Abednego" 585
"Shake Me and Wake Me" 13
"Shall We Dance?" 585
Shaller, Tony 488
Shannon, Ethel 248
Shannon, James Royce 336
Shar, Mildred 379
Shaw, C. Montague 170
Shaw, George Bernard 423, 424, 425
Shaw, Janet 499
Shay, Mildred 368, 435
Shayne, Tamara 506, 509, **515**
Shea, William 92, 101
Shean, Al 234, 228, 245, 288, 356, **358**, 365, 366, 556
Shearer, Douglas 117, 129, 166, 170, 172, 174, 198, 206, 228, 247, 288, 300, 315, 343, 356, 368, 380, 398, 412, 412, 423, 434, 464, 517, 530; Oscar for Best Sound Recording, *Naughty Marietta*, 175; Oscar for Best Sound Recording, *San Francisco*, 229; Oscar nomination, *Balalaika*, 369; Oscar nomination, *Sweethearts*, 317; Oscar nomination, *The Chocolate Soldier*, 424
Shearer, Norma 18, 115, 412, 413, 554
"She Didn't Say 'Yes'" 122, 127, 128
"She'll Love Me and Like It" 53, 60
Sheehan, John 170, 488
Sheeley, Elmer 274
Sheffield, John 530
Sheldon, Joan 172

Sheldon, Patti 488
Sheldon, Willard 498
Shelton, Marla 368
Sheridan, Frank 131, 228, 248
Sheridan, Michael J. 556
Sherlock, Charles 356
Sheron, Molio 506
Sherwood, Gale 114, 153, **540**, 541, **542**, 550, **551**, 560, 564, 565, 574, 575, 576, 578, 579, 580, 581, 583, 585, 586, 588, 589, 590
Shield, Leroy 562
Shilkret, Nathaniel 561, 562, 563, 564, 566, 567, 568, 569, 570, 571, 575, 577, 578, 581, 583, 584, 585, 587, 588, 589
"Ship Ahoy" 183
Shipman, Helen 174, 181, 228
Shirley, Florence 368, 376, 381
"Shoes" 397
"Shoo, Shoo Baby" 502
Shore, Dinah 500, 501, 502, 505, 541
Short, Dorothy 172
Short, Gertrude 356
"Shortnin' Bread" 162, 504, 505, 547, 568
"Shoulder to Shoulder" 67
Show Boat 10, 13, 33, 117, 277, 464, 560, 589
Show World 166
Shubert Theatre, NYC 248, 435
Schubert, J.J. (Jake) 13, 14, 337
Shubert, Lee 14
Shutta, Ethel 18
"Si Tu M'Aime" 379
"Si Tu Veux, Mignonne" 586
Sibley, John 502
"Sidewalks of New York" 169, 270, 336
Siegal, Bernard 356
"Sieh dort den kleinen Pavillion" 145
Sigaloff, Eugene 506
"Silent Night" 204, 376, 378, 379, 569
Silesu, Leo 422
Silverheels, Jay 506
Silvers, Louis 170

Simmons, Richard (Dick) 517, 521
Simpson, Ivan 381, 387
Simpson, Russell 228, 301
Sinatra, Frank 431, 555
"Sing Out" 495, 497
Sing Sing prison 9
"Singing a Song in Your Arms" 128
Singin' in the Rain 23, 246
Six Hits and a Miss 366
Skelly, Hal 8, 18, 88
Skipworth, Alison 14, 68, **69**, 70, 71
Slack, Freddie 500
Slaven, Buster 249
Slezak, Walter 435
"Slumber My Darling" 585
Smallens, Alexander 158, 178
"Smiles" 423
"Smilin' Through" 417, 421, 422, 423, 569, 586
Smilin' Through (1919 stage version) 412, 423
Smilin' Through (1922 film version) 412, 413
Smilin' Through (1932 film version) 412, 413
Smilin' Through ("Lux Radio Theatre") 413, 462
Smilin' Through 369, **412–423**, 434; Addenda, 591
Smiling Lieutenant, The 35, 92
Smirnova, Dina 506
Smith, A. Barr 172
Smith, C. Aubrey 102, **105**, **111**, 114, 368, 372, **376**, **377**, 379
Smith, Edgar 169, 170
Smith, Francis Carey 355
Smith, Frederick Y. 343
Smith, Harry B. 315
Smith, Jack 591
Smith, Jane 499
Smith, Leonard (Lennie) 412, 434, 499
Smith, Oscar 43
Smith, Pete 165–166
Smith, Queenie 10
Smith, Robert 170
Smith, Robert B. 315, 335, 336

Index

"Smoke Gets In Your Eyes" 574
"Snow Ballet" 170
Snow White and the Seven Dwarfs 502
"So Do I" 14
Sobol, Louis 540
Sock, Jasper 229
Soderling, Walter 436
"Softly, as in a Morning Sunrise" 387, 388, 396, 397, 569
Sohl, Marshall 451
Sokolskaya, Myra 506
"Soldier of the Czar" 379
"Soldiers of Fortune" 304, 314, 569
"Soldiers' Chorus" (*Faust*) 247, 269
Soloduhin, Gabriel 434
"Some Day" 37, 38, 40, 41
"Some Fine Day" (by Kern) 8
"Some Folks Say" 583, 586
"Some of These Days" 222, 502
Somers, Esther 530, 532
Somerset, Pat 92, 170, 248, 275
"Somewhere in the Night" 586
"Son of a Gun is Nothing But a Tailor, The" 112, 114
Sondergaard, Gale 500
"Song Is You, The" 586
"Song of Love" 569
Song o' My Heart 18
Song of My Heart 540
Song of Norway 267, 439, 578, 586
"Song of Paree, The" 104, 114
Song of the Flame 267
"Song of the Flea" 427, 432, 434, 569
"Song of the Mounties" – See "Mounties, The"
"Song of the Vagabonds" 37, 39, 40, 41, 569
"Song of the Volga Boatman" 372, 373, 378, 379, 569
Song of the West (Let Freedom Ring) 343, 344
"Songs My Mother Taught Me" 533, 537. 569
Sorcerer, The 581
Soray, Camille 590

Sorel, George 506, 513
Sosnick, Harry 561, 575, 579, 580, 581, 583, 584, 585, 586, 589
Soto, Alex 226
Sound of Music, The 250
Sousa, John Philip 299
Souter, Christine 541
South Broadway Theatre, Philadelphia 5
Spagnoli, Genaro 249, 590
Spanelská vyzvedacka (*The Firefly*) 274
Sparks, Ned 14
"Speak Low" 586
Spears, Paul Allen 488
Speer, Alan 432
Spela för mej (*Make Mine Music*) 502, **504**
Spence, Ralph 172
Spencer, Bob 129
Spencer, Robert 436
Spewack, Samuel and Bella 117
Spindola, Robert 275, 279, 287
Spivak, Charlie 500
Spøgelset i Operaen (*Phantom of the Opera*) 475, **476**
"Spring is Here" 436, 444, 448, 449, 450, 451. 569
"Spring Love is in the Air" 294, 299
"Springtide" (by Grieg) 527, 528, 529, 569
St. Brendan's Boys Choir 275
St. Helier, Ivy 398, 400
"St. Louis Blues" 220, 330, 336
St. Luke's Choristers 228, 275, 301, 314
St. Stephen's Church, Providence, Rhode Island 155
Stack, William 207
Stafford, Jo 560, 578, 587, 588
Stahl, Walter 476
"Stand Up, Stand Up for Jesus" 586
Standing, Wyndham 412, 413
Stange, Stanislaus 432
Stanley, Edwin 316, 499
Stanton, Harry 432
"Star Spangled Banner" 586

Stark, Georgia 410, 451
Stark, Tim 344, 355, 399
Starlight Theatre, Kansas City, Missouri 544
Starling, Lynn 68, 77
"Stars and Stripes Forever" 299
Stars in the Hollywood Walk of Fame 561
Steade, Doug 247
Steber, Eleanor 396, 424, 560, 563, 566, 567, 571
Stedman, Myrtle 229
Steele, Bill 207
Steele, Gile 380, 398, 412, 590
Steers, Larry 170
Steffe, William 247
Stein, Fritz 132
Stein, Leo 129
Stein, Paul L. (Dr.) 60, 61, **67**
Steininger, Franz 497
"Stella By Starlight" 586
Sten, Anna 195
Stephenson, Henry 412
Sterbini, Cesare 412, 505
Sterling, Andrew B. 365
Stevens, Cy 530
Stevens, Kenneth 356, 359, 366
Stevens, Risë **424**, **425**, 426, **427**, **428**, **429**, **431**, 432, **433**, 434, 560, 561, 562, 563, 566, 570, 577, 580
Stevens, Ted 315
Stevenson, Bob 368
Stevenson, Robert 172
Stewart, Cecil 465, 530
Stewart, Diane Lee 518, 529
Stewart, Donald Ogden 412
Stewart, James (Jimmy) 207, 208, **217**, 223, 224, 225, 555
Stewart, Marvin 247
Stewart, Melville 274
Stewart, Nicodemus 499
"Stille Nacht" ("Silent Night") 370, 376, 379
Stockdale, Carl 22, 172, 228
Stocking, Sybil 517
Stokowski, Leopold 161, 460
"Stolen Thunder" 68
Stoll, Freda 488

Stoll, Georgie 288, 464, 517, 528
Stone, Arthur 33
Stone, Lewis 530, **531**
Storey, June 172
Storm, Rafael 43, 369, 381, 436, **448**
"Story of a Starry Night" 586
Stössel, Ludwig 435, 452, 591
Stothart, Herbert 60, 117, 129, 145, 174, 178, 189, 206, 220, 228, 247, 266–267, 269, 274, 287, 288, 300, 314, 315, 355, 366, 366, 378, 379, 379, 379, 379, 380, 398, 412, 423, 434, 450, 464, 562, 563, 565, 566, 567, 568, 569, 571; Oscar nomination, *Maytime*, 249
"Stout Hearted Men" 381, 391, 396, 397, 556, 569
"Strange Music" (*Song of Norway*) 586
"Stranger in Paradise" 587
Stuart, Marvin 356, 380, 434, 464, 591
"Summer Serenade" 326, 335, 337, 569
"Summertime" 574
Sun Comes Up, The 267, **529–537**, 553, 565, 569, 570, 571; Addenda, 591
"Son of My Soul" 584, 586
"Sun-up to Sundown" 314, 570
Sunny Side Up 70, 88
Sunrise 267
"Surrey with the Fringe on Top, The" 586
Suss, Bernard 248
Sutherland, Eddie 498
Sutherland, Evelyn G. 51
Sutherland, Joan 271
Sutton, Grady 43
Sutton, Kay 368
Sutton, Paul 275, 368
Swailes, Harry 117
"Swan Lake" 299
"Swanee" 7
Swanson, Gloria 115, 462
Swarthout, Gladys **204**, 267
"Sweeping the Clouds Away" 41

"Sweet and Lovely" 586
"Sweet and Low Down" 10
Sweet Daddy 13
"Sweet Emerald Isle" 576, 579, 586
Sweet Kitty Bellairs 88, 313
"Sweetest Story Ever Told, The" 587
"Sweethearts" – See "Sweethearts Waltz"
Sweethearts (1913 stage version) 315, 317
Sweethearts 290, **315–337**; Oscar nomination, Best Score, 317; Oscar nomination, Best Sound, 317; *Photoplay's* Gold Medal Award, Best Picture, 317; "Screen Guild Theatre" (radio), 317; Special Oscar citation, Color Cinematography, 317
"Sweethearts Waltz" (by Herbert) 321, **325**, 328, 330, 333, 335, 336, 337, 525, 528, 529, 570
"Sweetheart, Sweetheart, Sweetheart" (by Romberg) – See "Will You Remember"
Sweetland, Sally 497
"Sweetly She Sleeps" 586
Swing Street 502
Swingtime 118
Sylvester, Henry 530
"Sylphides, Les" 269
"Sylvania's Queen" 32
"Sylvia" 587
Symes, Marty 355
"Sympathy" (by Friml) 282, 287
"Sympathy" (by Straus) 432, 570
Sysock, Claudia J. 423

Taggart, Ben 228
Taggert, Earl 228
Tailleur au Château, Le 101
"Take a Flower" 397
"Take Me Up with You, Dearie" 4
Talbot, Gloria 590
Talmadge, Norma 380, 412
Tamerez, Tom 172

Tamiroff, Akim 130, 146, **184**
Tang, Frank 172
Tangerine 8, 16
"Tango Bleu" 587
Tannen, Julius 398
Tannen, William 288, 356, 381, 385, **391**, 398, 465,
Tannhäuser 158, 179, 204, 269, 427, 429, 432
Tannura, Philip 488
"Tanya" 370, 378, 379
Tapfere Soldat, Der (The Chocolate Soldier) 423
"Ta-Ra-Ra Boom-dee-ay" 238
Tarantella (The Firefly) **274**
Tarkington, Booth 51, 60
Tausky, Herman 132
Taylor, Dennis and Pat 268
Taylor, Elizabeth 555
Taylor, Eric 475
Taylor, Forrest 167
Taylor, Kent 92
Taylor, Robert **201**, 290
Tchaikovsky, Peter Ilich 263, 270, 289, 299, 357, 366, 379, 485, 488, 540
Tchaikovsky's "Fourth Symphony" 527, 529
Tead, Phil 117
Teal, Ray 381, 506
Technicolor, 2-strip 18, 32, 33, 35, 60, 67, 166
Technicolor, 3-strip 117, 125, 315, 317, 333–334, 398, 412, 475, 478, 502, 517, 529
Ted Lewis and His Band 500
"Tell Me That you Love Me" 587
"Tell Me with Your Eyes" 509, 516, 517, 570
"Tell Me, What Is Love?" – See "What Is Love?"
"Temple Bells" 587
Temple University, Philadelphia 547
Temple, Shirley **204**
Templeton, Fay 166, 167, **169**, 170
"Ten Thousand Cattle Straying" – See "Dead Broke"

Index

"Ten Thousand Times Ten Thousand" 587
Tenbrook, Harry 175, 344
Tennent Presbyterian Church, Philadelphia 5
"Tennessee Ernie Ford Show" 541
Terry, Phillip 288, 368
"Tes Yeux" ("Thine Eyes") 220, 537, 570
Testör 424
Tetley Walter 499
Tevis, Carol 301, **304**, 315
Thalberg, Irving 115, 118, 129, 133, 134, 135, 251, 272, 273; death, 249–250
Thane, Dirk 368
"Thank the Lord the War is Over" 432, 434
That Lady in Ermine 144
That's Entertainment 554–555
That's Entertainment, Part II 555
That's Entertainment! III 167, 556
"That's the Rhythm of the Day" 171
Thayer, Ernest Lawrence 505
Theatre Guild 104, 424
Theby, Rosemary 229, 245
"Then You Will Know" 587
"There Is a Green Hill Far Away" 587
"There Is Magic in a Smile" 337
"There'll Be a Hot Time in the Old Town Tonight" 170, 246
"There's a Brand New Song in Town" 315
"There's a Long, Long Trail Awinding" 418, 423
"There's No Such Girl as Mine" 587
"There's Nowhere to Go But Up" 490, 496, 498
"They Didn't Believe Me" 574
They Shall Have Music 540
"This Is Your Life, Jeanette MacDonald." **539**, 541, 542
Thomas, Bernard 499
Thomas, Caroline 33

Thomas, John Charles 204
Thompson, Susanne 172
Thompson, Harlan 81
Thompson, Nick 301
Thompson, Ted 346
Thorpe, Richard 529, 531
"Three Blind Mice" 222
Three Caballeros, The 502
Three Cheers for the Boys 498
Three Daring Daughters 517–529; Addenda, 591
Three Musketeers, The 33, 35
Three Smart Girls 518
Three Stooges – See also Howard, Moe and Curley 167, 170, 171
"Three Times a Day" 96, 100
Threepenny Opera, The 65
Thrill of It All, The 539
"Through the Years" 587
Through the Years 413
Thursby, David 228
"Thy Beaming Eyes" 587
Tibbett, Lawrence 18, 40, 128, 134, 161, 165, 189, 204, 379, 380, 384
Tickle Me 267
Tierney, Harry 8
Tihmar, David 275
"Til the End of Time" 587
Tilbury, Zeffie 368
"Till I Wake" 587
"Till We Meet Again" 587
Tillie and Gus 71
Tillmany, Jack 11, 56, 179, 183, 210, 222, 241, 255, 447, 498
Tilzer, Harry von 365
"Time Changes Everything" 366
Time Magazine 87, 144, 189, 285, 334, 341, 421, 432, 448, 501, 537
Tin, Lee 131
Tiomkin, Dimitri 12, 170
Tip Toes 10
"Tira Lira La" (by Rodgers) 443, 450, 451,
"Ti-ra-la-la" (by Straus) 429, 432, 434, 570
"Tisket, A Tasket, A" 359, 365

TNT (Turner Network Television) 545
"To a Wild Rose" 474
"To Love or Not to Love" 297, 299
"Toast of the Town" 539
Tobey, Ruth 398, 404, 410, 488
Tobias, George 368, 371, **372**
Tobin, Charles 474
Tobin, Genevieve 92, **94**, 96, 100
"Today Show" 541
Today's Cinema 457
Todd, Ann E. 517, 518, **519**, **520**, **521**, **524**, **525**, **526**, 528
Todd, Fanny 16
Tokatyan, Armand 463, 537
"Tokay" 401, 403, 410, 412, 570
Tollaire, August 146
Tolle Marietta 174
Tolstoy, Count Andrey 288, 368
Toluboff, Alexander 117
Tom Jones (operetta) 369
Tom Nawn and Company 167
Tomarchio, Ludovico 117, 249, 259, 269
"Tomorrow" 587
Tombes, Andrew 368, 376
Tone, Franchot 170, 171
Tonight or Never (" Lux Radio Theatre") 462
"Tonight Show" (Jack Paar) 541
"Tonight We Love" 587
"Tonight Will Teach Me to Forget" 137, 141, 145, 570
Toomey, Regis 498
"Torna a Surriento" 41, 42
Tops, The, San Diego 540
"Toreador Song, The" 378, 379, 570
Torrence, Ernest 8
Torres, Luis 499
Tosca 217, 218, 223, **250**, 271, 475
Toscanini, Arturo 161, 163, 300, 302
Tosti, Sir Paolo 299
"Totem Tom-Tom" 206, 213, 214, 220, 222, 223, **224**, 570
Toukokuun päivää (*Maytime*) 247

Toumanova, Tamara 397
Tournament of Roses, 1956 542
"Tower Of Babel" 587
Townsend, Charles 275
Tracy, Spencer 228, 229, 230, 231, **235**, 245, 555; Oscar nomination, *San Francisco*, 229
"Trade Winds" 588
"Tramp, Tramp, Tramp" 181, 187, 189, 570
"Trample Your Troubles" 14
Traubel, Helen 397
Traviata, La – See *La Traviata*
Tree, Dolly 81, 288, 343
"Trees" 588
Trentini, Emma 174, 184, 274, 276, 368
"Tres Palabras" 505
Trial by Jury 588
Trilby. 13
"Trimmin' the Women" 56, 60
Tristan und Isolde 69, 71, 76, 77, 270, 504, 505
"Triumphal Chorus" (*Le Prophête*) 270
Troubetskoy, Maria 130
Trouble in Paradise 53
"Troubles of the World" 397
Troup, Bobby 529
Trovatore, Il 247, **251**
Trowbridge, Charles 530
Truesdell, Mary 192, 223, 315, 337, 379
Truex, Ernest 81
Truman, Harry 543
"Try to Forget" 125, 126, 128, 570
Tucker, Richard 288, 301, 316
Tucker, Sophie 211, 499, 500, 502
Turell, Saul J. 554
Turk, Edward Baron. 3, 6, 116, 338, 451, 462, 545
Turk, Roy 170, 502
"Turkey in the Straw" 446
"Turkish March" (by Mozart) 520, 528
Turner Broadcasting System 545
Turner Classic Movies 545

Turner Entertainment 247, 554
Turner Network Television 545
Turner, Lana 129, 135
Turner, Maude 316
Turner, Ted 545
Turner, William H. 102, 107
Turpin, Ben 22, 28
Twentieth Century Fox 334, 555
Twid, Cas 432
Twin Gables 341, 460, 543
"Twinkle in Your Eye, A" 446. 453
Two Can Play 81
"Two Silhouettes" 505
"Two Strong Men" 65, 67
Tynan, Brandon 301, 305
Tyroler, William 475

U.C.L.A. Film Archive 33, 34, 41, 81, 82, 102
U.C.L.A. Theatre Arts Collection. 205
U.C.L.A. – See Also University of Southern California
U.S.O. 460, 463, 499
UA Home Entertainment Group 545
Ulana, Elena 175
Ulric, Lenore 506, 513
"Un Bel Di" **362**, 363, 364, 366, 532, 537, 570
"Una Voce Poco Fa" 404, 410
"Uncle Ned" 581, 588
"Und nun das Glück gekommen" 145
"Une Dame Noble et Sage" 258, 269
"Une Heure près de toi" 570
Une Heure près de toi 91, 101
United Artists 33, 68, 113, 488
United Artists–British Dominion Films 115
United States Marine Corps 243
Universal Studios 464, 475, 498, 591
University of Southern California Thornton School of Music 553
University of Southern California, Los Angeles – See U.C.L.A.

Up in Central Park 560, 572, 573, 574
Uptowners, The 247
Urecal, Minerva 172
Usher, Guy 174

Vadja, Ernest 133
Vagabond King, The (1925 stage version) 32
Vagabond King, The 31, **32–41**, 208, 413, 560, 561, 564, 567, 570, 571; foreign versions, 33; restoration, 33, 34
"Vagabond King Waltz, The" – See "Huguette's Waltz"
Vajda, Ernest 21, 51, 129, 423, 590
Valentine, Joseph 172
Valentino, Rudolph 245
Valerie, Joan 518
Valetti, Lisl 436
Vallée, Marcel 146, 148
Vallee, Yvonne 91
Valles 343, 356, 368
Vallin, Rick 506
"Valse Tatiana" 32
Van Buren, Mabel 300
Van Dolsen, Roy 432
Van Dyke. W. S. II 174. 176, 177, 178, 179, 189, 194, 206, 221, 228, 237, 243, 245, 272, 287, 298, 315, 380, **382**, 398, 412, 434, **437**, 439, 448, 464, 465, 471, 472; death, 473; Oscar nomination, Best Director, *San Francisco*, 229
Van Eps, Robert 591
Van Patten, Joyce 517
Van Sickel, Dale 172
Vanaire, Jacques 117, 146, 435
Vanderveer, Ellinore 368
Variety 22, 41, 66, 76, 81, 86, 126, 144, 173, 220, 245, 267–268, 285, 298, 313, 334, 337, 354, 377, 396, 421, 448, 449, 473, 487, 501, 505, 528
Varney, Hal 477
Varno, Roland 368, 376, **377**, 591
Vaszary, János 434

Index

Vatori, Zeni 275
Vaverka, Anton 22
Ventura, Marcel 146
Vera-Ellen 555
Verdi, Giuseppe 247, 269, 270, 271
Verebes, Erno (Ernst) 369, **373**, 398, 506, 508
Vernell, Carl 499
Vernon, Wally 356
Verrier, André 146
Vervily, M. 564
"Very Thought of You, The" 588
Veuve Joyeuse, La 101, **146–152**
"Veux tu m'aimer," ("Love Me Tonight") 114, 570
Victor Record Review 560
Vienna Statsoper 369
Viktoria and Her Hussars 572, 573
"Vilia" 136, 145, 147, 152, 571
"Villanelle" 450
Victory Through Air Power 502
Villon, François 33
Vilonat, William 159,161
Virgil, Jack 172, 174
Virginian, The 355
Visaroff, Michael 61, 506
"Visi D'arte" 271
"Vision Fugitive" 588
Vitagraph 245
Vitaphone 2
Vivan, Percival 488
"Vive l'opera" 255, 269
Vlaskin, Jack 434, 435, **438**, 591
vocal doubles/stand-ins 399
Voelkel, Elda 33
Vogan, Emmett 498
Vogeding, Frederik 436
"Voice of Firestone" **542**
"Volga Boatman, The"– See "Song of the Volga Boatman"
Volk, George 368
von Eltz, Theodor 275, 498
von Flotow, Friedrich 270, 299, 487, 505
von Hardenburg, William 22
von Stroheim, Eric 3, 53, 129, 132, 133, 228

von Tilzer, Harry 365
von Wymetal, William 158, 206, 228, 247, 263, 475, 483, 487
Von, Elaine 229
Vorkapich, Slavko 43, 170, 206, 209, 247, 261, 271, 274, 283, 288, 300, 304, 315, 329
Vosselli, Judith 175

Wachner, Sophie 68, 77
Waggner, George 475, 480, 487, 488
Wagner, Charles L. 463
Wagner, Richard 269, 270, 432, 505
Wagner, Sidney 343
"Waiting for the Robert E. Lee" **468**, 469, 475
"Waiting for You" 9
Wakefield, Charles 474
Walburn, Raymond 316, **321**, **322**, 325, 343, 347, **350**, 355
Waldron, Edna 130
Wales, Ethel 102, 111
Walker, Nella 170
Walker, Ray 356, 381
Walker, Walter 82
Wallace, Beryl 436
Wallace, Earl 398
Wallace, Morgan 131, 356, **358**
Wallace, Nanette (Jeanette's great-niece) 206
Wallace, Oliver 505, 591
Wallace, Richard 115
Walsh, John 477
Walt Disney Productions 502, 503, 504
Walters, Luana 130
Waltz Dream, The 35, 423
"Waltz Huguette" – See "Huguette's Waltz"
"Waltz is Over, The" 474
"Wanting You," 389, 390, 396, 397, 571
Wanzer, Arthur 172
Warburton, Irvine 530
Ward, Dorothy 590
Ward, E. Clayton 68
Ward, Edward 366, 475, 487; Oscar nomination, Best

Scoring for a Musical Picture, *Phantom of the Opera*, 477
Ward, Dorothy 590
Warde, Anthony 499
Warner Bros. 91, 113, 192, 300, 357, 425, 539
Warner, H.B. 300, **303**, 304, **307**, **313**, 343, 345, 347, **348**, **354**, 381, 393
Warren, Betty 368
Warren, E. Alyn 117, 172, 301, 356
Warren, Leonard 539, 551
Warren, Ruth 81, 86
Warshauer, Allen 245
Warwick, Robert 381
Washburn, Bryant Jr. 172
Washington Irving High School, NYC 8
"Washington Post March" 299
"Water Boy" 588
Waters, Ethel 167, 464,465–466, 467, **469**, **470**, 473, 474, 475
Waters, John 166, 343
Watkins, Mary T. 68
Watkins, Pierre 288
Watson, Allan 270, 590
Watson, Bobs 249
Watson, Delmar 249
Watson, Lucile 316, 321, **322**, 336
Watson, Milton 275
Watts, Peggy 130
Watts, Richard Jr. 189, 196
Watts, Richard 31
Waverly, Frances 33
Waverly, Thora 33
"Way They Do It in Paris, The" 385, 397
Wayburn, Ned 6, 7, 8
Wayne and Warren 86
Wayne, Billy 499
Wayne, Joanee 518
Wayne, John 508
Wayne, Stephen 499
"We Are the Two Hacketts" 187
"We Belong to the Queen's Hussars" 125
"We Did It Before and We Can Do It Again" 474

We Must Have Music 434
We Were Dancing 410
"We Will Always Be Sweethearts" 96, 99, 100, 571
"Weary" 508, 516, 517
"Wedding March" (by Mendelssohn) 299
Weatherly, F.E. 246
Weatherwax, Rudd 530
Webb, Clifton 128
Webb, Ira S. 475; 591; Oscar, Best Color Interior Decoration, *Phantom of the Opera,* 477
Weber and Fields 166
Weems, Ted 505
Wegman, Jack 499
"Weib, Weib, Weib" 145
Weigel, Paul 248, 590
Weiler, A.H. 516, 537
Weill, Kurt 488, 492, 496, 497, 498; Oscar nomination, Best Scoring of a Musical Picture, *Knickerbocker Holiday,* 488
Weingarten, Lawrence 366
Weiss, Sid 505
Weissmann, Frieder 561, 570, 573
Welden, Ben 248
Weldon, Joan 397
Welles, Orson 500
Wentworth, Scott 424
Werba Theatre, Brooklyn 13
Werker, Alfred L. 81
"West Ain't Wild Anymore, The" 308. 315
West Philadelphia High School 6
West Side Story 581
West, Claudine 247, 272–273, 274, 423, 590
West, Emily [Wentz] 205, 413, **556**
West, Mae 7, 132
West, Pat 207, 220
West, Patricia 356
West, Vera 475, 591
Westcott, Gordon 102
Westcott, Helen 229

Western Electric Recording 2, 101, 475
Westman, Nydia 424, 425, 428
Weston, Paul 561, 569, 575, 578, 579, 580, 582, 587, 588
"Whale Who Wanted To Sing At The Met, The" 502, 503, 505, 571
"What a Little Thing Like a Wedding Ring Can Do" 95, 100
"What Could I Do?" 16
"What France Needs Is a King" 37, 40
"What is Love?" 402, 408, 410, **411**, 412
"What Is This Thing Called Love?" 588
"What Would You Do?" 99, 100, 101, 571
"What Ya Gonna Do When the Rent Comes 'Round?" – See "Rufus Rastus Johnson Brown"
"What's My Line?" 539
"Whatever It Is, It's Grand" 56, 60
Wheat, Lawrence (Larry) 172, 356
Wheeler, Lyle 464
"When a Felon's Not Engaged in His Employment" 584, 588
"When a Girl Marries" 349
"When a Maid Comes Knocking at Your Heart" 282, 287
'When I, Good Friends, Was Called to the Bar" 588
"When I Grow Too Old to Dream" 588
"When I Have Sung My Songs" 574
"When I Was a Lad" 588
"When Irish Eyes Are Smiling" 355
"When I've Got the Moon" 128
"When Old New York Was Young" 169
"When the Foeman Bares His Steel" 584, 588

"When You Walk in the Room" 574
"When You're Away" 574
"Whene'er I Spoke" 579, 588
"Where Else But Here" 344, 353, 355
"Where There's Love" ("The Rosenkavalier Waltz") 523, 528, 570, 571
"While My Lady Sleeps" 429, 430, 432, 434, 571
"Whispering Chorus" 128
White, Al 4, 5
"White Christmas" 588
White, Dave 288
"White Dove, The" 379
White, Francis 477
White, Jules 165, 166
White, Leo 117, 167
White, Marjorie 68, 70, **73**, 75, 77
White, Merrill 21, 32
Whiteman, Paul 18
Whiting, Jack 13
Whiting, Richard A. 51, 59, 60, 92, 100, 501
Whitman, Gayne 316, 381
Whitney, John 499
Whitney, Peter 506, 510, **512**, **515**
Whitney, Peter **515**
Whitson, Barbara 288
"Who Are We to Say" ("Obey Your Heart") 310, 312, 314, 315, 567, 571
"Who Knows?" 299, 590
Whoopee 88
"Whoopee-Ti-Yi-Yo" 588
"Why Should I Care?" 299
"Why Shouldn't We?" 220, 571
"Wie die Blumen im Lenz erblüh'n" 146
"Wie eine Rosenknospe" 145
Wie einst im Mai 248
Wigton, Anne 316
Wilber, Robert 275
Wilbur Theatre, Boston 8
Wilcox, Frank 499
Wilcox, Fred 517, 518

Index

Wilcox, Herbert   90, **91**, 115, 398, 400
Wild Flower   267
Wilder, Alec   505
Wilder, Billy   144
Wiley, Jan   499
Wilkerson, Guy   530
Wilkins, June   399
Will Tomorrow Ever Come   506
"Will You Remember?"   251, 252, 261, **266**, 269, 270, 271, 274, 571
Willenz, Max   435, 506
"William Tell Overture, The"   257, 269, 328, 329, 330
William Tell   269
William, Earl   541
William, Rhys   **472**
William, Warren   274, 280, **282**, **284**
Williams, Charlie   170
Williams, Esther   556
Williams, Geneva   117
Williams, Hannah   473
Williams, Kay   399
Williams, Lyman   172
Williams, Rhys   464
Williams, Thomas E.   270
Williams, Tudor   228, 247, 249, 269, 288, 451, 476, 487
Willie, the Operatic Whale   502
Willis, Edwin B.   117, 129, 166, 170, 172, 174, 206, 228, 274, 288, 300, 343, 356, 368, 380, 398, 412, 423, 434, 464, 517, 530
Willis, Leo   170
Willis, Norman   356
Willock, Dave   424
Willson, Meredith   553
Wilmot, D. Eardley   336
Wilshire Methodist Church   340
Wilson, Charles C.   170
Wilson, Clarence   102, 107, 248, 257
Wilson, Dooley   464, **469**, 470, 471, 475
Wilson, Dorothy   130
Wilson, Edwin   315
Wilson, Harry   344

Wilson, Howard   506
Wilson, Teddy   505
Wilton, Eric   92
Wiman, Dwight Deere   434
"Wind in the Trees, The"   305, 314
"Windy Day on the Battery, A"   273
Windheim, Marek   435, 477
Wing, Toby   316
Winkler, Ben   591
Winninger, Charles   13, 413
Winsten, Archer   285, 334, 421, 432, 448, 473
Winter, Hall   22
Winter, Keith   423
Winter, Philip   398
Winterhalter, Hugo   561, 581, 588
Winters [Winter], Shelley   488, 490, 497
Wir Schalten Um Auf Hollywood   166
Wise, Walter   451
Wister, Owen   355
"With These Hands"   588
"Without a Song"   589
"Without You" ("Tres Palabras")   505
Witmer, Thelma   502
Wizard of Oz, The   277, 290, 313
Woehler, Eddie   174
Wolcott, Charles   505, 591
Wolfe, Bill   499
Wolfe, Ian   248, 275, 517
Wolff, Gene   41
Wolfson, P.J.   170
Woman Commands, A   61
"Woman Needs Something Like That, A"   108, 114
"Woman With a Man, A"   475
"Woman's Kiss, A."   278, 287
"Woman's Smile, A"   287
"Wooden Shoes"   319, 335, 336, 337
Women's Voluntary Services   460
Wong, Anna May   549
WOO, Philadelphia   162
Wood, Douglas   248, 262, 590

Wood, Ercell and Clarice   172
Wood, Ernest   82
Wood, Peggy   248, 250, 398
Wood, Sam   117
Wood, Wilson   530
Woodbury, Eugenia   33
Woodbury, Mitch   335
"Woodland Sketches"   474
Woods, Buck   465
Woolley, Joan   337, 389, 398, 498
Woolley, Monty   301, 307
Worlock, Frederick   368
Worth, Bobby   505
Worth, Harry   275, 368, 376, 436, 464
Worthington, William   317
"Would You?"   235, 246
Wozzeck   161
Wray, Fay   340
"Wreck of the Julie Plante, The"   589
Wright, Armand "Curley"   249, 301
Wright, Bob   248, 267, 269, 270, 287, 315, 335, 336, 337, 355, 366, 378, 379, 379, 379, 439, 441, 449, 450, 529
Wright, Joseph   206, 315, 356
Wright, Ortho   228
Wrubel, Allie   505
Wulf, Ien   275
"Wunderbar"   589
Wynn, Ed   473
Wynn, Keenan   300

Xanrof, Leon   21
Xerxes   392, 397

Yaconelli, Frank   275
Yaconelli, Z.   300
Yankee Films   245
Yates, Herbert   506
Yearling, The   530
Yeckley, Molly   192
Yellen, Jack   502
Yeoman of the Guard   583
"Yes, Yes, Yvette"   13
Yes, Yes, Yvette   12, 13, 14
"Yip-I-Addy-I-Ay"   365

Yohalem, George 288, 300
York, Duke 207, 499
"You Ain't Got No Savoir Faire" 114
"You and I" 379
"You and the Night and the Music" 589
"You Are Free" 589
"You Are Love" 589
"You Be Nelson and I'll Be Jeanette" 195
"You Made Me Love You" 524, 529
"You've Got Me Up a Tree" 14
"You'll Love Me and Like It" 57
"Your Heart and My Heart" 379
"You're an Angel" 65, 66, 67

Youmans, Vincent 267, 413
Young, James 207
Young, Joe 222
Young, Rida Johnson 174, 247, 269, 366
Young, Robert 464, 465, **466**, **467**, **468**, **470**, 472, **473**, **474**, 475
Young, Roland 77, **78**, **80**, 81, 82, 83, **86**, 92, 96, 102
Young, Waldemar 101
Youssoupov, Prince 132
"Yubla" 62, 66
Yule, Joe 381

Zarco, Estellita 518
Zhukovsky, Vasili Andreevitch 379
Ziegfeld Theatre, NYC 398
Ziegfeld, Florenz 7, 89, 288
"Zigeuner" 404, **409**, 410, 412, 571
Zimmer, Dolph 368, 517
Zimmerman, Charles A. 299
Zinnen, Al 502
Zitt, Margaret 207
Zorina, Vera 435, 436, 498, 500, 592
Zucco, George 274, 283, 288, 293, 381, 389
"Zuyder Zee" 497
Zweifel, Harold 475

ELEANOR KNOWLES DUGAN (Author) is a San Francisco based writer, author of dozens of articles on films and film history, especially the early musicals and their relationship with musical stage forms. She started life as a theatrical and film costumer in New York and Los Angeles. More recently, she has written twenty-three books on business and communications topics.

JOHN COCCHI (Film Credits & Revisions) says he has "man and boy, known Eleanor Knowles since the 1960s, and we're still friends." He was a film reviewer-reporter for *Boxoffice Magazine*, a researcher for American Movie Classics, a contributor to over 200 film books, and the author of *The Western* and *Second Feature: The Best of the "B" Films*. He is a dedicated, lifelong movie buff.

J. PETER BERGMAN (Discography), a native New Yorker now living in western Massachusetts, is a journalist, theater critic, playwright and actor. His collection of short fiction, *Counterpoints*, received a Charles Dickens Award in 2002. His play, *Maids in the Mills,* about early 20th-century trade unions, is performed by schools throughout the Berkshire region. His newest play, *Hoping that You May Join with Us,* celebrates the work of Winnie Davis Crane, founder of the historic Pittsfield Community Music School. (Photo shows J. Peter Bergman as Bob Cratchit in his own play, *Clappertino's Christmas Carol*.)

www.ingramcontent.com/pod-product-compliance
Lightning Source LLC
Chambersburg PA
CBHW082017300426
44117CB00015B/2263